Bulgaria

the Bradt Travel Guide

Annie Kay

edition

2

www.bradtguides.com

Bradt Travel Guides Ltd, UK
The Globe Pequot Press Inc, USA

Belogradchik: over 50km² of dark red rocks in strange shapes and groups, the inspiration for many local legends
pages 148–9

Sofia: a pocket-sized capital with iconic gold-domed churches, layers of ancient history, fine museums, a yellow-brick road and even its own mountain
pages 75–102

Koprivshtitsa: this mountain town is famous for its revolutionary past and its beautiful and photogenic houses
pages 197–203

Rila Monastery: Bulgaria's finest monastery lies behind fortress walls; its church's frescoes are an explosion of colour, in contrast to the dark pine forests nearby
pages 103–8

Plovdiv: the UNESCO-listed Old Town has painted, timber-framed houses leaning across steep, cobbled streets: a photographer's dream
pages 227–35

ROMANIA

SERBIA

MACEDONIA

GREECE

AEGEAN SEA

Vidin
Lom
Drenovets
Belogradchik
Oryahovo
Nikopol
Knezha
Byala Slatina
Montana
Berkovitsa
Vrachanski Balkan National Park
Vratsa
Mezdra
PLEVEN
Levs
Pavliken
Lovech
Sevlievo
Boteygrad
Teteven
Troyan
Central Balkan National Park
Gabrov
Botev 2376m
Stara planina
SOFIA
Koprivshtitsa
Pernik
Cherni Vruh 2290m
Vitosha National Park
Panagyurishte
Vitosha Mountains
Kyustendil
Dupnitsa
Samokovo
Borovets
Pazardzhik
PLOVDIV
Malyovitsa 2720m
Musala 2925m
Rila Monastery Nature Park
Rila Mountains
Rila National Park
Krichim
Blagoevgrad
Velingrad
Razlog
Bankso
Rhodope Mountains
Vihren 2914m
Pirin National Park
Smolyan
Kurdzl
Sandanski
Gotse Delchev

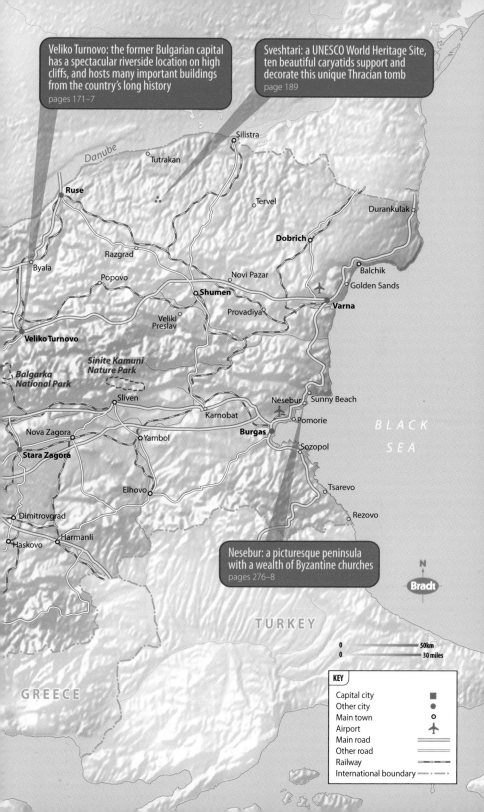

Veliko Turnovo: the former Bulgarian capital has a spectacular riverside location on high cliffs, and hosts many important buildings from the country's long history
pages 171–7

Sveshtari: a UNESCO World Heritage Site, ten beautiful caryatids support and decorate this unique Thracian tomb
page 189

Nesebur: a picturesque peninsula with a wealth of Byzantine churches
pages 276–8

Danube

Silistra

Tutrakan

Ruse

Tervel

Durankulak

Byala

Razgrad

Dobrich

Popovo

Novi Pazar

Balchik

Golden Sands

Shumen

Provadiya

Varna

Veliki Preslav

Veliko Turnovo

Sinite Kamuni Nature Park

Balgarka National Park

Sliven

Nesebur

Sunny Beach

Karnobat

Pomorie

Nova Zagora

Burgas

Yambol

Sozopol

Stara Zagora

Elhovo

Tsarevo

Dimitrovgrad

Rezovo

Haskovo

Harmanli

BLACK SEA

TURKEY

GREECE

N

Bradt

0   50km
0   30 miles

KEY

Capital city	■
Other city	●
Main town	○
Airport	✈
Main road	
Other road	
Railway	
International boundary	

Bulgaria
Don't miss...

Tomb at Sveshtari
Two of the ten elegant caryatids that support the roof of the Royal Tomb at Sveshtari, which dates from the 3rd century BC (BMT) page 189

Sofia
The lively capital Sofia has wonderful museums and varied architecture (such as the pretty Ivan Vazov National Theatre, pictured here), making it well worth a visit (NS/S) pages 75–97

Nesebur Harbour

One of Europe's oldest settlements, this ancient harbour is now busy with fishing and pleasure boats (ES/S) pages 276–8

Kukeri

The fearsome *kukeri*, men dressed in animal skins with several large bells strung on their bodies, form a colourful and very noisy procession intended to drive away evil spirits

(d/S) page 121

Belogradchik Fortress

This striking fortress makes use of the natural strategic defences of its rocky landscape, the result of millions of years of geological activity (I/S) page 149

Bulgaria in colour

above   The Roman Theatre in Plovdiv hosts operas and classical music concerts during the summer (m/S) page 231

below left   The sight of Veliko Turnovo's houses stacked above the River Yantra attracts artists and photographers alike (k/S) pages 171–7

below right   The striking building that housed Sofia's old mineral baths has now been restored, and is due to open as the new Museum of Sofia (NS/S) page 95

top   Originally built for a wealthy Greek merchant, this beautiful house is now home to Plovdiv's Ethnographic Museum (SP/D) page 231

above left   Colourful houses, cobbled streets and statues of heroes (here Todor Kableshkov): beauty and history combine in Koprivshtitsa (ND/D) pages 197–203

above right   The 19th-century Cathedral of the Assumption dominates the centre of Varna, and there are fine woodcarvings inside (AT/S) page 280

below   Bansko is Bulgaria's newest and liveliest ski resort, based in an old mountain town (PS/D) pages 115–22

Discover
an ancient
culture

BULGARIA

www.bulgariatravel.org

AUTHOR

Annie Kay first visited Bulgaria in 1974, and has been a regular visitor ever since.

For almost 20 years she has been the organiser of the special-interest tours of the British-Bulgarian Society, with themes such as birdwatching, butterflies and moths, wild flowers, folklore and festivals, wine and food, monasteries, music and architectural heritage. As a result she can take you to wonderful and little-known places not even mentioned in other guides!

She has written many newspaper and magazine articles about Bulgaria and a series of small photo-guides. She writes about Bulgarian wine for the best-selling *Mitchell Beazley Pocket Guide to Wine*.

Her favourite places are still Sofia and Koprivshtitsa.

AUTHOR'S STORY

My fascination for eastern Europe began when I was about four. My grandmother, with whom we lived as an extended family in a large house, offered accommodation to a refugee couple from Tito's Yugoslavia. The man was, at least to me, enormously tall, but every day he would bend down and shake my hand in a very polite way!

I studied Balkan history at university and made my first visit to Bulgaria as a student. Although this was the time of the Cold War, there was generous and welcoming hospitality to strangers, and this marked the beginning of my long relationship with this small, beautiful country.

Bulgaria has been a tourist destination for many years, and is deservedly popular for its coastal and ski resorts. I hope that this guide will encourage more people off the beaten track to discover some of its many other attractions, and that they too will experience Bulgarian hospitality at first hand.

PUBLISHER'S FOREWORD   *Hilary Bradt*

I approached the manuscript of the first edition of our guide to Bulgaria (published in 2008) with some trepidation. I felt ignorant about the country and indeed the whole region; like many other people I associated Bulgaria with cheap wine and crowded beaches on the Black Sea, and not much else. But before starting my reading I chatted to a neighbour pruning his buddleia. We talked about butterflies and their decline in England. 'You should go to Bulgaria,' he said. 'I've never seen so many butterflies!' After reading the book, I was hooked. Here's a country apparently unspoiled by industrialisation, with its nature and culture both intact. And here is an author who can describe it with an insider's knowledge and enthusiasm. Annie Kay has me convinced that Bulgaria is, for intelligent visitors, one of the most rewarding countries in Europe. I made a note of my final thought: 'People planning a holiday in Bulgaria would be mad not to buy this book!' The same of course applies to this second edition.

Second edition published June 2015
First published 2008

Bradt Travel Guides Ltd
IDC House, The Vale, Chalfont St Peter, Bucks SL9 9RZ, England
www.bradtguides.com
Print edition published in the USA by The Globe Pequot Press Inc,
PO Box 480, Guilford, Connecticut 06437-0480

Text copyright © 2015 Annie Kay
Maps copyright © 2015 Bradt Travel Guides Ltd
Metro map copyright © Sofiiski Metropoliten
Photographs copyright © 2015 Individual photographers (see below)
Project Manager: Laura Pidgley
Cover research: Pepi Bluck, Perfect Picture

ISBN: 978 1 84162 937 7
e-ISBN: 978 1 78477 125 6 (e-pub)
e-ISBN: 978 1 78477 225 3 (mobi)

British Library Cataloguing in Publication Data
A catalogue record for this book is available from the British Library

Photographs
Front cover Frescoes in the Nativity Church, Rila Monastery (CK/AWL)
Back cover Pirin National Park (ML/D)
Title page Aleksandur Nevski Cathedral, Sofia (m/S); The rose is Bulgaria's national flower (P/D); Freedom Monument, Shipka (EZ/D)

Photographers
Assen Ignatov (AI); AWL Images: Christian Kober (CK/AWL), Hemis (H/AWL); Bulgaria Ministry of Tourism (BMT); Balkania Travel (BT); Dreamstime.com: 2bears (2/D), Andrey Klimov (AK/D), Cylonphoto (C/D), Didreklama (D/D), Evgeny Zenkov (EZ/D), Julia Lazarova (JL/D), Nikolay Dimitrov (ND/D), Petarpaunchev (P/D), Psv (PS/D), Stoyo Petkov (SP/D), Todor Yankov (TY/D); Nick Greatorex-Davies (NGD); Michael Loveday (ML); Shutterstock.com: 2bears (2/S), Aleksandar Todorovic (AT/S), djumandji (d/S), Erni (E/S), Eugene Sergeev (ES/S), Giedriius (G/S), Jaroslav Moravcik (JM/S), Ilizia (I/S), kpatyhka (k/S), meunierd (m/S), Nickolay Stanev (NS/S), ollirg (o/S), Richard Whitcombe (RW/S), vicspacewalker (v/S)

Maps David McCutcheon FBCart.S; colour map base by Nick Rowland FRGS; some town plan maps include data © OpenStreetMaps contributors (under Open Database License)

Typeset by Wakewing, High Wycombe
Production managed by Jellyfish Print Solutions; printed in India
Digital conversion by www.dataworks.co.in

Acknowledgements

Many thanks to Julia Stoyanova, who has been a friend and colleague for almost 20 years, for answering umpteen questions and checking contact details of embassies, hotels, restaurants and Sofia transport.

I am very grateful to Rumyana Zafirova, an experienced guide with an in-depth knowledge of Bulgaria, who has checked the historical information and the contact details of hotels and restaurants.

Thanks are also due to the friends and past and present members of the British-Bulgarian Society tours team who shared their specialist knowledge for the first edition, which, with some updating, is again an important part of the second, especially Nick Greatorex-Davies, Assen Ignatov, Petar Iankov, Ina Kozhuharova, Tihomir Stefanov, Angela Pencheva, Mitko Popov, Kath Barker, Mrs Lilia Guerassimova, Mitko Petrakiev and Lyuba Boyanin.

Thank you to Anelia Genova and Annie Haralambieva of the Bulgarian Ministry of Tourism for their help with this new edition.

Apologies to family and friends neglected during the writing of the guide!

Finally, special thanks to Ognian Avgarski for driving many kilometres on research trips, for his contributions on language, the maps and recent political and economic developments, and most of all for his encouragement and support.

FEEDBACK REQUEST AND UPDATES WEBSITE

At Bradt Travel Guides we're aware that guidebooks start to go out of date on the day they're published – and that you, our readers, are out there in the field doing research of your own. You'll find out before us when a fine new family-run hotel opens or a favourite restaurant changes hands and goes downhill. So why not write and tell us about your experiences? Contact us on ☏ 01753 893444 or e info@bradtguides.com. We will forward emails to the author who may post updates on the Bradt website at www.bradtupdates.com/bulgaria. Alternatively you can add a review of the book to www.bradtguides.com or Amazon.

Contents

Introduction

Since the first edition of this guide, Bulgaria's attractions for visitors have grown both in number and diversity. There are award-winning golf courses, luxurious spas, five-star hotels and good-value budget accommodation for those wanting to explore the mountains and countryside. There are watersports and nightclubs on the coast and a wealth of birds, butterflies and wild flowers in the countryside. Food and wines are delicious and affordable. Museums, churches and monasteries are a window into Bulgaria's rich and turbulent history.

Sofia is the perfect destination for a relaxing city break: the centre is compact and can easily be covered on foot at a gentle pace in a couple of days, even allowing for coffee and lunch breaks. There are some familiar fast-food and retail outlets, but there is also an eclectic mix of Viennese-style boulevards, monumental set-piece communist official buildings and glorious gold-domed churches. The capital is very green with numerous parks, there are museums with recently unearthed treasures and a variety of colourful markets and stylish shops to discover. There are two exciting new museums due to open in Sofia: the Mineral Baths as the home of the Sofia City Museum, and the new art gallery complex dubbed Bulgaria's Louvre, because it too features an internal courtyard with a glass roof.

Outside Sofia there are several other rewarding towns and cities, such as Plovdiv, with its UNESCO-listed Old Town, and Veliko Turnovo, the former capital. The ski resorts of Bansko, Borovets and Pamporovo offer great skiing, great nightlife and great value. The Black Sea coast has fine beaches, watersports and nightclubs, but also quieter spots for family holidays, butterfly observation and birdwatching.

Rural Bulgaria has changed too: many young people have left for the cities or abroad, leaving an increasingly elderly population to work the land. However, investment in wineries, ecotourism and activity holidays should gradually attract more people back to the countryside. It is a wonderful place to drive; roads are quiet, wildlife is rich, the mountain scenery is unrivalled and there are monasteries, archaeological sites, caves and rock formations, as well as picturesque villages and vineyards to visit.

Hospitality to strangers is as generous as ever – on my most recent visit a month ago, we asked a man just emerging from his house in a side street of Veliko Turnovo how to reach the tourist information centre. Obviously it was a tricky route to describe so he solved it by getting into his car and urging us to follow him in ours. He took in several of the main tourist sites waving his arm helpfully out of the car window at them. When we reached the destination, he pointed, did a swift U-turn, waved and departed before we could properly thank him. Contrast this with a similar request made in New York, to which the response was 'Buy a map!'

Bulgarians tell a nice story against themselves: God was dividing up the earth between all the different peoples; characteristically the Bulgarians arrived late and God had nothing left. So he gave them a piece of Paradise.

SEND US YOUR SNAPS!

We'd love to follow your adventures using our Bulgaria guide – why not send us your photos and stories via Twitter (@BradtGuides) and Instagram (@bradtguides) using the hashtag #bulgaria. Alternatively, you can upload your photos directly to the gallery on the Bulgaria destination page via our website (*www.bradtguides.com*).

FOLLOW BRADT

For the latest news, special offers and competitions, subscribe to the Bradt newsletter via the website www.bradtguides.com and follow Bradt on:

- www.facebook.com/BradtTravelGuides
- @BradtGuides
- @bradtguides
- pinterest.com/bradtguides

There are some variations in the standard Latin spelling of Bulgarian words, centring on the letter ъ which is pronounced like the 'u' in 'up', although others define this as the sound of 'a' as in 'across'. The result is that when transliterated it varies. I have used the former throughout the book.

The Bulgarian alphabet does not include the letter x, and its sound is instead represented by 'ks', for example in 'Aleksandur'. The letter ж is equivalent to the 's' in 'measure' and represented by the letters zh. The letter ц is the sound of 'ts' as in 'tsar'.

Hotel websites and email addresses are usually individual interpretations and may vary from these examples!

The correct practice for naming churches dedicated to two saints is to repeat the abbreviation for saint. Hence Sv Sv Konstantin and Elena – **Св Св Константин и Елена**.

MAPS
Keys and symbols Maps include alphabetical keys covering the locations of those places to stay, eat or drink that are featured in the book.

Grids and grid references Several maps use grid lines to allow easy location of sites. Map grid references are listed in square brackets after the name of the place or sight of interest in the text, with page number followed by grid number, eg: [88 A3].

LISTINGS Accommodation and restaurants are listed alphabetically and marked with a price code. The prices are fairly similar throughout the country except in Sofia and the ski and beach resorts, where prices are higher.

MUSEUMS AND HISTORIC SITES Prices and opening hours are listed where applicable. Monasteries and churches are free to enter, though donations are obviously welcome. They are generally open during the day; if closed, a mobile number to contact the key holder is sometimes offered. Some larger monasteries have museums or special exhibitions for which there may be a charge.

For additional online content, articles, photos and more on Bulgaria, why not visit www.bradtguides.com/bulgaria.

Part One

GENERAL INFORMATION

Location Southeast Europe

Neighbouring countries Romania, Turkey, Greece, Macedonia and Serbia

Size 110,910km²

Climate Temperate: cold, damp winters; hot, dry summers

Status Republic

Population 7.265 million in 2013

Life expectancy 78 for women, 71 for men in 2013

Capital Sofia (population 1.4 million in 2013)

Other main towns Plovdiv, Varna, Burgas, Ruse, Veliko Turnovo

GDP US$53.01 billion in 2013

Official language Bulgarian

Religion Bulgarian Orthodox (81%), Muslim (12%), others (7%)

Currency Leva, divided into 100 stotinki

Exchange rate €1 = 1.96lv; £1 = 2.70lv; US$1 = 1.83lv (March 2015)

National airline Bulgaria Air

Airports Sofia, Varna, Burgas and Plovdiv

International telephone code +359

Time GMT+2 and BST+2

Electrical voltage 220V

Weights and measures Metric

Flag A rectangle divided horizontally into three colours, of equal size, white, green and red from top to bottom

National anthem *Mila rodino*

National flower Rose

National sports Football, basketball, volleyball

Public holidays 1 January (New Year's Day), 3 March (National Day of Liberation), Easter, 1 May (Labour Day), 6 May (Sv Georgi Day – Day of Valour and Bulgarian Army), 24 May (Sv Sv Kiril and Metodii Day – Day of Slavonic Culture and Literacy), 6 September (The Unification of Bulgaria), 22 September (Independence Day), 24–26 December (Christmas)

Background Information

GEOGRAPHY

Bulgaria is in the eastern part of the Balkan Peninsula, which is itself named after the range of mountains which runs from west to east across Bulgaria. The country has an area of 110,910km², of which 360km² is water. It has a coastline on the Black Sea which is 354km long and has borders with Romania (608km), Turkey (240km), Greece (494km), Macedonia (148km) and Serbia (318km).

The terrain is mainly mountainous; indeed, Sofia is one of Europe's highest capital cities. The whole country averages 470m above sea level. The principal mountain ranges are Stara Planina (the Balkan range) and the lower Sredna Gora, Rila, Pirin and the Rhodopes. At 2,925m, the highest peak in the Balkans is Mount Musala, in the Rila Mountains. The major rivers are the Danube, the Struma, the Iskur and the Maritsa.

CLIMATE

Bulgaria is very diverse geographically, and this is reflected in the climate, which is quite extreme. It can be bitterly cold in winter and uncomfortably hot in the cities in summer. The southwest has higher temperatures in both summer and winter, as warm air from the Aegean arrives via the Struma Valley. Places such as the ski resort of Pamporovo in the southern part of the Rhodope Mountains are noted for their mild sunny winters. The coast is hot in summer, though with pleasant sea breezes, and is usually damp and often misty in winter, but snowfalls, even of significant amounts, are possible. Sofia is frequently foggy in winter with below-zero temperatures by day and night common, while in summer it is hot and sunny. The area north of the Balkan Mountains on the Danube Plain can be particularly bleak in winter, whereas to the south of the same range the Valley of the Roses and Thracian Plain are protected from the worst of the cold weather coming from the north.

NATURAL HISTORY AND CONSERVATION

FLORA Bulgaria is situated between 41°30′ and 44°20′ north latitude and 22° and 28° east longitude on the central part of the Balkan Peninsula. In its comparatively small territory more than 3,800 higher (vascular) plant species are recorded.

The reasons for this incredible wealth of plant life are complicated. Not only is there a rich geological and palaeo-climatic history but geographical position is also influential as it is where several phyto-geographic regions meet. There are records of two glaciations that have influenced both the relief and the flora of the highest mountain ranges, Rila and Pirin. There are many glacial relicts, their distribution being related to the glacial processes: **globe-flower** (*Trollius europaeus*), **narcissus-flowered anemone** (*Anemone narcissiflora*), **blackcurrants** (*Ribes nigrum*), **bog bilberry** (*Vaccinium uliginosum*), **spring gentian** (*Gentiana verna*) and **snow gentian** (*Gentiana nivalis*). The valleys in the Rhodopes and other mountains, with their milder climate, were refuges for many Tertiary relicts like **haberlea** (*Haberlea rhodopensis*), **ramonda** (*Ramonda serbica*), **yew** (*Taxus baccata*), **Judas tree** (*Cercis siliquastrum*), **horse chestnut** (*Aesculus hippocastanum*), **cherry laurel** (*Laurocerasus officinalis*) and **medlar** (*Mespilus germanica*).

Bulgaria is divided into three more or less distinct phyto-climatic districts: the southeastern part of the central European region, the Mediterranean district and the Euro-Asian steppe and forest-steppe district. This division is based on the species composition of plants in these areas and their specifics of distribution. It shows the connections of the flora and vegetation here with that of central Europe, the Mediterranean and the Euro-Asian steppe. In other words here, in a comparatively small area, keen botanists can see plants that originated in different and distant parts of the world.

The southeastern part of the central European region is characterised by deciduous forests rich with south European species. In southeast Bulgaria and on the Black Sea coast there are many species with Asia Minor (colchid) origin: **oriental beech** (*Fagus orientalis*), **Caucasus nettle-tree** (*Celtis caucasica*), **cherry laurel** (*Laurocerasus officinalis*), **blueberry** (*Vaccinium arctostaphylos*), **squill** (*Scilla bythinica*), **pontian fritillary** (*Fritillaria pontica*) and the relicts – **pontian rhododendron** (*Rhododendron ponticum*) and **pontian daphne** (*Daphne pontica*). The Balkan subdistrict includes the mountain areas of Pirin, Rila, the Western and Central Rhodopes, Osogovo, Kraishte, the western border mountains, the west and central Stara Planina and the west and central Sredna Gora and the hilly region of Ludogorie. Vegetation belts change with the increased elevation as follows: oak and beech forests of the central European type, spruce forests of the subarctic type, and arctic-alpine non-arboreal vegetation. Above 2,500m are plants like **netted willow** (*Salix reticulata*), **mountain avens** (*Dryas octopetala*) and **lesser primrose** (*Primula minima*). The mountain ridges have been migration routes for boreal species from the Alps and the Carpathians.

The Mediterranean district is characterised by patches of evergreen arboreal vegetation localised in the southernmost parts of the country. Plants that are distributed mainly in the Mediterranean region penetrate from the Aegean coast northward to the Eastern Rhodopes, the Thracian Plain, the Tundzha hilly region, the Struma Valley, the Mesta Valley, south Pirin, Slavyanka, Belasitsa and also along the Black Sea coast. Examples include: **kermes oak** (*Quercus coccifera*), **phillyrea** (*Phillyrea latifolia*), **Grecian juniper** (*Juniperus excelsa*), **bladder senna** (*Colutea arborescens*), **wild jasmine** (*Jasminum fruticans*) and **hop-hornbeam** (*Ostria carpinifolia*). There are two barriers for the Mediterranean climate. The first one is the Rila-Rhodopes Massif. These mountains stop the distribution to the north of plants such as **laurel** (*Laurus nobilis*), **myrtle** (*Myrtus communis*), **strawberry tree** (*Arbutus unedo*), **eastern strawberry tree** (*Arbutus andrachne*) and **tree heath** (*Erica arborea*). The second barrier is Stara Planina. This restricts the distribution to the north of species like **prickly juniper** (*Juniperus oxycedrus*), **clover** (*Trifolium purpureum*), **asphodel** (*Asphodeline lutea*) and **anemone** (*Anemone pavonina*). There are some Mediterranean plants that do reach north of the ridge of Stara Planina, but only on calcareous basic rocks and along the Black Sea coast.

The Euro-Asian steppe and forest-steppe district is in northeast Bulgaria. The steppe vegetation is characterised by herbaceous plants. Primary steppe communities with no natural forests since the glaciations occur in south Dobrudzha and on the north Black Sea coast. The steppe communities of Dobrudzha are characterised by **grasses** (*Festuca pseudovina, Koeleria brevis, K. splendens*), **sweetvetch** (*Hedysarum grandiflorum*), **pinks** (*Dianthus nardiformis, D. palens*), **catchfly** (*Silene pontica*), **mullein** (*Verbascum crenatifolium*), many species of **knapweed** and many chalophytes, as well as the steppe shrubs **little almond** (*Amygdalus nana*), **blackthorn** (*Prunus spinosa*) and **Christ's thorn** (*Paliurus spina-christi*). This is unlike the Russian and Ukrainian steppes where **feather grasses** dominate. Where forests have been cleared by man, secondary steppe communities have developed. Such interesting vegetation can be seen on calcareous basic rock all over the country.

In total there are 705 Balkan endemics (plant species localised only on the Balkan Peninsula), and 600 of them are distributed in Bulgaria. For example, several **yellow lilies** (*Lilium rhodopaeum, L. jankae, L. albanicum*), **haberlea** (*Haberlea rhodopensis*), **ramonda** (*Ramonda serbica*) and **saxifrages** (*Saxifraga stribrnyi, S. ferdinandi-coburgi, S. spruneri*). Bulgarian endemics or plants distributed only in a small, particular territory within Bulgaria number about 170 species and 100 subspecies such as an endemic pink **primrose** (*Primula frondosa*) found only in the Stara Planina, **mullein** (*Verbascum davidoffii*), **rattle** (*Rhinanthus javorkae*; only in Pirin) and an endemic purple **primrose** (*Primula deorum*), which is found only in the Rila Mountains.

Bulgaria's mountains are so richly endowed with endemics partly because of the mild climate, but also because of various ecological conditions related to the altitude, limestone or silicate rock and relief, as well as their rich geological history.

FAUNA
Birds Bulgaria has one of the richest ranges of birdlife in Europe. Occupying only 1.1% of the territory of the continent, it is home to about 47% of its bird species. One reason for this is the special geographical position of Bulgaria at the crossroads of Europe and Asia Minor and at the joining point of the continental, steppe and Mediterranean biomes. Also important is the presence of a large internal sea, putting the country on one of the major migratory flyways on the continent. The landscape richness, including habitats from sea dunes to alpine rocky peaks of almost 3,000m, is also a contributory factor. Last, but by no means least, the weak economic development of the country during the second half of the 20th century allowed the self-preservation of wildlife on most of the territory, but especially in the mountains. Most of the country's territory remains unspoiled even at the beginning of the 21st century, in spite of the rapid development of the country during recent years.

Bulgaria offers extraordinary opportunities for birdwatching and twitching. In a week at the appropriate time (April–May and August–October) and in an appropriate combination of sites (Black Sea coast and Rhodope Mountains) it is easy to have over 200 species in the list or even 240 species in two weeks! It is quite typical in Bulgaria for all the European species of a certain bird group to be present, sometimes at the same time.

In late autumn and winter all species of **grebes**, as well as the **cormorant, pygmy cormorant** (in winter time you may see thousands of them roosting, including actually within the city of Plovdiv) and **shag** can be seen along the coastline and coastal wetlands. All year round you may see both the **Dalmatian** and the **white pelicans** (usually as many as hundreds or thousands of birds!). Sixteen species of **bitterns, herons, egrets** and **storks**, as well as **spoonbill, glossy ibis** and **greater**

flamingo, can be seen in the country. You can see and take a photo of the **white stork** in most lowland villages; sometimes the nests are situated on very picturesque sites (for example, the well-known ruins of the church in Rudina village in the Eastern Rhodopes). You can also easily see the **black stork** (including several nests from just one observation point) in the Eastern Rhodopes.

At first glance it would seem unlikely to be the same for **waterfowl**, as Bulgaria is not abundant in wetlands. But, in fact, almost all European **geese** and **duck species** may be seen in wintertime, including the **red-breasted goose** (mainly around the northern coastal wetlands of Durankulak and Shabla) and **white-headed duck** (mainly at Burgas Wetlands) and often all three swan species together at the same site.

In one area, the Eastern Rhodopes, you can even hope to see 37 of the 39 European **birds of prey**, including **griffon** and **black vultures**, **Levant sparrowhawk** and **Bonelli's eagle**. Almost all of them pass over the Black Sea coast every autumn and the only thing you need to do is to sit and watch at some of the migration watching points there (near Atanasovsko Lake and Balchik are two of the best).

Nine game species of a wide spectrum have been recorded in Bulgaria – from the typical forest species such as the **hazel hen** (easily seen in the Rila Monastery Nature Park) and the **capercaillie**, to the rock lovers such as **chukar** and **rock partridges**. Although some of them have been lost as breeders, all European **rails**, **crakes**, **cranes** and **great** and **little bustards** can still be seen, though some special efforts may be needed. More easily viewed are the **corncrake** (often just near the road), **water rail**, **little crake** and the **common crane** (especially in October on the northern Black Sea, but also in March and April there too).

Fifty-one **wader**, twenty-two **gull** and nine **tern** species occur in the country and most of them are not difficult to see even on one trip. It is also possible to see **collared** and **black-winged pratincoles**, **broad-billed sandpiper**, **marsh sandpiper** and **red-necked phalaropes** (the best time is July to September at Atanasovsko Lake, for example). The same is true for the **slender-billed gull, gull-billed tern** and the three species of **'marsh' terns**, which can often be seen together. There is a good chance of seeing the **great spotted cuckoo** as well as the ten species of owl; even the impressive **eagle owl** often breeds close to places where it may be seen just from the road (along the cliffs between Balchik and Cape Kaliakra). **Scops owls** are a common sight in the towns and villages, while **little owls** breed in every Bulgarian settlement. In many of them the **pallid swift** breeds near to the **common**, and sometimes even with the **Alpine swift**, giving excellent opportunities for comparison of the identification features. Huge colonies of hundreds of nests of **bee-eaters** (especially along the Danube River), and also very common **hoopoe** and **roller**, provide an exotic aspect of bird fauna almost everywhere in the lower parts of the country.

There are ten species of woodpecker in Bulgaria, including the very common Syrian woodpecker which lives in virtually every village. **Black-** and **grey-headed woodpecker**, as well as the misanthropic **white-backed** and **three-toed woodpecker**, can be seen in the higher mountains. It is quite easy in just a few hours to see as many as six **woodpecker species**.

The rich variety of **passerine species**, predetermined by the various geographical conditions, makes the country a twitcher's paradise. Eastern specialities such as **paddyfield warbler** (easily seen at Durankulak and Shabla lakes) and **pied wheatear** (abundant at Cape Kaliakra) within a few hours' drive are replaced by southern ones such as **semi-collared flycatchers** (in the forests of the Balkan Range) or **masked shrike** and **olive-tree warbler** (in Sakar, Eastern Rhodopes or Strandzha).

Butterflies and moths One of the things that quickly strikes you when travelling about Bulgaria is the variety of its beautiful landscape and the abundance of seminatural habitats. There are high mountain peaks, forest-covered hills which stretch across the horizon, mile after mile of rocky scrubby hillsides, rocky gorges, smooth grassy (almost steppe-like) hills and lowland wetlands. During the spring and summer, the flower-rich meadows are stunning, and they are everywhere – and *buzzing* with insects! If it were in Britain, it would be like stepping back in time a hundred years or more, except for the general lack of hedgerows. Bulgaria is a country that has so far largely escaped the excesses of modern intensive agriculture and its damaging effects on wildlife. Traditional farming methods, such as scything, hand-hoeing and extensive grazing, have maintained species-rich habitats. However, much of this is changing now that Bulgaria is part of the European Union and funds are made available for large-scale modern agriculture. Rural communities are becoming depleted of their young people, as they move away to towns and cities, or even emigrate, seeking a different life. Agricultural land is now either abandoned or more intensively farmed.

Some 212 butterfly species are currently known to occur in Bulgaria, comparing favourably with other European countries that support a rich butterfly fauna. Many of Europe's more spectacular species are common or frequent in the right habitat here, including the **swallowtail** and **scarce swallowtail**, the **eastern** and **southern festoons**, **black-veined white**, the **large tortoiseshell**, **Camberwell beauty** and the **southern white admiral**. Three species of emperor butterfly occur here, including **Freyer's purple emperor**. The spectacular **poplar admiral** can also be seen here, sometimes in significant numbers in the right locations. In the mountain areas **Apollo** and **small Apollo** can be common. A good selection of species whose European distribution is restricted to southeast Europe can be found in Bulgaria; some are widespread and in places common. The mountains provide habitat for a range of alpine species including 14 species of *Erebia* (mountain ringlets). Bulgaria holds important populations of many species that have seriously declined in other parts of Europe. An example is the subspecific form '*rebeli*' of the **Alcon blue**, formerly regarded as a distinct species – the **mountain Alcon blue** – which lays its eggs on cross gentian and whose larvae complete their development in the nests of ants, feeding on the ant larvae. Many of the species that were once considered common and widespread in Britain still hold that privileged status here. Almost anywhere you care to stop in Bulgaria you can soon find 30 or more species of butterfly at the height of summer, but totals of 40–50 species are not uncommon, even recording 80 or more species in a day in July in the richest places. There is just so much 'habitat' everywhere.

Over 1,400 species of macromoths have been recorded in Bulgaria, the majority of which fly at night and include such spectacular species as the **giant peacock moth**, the **oak**, **willowherb**, **convolvulus**, **spurge** and **striped hawkmoths**, the **plum** and **pine-tree lappets**, and many *Catocala* species such as the **rosy** and **light crimson underwings** and the **oak yellow underwing**. Many species of day-flying moth (or those easily disturbed in the day) which the British lepidopterist mostly only dreams of are a common sight in the right habitats in Bulgaria.

These include the **Essex** and **Sussex emeralds**, **rest harrow**, the **bright** and **Lewis waves**, **black-veined moth**, **feathered footman**, **nine-spotted**, **spotted clover**, **spotted sulphur**, **pale shoulder** and **geometrician**, as well as many **burnets** and **foresters**; and of course, there are a host of species that are not known at all in Britain, both night- and day-flying. Many species still await discovery, as the number of serious entomologists working in Bulgaria over the years has been relatively few.

Insects The rich variety of landscapes and climatic regions is the source of the great diversity of over 20,000 species of insects, of which 750 are endemic.

The 68 species of dragonflies and damselflies are very attractive. Several years ago, a new one, **Bulgarian emerald** (*Somatochlora borisii*), was discovered in southern Bulgaria.

If your prime interest is beetles, here you will be able to see **European stag beetle, blue longhorn beetle** with **black spots (Rosalie beetle), Calosoma beetle, inquisitor carabus, gigas ground beetle, ground beetle** and **European rhinoceros beetle**.

Orthopterans (grasshoppers, locusts, crickets, bush crickets) are a moderately large order of insects with more than 200 species in Bulgaria. The group includes middle-sized to very large insects. The big carnivorous **saga**, the largest insect in Europe, occurs in xerothermic scrubs in the low southern parts of the country. Orthopterans can be found everywhere, from the caves to the highest mountains, but exhibit the greatest diversity in the lowland and hilly dry bushes and steppe habitats. The totally black **bush cricket** (*Bradyporus dasypus*) has completely lost the ability to jump and reaches a weight of 30g.

Many insects, such as mayflies, stonefly, scorpionfly, snakefly and lacewings, can be seen in their typical habitats. Of the large and eye-catching insects you can see ascalaphids (such as **owlfly**), myrmeleontids, nemopterids, the rare **bubopsis** and **deteproctophylls** (only near the Ropotamo River). Some local libelloides look like dragonflies. Don't miss other delightful species such as the **thread-winged lacewing** and **mammoth wasp**. **Wood ants** are not very common, but they have an exciting – and little-known (except to experts) – rich social structure and rigid, chemically mediated hierarchy. Undoubtedly, they hold more secrets for the biologist to discover.

Fish The fish fauna of Bulgaria is also one of the most interesting and rich in species in Europe. More than 220 species of marine and freshwater have been recorded. The ichthyofauna of the Black Sea contains many Ponto-Caspian relic species, which makes it quite exotic. Some of them are the **toad goby** and **grass goby**, which can often be seen for sale in coastal fish markets. Another relic species is **Caucasian goby**, the smallest fish in the Black Sea. Other important species for the marine fisheries are **sprat, anchovy, scad** and **spurdog**. The population of the **turbot** has dramatically decreased in recent years and it is now forbidden to catch them.

The diversity of freshwater fish in the country is also amazing. The Danube River, the richest river in Europe for fish species, is in its lower course in Bulgaria which determines the predominance of the cyprinids like **common carp, bream** and **roach**. Typical of the Danube are the **pike, wells catfish** and the only freshwater representative of the cod family, **burbot**. Every spring the sturgeons, a globally threatened group of fish, come to the Bulgarian stretch of the river for spawning. These extremely interesting, large, primitive fish spend most of their life in the Black Sea. Overfished because of their caviar and meat, they are now on the edge of extinction. The most typical among them is the **Beluga sturgeon**. The lifespan of this fish is more than 50–60 years and it can grow to more than 4m and 1,000kg, which makes it the biggest freshwater fish in Europe. At the other extreme is the very small but equally interesting Danubian fish, **Bulgarian loach** (*Sabanejewia bulgarica*), an endemic species for this region. There are some other Balkan endemic fish in Bulgaria: **Struma loach** (typical only for the rivers Struma and Mesta), **dark vimba, Vardar nase** and some others. The upper parts of the rivers, in the mountain areas, are inhabited by an interesting complex of rheophilic species including **brown trout, bullhead, stone loach, small gudgeon** and **golden loach**.

Amphibians and reptiles A total of 18 species of amphibians can be found here. They include five species of newt, the most numerous of which is the **common newt**. The **Alpine newt** is hard to find, because it is a glacial relict species, distributed only in the higher parts of the mountains in the country. The **fire salamander** is also a widespread species, especially in the deciduous forests. It can often be seen crossing the roads after rain.

A great diversity of frogs and toads – a total of 12 species – makes the wetlands in the country quite a noisy place during the spawning period. The biggest of them, the **common toad**, is mainly nocturnal and is widespread, but more numerous is the **green toad**, often found even in cities. Both species can be found quite a long way from water. An interesting species, which lives in the sandy areas in the lowlands of Bulgaria, is the **eastern spadefoot**, distributed only in the eastern and southern Balkans. The smallest representatives of the group of amphibians are the **fire-bellied toad**, which lives in low-lying areas, and **yellow-bellied toad**, found in more upland areas. Both are very small, usually under 4cm in length, with a dark back and bright spotted belly. Another small but very noisy species is the **European tree frog**. It lives all over the country, sometimes a long way from water bodies, where it spawns. It is not difficult to find this species – just follow its loud song. It is amazing how such a small creature can produce such a sound. The most common amphibian in Bulgaria is the **marsh frog**, which lives and makes 'concerts' in almost every area with open water. Their croaking is the usual background sound in the countryside.

The geographical position of Bulgaria and its highly varied relief determine the diversity of reptiles in the country. A total of 37 species can be found, making Bulgarian herpetofauna one of the richest in Europe.

A typical inhabitant of the wetlands in the country is the **European pond terrapin**, though the **Balkan terrapin** can be found only in the extreme south. Both species are shy but can sometimes be observed sunbathing on some floating objects or on the banks. There are also two species of tortoises roaming the lowlands of Bulgaria: **Hermann's tortoise** and the **spur-thighed tortoise**. Although they can be found anywhere in the country, their populations are decreasing and now they are both strictly protected.

There is also a wide diversity of lizards: gecko, skink, limbless lizards and lacertids. **Kotschy's gecko**, a typical species in southeast Europe, can be found in many places in Bulgaria, especially in the south and always close to people, in cities and villages. It usually creeps up the walls of the houses, hunting insects attracted by the house lights. The only skink species in Bulgaria, the **snake-eyed skink**, is widely distributed in the lower parts of the country. The snakelike **European glass lizard** is the most unusual and bizarre creature among this group; it is a heavy-bodied, legless lizard with a prominent groove on each side of the body and yellowish to brown colouring, which can be up to 140cm long. It is usually found close to the Black Sea coast. There are a total of nine lacertid lizards in Bulgaria, the most common among them being the **green lizard** and the **wall lizard**, but the most interesting being the **snake-eyed lacertid**, distributed in just a few localities in the extreme south part of the Eastern Rhodopes.

Bulgaria is one of the richest countries in Europe for snakes, being home to 18 species including four vipers. The **sand boa**, the only boa species in Europe, can be found in Bulgaria, in sandy areas of the southernmost lowlands. Most of the time it hides in the sand or under big stones, so visitors need to be lucky to see it. The same applies to another peculiar species, the **worm snake**. This is the smallest snake in Bulgaria (about 20–30cm), with a slender cylindrical body, very small eyes on the top of the head, and scales underneath. It eats mainly ants and their larvae. There are 12 species of colubrids, the biggest snake group in Bulgaria. The most common among them are the **dice snake** and the **grass snake**, both associated with water but which can sometimes be seen a long way from wetlands or rivers. They can often be seen warming their bodies on riverbanks or swimming gently on the surface of the water. The dice snake is primarily a fish eater while the grass snake mainly hunts frogs. The biggest snake in Bulgaria, the **large whip snake**, can be more than 2m in length. It is common everywhere except in the mountains. The **leopard snake** is probably the most beautiful snake in Europe; lucky visitors might see it in the southern Struma River Valley, especially in Kresna Gorge. There are two colubrid species in Bulgaria which are poisonous: the **Montpellier snake** and the **cat snake**. However, both of them are harmless to people because the venom fangs are at the very back of the upper jaw. The really venomous snakes are the vipers: the **nose-horned viper** is distributed in the dry lowlands all over the country, while the **adder** is found only in the mountains.

Mammals About 100 species of wild mammals are known to inhabit Bulgaria, some of which are not native, but have adapted well to live here. For example, the **racoon dog** (which has been observed along the Danube River and the Black Sea coast since the 1970s), the **muskrat** (along the Danube River) and **coypu** (most numerous on the Black Sea coast and the Maritza and Tundzha rivers). Other mammals, such as the **fallow deer** and the **mufflon**, have been introduced into the country, but their existence here depends on human help.

The insectivores are represented by the **eastern hedgehog** (widely distributed in Bulgaria, often being the main food of the eagle owl), and two species of moles, **common** and **Black Sea**. Of the six species of shrew, the most interesting, and also one of the smallest mammals in the country, is the **pygmy white-toothed**, which occurs in the southeast. With 32 bat species, Bulgaria is one of the richest countries in Europe. Very stable populations consisting of thousands of bats live in the caves of the Rhodope and Balkan mountains.

What about the lagomorphs? It is possible to see two species: during the 1930s the **rabbit** was introduced but it occurs only on St John Island near Sozopol, and the **brown hare**, which is distributed throughout the country.

The **red squirrel** and **European suslik**, the main prey of imperial eagle and long-legged buzzard, represent Sciuridae. When it comes to rodents, there are five species of Gliridae, 11 species of Muridae, three of Cricetidae and eight of Arvilolidae, as well as the **southern birch mouse** (Zapodidae) and the **lesser mole** (Spalacidae).

Sixteen species of carnivore occur in Bulgaria: the **wolf** (Canidae, four species) is concentrated in the mountains and in the forests of the northeast; the **brown bear** (Ursidae) can be found in Rila, Pirin, Central Balkan and Western Rhodopes; the **badger**, **otter** (rare), **weasel**, **western polecat** and **beech marten** (all Mustelidae) are common throughout, while other Mustelidae, the **marbled polecat** and **pine marten** are only found in the mountains; the **wild cat** (Felidae) is widespread, but the **lynx** was thought to be extinct, though some footprints have been found and many sightings have been reported during the last couple of years.

Artiodactyls are represented by **wild boar** (Suidae) and **red**, **fallow** and **roe deer** (Cervidae). There are four species of Bovidae: **European bison** (about 50–60 individuals in Razgrad region), **mufflon**, **Alpine ibex** (several individuals in the Rila Mountains) and **chamois** (Rila, Pirin, Rhodopes and Stara Planina). The Odonceti are represented by two dolphins: **common** and **bottle-nosed**. The member of the Phocoenidae family distributed in the Bulgarian Black Sea is the **porpoise**. No **Mediterranean monk seal** has been observed since the 1990s.

NATIONAL PARKS, RESERVES AND OTHER PROTECTED AREAS IN BULGARIA There are six categories of protected areas in Bulgaria: strict reserves, national parks, managed reserves, nature parks, protected sites and natural monuments. In **strict reserves** you can walk only on the specially marked paths. There are also quite strict rules in the large territories of the **national parks** (Central Balkan, Rila and Pirin), while in the **managed reserves** various activities are possible, provided they maintain or improve the conditions of the wildlife under protection there. The **nature parks** (11 in total) are among the largest protected areas in the country and have a relatively 'soft' regime. All traditional and sustainable economic activities are allowed, though large-scale activities such as opencast mining or huge dams are not permitted. In many cases they are examples of the coexistence of the wise use of resources along with biodiversity conservation. The **protected sites** usually preserve something specific: important bird colonies such as the Poda and Pomorie Lake protected sites, or wintering sites of waterfowl as at Durankulak and Shabla lakes. The **natural monuments** preserve unique rock formations such as the Melnik Pyramids and Trigrad Gorge, and also the numerous caves, which occur in many areas of the country. Usually every protected area is marked with special information panels in both Bulgarian and English, giving details of the name, territory, status and biological elements of the site. There is no legal requirement to have permission to visit a protected area, but where there are marked paths in the reserves you must follow them. Other entrance requirements, if any, may be shown on information panels at the site.

NATURE CONSERVATION ORGANISATIONS The first biodiversity conservation organisation was the **Bulgarian Society for the Protection of Birds (BSPB)** (*BG-1111, Sofia, PO Box 50;* \ *02 9799500;* e *bspb_hq@bspb.org; www.bspb. org*) established in 1988. This is the National Partner for Bulgaria of **BirdLife International** (*Wellbrook Ct, Girton Rd, Cambridge CB3 0NA;* \ *01223 277318;* e *birdlife@birdlife.org; www.birdlife.org*), an international organisation uniting the strongest bird conservation organisations in over 110 countries throughout the world. Since 1992 it has actively contributed to the development of modern nature conservation with finance, experience and logistical support. By strengthening BSPB, BirdLife has built the basis for the long-term and sustainable preservation of birds, Important Bird Areas (and through them, other wildlife) and the habitats. Among the most significant achievements is the introduction in Bulgaria of the most contemporary conservation approaches, such as the Species Action plans, Important Bird Areas concept, Habitat Conservation strategies and others.

Despite its name, BSPB works for the preservation of wildlife as a whole. It has activities for the preservation of forests, rivers and other wetlands, wet meadows, and mountain areas with all their biodiversity, including preservation of tortoises, otters, susliks and even some rare plants. BSPB is very active in conservation education, public awareness and ecotourism as a way to promote more careful attitudes towards nature. BSPB and Green Balkans (see below) were authorised by the government to identify and prepare the documentation for the Bulgarian part of the EU ecological network Natura 2000 under the EU Bird Directive, which includes the most significant bird areas in the country.

Green Balkans is also active in biodiversity conservation (\ *032 626977;* e *office@ greenbalkans.org; www.greenbalkans.org*). Its main activities are connected with the conservation of different species of birds, mammals (bats and marine mammals) and their habitats, forests, wetlands and grassland. Successful reintroduction projects have been implemented for vultures and lesser kestrels that were extinct in

1

Bulgaria. Green Balkans operates the only Wildlife Rescue Centre in the country, based at Stara Zagora. The organisation is active in the designation of protected areas and the development of management plans. Programmes for environmental education and public awareness are also carried out, including running the state-of-the-art Pomorie Lake visitor centre.

Balkani Wildlife Society (✆ *02 9631470;* e *office@balkani.org; www.balkani. org*) concentrates mainly on the conservation of particular species (for example, the wolf) and sites (Dragoman Marsh, western Balkans), but also co-operates with other NGOs in campaigns, for example on Natura 2000 issues.

Another active organisation working mainly in southwest Bulgaria and the eastern Balkans is the **Fund for the Wild Flora and Fauna** (e *pirin@fwff.org; www. fwff.org*). Its main activities are directed at minimising the conflict between the sheep breeders and some large predators (for example, the wolf), reducing the use of poisons and vulture conservation.

Birds of Prey Protection Society (✆ *02 9634037;* e *bpps@abv.bg; www.bpps.org*) is a small organisation dealing with specific issues regarding the conservation of some raptor species (such as artificial up-feeding and nest guarding) in the country, and is also active in the western Balkans.

Bulgarian Biodiversity Foundation (✆ *02 9316183;* e *bbf@biodiversity.bg; www. bbf.biodiversity.bg*) is a Swiss-funded organisation supporting the conservation activities of different NGOs, student groups and others.

NATURE CONSERVATION EVENTS In Bulgaria there are several national events connected with birds. In January every year the **Mid-Winter Census of Waterfowl** takes place. It is organised by BSPB and Green Balkans and for several days around 15 January all the wetlands in the country are visited and the birds there are counted. This is part of an international waterfowl monitoring scheme, intended to note any changes in the state of the birds (especially the rare ones), and also of the wetlands. The event is traditionally covered very well by the media.

The **International Wetlands Day** is celebrated on 2 February with events for school students, visits to some wetlands and media broadcasts about their importance. Every 1 April is celebrated as the **Day of Birds** with some media broadcasts, using birds as a way to attract public attention to nature conservation issues.

International Bat Night (last weekend in August) has in recent years become a regular occasion, raising public awareness. It usually takes the form of a series of events in towns nationwide.

Once every five years, over the first weekend of October, the BSPB organises, under the BirdLife International initiative, the national section of the **World Birdwatch** festival, and in the other years the Bulgarian section of the **European Birdwatch** festival. It has already become a tradition to organise a set of public events (birdwatching excursions, children's performances and competitions, 'bird' desks in the parks and squares, for example), and these activities are very well covered by the media. It is exciting that similar events are organised at the same time in most of the countries of the world or Europe by the other BirdLife Partners, and a common list of the birds observed during these days is prepared every year.

ARCHAEOLOGY

The Balkan Peninsula has always been a crossroads of different civilisations because of its location. The mild climate and the opportunities for agriculture near the rivers, the plentiful wildlife in the forests, and the natural hills, suitable for fortified settlements, were always the requirements for a good and secure life in ancient times. This is the reason why nowadays in Bulgaria there are so many preserved monuments representing almost every stage of human progress.

The first signs of settlements and necropolises date from the Neolithic Age, approximately 6000BC. From the following Eneolithic Age, around 4400–4100BC, dates the oldest worked gold in the world, which was found in the famous necropolis of Varna. The Bronze Age (3500–1100BC) introduced the use of metal and left rich and varied archaeological evidence. In the subsequent Iron Age, influenced by neighbouring Greeks and Scythians, a monumental style of architecture developed.

So, who were the inhabitants of the modern Bulgarian lands? Most probably, they were the mysterious Thracians. Archaeologists still debate whether they originated here or whether they moved to the region later. One fact is certain: from them we have inherited an extremely rich and developed culture. Nowadays, every archaeological season uncovers more and more Thracian treasures – monolithic tombs, temples, necropolises and sometimes even whole towns. Furthermore, many gold and other valuable objects have been found, some of them locally produced, and some imported through trade.

The biggest problem in understanding the culture and the history of the Thracians is the fact that their language is still undecipherable. The sources of information available to us are all Greek, such as Herodotus, and Homer's *The Iliad* and *The Odyssey*. After the 7th century BC, Greek influence increased and contacts between Greeks and Thracians became even closer, with the establishment of the Greek colonies on the Black Sea coast. The most important were Apollonia Pontica (Sozopol), Messambria (Nesebur) and Odessos (Varna). In some parts of these modern towns you can still see some architectural details preserved, and there are expositions in many museums with contemporary artefacts. From this period onward we know more about the existence of different Thracian tribes and kingdoms and the relationships between them and the Greeks. The most famous example is the Kingdom of the Odrysae, which was powerful around the time of Alexander the Great. Sevtopolis, situated near the modern town of Kazanluk, was the capital of this kingdom, but unfortunately today it is covered with the waters of Koprinka reservoir.

Recent excavations show another side of Thracian life. It seems that the valley near Kazanluk was chosen as a necropolis for the Thracian kings and aristocrats, probably the Odrysae. Numerous tombs and rich graves have been discovered, usually covered by earth mounds of varying sizes. The tombs are massive architectural constructions, sometimes decorated with colourful wall paintings. One of the most impressive and famous of these is the Kazanluk tomb, an exact copy of which is available to visit. Some of the other tombs in the region which are also open for visitors are: Golyamata Kosmatka, Ostrusha, Shushmanets, Golyama Arsenalka, Helvetia and Griphonite: the last five can be visited after a prior request; the tomb of Muglizh was studied and the artefacts are exhibited in the local history museum. In other parts of the country similar tombs have been excavated, the most spectacular of which are Sveshtari (UNESCO site), Starosel and Mezek. The findings include unique items of gold and silver jewellery, metal and ceramic vessels, weapons and armour. Some of these are displayed in the National History Museum, the Archaeological Museum in Sofia and the Kazanluk Museum.

In the 1st century BC the modern Bulgarian lands became part of the Roman Empire and the process of Romanisation of the Thracian lands began. Many Roman towns were founded on the sites of old settlements while others were completely new. That is why in the centres of most large Bulgarian towns, such as Sofia, Plovdiv,

Stara Zagora and Varna, Roman remains can be found. The Danube border was of particular importance to the empire, as it was a vital defence against the barbarians coming from the north and northeast. This was the reason for the numerous military camps along the river such as Eskus at Gigen village, Ratiaria at Archar, Novae near Svishtov and Durostorum at Silistra.

The road links in Bulgaria to the other parts of the empire were particularly important for the Romans. In the interior part of Thrace, for example, was the main road from central Europe to Asia Minor: the Via Diagonalis, which went from Sigidunum (Belgrade) via Naisos (Nis), Serdika (Sofia) and Filipopolis (Plovdiv) to Byzantium (Istanbul).

The Byzantine Empire succeeded the Romans, and barbarian invasions continued to be a serious problem for this border zone of the empire, even though most of the barbarian tribes only crossed through the region. In the 5th and 6th centuries AD the Slavs arrived, followed, in AD681, by the Proto-Bulgarians, who eventually united with the majority of the Slav tribes and founded the First Bulgarian Kingdom. From this time on, a new culture with its own architectural traditions developed, although until the Ottoman conquest in 1396 it was mainly influenced by Byzantine trends. After their conversion to Christianity in the 9th century the Bulgarians began an intensive process of church building. The old town on the Nesebur Peninsula is an excellent example, with nine churches built between the 5th and 14th centuries still in a well-preserved state. From the establishment of their state until the time of the Ottoman invasion, Bulgaria had four capitals in succession, Pliska, Preslav, Ohrid (in present-day Macedonia) and Veliko Turnovo, all of them of great architectural interest to visitors.

BRIEF CHRONOLOGY

6000BC	Evidence of Neolithic sites.
3000BC	Thracians settle in the whole region.
7th century BC	Greek settlements on the coast.
AD50	Thrace becomes a Roman province.
5th century AD	Slav tribes begin to settle here.
7th century AD	The Bulgars arrive.
681	The First Bulgarian Kingdom is established by Khan Asparuh.
855	The Bulgarian alphabet is devised.
865	Christianity is adopted as the official religion.
1018	Bulgaria is defeated by the Byzantine Empire.
1185	Establishment of the Second Bulgarian Kingdom.
1396	Bulgaria becomes part of the Ottoman Empire.
1762	Beginnings of Bulgarian National Revival.
1876	The April Uprising.
1877–78	The Russo-Turkish War.
1878	**March:** the Treaty of San Stefano.
	July: the Treaty of Berlin.
1879	Sofia becomes the capital of the new country, with Aleksandur Batenberg its ruler.
1885	Unification with Eastern Rumelia.
1887	Prince Ferdinand of Saxe-Coburg-Gotha becomes new ruler.
1908	Declaration of independence from Ottoman rule.
1912	First Balkan War.
1913	Second Balkan War.

1915	Bulgaria joins World War I on German side.
1918	Ferdinand abdicates in favour of his son, Boris.
1919	Punitive Treaty of Neuilly.
1941	Bulgaria joins World War II on German side.
1943	Boris dies and is succeeded by his son, Simeon.
1944	Fatherland Front takes control in Sofia.
1945	The Bulgarian Communist Party wins elections.
1946	The republic is established after a referendum on monarchy.
1954	Todor Zhivkov becomes First Secretary of the Bulgarian Communist Party.
1989	Zhivkov is deposed.
1996	Economic crisis.
1997	UDF (Union of Democratic Forces) government and IMF stabilise the economic situation.
2001	Surprise electoral victory for Simeon Saxe-Coburg-Gotha.
2004	Bulgaria joins NATO.
2007	Bulgaria joins EU.
2014	Plovdiv is chosen as European Capital of Culture for 2019.

HISTORY

NEOLITHIC AND THRACIAN BEGINNINGS Archaeologists estimate that present-day Bulgaria was inhabited in Neolithic times, around the 6th millennium BC. Much more is known about the new wave of settlers, the Thracians, who probably arrived about the 2nd millennium BC. It seems that theirs was already a highly developed civilisation; they were horsemen and warriors, vine-growers and winemakers, and recent discoveries of gold treasures indicate that their metalworking skills were very advanced.

From about the 7th century BC the **Greeks** began trading with the Thracians and settling at a few places on the Black Sea coast: present-day Nesebur, Sozopol, Varna and Balchik, for example. The situation was fluid, and there were incursions by powerful neighbours, the **Persians** and the **Macedonians**, but eventually Thrace became a **Roman** province around AD50. The Romans built towns and strongholds, particularly along their northern frontier, the Danube. The empire was always under threat from the north, and even its division into two more manageable halves, with the eastern part being ruled from Constantinople, only delayed, but could not prevent, its fall.

THE SLAVS AND BULGARS ARRIVE Into the power vacuum newcomers arrived, the Slavs. They came from the north and seem to have been numerous enough to absorb the Thracians. They were peaceful settlers, farmers rather than fighters. They were soon followed by the Bulgars, or Proto-Bulgarians, who probably originated in Asia. They were a nomadic people and powerful warriors who, in the middle of the 7th century AD, united and established their kingdom, recognised by Byzantium and named Great Bulgaria. It spread from the Kuban in the east to the rivers Donets and Dnieper in the north and west and to the Sea of Azov and the Black Sea in the south. Later their kingdom was attacked by the Khazars and disintegrated. One of the Bulgarian tribes, under the leadership of Khan Asparuh, crossed the Danube into the Dobrudzha area. They made a union with seven Slavic tribes and, after victorious battles over Byzantium, the newly formed Bulgarian kingdom was recognised. In the melting pot, the military energy and superiority of the Bulgars was absorbed by the Slavs, whose language also prevailed. However, the name of the Bulgars was retained.

THE FIRST AND SECOND BULGARIAN KINGDOMS Their position of strength allowed the Bulgarians to negotiate a peace treaty with the Byzantine Empire and led to the foundation of the First Bulgarian Kingdom in AD681. This kingdom was independent of Byzantium and occupied the land between the Balkan range and the Carpathian Mountains, with its capital at Pliska. Under Tsar Simeon (AD893–927) it reached its greatest size and was known as the 'Kingdom of the Three Seas', because it bordered the Black, Aegean and Adriatic seas.

In the 9th century Khan Boris I converted to **Christianity** and subsequent rulers were known as tsars, following the Byzantine tradition. Around this time, two monks, Kiril and Metodii, devised an alphabet better suited to the sounds of the Bulgarian language; it was thought that this would help to develop national unity and hasten the expansion of Christianity as the official religion. It would have the additional benefit of reducing Byzantine religious influence. Indeed, it proved to be the basis for a great cultural flowering.

A new and magnificent capital was constructed at Preslav, but, with Tsar Simeon's expansion to the west, Ohrid (in present-day Macedonia) became the second and very important centre of religion and culture. Within a hundred years the Bulgarian Kingdom had been defeated militarily by its old rival, the **Byzantine Empire**, and made a Byzantine province. However, Byzantium also had its problems, both internal and from external attacks across the Danube, and the Bulgarians were able eventually to break away again, in 1185 under the leadership of the brothers Petur and Asen. This Second Bulgarian Kingdom lasted for more than 200 years and became, once more, the strongest state in southeast Europe, regaining its borders on the three seas. The capital was established at Veliko Turnovo, and the splendour and magnificence of the former capitals was once again achieved.

The Second Kingdom suffered frequent attacks by **Tatars** from the north, which, together with internal difficulties, eventually weakened it so that when the Ottoman Turks arrived they proved unstoppable. Five centuries as part of a Muslim empire began. However, there was plenty of resilience in the Bulgarians, and their religion, customs and culture survived even this.

THE OTTOMAN YOKE The Ottoman Empire ruled an enormous territory, which at different stages reached the gates of Vienna, the Pyramids, the Holy Land, the Persian Gulf, the Caspian Sea, Sudan, Yemen and Ukraine. It enslaved and heavily taxed its conquests and stamped out resistance with punitive massacres. Only really remote areas avoided its heavy presence. The powerful were stripped of their property; the church was put under the control of the Greek Orthodox Church so that Bulgarian was no longer the language of religion; and the educated, such as monks and scribes, were massacred or else fled to avoid such a fate. It was left to the monasteries and remote villages to remember that they were Bulgarians.

The country was effectively isolated from Europe and reduced to a condition of **serfdom**; the Turks referred to the Christians as *raya* (the herd). One possible escape was to convert to Islam and some, particularly in the Rhodope mountain villages, did so. One major advantage was not to be subject to the blood tax. For this the Turks forcibly recruited young males (one boy in five) from all over the empire, converted them to Islam and trained them to be fiercely loyal administrators and soldiers known as janissaries.

The geographic position of the Bulgarians meant that they suffered the worst fate, as they were conquered first and were the last of the Balkan countries to win their freedom. A weakening Ottoman Empire might ignore some loss of influence in Montenegro, Serbia or Greece, but Bulgaria was on the doorstep and needed to remain under control. Of course, there were **uprisings** whenever the Turks lost a significant battle, but they were always swiftly suppressed. There were, however, long periods of comparative stability when local Bulgarians, especially in mountain regions, won some privileges in exchange for some responsibilities.

THE NATIONAL REVIVAL One of the triggers for the eventual **National Revival** did indeed come from the church, as in 1762 the monk **Paisii** wrote and circulated a history of the Bulgarian people, which was a reminder of their past glories. By the 1840s the provision of education was spreading and in 1870 the **Bulgarian Exarchate** was granted, allowing an autonomous church. This encouraged the hope of eventual political freedom, too. Throughout the 19th century there was a gradual weakening of central control in the empire.

After the Crimean War, the French and British extracted promises from the Turks that the Ottoman Empire would be opened up to European trade. The new Bulgarian middle classes who benefited from this trade, led the movement for religious freedom, endowed schools and sponsored the architects and the artists who built the beautiful houses and churches of the National Revival.

In the 19th century there was a movement known as **Panslavism**, which Russians perceived as a natural empathy between fellow Slavs and a willingness by them to protect their oppressed brothers, particularly those in the Ottoman Empire. Other great powers were suspicious of this altruism, imagining Panslavism to be a sort of Trojan horse through which Russia would extend its influence in the Balkans. When the Turks refused to allow Russia to protect Christians in the Ottoman

VASIL LEVSKI

Vasil Levski was born Vasil Ivanov Kunchov in Karlovo in 1837. He studied in Karlovo and Stara Zagora and he gave his vows as a monk in 1858. He became Deacon Ignatii in 1861. Though he considered both medicine and the priesthood, he decided to dedicate himself to the fight for liberation. He joined Rakovski's Bulgarian legion (see box, page 183) and, after it disbanded, he took refuge in Romania together with fellow revolutionary Hristo Botev, living in poverty and almost starving (see box, page 143). He took part in several actions against the Turks, including the unsuccessful one in 1867. He was nicknamed Levski (the Lion) for his bravery.

He realised that these raids hardly bothered the Turks, nor did they arouse local support. He therefore concluded that a core of sympathisers had to be created in Bulgaria itself and set himself and others the task of building this support. They began in 1868, funded by Bulgarian merchants in Bucharest. They were often assisted at monasteries, where they could rely on shelter and support. They did succeed in building a strong network of activists, but unfortunately one member decided to raise funds by a bungled raid on a post wagon, and when captured revealed everything in the hope of saving himself. There were many arrests, among them Levski, who was hanged in Sofia in 1873, several years before Bulgaria became free. He remains one of the country's most popular heroes, and is always described as the Apostle for Freedom.

Empire the Crimean War was sparked off. Britain, France and Austria supported Turkey, now universally known as the 'Sick Man of Europe'. Russia's defeat in the war did not slow Bulgarian aspirations and, urged on by an increasingly active group of revolutionaries, they finally rose in rebellion in 1876.

THE APRIL UPRISING OF 1876 AND ITS AFTERMATH The members of the **Bulgarian Revolutionary Central Committee** established by Vasil Levski believed that guerrilla-style action would either rouse the whole nation or attract the military support of Serbia or Russia. There were intensive practical preparations: uniforms were sewn and homemade cannons constructed. However, a spy who infiltrated one of the final meetings revealed the plans to the Ottoman authorities who went to **Koprivshtitsa** to arrest Kableshkov, the local leader. Learning of his impending arrest, Kableshkov launched the uprising earlier than planned.

In the event, the insurgents were not sufficiently well prepared and their revolution was short-lived, but the ferocity with which it was suppressed by out-of-control irregular Muslim armed troops shocked the whole of Europe. The decaying empire immediately regained its earlier image of being vicious and repressive. Bulgarian liberation quickly became a cause célèbre, taken up by influential politicians and writers. After an attempt at negotiation with Constantinople had failed, the Russians declared war in April 1877. The Turks were defeated and, in the **Treaty of San Stefano** signed in March 1878, a large independent Bulgarian state was set up. This alarmed the other European powers, who still feared Russian expansion into the Balkans; the Austrians indeed had their own ambitions in this direction.

A new peace conference was called and the resulting treaty of the **Congress of Berlin** divided Bulgaria into three: it completely restored Macedonia and southern Thrace to Turkey; the independent principality of Bulgaria was established to the north of the Balkan Mountains, still owing nominal suzerainty to the Turks and paying an annual tribute to the sultan; and south of the Balkan Mountains, Eastern Rumelia was set up as an autonomous province of the Ottoman Empire.

The Ottoman occupation of half a millennium obviously varied in its severity at different times and in different places; although the conquest and early years imposed a fierce regime, there were more enlightened sultans and there were periods of calm. Historians have given this a name: Pax Ottomanica. By the 19th century the Ottoman Empire was in decline, as its subject peoples were increasingly prosperous and better educated, and ready to throw off the yoke. Weak sultans with little control allowed irregular soldiers to suppress uprisings with violence and cruelty. With these memories fresh in their minds the newly liberated Bulgarians were not ready to concede that the occupation had ever been anything but onerous.

INDEPENDENT BULGARIA The small independent new country was allocated as its new constitutional ruler an unemployed royal, **Aleksandur of Batenberg**. The arrangements of the Treaty of Berlin were not expected to last, as there was a big demand in both Bulgaria and Eastern Rumelia for **unification,** which indeed took place in 1885 and was announced to the world as a *fait accompli*. Russia was offended at not being consulted, but both Britain and Turkey soon recognised the new union. The apparent British volte-face was a result of their realisation that the new Bulgarian state was not as subservient to Russia as they had feared it might be. However, the neighbouring Serbs promptly declared war on Bulgaria, and though the Serbs were quickly defeated, they were rescued when the Austrians threatened to intervene. The Russians also meddled by supporting the kidnap and abdication of Aleksandur, whose failure to consult them about unification still rankled. The

Bulgarians found an alternative ruler, **Prince Ferdinand of Saxe-Coburg-Gotha**, of whom the Russians also initially disapproved.

Opinions about Ferdinand vary – he was often referred to as Foxy Ferdinand, indicating something sly! Although Bulgaria took steps towards becoming a modern state under his rule, it also participated in various disastrous wars. In 1912 Bulgaria allied with Serbia and Greece to reclaim territory lost to the Turks in the Treaty of Berlin. Although they were successful in the battles of the First Balkan War, the victors squabbled over the spoils, and in the Second Balkan War Bulgaria was defeated and lost much of what it had gained.

At the start of **World War I** Bulgaria declared itself neutral, but that neutrality was not to last. Public opinion favoured the British, French and Russian side, but as these countries supported the recent enemy, Serbia, and the Germans made tempting offers of border changes with Macedonia, Bulgaria was drawn into the war on the German side. They were defeated, lost valuable territory and made to pay heavy indemnities. The country was then in such a poor state that in 1918 Ferdinand wisely abdicated in favour of his son Boris. At elections in 1919 the agrarians and communists were the most popular. The **inter-war years** were an unstable period, when the terrorist activities of the **Internal Macedonian Revolutionary Organisation** were at their height. The repression, following a communist bomb attack in Sv Nedelya Church in Sofia in 1925, virtually annihilated all opposition and political life, leaving Boris as a sort of dictator. Communist uprisings were fiercely suppressed and there was severe economic depression, which further increased support for the communists.

Bulgaria remained a monarchy until after World War II, but the only real achievement of Boris's reign was to save Bulgaria's Jews from being sent to death camps.

At the beginning of **World War II**, Bulgaria had once again declared itself neutral, but was wooed into the German camp by the promise of Macedonian territory and the offer of the return of Dobrudzha, which was lost to Romania in the Balkan Wars. The communists were active during the war and ready to move quickly at its end, overthrowing the fascist government in 1944 and the monarchy, by referendum, two years later.

THE PEOPLE'S REPUBLIC From the mid-1950s **Todor Zhivkov** was the Bulgarian leader, and he kept close to the Soviet Union and its policies. The wartime communist leader, Georgi Dimitrov, was honoured with a Lenin-style mausoleum, which was besieged by queues of eager visitors when it was open. Zhivkov was a clever politician who seemed to have a real knack for staying in power. Indeed, in a curious way he was regarded as an avuncular figure and there was never any likelihood of a Ceaucescu-style demise. Possibly the only major political mistake he made was to launch the infamous **name-changing campaign**. This was an attempt to homogenise the country's inhabitants by forcing Turks to adopt Bulgarian names. The campaign resulted in some violence and even deaths and the spectacular departure of over 300,000 ethnic Turks to Turkey in 1984–89, with considerable economic consequences in the countryside.

THE POST-COMMUNIST PERIOD The **Gorbachev** phenomenon caught Zhivkov unawares, and an in-party coup in 1989 replaced him in the hope that this would appease the reformers. He lived out his life under house arrest in the no-doubt considerable comfort of his own home. Despite massive Western interference by financing the right-wing coalition, the socialist successors to the communists won the 1990 elections. However, the situation remained unstable: there were protests and rallies, and tent cities of protesters, and more elections had to be held. The early 1990s were a very hard time economically for Bulgaria and successive governments seemed more concerned with exercising their new political freedom than sorting out the country's economy. The lowest point came in 1996 with massive inflation leading to strikes and demonstrations. Finally action was taken, the IMF became involved, stringent economic measures were taken and eventually economic and hence political stability resulted.

The political surprise of the new millennium was the **landslide victory** of Simeon Saxe-Coburg-Gotha in 2001. The UDF (Union of Democratic Forces) had failed to deliver the long-awaited improvement in living standards, and the BSP (Bulgarian Socialist Party) was still under a cloud from the financial incompetence of the Videnov government forced from office in 1997, so was unable to profit from the disillusion. A new party was likely to succeed, especially if it was seen as untainted by the problems since 1989. Simeon's programme of careful housekeeping and progression towards membership of NATO and the European Union was not particularly innovative but it produced an electoral victory and, with the co-operation of the Turkish party, the Movement for Rights and Freedoms, he had an absolute majority.

Many of those who voted for Simeon did so because they hoped he would set an example of correct behaviour in public life. The disintegration of the communist framework amid astonishing corruption and money-grabbing was an upsetting phenomenon for many. Bulgaria needed and wanted morality in public life, and guidance as to how it could be achieved. The transfer from socialism to capitalism was a massive undertaking, for which no leaders had the right experience. It was in this confused period that shady deals were done and organised crime gained a foothold.

Much was made of Simeon's promise to turn the country round in **800 days**, a pledge which was hedged with more and more ifs and buts as the time for its fruition grew closer. Once again the failure to deliver improved living standards caused a politician's support to vanish, and in 2005 the country slipped back into the comfy old shoe of a Socialist prime minister, Sergei Stanishev, who was young and energetic, and worked in a coalition with some of Simeon's team and the Turkish party. The existing right-wing parties were unimpressive and fragmented.

Into this gap in 2006 came a **new right-wing party** – GERB (Citizens for the European Development of Bulgaria) – led by Boyko Borisov, a karate expert and former bodyguard (including of Simeon). The party quickly became popular and within a year second to the socialists, with 14% approval in opinion polls. It applied for membership of the European People's Party of the EU and was admitted in 2008. By 2009 GERB had won two consecutive elections: Bulgaria's election of MEPs and the election for the National Assembly. Disillusioned by the tripartite coalition of socialists, Simeon's party and the Turkish party, voters placed GERB first, and Borisov formed a minority government supported in Parliament by a right-wing coalition. In 2011 GERB also won the Presidential elections, and at the time of writing (January 2015) its candidate, Rosen Plevneliev, was still in office.

However, the GERB government resigned in February 2013 after nationwide protests. In the following elections GERB still came first but with a reduced majority, so Borisov refused to form a government. The socialists, placed second, took up the challenge and formed a coalition with the support of the Turkish party. In the face of Stanishev's falling popularity, Plamen Oresharski was nominated as Prime Minister. This government quickly lost public trust: ill-judged appointments to office and allegations of behind-the-scenes shady deals and the giving of undue privileges to the Turkish party and its own inner circle led to a summer of continuous (but peaceful) protests. A rift between the coalition partners finally brought the government down in August 2014.

Five governments in under two years have jaded voters and worried investors. The early elections of October 2014 have produced an extremely fragmented Parliament, with a record number of parties entering the National Assembly; GERB won the most seats, but has no absolute majority. Perhaps this indicates a tentative move away from the long-held Bulgarian belief that a big strong hero (Krali Marko, Simeon Saxe-Coburg-Gotha, 'Bate Boyko') will appear to save them. The situation is serious and politicians need to make the next coalition work, as most Bulgarians wish.

GOVERNMENT AND POLITICS

The Republic of Bulgaria is a parliamentary democracy. It is administratively divided into 28 districts (*okrazi*): Blagoevgrad, Burgas, Dobrich, Gabrovo, Haskovo, Kurdzhali, Kyustendil, Lovech, Montana, Pazardzhik, Pernik, Pleven, Plovdiv, Razgrad, Ruse, Shumen, Silistra, Sliven, Smolyan, Sofia City, Sofia District, Stara Zagora, Turgovishte, Varna, Veliko Turnovo, Vidin, Vratsa and Yambol.

The head of state is a president, currently Rosen Plevneliev, the GERB candidate, elected in 2011. A president is directly elected for a five-year term with the right to one re-election. He is both the head of state and commander-in-chief of the armed forces.

The prime minister is the chairman of the Council of Ministers, the executive body of about 20 ministers. The prime minister is chosen from the largest group in Parliament, which usually works with the co-operation of one or more other parties.

A caretaker government between August and October 2014 oversaw early general elections, won by GERB (page 20). The (mega) Ministry for the Economy has now been split and new ministries for Energy and Tourism have been created.

The main parties are GERB (Citizens for the European Development of Bulgaria), a centre-right party founded in 2006 by Boyko Borisov; the socialist BSP; DPS, the Movement for Rights and Freedoms; the new grouping Reformers' Block (RB), a loose election coalition between fragments of former right-wing and nationalist parties; the new populist party Bulgaria Without Censorship (BBC) of Nikolay Barekov; a number of nationalist parties, ranging from the milder VMRO (Inner Macedonian Revolutionary Organisation – a name borrowed from 19th- and early 20th-century movements) to ultra-nationalist Ataka, led by Volen Siderov, which has recently embraced the restoration of closer ties with Russia and the expulsion of large multinational companies from Bulgaria as some of its main policies.

After the elections of October 2014, eight parliamentary groups are represented in the National Assembly: GERB, BSP, DPS, RB, PF (Patriotic Front consists of VMRO and NFSB (National Front for Salvation of Bulgaria) and is part of RB), BBC, Ataka and ABV (a breakaway group from BSP, founded by former Socialist President Georgi Purvanov). NDSV (today meaning National Movement for Stability and Progress), founded by Simeon Saxe-Coburg-Gotha as his vehicle for entry into Bulgaria's politics, has all but disappeared.

The National Assembly or *Narodno Subranie* is a single-chamber parliament. It is housed in a prominent white building in the centre of Sofia, which bears the motto 'Обединението Прави Силата' ('Strength Through Unity'), although unity is not one of the characteristics displayed by its members, who are turbulent and prone

1

to walking out and boycotting proceedings, defecting from one party and setting up another.

The 240 MPs are elected for four-year terms. Parliament makes laws, approves the budget, selects or dismisses prime ministers, declares war, deploys troops outside Bulgaria and ratifies international agreements.

The judicial system has regional, district and appeal courts and a Supreme Court of Cassation. There are also military courts.

The three armed services are Land Forces, Navy and Air Forces. The patron saint of the army is Sv Georgi, who is celebrated on 6 May, which is also the Day of Valour and Bulgarian Army. Bulgarians are rightly proud that, despite their participation in every major war of the last century, they have never lost a flag in conflict, the only army in the world of which this is true.

Since 1989, troop numbers have been steadily reduced (currently about 37,000). Since 2007, all three services are fully professional. A defence co-operation agreement with the United States allows the development of two air bases, a training range and a logistics centre as joint US-Bulgarian facilities.

Since 1992 Bulgaria has been a member of the Council of Europe, and since 2004 a member of NATO and a participant in international peacekeeping exercises. In January 2007 Bulgaria joined the European Union, fulfilling the long-term aims of its various governments throughout the 1990s.

Bulgaria's recent political instability, judicial failings, flagging economy, health-care issues and demographic crisis have rekindled debates about constitutional change, with the idea of a presidential republic being mooted, playing on remnants in the national psyche about the idea of 'strong man' rule.

EU membership seems likely to continue to expand the numbers of young people working abroad. The challenge for all future governments, apart from the obvious ones of improving living standards and fighting crime, will be to give them a good reason to come home.

ECONOMY

The first few years after the changes of 1989 were particularly difficult. The Bulgarian economy had been closely tied to COMECON (the Council for Mutual Economic Assistance, which was the communist equivalent of the Common Market). The loss of this market caused the economy to contract considerably. It is estimated that the standard of living fell by as much as 40%, and that it took over ten years to recover. An additional blow was the imposition of UN sanctions on Yugoslavia and Iraq, two of Bulgaria's trading partners, which had very negative effects on Bulgaria's recovery.

In those early years after 1989, inefficient state firms were no longer propped up financially and many of the enthusiastic but inexperienced new entrepreneurs did not succeed. The birth of capitalism was a painful one for many, and for the elderly, particularly those with no family to support them, it was a catastrophe as prices rose and their pensions shrivelled in value.

In 1994 there was a brief flowering as inflation fell and GDP grew, but the banking system was not yet stable and Bulgaria had no real international support, with the result that 1996 witnessed an economic collapse and the fall of a weak socialist government. This concentrated minds, and economic reforms were put in place and responsible fiscal planning was adopted. Since then macroeconomic stability has been for long periods a consensual cornerstone of government policies. From 2000, public debt was reduced from 70% of GDP to 22.8% in 2006 and 16.3%

in 2010, one of the lowest in the EU today. Average annual growth reached 4.7% before the effects of the Russia–Ukraine gas dispute, which stopped all supplies to Bulgaria in 2009 and caused industrial output to suffer. The global financial crisis hit hard from the second part of that year and has been slow to recover in the years since. Inflation remained low to negative in the year to July 2014.

Transfers from expatriates working abroad reached 1.7 billion leva in 2013 (based on official statistics), making them the number one source of foreign money injection into the Bulgarian economy that year. GDP per capita reached €5,518 in 2013. Exports have helped the economy expand in 2014, with GDP forecast to grow 1.6% in 2014 and over 2% in 2015. However, the war in Ukraine, with US and EU sanctions against Russia, is hitting Bulgarian agriculture, tourism, real estate, the wine industry, exports, investment and new jobs in the South Stream gas pipeline project, with yet another gas crisis looming. These negative external factors, coupled with resilient internal problems, such as corruption, a weak judiciary and the presence of organised crime, are significant challenges facing the Bulgarian economy and society in general. There is hope and a declared determination to improve the absorption of significant EU funding, planned at €16 billion for Bulgaria for the period between 2014 and 2020.

Bulgaria's agricultural products include vegetables, fruits, tobacco, wine, rose oil, livestock, wheat, barley, sunflowers and sugar beet. Industries are electricity, gas and water, food, beverages, machinery and equipment, base metals, chemical products, coke, refined petroleum and nuclear fuel. Export business partners include Italy, Germany, Turkey, Belgium, Greece, the US, the UK and France. The traded commodities are clothing, footwear, iron and steel, machinery and equipment and fuels. Import partners include Germany, Italy, Russia, the UK, Greece, Turkey and France, trading in machinery and equipment, metals and ores, pharmaceuticals, chemicals and plastics, fuels, minerals and raw materials. Minerals such as copper, coal and zinc are important assets.

PEOPLE

The Bulgarian lands have been inhabited by a variety of peoples, and those of today are descended from Thracians, Slavs and Bulgars. They are often dark-haired and dark-eyed, but some are fair and blue-eyed. They are generally peaceful and tolerant, though there is visible discrimination against Roma or gypsies, who are blamed for most petty crimes. There are very few people of African or Asian origin here and so some racial intolerance may be experienced. Overtly gay people are still something of a novelty even in Sofia, and will be treated with some suspicion outside the capital. Relations with the Turkish minority are generally harmonious.

So what are the Bulgarians really like?

It has been said that they live with pleasure and, despite the fact that their lives are often hard, this does seem to be the case. Watch as you walk in the streets. In a city like Sofia with a comparatively small centre you bump into people you know very often. Bulgarians enjoy this enormously; they shake hands, embrace, smile and catch up on the news. Like the Italians, they always try to look good, and they appreciate seeing a pretty girl, a well-dressed woman or a smartly dressed man. When they throw a party, it's a good one; if they eat out they do it in the best style they can afford (or sometimes more than they can afford!). It's a far cry from the oft-quoted remark about the British 'taking their pleasures sadly'.

The Bulgarians can laugh at themselves, and seem to take a perverse pleasure in observing how bad things can get. A visiting wine importer from a British supermarket chain was invited on a VIP inspection of some wineries in the southeast. Despite the best-laid plans of his hosts, who used a private plane to get him as close to the wineries as they could, he soon discovered the strength in depth of Bulgarian pot-holes, and announced that Bulgarian roads were the worst he had ever encountered. Everyone took this as a sort of back-handed compliment and kept delightedly telling everyone else connected with the visit what he had said.

Bulgarian hostesses are noted for their extreme generosity and desire to feed their guests everything they could wish for. So it is wise to temper your expressions of gratitude and enthusiasm, and leave some food on your plate, otherwise the extra helpings will keep coming!

Two anecdotes will introduce you to some Bulgarian characteristics. There is a tendency in Bulgaria to leave arrangements to the last minute, and I mean the last minute. I was staying in Koprivshtitsa before the big folklore festival which takes place every five years. The day before the festival, the roadmen came and laid fresh tarmac on the last 5km of road into the village, and it was still steaming as the first coaches of visitors arrived. At the Kazanluk Rose Festival I met a journalist who had been put in the VIP seats at the front of the stadium – she turned round and showed me proudly three stripes of white paint on the seat of her jeans.

There are a number of well-known Bulgarians: opera singers such as Boris Hristov, Nikolai Ghiaurov, Raina Kabaivanska and Anna Tomova-Sintova have all sung in the world's most famous opera houses. The clarinettist Ivo Papasov is internationally renowned, and a winner of the BBC World Music Award; there is also the musician Theodosii Spassov, who plays the shepherd's pipe (*kaval*); Christo, the eccentric wrapper-upper of buildings; the tennis player Grigor Dimitrov and a host of sports stars in the fields of athletics, ice-dancing, skiing and skating. In 1988 Bulgaria had *ten* Olympic champions at the Seoul games, giving it the rank of eighth in the world. (Yes, it is a while ago, but the English still remember 1966, don't they?)

LANGUAGE

Bulgaria has the unique distinction of being both the first, and currently the only, member of the European Union to use the Cyrillic alphabet. Bulgarians are proud of their alphabet, and have a national holiday celebrating it, the Day of Slavonic Culture and Literacy on 24 May.

The holiday is also known as Cyril and Methodius (Kiril and Metodii) Day after the missionary brothers who devised the Cyrillic alphabet in the 9th century. The purpose was to equip the Bulgarian language with an alphabet to suit it, rather than using the Greek alphabet. Bulgarian was, in fact, the first Slavic language to be written. The possession of a written and spoken language using the same alphabet was one of the earliest ways of developing national identity and unity.

It is a South Slavonic language with similarities to others such as Serbian, Croatian and Russian. There are 30 letters with consistent phonetic pronunciation. The Bulgarians have no equivalent of the dreadful complications of English: bough, cough, dough, enough! Some letters are the same as in English; some only look the same; and others neither look nor sound the same. Even so, if you can make the effort to learn 30 letters, many signs will be immediately comprehensible.

If you feel inspired to learn more than a few phrases, try *Complete Bulgarian* by Michael Holman and Mira Kovatcheva, in the Teach Yourself series, published in 2011. There is a textbook and two helpful audio CDs.

RELIGION

Over 80% of the population are at least nominally Bulgarian Orthodox. The Church was founded in the 9th century but at various times in its history has been subordinate to the Greek Orthodox Church and the Ottoman Empire. The Church played a very important role in the preservation of national consciousness during the Ottoman period and was at the forefront of the National Revival during the 18th and 19th centuries. For this reason it is felt that Bulgarians owe the Church a debt of gratitude, and it was respected even during communist times, when atheist propaganda tried to undermine it. Since 1989 Bulgarians have shown increased interest in religion, or at the very least in the celebration of religious festivals and the sacraments of baptism and marriage. However, they have never been noted for their religious fervour. (Poor people traditionally said a grace before meals, inviting God to their table, but with the cautious proviso: 'Bring your own bread!') There is a growing trend for the newly wealthy to endow churches and monasteries or to pay for their restoration. Confiscated church property has been returned and the option of religious education is available.

If you visit some churches while you are in Bulgaria you will immediately notice quite different rituals taking place. Like Catholics, Orthodox believers cross themselves on entering the church, though the sequence is different and ends at the heart. They then normally buy a few candles and light them before placing them in the candelabras. Those above are for the living, and those below are for the dead. Orthodox visitors also normally go to one or more icons, cross themselves, kiss the icon and sometimes leave a coin or even a flower next to it.

You will see that in most churches there are huge empty spaces where you might expect pews. It is normal to stand for the service, except for the elderly who may sit around the edge or lean against the wall. This is said to be the origin of the phrase, 'the weakest go to the wall'. Some Orthodox services are very long, but it seems to be acceptable to stay for part of them and then leave.

The music is invariably magnificent – just the unaccompanied singing of the priests, sometimes with a choir.

If you are visiting a big church like Sv (*Sveta*, Saint) Nedelya in Sofia on a Saturday, the chances are that you will witness a baptism or a wedding. Babies are baptised naked, and immersed three times in holy water. Afterwards they are dressed in new clothes, provided by their godmother, as a symbol of their new life.

Weddings are very majestic ceremonies: the bride and groom wear crowns which their best man or *kum* symbolically ties together before holding them up to demonstrate the equality of the couple before God. The bridesmaid or *kuma* crosses the rings before they are put on the couple's fingers. A stately perambulation three times around the ceremonial table is made by the bride and groom, then the drinking of wine and breaking of bread completes the marriage.

No-one who has walked about in any Bulgarian town can have failed to see that doors and lampposts have necrologies or death notices pasted on them. These may either be the announcement of a recent death or some anniversary of it: 40 days, a year or any number of years. There are also similar notices in the newspapers. At funerals the coffin is usually open. At the wake, and on many subsequent occasions, it is traditional to pour a little of your drink on the floor in memory of the deceased.

In Bulgaria 12% of the population are Muslims and a small number profess other faiths: Roman Catholicism, Protestantism and Judaism. The Muslims are made up of ethnic Turks, some Roma and Pomaks (Bulgarians who converted to Islam during the Ottoman rule). Some say these were forcible conversions, others that they converted to have an easier life and a few privileges, and that their name comes from the Bulgarian word *pomagam* (to help); as with many historical conundrums there is probably some truth in both explanations. Present-day Muslims are mainly in the northeast, the south and the southeast, with some in Sofia.

Bulgaria's achievement in saving its Jews from the Holocaust, despite being, at that time, allied to Germany, is particularly admirable and has recently been properly acknowledged. The small Jewish community now lives in Sofia, Plovdiv and Ruse, though most emigrated to the new state of Israel when it was set up after World War II.

RELIGIOUS FESTIVALS In a rural country many traditional occasions are connected with the farming year, though these have gradually joined in a sociable coexistence with saint's days and religious festivals. Many are still celebrated, often with local variations and some differences according to whether the old or new style calendar is being followed. Occasionally, in mixed areas like the Rhodopes, when Muslim and Christian festivals are on the same day the festivities are shared too.

Because of this link with farming, many festivals take place around the **winter** and **summer solstices** in December and June, and the vernal equinox in March. Popular wisdom has it that these are the times of pivotal changes in nature and the best times for rites and magic that could influence the harvest.

Though the British tend to think of **Christmas** as coming at the end of the year, Bulgarians believe it signifies the rebirth of the sun, so is in a sense the beginning. Budni Vecher, Christmas Eve, is celebrated as a family. Traditionally a *budnik*, or Yule log, was kept burning all night, fire being the substitute for the sun, which protected the house against evil and sickness. Its ashes were scattered in the fields for fertility and a handful mixed with the seeds for planting.

Christmas fare was set out on hay as a reminder of Christ in the manger and consisted of an uneven number of vegetarian dishes to ensure the following year would provide plentiful harvests. Dishes might include beans, stuffed vine leaves, nuts, grapes, honey and wine. The table would not be cleared in case dead ancestors came and wanted something to eat. Elements of these traditions, mainly the Christmas Eve dinner, are maintained by many families.

Midwives, important assistants in the birth of a new life, are celebrated on 8 January. There are some residuary elements of the Thracian worship of a mother goddess in this. Sv Trifon Zarezan, literally the trimmer of vines, is celebrated on either 1 or 14 February. This too is associated with the Thracian feasts dedicated to Dionysus, and so the tradition is still to celebrate the day for vine-growers and winemakers. Vines are ritually trimmed by a respected winemaker who sprinkles the vine with wine and makes a wreath of the prunings to wear on his hat. Everyone is expected to drink wine to ensure a plentiful harvest.

The **last Sunday before Lent** is also celebrated to mark the end of winter. *Koukeri* (mummers) perform folk plays and make a noisy procession with their clanging bells and ritual dances. The masks they wear are real works of art, made of wood and decorated with feathers and beads. Traditionally, the goat, ram and bull are the oldest designs. Various scenes are played out to ensure fertility and drive away evil spirits.

March is the transitional month between winter and spring, sometimes mild and pleasant, sometimes severe and cold. According to Bulgarian folklore only an old woman could be so changeable, so March is known as **Granny March**, and on her first day one of the most widespread, if not universal, traditions is carried out. To this day Bulgarians give one another a *martenitsa* on 1 March, with the greeting

'Chestita Baba Marta!'('Happy Granny March!'). Originally the mistress of the house made these tokens by twisting red and white threads together, and gave them to everyone. They were believed to help nature to be fruitful, so were traditionally tied around the wrist of the youngest child and on to newborn animals, fruit trees, beehives and vines. They are still seen as a symbol of good wishes and good fortune, and are generally worn until the first stork returns from migration, after which they are variously tied on trees or buried under stones.

St Lazar's Day (Lazarovden) is on the Saturday eight days before Easter; it is an important occasion for girls, signifying their transition from child to young woman. The songs and dances (known as Lazaruvane) are performed at each house in the village by the girls in national dress. This brings good fortune to the household and in return the girls receive small gifts. Traditionally, in the evening, the celebrations culminated in a dance attended by single men and their mothers, who chose the girl they wished to have as a bride and a daughter-in-law.

Palm Sunday, the Sunday before Easter, is called Tsvetnitsa or Vrubnitsa in Bulgaria. The first means the day of flowers, the second the day of the willow tree, and both form part of the rituals. Willow twigs are taken to church to be blessed and then taken home and placed on the family's icon. It is believed they keep the healthy people well and can help to cure the sick. They also protect from evil. In the past, young girls wove wreaths of willow on their heads and young men wore them round their waists to keep them strong. There are many songs about this day, about the young girls planting their gardens and the flowers competing to be the first in bloom so they will be picked for the girls' posies and garlands.

Easter or Velikden ('Great Day') is seen as the main religious holiday. Colouring eggs is one of the prettiest customs: some are just boiled in coloured water, red being the most popular, but others are hand-painted, usually with flowers. In the past, girls gave their chosen young men a painted egg as a love token. Easter is another occasion when a special bread is baked. Traditionally in villages a *horo* was danced at Easter after the long days of Lent when no dancing took place. Nowadays the eggs seem to have become like English children's conkers, and are smashed against each other after the Easter service.

Gergyovden, the day of Sv Georgi, is on 6 May, the beginning of the new year in farming, and traditionally celebrated by eating whole roast lamb. In villages there were rituals connected with the blood sacrifice of the lamb, including making the sign of the cross in lamb's blood on children's foreheads, dancing particular dances and swinging on special swings tied to a green tree. Nowadays the lamb feast is the main event.

Midsummer, Enyovden, is the turning point of the year, when it begins to move back to winter. Herb gatherers believed that herbs had supernatural powers if gathered on Midsummer's Eve but that they shouldn't be gathered at all after that as they were possessed by evil spirits.

The **Dormition of the Holy Virgin**, Ouspenie Bogorodichno, is a major Christian festival on 15 August, though many of the rituals associated with it are pagan. Traditionally, village women dressed in their finest clothes went to church taking bread made from the first flour milled from the new crop, melons, grapes and the first honey of the year. There are obviously some similarities here between the worship of the Virgin Mary and the cult of the Goddess of Fertility and Earth. This was the last major ritual before Christmas.

In addition to these major festivals there are also many **saint's days** celebrated or at least noted, sometimes in connection with the name days that Bulgarians like to celebrate as a kind of additional birthday. Yordanovden (6 January), Todorovden (first Saturday of Lent), Dimitrovden (26 October) and Nikulden (6 December) are just a few examples of these.

Muslim festivals are decided by the lunar calendar so they are not on the same dates each year. Ramadan is the month of daylight abstention from food, water and tobacco, the observance of the fast varying according to individual preferences. It ends with Sheker Bayram, the Sugar Holiday, which as its name implies involves the giving of sweets and presents at a family gathering. Kurban Bayram is another major festival, this time meaning sacrifice. Sheep and goats are ritually slaughtered and then eaten at a feast with dancing. Outdoor picnics and feasts are part of Muslim culture in Bulgaria and sometimes both Christians and Muslims share such occasions informally.

EDUCATION

Bulgarians are noted for their expertise in mathematics, chess and IT, as well as having numerous Mensa members. In international competitions in mathematics they invariably win gold or silver medals. Most attend the state schools which are free, though parents have to buy books and equipment. There are also a small number of fee-paying schools, but for most people these are too expensive. However, private tuition is something parents invest in, mainly in mathematics and Bulgarian language and literature as these are obligatory matriculation exams. There are also private courses which pupils may attend to improve their performance in school and also to gain certificates and qualifications recognised abroad.

Children start school at the age of seven, and are in the primary stage for grades one to four, then the basic stage for grades five to seven, and the secondary stage for grades eight to 12. Most school buildings provide two shifts, with morning children from 08.00 until 13.00 and afternoon children from 13.00 to 18.00.

The standard of academic achievement is high, indicating that so-called old-fashioned teaching methods may actually be superior. A Bulgarian child at a London primary school was regarded as a mathematical genius, his ability being greater than that of children four or five years his senior. When he and his diplomat parents returned to Sofia, they found he was nowhere near the top of the class, even for his own age group!

As in every country, competition to enter one of the top schools is keen, and parents increasingly invest in extra tuition in the hope of their child securing a place. Many children go on to higher education, and nowadays the brightest often study abroad, though many later return home.

Leaving school has for some reason now turned into a major celebration lasting for days, with non-stop partying, drinking and roaring about in cars with horns blaring. Ironically, the same day (24 May) has long been celebrated as the Day of Slavonic Culture and Literacy, though traditionally with rather less gusto!

CULTURE

At the time of its liberation in 1878, Bulgaria had been cut off from the main stream of European culture for half a millennium. Visitors described it as a backward, 'oriental' country. However, a pent-up energy and enthusiasm soon made themselves felt in every sphere.

LITERATURE Literature was in the forefront of the art forms and here there was a lively debate between the supporters of Ivan Vazov, author of Bulgaria's national novel *Under the Yoke*, who thought that critical realism applied to tradition and folklore should be the leitmotif of Bulgarian literature, and a group centred on the magazine *Misul* (*Thought*), including the famous poet Pencho Slaveykov, which was more influenced by western European trends. It was a productive rivalry and the work of poets such as Dimcho Debelyanov and Peyo Yavorov has been published in many countries. However, until recently it was unusual for any contemporary Bulgarian literature to be translated into English, so its authors and poets were little known outside the country. This situation is now changing, due largely to the Elizabeth Kostova Foundation, which has opened up a treasure trove for others to enjoy through its literary events, assistance with translation and its website www. contemporarybulgarianwriters.com.

MUSIC Bulgaria's **opera** singers are world class: Boris Hristov, Nikolai Ghiaurov and Raina Kabaivanska, for example. The country's folk singers have also become well known for their extraordinary rhythms, harmonies and sudden contrasting dissonance, captivating lovers of world music. Folk musicians such as Theodosii Spassov, who plays the shepherd's flute, have taken Bulgarian music all over the world. *Newsweek* described him as a musical ambassador who, through his fusion of the traditional wooden flute and folk music with jazz, and classical music with pop, has created a whole new genre.

Ivo Papasov is the foremost exponent of so-called **Wedding Band Music**, a fast, exciting rhythm in which the dignified clarinet takes on a dramatically different role and produces more notes to the second than you would have thought possible.

The music you are most likely to hear in nightclubs is *chalga*, which combines modern dance beats with Balkan, Gypsy and Middle East rhythms. The lyrics and videos are explicit, and glamorise aggressive men and promiscuous women.

In **classical music**, two generations of the Vladigerov family, Pancho and his son Alexander, have dominated in the spheres of performance and composition. The former's *Vardar Bulgarian Rhapsody* is one of the best-known and best-loved works. A chance encounter at the Riviera Holiday Club with Alexander Vladigerov gave my then eight-year-old son the opportunity to play an (improvised!) piano duet with the famous performer. A third generation of the same family, brothers Alexander and Konstantin, who spell their surname Wladigeroff, are a trumpeter and a pianist, who, with their band, take Balkan jazz around the world.

TRADITIONAL FOLK DANCE AND MUSIC Bulgaria is a country with an ancient, rich musical tradition which was sheltered during the rule of the Ottoman Empire. Since 1945 it has gradually been exposed to pervasive Western influences to the extent that now the only pure folk culture on show for tourists is at festivals such as Koprivshtitsa (every five years), Pirin Sings and Rozhen (annually). In the past the chain dance, *horo*, led by a dancer waving a cloth or other object, was purely a social village-bonding activity usually related to rituals like sowing in spring, when fertility was invoked, or at harvest time, and was often where matches were made – hence the showing-off element. Some dances were in an open crescent, others were performed in a straight line or a closed circle. Many were danced to sung accompaniment, often with the mysterious unique harmonies found in Bulgarian choral work.

A number of dance and choral ensembles, mostly no longer state-funded, exist in many towns and some large villages, as well as in a vulgarised form at Black Sea holiday resorts. Most of these groups depend on devoted choreographers trained at former state academies. Otherwise, at any large social occasion, particularly weddings or public holidays, some local folk dances, possibly played in a very jazzed-up style on electronic keyboards, will be actively participated in by all age groups.

The varied and asymmetrical rhythms found almost exclusively in the Balkan region are echoed by the variety of styles of music and dance in the different ethnic areas of Bulgaria. These are all influenced by neighbouring countries: expect earthy stamping in Dobrudzha, nimble-footed dances in northern Severnyashko, stately movements in the Rhodopes, smooth but powerful action in Thrace, graceful balancing in Pirin, and around Sofia enjoy the manic Shopluk in which dancers seem to hover above the ground while shaking it at pneumatic speed! To learn how to emulate these precise athletics is the study of a lifetime, but is a rewarding way for foreigners to earn great respect from everyday Bulgarians who may barely know one or two local steps.

BULGARIAN NATIONAL COSTUME AND EMBROIDERY

Bulgarian **embroidery** is an intrinsic part of the national costume. It is one of the most significant and brilliant expressions of folk art in the world, striking in its detail, richness of pattern and numerous colour combinations. These skills have been handed down from mother to daughter for many generations. From the age of about six years old a girl was expected to start preparing her trousseau: embroidered dresses, woven blankets, a chemise for her future husband, all to demonstrate her potential as a good wife. From Thracian times examples can be found in wall paintings of women dressed in exquisitely embroidered gowns. Contemporary Bulgarian embroidery is the result of a long and complicated process, enriched to some extent by other, outside influences over the centuries, and reaching its highest point during the National Revival in the 18th and 19th centuries. The borrowed elements and patterns have always been interpreted in a particular Bulgarian way.

Embroidery was a decoration used exclusively on the national costume, particularly for the women. Some embroidery was worked on a man's clothing, especially on costumes worn at festivals, but not to the same extent. Women wore a chemise, *riza*, with its decoration, over which a long, narrow apron would be worn. This developed into a chemise and a *sukhman*, a tunic-like dress, usually sleeveless and with no front opening, worn mainly in the south and central areas, or a *saya*, which is open all the way down and usually has short sleeves, worn mainly in the north. On top of this is an apron worn at the front. The apron has evolved from a long thin garment to a much shorter one. In some parts of the country, mainly in the north, another apron is also worn at the back, and this is very closely pleated. These pleats are pressed in and become permanent. On top of this costume would be worn many additional items of dress including a heavy metal belt to ward off the eagle eye, socks, felt or leather shoes (*tsurvali*), a headscarf and various pieces of jewellery to show off the wealth of the family. There are numerous ways of tying the scarf. Young, single girls might show their hair, but once married the hair was always covered. The headdresses for weddings and festivals are sometimes very elaborate indeed.

The man's costume was originally white, natural wool, but later black (or dark blue or brown) was introduced, and now the white costume is mainly worn in the Sofia region. The shirt would be embroidered at the neck and the cuffs, but the jacket and trousers were decorated with braiding (*gaytan*) along the seams and pockets. The costume would include a red cummerbund, a black lambskin hat (*kalpak*), socks, gaiters and shoes made of ox-hide or pigskin. When out in the fields a long cloak woven from sheep and goats' wool would be worn (the goat hair would make it weatherproof).

The embroidery on the woman's chemise would be concentrated on the sleeves, round the neck, front and hem (the parts that show) on the front of the tunics, and on the front apron. The amount of embroidery varied according to the usage of the costume, the most elaborate being wedding and festival clothes and the least for everyday working clothes. The costume itself denoted the age, and marital and social standing of the wearer. The brightest colours and most flamboyant stitching were reserved for young, single girls, and the colours became progressively darker with the age of the wearer, reaching their most sombre in widowhood.

Embroidery **patterns** are mainly geometrical. They started off as imitations of natural phenomena – flowers, plants, animals, the human body – but over time they became very stylised. Human and animal figures are now almost completely unrecognisable, although occasionally you can glimpse in the pattern a trace of a human figure or a bird (a favourite design and perhaps more easily recognisable). The tree of life (used throughout the world) has great symbolic significance, as does the swastika. Also incorporated into many designs is the national dance (the *horo*) and often the designs along the hem of a chemise represent this dance.

The **material** used varied by region depending on local conditions. Obviously in sheep-rearing areas wool was the cloth most commonly used for *sukhman* and *saya*, but linen or hemp was used for the chemise. A small area in the southwest produced silk, but this was very expensive and used only in small quantities on special costumes, usually as silk thread.

The type of material was not only determined by the region in which the wearer lived, but also by social standing, the wealthier using scarcer resources from other regions, or even imported from other countries by their merchant husbands. Occasionally the costume of a wealthy woman was trimmed with velvet or fur.

The fabric was spun and hand-woven in the home, and the various garments for both men and women were assembled using a single loom-width of cloth. The chemise was folded at the shoulders and slashed at the neck to allow the head to pass through. The sleeves were sewn on at right angles to the body, and various gores and gussets inserted to provide extra width, with maximum usage of material and no waste.

Each region had its main colour scheme, although throughout Bulgaria red is the dominant colour, as this is considered the colour of life, good health and fertility. It is said that Bulgarian women knew of some 300 or 400 colour ranges which could be produced from natural dyes. In the late 19th century aniline dyes were introduced, although spinners and weavers also use traditional, natural dyes. It is the unusual combination of colours that often makes the embroidery so striking. In some areas the pattern is woven into the fabric and embroidery stitches worked over, wool on wool, cotton on cotton, creating a double embellishment.

While each region has its own particular colour and theme which has developed because of the isolation of villages and towns imposed by the mountainous terrain and lack of roads and transport, there are a great many variations within that theme from village to village.

The **stitches** used are very simple: straight stitch, filling, cross, half, running and back stitches, single and double fishbone (herringbone) and split stitch are the main ones used, although there are many variations. Sometimes you come across chain stitch. The straight stitch (filling stitch) is 'trammed' to give a raised effect and often the pattern is outlined with contour stitch to give it emphasis. Pulled and drawn threadwork is also used. With these few simple stitches the Bulgarian embroiderers create an extraordinary variety of intricate designs. Most of the patterns are worked by counting threads and this is quite easily done with the coarse woven linen or *panama*. On the finer material they use an overlay of canvas (*kanava*), which we call waste canvas, of differing thickness, and then pull out the threads after sewing the pattern. This fine *kanava* is used particularly when working on silk, although I have watched women sew without it.

While many costumes are still made and embroidered by hand in the villages, mainly by older women, small workshops still exist in the towns to produce this work, and many women belong to the **Zadruga na Maistorite**, the Bulgarian equivalent of Britain's Embroiderers' Guild. These women might specialise in some particular aspect of needlecraft: embroidery, *kene* (which is the delicate edging on work), braid-making and sewing (*gaytan*), or lacemaking (bobbin, crochet and knitted – at which the Bulgarians excel). I was delighted on my last visit to come across an old woman in a small village spinning with distaff and spindle. She was preparing wool from local sheep to be woven into cloth for a neighbour. Weaving is still done in the home, both on horizontal and vertical looms, and while the traditional patterns and weaves are still being copied, the articles produced are of a more modern concept. On a visit to Etur (the Ethographic Museum near Gabrovo), where all the crafts demonstrated use only water power and traditional tools, I came across an old fulling mill (used to clean and thicken the cloth), a braiding machine workshop and a weaver of goat-hair bags. Here I was able to see the whole of his process, from beating the raw hair with a flail on a board, to spinning and then weaving it into a shepherd's bag, in what is now becoming a dying art.

Although originally embroidery patterns were used exclusively on the national costume and articles associated with festive occasions, nowadays the tradition is carried on in domestic embroidery in the form of tablecloths, cushions and small pieces for use in the home.

There are many excellent ethnographic museums in all the major centres in Bulgaria where examples of regional costumes can be seen. These are well displayed alongside examples of local traditional crafts. The Ethnographic Museum and National History Museum in Sofia both have fine examples of national costumes (pages 93 and 98–100), but in other towns the displays will generally be confined to their particular area. It is invidious to pick out any particular place, but Smolyan's Historical Museum (page 242), with its well-arranged artefacts demonstrating development of the Rhodope region, the National Ethnographic Museum in Pazardzhik (page 227), with its comprehensive display, and the excellent Ethnographic Museum (in a splendid National Revival-period house – page 231) in Plovdiv are all well worth a visit.

CULTURAL TOURISM Cultural tourism specialists will be able to show you Bulgaria from the inside. They want to explore the beauty of Bulgaria with you, and introduce you to the real Bulgaria, a world far removed from the mass tourism market. You can experience colourful local village markets, participate in cultural performances and sample local dishes.

For example, if you take an archaeological tour, focusing on a particular period, specialist tour operators can arrange your participation in excavations. It could be you who makes the next big discovery! These archaeological tours include visits to both well-known and newly excavated sites, guided tours of museums with their unique artefacts, and even meetings with archaeologists.

Trips to caves with evidence of human occupation from the Neolithic to the Bronze Age can be arranged, or, for the more adventurous, cave exploration and expeditions. Walks and hikes to remote holy places, dolmens and ruins are another aspect of such cultural activities.

Bulgaria's nine entries on UNESCO's World Heritage list are obviously the foundation for any cultural tour, and these can be enhanced by visits to monasteries, churches and stone and wooden houses from the Ottoman period and the subsequent National Revival.

Folklore and traditions also make interesting excursions, which are offered all year round, visiting villages where the authentic rituals are still alive. From Christmas to Easter, from the day of Sv Georgi (6 May) to the day of Sv Dimitur (26 October), guests can enjoy the village rituals where the pagan and Christian are mixed in a very charming way. The stories of dragons, fairy tales and witches are still alive.

Tours revealing the ethnic mosaic, the multifaceted life of Bulgaria, are very popular too. Turkish Muslims and Pomaks (Bulgarian Muslims), Roma, Jews, Armenians, Old Believers and Gagauzi (Turkish Christians) all form part of the mixture. These trips can be specially organised on request or be part of other Bulgarian sightseeing tours.

Wine and gourmet tours are increasingly popular. Specialist tour operators keep themselves up to date with the best-quality wines produced in private wine cellars as well as with the best restaurants (established or newly opened), where young chefs will offer delicious food, based on the best of traditional cuisine. For more information on this, see pages 40–1.

2

Practical Information

WHEN TO VISIT

Bulgaria has something to offer all year round. In spring the towns and cities blossom as parks and gardens reawaken and outdoor eating at cafés and restaurants begins again. For nature lovers this is the most spectacular time to come as plants flower and migrant birds return.

The Black Sea coast is the destination of most summer visitors, though increasingly the mountain resorts are attracting people to their new golf courses, as well as to more traditional summer activities such as hiking, biking, climbing and horseriding. The summer is a good time to visit if you enjoy folklore and traditional festivities, as many small towns and villages organise local celebrations. It can be almost too hot for sightseeing in Sofia and Plovdiv in summer, so it's best to time a cultural visit in spring or autumn.

The winter is beautiful in the mountains and Bulgaria has some fine ski resorts. Music lovers might like to visit some of the big cities in winter, as there is a busy programme of operatic and classical performances.

The choice is yours. For a list of public holidays and festivals, see pages 63–5.

SUGGESTED ITINERARIES

If you are only in Bulgaria for a few days, it is best to stay mainly in Sofia with a day or half-day at nearby Boyana.

If you have a week then you could do the same, but add a day trip to Rila Monastery and perhaps a two-day visit to Plovdiv with an overnight stay there.

In a ten-day stay you could expand on this core programme with extra time at Plovdiv to allow a visit to Bachkovo Monastery and a return drive via Koprivshtitsa. The day visit to Rila could become two days with an overnight stay in the southwest to allow a visit to Melnik, Rozhen and Bansko. Or in ten days you could visit Sofia and Plovdiv and then travel to the resorts around Burgas for some relaxation on the beach.

In two weeks you could make a round trip: Sofia, Rila, Plovdiv, Bachkovo, Nesebur and Varna on the coast and return through Veliko Turnovo, Kazanluk and Koprivshtitsa.

Each region has a lot to offer, so you really need a longer stay!

SCENIC ROUTES The following routes are recommended, so try to build them into your travels if you can. I have arranged them according to the chapters in the book. Some of these routes are along minor mountain roads – you really need to use a detailed map for checking your progress. Winter weather plays havoc with the summer-mended pot-holes, so be particularly careful in spring.

Sofia
* Sv Sofia Church – the ancient basilica that gave Sofia its name.
* Sv Aleksandur Nevski Memorial Church – the iconic gold-domed symbol of Sofia.
* Boyana Church – unique medieval art in a mountain setting.
* Vitosha Mountain – Sofia's own mountain!

The Southwest
* Rila Monastery – UNESCO World Heritage listed, colourful guardian of Bulgarian culture and history.
* Pirin National Park – also UNESCO listed, outstandingly beautiful mountains.
* Melnik – a picturesque town, home of the famous wine.

The Northwest
* Belogradchik rock formations – a huge area of fantastic shapes and legends.

Central Stara Planina and the Danube Plain
* Sveshtari (Thracian tombs) – UNESCO-listed, beautiful caryatids.
* Bozhentsi village – a visit to the past, a traditional old village.
* Veliko Turnovo, the former capital – spectacular location and a wealth of historic buildings.
* Arbanasi village – traditional architecture and a church bursting with frescoes!

The Valley of the Roses and Sredna Gora
* Koprivshtitsa (a mountain town) – combines beauty and historical importance.

Plovdiv, the Rhodopes and the Thracian Plain
* Plovdiv Old Town – UNESCO listed, one of the oldest continuously inhabited cities in Europe.
* Bachkovo Monastery – beautiful monastery in a beautiful location.
* Perperikon archaeological site – striking ancient monument in a remote location.
* Chudnite Mostove rock bridges – magnificent creation by nature!
* Madzharovo Nature Reserve – see rare vultures on their home ground.

Strandzha, the Black Sea Coast and Dobrudzha
* Nesebur Peninsula – numerous medieval churches on a tiny peninsula.
* Cape Kaliakra – bird migration, archaeology and legend combined.

The Southwest *Map, page 104*
* Rila Monastery is signed off the main road via Kocherinovo; this is a good road and an attractive one. A quieter approach is to turn off for Rila a little further north at the Boboshevo crossroads. There are fine views of the Struma Valley and across to the sand pyramids at Stob, and then this joins the other route to the monastery. Continue on to Kirilova Polyana, beyond the monastery for more fine mountain views.

- By rail on the Sofia to Kulata route, the stretch from Blagoevgrad to Kresna is particularly attractive. Watch out for bird migration if you are travelling in spring or autumn. This is the Via Aristotelis which crosses the Tisata Reserve and heads south to the Aegean.
- South from Dobrinishte to Gotse Delchev is a beautiful route through the mountains. This is an area rich in legend and history, an old trading route to Drama in Greece and haunt of Macedonian freedom fighters.
- Also in the Gotse Delchev area, the road via Gurmen to unforgettable Kovachevitsa village is worth the drive.
- If you plan to travel east into the Rhodope Mountains, the road from Dupnitsa to Satovcha is on your way, and here you can see Mediterranean-type vegetation and views of the Mesta Valley and Pirin National Park.
- By rail from Dobrinishte or Bansko, the narrow-gauge railway goes at photographers' speed, allowing leisurely views of the three mountain ranges it passes: Rila, Pirin and Rhodope.

The Northwest *Map, page 138*
- The route to Belogradchik via Gavril Genovo and Dolni Lom is very picturesque.
- The route to Berkovitsa over the Petrohan Pass and through the village of Gintsi is a very beautiful drive.
- If you are driving, you can take the scenic route from Lakatnik, north of the Iskur Gorge, to Milanovo, and then on to Vratsa on a minor and very winding road, passing by Vratsata, the rock-climbing cliffs. However, even the main road from Novi Iskur via Lakatnik to Mezdra and on to Vratsa passes through some beautiful northwestern Bulgarian scenery.
- By rail the route from Sofia to Mezdra passes the Lakatnik rocks, the Ritlite at Cherepish, and 23 tunnels as it crosses the Balkan range!

Central Stara Planina and the Danube Plain *Map, page 154*
- From Etropole, the drive east, with a detour to the Etropolski Monastery, to Yamna and Cherni Vit is almost deserted, and offers a chance to see the beautiful Balkan Mountains at close quarters.
- The road from Troyan to Lovech is an attractive drive whichever direction you take it. It follows the gentle Osum River.
- The short side road from Sheremetya, east of Veliko Turnovo, north to Arbanasi, gives wonderful views across to Tsarevets, Trapezitsa and Asenova mahala, and the whole city of Veliko Turnovo.
- Approaching Veliko Turnovo from the north, beside the River Yantra, gives a panoramic view of the city.
- East of Veliko Turnovo a pretty riverside road takes you from Zlataritsa to the lovely small town of Elena. This route can also be followed by rail.

The Valley of the Roses and Sredna Gora *Map, page 198*
- The drive south from Koprivshtitsa to Strelcha shows you the best of the Sredna Gora, with distant views to the Thracian Plain, the Balkan range and even the Rhodopes on a clear day.
- Another short stretch of road with wonderful views is Banya to Pesnopoy, which gives superb views of the Balkan range and the Valley of the Roses.
- By rail from Karlovo to Sofia, the stretch from Rozino to Gara Stryama gives lovely views of Klisura and the major peaks of the Balkans.

- Driving down from Shipka Church to Kazanluk is a very pleasant drive. However, a side route from just north of Shipka, via Buzludzha and the very bendy onward road to Krun, reveals ancient beech forests, wonderful views down to the Valley of the Roses and the Shipka Monastery.
- Further east, from Sliven there is a nice circular route to Karandila above the town; you can go and return by different routes with interesting views.

Plovdiv, the Rhodopes and the Thracian Plain *Map, page 226*

- There are various roads off the old Sofia–Plovdiv road that lead up into the mountains; Sestrimo to Yundola by way of the Belmeken Reservoir is pretty, with spruce and deciduous forests and mountain pastures.
- By rail the narrow-gauge railway mentioned above, under *The Southwest*, starts from Septemvri and goes up into the Pirin Mountains.
- Travelling south from Batak to Dospat you pass four huge reservoirs in a wild and almost deserted forest landscape.
- Another turn off the old Plovdiv road is via Stamboliiski to Krichim and then a scenic drive to the spa town of Devin.
- Travelling south of Devin to Teshel and from there to the fantastic Trigrad Gorge is a wonderful experience; a parallel road from Teshel to the Buinovo Gorge, longer and narrower than Trigrad, is also worthwhile.
- North of Smolyan there is a good road which follows the Shirokolushka River Valley from Stoikite to Devin via the attractive mountain village of Shiroka Luka.
- The road from Luki to the observatory at Rozhen, near Pamporovo, gives lovely panoramic views.
- The railway from Momchilgrad to Podkova (the end of the line) follows the River Varbitsa and gives lovely views of the Eastern Rhodopes.
- Krumovgrad to Ivailovgrad is the archetypal Eastern Rhodope road, with numerous villages and hamlets, broad views, rich wildlife.

Strandzha, the Black Sea Coast and Dobrudzha *Map, page 262*

- The route from Burgas to Malko Turnovo leaves the scenic coastline, crosses a plain and gradually approaches the Strandzha Mountains, passing through two climatic belts with a resulting diversity of vegetation.
- A very pretty route leaves the coast at Tsarevo and passes through big oak forests and the valley of the Veleka River to Malko Turnovo.
- Another possibility is the coastal route from Burgas almost to the edge of Bulgaria at Sinemorets, famous for its wonderful beach; there are coastal reserves, scenic bays and the estuaries of the Ropotamo and Veleka rivers.
- Travelling south from Banya to Sv Vlas gives wonderful views as you descend, to Nesebur, Sunny Beach and Burgas Bay, even as far as Sozopol on a clear day.
- The road from Bulgarevo to Kaliakra crosses an area of steppe with views of almost the whole of the north coast: Balchik, Albena and Golden Sands. This drive can easily be joined on to…
- … Shabla town to Cape Shabla and Bulgaria's oldest lighthouse, then south along the coast to Tyulenovo and Kamen Bryag. The coast here is quite different from other parts, with rugged red rocks and cliffs. Beautiful and (still) quiet.

TOURIST OFFICES

ABROAD Tourist information is currently handled by a department within Bulgarian embassies. They have maps and brochures. Some useful sites are:

www.bulgariatravel.org Official Tourist Portal of Bulgaria.
www.booking.com The best website for booking hotels & private rooms.
www.mybulgaria.info Property, travel & tourism information.
www.hotelsbulgaria.com Online hotel bookings & late deals.

www.sofiacityguide.com Practical information & listings.
www.novinite.com Online daily newspaper in English.
www.travel-bulgaria.com Regularly updated travel information.

IN BULGARIA Coverage is rather patchy, but most places, including some small and remote ones, have a tourist information office. Usually these offices can also advise about private rooms and other accommodation. Most will have free maps and local brochures, while others have booklets for sale.

MAPS

Domino (*www.domino.bg*) maps of Bulgaria and street maps of many towns and cities are excellent and readily available at bookstalls and petrol stations in Bulgaria. There are Cyrillic and Latin versions, and they incorporate lots of useful tourist information and town plans on the reverse. You'll easily pick out their distinctive red covers.

More old-fashioned in presentation, but useful particularly for the series covering mountains and national parks, are the **Kartografiya** maps in Cyrillic.

In addition, **www.bgmaps.com** is a useful website which offers town plans and route searches. It has English and Bulgarian versions.

UK
Blackwells Map and Travel Shop 53 Broad St, Oxford OX1 3BQ; ☎01865 793550; www.blackwell. co.uk
National Map Centre 22–24 Caxton St, London SW1H 0QU; ☎020 7222 2466; www.mapsnmc.co.uk
Stanfords 12–14 Long Acre, London WC2E 9LP; ☎020 7836 1321; 29 Corn St, Bristol BS1 1HT; ☎0117 929 9966; Stanfords Business Services, Suite 302A, Triangle Business Centre, Fennel Street, Exchange Square, Manchester M4 3TR; ☎0845 880 3730; www.stanfords.co.uk

US & CANADA
Globe Corner Bookstore 28 Church St, Cambridge MA 02138; ☎1 800 358 6013; www. globecorner.com

Map Link Inc 30 S La Patera Lane, Unit 5, Santa Barbara, CA 93117; ☎1 800 962 1394; www. maplink.com
Rand McNally Numerous outlets; check the website: www.randmcnally.com or ☎1 800 333 0136
World of Maps 1235 Wellington St, Ottawa, Ontario K1Y 3A3; ☎1 800 214 8524; www. worldofmaps.com

AUSTRALIA & NEW ZEALAND
The Map Shop 6 Peel St, Adelaide; ☎08 8231 2033; www.mapshop.net.au
Mapworld 35 Moorhouse Av, Christchurch 8011; ☎03 374 5399; www.mapworld.co.nz

TOUR OPERATORS

UK
Specialist
ACE Cultural Tours (Association for Cultural Exchange) Stapleford Granary, Bury Road, Stapleford, Cambridge CB22 5BP; ☎01223

841055; e ace@aceculturaltours.co.uk; www. aceculturaltours.co.uk. Monastery tours.
Andante Travels The Clock Tower, Unit 4, Oakridge Office Park, Southampton Road, Whaddon, Salisbury SP5 3HT; ☎01722 713800;

e tours@andantetravels.com; www.
andantetravels.co.uk. Lecture tours of
archaeological sites & medieval monasteries.
Balkania Travel Ltd Avanta Harrow, 79 College
Road, Harrow-on-the-Hill HA1 1BD; 020 7536
9400; e ognian@balkaniatravel.com; www.
balkaniatravel.com. City breaks, short breaks,
special-interest tours (including Taste of Bulgaria
wine tours) & tailor-mades. Tour operator for the
British-Bulgarian Society. See ad, 3rd colour section.
British-Bulgarian Society Postal address as
Balkania Travel above; 020 7237 7616;
e annie.kay@btinternet.com; www.b-bs.org.uk.
Special-interest tours including birdwatching,
flowers, butterflies and moths, natural
history, archaeology, folklore & culture, led by
British & Bulgarian experts. Also tailor-made
arrangements. See ad, page 71.
Exodus Travel Grange Mills, Weir Rd, London
SW12 0NE; 0870 240 5550; www.exodus.co.uk.
Mountain walking & snowshoeing tours.
Explore Worldwide Ltd Nelson House, 55
Victoria Rd, Farnborough, Hants GU14 7PA; 0843
634 6213; www.explore.co.uk. Walking tours.
Limosa Holidays West End Farmhouse,
Chapelfield, Stalham, Norfolk NR12 9EJ; 01692
580623; e enquiries@limosaholidays.co.uk; www.
limosaholidays.co.uk. Birdwatching tours in spring
& autumn.
Regent Holidays (UK) Ltd 6th floor, Colston
Tower, Colston St, Bristol BS1 4XE; 020 7666
1244; e regent@regent-holidays.co.uk; www.
regent-holidays.co.uk. Fly-drive arrangements.

General: beach & ski packages

Balkan Holidays Sofia House, 19 Conduit
St, London W1S 2BH; 020 7543 5555; www.
balkanholidays.co.uk. The widest range of beach &
ski packages, also flight-only deals.
Cosmos Holidays Wren Court, 17 London Rd,
Bromley, Kent BR1 1DE; 0843 227 1464; e mail@
cosmos.co.uk; www.cosmosholidays.co.uk
Crystal Ski Holidays DST House, St Mark's Hill,
Surbiton, Surrey KT6 4BH; 020 3468 3016; www.
crystalski.co.uk
First Choice Holidays Wigmore House, Wigmore
Lane, Luton LU2 9TN; 020 3451 2720; www.
firstchoice.co.uk
Neilson Active Holidays Locksview, Brighton
Marina, Brighton BN2 5HA; 0333 014 3351;
e admin@neilson.com; www.neilson.co.uk

Thomas Cook Unit 17, Coningsby Rd,
Peterborough, Cambs PE3 8SB; 0844 412 5959;
www.thomascook.com
Thomson Holidays Wigmore House, Wigmore
Lane, Luton LU2 9TN; 020 3451 2688; www.
thomson.co.uk

US & CANADA

Adventures Abroad Worldwide Travel 2148–
2080 Westminster Highway, Richmond, BC V6V 2W3
Canada; 1124 Fir Avenue, Blaine WA 98230 USA;
1 800 665 3998 (US & Canada); www.adventures-
abroad.com. One-week tour of highlights.
Avia Voyages Montreal office, 2021 Union, Suite
830, Montreal, Quebec H3A 2S9; 514 284 4400;
www.aviavoyages.ca
Canadian Travel Abroad 1193 Ashland Drive,
Cobourg, ON K9A 5S4; e info@cantravel.ca
Cinderella Travel 97-11 64th Rd, Rego Park, NY
11374; 1 800 821 9223; e juja@cinderella.com;
www.cinderellatravel.com
Glavs Travel 55 W 39th St, #808, New York
10018; 1 212 290 3300; e info@glavs.com;
www.glavs.com

AUSTRALIA & NEW ZEALAND

Adventures Abroad PO Box 812, Round Corner,
NSW 2158, Australia; 1800 147827 (Australia);
0800 800434 (NZ); www.adventures-abroad.
com. One-week tour of highlights.
Eastern Eurotours 1-66 Appel St, Surfers
Paradise, QLD 4217 Australia; 1755 262855
(Australia); www.easterneurotours.com. Flights,
hotels, short breaks & guided tours.

SPECIALIST TOUR OPERATORS IN BULGARIA

Note Bulgarian addresses are written with the
word for street, square or boulevard first, that is
ulitsa (ul), *ploshtad* (pl), and *bulevard* (bul). This is
followed by the name and then the number.

Explorer 2000 bul Evlogi Georgiev 120, Sofia
1505; m 0888 716775; e explorer2000ltd@gmail.
com; www.explorer2000.com. Birdwatching, natural
history & sightseeing tours. See ad, page 33.
Lyuba Tours ul Tsanko Tserkovski 22, Sofia 1164;
02 9633343; e info@lyubatours.com; www.
lyubatours.com. Cultural short breaks, folklore,
archaeology & rural events. Also tailor-made
itineraries.

Odysseia-In/ZigZag Holidays bul Stamboliiski 20; ✆02 9890538; e odysseia@omega.bg; www. hiking-bulgaria.com; ⊕ 09.00–18.30 Mon–Fri & 09.00–17.00 Sat–Sun in summer. These travel agents can arrange accommodation in Sofia & all over the country & advise on rural & activity tourism. They also sell a variety of maps.

ACTIVITY AND SPECIAL-INTEREST HOLIDAYS

HIKING The Rila, Pirin, Rhodope and Balkan ranges are the best destinations for hiking in Bulgaria, with well-marked, well-maintained trails, and accommodation and services for visitors.

Popular starting points for the **Rila Mountains** are Samokov and Borovets, from where Mount Musala (2,925m) can be attempted. Nearby, Govedartsi village and the Malyovitsa area offer good accommodation, making them the preferred base for Mount Malyovitsa, the Seven Rila Lakes, Rila Monastery, Ribni Lakes Hut, Makedonia Hut and Predela Pass. A typical hike from one hut to another takes up to 7 hours along marked footpaths surrounded by beautiful scenery and mountain lakes in all directions.

Beyond Rila, a classic hiking itinerary may extend into the **Pirin Mountains** through Predela Pass, 6 hours from Yavorov Hut, which is a good base for the main ridge of Pirin and Vihren Hut. From here trails lead to Sinanitsa Hut and then continue to Kamenitsa or Popina Luka huts and the towns of Sandanski and Melnik. Another option is to hike to Tevno Ezero Hut, and continue on to Pirin Hut, Rozhen Monastery and Melnik. Good hikes also start from Dobrinishte village to Popovo Lake, the largest high-mountain lake in Bulgaria, from where the Damyanitsa River Valley and Bansko are good alternatives. Pirin's karst ridge is the most attractive scramble in Bulgaria, with sheer drops and dramatic views on both sides. Walking in Pirin is a physical challenge because of its sharp, alpine terrain.

Most of the above-mentioned paths in both mountain ranges are on the **E4** trans-European hiking route.

Alongside the Pirin and Rila mountains lie the **Rhodope Mountains**, normally reached from the city of Plovdiv on the road to Bachkovo Monastery. From the monastery, the path leads to Martsiganitsa Hut, Krustova Gora and the ancient sanctuary of Belintash. Orehovo village, Chudnite Mostove (the wonderful bridges) and Shiroka Luka village is another possible itinerary. Starting from Byala Cherkva past Orehovo village will bring you on the Roman road to Persenk and Izgrev huts and down to the town of Chepelare or to Shiroka Luka village. From Shiroka Luka there are trails heading on to Gela and Trigrad, or Yagodina and Borino villages. Good hiking is also possible in the vicinity of Kovachevitsa village. Walking in the rounded hills of the Rhodopes is less strenuous than in other Bulgarian mountains as there are only moderate altitude differences and high-quality paths or forestry roads.

The **Balkan Mountains** run right across the country; their main ridge is the longest trek in Bulgaria and part of the **E3** trans-European hiking route. It takes at least 20 days to hike the whole ridge, which is exposed to climatic extremes all year round, so be cautious. A significant part of the route passes within the Central Balkan National Park, famous for its rich biodiversity and the best-established network of hiking trails and huts. One suggested itinerary starts from the town of Teteven and continues on to Benkovski, Vezhen, Eho and Kozya Stena huts, then descends to Beklemeto Pass and on to Dermenka and Levski (for the town of Karlovo) huts or continues on to Mount Botev and Pleven or Rai huts. Pleven Hut is an ideal spot to surrender to the conveniences of civilisation

2

in Apriltsi village or continue the ridge walk, resting at Tuzha, Mazalat and Uzana huts along the way to Shipka Pass.

The numerous huts, guesthouses and hospitable family hotels are excellent bases for hiking. Bilingual maps for all Bulgarian mountain ranges at a scale of 1:55,000, as well as guidebooks, have been published. There are hiking maps for Rila, Pirin and the Western Rhodopes. The paths are marked on the map and on the route in the same colour. Mountain huts and villages offering accommodation are also marked. They can be bought from Odysseia-In (page 82), the book market in pl Slaveykov, Sofia, and often at newspaper kiosks in the mountain towns and villages, though it's safer to stock up in Sofia. Professionally trained guides are also available.

BIRDWATCHING, BUTTERFLIES AND PHOTO SAFARIS Bulgaria's rich wildlife is described on pages 5–10. The main areas for observation are the southwest, especially the border regions, the southern mountains of Pirin and the Rhodopes, the Black Sea coast and the various nature parks and reserves. Many companies offer specialised tours (pages 39–41).

CYCLING AND MOUNTAIN BIKING The vast network of paths and mountain roads in Bulgaria is an immense bonus for mountain bikers. Many places in the Balkan, Rhodope and Rila mountains offer bikes to rent. The most popular routes are those connecting high mountain villages. There are two biking maps covering areas in the Central and Western Rhodope Mountains.

GOLF Several golf courses have been created in recent years – those within reach of the capital are the Sv Sofia Golf Club, Pravets Golf Club and the long-established Ihtiman, all to the east of Sofia. To the south, in a picturesque mountain setting at Bansko, is the Pirin Golf and Country Club. The other cluster of golf courses is between Balchik and Kavarna, north of Varna on the Black Sea coast: they are Black Sea Rama, Thracian Cliffs and Lighthouse. Thracian Cliffs was awarded European Golf Resort of the Year 2014.

HORSERIDING The largest Bulgarian horse-breeding farm, Kabiyuk, established in 1864, is in the northeast near the town of Shumen. It produces high-class horses of Arab and eastern Bulgarian breeds, English thoroughbreds and Scottish ponies. There is a wide range of horseriding holidays available, from gentle treks through the plains to week-long expeditions into the mountains. The most popular places in northern Bulgaria are Sevlievo, Uzana, Arbanasi and Botevgrad. There are many places in the Rhodope Mountains offering horseback riding: Trigrad, Arda and Debrashitsa, for example. The village of Beli Iskur, at the foot of the Rila Mountains, has an equestrian club that offers trips in the area. Not far from Sofia, in the Lozenska and Rila mountains, there are horseriding facilities at Iskur hunting lodge.

HUNTING AND FISHING There are about 30 hunting farms in different parts of Bulgaria; participants have to be properly licensed and abide by the correct seasons for the game or deer. Fishing is permitted anywhere except in nature reserves. The Black Sea coast offers boat hire for fishermen, and inland there are many rivers, dams and marshes for enthusiasts to try their luck.

MEDICAL AND DENTAL VISITS Choosing Bulgaria as a destination for medical tourism has definite financial advantages – both the treatments and your living expenses will be cheaper. The private facilities are usually of high quality, and the prices surprisingly low. The treatments on offer include fertility treatment, cosmetic surgery, dentistry and prostate laser surgery.

MedspaBG bul Cherni Vruh 1–3, 1420 Sofia; www.medspa.bg. See ad, page 71.

Nadezhda ul Blaga Vest 3, 1330 Sofia; www.nadezhda.bg/index.php?lang=en

RURAL AND ECOTOURISM Village life can be very interesting and you can still experience the true meaning of the word 'hospitality' here. It is difficult to imagine that there are still places in Europe untouched by modern civilisation, but Bulgarian villages have managed to maintain their traditions and history. You'll feel as if you've stepped into the past as you wander past the traditional architecture, watch the villagers do their daily chores, and experience their welcoming attitude towards visitors.

In some villages you can learn more about Bulgarian handicrafts: for example, carpet-weaving in Chiprovtsi, woodcarving and icon painting in Tryavna, winemaking in Osmar or Melnik, pottery in Troyan, carpentry in Bukata, or handicrafts in Zlatograd.

In many villages and small towns, the owners of family pensions, guesthouses and hotels welcome guests and reveal the interesting world of their region. **Eco-trails** have become a popular feature of a stay in the country. These are specially designed paths, using wooden bridges to reach viewpoints, so that visitors can become familiar with local biodiversity and unspoiled nature. They are spread throughout Bulgaria, mainly in mountain regions, and are well signposted. The Ministry of Tourism recently published a map of the eco-routes in Bulgaria, and this can be found in most tourist offices.

SKI MOUNTAINEERING This is an adventurous sport in the high mountain ranges, using light heel-free skis. Circular or through tours, with a few stopover nights at guesthouses or mountain huts, give a memorable experience. The beauty of winter in the Pirin and Rila mountains makes them the best places in Bulgaria for this activity.

SNOWSHOEING This is a popular, non-technical winter sport comparatively new to Bulgaria. It is an excellent alternative to skiing or when the route goes though terrain too difficult to ski on. Snowshoeing in Bulgaria can be practised anywhere in the mountains and can be as adventurous as you like. Try this sport in the Rila or Rhodope mountains.

SPA TOURISM Bulgaria's wealth of mineral springs have until recently only been used in a few spas, and then often in sanatoria and convalescent homes. More recently their use for pleasure and well-being has been recognised, and now old spas are being revitalised and new ones are opening. Spas in Sofia, Sandanski, Hisarya, Velingrad, Devin and Pomorie are well established. Many of the new golf courses (page 42) offer luxury accommodation and spa facilities. Check the Tourism Authority website: www.bulgariatravel.org.

VISAS AND ENTRY REGULATIONS

Entry requirements for **UK nationals**: UK passport holders, endorsed British Citizen, do not need a visa to visit Bulgaria for a period of up to 90 days in a six-month period. Passports should be valid for the period of the intended stay. Other UK passport holders require a visa and a passport that is valid for at least six months.

Entry requirements for **Irish nationals**: Irish nationals do not need a visa to visit Bulgaria for a period of up to 90 days within a six-month period. A passport valid for the period of intended stay is required.

Citizens of the **USA**, **Canada**, **New Zealand** and **Australia** do not need a visa to visit Bulgaria for a period of up to 90 days within a six-month period. Passports must be valid for at least three months after entry.

South Africans, however, do need a visa to enter Bulgaria. A passport valid for at least six months on entry is required and a visa will only be issued if blank pages are available.

REGULATIONS Visitors must have proof of sufficient funds or onward or return tickets in addition to other documents needed for the next destination. Valid health insurance is required. All visitors to Bulgaria are **required** to register as foreigners at a local police station within five days of arrival. This registration is usually done as a matter of course through the hotel or accommodation establishment. Immigration and entry regulations are strictly enforced. Passports of all visitors should be valid for at least six months on entry for those requiring a visa, and three months on entry for visa-exempt nationals other than those from EU countries, whose passports must be valid for the period of stay.

For stays longer than 90 days or for those travelling on diplomatic or official passports, a visa is required and must be obtained in advance.

Passengers (over 16 years of age) can import with **no customs duty** 200 cigarettes or 250g of other tobacco products, two litres of wine and one litre of spirits. There is no age restriction for the perfume (50ml) and toilet water (25ml) allowance. These regulations do not apply to EU citizens.

EMBASSIES

IN SOFIA

Ⓔ Australia Consulate ul Trakia 37; ☎02 9461334

Ⓔ France ul Oborishte 27–29; ☎02 9651100; e press@ambafrance.bg; www.ambafrance-bg.org

Ⓔ Germany ul Frederic Joliot-Curie 25, Izgrev; ☎02 918380; e gemb@vilmat.com; visa enquiries: www.sofia.diplo.de

Ⓔ Greece ul San Stefano 33; ☎02 9461030; e gremb.sof@mfa.gr; www.mfa.gr/bulgaria

Ⓔ Japan ul Lulakova Gradina 14, Izgrev; ☎02 9712708; e emb-jp-bg@sf.mofa.go.jp; www.bg.emb-japan.go.jp

Ⓔ Macedonia ul Frederic Joliot-Curie 17, Izgrev; ☎02 8701560; e sofia@mfa.gov.mk

Ⓔ Romania bul Michai Eminescu 4, Oborishte; ☎02 9712858; e ambsofro@exco.net; http://sofia.mae.ro

Ⓔ Russia bul Dragan Tsankov 28, Izgrev; ☎02 9630914; e info@russia.bg; www.russia.bg/en

Ⓔ Serbia ul Veliko Turnovo 3; ☎02 9461633; e sofia@emb-serbia.com; http://sofia.mfa.gov.rs/cir/

Ⓔ South Africa 2nd floor, ul Bacho Kiro 26; ☎02 9395015; e sofia.consular@dirco.gov.za; www.dfa.gov.za/sofia/contact.html

Ⓔ Turkey bul Vasil Levski 80, Sredets; ☎02 9355500; e embassy.sofia@mfa.gov.tr; http://sofia.emb.mfa.gov.tr/

Ⓔ UK ul Moskovska 9; ☎02 9339222; e BritishEmbassySofia@fco.gov.uk; www.gov.uk/government/world/organisations/british-embassy-sofia

Ⓔ USA ul Kozyak 16; ☎02 9375100; e sofia@usembassy.bg; http://bulgaria.usembassy.gov

BULGARIAN EMBASSIES ABROAD

Ⓔ Australia 29 Pindari Crescent, O'Malley, Canberra, ACT 2606; PO Box 6096, Mawson, ACT 2607, Canberra; ☎+61 2 6286 9711; +61 2 6286 9700 (consular); ☎+61 2 6286 9600; e Embassy.Canberra@mfa.bg; www.mfa.bg/embassies/australia

Ⓔ Canada 325 Stewart St, Ottawa, Ontario K1N 6K5; ☎+1 613 789 3215, +1 613 789 3523 (consular); ☎+1 613 789 3524; e Embassy.

Ottawa@mfa.bg; www.mfa.bg/embassies/
canada
e France 1 av Rapp, Paris 75007; ☏ +33 1 45 51
85 90; e Embassy.Paris@mfa.bg; www.mfa.bg/
embassies/france
e Germany Mauer Str 11, Berlin 10117;
☏ +49 30 201 0922, +49 20 604 8936 (consular);
e Embassy.Berlin@mfa.bg; www.mfa.bg/
embassies/germany

e UK 186–188 Queen's Gate, London SW7 5HL;
☏ 020 7584 9400; e consular@bulgarianembassy.
org.uk; www.bulgarianembassy-london.org
e USA 1621 22nd St, NW, Washington DC 20008;
☏ +1 202 387 0174; e office@bulgaria-embassy.
org, consulate@bulgaria-embassy.org (consulate);
www.bulgaria-embassy.org

GETTING THERE AND AWAY

BY AIR The main international airport is **Sofia Airport** (*www.sofia-airport.bg*).
Terminal 2 opened in 2007 and is for international scheduled services. Terminal 1
is used for domestic, budget and charter flights. The three other airports, Plovdiv
(*www.plovdivairport.com*), Varna (*www.varna-airport.bg*) and Burgas (*www.
bourgas-airport.com*), mainly operate with charter and budget flights.

Bulgaria's national carrier is **Bulgaria Air** (☏ *02 4020400;* e *callFB@air.bg; www.
air.bg; at Heathrow* ☏ *020 8745 9833;* e *LHR@bulgaria-air.co.uk*).

There are regular flights between Sofia and Amsterdam, Alicante, Barcelona,
Berlin, Brussels, Cologne, London, Madrid, Malaga, Manchester, Milan, Moscow,
Palma de Mallorca, Paris, Prague, Rome, Tel Aviv, Vienna and Zurich, as well as
internal flights to and from Burgas and Varna. There are also international flights
to Burgas and Varna, but these are mainly holiday charters and mainly in summer.
However, the budget airline WizzAir flies to both coastal airports several times
weekly all year round from Luton airport.

There are no direct flights from Australia, New Zealand or Canada, so travellers
from there will need to connect via a European hub. For Australia check www.
flightcentre.com.au or www.mgtravel.com.au; for Canada www.travelocity.ca and
for New Zealand www.flightcentre.co.nz. The STA Travel website (*www.statravel.
com*) has information on all these, as well as US connections.

International airlines

✈ **Aer Lingus** Ireland; ☏ + 353 1886 8202; www.
aerlingus.ie
✈ **Air France** UK; ☏ 0870 142 4343; Ireland ☏ 01
605 0383; www.airfrance.co.uk
✈ **Alitalia** UK; ☏ 0870 544 8259; Ireland ☏ 01
677 5171; www.alitalia.com
✈ **Austrian Airlines** UK; ☏ 0845 601 0948;
www.aua.com
✈ **British Airways** UK; ☏ 0845 773 3377; Ireland
☏ 0141 222 2345; www.britishairways.com
✈ **Bulgaria Air** UK; ☏ 020 7637 7637; http://
bulgaria-air.co.uk
✈ **Czech Airlines** UK; ☏ 0870 444 3747; www.
czechairlines.co.uk
✈ **easyJet** www.easyjet.com
✈ **Lufthansa** UK; ☏ 0845 773 7747; Ireland ☏ 01
844 5544; www.lufthansa.com
✈ **Ryanair** www.ryanair.com

✈ **Sky Europe** UK; ☏ 020 7365 0365; www.
skyeurope.com
✈ **Turkish Airlines** UK; ☏ 020 7766 9300; www.
turkishairlines.com
✈ **WizzAir** Hungary; ☏ UK 09072 920102;
Bulgaria ☏ 0900 63022; www.wizzair.com

Flight & travel agents in the UK & Ireland

This is now a very competitive market & there are
bargains to be found at ticket shops & online.

Balkania Travel Avanta Harrow, 79 College
Road, Harrow-on-the-Hill HA1 1BD; ☏ 020 8515
1140; e vania@balkaniatravel.com; www.
balkaniatravel.com. IATA flights agency, ticket
agents, London hotel bookings. Specialists to
Bulgaria. See ad, 3rd colour section.
Expedia www.expedia.co.uk

2

Opodo www.opodo.co.uk
STA Travel UK; ☎0333 231 0099; www.statravel.
co.uk. Low-cost flights primarily for students &
under-26s. Branches all over the UK.

Top Deck UK; ☎0845 257 5212; www.topdeck.
travel. Discount flights.
Trailfinders UK; ☎020 7937 1234; www.
trailfinders.com; ☎Ireland: 01 677 7888; www.
trailfinders.ie. Branches all over the UK & in Ireland.

BY LAND

By train There are trains from Belgrade, Bucharest, Istanbul, Munich, Thessalonika, Venice, Vienna, Zagreb and Zurich. From elsewhere in Europe you need to make a connection via these stations or along the route.

Customs formalities and passport control are carried out on the train. It is worth booking a sleeper, which is both safer and more comfortable. Tickets can be booked from any European rail agency. In Bulgaria, international train tickets are sold by **Rila Railway Ticket Agency** (*ul Gurko 5;* ☎ *+359 2 9870777;* e *info@bdz-rila.com; www.bdz-rila.com*). There are other offices at NDK (*the National Palace of Culture;* ☎ *+359 2 8657186*) and Sofia central railway station (☎ *+359 2 9323346*).

By bus Buses from all the major European cities run to Sofia, Plovdiv, Varna and Burgas. The biggest bus company is **Eurolines** (*www.eurolines.com or www.eurolines. bg in Bulgaria*). From the UK there is also **Balkan Horn** (☎ *020 7630 1252; www. balkanhorn.com*) and its number in Sofia at Serdica bus station is ☎02 9808840.

Several Bulgarian companies have lines to Europe. All the buses arrive at or depart from the international bus station in Sofia. The shortest routes to western Europe are via Serbia and Romania. Normally a bus trip from Paris to Sofia takes about 36 hours and the cost of the ticket is about €100.

Long delays can be expected at the borders. The passenger is expected to get off the bus and take his passport to the customs officer for a stamp and check.

By car It is very convenient to have a car in Bulgaria for travelling around the country, as there is a well-developed network of roads, although some are in poor condition. It is, however, a long drive there, so unless it is part of some extended travelling, it may be easier to hire a car on arrival.

The main border crossing points are via Serbia: Kalotina to Dimitrovgrad (the Belgrade road). Most traffic crosses here, so it can be time-consuming in the holiday season. Smaller, but not well signposted and with bad roads, are Vrushka Chuka to Zaichar (Serbia), Bregovo to Negotin (Serbia), and Strezimirovtsi to Klisura (Serbia).

INTERNATIONAL TRAINS TO/FROM SOFIA

To/from	No daily	Length of journey	Approximate fare
Belgrade	1	7hrs 20mins	55lv
Bucharest	2	11hrs	70lv
Istanbul	1	12hrs 30mins	63lv
Thessalonika	1	9hrs 30mins	35lv
Moscow	1	50hrs	287lv

There are also trains to Bratislava, Kiev, Ljubljana, Minsk, Munich, Venice, Vienna, Zagreb and Zürich.

For more information and timetables, contact ☎02 9870777, 02 9325273; www.bdz-rila.com/index.php?page=home

From Romania, there is the New Europe Bridge between Vidin and Calafat (€6 toll). The Ruse to Giurgiu (Romania) bridge is in northeastern Bulgaria (€6 toll).

There are a few other border crossings from Romania but the roads are poorly marked and in bad condition: Oryahovo to Beket, Kardam to Negru Voda, Durankulak to Vama Veche, Silistra to Calarashi, Svishtov to Zimnicea, Tutrakan to Oltenita and Nikopol to Turnu Magurele (all by boat).

From Greece, the major border checkpoints are Kulata to Promahon (Greece). This is the main road from Thessalonika to Sofia passing through southwestern Bulgaria. Ilinden to Eksochi, along the valley of the Mesta River, links northeastern Greece to the Rhodopes and Pirin. Kapitan Petko Voivoda to Ormenion is in southeastern Bulgaria. Zlatograd to Xanthi, Ivailovgrad to Kyprinos, Hadzhidimovo to Kato Nevrokopi and Makaza to Komotini are all minor crossings.

From Turkey, Kapitan Andreevo to Kapikule (Turkey) is on the main road from Istanbul which enters Bulgaria in the southeast. Malko Turnovo to Derekoy is further east. Lesovo to Hamzabeili in the Rhodope Mountains is the newest checkpoint.

From Macedonia there are crossings between Gueshevo and Kriva Palanka, Dechevo and Stanke Lisichkovo and Zlatarevo and Novo Selo.

To cross any of these borders you'll need your personal documents and those proving the ownership of your car.

In Bulgaria there is a compulsory road tax (which takes the form of vignette stickers which you have to display on your windscreen). They cost about 10lv for a week. They are available at the border and the major petrol stations.

BY SEA Currently there are no regular passenger ships to Bulgaria, although the two main Black Sea ports of Varna and Burgas have the facilities to accommodate them, and cruise ships do visit during the tourist season. Ruse also has facilities for passenger ships.

HEALTH *with Dr Felicity Nicholson*

There are state-run hospitals, private medical centres and local polyclinics. Doctors are extremely well qualified and able, but they are often let down by poor equipment and facilities. Nurses are efficient but often without the friendly, personal touch which makes hospital treatment bearable. You will not find many English speakers, so try to take a Bulgarian friend with you if you do need hospital treatment.

You are entitled to free medical and dental treatment, but all visitors must pay for medicines. The availability of private medical treatment is on the increase and it is not expensive for foreigners; keep your receipts if you intend to claim on your travel insurance. The E111 form is no longer valid and citizens of EU countries need to obtain a European Health Insurance Card (EHIC). This is NOT a substitute for comprehensive medical and travel insurance which you are recommended to obtain. The EHIC entitles citizens of EU countries to medical treatment on the same terms as Bulgarian nationals. You can get your EHIC online at www.ehic.org. uk or from post offices using form T7.

As in any hot country, visitors should be cautious, at least for the first few days, about what they eat, especially if prone to upset stomachs. Avoid seafood, ice in drinks and ice cream, and always wash fresh fruit. It is wise to pack some Imodium or similar tablets, as well as insect repellent and treatment for bites, stings and minor cuts.

While the chances of getting any serious illness are remote, it should be noted that in certain districts, hepatitis A, tick-borne encephalitis and other conditions may be encountered. There are currently no compulsory vaccinations, but check on the Foreign Office's Know Before You Go website (*www.fco.gov.uk*) before travelling. It is recommended that you are up to date with tetanus, diphtheria and polio according to the British Vaccination Schedule, and hepatitis A would also be recommended as Bulgaria is considered to have a moderate to high prevalence of the disease. Hepatitis B vaccine would be recommended for those working in health care, working with children, or playing contact sport. The course comprises three doses of vaccine and can be done over as little as 21 days (Engerix only) for those aged 16 or over. Ambirix, a combination of hepatitis A and B, can be used for those aged 15 or under and only one dose is needed with a booster in 6–12 months.

Those planning to spend their holiday in mountain or rural areas are at some risk from ticks. This is especially important to bear in mind during the spring and summer months, when there is a risk of tick-borne encephalitis. You should dress defensively, wearing long trousers tucked into socks or boots, and long-sleeved shirts. Also apply tick repellents to your skin. You should check warm areas of the body (armpits, groin, behind the knees and ears) after walking through forests or long grass. If you do find a tick you should use tweezers to pull it out without twisting it. Do not use irritants such as olbas oil or lit cigarettes, as this will encourage the tick to regurgitate its stomach contents and will increase the risk of infection. Remember, if you have been bitten by a tick you should seek medical advice as soon as possible for treatment. Tick-borne encephalitis vaccine is available in the UK for those who prefer to protect beforehand. A primary course consists of three vaccines over several months but, if time is short, two doses given a minimum of two weeks apart will do.

If you are unfortunate enough to be bitten by a stray dog (very rare) you need to get medical attention straight away as there is a small risk of rabies, and any animal bite could potentially lead to other infections. Whether it is a bite, a scratch or a lick over an open wound, wash it immediately with soap and water, apply an antiseptic and then go to a doctor.

Water is perfectly safe to drink everywhere in Bulgaria, but if you are anxious about it there are many inexpensive and pleasant bottled mineral waters for sale.

TRAVEL CLINICS AND HEALTH INFORMATION A full list of travel clinic websites worldwide is available on www.istm.org. For other journey preparation information, consult www.nathnac.org/ds/map_world.aspx (UK) or http://wwwnc.cdc.gov/travel/ (US). Information about various medications may be found on www.netdoctor.co.uk/travel. All advice found online should be used in conjunction with expert advice received prior to or during travel.

PHARMACIES Every town will have several pharmacies (look for the sign 'Аптека'). Most have familiar proprietary brands on sale and can offer advice.

SAFETY

Despite Bulgarians themselves believing that crime is at a high level, it is actually much lower than in the UK. Theft, particularly of cars, is the most common crime in cities, but very rare in the countryside. However, there are plenty of inexpensive guarded parking lots available in cities.

Obviously you should behave with reasonable caution, particularly in crowded places, such as markets and bus and train stations, as you should in any country. Keep money and expensive belongings out of sight, wear a money belt, and have your handbag across your body rather than on the shoulder.

There have been reports of drivers being stopped by con men posing as policemen, and being asked to pay on-the-spot fines. You should play dumb and ask to be taken to the police station to have someone translate what you have apparently done to break the law. Similarly, it is probably best to be cautious if someone tries to flag you down to help with a breakdown, or, in the case of single male travellers, to be cautious if a 'damsel in distress' tries to attract your attention. Talk of the Mafia and organised crime, and related judicial and police corruption, is of course bad for Bulgaria's image and certainly more resources have to be directed at solving these problems. They are not, however, ones which will impinge on tourists or even foreigners setting up home here.

There is a global risk of terrorism in all public places, so always be vigilant, but there is no specific threat to Bulgaria.

Bulgaria regularly experiences earth tremors, normally minor, registering up to 4.5 on the Richter scale.

Regarding general safety, be careful, but don't be worried. I have been travelling in Bulgaria for over 30 years, during which time I have had just one negative experience involving money-changing, which could easily have been avoided if I had taken my own advice: don't change money on the streets, you will always be the loser!

WOMEN TRAVELLERS

In Sofia and on the coast the dress code for women is much the same as elsewhere in Europe, but in rural areas people are more conservative and if you plan to travel alone you should certainly dress to camouflage rather than impress. You will certainly be stared at and commented on or even propositioned, but a firm rejection should suffice. As always, it is much better to avoid awkward situations than to have to get out of them. Travel with friends, or join forces with another solo traveller, especially in potentially hazardous places like overnight sleepers on trains.

Generally you will find Bulgarian men gallant in a way we have become unused to in the UK, opening doors and seating you at the table, for example.

GAY TRAVELLERS

Although homosexuality is no longer illegal, outside the main cities and resorts there is little tolerance towards gay people, who should avoid overt displays of affection and flamboyant dressing.

TRAVELLERS WITH A DISABILITY

Travellers with a disability, particularly those in wheelchairs, will find Bulgaria difficult. Few places have disabled access, and many pavements are in poor repair. Many of the attractive old towns have steep and/or cobbled streets. New buildings are obliged to provide suitable access, but until the roads and pavements leading to them are better, there will still be problems.

Public transport such as trams and buses are not adapted for wheelchair users, or those with walking difficulties.

TOILETS

There are not many public toilets (*тоалетни*) around; the newer ones are OK but some of the older ones are best avoided. There is usually a caretaker who collects a small fee, in exchange for which you get a very small square of thin paper. It's worth carrying some tissues with you. If there is a wastepaper basket you should use it for paper rather than the toilet, which may get clogged up. The signs are 'М' (*muzhe*) for men and either 'Д' (*dami*) or 'Ж' (*zheni*) for women. Toilets in hotels, restaurants, cafés and bars are usually acceptable, though a few still make a small charge.

WHAT TO TAKE

If you bring any electrical equipment such as hairdryers, mobile-phone chargers, laptops or heating elements you will need the usual two-pin continental adaptor. Travelling elements are useful if you like late-night or early morning hot drinks, as Bulgarian hotels don't normally provide kettles. You'll also need sachets of coffee, powdered milk and teabags.

You should bring Imodium or similar, as mentioned in *Health* above, plus insect repellent, sun protection and treatment for bites or stings. Any personal medication should be kept in the package identifying the dosage.

Sweaters or a fleece are useful even in summer, as it can be cool in the early morning and evening, particularly in the mountains. Two or three light pullovers are better than one thick one. You can put them on in layers, or all together if it is really cold!

Anyone planning on hiking or rambling should have good broken-in boots, waterproofs and a rucksack. Birdwatchers will need their optics and identification guides. If you're off the beaten track you may take picnics for lunch, so you could bring something to sit on (plastic sheet), a camping cutlery set or plastic cutlery, and wet wipes. Tissues or toilet paper, sunglasses and a sunhat might also be useful.

Many hotels offer swimming pools, so it's worth taking your costume.

Bulgarian shops are well stocked nowadays, so you should be able to buy anything you have forgotten to bring.

MONEY

The currency is currently the lev (plural leva), divided into 100 stotinki. Coins are 1, 2, 5, 10, 20 and 50 stotinki, and 1 lev. Notes come in 2, 5, 10, 20, 50 and 100 leva denominations. Prices for properties are often quoted in euros.

Bulgaria is a cash-based society; credit cards are rarely used (except for hotel bills and in some Sofia restaurants). **ATM** machines are widely available in all town centres and UK bank cards can be used to draw cash (for a fee), though the daily amount that can be withdrawn is limited to 400lv (about £140) and is always at a poor rate of exchange. If you plan to travel off the beaten track, it is best to change money in advance.

In the past, money-changing was constantly offered to foreigners on the street, and many exchange bureaux had overtly good exchange rates in order to tempt customers in, but these somehow never quite materialised in practice due to hidden surcharges and commissions. The whole process is now well regulated; bureaux are not allowed to charge commission and the figures displayed are what you should receive. As an additional safety measure, the customer has to sign for the money, so if it is not what you expect you can refuse to sign and get your money back. Banks and exchange bureaux give better rates than hotels or airports. Rates vary but for £1 you get about 2.54 leva, usually written in this context as 2.54BGN. The US dollar equals 1.67BGN but fluctuates. The euro rate is pegged at 1.95BGN. Banks are obviously the safest bet.

When exchanging foreign currency for leva, you should offer clean, undamaged notes. Travellers' cheques are still not easy to change, especially away from Sofia and the resorts, and only a minority of restaurants will accept payment by credit card.

There are still a few street touts offering 'great rates' and the simple rule is **never** to deal with them, because you will always be the loser!

If you wish to export cash (in any currency) amounting to more than 25,000lv you will need documentation showing its origin, and proof that no money is owed to the National Revenue Agency.

At present you can import up to the equivalent of 8,000lv without question; if you bring more it is not a problem, but you have to indicate its provenance, such as savings, inheritance, lottery win!

BUDGETING Sofia has a good spectrum of prices and it is easy to have either a budget or an expensive day out. It is generally more expensive than other towns, and definitely more expensive than rural areas, but the highest prices will be found in high season on the coast and in the mountains.

Low-budget day
Breakfast A take-away *banitsa* 1.20lv; *ayran* or tea: 1lv
Lunch Bean soup, *kavarma*, mineral water at **Trops Kushta** (page 84): 9lv
Afternoon coffee break Coffee: 2lv
Dinner Large pizza at **La Cattedrale** (page 85) 7lv, salad 3lv and a drink: 3lv
Overnight stay Internet Hostel (page 83): 16lv
Transport tickets 3 tickets: 3lv
Evening 2 drinks at **Bilkovata**: 5lv
Total 50.20lv (about £20)

Money-no-object day!
Breakfast This will be provided by the hotel.
Coffee break At a smart hotel, coffee and a mineral water: 10lv.
Lunch Try **Lebed** (page 85): starter 10lv, glass of wine 10lv, main course 15lv, coffee and dessert 10lv. Total: 45lv plus 2 taxi fares 60lv.
Dinner At **La Terrazza di Serdica**, 100lv with a bottle of wine.
Overnight stay For example at the **Grand Hotel Sofia** (page 83), 370lv.
Taxis Two or three short trips 15lv.
Nightlife Meet at **Upstairs** for a drink or two, 20lv. At Chervilo at the Military Club entrance, a few cocktails or whiskies is 60lv.
Total 680lv (about £272.50)

GETTING AROUND

The website www.bgrazpisanie.com has bus and train timetables, tickets and all the travel and general information you need, including car rental and hotels.

BY TRAIN There are different categories of train. **Passenger** trains (*Putnicheski vlak*) are the slowest and least comfortable, usually only covering short distances or connecting to remote places. They are the cheapest.

Rapid trains (*Burz vlak*) are the regular trains that connect major cities. They are more expensive than passenger trains and less uncomfortable.

Express (*Expresen vlak*) are the most expensive trains. They are also faster and

To/from	No daily	Length of journey	2nd class	1st class
Blagoevgrad	7	2hrs 35mins–3hrs 45mins	7.50lv	9.40lv
Burgas	4	6hrs 30mins–8hrs 50mins	25.00lv	31.10lv
Kazanluk	1	3hrs 30mins–5hrs 20mins	11.40lv	14.30lv
Koprivshtitsa	1	1hr 45mins–2hrs 45mins	5.20lv	6.50lv
Pleven	10	2hrs 50mins–5hrs 15mins	10.60lv	13.30lv
Plovdiv	13	2hrs 20mins–3hrs 45mins	9.00lv	11.30lv
Ruse	5	7hrs–10hrs	18.90lv	23.60lv
Varna	5	7hrs 30mins–9hrs 30mins	23.60lv	29.50lv
Veliko Turnovo	9	4hrs 45mins–6hrs 45mins	20.30lv	25.30lv
Vidin	4	5hrs 30mins	13.80lv	17.30lv

For more information and timetables: ☎ 02 9311111; m 0884 139481; http://bdz.bg.

more comfortable. They are not very common; usually there is just one a day from Sofia to Burgas, Varna and Plovdiv or on international services.

Listings in this guide give a range of times for a journey where known, as obviously the time will depend on the service you choose.

Train tickets on main routes (Sofia to Plovdiv, Varna and Burgas) can be purchased online at www.bdz.bg. Timetables are now available online at www.bgrazpisanie.com/en. For examples of routes and prices see box, *Travelling by public transport in Bulgaria*, below.

TRAVELLING BY PUBLIC TRANSPORT IN BULGARIA

The current restructuring of Bulgarian railways means that routes may be suspended or cancelled and prices changed. There are numerous bus companies meaning that fares are competitive with promotions and offers lowering prices. The prices listed below are a guide and were correct at the time of writing, but check before you travel. All prices quoted are standard class.

THE SOUTHWEST
Rila Monastery From Sofia to Dupnitsa: train 5.20lv; bus 8lv (then bus connection from Dupnitsa to Rila village 5lv, onward bus connection to the monastery 2lv).
Kulata/the border with Greece From Sofia: train 11lv; bus 17lv.

THE NORTHWEST
Vidin/bridge crossing to Romania From Sofia: train 13.80lv; bus 20lv.
Vratsa From Sofia: train 5.70lv; bus 8lv.
Mezdra About 15–20 mins south of Vratsa by train (3lv), this is a useful hub for onward travel in northern and eastern Bulgaria.

CENTRAL STARA PLANINA AND THE DANUBE PLAIN
Veliko Turnovo From Sofia: train 20.30lv; bus 30lv (several bus companies serve this route, so shop around for the best price).
Ruse From Sofia: train 18.90lv; bus 23lv. From Varna: train 10.50lv; bus 33lv.

Central Railway Station
Train tickets (internal) m 0884 193758, 0884 570515
Sleepers (internal) m 0884 193758; www.bdz.bg

Rila International Passenger Office
Information ul Gurko 5; ☎02 9870777, 02 9325273; www.bdz-rila.com/index.php?page=home
Train tickets (internal) ☎02 9870222, 02 9325531

CCTS at the National Palace of Culture
Internal lines information ☎02 8658402, 02 9324280
International lines information ☎02 8657186, 02 9324293
Train tickets and sleepers on internal lines ☎02 8659108

BY BUS Bus transport is generally a little more expensive than trains but it is faster and in many ways better. The buses are new and air-conditioned and provide a good service. Most of the bus routes to the major cities and international lines start from Sofia's central bus station (*next to the central railway station; bul Knyaginya Maria Luiza 100;* ☎ *0900 21000 (24hr information); www.centralnaavtogara.bg*). Numerous companies are licensed to operate here. You should check bus journey routes, times and prices locally. For some journeys the actual route may vary, taking in different towns and taking longer.

A helpful website for bus information is www.avtogari.info/index_en.php.

DRIVING IN BULGARIA In the countryside where the pace of life is slow, there are no particular difficulties about driving, but it becomes more complicated in the big cities; everyone declares Varna drivers to be the worst! Busy main roads, especially in summer, are also hazardous. Many are single carriageway and full of drivers impatient to overtake slow-moving lorries. Even on the motorway it can be difficult because there are still some old cars whose top speed is very slow, and

Shumen From Sofia: train 26.20lv; bus 31lv. From Ruse: train 8.90lv; bus 11lv.
Gorna Oryahovitsa About 20 mins by train from Veliko Turnovo (2lv) this is a busy railway hub on the route between Sofia and the coast, and for Ruse in the north and Stara Zagora to the south.

THE VALLEY OF THE ROSES AND SREDNA GORA
Koprivshtitsa From Sofia: train 5.20lv (onward connection by bus takes 15 mins (2lv), but is not always reliable); bus 14lv.
Stara Zagora From Sofia: train 13.80lv; bus 28lv. From Burgas: train 15.70lv; bus 21lv.
Sliven From Sofia: train 14.60lv, bus 28lv. From Plovdiv: train 17lv, bus 19lv.

PLOVDIV, THE RHODOPES AND THE THRACIAN PLAIN
Plovdiv From Sofia: train 9lv; bus 14lv. From Stara Zagora: train 6.50lv; bus 10lv. From Burgas: train 14.60lv, bus 24lv.
Smolyan From Sofia: bus 28lv. From Plovdiv: bus 17lv.
Svilengrad/border crossing to Turkey From Sofia: train 18lv; bus 45lv. From Plovdiv: train 10lv; bus 25lv.

STRANDZHA, THE BLACK SEA COAST AND DOBRUDZHA
Burgas From Sofia: train 25lv; bus 30lv. From Varna: bus 15lv.
Varna From Sofia: train 25lv; by bus 32lv. From Ruse: train 16.80lv; bus 20lv.

they occasionally pull out to overtake trucks, causing all the speedy BMW and Mercedes drivers to brake dramatically. On minor roads there may be slow-moving agricultural machinery and donkey carts.

Road conditions vary enormously: there are smooth stretches of dual carriageway (a few!), plenty of reasonably well-kept roads, and some seriously pot-holed roads, a pot-hole being 20–40cm deep and maybe 1m across! In remote areas there are unmade roads, which appear on maps but have no tarmac at all; some are fairly smooth and some almost impassable. So although Bulgaria is not a large country, it is important not to assume you can cover distances in the time it would be possible in the UK. Apart from the lack of road maintenance, much of the country is mountainous with winding roads where traffic speed is regulated by the slowest trucks.

A **vignette** (a sort of road tax) is needed to drive on main highways. A hire car will be equipped with one but if you are travelling in your own car you will need to buy one at the border or at some petrol stations, and display it on your windscreen. Prices vary according to your length of stay – it's about 10lv for a week.

OMV **petrol stations** and Happy restaurants are good places to stop for clean loos, good coffee or a meal. They are on motorways and some main roads.

Car rental is available everywhere although, if you wish to collect in one place and hand over in another, your best bet will be the larger companies. Online booking often provides the best deals, so it is well worth checking there first. The largest Bulgarian car-hire company is www.rentacarbulgaria.com.

The following big names all have offices in Bulgaria: Avis, Hertz, Thrifty, Budget, Alamo, Sixt and Europcar. Online prices vary from a cheap €16 per day (check the small print!) to over €80 per day for large four-wheel drives such as Toyota Land Cruiser, VW Tuareg or Range Rover. The website www.carrentals.co.uk/car-hire/bulgaria-guide.html compares the prices of the major car-hire companies. For holiday hire, your UK licence will be fine, but for longer stays (over 12 months) you will need a Bulgarian licence and will have to take a test to get one.

Bulgarians drive on the right; there are strict speed limits and many traffic police devoted to catching you out. Oncoming motorists usually flash to indicate police ahead or a radar trap. In towns the speed limit is 50km/h, 90km/h on main roads and 120km/h on motorways. You should always have your driving licence with you. Seat belts are compulsory for front and rear passengers. The alcohol limit for drivers is 0.05% so it is safest not to drink and drive. On-the-spot fines can be levied for offences.

In general it is probably best to avoid driving at night, as unlit roadworks and pot-holes are a danger.

No Bulgarian drivers stop for pedestrians to cross at zebra crossings; and confusingly, a green light for pedestrians to cross at junctions may also be a green light for drivers turning right. There's safety in numbers so, as a pedestrian, try to cross with a crowd!

On main roads, in large cities and at the coast and ski resorts, Latin script will usually appear alongside Cyrillic on signs. In rural areas this will not be the case. However, it is a simple thing to have the two alphabets written on a sheet of paper for comparison, or to keep two maps, one in Latin, one Cyrillic, in the car. A useful tip if you are looking for a particular turning, and are concerned by lack of signs, is to pull up, turn your head round and check whether the village is signed from the other direction. Sometimes it is!

On main roads there are several well-known roadside markets where you will see peppers, apples, yoghurt, homemade wine and *rakiya*, or *halva*. In general if you see a busy lay-by, it's probably worth a look.

If you are driving in border regions, especially after dark, it is likely that you will be stopped while the police check your documents. This is quite routine, takes only a few minutes and is nothing to get alarmed about.

A useful recent innovation is that tourist attractions are now indicated with the same brown signs in use all over Europe.

ACCOMMODATION

As with so many aspects of Bulgarian life, accommodation is changing very rapidly. In communist times every town had a central, state-owned hotel, but during the 1990s these often became dilapidated. However, most have now been sold off and new owners have partly or fully refurbished them; they are worth considering if you want a convenient location.

Also a leftover from pre-1989 are the rest homes (*pochiven dom*) which were owned by trade unions, professional associations and factories, and which provided inexpensive holidays for their members or employees. Many were fairly basic, though some were very grand, and these are now open to anyone.

Privately owned new hotels are numerous, varying from small and family-run to the Vegas-style monsters on the coast. In general, these are better managed and more friendly and comfortable than the old-style places, but there are exceptions. Both ratings and rates present problems; the international star rating has been introduced by the state tourism authority and facilities corresponding to international standards can be expected. Some owners of accommodation shy away from government licensing though, and they fall outside the star system. Owners of new hotels quite often decide how many stars they'll award themselves! You can always ask to be shown a room before you commit to it. It is important to realise that infrastructure development lags behind that of hotels, and local roads and services may be poorer than the hotel rating implies.

With the exception of old ex-state-owned hotels, most new **hotels** have larger rooms (than, for example, the usual UK ones). Generally, the majority of hotels in Bulgaria are purpose-built rather than conversions, the latter only coming into the market recently. Hotels increasingly offer double beds, although the old-style head-to-foot twin single beds in a room are still offered. Bathroom standards are improving gradually. There is, however, an old resilient Bulgarian concept that a washed floor is a clean floor. This may mean you are greeted by wet and potentially slippery floors. Sink plugs are not always offered; Bulgarians prefer to wash themselves and their dishes in running water. Kettles and tea- or coffee-making facilities are very rare. Air conditioning is increasingly available. Bulgarians' own increasing foreign travel experience has had a positive effect on standards, as has the arrival of several international hotel chains such as Novotel, Hilton, Kempinski and Best Western.

Rates are another area of uncertainty as some hotels charge single travellers almost the double room price, while others have a rate per person, and some, but not all, include breakfast. Only Sofia, large cities and Black Sea coast hotels will accept credit cards, and most places prefer cash. The least expensive small hotel, away from Sofia and the coast, costs about 50lv per room per night, rising to 500lv or more for a suite in a city-centre de luxe hotel.

Private rooms are available in Bulgaria's largest cities, on the coast and in some other tourist destinations. In towns they can be booked at special agencies (*kvartirno byuro*) or through the tourist information offices. Obviously the rooms vary and you probably won't have the chance to see them first, unless they are very close to the booking agency. However, the staff there may be able to advise you. Breakfast is not normally included, though you can usually offer to pay extra for it. The price outside Sofia and away from the coast should be about 15lv per person. Private rooms can also be booked at www.rooms.bg.

There are an increasing number of **backpacker hostels** in Sofia, Plovdiv and on the coast, which charge about 20lv for a bunk. There are a few remaining old tourist dormitories (*turisticheski spalnya*) which tend to be cheaper (10–15lv) but more basic.

Mountain huts (*hizhi*) vary: some deserve the name, others are chalets and much more comfortable. Prices are about 15lv per person per night. Book them in advance through Odysseia-In in Sofia (page 82).

Some monasteries also offer accommodation. Often it is basic but some are seeing the benefits of additional income and are providing more comfortable options. Prices range from 10 to 25lv. Find out more at www.bulgarianmonastery.com.

Camping is only allowed at campsites, and away from the coast there are very few. In general there seem to be fewer and fewer campsites, as developers buy the land for construction.

The charge is about 5–8lv for pitching your tent.

EATING AND DRINKING

BULGARIAN CUISINE There are said to be three great cuisines in the world: French, Chinese and Turkish. Bulgarian cuisine is very similar to Turkish. Its strengths are the wonderfully tasty salads, vegetables, herbs and fruits. There are slow-cooked meat dishes, grilled meats and plenty of meat-free dishes based on eggs and cheese. Nowadays many vegetables are available all year round from imported sources, but stay with the local seasonal produce to get the best flavours!

Bulgarians always start a meal with a salad and, usually, a *rakiya* or two. They may then order a main course, but often a hot starter will precede that, or a soup, sometimes both! For obvious reasons, after all this they are not very interested in desserts!

So already a few explanations are needed. *Rakiya* is a spirit drink made of grapes or plums, often called a brandy, but quite different from the English meaning of the word, and *never* drunk at the end of the meal. In summer, *mastika*, an aniseed-flavoured drink served with ice, which can also be diluted with water, is an alternative. Unless you specify 'small' (50g) you will be served what is considered a normal measure (100g). Beware! 50g is roughly a British double measure. The normal order for 100g is a quadruple. There is a story, which may be true, of a Bulgarian diplomat in London, knowing about British pub measures, asking for four whiskies, and adding politely, 'And please put them in one glass!'

Often folk-style restaurants (*mehanas*) have a choice of dried herbs and spices on the table, which you can use to dip your bread in. *Choubritsa* (a Bulgarian dried herb), *sharena sol* (*choubritsa* and salt) and paprika are the usual ones. Herbs are frequently used in cooking; local ones include savory, parsley, dill, mint, paprika and basil. The dipping of bread in this way is part of a traditional welcome; indeed, some restaurants have a waiter outside greeting guests by offering bread and herbs.

Salads are arguably the best part of the meal. The most popular is *Shopska salad*, named after the Shops who are the people from around Sofia. This is a mixture of chopped tomatoes, cucumber, onion and fresh or preserved peppers, sprinkled with grated or crumbled white cheese (*sirene*) made from the milk of sheep or cows. There are many variations, and also single-ingredient salads of just tomatoes or baked peppers, for example. *Snezhanka* is made from chopped cucumber in strained yoghurt with garlic and chopped walnuts added. In summer the popular *tarator* (a cold soup) is essentially the same ingredients in a more liquid form and it's very refreshing. In winter try *turshiya*, made from pickled vegetables such as cauliflowers, carrots, peppers and green tomatoes. *Kyopolou* is made by roasting aubergines and peppers and mixing them, minus their skin, with garlic, parsley and oil. Smart restaurants, particularly in Sofia, have begun to offer Caesar salad and Italian-style salad with mozzarella, and other variations.

Bulgarian **yoghurt**, or *kiselo mlyako*, meaning 'sour milk', is world famous. It has a long history: the Thracians were very good at stockbreeding and produced a number of dairy products, and the word yoghurt is believed to be from the Thracian language. In 1905 the secret of Bulgarian yoghurt, a special bacteria named *Lactobacillus bulgaricus*, was discovered. There are different varieties made from the milk of cows, sheep, goats and buffaloes, and blends of these. In Bulgaria, they are all used for the preparation of various healthy dishes such as *tarator* (the cold summer soup mentioned above), *banitsa* (a traditional snack) and *ayran* (the ultimate drink for thirsty people – a mixture of yoghurt, water and salt).

Hot starters are very varied and delicious; braised liver, tongue and chicken hearts are popular. *Mishmash* is something like an omelette – tomatoes, red peppers and white cheese held together by scrambled eggs. *Surmi* are stuffed cabbage or vine leaves, usually with meat and rice, but they can be just rice. If you want vegetarian options ask for *postno yadene*, which means fasting food; this will make it clear you don't want meat. *Pulneni chushki* are stuffed peppers (meat and rice) and *chushki byurek* are peppers stuffed with cheese and herbs and then fried in breadcrumbs or batter. Particularly delicious when in season are courgettes (*tikvichki*), which are served either stuffed like the peppers or fried and served with a garlic and dill sauce as *podlucheni tikvichki*.

Aside from *tarator*, there are the usual selection of vegetable and chicken **soups**, and local specialities such as *supa otkopriva* (nettle soup), *bob chorba* (bean soup) and the local favourite, tripe soup. This last is sometimes eaten at breakfast, maybe because it is a famous hangover cure. Readers of *The Times* in London were asked to suggest effective hangover cures and one expatriate wrote in with a recipe for Bulgarian tripe soup.

Main courses divide into simple grilled meats, often now called BBQ rather than *skara* (grill), and dishes such as moussaka or stews. Chicken, pork and lamb are the usual meats on offer. Fish is available in Sofia and on the coast, but unless you go to a specialist restaurant it is unlikely to be anything but fried.

Grills include *kebapcheta* (sausage-shaped and similar in taste), *kyufteta* (burger-shaped and spicier), skewers (*shish*) of chunks of meat interspersed with onions, mushrooms and peppers, and chops of pork or lamb. *Kavarma*, a stew, is served in a special pot with a lid, cooked for a long time and sometimes topped with a fried egg. *Gyuvech* is a similar stew usually of just vegetables, and moussaka we all know, though in Bulgaria it is usually with potatoes not aubergines. Garnish, meaning potatoes and other vegetables, is normally ordered separately and will not appear automatically.

Desserts might be ice cream, crêpes or fruit. Delicious pastries such as *baklava* are not usually eaten as a dessert but in the afternoon with a cup of coffee. Tea, as you will notice, is not drunk much; if you ask for tea, Bulgarian friends may ask with concern if you are feeling ill! They drink tea, usually herbal, for medicinal purposes. It is served without milk unless you ask for some.

There are lots of **snacks** available on the streets – currently the most popular and usually most horrible is pizza. Freshly baked pizzas in restaurants will be fine,

Here are a few favourites you might like to try when you get home, or before or after you go. I am honoured that Lilia Guerassimova, the doyenne of Bulgarian cuisine, has given me permission to share some of her recipes with you.

SHOPSKA SALAD
Ingredients

5 peppers	parsley (flat-leaf)	150g white cheese
3 tomatoes	40ml vegetable or	(feta is a good
1 cucumber	olive oil	substitute)
1 onion	salt to taste	1 chilli pepper

Method Cut the peppers in strips lengthwise and arrange in a salad bowl, add cubed tomatoes, cubed cucumber and finely chopped onion and parsley. Pour the oil over the mixture and sprinkle salt over it. Top with crumbled or grated white cheese and the chilli pepper.

TARATOR
Ingredients

2 small cucumbers	1 spoonful of vegetable oil	3–4 cloves of garlic
salt to taste	2–3 crushed walnuts	1 glass of water
½kg of yoghurt	1 bunch of dill	

Method Peel and cut the cucumbers into small pieces. Add salt and leave for a while. Beat up the yoghurt in a big glass bowl, add the cut cucumbers, the oil, the walnuts and the dill (finely chopped). Add the crushed cloves of garlic and the water or (on a hot summer day) some ice. (This is a soup – it can be thicker or thinner according to how much water you add.)

MISHMASH
Ingredients

1 onion	2–3 tomatoes	2 eggs
2–3 tbsp of vegetable oil	pinch of salt	parsley (flat-leaf)
3–4 peppers	200g white cheese (feta is a good substitute)	

Method Chop the onions and fry in the vegetable oil until brown; add the peppers (cut into strips), the chopped tomatoes and the salt. When fried, add the grated cheese, eggs and parsley and cook to taste (it should look like an omelette). Serve hot.

FRIED COURGETTES
Ingredients

3–4 medium-sized courgettes	150ml vegetable oil	yoghurt
	15g salt	garlic

Method Wash and cut the courgettes into thin circles. Fry in hot oil. Arrange the browned circles in a serving dish, sprinkle with salt and garnish with yoghurt flavoured with crushed garlic.

BEAN SOUP (old monastery recipe)
Ingredients

150g white beans	1 onion	2 tomatoes
1 chilli pepper	2–3 carrots	peppermint
5 tablespoons vegetable oil	½ celery heart	salt to taste
	2 peppers	

Method Soak the cleaned and washed beans in cold water overnight or for 6–7 hours, throw away the water, wash them again, then pour more water over them and boil with the whole chilli pepper at a moderate heat. Add the oil and the finely chopped onion, carrots and celery. Later add the peppers, also finely chopped. Towards the end of the cooking add the peeled and finely chopped tomatoes and the peppermint. Season to taste.

TRIPE SOUP
Ingredients

1kg tripe (beef or pork)	80g butter or vegetable oil	6 cloves of garlic
black and red pepper	paprika	vinegar
250ml milk	salt	

Method Thoroughly clean and wash the tripe and scrape with a knife. Simmer for several hours in slightly salted water until the tripe is soft. Season with black and red pepper while cooking. Remove from the stock and cut into very thin strips. Simmer the strained stock for another 20 minutes with the milk, butter or oil, and paprika. Serve the sliced tripe in a bowl and pour over the hot stock. Season to taste with garlic vinegar, made by crushing the garlic and soaking it in vinegar. This is usually served separately. Coarsely crushed hot chilli pepper can also be added.

CHICKEN LIVERS (STRANDZHA STYLE)
Ingredients

100g onions	75g butter	1 glass of dry white wine
80g spring onions	10g black pepper	salt to taste
500g chicken livers	100g mushrooms	

Method Cook the onions and spring onions with the chicken livers in the butter, add the black pepper, the mushrooms, the white wine and salt to taste. Cover the dish and bake for about 40 minutes in a moderate oven.

SHISH (GRILLED PIECES OF MEAT ON A SKEWER)
Ingredients

1kg meat (veal or pork)	3 long peppers	salt
2 onions	3 tomatoes	10g black pepper

Method Cut the meat into cubes and the onions and peppers into small pieces. Skewer a piece of meat, tomato, pepper and onion successively. Season to taste. Grill until tender.

continued overleaf

RED PEPPERS STUFFED WITH MEAT AND RICE
Ingredients

12 peppers	1 small cup of rice	600g minced meat
salt	½ bunch of parsley (flat-	(300g pork and
1 onion	leaf)	300g veal)
2 tablespoons	2–3 peppermint sprigs	black pepper
vegetable oil	1 tomato	beef stock or water

Method Prepare the peppers to be stuffed by cutting off a 'lid' from the top and keeping it to put back on the pepper after you stuff it. Rub a little salt on the inside of each pepper and prick it with a fork. Prepare the stuffing by frying the onion in the vegetable oil, then add the rice and the herbs. Add the raw meat to the mixture and season to taste. Fill the peppers and arrange them close together, dividing them by a slice of tomato. Pour a cup of hot water or beef stock over them and bake at 220°C for about 45 minutes.

GYUVECH (from Stara Zagora)
Ingredients

1kg meat (veal or	3 long peppers	10g black pepper
pork)	3 tomatoes	
2 onions	salt	

Method Cut the meat into chunks, salt it and put it in a saucepan. Add the finely chopped onion, peppers and black pepper and simmer till all water evaporates. Place the meat in an earthenware dish (called *gyuvech* in Bulgarian) and cover it with the vegetables cut in fairly large pieces. Place in the oven and bake till golden-brown on top. Sprinkle with parsley. Serve in the baking dish. (This dish can be made without the meat as a satisfying vegetarian 'stew'.)

BAKLAVA (Plovdiv style)
Ingredients

300g butter	2 teacups ground walnuts	800g sugar
800g filo pastry	1 lemon	3 teacups water
sheets	1 teaspoonful cinnamon	

Method Grease a rectangular tin with melted butter. Start arranging the pastry sheets in the tin, buttering each one. Having arranged half of the sheets, sprinkle evenly with ground walnuts mixed with lemon peel and cinnamon. Arrange the remaining pastry sheets on top. Using a heated knife cut the *baklava* into square or diamond-shaped (traditional style) pieces. Pour over the remaining melted butter, and bake in a very hot oven at first, then reduce the heat to moderate, until the *baklava* is browned. Leave it to cool, then pour hot syrup made from sugar, water and lemon juice over it. Leave to soak in the syrup at least 4–5 hours. Experienced pastry-cooks recommend letting *baklava* mature for at least 24 hours.

but the ones keeping warm in a kiosk are likely to be greasy and tasteless. Another snack which can veer between the delicious and the dull is *banitsa*, a popular breakfast take-away. When freshly made, or even better homemade, it is a crisp light pastry filled with cheese, or pumpkin and walnuts, or leek or spinach. At its worst it is heavy and greasy.

Other street foods include nuts and seeds, *gevrek* (like a bagel) sold from paper sacks on street corners, chestnuts and sweetcorn on open-air grills, and *mekitsi*, which are fried and rather like doughnuts served with a dusting of icing sugar but without any jam filling.

In summer you can buy huge quantities of cherries, grapes, strawberries and raspberries very cheaply, but remember to wash them before you indulge.

Many restaurants, even outside Sofia, have English-language menus. Something to look out for is the weight given in grams of the dish you are ordering. Recently salads have begun to be served in huge quantities, so choose the lighter-weight ones if you are not very hungry. Normally food is served warm rather than hot, and particularly in smaller restaurants may arrive in quite a random order, so that in a group someone may have a starter and a main course and someone else may have nothing!

One of the pleasures of travelling round the country is discovering local dishes which are unfamiliar to you; the Rhodopes and Pirin are particularly rich in regional specialities.

Restaurants generally operate between 11.00 and 23.00, while cafés open earlier (07.30 or 08.00) and may close earlier, though some morph into bars in the evening.

WINE Although Bulgaria is a small country, it has a great variety of terrains and microclimates, and can produce many wines of distinctive characters. The climate and nutrient-rich soil are perfect for viticulture.

In the Danube Plain region in the north, the river moderates extremes of temperature, and local wineries include Borovitza, Chateau de Val and Leventa. The Black Sea region has a moderate climate all the year round, and specialises in the production of white grapes, for example at Varna, Vinex Preslav and Pomorie wineries. The Thracian Plain and the foothills of the Rhodope Mountains make up the most productive region, mainly of red wines, and include the well-known wineries of Bessa Valley, Castra Rubra, Katarzyna, Edoardo Miroglio, Minkovi Brothers and Midalidare Estate. The climate is hot in summer, but with good annual rainfall. Finally there is the Struma Valley region in the southwest, a comparatively small area noted for its very hot climate and hence its rich and fruity wines. The dark red wine of Melnik, reputedly Winston Churchill's favourite, is made here.

Bulgaria has a long historical connection with wine; there is evidence of viticulture and winemaking in Thracian times. Archaeologists have proved this theory with their numerous finds of stone troughs which were used for winemaking and ageing. The wines of Thrace are mentioned by Homer in both *The Iliad* and *The Odyssey*.

The Romans continued the winemaking tradition and expanded the area under cultivation. Throughout the Middle Ages wine production thrived in Bulgaria, and even when the Ottoman Turks conquered the country it continued to prosper. Despite wine drinking being forbidden in the Koran, the Turks saw the financial benefits of allowing the successful business to continue. They even introduced dessert grapes from Asia Minor to develop the production of sweet wines.

However, in the 19th century, disaster struck. Phylloxera spread east across Europe and reached Bulgaria in the last decades of the century. The disease is spread by an aphid (a tiny insect) which feeds on vine roots, thus killing the plant.

Thousands of vines were affected, so growers had to replace their stocks with new disease-resistant ones.

Under the post-war communist government, wine production was nationalised. Winemaking became an industry as massive wineries, supplied by huge new vineyards, dramatically increased production levels. During the 1960s a more scientific approach was adopted, as varieties of grape were more carefully matched to the areas which provided the best growing environment for them. At this time too the classic grapes (mainly French) were introduced with resounding success.

Nowadays Bulgaria's winemakers are still fascinated by experiments with new grape varieties, but often blend them with indigenous grapes. Some older, almost forgotten varieties are being revived. Of the new varieties, Cabernet Franc has proved particularly successful. Cabernet Sauvignon remains the dominant grape, but Merlot is increasingly popular. Other classic varieties include Chardonnay, Riesling, Sauvignon Blanc and Ugni Blanc. The indigenous grapes are Dimiat, Misket, Pamid, Gamza, Mavrud and Melnik.

In Bulgaria today, regional characteristics and the long winemaking tradition, coupled with investment and new technology, are producing stylish and excellent-value wines. Alongside this, boutique wineries have demonstrated that the production of small quantities of really good quality wine, at a much higher price level, has also got potential.

The best dry Bulgarian red wines include Enira from Bessa Valley; Merlot from Strymon and Santa Sarah; Gamza from Novo Selo; Mavrud from Asenovgrad; and Melnik Uniqato from Damianitsa.

Chardonnay from Leventa and Sauvignon Blanc from Vinex Preslav are good quality Bulgarian white wines. The latter also makes a fine and well-known brandy. The sparkling wine of Edoardo Miroglio is Bulgaria's best fizz.

As a novelty you might like to try aromatic Pelin from Osmar, near Shumen, which is made to a 120-year-old secret recipe using 34 different herbs in the red wine and 28 in the white. There are also some quinces and apples in the mixture!

Wine tastings can be arranged at most wineries around the country; some have regular opening times while others need an appointment. Already there are several wineries with an adjoining hotel and the number seems certain to increase. There is a useful guidebook, *The Wine Routes of Bulgaria*, published in 2014 by VinoZona.

OTHER ALCOHOLIC DRINKS Bulgarian **beer** is lager style; the best brands are Astika from Haskovo, Zagorka from Stara Zagora and Kamenitza from Plovdiv, all about 5% alcohol.

Rakiya is the traditional drink of Bulgaria: it has a high alcohol content, anywhere between 40% and 95%. Winemaking and *rakiya* distillation (not illegal!) are a popular hobby, but nowadays distilleries produce more and more of the *rakiya*. Grapes are the most popular ingredient, but other fruits such as plums, pears and apricots are used. *Rakiya* and salad complement each other perfectly and are part and parcel of everyday Bulgarian life.

Mastika is a strong aniseed-flavoured drink, also with a high alcohol content, but usually served with ice and water as a very refreshing summer drink.

Liqueurs are made from a variety of ingredients, including rose petals, peaches, almonds and mint. These are typically very sweet and served either after meals, or with coffee and cakes in the afternoon.

Some of these unusual drinks might make a nice present or souvenir!

SHOPPING

Shops normally open from 09.00 till 18.00, though convenience stores are often open till 22.00.

Arts and crafts make some of the best souvenirs, and away from the coast the prices are reasonable and the quality high. Embroidered items are often exquisitely made. Modern homes tend not to have much use for embroidered tray cloths and place mats, but imagine them stylishly mounted and framed as a set of four or six, and you may change your mind. Ceramics, woodcarvings, metalwork and jewellery are all unusual and beautifully crafted.

Music CDs, particularly of folk and classical recordings made in Bulgaria, are often good value. Coffee-table illustrated books about Bulgaria are widely available, with good quality photographs. Many tourist attractions have a few local artists working nearby, and most have works to sell, so you may well find something unusual and original.

Museum shops, particularly those attached to Ethnographic Museums, often have interesting souvenirs for sale.

ARTS AND ENTERTAINMENT

Western European and American films arrive soon after release in Bulgaria; some are dubbed but many are shown in the original format with Bulgarian subtitles.

Theatre performances are of a high standard but being in Bulgarian are not accessible to most visitors. Sofia has several theatres and most large towns at least one. Opera performances are world class and rely much less on understanding the language. Several towns have opera houses. Orchestral and chamber music concerts are very popular and performances are of a high standard.

Many large towns have a festival lasting one, two or more weeks, with a busy cultural programme. Videos of many of these unusual traditional events can be found on YouTube.

It is always worth checking at tourist information offices for local art exhibitions and events.

CULTURAL EVENTS AND FESTIVALS Always check before travelling, as dates sometimes change.

January

Early January	Orchestral Music Festival, Plovdiv.
1 January	*Kukeri* (mummers/performers of seasonal folk plays) in western Bulgaria, Razlog, Sandanski, Pernik and Petrich (dates vary locally).
6 January	Yordanovden celebrations in Koprivshtitsa and Kalofer. Young men leap into icy waters to retrieve a cross; the winner will have health and happiness.

February

1 February	Sv Trifon Zarezan – Wine Day! Traditionally on 14 February, it now varies, due to the encroachment of the alien St Valentine.
14 February	Another Wine Day! Yes, you can celebrate it twice in February!
18–19 February	*Kukeri* in Karlovo and neighbouring villages.

March

Sofia Film Festival.
Pancho Vladigerov Days of Music, Shumen.

First weekend	Carnival of masks in Shiroka Luka.
Last two weeks	Classical Music Festival in Ruse.
First Saturday of Lent	Todorovden: horse races at Koprivshtitsa, Dobrinishte and Katarino near Razlog. Celebration of the horse: police and army horse displays, various venues.

April

Orthodox Easter	Main services on Thursday and Saturday nights, the Great Easter Concert at Bansko.

May

Gabrovo Festival of Humour and Satire, every two or three years.
Re-enacting of scenes from the April Uprising, Koprivshtitsa.

25 days after Easter Sunday	Procession of icons from Bachkovo Monastery to Ayazmoto.
6 May	Gergyovden. The most popular holiday. Events include sacrifices and feasts at Chiprovtsi, Slatolin (near Montana) and Sv Georgi Monastery at Hadzhidimovo (near Gotse Delchev). Christian and Muslim gatherings at Ak Yazula Baba Tekke (near Obrochishte) and Demir Baba Tekke (near Sveshtari).
17–24 May	Celebration of Bansko traditions.
21 May	Measuring of the milk: festivals in various Rhodope villages. Fire-dancers (*nestinari*) at Bulgari in Strandzha.
Last weekend	Thracian Folklore Festival in Haskovo.
Late May– late June	Sofia Music Weeks: festival of classical music and ballet.

June

Orpheus International Youth Folklore Festival, Smolyan.
Rockers' Festival: classic cars and bikes between Pazardzhik and Plovdiv.

2 June	Nationwide pilgrimage to Okolchitsa peak in commemoration of the death of Hristo Botev and all who died for Bulgaria, also a Memorial Day at his birthplace in Kalofer.
First weekend	Rose Festival in Karlovo and Kazanluk.
Mid-June	Chamber Music Festival, Plovdiv.
24 June	Day of Herbs, Enyovden.
Late June or early July	Roma Music Festival, Stara Zagora.
June–August	Varna Summer: festival of classical music, folklore and jazz.

July

Yoghurt Fair: festival of folk traditions, arts and crafts, Razgrad.
Film Nights in Philippopolis: summer film panorama, Plovdiv.

Last weekend	Macedonian Subor (gathering) at Rozhen, near Melnik.
July/August	Sv Iliya Day, celebrated variously on New Style dates in late July or Old Style early in August at churches and monasteries named after Sv Iliya. Ilindenski Subor at Popovi Livadi, near Gotse Delchev.

August

Pirin Sings (Pirin Pee): Folklore Festival at the Predel Pass, Pirin Mountains.

First Sunday	Ilinden Bagpipe Festival at Gela, near Shiroka Luka.
First Sunday	Folklore Festival of Macedonian, Vlach and Pomak traditions at Dorkovo.
Nearest weekend to 15 August	Annual folk music festival at Koprivshtitsa. Every 5 years (the next in 2015) on the first or second weekend in August: the Great Koprivshtitsa Folklore Festival.
15 August	Golyama Bogoroditsa: parade of icons at the monasteries of Rila, Bachkovo, Troyan and Rozhen, and celebrations at all churches dedicated to the Virgin Mary.
Third weekend	Karakachani Festival at Sinite Skali, Sliven.
Late August	International Folk Music Festival, Burgas.
Last weekend	Rozhenski Subor at Rozhen in the Rhodopes.
Last weekend	Milk Festival at Smilyan in the Rhodopes.

September

First 7–10 days	Apollonia Arts Festival, Sozopol: literature, theatre and classical, jazz, rock and folk music.
First week	Thracian Festival, in Madzharovo: music, dancing and wrestling.
Second weekend	Pirin Folklore Festival, Sandanski.
14 September	Krustovden pilgrimage to Krustova Gora.
September–October	Katya Popova Laureate Days, International Music Festival, Pleven.

October

Golden Dolphin: International Puppet Theatre Festival, Varna.

18 October	Wine Harvest Festival, Melnik.
19 October	Sv Ivan of Rila Feast Day.
Last week	International Jazz Festival, Ruse.

November

Second week	International Jazz Festival, Sofia.

December

International Book Fair, Sofia.

SPORT

Bulgarians are passionate about their **football** and take an interest not only in their own team but also in football in other European countries. Sofia has two teams, CSKA and Levski. Hristo Stoichkov, in the not-too-distant past, and Dimitar Berbatov, more recently, are some of the better-known faces of Bulgarian football.

Basketball is popular as a school game. **Volleyball**, somewhat surprisingly, is the one group sport which has most consistently scored high international results and placings. Bulgaria's greatest achievements, including many world and Olympic titles, are in sports such as **wrestling**, **gymnastics**, **weightlifting**, **track and field** and, more recently, **ice skating**, all individual events. Perhaps this tells us something about the Bulgarian national character!

PHOTOGRAPHY

Most international brands of film are readily available, but more unusual items such as black-and-white film may not be. So enthusiasts should take specialised equipment with them. Shops in Sofia and the resorts can develop film in a few hours.

Digital cameras eliminate the need for film, though if you take a lot of photos you may need to clear space on the memory card by emailing them home.

At some tourist attractions photography is not permitted, and at others there may be a fee for taking photos. Photography of military and naval bases, airports, border posts and railway stations is not allowed. It is courteous to check before photographing people.

MEDIA AND COMMUNICATIONS

After 1989 the (mainly) serious newspapers were replaced by a wider variety and greater number of publications, which at first had definite party affiliations. This is no longer the case, and the economic and business connections of the owners play more of a part in determining the content. *Duma* and *Novinar* do have party affiliations and *Dnevnik* and *Kapital* offer serious political and economic analysis. There are also papers which contain mainly celebrity gossip and naked women. Sports newspapers such as *Meridian Match* and *7 Dni Sport* are very popular. There are also a large number of magazines devoted to computers, home furnishing and wine and food. There is an online newspaper in English: www.novinite.com.

Currently one of the most discussed issues in Bulgarian media is the question of deteriorating media freedom. Monopolies in ownership, advertising and distribution are often cited and Reporters Without Borders consistently ranks Bulgaria last among EU members in its Press Freedom Index.

TV Bulgaria's state-owned channel BNT1 has now been joined by BNT2 and Kanal3. Popular stations include bTV, Nova and News7. Cable and satellite channels show a lot of sport, including football from England, Italy and Spain, and National Geographic, Discovery, CNN, BBC World and Disney are all available.

There is little home-produced drama or documentary material.

RADIO Horizont and Darik Radio are popular Bulgarian stations. If you want to hear the BBC, check its schedules on www.bbc.co.uk/worldservice.

POST OFFICES (ПОЩА) Most are open from Monday to Friday 08.00–17.00, Saturday 08.00–13.00. There are usually several counters and it is not always clear which counter you need. Most visitors will only need stamps (*марки*) or poste restante, for which you'll need to show your passport. Letters within Europe take about 5–7 days, and 10–14 days from the US. Of course travellers nowadays have less need for stamps or poste restante, as they have been superseded by emails and texts.

FAX Most hotels and post offices have fax services, but they are rapidly being superseded by emails.

ADDRESSES Bulgarian addresses are written the opposite way to British ones. The country comes first, then the town with its postcode. The abbreviation for street (*ul/ulitsa*), square (*pl/ploshtad*) or boulevard (*bul/bulevard*) comes next, followed by its name in inverted commas, and the number. On housing estates additional information will be the number of the block (*bl*), the floor (*et*) and the flat number (*ap*). For larger blocks there is sometimes an entrance number too (*vh*). The name of the addressee comes last.

INTERNET Free Wi-Fi is available in many cafés, bars, hotel lobbies and even parks.

TELEPHONE Public telephones may be in special shops in town centres; there are also phones in hotel lobbies and on the street. They are card operated; phonecards (*фонокарти*) can be purchased in post offices and at newspaper kiosks. The area code for Bulgaria is 359. You should omit the following zero when dialling from **outside** the country.

MOBILES There is good coverage in general, though some remote mountain areas are not covered. Roaming charges are under review in Europe, so it is best to check before you go. A pay-as-you-go Bulgarian SIM card is a good solution. There are numerous phone shops where you can buy these.

BUSINESS IN BULGARIA

In general, Bulgarians do business in a similar way to other European countries. Their approach is friendly and welcoming.

LANGUAGE English is widely spoken in Sofia and the other main towns (Plovdiv, Varna and Burgas), particularly among young people. Most businesses will have at least one member of staff who can speak English and act as interpreter during meetings. In government ministries and agencies, knowledge of English is less widespread and it may be necessary to take your own interpreter to meetings. The British Embassy in Sofia can provide a list of agencies if necessary. If you develop a long-term relationship with Bulgaria, it is worth learning the alphabet and some words and phrases, or even trying a teach-yourself language course (see page 24 and *Appendix 1*). English–Bulgarian dictionaries are widely available locally.

DRESS CODE This is generally smart: suit and tie or jacket and tie for men, suits or trouser suits for women. In winter, sturdy non-slip footwear will be essential for snow-covered pavements, which are not usually cleared. Evening parties require business-style dress. Black tie is rarely required, even in cases where it would be expected in the UK. In general Bulgarians are relaxed about the dress code.

APPOINTMENTS Appointments should be made in advance by email; English is usually acceptable, if the message is simple. At government ministries and agencies, they will usually agree to an appointment only after a written request outlining the purpose of the meeting. It is possible to arrange appointments by telephone at short notice, but it is considered more courteous to arrange them in advance. It is common practice for companies not to respond, especially to a first contact, if they do not think a meeting will be beneficial to them, or if you have not been introduced by a mutual friend or business partner. This is how Bulgarians prefer to work. You therefore have to be persistent and get a definite 'yes' or 'no' in arranging an appointment.

2

LOGISTICS Travelling between appointments in the cities of Sofia or Plovdiv may be possible on foot if you stay in a centrally located hotel and are visiting ministries and other businesses located downtown. Hotels can provide a street map and advice on finding particular streets. Otherwise use a yellow taxi; see page 79 for advice on these.

TIMEKEEPING Bulgarians expect punctuality from British business people, because that is their reputation. This does not mean that they will be punctual in return!

MAINTAINING BUSINESS CONTACTS Undertakings and promises are meant when given, but not always honoured in practice. For example, if you receive a promise to receive some information within a week, you may still be waiting after one month. Polite and regular contact to establish a good working relationship can help to overcome such problems, which are not exclusively Bulgarian!

OFFICIAL BUSINESS Dealing with government ministries and agencies requires patience and persistence. Lack of decision-making (particularly when the decision is perceived as difficult) prevails, as well as a culture of not wishing to take responsibility. Officials may hide behind bureaucratic procedures or the need to refer a decision to a higher level (though the latter is indeed often the case).

WOMEN IN BUSINESS Foreign and local businesswomen are treated in the same way as their male colleagues, often with a gallantry no longer seen in Britain. In both the private and public sectors there are many successful Bulgarian women, though attitudes to women are in general a little more conservative than in the UK, particularly among the older generation.

HOSPITALITY Entertaining is often a feature of business life, and invitations to lunch or dinner may help build the foundations of a good working relationship. Contacts may return the invitations but entertainment is almost always in restaurants, of which there are plenty to suit different budgets and tastes in Sofia and the other main cities. Meals follow a similar time and pattern to those in Britain, though the pace tends to be considerably more leisurely. Bulgarians particularly enjoy their starter salads, and the accompanying *rakiya(s)* (see page 62).

BUYING PROPERTY IN BULGARIA

INVESTMENT OR RELOCATION The property market for foreigners still divides essentially into two groups: the investors with no particular knowledge of or interest in Bulgaria unless there is a profit to be made, and those who, even if they don't yet know the country very well, do genuinely like the place and want to spend time here.

The former will be mainly interested in new developments on the Black Sea coast, in the ski resorts and possibly in new developments in Sofia. The latter are mainly looking for village houses at bargain prices, which they plan to restore.

Both groups need to be aware that, although they are in the Bulgarian property market, in most cases they are also out of it! By this I mean that, whether it is a well-restored village house or an apartment with a sea view, it is unlikely that when you sell you will be selling to a Bulgarian.

For many early investors, the idea was to buy before Bulgaria joined the EU in order to reap an expected profit when it did so, but then there was a second wave who were previously rather timid about buying here, and who are now reassured by EU membership. At the very least, buyers should like what they are buying, and be ready to use it and keep it for a while, because a lot of those promises about quick profits and high rental income for several months a year will never happen. The coast does not have a long season; it is very quiet between late September and early May, and there is no villa-letting culture as there is in Spain and Portugal. There is only a basic airline service to the coast in winter and no, despite what some villa ads declare, you can't drive from Sofia to the coast in under 3 hours. Villages may be set in glorious scenery but they are not Italian villages with charming cafés and eateries; they are basic and in many cases poor. You may have improved your house tenfold, but who will buy it? Not local Bulgarians who can't afford it; not wealthy Bulgarians who are not interested in little village houses, only lavish villas; and maybe not other foreigners, as they will be looking to do their own restoration. As always, caveat emptor!

WHERE TO BUY Once you have decided to buy in Bulgaria you must do some research. It looks small on the map, but the roads aren't good and those tales of skiing in the morning and sitting on the beach in the afternoon are just that, tales. So you have to decide if it's sea or ski, how far you are willing to travel from an airport and how close to your chosen place you can afford to be. Or if it is a village, are you ready to learn Bulgarian? Because if not you will be very isolated.

LEGAL PROCEEDINGS Make sure you set a budget and include all the peripheral costs of buying: legal costs, estate agents' fees, stamp duty, bank fees, translators, notaries, travel expenses for visits, car hire, renovation costs if applicable and furniture. You will need a solicitor, especially if you are buying an existing property, as there will be searches to do to make sure the vendor is the sole owner or is selling in agreement with his co-owners, and to make sure there are no debts connected with the property.

Your estate agent may suggest a solicitor or you may like to choose your own; obviously an English speaker is an advantage. The British consulate website (*www.britishembassy.gov.uk*) has a list of English-speaking lawyers.

The legal activity takes place in two main bursts: when you sign a preliminary contract and about a month later when everything has been checked, a final signing. At the first stage you will need to pay a deposit of at least 10%, higher for off-plan arrangements. The estate agent often draws up the basic contract but you should definitely get your lawyer to check it, and probably it's wisest to have it translated too. You'll find yourself spending a lot of time at the notary's office: contracts, translations and power of attorney (if required) all need to be stamped.

FINANCE For the second stage you will need to have all your funds in place; your bank will show you how to arrange a transfer, which costs about £20. On completion day you meet the vendor or the developer or their representative, lawyers from both sides and a translator at the notary's office. The notary authenticates the identities of buyer and seller, foreigners use their passports, Bulgarians show their EGN or citizen's registration document. The contract may then be read out and a translation made simultaneously (or written if you prefer) and the two parties sign the notary act and the notary stamps all the documents. Once the money and keys have been exchanged the notary will register you as the new owner on the Land Registry. Your lawyer must register the property with the tax authorities within seven days.

2

You should speak to your UK bank before you start your search so that you understand the timescale and costs of moving money around. Obviously you will need a Bulgarian bank account to receive the money and for future general use, arrange such as paying all your utility bills by direct debit.

LIVING IN BULGARIA If you intend to make Bulgaria your permanent home you will need to check out the latest regulations about visas. There is plenty of helpful information on www.bulgarianembassy.org.uk. The passport office in Sofia is at bul Maria Luisa 48.

Take advice from your bank if you need to raise a mortgage, as some Bulgarian banks offer these but UK interest rates are lower. It's much better to have discussed this before you go house-hunting, as it's easy to get carried away and overcommit yourself.

Be prepared, take advice, check everything and then enjoy the experience!

CULTURAL ETIQUETTE

TIPPING Tipping is expected by porters, taxi drivers, waiters and tour guides; 10–15% is about right for someone who has served you a meal, so long as you are satisfied with the service. When paying with a large denomination note in a restaurant, put the money on the plate but do *not* say 'Thank you' unless you intend the waiter to keep all the change. If you say nothing he will bring the change and you can use some of it to leave as your tip. For taxi drivers and those who've served a beer or a coffee, just round up the bill. For porters, depending on the task, give 2–5lv.

SMOKING Smoking is very widespread, but smoking in restaurants and public buildings is now illegal, and this is generally, but not always, adhered to.

IN COMPANY The word '*Nazdrave!*' ('Your Health!') is often the only one foreigners learn. Bulgarians at a table will make quite a ceremony of beginning to drink and expect to greet and make eye contact with everyone at the table individually and clink glasses with them. At intervals throughout the evening, and not just when a new round of drinks arrives, someone will initiate a repeat performance; it is a very sociable tradition.

If you visit Bulgarians at home you should take a present: a bottle of good wine and some flowers, for example. The flower stems should be an uneven number – even numbers are for funerals. Bulgarians normally take off their shoes when entering someone's house or flat, though they won't expect you to. However, if it is midwinter and Sofia's streets are covered in old dirty snow, you could leave your boots at the door and put on clean shoes.

Most Bulgarians earn less than their western European counterparts, so be sensitive to this in conversation. Remarks about how wonderfully cheap restaurants and shops are would be tactless.

TRAVELLING POSITIVELY

Visitors to Bulgaria will all be aware of two things: one is that its people are extraordinarily generous, and the other is that many of them are very hard up.

There are many other worthwhile causes but I have included ones which I personally know about and support.

The **Karin Dom Foundation** (*Sv Nikola, Varna 9010, PO Box 104;* ✆ *052 302517;* e *karindom@bta.bg; www.karindom.org*) was set up by a former Bulgarian Ambassador to the UK and the Republic of Ireland, Ivan Stancioff. He offered his family house, which had been built in 1908, nationalised in 1944 and restituted in 1993, to a foundation named after a cousin, Karin, who had suffered from cerebral palsy. The **Centre for Rehabilitation and Social Integration of Children with Special Needs** is the first such centre in Bulgaria. Each year it is possible, after successful rehabilitation, to transfer some children to mainstream kindergartens and schools. The multidisciplinary team of specialists work with about 150 children on average in a year. Karin Dom serves as a day centre for children with physical disabilities, mental or behaviour problems, autism and learning difficulties. The objective is to help children with special needs and their families, so that they are not abandoned in institutions but included in the life of the community. There is more information on the website and details of how to help by making a donation.

Any visitor to Sofia will be aware of the plight of the street dogs. Residents are ambivalent about the dogs, seemingly believing that sterilisation is cruel, but that to abandon unwanted pets on the street is 'giving them a chance'. **Animal Rescue Sofia** (m *0879 022675; www.arsofia.com*) rescues, treats and rehomes stray and/or injured animals. It ran a successful fund-raising campaign in 2013, resulting in the purchase of land and buildings for the home of the rescue centre. Dogs are vaccinated and neutered before being offered for rehoming. The Farm is accessible by public transport from Sofia.

Part Two

THE GUIDE

3

Sofia (София)

Telephone code: 02

Sofia has the buzz of a capital city and the convenience of a compact centre where all the main sights can be visited on foot. For those averse to map-reading, a simple rule of thumb is to follow the yellow brick road!

The city has a good selection of museums, religious buildings of several faiths and in many styles, from the ancient and unassuming Sv Sofia to the iconic Sv Aleksandur Nevski, and numerous good restaurants, cafés and bars. It has a UNESCO World Heritage Site, Boyana Church, and its own mountain, Vitosha, right on the edge of the city, providing skiing in winter and wonderful walks, flowers, birds and fresh, cool air in summer.

It has only been Bulgaria's capital since 1879 so its main boulevards are from the late 19th century, but in among them are some older sites: the Neolithic settlement at Slatina; the Roman rotunda of Sv Georgi and several newly excavated Roman buildings discovered during the construction of the metro; and the sunken Church of Sv Petka Samardzhiiska, which was built in Ottoman times. There are several monuments and buildings reflecting Bulgaria's long and close relationship with Russia: the fine statue of Tsar Alexander II the Liberator, the Russian Church of Sv Nikolai and the Sv Aleksandur Nevski Memorial Church, for example. There is a mosque and a synagogue; indeed in the central pl Sv Nedelya you can see the Orthodox Church, the Banya Bashi Mosque, the newly built Catholic Cathedral of St Joseph and the Synagogue within a few hundred metres of each other.

Sofia in the 21st century has a real energy and a feeling of being a city that is on the up. It is also a rather relaxed city, especially in summer, when people-watching while strolling and sitting at pavement cafés are favourite evening occupations. However, there's plenty of culture available too: affordable opera, classical music and theatre (if your Bulgarian is good enough!). Bars, clubs and a wealth of excellent restaurants make spending a few, or indeed many, days in Sofia a pleasure.

HISTORY

The history of Sofia is clearly inextricably linked to the history of the whole of Bulgaria (pages 15–21), so it is told here with reference to some buildings which have witnessed the different eras.

As with many Bulgarian towns and cities, Sofia is built on ancient foundations. Excavations of Slatina, the Neolithic village beneath a modern suburb, have produced female terracotta figures, ceramics and beads from a large dwelling area of 1,500m². There were also signs of cult burials from which a terracotta bull, arrowheads, weights for vertical looms and many other domestic objects have been discovered. When the Museum of Sofia finally opens, these will be among the first exhibits.

The Thracian tribes lived in much of the territory of Bulgaria, at least as early as the 8th century BC and probably much earlier. They spread to other parts of southeast Europe and the Caucasus, and were further dispersed by the campaigns of Alexander the Great and the division of the Roman Empire into its western and eastern parts. It seems that their tribal structures were fluid, some historians claiming there were as many as 80 tribes, whereas Homer refers to only three.

In the context of Sofia's history, the fact that the tribe in this area was called Serdi provided the Romans with the place name Serdika. By the 5th century BC, Thracian culture had developed to its highest point and was in no way inferior to the better-known achievements of the Greeks. But here in Sofia, from the 1st century AD Thracians ceded to Romans. Serdika was equipped with the usual Roman necessities: baths, theatres, basilicas and amphitheatres, wide roads and villas. The most complete remaining Roman building is behind the Sofia Hotel Balkan, the rotunda of Sv Georgi.

The oldest parts of Sv Sofia were built as a basilica for burials in the 4th century. It was destroyed by the Huns, but rebuilding on the old foundations quickly began. During the Second Bulgarian Kingdom there was more damage and reconstruction. It survived as a mosque during much of the Ottoman occupation, but the two earthquakes of the 19th century, which caused the loss of its minaret and other damage, were seen as ill omens and the Turks abandoned it. Now, after a very prolonged restoration, it is the most beautiful simple building, with dignity and charisma.

The almost 500 years of Ottoman subjugation have left some visible Muslim buildings and a few barely visible Bulgarian buildings constructed during Ottoman rule. One such is the Church of Sv Petka Samardzhiiska, built low on the ground in order to demean it and not to rival Muslim buildings. The original Sv Petka probably dates from the 14th century, but this was demolished by the Turks because it was near their city centre. The Guild of Saddlers paid for the reconstruction, hence its name, from the word *samar* (a kind of saddle). The outside is plain in order to avoid offence but inside there are vibrant and expressive murals from the 16th century, as well as later, less passionate, additions.

From the same period, but from the Ottoman rather than Bulgarian side, is the Great Mosque, an impressive nine-domed square building completed in 1494. This is now the Archaeological Museum.

The liberation of a large part of Bulgaria in 1878 caused a building frenzy in the new capital, Sofia, as infrastructure projects such as water supplies and drainage were undertaken, and projects for building suitably dignified bridges and boulevards were initiated. From this period date the Eagles and Lions bridges (Orlov Most and Lavov Most) and the beautiful Ivan Vazov Theatre. The establishment of the new capital had two functions: to draw a line under the Ottoman period, and to indicate that Bulgaria was not satisfied with the boundaries allocated to it in 1878. It was particularly important that Macedonia, which many considered to be an integral part of the country, remained outside its borders. Choosing a capital on the western edge of the country was a clear demonstration that one day, with Macedonia included, it would be a central capital.

Under communism many monumental Stalinist-style edifices were constructed: TSUM, the Sofia Hotel Balkan and other buildings around and near to the Largo. In the post-communist era there have been some good restorations of old buildings, some stylish new ones and also some inappropriate monstrosities. Many new apartment blocks are crammed far closer together than the old, much-maligned, communist ones.

GETTING THERE AND AWAY

BY AIR There are daily internal flights (taking about an hour) between Sofia and the Black Sea airports of Varna and Burgas operated by Bulgaria Air (*www.air.bg*).

BY TRAIN The central railway station is at bul Maria Luisa [80 D1], next to the bus station. See page 46 for examples of international trains to Sofia, including journey times and prices. Same-day tickets for Bulgarian destinations are sold on the ground floor; allow time for queues and finding the right platform. The large screen has departure and arrival information in English. Advance tickets and international tickets are sold by Rila Bureau at the station (✆ 9323346) and other Rila offices such as the one at ul General Gurko 5 (✆ 9870777). For timetables and online tickets, see www.bdz.bg.

BY BUS Sofia's central bus station is at bul Maria Luisa [80 D1] (✆ 0900 21000; *www.centralnaavtogara.bg*), and information is in English and Bulgarian. There are several different operators so prices on the same route can vary. Intercity buses are clean and comfortable, but those to small village destinations are often old and uncomfortable.

Sofia has other bus stations at Ovcha Kupel, bul Tsar Boris III (*also called Zapad (west) bus station;* ✆ 9555362). Buses from here leave for the southwest of the country, an area also served by buses from the central bus station. Yug (south) station (✆ 8722345) has buses for Samokov, and Poduene bus station (✆ 8474262) has buses for central Bulgaria.

GETTING AROUND

Public transport is well organised and efficient. The first tram (*tramvai*) line opened in January 1901, the first bus (*avtobus*) route in 1935, and the first trolley bus (*trolley*) in 1941. The same fare structure applies to all three.

Ticket type	Cost
Single (all kinds of public transport)	1lv
Ten trips (for underground loaded on a smart card)	8lv
Ten trips (for trams, trolley buses and buses loaded on a smart card)	8lv
Ten tickets for ten single journeys on ground transport (use in order, keeping ticket no. 10 until the end)	8lv
One-day pass (all kinds of public transport)	4lv
One-month pass (ground transport; one line)	28lv
One-month pass (underground)	42lv
One-month pass (all lines)	60lv

Single-trip tickets are sold at kiosks and newspaper stands at the major stops, at onboard ticket-vending machines or by the driver of the vehicle. You have to validate the ticket using the metal punchers located near the windows. The electronic smart cards are issued in Sofia Urban Mobility Centre's ticket offices. The fare is collected from the smart card at touch screen validators in the vehicle. There are frequent ticket inspections. The fine for not having a ticket is 20lv. If you are travelling with a suitcase or large rucksack you should buy an additional ticket.

Public transport runs from 04.30 to 23.30.

MAJOR TRAM LINES

1, 7   Central railway station to bul Hristo Botev to National Palace of Culture (NDK). Tram 1 continues to Ivan Vazov residential district; Tram 7 drives along bul Bulgaria.

12   Central railway station to ul Graf Ignatiev to Lozenets district (pl Jurnalist).

6   Central railway station to National Palace of Culture underpass to Lozenets district (ul Arsenalska).

5   Ul Alabin (centre) to pl Makedonia to Rodina Hotel to bul Tsar Boris III to Knyazhevo district.

19   Knyazhevo district to bul D. Petkov to metro station Vardar to overpass Nadezhda to Railway station (north).

MAJOR BUS ROUTES

84   Sofia University to Sofia Airport Terminal 1.

384   Sofia University to Sofia Airport Terminal 2 via bul Chr Columbus to bul Tsarigradsko Shose (Metro Shop 1).

94   Sofia University to National Soccer Stadium to National Palace of Culture to Hemus Hotel to Darvenitsa district to Studentski grad (students' town).

213   Central railway station to Lavov Most (Lions Bridge) to bul Tsarigradsko Shose to Mladost 4 district.

64   Hladilnika district to Dragalevtsi to Boyana to bul Bulgaria, Centre for Hygiene

98   Hotel Hemus to Hladilnika, Sofia Zoo to Dragalevtsi district to Simeonovo, Bistritsa and Zheleznitsa.

122   Hladilnika district to Sofia Zoo to Simeonovo cable-car station.

93   Hladilnika district to Dragalevtsi chair-lift station.

63   Tsar Boris III to bul Bukston to Belovodski Put (for the National History Museum).

111   Lyulin 1, 2 district to ring road (stops at National History Museum) to Business Park Sofia to Mladost 2 district to Mladost 1 district

MAJOR TROLLEY BUS LINES

1   Peta Gradska Bolnitsa (City Hospital 5) St Klementina (near the central railway station) to Opalchenska metro station to National Palace of Culture underpass to Sofia University to Hadzhi Dimitur district to Vasil Levski district.

2   Hadzhi Dimitur district to Sofia University to bul Patriarh Evtimii to Medical Academy to Borovo district to Bukston district.

5   Nadezhda overpass (near the central railway station) to Opalchenska metro station to National Palace of Culture underpass to Mladost 1 district.

UNDERGROUND TRANSPORT The metro opened in 1998 with a 10km line from Serdika station, by the Sofia Hotel Balkan, to Lyulin district. It is being rapidly developed. Line 1 is orientated east–west. It now reaches Mladost residential area and the last station is in front of Expo Centre and Metro Shop 1.The second line started to operate at the end of August 2012 and it is orientated north–south. The two lines cross at Serdika station in the centre and passengers can pass from line to line without paying for a second ticket. In 2015 the construction of more extensions to the lines will be completed and line 1 will reach Sofia Airport Terminal 2.

Metro tickets are different from other transport tickets. They cost 1lv and are sold at cash desks at the entrance to the station. They are not valid on other forms of transport.

MINIBUS TRANSPORT In addition to the regular lines there are also minibus services (*marshrutni taxita*) which are part of the city transport. The tickets are sold by the driver and the cost of a single ticket is 1.50lv (no passes).

It is quite confusing for non-Bulgarian speakers, as there are no fixed stops nor clear information about the numbers or destinations of the minibuses. Regulars just wave at a crossroads or boulevard and the driver stops. So you need to know the number of the minibus and where it is going. Minibuses run from 05.30 to 22.30.

5	Central railway station to Studentski Grad.
10	Pl Ruski Pametnik to Bankya.
12	Pl Ruski Pametnik to Zlatnite Mostove, Vitosha.
27	Ovcha Kupel to Nov Bulgarski Universitet (New Bulgarian University) to NDK to Studentski Grad.
35	Vruzhdebna to ul Gurko to Lyulin 1 district.
37	Novi Iskur to Levski Monument to Park Vrana to Lozen village.

TAXI SERVICES Taxis are quite cheap and that makes them a good form of transport in Sofia. You should be aware, though, that some drivers will try to cheat you. The most 'dangerous' places are the airport, bus and train stations and outside embassies and expensive hotels. Always check the rates displayed on the dashboard and use only reputable companies (such as those listed below). Avoid getting into an argument with the driver.

Since June 2000 all legal and registered taxicabs must be yellow and operate with meters. The rates per kilometre are regulated. The average rate is 0.79–1.30lv per kilometre. The daytime tariff (*06.00–22.00*) and night-time tariff are different, the latter usually being 15 stotinki more per kilometre.

You can order taxis by phone. When you do that they will give you the three-digit number of the taxi which will come to pick you up. An additional fee of 0.70–1.00lv has to be paid for this service.

When hailing a taxi, the green or red light at the front window indicates whether or not it is free. Most drivers don't speak English so it is a good idea to know the Bulgarian name of the place you want to go, or have it written down in Cyrillic.

Taxi companies

🚕 **OK Supertrans** ☏ 9732121

🚕 **Radio SV Taxi (Радио СВ Такси)** ☏ 91263; m 1263

🚕 **Taxi S Express** ☏ 91280; m 1280

🚕 **Yellow Taxi** ☏ 91119

GETTING FROM THE AIRPORT TO THE CENTRE Bus number 84 goes from the airport Terminal 1 to the university; from Terminal 2 bus 384 also goes to the university, or you can take a taxi. On buses you'll need to buy an **additional ticket for your luggage**. The metro station at the airport is due to be completed in spring 2015, when it will provide a very convenient and inexpensive transport option.

PARKING If you have a hire car you will need to understand about parking. This may be provided by your hotel, at a price, or you may leave the car in a guarded car park nearby, also at a price. There are a few central multi-storey-type car parks

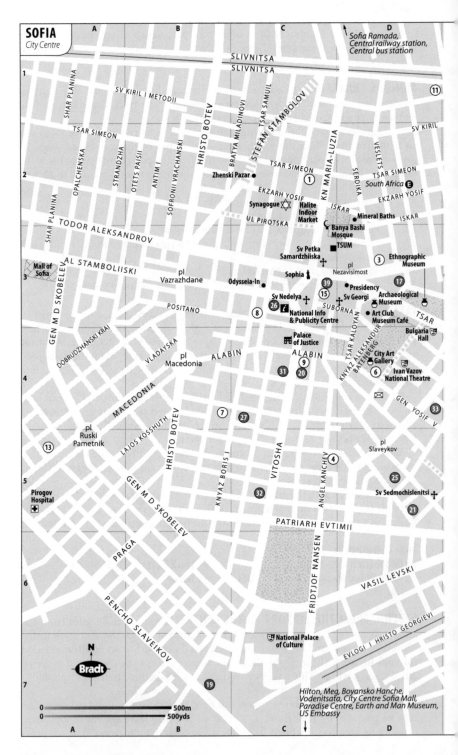

SOFIA
City Centre

Sofia Ramada,
Central railway station,
Central bus station

SLIVNITSA
SLIVNITSA

SHAR PLANINA
SV KIRIL I METODII
TSAR SIMEON
OPALCHENSKA
STRANDZHA
OTETS PAISII
ANTIM I
SOFRONII VRACHANSKI
HRISTO BOTEV
BRATYA MILADINOVI
TSAR SAMUIL
STEFAN STAMBOLOV
SV KIRIL
VESLETS
SERDIKA
KN MARIA–LUZIA
ISKAR
TSAR SIMEON
TSAR SIMEON
EKZARH YOSIF
South Africa (E)
EKZARH YOSIF

Zhenski Pazar ●

SHAR PLANINA
TODOR ALEKSANDROV
Synagogue ✡
Halite Indoor Market
UL PIROTSKA
⚲ Banya Bashi Mosque
Mineral Baths
ISKAR
TSUM ■

Mall of Sofia
AL STAMBOLIISKI
GEN M D SKOBELEV
DOBRUDZHANSKI KRAI
pl Vazrazhdane
POSITANO
Odysseia-In ●
Sv Petka Samardzhiiska ✝
pl Nezavisimost
Sophia ⚲
Sv Nedelya ✝
26 ⓘ
National Info & Publicity Centre
8
Sv Georgi
SUBORNA
③ Ethnographic Museum
⑰
Presidency ●
Archaeological Museum
Art Club Museum Café ●
TSAR
Bulgaria Hall 🎵
VLADAYSKA
pl Macedonia
ALABIN
Palace of Justice
ALABIN
9
31 20
TSAR KALOYAN
KNYAZ ALEKSANDUR BATENBERG
City Art Gallery
6
Ivan Vazov National Theatre
MACEDONIA
LAJOS KOSSHUTH
HRISTO BOTEV
7
27
VITOSHA
GEN YOSIF V
33
pl Ruski Pametnik
13
KNYAZ BORIS I
ANGEL KANCHEV
4
pl Slaveykov
25
Pirogov Hospital ✚
GEN M D SKOBELEV
32
Sv Sedmochislenitsi ✝
21

PRAGA
PATRIARH EVTIMII
FRIDTJOF NANSEN

PENCHO SLAVEIKOV
VASIL LEVSKI
EVLOGI I HRISTO GEORGIEVI

N
Bradt

🏰 National Palace of Culture

19

0   500m
0   500yds

Hilton, Meg, Boyansko Hanche,
Vodenitsata, City Centre Sofia Mall,
Paradise Centre, Earth and Man Museum,
US Embassy

80

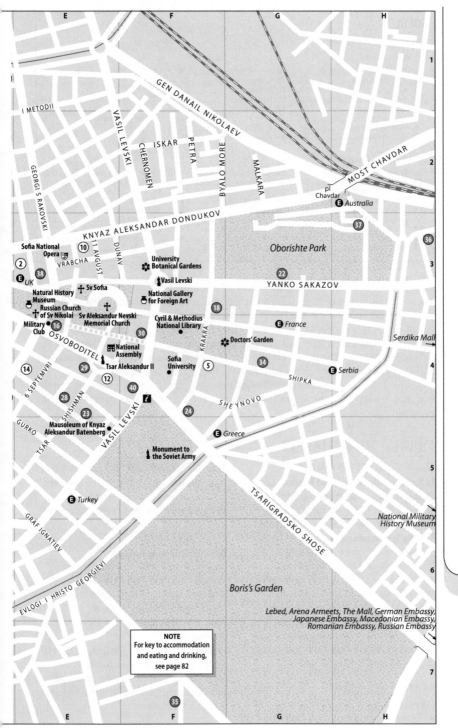

in Sofia, and a lot of small open spaces which have been turned into car parks. These will have attendants to sell you tickets, and arrange for the dreaded 'spider' to come and lift your car on to a truck and take it to a car pound if you overstay. It is worth carrying a supply of the scratch-card-style tickets in case there is no visible attendant when you arrive. You can buy them from kiosks, petrol stations and the parking attendants. The prices vary but are 2lv per hour in the centre, the blue zone; and 1lv per hour in the green zone, which is slightly less central.

There is also street parking with regulations displayed on signposts; be careful that you understand the instructions or you may return to a space where you expected your car to be.

TOURIST INFORMATION

TOURIST INFORMATION CENTRES
🛈 National Information and Publicity Centre (Информационен център) [80 C3] pl Sv Nedelya 1; ☎9879778; www.bulgariatravel.org; ⊕ 09.00–17.00 Mon–Fri. Has useful brochures.
🛈 Sofia Tourist Information Centre [81 F4] In the underground pass in front of Sofia University; ☎4918344; e tourist@info-sofia. bg; www.visitsofia.bg; ⊕ Jul–Sep 08.00–20.00 Mon–Fri & 10.00–18.00 Sat–Sun, Oct–Jun Mon–Fri 09.30–18.00. There are leaflets here about free walking tours, pub crawls & food tours, as well as free maps & information about opening times. Additional centres are due to open near the National Theatre & Sv Petka Samardzhiiska.

TOURIST MAGAZINES
Sofia In Your Pocket Free map & mini-guide to the capital & events. Available in hotels & shops.

Sofia: The Insider's Guide This quarterly listings magazine, available in hotels, shops & elsewhere, is a useful resource for up-to-date information on eating out, nightlife & special events. Price: 3.60lv.

TOUR OPERATORS
Odysseia-In/ZigZag Holidays bul Stamboliiski 20; ☎9805102; www.zigzag.dir.bg; ⊕09.00–18.30 Mon–Fri & 09.00–17.00 Sat–Sun in summer. These travel agents can arrange accommodation in Sofia & all over the country & advise on rural & activity tourism. They also sell a variety of maps.
Lyuba Tours ul Tsanko Tserkovski 22; ☎9633343; e info@lyubatours.com; www.lyubatours.com. Consult this company for something more unusual, with the focus on special events such as folklore festivals & wine-tastings.

UPMARKET €€€€–€€€€€

🏠 **Arena di Serdica** (64 rooms) ul Budapesta 2–4; ✆8107777; e hotel@arenadiserdica.com; www.arenadiserdica.com. Roman ruins discovered during the hotel's construction can be seen in the hotel lobby. Stylish, modern boutique hotel with a popular terrace restaurant. Wellness club.

🏠 **Grand Hotel Sofia** (105 rooms) ul Gurko 1; ✆8110800; e reservations@grandhotelsofia.bg; www.grandhotelsofia.bg. Located in the heart of Sofia, overlooking the City Garden & the National Theatre. De luxe business hotel in a modern glass building housing smart restaurant, piano & cigar bars & cafés.

🏠 **Hilton** (245 rooms) bul Bulgaria 1; ✆9335000; www.hilton.com. Pleasant but not central location, with business centre, health club, swimming pool & modern in-room facilities.

🏠 **Radisson BluGrand Hotel** (136 rooms) pl Narodno Subranie 4; ✆9334334; e info.sofia@ radissonsas.com; www.sofia.radissonsas.com. In the most attractive part of the city, opposite the National Assembly & Sv Aleksandur Nevski Church; terrace café in summer, health club & casino.

🏠 **Sofia Hotel Balkan** (188 rooms) pl Sv Nedelya 5; ✆9816541; www.sofiabalkan.net. Very grand hotel, & an architectural landmark in the heart of Sofia. Casino, business centre, conference facilities, excellent restaurant & café.

MID-RANGE €€€

🏠 **Crystal Palace Boutique** (63 rooms) ul Shipka 14; ✆9489489; e hotel@crystalpalace-sofia.com; www.crystalpalace-sofia.com. Unique combination of architectural monument & modern hotel. Business centre, health club, restaurant & bar.

🏠 **Rodina** (506 rooms) bul Totleben 8; ✆9179999; e reservation@rodina.bg; www.rodina.bg. Older-style high-rise building with a panoramic view of the city; excellent facilities, 4 restaurants, congress centre, sports centre, swimming pool.

🏠 **Sofia Ramada** (603 rooms) bul Maria Luiza 131; ✆9338888; www.sofia-princess-hotel.com. Biggest hotel in the city; largest casino in the country, with a great variety of gambling facilities. Near railway & bus stations, but not in an attractive part of the city.

BUDGET €€

🏠 **Amethyst** (27 rooms) ul Tsar Simeon 67; ✆9835475; e hotel_amethyst@abv.bg; www.hotelamethyst.com. Central location, just round the corner from Halite. Clean, basic but welcoming.

🏠 **Arte** (25 rooms) bul Dondukov 5; ✆4027100; e reception@artehotelbg.com; www.artehotelbg.com. Bright, stylish & central hotel with welcoming & helpful staff.

🏠 **L'Opera** (9 rooms) ul Parizh 8; ✆9806126; e hotel_opera_sofia@yahoo.com; www.hotel-lopera.eu. Large rooms, convenient (& quiet) location, friendly staff. In an old building with antique furniture.

🏠 **Meg** (17 rooms) ul Krum Popov 84; ✆9651970; www.meg-lozenetz.com/en. Popular modern hotel near the National Palace of Culture. Good-value business hotel with spacious rooms.

🏠 **Slavyanska Beseda** (91 rooms) ul Slavyanska 3; ✆9801303; e reception@slavyanska.com; www.slavyanska.com. Very central location; good value for money, but otherwise a rather basic standard of accommodation.

SHOESTRING €

🏠 **Pop Bogomil** (10 rooms) ul Pop Bogomil 5; ✆9837065; e hotel@popbogomil.com; www.popbogomil.com. A small, welcoming hotel, with nice rooms. Handy for train & bus stations.

HOSTELS €

🏠 **Art Hostel** ul Angel Kunchev 21; ✆9870545; e art-hostel@art-hostel.com; www.art-hostel.com. The owners of this centrally located hostel organise art performances, exhibitions & live music during the summer, so it can be interesting to stay here.

🏠 **Hostel Mostel** bul Makedonia 2A; m 0889 223296; e info@hostelmostel.com; www.hostelmostel.com. One of the most popular hostels in Sofia, with friendly staff & a nice atmosphere. Discounts for more than 2 nights; organised tours.

🏠 **Hostel Sofia** ul Positano 16; ✆9898582; e hostelsofia@yahoo.com. Nice accommodation in the centre; communal kitchen, lounge. Very friendly.

🏠 **Internet Hostel** ul Alabin 50A, 2nd floor; m 0889 138298; e interhostel@yahoo.co.uk. Very central, basic accommodation.

Sofia has a lively restaurant scene, having seen a complete transformation in the last decade. At last Bulgaria's own fantastic fresh and tasty ingredients are appreciated and used in exciting dishes. No longer do restaurants attempt and fail at foreign cuisine; many chefs now realise the strengths of their own traditional recipes and use them with confidence. Some young chefs are even updating old favourites and presenting them in a new way. Those restaurants which offer foreign cuisine now do so at the highest level. Italian food is particularly popular and well presented.

Inevitably if the scene is lively, it is fast changing, so I have included some established restaurants which should continue to stand the test of time, alongside some exciting new ones. Prices for a main course range from 3lv for the most inexpensive up to 45lv for the most expensive, that is between £1.20 and £18 approximately.

The following suggestions are just a small selection of the possibilities. In general, I would recommend you avoid hotel dining, because in Sofia there are so many more exciting possibilities. However, outside the capital the restaurant in the main hotel of a small town may well offer the best meals.

In Sofia most restaurants are open daily 11.00–23.00, though some close on Sundays. I have only marked exceptions.

RESTAURANTS

✕ **Gloria Mar** ul Slavyanska 29; m 0890 555111. Recommended for its fresh & varied seafood dishes. Service is attentive & helpful. Extensive wine list. €€€€

✕ **Grozd** bul Tsar Osvoboditel 21; ✆9443915. This smart restaurant, with views across to the Soviet Army Monument & park, has an extensive menu with some unusual specialities. €€€€

✕ **Krim** ul Slavianska 17; ✆9886951. Often called the Russian Club, Krim has the best of summer & winter dining. Centrally situated in an old house, in winter you dine indoors in one of several rooms, & in summer in a wonderful tree-shaded garden. A favoured restaurant before 1989, this is still popular with businessmen & politicians. It has an air of elegance, like a gentleman's club, making it ideal for that special occasion. Bulgarian dishes & some Russian specialities. €€€€

✕ **La Capannina** pl Narodno Subranie 9; ✆9804438. Lovely view, excellent Italian food, shady outdoor dining in summer. €€€

✕ **Made in Home** ul Angel Kanchev 30A; m 0876 884014. Mediterranean-style cuisine, stylish & quirky interior, good food & service. €€€

✕ **Pri Miro** ul Murphy (Murfi) 34; ✆9437127. A carnivore's paradise serving enormous helpings of delicious Serbian specialities in a well-presented old house, with a garden for summer

dining. Chef Miro comes to check that no-one is going hungry! €€€€

✕ **Skara Bar 1** ul Dimitar Grekov 2, by the Sfumato Theatre; ✆4830696. Along with its sister establishment (below), this serves huge portions of excellent grills, salads & delicious & unusual puddings. It has a lot of outdoor seating & is very popular with families in summer as it is in a park. Stylish décor in both. €€–€€€

✕ **Skara Bar 2** ul Benkovski 12; ✆4834431. Same as the Skara Bar 1, but a more central location. €€–€€€

✕ **Trops Kushta** bul Maria Luisa 26. Budget option, several branches in central Sofia. Grills, soups & stews, mains from 3lv. €

TRADITIONAL FOLK-STYLE RESTAURANTS

✕ **Chevermeto** pl Bulgaria 1; ✆9630308; m 0885 630308. This somehow succeeds in taking you from a busy Sofia street to a Bulgarian village. Inside are a watermill, a well & trailing plants & vines; there is a lengthy folklore programme of a high standard & well-presented traditional Bulgarian dishes. €€

✕ **Pod Lipite** ul Elin Pelin 1; ✆8665053; www. podlipitebg.com. A simple, old-fashioned setting with a very reliable & good kitchen. This is a restaurant from a different era, a meeting place for writers, artists & musicians for over 80 years. Very popular, so booking is recommended. €€

✗ **Vodenitsata (The Watermill)** [map, page 99] Vitosha Park by Dragalevtsi cable-car; ☎9671058; http://vodenitzata.com. This stylish traditional restaurant, with a garden & indoor eating, is just 20mins from central Sofia. It has a folklore programme. €€

PIZZERIAS

✗ **Dobro** bul Yanko Sakazov 23A, in the park; ☎9433101. Very popular for lunches; pizzas plus a few specialities. Has a garden. €€

✗ **La Cattedrale** ul Oborishte 1; m 0888 040404. Indoor & outdoor dining, mainly pizzas; views of Aleksandur Nevski. €€

✗ **O!Shipka** ul Shipka 11; ☎9449288. Cheap & tasty pizzas; busy. There is a nice garden at the rear. €€

✗ **Victoria** bul Tsar Osvoboditel 7; ☎9863200; www.victoria.bg. Stylish surroundings, very central, lovely outdoor eating in summer. €€

BUDGET

✗ **British Council Café** ul Krakra 7, basement. Salads & sandwiches. Good tea & coffee. €

✗ **Divaka** ul 6 Septemvri 41a; ☎9866971. Large, busy & popular for Bulgarian meats, salads & desserts at very reasonable prices. €

PUBS

♫ **Irish Harp** ul Sv Sofia 7; ☎9898737. Near Sofia Hotel Balkan, this has a British pub atmosphere, so something of a novelty in Sofia, & food. €

♫ **J J Murphy's** ul Karnigradska 6; ☎9802870. Sofia's main Irish pub, with food specialities & live music at w/ends; full of expatriates. €

OUT OF TOWN

✗ **Lebed (Swan) Restaurant** [map, page 99] Samokovsko Shose 83, Pancharevo; ☎9921111; http://restaurantlebed.com. This is less than half an hour's drive from central Sofia. It has huge outdoor & indoor dining spaces with great views of the lake; excellent for fish & grills. Very well presented & served. €€–€€€

ENTERTAINMENT AND NIGHTLIFE

All Bulgarian towns and cities have a thriving cultural life, with music being the most obviously accessible to visitors. Bulgaria has had a host of world-class opera singers; most of them make occasional return visits to perform and this is a wonderful opportunity to see them at very affordable prices. Audiences in Sofia make an effort when going out to the theatre and dress is often quite formal. There are several excellent venues. **Bulgaria Hall** [80 D4] (*ul Aksakov 1*) is actually two halls, one large seating over a thousand people, and a smaller one used for chamber concerts, both of which have a programme of concerts throughout the year. It is close to the Ethnographic Museum. This is the home of the Sofia Philharmonic Orchestra and the acoustics are of a very high quality.

The **National Palace of Culture** [80 C7] (*Националния дворец на културата; pl Bulgaria 1, ticket office on right of main entrance facing bul Vitosha;* ☎ *9166300, 9166400*) is the high-visibility 1980s construction which houses pop and classical concerts, exhibitions, fashion shows, arts festivals, international academic conferences and film premières. It's worth checking in the press. There are numerous halls and exhibition spaces which are quite hard to navigate.

The **Sofia National Opera** [81 E3] (*Софийската народна опера; ul Vrabcha 1; ticket office* ☎ *9811549, 8006266*) is the most elegant of the venues, a little faded but still glamorous. The plush interior seems suitable for the setting of some romantic costume drama. The operas are usually sung in Bulgarian, or sometimes Italian. The programmes now have English-language explanations of the story, and there are English-language subtitles above the stage. Prices range from about 13.50lv to 40lv.

Arena Armeets [map, page 99] (*Арена Армеец; bul Asen Yordanov 1;* ☎ *9033749*) is a large indoor arena seating about 12,000 that hosts shows and concerts, as well as sporting events.

BARS AND CLUBS In the fast-moving world of fashionable nightlife it is likely that suggestions in a book will seem outdated. Check in *Sofia: The Insider's Guide*, listed above under tourist information. *Programata* is a what's-on listing of almost all places of entertainment in Bulgaria's largest cities, available free in most restaurants and hotels. It is also available online (*www.programata.bg*), where it is updated daily.

♬ **Black Label Whisky Bar** [81 E4] bul Tsar Osvoboditel 7; m 0884 143451; ⊕ 20.00–04.00. In the Military Club, so the décor is splendid.

☆ **Brilyantin** [80 D3] ul Moskovska 3; m 0889 245415; ⊕ 17.00–04.00. The classic disco club of Sofia, with mirror balls hanging from the ceilings. It gets full easily & it is hard to get in so a reservation may be a good idea.

☆ **Chervilo** [81 E4] Also in the Military Club; m 0892 000999; 0895 123456; ⊕ 22.30–06.00, closed Sun–Mon. This is the most fashionable Sofia club with leading DJs from Bulgaria & abroad; it is divided into 3 halls.

☆ **Hambara** [80 D5] ul 6 Septemvri. Eccentric, Bohemian, love-it-or-hate-it club. No contact details, no opening times, candle-lit & smoky.

☆ **Life House** [80 C4] ul Denkoglou 12; m 0888 241016; ⊕ 23.00–06.00, closed Sun–Tue. The best place for house music.

☆ **My Mojito** [80 D4] ul Ivan Vazov 12; m 0895 490691; ⊕ 21.00–05.00. Small place in the centre; soon gets crowded in the evenings. Two separate rooms with DJs.

☆ **Yalta** [81 F4] bul Tsar Osvoboditel 20; m 0897 870230; ⊕ 20.00–06.00. The longest-running nightclub in town, featured in *DJ Mag*'s 'Best 100 Clubs in the World'. International DJs star every w/end. Fashionably minimalist décor. One of the best nights out in Sofia.

SHOPPING

Most shops are open 09.00–18.00 or 10.00–19.00 from Monday to Saturday. Some also now open on Sundays for a more limited time.

Recent years have seen huge change and expansion of the shopping scene in Sofia. Much is mainly of interest to locals, such as the out-of-town supermarkets, furniture emporia, DIY supplies and electrical superstores, which have made a large range of goods easily available.

There are also eight shopping malls, which again are perhaps more interesting for residents, though the **City Centre Sofia** [80 C7] (*bul Arsenalski 2*) has a six-screen cinema, some fast-food outlets, bars and restaurants. The **Mall of Sofia** [80 A3] (*bul Stamboliiski 101*) is more upmarket, with a wider choice of shops, a 12-screen cinema and an IMAX screen. Newer ones include: **Serdika Mall** [81 H4] (*bul Sitnyakovo 48; www.serdikacenter.bg*), **The Mall** [81 H7] (*bul Tsarigradsko Shose 115; www.themall.bg*) and **Paradise Centre** [80 C7] (*bul Cherni Vrach 100; www.paradise-center.com*). All have on-site parking.

The traditional smart shopping area of **bul Vitosha** remains popular and for visitors seems a lot more atmospheric and typical of Sofia than any mall. There are restaurants, cafés and innumerable fashion outlets. It is pedestrianised and nicely landscaped, though cars can cross at three junctions.

The **flea market** in front of Sv Aleksandur Nevski Church is a big tourist attraction, though the prices are artificially high – you should try to negotiate. It is fascinating to see the old military paraphernalia, often from the Soviet Union, old cameras and new (fake) Rolexes. There is an art section which is worth browsing through, with a huge range of oils and watercolours. Across the square, elderly ladies display incredibly fine needlework – mainly tablecloths and mats, but also some nice embroidered blouses, and sometimes knitwear for children. The prices are generally reasonable.

TSUM [80 C3], previously the showpiece department store in communist times, now houses an assortment of shops and has an excellent café for shoppers wanting a rest.

Across the road is the restored **Halite** [80 C2] or indoor market, selling fruit, vegetables, fish, bread, delicatessen food, sweet pastries, herbal teas, wines and spirits, and upstairs some inexpensive shops for bags and leather goods and a large pharmacy and cosmetics store, Elitis; in the basement there are the ruins of a section of the old fortress wall of Serdika.

Ul Pirotska is pedestrianised and has plenty of budget shops for clothes, and particularly shoes. It leads you close to **Zhenski Pazar** [80 C2], or Ladies Market, where you can buy almost anything! **Ul Graf Ignatiev** is also a good shopping street, with a variety of stores for clothes, shoes and bags, as well as some cafés and fast-food places.

For visitors wanting to take home souvenirs of Bulgaria, among the most useful resources are the various **museum shops**. The Ethnographic Museum (*pl Aleksandur Batenberg*) has a real Aladdin's cave of a shop where you can buy books, jewellery, rugs, woodcarvings, pottery and embroidery. An unusual selection is available at the National Military History Museum (*ul Cherkovna 92*) where replica KGB hip flasks are on offer alongside well-worn pieces of clothing and equipment.

Clothes sizes are different from European, British or American, with, for example, the British size 12 equalling the American size 10, the European size 40 and, depressingly, the Bulgarian size 46! All increase in increments of two and larger sizes are often not in stock. Most shops are not keen on refunds, so be sure that you are happy with your choice. Customer service varies from very helpful to very offhand, but is generally better in the newer modern shops.

OTHER PRACTICALITIES

BANKS Banks are closed on public holidays (though ATMs will be working) but restaurants, bars and cafés are open. Large shops are often open during holidays, except on Easter Sunday, Christmas Day or New Year's Day, and you will probably find that small corner shops are also open.

COMMUNICATIONS
Internet The internet is available in cafés; both the new and the large hotels provide it, and so does the post office. Free Wi-Fi is widely available in hotels, cafés and even parks.

Post Postal services are not noted for their speed. Christmas cards and holiday postcards seem to be particularly slow, while business letters seem to fare better. Companies such as EMS/BulPost (*ul Gurko 11;* \ *0700 19666, 9815621; www. bgpost.bg*) offer very quick, even overnight, packages to the UK, but at a price.

The **central post office** [80 D4] (*Пощенската палата; ul Gurko 6*) is a large and confusing building. Smaller post offices are fine for buying stamps and local post, but the main office is unavoidable for international parcels. These have to be inspected by customs before they are sealed. Large tables are available for you to complete the wrapping process after inspection. Mysterious distinctions are made between parcels and large envelopes, even if these both contain, for example, a paperback book. Go with a Bulgarian friend! **International parcel collection** is elsewhere, near the railway station at ul Veslets 84. Other express delivery services are SPEEDY (*www.speedy.bg*) and DHL Bulgaria (*www.dhl.bg/bg.html*).

Telephone Public telephones work with prepaid phonecards which are on sale at post offices and kiosks. Another option is to buy a Bulgarian pay-as-you-go SIM card for your mobile phone. MPrima from MobilTel is a popular one, often with special offers. Two other GSM operators are Telenor and Vivatel.

MEDIA English newspapers can be read online, and www.novinite.com is a Sofia-based online English-language newspaper.

MEDICAL The options when dealing with medical emergencies will depend on their seriousness and your medical insurance. For minor problems the staff at **chemists** (*аптека*) can often help, or one of the many private polyclinics. Major emergencies will be taken straight away to the **Pirogov Hospital** [80 A5] (*bul General Totleben 21*). Bulgarian doctors and nurses are very well trained but poorly paid and often ill equipped. If you do need to stay in hospital it would be wise to take some advice from Bulgarian friends or your embassy. The **emergency number** is ☏112.

PRICES The entrance fees for national museums are the highest (usually 10lv) whereas regional museums are governed by local municipalities and vary between 2lv and 5lv. There are only a very small number of private museums, but these tend to be more expensive than national or local ones. Children under seven are admitted free, and schoolchildren, students and pensioners are entitled to a variety of discounts of 50–70% of the standard adult entrance fee.

WHAT TO SEE AND DO

The highlights of a visit to Sofia include the Sv Aleksandur Nevski Memorial Church; Sv Sofia Church; a day or half-day out to the National History Museum and Boyana Church, possibly extending to a walk on Vitosha Mountain if the weather is suitable; the restored Halite (indoor market) and the Ethnographic Museum in the former Royal Palace.

There is a rather nice little booklet called *100 National Tourist Sights* and subtitled 'Bulgaria – this is my country' (100 национални туристически обекта. България – това е моята Родина). It is useful if you are planning to do some sightseeing in Sofia and in other parts of Bulgaria as it gives the names of local places of interest, and if you visit the attraction you can get your booklet stamped. All the stamps are different, and some are particularly well designed. The booklet costs just 1lv and is available at any participating attraction. Fun for children of all ages!

WALKING TOUR *Map, page 89*

The following walking tour is devised as a (very) rough figure of eight, with the crossing point at a pleasant café, the Art Club Museum Café.

There are one or two possible extensions for those with more time, and the compactness of the city centre means that you can break off and rejoin anywhere. Ideally spread the walk out over a couple of days, to allow time for visiting those museums that interest you.

Weekends are a lovely time to walk in Sofia – the traffic is lighter and there are fewer parked cars. Pavements and roads are often uneven, so do take care.

It's probably best to start your walking tour at ① **Sv Aleksandur Nevski Memorial Church** [89 F2] (*Храм-паметник Св Александър Невски*; ☉ *daily*) as it is the largest and most visible building in Sofia. This is Sofia's set-piece square for

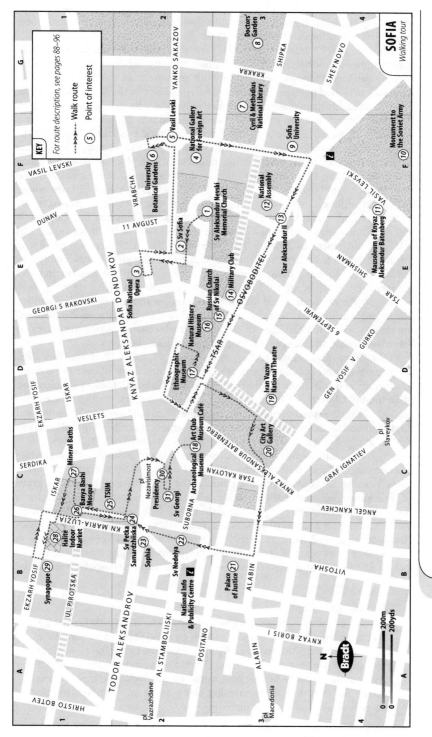

KEY

For route description, see pages 88–96

➤➤➤ Walk route

⑤ Point of interest

SOFIA
Walking tour

Doctors'
Garden
⑧

SHIPKA

Cyril & Methodius
National Library
⑦

SHEYNOVO

⑤ Vasil Levski

National Gallery
for Foreign Art
④

University
Botanical Gardens ⑥

VRABCHA

VASIL LEVSKI

DUNAV

11 AVGUST

Sv Sofia ②

① Sv Aleksandur Nevski
Memorial Church

National
Assembly
⑫

Sofia
University
⑨

VASIL LEVSKI

Monument to
the Soviet Army
⑩

GEORGI S RAKOVSKI

Sofia National
Opera ③

Military Club
⑭

Tsar Aleksandur II
⑬

Mausoleum of Knyaz
Aleksandur Batenberg
⑪

SHISHMAN

TSAR

Russian Church
of Sv Nikolai ⑮

Natural History
Museum ⑯

TSAR

6 SEPTEMVRI

GURKO

GEN YOSIF V

Ethnographic
Museum ⑰

Ivan Vazov
National Theatre ⑲

pl
Slaveykov

Art Club
Museum Café

Archaeological ⑱
Museum

City Art
Gallery ⑳

KNYAZ ALEKSANDUR BATENBERG

GRAF IGNATIEV

ANGEL KANCHEV

Mineral Baths
㉗

Banya Bashi
Mosque ㉖ ㉕ TSUM

pl
Nezavisimost
㉚

Presidency

㉛

Sv Georgi

SUBORNA

TSAR KALOYAN

SERDIKA

ISKAR

EKZARH YOSIF

ISKAR

VESLETS

KNYAZ ALEKSANDAR DONDUKOV

Synagogue ㉙

Halite
Indoor
Market ㉘

Sv Petka
Samardzhiiska ㉓

Sv Nedelya
ℹ

KN MARIA-LUIZA

Sophia ㉔
㉒

Palace
of Justice ㉑

ALABIN

VITOSHA

UL PIROTSKA

EKZARH YOSIF

TODOR ALEKSANDROV

AL STAMBOLIISKI

National Info
& Publicity Centre ℹ

POSITANO

ALABIN

KNYAZ BORIS I

HRISTO BOTEV

pl
Vazrazhdane

pl
Macedonia

N
Bradt

0   200m
0   200yds

impressing visiting delegations, and political and religious leaders. It is also where public demonstrations and celebrations take place.

Although the Church of Sv Sofia gave the capital its name, this much-photographed memorial church is the symbol of the city. Sofia's skyline is dominated by its gleaming golden domes. It was built in honour of the 200,000 Russian casualties who died fighting for Bulgaria's independence in the Russo-Turkish War of 1877–78 and is named after Sv Aleksandur Nevski, a Russian prince who saved his country from invasion in the 13th century, and was the patron saint of Tsar Alexander II, Bulgaria's liberator. The foundation stone was laid in 1882, but the real construction works started in 1904 and finished in 1912 when a period of wars started in Bulgaria, so the official consecration only took place in 1924. Craftsmen and artists worked for many years to create this enormous church, which is said to hold over 5,000 people. The belfry is 52m high and contains 12 bells, whose clamour is audible across the city. Its lavish exterior is, even so, surpassed by the frescoed interior and splendid iconostasis and the golden mosaics. There are nearly 300 mural paintings, including a dramatic vision of God in the main cupola and a Day of Judgement as a timely reminder above the exit. There are decorative finishes in Siena and Carrera marble, onyx, alabaster and gold. It was financed by public subscription and designed in neo-Byzantine style by the Russian architect Pomerantsev. Services are held daily, usually at 09.30 and 17.00; it's well worth witnessing the elaborate ritual with incense, candles and unforgettable chanting. The sounds of this great choir can be purchased on CDs from the women who sell the candles. There is a very famous church choir which sings during the liturgy on Saturday evening and Sunday morning and on religious holidays.

In the Crypt (*Крипта; pl Aleksandur Nevski;* ⊕ *10.00–17.30 Tue–Sun; adult 10lv*), entered from outside, a large exhibition of icons from all over the country is superbly and effectively displayed. This is the **National Gallery's Collection of Orthodox Church Art** from its origins in the 4th century through to the 19th-century National Revival period. There is an illustrated guidebook in Bulgarian and English to help to identify and explain the most significant exhibits. Guided tours can also be arranged, but they are for the real enthusiasts as they last 1–1½ hours.

Across the square to your right as you leave Sv Aleksandur Nevski is the outwardly unassuming ② **Church of Sv Sofia** [89 E2] (*Св София*) from which the capital takes its name. To reach it you pass, among the trees, the simple, moving **grave of Ivan Vazov**, Bulgaria's national writer, who asked to be buried here, in order to continue to be part of the everyday life of the people. The boulder was brought from Vitosha Mountain and inscribed with his name. Walk on to the bronze lion which guards Sofia's eternal flame in memory of the **Unknown Soldier** and continue to the entrance to Sv Sofia. It is ancient and faded but somehow impressive despite its lack of flamboyant flourishes. A new attraction is the **Necropolis** beneath the

CAMPANOLOGY

Few visitors will know that the 12 bells of the Aleksandur Nevski Church are rung every day of the year, single-handedly by an 84-year-old woman, Maria Zabova. She climbs 220 steps up a winding stair to the belfry. This is of course open to the elements so that the sound of the bells can be heard across the city. In winter it can be bitterly cold, but Maria has performed this amazing task for 30 years now in the morning and evening on weekdays, and on Saturday evening and Sunday morning.

basilica. Archaeological investigations revealed 56 tombs and the ruins of the four preceding churches, including some mosaic floors. A staggering 23 centuries of history lies below the church which gave Sofia its name (🕘 *10.00–17.00 daily; adult 6lv, guided tour*).

Two optional extra routes

1 You might like to turn right out of Sv Sofia and continue along Parizh, cross over ul Moskovska, and at the next crossroads with ul Vrabcha, you will see the opera house on your left. The ③ **Sophia National Opera** [89 E2] (*Народната опера*) is based on the design of the Paris Opera. The first operatic performance in Bulgaria, though not in this building, was in 1891. No opera lover will be unaware of Bulgaria's wealth of world-class opera singers (page 29).

Retrace your steps to Moskovska and turn left towards bul Vasil Levski for another optional loop.

2 Leaving the square in the direction of bul Levski, you see the handsome building which used to contain the ④ **National Gallery for Foreign Art** [89 F2]. It has been restored and linked to its neighbouring buildings to form a new (as yet unnamed) museum complex, which will house exhibits from the collection of the Gallery for Foreign Art and the National Art Gallery. Three of the four wings are complete and due to open in autumn 2015. The intention is for the complex to be a national cultural centre and a prestigious venue for visiting exhibitions from abroad.

Beyond it is the monument to revolutionary ⑤ **Vasil Levski** [89 F2], rather beleaguered in the middle of a busy traffic island. The obelisk marks where he was hanged by the Turks in 1873 (see box, page 17). On 19 February each year the people of Sofia pay homage here to Levski, who is the symbol of Bulgarian liberty.

To your left along bul Levski you will find the entrance to the ⑥ **University Botanical Gardens** [89 F2] (*Университетски Ботанически Градини;* 🕘 *09.00–17.00 Mon–Fri & 09.00–18.00 Sat–Sun; adult 2lv*), cleverly disguised as a flower shop. There is a small sign by the door, easily missed. You pay at the counter then pass behind it into a really magical small space in the very centre of Sofia. The gardens are extremely well kept, and labelled with Bulgarian and Latin names. There is a useful small pamphlet in English. In the centre of the garden is a huge oak tree, planted by Tsar Ferdinand in 1892. There is also a large collection of roses, herbaceous plants and palms. There are greenhouses for more exotic species such as orchids, cacti and succulents; a Greek garden with citruses, myrtle and bay; a rock garden and a vegetable patch to show visitors how easy it is to grow your own.

Turn to your right along bul Vasil Levski, and on the left-hand side is the ⑦ **Cyril and Methodius National Library** [89 G3], named after the two brothers responsible for the creation of the Bulgarian alphabet. Their statues are in the small garden in front. It was opened in 1953, though work on the building began before World War II. Behind the National Library is the lovely small park known as the ⑧ **Doctors' Garden** [89 G3], bounded by the streets Oborishte, Shipka and San Stefano. It is named after the monument in its centre, which was erected in 1883 to honour the Russian doctors and medical orderlies killed in the Russo-Turkish War of 1877–78. In 1896, the garden was given to Sofia University for the purpose of creating a botanical garden, and some rare varieties of oak and sycamore were imported. Dotted around are a miscellaneous assortment of archaeological finds, capitals, columns and decorative friezes. It is a very restful and relaxing place. Beyond the National Library is the imposing building of ⑨ **Sofia University** [89 F3], built in the 1920s. At the entrance are the seated figures of the donors of the land and building, Evlogi and Hristo Georgiev.

At street level, you can see the tall ⑩ **Monument to the Soviet Army** [89 F4] (*Паметника на Съветската Армия*). This powerful monument remains controversial. Its base is normally home to skateboarders resting from their spectacular exertions on the adjacent halfpipe, but at times of political tension it becomes either a meeting place for supporters of the Left or a target for graffiti artists. In 2011 the figures on the base were painted as Batman, Robin, Joker, Ronald McDonald and others; there have been several more paintings since then, apologising for Bulgaria's role in the suppression of the Prague Spring, and, recently, painting it in the colours of the Ukrainian flag as a gesture of support.

Before rejoining the main walk you might like to continue along bul Levski (away from the university) to see the ⑪ **Mausoleum of Knyaz Aleksandur Batenberg** [89 F4] (*Мавзолеят на Княз Александър Батенберг; bul Vasil Levski 81; ⊕ 09.00–17.00 Mon–Fri*), which sits in a small garden next to ul Slavyanska. Aleksandur was deposed in 1886 and died in exile, but asked to be buried in Sofia. His successor Ferdinand agreed to build this mausoleum in honour of Bulgaria's first ruler after the liberation. It was built in 1897 by a Swiss architect, and contains his marble sarcophagus. It is set back from the busy road in a shady garden.

This optional loop is completed by returning to the university via the underpass, where you can find the entrance to the metro station Sv Kliment Ohridski, which serves the university and surrounding area (see metro map, 2nd colour section). The **Sofia Tourist Information Centre** is also here (page 82).

Along bul Tsar Osvoboditel
Walk along bul Tsar Osvoboditel back towards Sv Aleksandur Nevski; the Parliament building will be on your right.

If you didn't do the optional loop along bul Levski, leave pl Aleksandur Nevski to the south and walk to the ⑫ **National Assembly** [89 F3] (*Народното събрание*). This is a dignified white building, built and extended during the period 1884–1928. Facing it is a really fine ⑬ **equestrian statue of Tsar Aleksandur II** [89 E3], known as the Liberator. It was erected as a gesture of gratitude for the part he and his troops played in Bulgaria's liberation from the Ottoman Empire in 1878. Around the pedestal are bronze scenes commemorating the battle for Stara Zagora in 1877, the treaty of San Stefano in 1878 and the parliamentary assembly at Veliko Turnovo in 1879.

If you now walk to the west along bul Tsar Osvoboditel, you will see on the right-hand side, facing a small park, a rather grand building, the ⑭ **Military Club** [89 E3] (*Централен военен клуб*). Before 1944 this was the haunt of Sofia's fashionable élite, attending balls and receptions. It has been wonderfully restored and is once again a social hub with bars, clubs and a popular pizza restaurant occupying the grand surroundings.

Immediately beyond it is the exuberant ⑮ **Russian Church of Sv Nikolai** [89 E3] (*Руската черква Св Николай*). With its bright yellow tiles, gilded onion domes and emerald-green spire, it looks like something from a fairy story, the church equivalent of Hansel and Gretel's gingerbread house perhaps! It was built around 1912 by a Russian diplomat who feared for the fate of his soul if he worshipped in the schismatic Bulgarian churches. Sv Nikolai traditionally works miracles, and it is customary for worshippers to write requests on pieces of paper and put them in the box in the basement next to the tomb of the revered Bishop Serafim, who died in 1950.

Next to the church is the ⑯ **Natural History Museum** [89 D2] (*Природонаучен музей; bul Tsar Osvoboditel 1;* \ *9885115;* ☻ *10.00–17.00 daily; adult 4lv*), which is a large collection of stuffed and preserved creatures, plus a few in cases on the stairs which are alive (if dormant!). The collection was started by Knyaz Ferdinand, a keen entomologist. The ground floor is dedicated to minerals from Bulgaria and around the world. The first floor is devoted to the history of Earth and the life on it. The second floor is for mammals, and the third for insects. The museum shop sells semi-precious stones, some mounted as modern jewellery.

Continuing along bul Tsar Osvoboditel and into pl Aleksandur Batenberg, the beautiful building on the right, facing a big open space (sadly, usually full of parked cars), is the ⑰ **Ethnographic Museum** [89 D2] (*Етнографски музей; pl Aleksandur Batenberg 1;* \ *9881974;* ☻ *10.00–17.30 Tue–Sun; adult 6lv*) and **Art Gallery** (*Художествена галерия; pl Aleksandur Batenberg 1;* \ *9803320;* ☻ *10.00–18.00 Tue–Sun; adult 6lv*). It was originally the Turkish *konak* and then, after 1878, the Royal Palace. It was used as the governor's residence as well as for administrative offices. It was here that Levski was tried and sentenced in 1873. The building was reconstructed for Knyaz Aleksandur Batenberg between 1880 and 1882, and was further expanded by Knyaz Ferdinand (1894–96). After World War II it was taken over by the Council of Ministers and opened in 1954 as the Art Gallery and Ethnographic Museum.

The Art Gallery shows the development of Bulgarian art from the late 18th to the 20th century. The collection has more than 30,000 paintings, prints and sculptures.

The Ethnographic Museum has lovely displays of costumes from a variety of regions. Indeed, it has more than it can display, and the serious enthusiast can arrange by appointment to see reserve collections. It is not well displayed or labelled, so if you are interested it's worth paying extra for a guide to show you around. The souvenir shop is extremely well displayed, cramming lots of desirable objects into a small space (page 87).

Time for a break? Continue across the square, passing the Bulgarian National Bank on the left. Soon, also on the left, you'll see the ⑱ **Archaeological Museum** and adjoining it the popular **Art Club Museum Café** [89 C2] (*ul Suborna 2;* \ *9806664*). You might like to take a rest here!

A slightly longer option is to turn left out of the Ethnographic Museum, and immediately left into the park, then cross the small park behind the museum and emerge on to Moskovska. On 4 January 1878, the citizens of Sofia welcomed the liberation army of General Gurko in this street, and spontaneously renamed it Moskovska. Its closeness to the Royal Palace attracted wealthy citizens to the area and soon various beautiful houses, designed by the best Bulgarian architects, were built here. Some of them still remain, and generally this is one of the loveliest streets in Sofia, with a feeling generally of more tranquil times, marred now by the security arrangements of the British Embassy, itself something of a modern carbuncle.

Turn left along Moskovska and left again to return the short distance to pl Aleksandur Batenberg; across the road you will see the Archaeological Museum and café mentioned above.

The City Garden and towards bul Vitosha If you stopped earlier, you might like to continue the walk from the Ethnographic Museum by crossing the road into the City Garden. You will quite quickly reach the fountains and lovely vista of the ⑲ **Ivan Vazov National Theatre** [89 D3] (*Народния театър Иван Вазов*). This was built in 1907 by Austrian architects and is one of Sofia's most elaborate buildings. Above the six white marble columns in the pediment is a scene of Apollo and the Muses, and on the two towers behind that the muse of tragedy Melpomene and the muse of dance Terpsichore are on chariots, drawn by lions. The theatre has a capacity of 850 people. Inside there are colourful hangings woven by women from Panagyurishte and a vivid fire-bird on the stage curtain taken from Stravinsky's ballet. In summer, lovely outdoor cafés are created in this area.

Keep the theatre and the fountains on your left to reach, at the far end of the gardens, the ⑳ **City Art Gallery** [89 C3] (*Градската художествена галерия;* ⊕ *10.00–19.00 Tue–Sat, 11.00–18.00 Sun; free*), with a collection of mainly 20th-century paintings and sculptures. Recitals and exhibitions are sometimes held here.

The gardens are a popular venue for groups of elderly men who seem to be participating in never-ending chess and backgammon tournaments, sometimes watched admiringly by keen young children, maybe dreaming of following in the footsteps of Bulgarian Grand Master and 2005 World Champion Veselin Topalov!

Leaving the gardens by the gallery you will be near the corner of ul Gurko and ul Aleksandur Batenberg; leaving the latter on your right walk along ul Alabin towards the main shopping street, bul Vitosha. If you want a break from sightseeing or some refreshments there are plenty of possibilities around here.

As you reach the main boulevard you will see the imposing ㉑ **Palace of Justice** [89 B3] (*Съдебна палата*) facing you. This huge, purpose-built Neoclassical building was constructed between 1928 and 1936. From 1980 to 1999 it was taken over and used as the National History Museum, when the two large bronze lions, symbols of Bulgaria, were placed outside its main entrance. It has now been restored to its original judicial purpose. Turn right towards pl Sv Nedelya, the centre of another cluster of interesting buildings.

Or turn left and go shopping on bul Vitosha!

Pl Sv Nedelya and beyond Now you can see ㉒ **Sv Nedelya** [89 B2] (*Св Неделя*), a 19th-century church built on the ancient site that was the hub of Serdika. There have been several churches on this site over the years. In 1925, it suffered destruction in a bomb blast, which was an assassination attempt on Tsar Boris III. The 19th-century iconostasis survived, but otherwise the interior is rather disappointing and the modern frescoes are not particularly appealing. Sv Nedelya is, however, a favourite place of worship and is invariably busy with baptisms, weddings and funerals.

Walking towards the Sofia Hotel Balkan, now rendered almost invisible at street level by a line of shops occupying what was once an elegant façade, you will see the towering modern ㉓ **statue of Sophia** [89 B2], a replacement for the statue of Lenin which was removed from here after the 1989 changes. Made of bronze and copper, and 24m high, it was created by Bulgarian artist Georgi Chapkanov and architect Stanislav Konstantinov, and placed here in 2001. Sophia is not universally popular, as she is considered to be rather improperly dressed for her serious role. She supposedly combines the symbols of power (her crown), fame (the wreath in her hand) and wisdom (the owl perched on her wrist); her name also means wisdom. The statue is intended as an apolitical symbol of the city.

Continuing forward you need to cross the busy Largo by way of the underpass. The advantage of this is that as you walk down the steps and keep left you see the little low ㉔ **Church of Sv Petka Samardzhiiska** [89 B2] (*Църквата Св Петка*

Самарджийска; admission by donation), dating from the 14th century (page 76). The entrance to the metro station Serdika is on the left, but continue straight on up the steps and you will see in front of you the excavations of Roman Serdika uncovered during the building of the metro. In Sofia it seems that whenever the earth is disturbed, yet more discoveries are made. There are some helpful noticeboards explaining what you can see, but this is still a work in progress. To your right is the huge building known as ㉕ **TSUM** [89 C1], the former state-owned department store, now reinvented as a shopping mall with small shops and cafés.

Beyond is the ㉖ **Banya Bashi Mosque** [89 C1] (*Джамия Баня Баши*), Sofia's only working mosque, which was built in 1576 by Hadzhi Mimar Sinan, the chief architect to the Sultan, whose works include the Selim Mosque in Edirne and the famous Blue Mosque in Istanbul. The *muezzin* calls the faithful to prayer every day on his loudspeaker. The brick-built mosque has a single minaret, and a large dome with a diameter of 15m, the only example in Bulgaria of a dome on a square base. It stands in good repair on the edge of a restored garden with a fountain at its centre.

Across the garden are the ㉗ **Mineral Baths** [89 C1] (*Минералните бани*). Bulgarians are generally rather interested in the different types of mineral water; sometimes in the most remote of places you will see a line of parked cars and a queue of people waiting beside a water spout with their plastic containers. The mineral baths in Sofia are no exception, and there are often long queues of people waiting to collect water from the tapped springs. This spectacular building was for a long time in a state of extreme decrepitude, but it is now being painstakingly refurbished to its original condition. There will be a small spa and the larger rooms will become the exhibition space of Sofia City Museum, which has long had a collection but never a home. The exhibits include materials from archaeological excavations, coins, jewellery, weapons, clothing and belongings of some famous figures such as Stefan Stambolov and Tsar Ferdinand. Occasionally some of these exhibits are displayed temporarily in subway installations but it will be genuinely exciting to see a properly dedicated museum reflecting Sofia's rich history.

Retrace your steps and cross the road and tramlines to ㉘ **Halite** [89 C1] (*Халите*; ⊕ *07.00–midnight daily*), the indoor food market which was built in 1909–11 and completely renovated at the end of the 1990s. Its style is reminiscent of medieval Bulgarian and Byzantine architecture. By a happy coincidence it seems, from archaeological excavations, that this was a marketplace thousands of years ago. You can see some ancient walls in the basement. There are several cafés and places for a quick snack or a sit-down after all that sightseeing (page 87).

Just beyond the market to the west is the ㉙ **Synagogue** [89 B1] (*Синагогата; ul Ekzarch Yosif;* ⊕ *09.00–17.00 Mon–Fri, 09.00–13.00 Sat; ring the bell for access*), yet another lovely building that has recently been restored. It was built between 1905 and 1909 as a replica of the Viennese synagogue (destroyed during World War II) and is now the largest Sephardic synagogue in Europe. The interior is dominated by the huge star-spangled dome, which in turn is dominated by 2,000kg of brass chandelier.

Sofia first welcomed Jews in Roman times but only developed as a significant centre after the expulsions from Spain, Sicily and Portugal in the 15th century. In the 16th century, many other towns and cities had Jewish communities: Plovdiv, Ruse, Varna, Shumen and Kazanluk, for example.

Along the yellow brick road
Walk back to TSUM, then turn left along the yellow brick road, keeping TSUM on your left. Ahead of you is the old Communist Party building and the offices of the Central Committee, now red star-less; the yellow

brick road leads there and beyond towards the Parliament and Aleksandur Nevski. The yellow bricks were produced in the Austro-Hungarian Empire by a factory near Budapest from a special kind of stone 'marl'. The decision for the pavement of the central part of Sofia was taken and the financing of the project was implemented by the Bulgarian government in 1906–07.

Use the underpass to cross the busy road. In front of you is the Archaeological Museum, in a former mosque, but first look to your right. This is the entrance to the ㉚ **Presidency** [89 C2] (*Президентството*), which has beautifully attired guards of honour at its entrance. No lover of Tintin can fail to recognise them from *King Ottokar's Sceptre*. It is pleasant to sit in the shade on the low wall round the fountains as you wait for the hourly ceremony of the changing of the guards.

Enter the courtyard which the soldiers are guarding. In front of you is the ㉛ **Church of Sv Georgi** [89 C2] (*Черква Св Георги;* ⊕ *in summer 08.00–19.00 daily, variable times in winter; entrance by donation*), also known as the Rotunda. It is surrounded by the Sofia Hotel Balkan and some official buildings, which dwarf it. It is Sofia's oldest preserved building, dating from the 4th century, and was opened to the public in 1998 after lengthy restoration. It stands among various excavated ruins like a little mushroom. In the dome there are wonderful frescoes depicting Christ Pantocrator, surrounded by a frieze of prophets. These are 14th century, but there are older ones too, including some floral patterns which are from the 9th century. There is a particularly compelling fragment of an angel's face in the inner vault which experts link to the same realistic style displayed at Boyana.

Leave the courtyard by the same archway and admire the beautiful nine-domed Buyuk or 'Great' Mosque, now the ⑱ **Archaeological Museum** [89 C2] (*Археологическия музей; ul Suborna 2;* ⊕ *May–Oct daily 10.00–17.00, Nov–Apr Tue–Sun; adult 10lv*). It is the oldest museum in Bulgaria as it opened in 1899, but the mosque itself was built in the late 15th century. Originally it would have stood as part of an ensemble of buildings, including a *madrasa* (theological college), caravanserais and administrative offices. It has recently been restored, like so many Sofia buildings, and is now an excellent, well-displayed and well-labelled (in Bulgarian and English) museum. The interior is light and an ideal setting for displaying the extensive collections. There are terracotta vessels, silver and bronze figures, and Thracian and Roman artefacts. There are tombstones and plaques, and frescoes from all over Bulgaria. The Vulchitrun gold treasure from the 16th–12th century BC is here, as well as coins and newly discovered finds from the Valley of the Thracian Kings, including the amazing solid gold mask of the Thracian King Teres and his ring and the finely wrought gold wreath. These caused such excitement when they were first exhibited that enthusiasts queued around the building.

So our walk ends at the nice Art Club Museum Café.

On the way you may have noticed that Sofia street names are rather interesting. They usually refer to people or historical events, and tend to come in connected clusters. East and west of bul Vitosha, there are streets named after khans and tsars from the earliest years of the Bulgarian state: Asparuh, Boris, Krum, Samuil and Ivan Asen. Near the railway station is an area previously designated as an industrial area, and the street names reflect this: Kamenodelska (stone-carving), Kozhuharska (coat-making), Gruncharska (pottery), Zavodska (factory) and Industrialna (industrial). Around the Doctors' Garden the struggle for liberation from the Ottoman Empire is recalled in Shipka (the battle at the pass), San Stefano (the treaty after the war), Veliko Turnovo (the town where the constitution was adopted) and Oborishte (the place where the uprising was planned).

There are many more such groups of names: history on the hoof!

OTHER SIGHTS The following sights are off our route but you can add them if you have time.

National Military History Museum [map, page 99] (*Националния военно-исторически музей; ul Cherkovna 92;* ✆ *9461805;* ☉ *10.00–18.00 Wed–Sun; adult 10lv*) Although not within walking distance of the central sights, this well-displayed museum is worth the detour not only for those with military interests but also for anyone interested in Bulgaria's history. There are some excellent sections with sound effects illustrating particularly important events, as well as captions and detailed explanations in Bulgarian and English. Outside there is a huge array of tanks, field guns, troop carriers and helicopters. There is also a good museum shop. The museum was recently awarded a Certificate of Excellence by TripAdvisor.

Earth and Man Museum [map, page 99] (*Национален музей земята и хората; bul Cherni Vruh 4;* ☉ *10.00–18.00 Tue–Sat; adult 4lv*) Behind the Hilton Hotel and quite far from the centre, this has a collection of huge crystals and gems from all over the world, donated by a Bulgarian expatriate collector. It is situated in a well-restored 19th-century building, which is a former arsenal. Opened in 1987, it contains seven expositions of more than 20,000 minerals from around the world, including some giant crystals, although, unfortunately, the explanations are only in Bulgarian. Mainly of interest to geologists, the museum sometimes hosts visiting exhibitions, recitals and musical events.

Museum of Socialist Art [map, page 99] (*музей на социалистическото изкуство; ul Lachezar Stanchev 7;* ☉ *daily 10.00–17.30; adult 6lv*) This is part of the National Gallery of Bulgarian Art, and collects and preserves art from the period 1944–89. Outside is a sculpture park where statues of historical heroes from the communist era are displayed. In the exhibition hall are paintings and a small cinema where propaganda films of the time are shown. There is a souvenir shop. The big red star at the entrance was once on top of the Party House on the Largo.

Pl Slaveykov [80 D5] This is a must if you are a book lover, as the whole large square is full of bookstalls. There are several specialising in maps and glossy coffee-table books about Bulgaria at very good prices. There is also a lovely statue of the father-and-son writers and poets, Petko and Pencho Slaveykov, sitting on a bench, no doubt pleased to see so many bookworms! Maybe join them for a photograph.

Sv Sedmochislenitsi [80 D5] (*Св Седмочислеwaници; ul Graf Ignatiev*) Another former mosque which has survived is the Black Mosque built in 1528, so called because of the colour of the granite used in its construction. It has been converted into a church known as Sv Sedmochislenitsi – which translates as 'the Holy Seven'; that is Cyril and Methodius and their five disciples: Kliment of Ohrid, Naum, Gorazd, Sava and Angelairi. The conversion made few changes to the mosque apart from adding a porch.

Museum Park Vrana [map, page 99] (*парк-музей врана; also known as Vrana Residence, bul Tsarigradsko Shose;* ☉ *10.00–16.00 Sat–Sun; adult 6lv*) On the outskirts of Sofia near the junction with the ring road, this looks like a western European park, although it was established before Bulgaria's liberation from the Ottoman Empire. After 1878 a Bulgarian, Hadzhi Bone Petrov, developed it as a model farm. In 1889 Tsar Ferdinand bought the farm and some neighbouring land to create the mansion and grounds of Vrana. There are over 800 tree, shrub and herbaceous species. It is a very pleasant and peaceful place.

BOYANA (БОЯНА) Further afield but an essential excursion from Sofia is Boyana, on the outskirts of the city in the foothills of Vitosha Mountain. Here is the relocated National History Museum, no longer in the Palace of Justice but in a splendid former government residence where it has plenty of space and has been beautifully arranged. By good fortune Sofia's other star attraction, Boyana Church, is in the same suburb. The UNESCO-listed medieval church has frescoes of astonishing brilliance.

Getting there and away Buses 64 and 107 go to Boyana. It is about 10–15 minutes' walk from the stop Boyansko Hanche to the church.

Taxis are a convenient option costing about 10lv (one-way) depending on your starting point.

By car, Boyana is to the southwest of the centre, and accessed by a signposted turning off the ring road.

✖ Where to eat and drink
✖ **Chepishev Perfetto Restaurant** ul Ivanitsa Danchev 27; m 0888 630630; http://perfettobg. com. Italian, other European & Bulgarian options, good service & terrace. €€

What to see and do The **National History Museum** (*Национален исторически музей; ul Vitoshko Lale 16, Okolovrustno Shosse;* 9554280; *www.historymuseum. org;* ◔ *09.30–17.30 daily; adult 10lv*) has over 20,000 exhibits charting the social and political life of Bulgaria from prehistory to the end of World War II. There are amazing gold treasures such as those from Panagyurishte and part of the Rogozen hoard.

There was much controversy when the museum was moved out of the centre in 2000; pessimists decreed that tourists would no longer visit. However, the wealth of the collection, and its proximity to Boyana Church, means that visitors do indeed come. The museum is well labelled in Bulgarian and English and the shop sells guidebooks in several languages.

The first hall begins with Neolithic artefacts, which feature various decorated stone figures of the mother goddess. The second hall has the gold and silver hoards for which Bulgaria is famous. The Thracian treasures, such as that found at Panagyurishte, include drinking vessels shaped like animal heads. Each *rhyton* has detailed and intricate mythological scenes around it. The third hall has mainly replicas of medieval artefacts – useful to see if you don't have time to travel all over Bulgaria to see them *in situ*.

The fourth hall demonstrates how the Bulgarian Church preserved a sense of national consciousness during the half-millennium of Turkish rule. There are icons from the various schools and some frescoes from monasteries, including some fine examples from the master of the skill, Zahari Zograf. The fifth hall covers the Third Bulgarian Kingdom, that is the period 1878–1946. Two halls are reserved for temporary exhibitions. The eighth hall is dedicated to finds from the Sozopol necropolis, the ninth to traditional calendar feasts and festivals and national costumes, and the tenth to an impressive collection of coins. Another hall visits a typical Bulgarian house during the National Revival period, based on a house in Teteven.

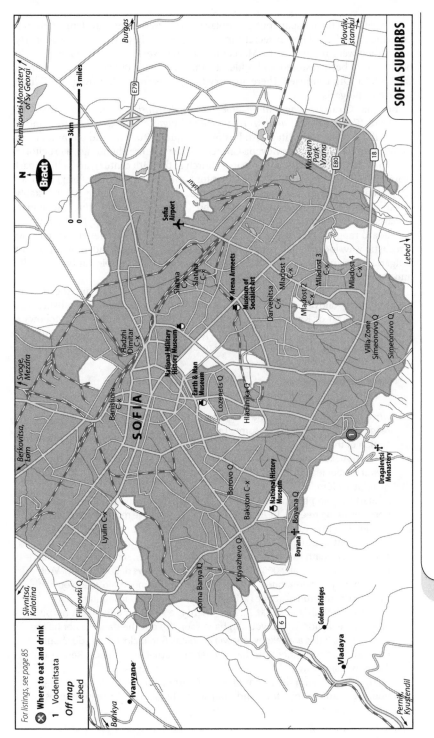

SOFIA SUBURBS

For listings, see page 85

Where to eat and drink

1 Vodenitsata

Off map
Lebed

In May 2006, the museum put on display for the first time unique items of church art which had been kept in secret for over 70 years. They became state property when they were rescued from Macedonia during World War I in 1916. All 400 objects have been restored and added to the collection 'Bulgarian Culture from the 15th to 19th centuries'. There are very fine pieces from Chiprovtsi and Edirne (Odrin to Bulgarians).

Boyana Church (*Боянската църква; ul Boyansko Ezero 3;* \ *9590939;* ☉ *09.00–17.00 Tue–Sun; adult 10lv*) is one of Bulgaria's greatest treasures, and is on UNESCO's World Heritage list. It is picturesquely situated amid old pines in an exclusive Sofia suburb. The Boyana Church consists of three buildings: a cruciform church of the 11th century, a two-storey church of the 13th century, and a third part from the 19th century. In 1259, Sevastocrator (a title second to that of tsar) Kaloyan expanded the church and commissioned the murals. They display a remarkably advanced approach to portraiture (see box, page 178), pre-dating the Italian Renaissance by a century. Contemporary art depicted stiff and stylised figures in a standard range of colours, but at Boyana 240 figures in 89 scenes are depicted in a realistic way, looking like people not images. They are surrounded by aspects of Bulgarian life; they are eating Bulgarian food, the peasant staples of bread, garlic and radishes; their skin has lifelike tones; the colours are varied.

The portraits of Tsar Konstantin Asen and his wife Irina, and the donors Sevastocrator Kaloyan and his wife Dessislava, are astonishingly realistic. The famous portrayal of Kaloyan with the model of the church in his hand follows a traditional way of representing the donor, but nothing else about it is traditional.

Visits to the church are restricted to 10 minutes due to concerns about pollution, and only possible with a guide.

A VITOSHA WALK

Drive from Sofia to Aleko, via Dragalevtsi. After about 40 minutes, you will reach Aleko at a height of some 1,800m; you can park your car near the station of the gondola lift.

From Aleko a typical walk might be to the plateau. And if there is more power in your legs then why not aim for the top of the mountain, Cherni Vruh peak, at 2,290m.

Start by going behind the building, and then follow the path, which soon goes above the treeline. In 20 minutes or so you will have reached the plateau. Continue on in a westerly direction until you reach a mountain road. Here you can turn left and start ascending to the higher level of the plateau, which is also the main path to Cherni Vruh. Just follow this mountain road and after 30 minutes you will be at 2,000m and enjoy stunning views of Sofia, Cherni Vruh and other mountain ranges. If you continue on this mountain road you can climb to Cherni Vruh in about 1½ hours, depending on your strength!

At Cherni Vruh you are at 2,290m. There is a small mountain rest house, open at weekends, where you can have soup, try out the pancakes or have a herbal tea. If it is a weekday you will probably find it closed, so you should pack some snacks, chocolate bars, water and other sustenance. Return to Aleko the same way.

The total walking time from Aleko to Cherni Vruh and back is about 4–5 hours, excluding any stops and your lunch break. Height gain and loss: 490m.

VITOSHA MOUNTAIN NATURE PARK

Vitosha Mountain is a non-erupted volcano which consists mainly of silicate basic rock. Only part of its southern slopes are formed of marble, and as a result of karst processes the longest cave in Bulgaria, named Duhlata, is located here. It is a labyrinth of 18km. Cherni Vruh, the highest peak, is 2,290m.

The UNESCO biosphere reserve Bistrishko branishte is a refuge for native spruce forest and subalpine meadows dominated by juniper (*Juniperus sibirica*), grass (*Sesleria commosa*) and the Balkan endemic grass (*Festuca valida*). Many interesting plants occur here such as the Balkan endemics: **yellow lily** (*Lilium jankae*), **yellow columbine** (*Aquilegia aurea*), **ragwort** (*Heracleum verticillatum, Senecio pancicii*), **bellflowers** (*Campanula moesiaca, Campanula velebitica*), **louseworts** (*Pedicularis orthantha, P. hoermaniana*), **Balkan butterwort** (*Pinguicula balcanica*), **pink** (*Dianthus microlepis*) and **crocus** (*Crocus veluchensis*). There are also *Red Data Book* plants: **great yellow gentian** (*Gentiana lutea*), **spotted yellow gentian** (*Gentiana punctata*), **globe-flower** (*Trollius europaeus*), **narcissus-flowered anemone** (*Anemone narcissiflora*), and simply spectacular plants: **scarlet avens** (*Geum coccineum*), **alpine coltsfoot** (*Homogine alpina*) and **orchids** (*Dactylorhyza cordigera, Nigritella nigra*). Astonishingly these wonders can all be found on walks from the capital city, Sofia.

The Boyana Church is not an isolated phenomenon, but part of a whole host of pioneering artistic developments that took place in Bulgaria on the eve of the Ottoman invasion.

VITOSHA Sofia is very fortunate to have Vitosha Mountain on its doorstep. However, the desirability of its lower slopes as smart residential areas means that some planning restraints need to be implemented, or it will become overdeveloped. Vitosha is accessible by public transport in half an hour (see bus routes, page 79), so at the weekend it can be busy. There are plenty of signed trails to explore in summer and good, if limited, skiing in winter. The Boyana waterfall and lake are popular destinations.

The **Golden Bridges** (*Златните мостове*) are a stone moraine moved here by glaciers aeons ago. The reference to gold is that at one time some gold-panning took place in the stream that runs beneath the huge boulders.

SOFIA'S HOLY MOUNTAIN Dragalevtsi Monastery (*Драгалевския манастир*) dates from the 14th century. It is part of the group of monasteries built at this time which roughly circle Sofia, and were known as Little Mount Athos, or Sofia's Holy Mountain. Only the church and some cells around the courtyard survive from the original monastery complex. It is a tranquil place, and the summer residence of the Bulgarian Patriarch is nearby.

There are interesting frescoes from the original period, but only fragments of scenes, such as Judas and the pieces of silver and Peter's denial; most of the frescoes are more recent. The monastery's feast day is 15 August, the Feast of the Assumption (*Голяма Богородица*), and many people come then to pray, to celebrate and to picnic.

Boyana (pages 100–1) and Dragalevtsi are two of the best-known of the monasteries and churches which together form a circle around Sofia. Another, the

Kremikovtsi Monastery of Sv Georgi (*Кремиковски Манастир Свети Георги*), is on a hillside northeast of Sofia. It was founded during the Second Bulgarian Empire (12th–14th century), destroyed during the Ottoman Conquest, and re-established in 1493 by a local nobleman, Radivoy, who dedicated the church to his two children. As is traditional, the paintings include one of the benefactor and his family, presenting a model of the church. These frescoes are among the most valuable surviving examples of 15th-century Bulgarian art.

Other monasteries are nowadays just ruins, though some have more modern monasteries (or convents) on the old sites. For those who are particularly interested, there is a free map from tourist information centres listing 17 monasteries around Sofia. You would need a car to reach many of them.

4

The Southwest

The highlights of the southwest, one of the most visited parts of Bulgaria, are **Bansko**, the fast developing ski resort, and **Rila Monastery**, which together with the **Pirin National Park** is included in UNESCO's World Heritage list. There are several attractive monasteries and small towns, and countless opportunities for walking, hiking, birdwatching and botanising, making this a favoured destination for both Bulgarian weekenders and visitors. The region is often referred to as Pirinska-Makedoniya to denote the physical, geographical and ethnographical home of the folklore most Bulgarians love. In political terms it refers to the Bulgarian region in the southwest, as opposed to Vardarska Macedonia, which is the present-day Republic of Macedonia across the border. The drive south along the Struma Valley has views across to the jagged peaks of the Pirin Mountains on one side, and pastoral scenes of fishermen trying their luck in the river valley on the other. This is tobacco country, and at harvest time there are lines of leaves on strings drying in makeshift shelters or under the eaves of houses.

IN THE RILA MOUNTAINS *Telephone code: 07054*

The Rila Mountains are home to Bulgaria's oldest ski resort, Borovets, which in summer can be the base for mountain walks or the ascent of the Balkan Peninsula's highest peak, Mount Musala. There are famous attractions like the Seven Lakes, with well-marked hiking trails. Despite development at Borovets, the Rila National Park is in many parts untouched and home to a huge variety of birds, butterflies, wild flowers and wild animals.

RILA MONASTERY (РИЛСКИ МАНАСТИР) (*www.rilamonastery.pmg-blg.com;*

🕓 *dawn till dusk daily; museum* 🕓 *08.30–17.00 daily; adult 8lv*) The road to Rila Monastery runs beside the River Rilska through beautiful wooded mountains. In summer and at weekends it is exceptionally busy, and, surrounded by buses and cars, it is hard to remember what a remote and quiet place this was for most of its history. If you can arrive early, perhaps on a winter morning when a dusting of snow picks out the architectural features, then you may have that feeling of awe at the immense walls and astonishment at the vibrant colours in the courtyard. Perhaps you will begin to understand what importance the place has for Bulgarians.

The first sight of the monastery's towering exterior gives the impression of a fortress; in the past this security was necessary, as the wealth of the monastery attracted bandits and robbers, though its remote situation in the mountains and its altitude, 1,150m, helped to protect it. The founder, **Ivan Rilski** (880–946), was a hermit who sought enlightenment in the solitude of this place, but his reputation as a wise man with healing powers generated followers. In response to their requests

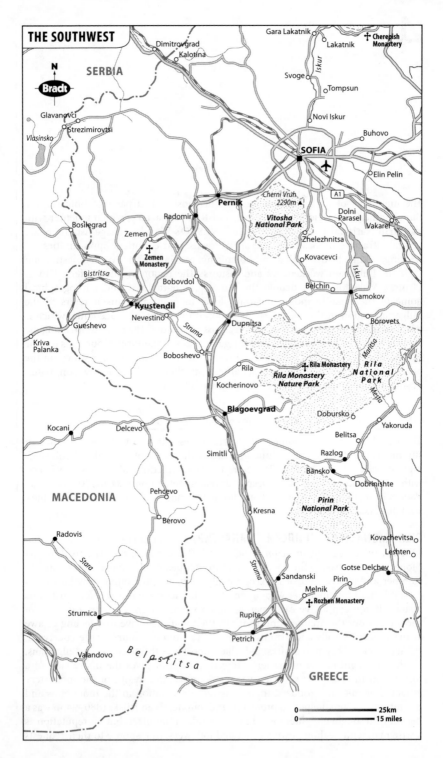

THE SOUTHWEST

N

Bradt

SERBIA

Dimitrovgrad
Kalotina

Gara Lakatnik
Lakatnik
† Cherepish
Monastery

Glavanovci
Strezimirovtsi

Vlasinsko

Svoge
Tompsun

Novi Iskur

Buhovo

SOFIA

Elin Pelin

Pernik

Cherni Vruh
2290m ▲

Dolni
Parasel

A1

Vakarel

Radomir

Vitosha
National Park

Zheleznhitsa

Bosilegrad

Zemen

Kovacevci

† Zemen
Monastery

Bobovdol

Belchin

Bistritsa

Samokov

Kyustendil

Nevestino

Struma

Dupnitsa

Borovets

Gueshevo

Kriva
Palanka

Boboshevo

Rila

Rila Monastery
Nature Park

† Rila Monastery

Rila
National
Park

Marisa

Kocherinovo

Blagoevgrad

Doburско

Mesta

Kocani

Delcevo

Belitsa

Yakoruda

Simitli

Razlog

Bänsko

Dobrinishte

MACEDONIA

Pehcevo

Berovo

Kresna

Pirin
National Park

Radovis

Kovachevitsa

Leshten

Stara

Struma

Sandanski

Pirin

Gotse Delchev

Melnik

† Rozhen Monastery

Strumica

Rupite

Petrich

Valandovo

B e l a s t i t s a

GREECE

0 ——— 25km
0 ——— 15 miles

he founded a religious community, which soon became a place of pilgrimage for people from all over the Balkans.

Rila was refounded in 1335, a few kilometres southwest of the original hermitage, under the patronage of the *bolyar*, Stefan Hrelyo Dragovol. The oldest of the buildings visible today, **Hrelyo's Tower**, was built then. It is five storeys high, and would originally have been a lookout point. At the top there is a small chapel, with vestiges of frescoes. There was damage and destruction to the monastery during the Ottoman conquest and the subsequent occupation, but after each setback renovation soon began again. The return of the relics of the founder Ivan Rilski from Veliko Turnovo in 1469 was a significant event for the growing importance of the monastery.

After the great fire of 1833 the Ottoman sultan allowed the rebuilding of the monastery, and plentiful financial donations from the people, together with the gifts of time and skills by many great artists and craftsmen, resulted in the splendid building we see now.

Getting there and away Leaving Sofia in the direction of Pernik, the road skirts Vitosha Mountain and then, as the E79, heads directly south. The road to Kulata (for the border crossing to Greece) gives easy access to the area for drivers and bus passengers. The route follows the River Struma for much of the way, and the railway line crosses and recrosses the road and river. It is a busy road; many stretches have been upgraded to motorway, but road building continues, resulting in some diversions and delays, but with the prospect of easier and safer journeys in the future.

Rila Monastery is a popular day trip from Sofia. The drive will take a couple of hours and the easiest option is to hire a car, with or without a driver/guide. Most of the Sofia travel agencies can arrange this for about €80–100 for an individual with a private guide – it's worth looking online and shopping around. Joining a group tour will be much less expensive. A good guide will definitely make the whole experience more interesting.

The route from Sofia to Kulata is well served by **buses** (*page 52; Sofia central bus station (Централна Автогара София);* ◈ *0900 63099; www.centralnaavtogara.bg; some buses to places in southwest Bulgaria also leave from Bus Station Zapad (West), bul Ovcha Kupel 1;* ◈ *02 9555362).*There are hourly buses from Sofia to Dupnitsa, a journey of about 1½ hours, then it is a further 1 hour 20 minutes on a twice-daily bus to the monastery. Connections to Rila and the monastery beyond are not always conveniently timed and it is important to check the timetables. Local taxis will be inexpensive. There are five buses a day from Rila village to Blagoevgrad (*45mins*). Buses from Kyustendil (*2 daily; 50mins*) and Samokov (*4 daily; 1hr*) also serve Dupnitsa.

There are also three daily **trains** (*page 52; central railway station* ◈ *02 9323333*) from Sofia to Dupnitsa but you will still need a bus connection to the monastery. The train journey tends to be slower, taking 2 hours 35 minutes from Sofia to Dupnitsa. There are also trains from Blagoevgrad (*hourly; 45mins*) and Kulata (*5 daily; 2–3hrs*).

Where to stay The accommodation in the **monastery** itself has been upgraded. There are still some sparsely furnished rooms in the west wing, each with three or four beds, communal toilets and no showers. New rooms have their own bathroom with shower, but are often already booked by midday. If you can arrange it, it is a magical experience to be in the monastery after the tourist crowds have left. You need to enquire at the **lodging office** (*in the courtyard;* ◈ *2208*).

Near the monastery

⌂ **Rilets** (90 rooms) ☏2106. Former state-run hotel, rather gloomy, but the only option near the monastery if Tsarev Vruh is full. Reopening in 2015 after refurbishment. €

⌂ **Tsarev Vruh** (65 rooms) See below; ☏2280; www.tzarevvrah.com. Newer hotel, built in the early 1990s. Clean, comfortable, budget option. Plain & basic but rooms have en suites. Restaurant..€

In the vicinity

⌂ **Bor camping** (20 beds in chalets) ☏2106. Also has camping facilities. Pine forest location, but showers & facilities are basic. €

⌂ **Gorski Kut** (15 rooms) See below; 5km before you reach the monastery; ☏2170;

e gorskikut@abv.bg; www.gorski-kut.eu. Plain basic rooms, clean & comfortable. Restaurant overlooking the river. €

⌂ **Pchelina** (20 beds in dbl, trpl and studios) See below; 3km from the monastery near Pchelina cloister; m 0888 393058; e hotelpchelina@abv. bg; www.pchelina.com. Stylish new hotel, in a rural setting. All rooms with modern en suites. Restaurant. €

⌂ **Pri Chicho Kiro** (20 rooms) Kirilova Polyana, 7km east of the monastery; ☏0738 33987; e chkiro@hotmail.bg; www.chkiro.hit.bg. Motel-restaurant; accommodation in rustic-style chalets with en suites. €

⌂ **Zodiak camping** (20 beds in chalets); ☏2291. Idyllic forest setting, basic showers. Café. Also has camping facilities. €

✖ **Where to eat and drink** There is a much bigger choice of places to eat than to stay, reflecting the fact that most visitors come just for the day. Restaurants are normally open between 11.00 and 22.00, with cafés opening earlier at 07.30 or 08.00. There is just one menu, with no distinction between lunch and dinner options.

Near the monastery

✖ **The Bakery** Monks run a bakery just outside the east gate, where delicious bread, sheep's yoghurt & doughnuts can be purchased. €

✖ **Drushlyavitsa** m 0888 283864. Close to the monastery, with terrace overlooking the river, serving local freshly caught trout as a speciality. Traditional Bulgarian food & grills, soups & salads. Always popular & busy. €€

✖ **Rila** Just outside the Samokov Gate; ☏2290. Attractive old building, traditional cuisine. €€

In the vicinity

✖ **Gorski Kut** 5km before the monastery; ☏2170. Restaurant with nice garden, offers fresh trout, grilled meat, Bulgarian food. €€

✖ **Pchelina** See above. Folk-style tavern, fireplace for winter dining & attractive summer garden for 60 guests. Traditional Bulgarian cuisine. €€

✖ **Ribarnika** 4km before the monastery; ☏0985 04284. Nice location by meadows & Rilska River. There's a fish farm here – a guarantee of good fresh trout. Also grilled meat, salads, Bulgarian cuisine. €€

✖ **Tsarev Vruh** See above. Rustic setting with traditional cuisine & the local speciality of trout. €

What to see and do

The monastery Passing through the huge gates of the monastery for the first time is one of life's special moments: the scene changes from grey severity to a carnival of colour. All round the enormous courtyard are tiers of monks' cells behind boldly decorated, arcaded balconies. In the centre, the church itself, with richly coloured frescoes in the shelter of its porch, is the focus of attention, its lavishness emphasised by the simplicity of the 14th-century tower alongside it.

The temptation to conclude the visual feast by going straight into the **Church of the Nativity of the Virgin Mary** (Черквата на Рождество Богородично) should not be resisted. The iconostasis is a splendid mass of intricate carvings, heavily decorated with gold leaf. It is made of walnut wood and its subjects are from nature: flowers, fruits and birds. The pulpit and bishop's throne echo its magnificence and the colours are repeated and strengthened in the frescoes covering every available wall, ceiling and arch. Zahari Zograf, perhaps Bulgaria's most famous mural painter, was one of the artists who worked here. The theme of the frescoes is the triumph of good over evil and light over darkness. The mood is optimistic and the colours light. The external frescoes have particularly lively depictions of the seven deadly sins and the descent of their perpetrators into hell.

At the time of its completion it was the largest monastery church in the Balkans. It is a cruciform shape with several altars and two chapels. The acoustics are excellent, and hearing a service there is a wonderful experience. The service is preceded by a monk walking round the outside of the church banging a wooden stick, a ceremony said to be a reminder of Christ being nailed to the cross.

The monastery **museum** has many treasures, the most memorable being the double-sided Rafael cross, carved in wood with 36 Biblical scenes with more than 200 miniature three-dimensional and remarkably detailed figures, each about the size of a grain of rice. No figure is repeated, and each has distinctive and expressive features. There are also coins, religious artefacts, costumes and various documents significant to the monastery's history, as well as an extensive library. Some English-language information signs are dotted around the monastery and you can also buy useful leaflets at the souvenir shop for a small price.

An indication of the importance of the monastery as a spiritual centre is: the **kitchen**! Here cooking pots capable of holding 2,500 litres can be seen. The largest oven in Bulgaria could bake 1,500 loaves, enough for the 5,000 worshippers who attended religious festivals and holy days. In the 18th and 19th centuries the monastery functioned as a virtually self-sufficient small town. It had a watermill working all year round and a grain store, over 2,000ha of forests providing wood for fuel, over 100 beehives allowing the production of honey, and over 15,000 sheep and 200 goats providing meat and milk from which cheese was made.

As you walk around the arcaded galleries, admiring the views of the magnificent Rila Mountains, you will find some beautifully furnished **guest rooms**, which were endowed by neighbouring towns for the use of their citizens and which bear their names. These are not the rooms present-day visitors use, but it is possible to stay in some of the monastery's more spartan accommodation. Rila is typical of many of Bulgaria's monasteries with its remote location, where it was possible to preserve a sense of national identity during the 500 years of Ottoman occupation. As national awareness gradually grew, they served as local centres for rallying support for Bulgarian religious, educational and, eventually, political freedom. Their role is therefore an important one.

James Bourchier's grave

Quite hidden away, and not signposted, is the grave of a remarkable British man whose affection for Bulgaria made him wish to be buried here. **James David Bourchier** (1850–1920), from an Anglo-Irish family, was destined for a career as a barrister, but after contracting first measles and then a cold, he became increasingly deaf. He was offered a post as a beak at Eton College, teaching classics, but this was not a success, his deafness proving too much of a handicap in dealing with high-spirited boys. He was also unconventional and himself lacked the punctuality the boys were encouraged to show.

For recreation he began writing occasional articles for the press, which attracted the attention of *The Times* and led to his appointment as their foreign correspondent in the Near East. He travelled extensively in the region, learned Greek and Bulgarian and a working knowledge of the other Balkan languages, and was as ready to write about village life as political congresses. It seems that Bulgaria became his favourite place, and his descriptions of its countryside are both affectionate and vivid.

He formed a strong friendship with Prince Ferdinand and his mother Princess Clementine, bonding with the latter because she too was deaf. The prince showed him much kindness, not because he was *The Times* correspondent, but because he was a cultured and entertaining person, and they visited Rila together many times.

> To share a meal at Rila, or to travel in the country with Mr Bourchier as host, was a delightful experience, for he was honoured and loved in every village in which we stayed. And the secret of his strength and power lay in that remarkable gift of sympathy and his transparent sincerity, which won alike the hearts of kings, ecclesiastics, statesmen and peasants. He was to all of them 'Uncle James.' (From *The Times*, 3 January 1921)

Bourchier was a highly influential person, partly because of his knowledgeable reports but also because his advice was sought by the decision-makers of the Balkans. One of his former students recalled: 'That is the man whose word controlled the destinies of nations and the guns of three continental armies; and that is the master in whom we saw nothing but inability or unwillingness to force us through the round of school routine' (*Eton in the Eighties* by Eric Parker, 1914). Bourchier's great love of Bulgaria and its people was reciprocated and an important boulevard in Sofia continues to be named after him, despite many other 'road heroes' having been demoted! Sadly, his grave is no longer well cared for.

The Chapel of Sv Ivan of Rila About an hour's walk north of the monastery is the cave where the founder of Rila Monastery lived and is buried. It is said that only those who haven't sinned will be able to enter through the narrow opening.

RILA NATIONAL PARK This is the largest national park in Bulgaria, located about 100km south of Sofia, in the central and highest regions of the Rila Mountains. It

BOTANY IN THE RILA NATIONAL PARK

The Rila and Pirin mountains were glaciated and the relief shows obvious signs of this process. The highest mountain on the Balkan Peninsula, Musala, reaches 2,925m and is formed predominantly of silicate base rock. The alpine flora and vegetation belt above 2,500m is really impressive. Many plants here are listed in the Bulgarian *Red Data Book*: **globe-flower** (*Trollius europaeus*), **great yellow gentian** (*Gentiana lutea*), **spotted yellow gentian** (*Gentiana punctata*), **yellow lousewort** (*Pedicularis oederi*) and **saxifrages** (*Saxifraga retusa, S. androsacea*). There are lots of Balkan endemics: **Bulgarian avens** (*Geum bulgaricum*), **ragwort** (*Senecio pancicii*), **pink** (*Dianthus microlepis*), **yellow columbine** (*Aquilegia aurea*), **yellow lily** (*Lilium jankae*) and **louseworts** (*Pedicularis orthantha, P. hoermaniana*) occur here. On the damp habitats around the beautiful glacial lakes and crystal-clear streams the incredible deep magenta flowers of the local endemic **Rila cowslip** (*Primula deorum*) can be seen. The total number of endemic species in this park is 54 (18 of which are endemic to Bulgaria, 36 to the Balkans).

The towns from where you can start walks into the mountains are Samokov (for Malyovitsa and the Musala trogue [U-shaped] valleys), Simitli (for the Seven Lakes trogue valley), and the town of Rila (for Rila Monastery and some glacial lakes).

This is the kingdom of the forest birds; species such as **wryneck, Syrian** and **middle-spotted woodpeckers** keep to the lowest parts of the mountain, and are replaced at the middle altitudes by **grey-headed** and **white-backed woodpeckers** (of the Southern subspecies *lilfordi*) and by the **three-toed woodpecker** in the highest coniferous forests. In the mixed middle-altitude belt the **hazel hen** is quite abundant, as is the **dipper** along the mountain streams, and in the highest and most remote woodland parts are the **capercaillie** lands. Quite often around the mountain huts you will find **pallid swift, red-rumped swallow** and in great abundance the **black redstart**. In the alpine zone of the mountain, the **alpine chough, rock partridge, golden eagle**, numerous **alpine accentors** and abundant **horn larks** (of the race *balcanica*) can satisfy even the most demanding birding taste. Some of these birds can even be seen from the areas where car access is allowed (for example, Kirilova Polyana near the Rila Monastery). On the walls of the monastery itself **wallcreeper** can sometimes be observed, and nearby, grazing **chamois** from Kirilova Polyana. For information on the park and conservation activities, contact Rila National Park Directorate (e *office@rilanationalpark.bg*).

was designated a park in 1992 with the aim of preserving the natural heritage of the area and the local traditions, culture and skills. It covers a total area of 81,046ha and there are four nature reserves, with a combined area of 16,222ha.

Rila Monastery Nature Park, within the Rila National Park, covers some 25,000ha of forest, alpine meadows and mountain peaks. There are 28 alpine lakes, mainly of glacial origin, and 36 peaks above 2,000m. The forests are of beech, spruce and pines, which are home to wild goats and brown bears. More information can be obtained from Rila Monastery Nature Park Administration (*ul Benkovski 2, Rila;* ☏ *2293*).

BELCHIN (БЕЛЧИН) The road from Dupnitsa into the Rila Mountains on the way to Samokov reaches first the restored fortress at Belchin, near the small spa of Belchin Banya.

Getting there and away This is a trip best made by car. From Sofia it will take about 1–1½ hours. Leave the main route south (E79) at Dupnitsa, on the way to Samokov. A bus or train from Sofia to Dupnitsa would need a taxi ride of about 45 minutes to continue to Belchin.

⌂ **Where to stay and eat**

⌂ **Spa Hotel Belchin Garden** Belchin Banya; ☏ 0722 98750; e office@belchin-garden.com; www.belchin-garden.com. The spa & facilities are all new; helpful friendly staff, idyllic peaceful location. €€

What to see and do The newly opened historical site **Tsari Mali Grad Fortress** (m *0886 614814;* e *carimaligrad@yahoo.com;* ⊕ *09.00–17.30 Tue–Fri & 09.00–18.00 Sat–Sun; funicular* ⊕ *09.00–17.00 Wed–Fri & 09.00–17.30 Sat–Sun, closed noon–13.15; adult 4lv*) sits on Sv Spas Hill, above Belchin. Its name means the 'Tsar's Small Town', because its area of 4ha rivals that of the famous Tsarevets Fortress in Veliko Turnovo. Excavations began in 2007 and revealed a Roman fortress with six watchtowers and 400m of walls, constructed in the 4th century AD to guard the valley and the crossroads of Roman routes connecting Sofia, Plovdiv, Samokov and Kyustendil. The original fortress expanded into a busy fortified settlement with several churches. There are small exhibitions in the towers of coins, ceramics and other finds.

Two paths lead to the top of the hill. The one to the right is shorter but steeper, while the one to the left is more gradual with plenty of benches to rest on, and may be your best option if there are children with you, as it passes by the adventure playground. There is a funicular to take you to the top, but it is very small and, especially at weekends, the queues can be very long.

The area has always been known for its healing thermal springs and nowadays there is a luxury spa hotel nearby (page 109).

SAMOKOV (CAMOKOB) *Telephone code: 0722*
The town is most famous for its woodcarvers and icon painters, whose work decorates many Bulgarian churches, particularly those built during the National Revival. It is reached from Sofia along the wooded valley of the Iskur River. During the Ottoman occupation, Samokov was a flourishing town whose weavers and tailors made army uniforms, but nowadays it is mainly known for its potato-growing.

Tourist information The tourist information office is in the Municipality Building, to the right of the main entrance (*ul Macedonia 34;* ✆ *60019;* e *samokovtouristcenter@mail.bg;* ⊕ *09.00–17.30 w/days, 09.00–17.00 w/ends).*

Getting there and away Buses (*Sofia bus station Yug (south);* ✆ *02 8722345*) leave from Sofia every half-hour, taking 1 hour. There is a connection up to Borovets every 20 minutes, taking 15 minutes. There is one daily bus from Plovdiv (*1hr 45mins*), one daily from Blagoevgrad (*2hrs*) and two daily buses from Malyovitsa (*50mins*).

🏠 Where to stay
🏠 **Sonata** (10 rooms) ul Petar Beron 4; ✆ 60334; e hotel_sonata@abv.bg; www.hotelsonata.com. Smart modern central hotel with spa & gym in a good location with a popular restaurant (see below). Welcoming, helpful staff. €

🏠 **Zodiak** (9 rooms) ul Rilska Malina 29; m 0878 510033; e zodiac@abv.bg; www.zodiac-bg.com. Small, welcoming, family-run hotel. Light & clean rooms. €

✕ Where to eat and drink
✕ **Golyamata Cheshma** See above; ul Turgovska; ✆ 66617. Offers Bulgarian specialities in a traditional rustic atmosphere. Friendly & efficient service. €€

✕ **Madarova House** ul Dimitur Talev 3; ✆ 60022; e madarova.house@abv.bg; www.madarovahouse.eu. The building is a 19th-century cultural monument, beautifully restored. The cuisine is stylish, modern & international. €€€

✕ **Sonata restaurant** See above. Traditional food, well presented, friendly service & good value. €

✕ **Starata Kushta** ul Zahari Zograf 13, on corner with ul Kliment; m 0885 882828. Traditional atmosphere, Bulgarian cuisine & excellent service. Hard to find but worth the effort. €€

✕ **Zodiak restaurant** Regional dishes in the popular restaurant. €

What to see and do There are a few interesting sights, of which the mushroom-like fountain, or *cheshma*, on the main square is one, a reminder of the Ottoman fondness for running water. Its elaborate appearance looks quite incongruous on the cracked concrete. The mosque nearby, **Bairakli Dzhamiya** (*Байракли Джамия; ul Turgovska 49;* ⊕ *09.00–noon & 13.00–16.00 Mon–Fri; adult 3lv*) is now a museum.

It shows the quality of the local builders' workmanship. There is a splendid sun motif on the ceiling and flower and plant decorations.

The **History Museum** (*Исторически музей; east of the main square, ul Professor V Zahariev;* ① *08.30–12.30 & 13.30–17.30 daily; adult 2lv*) has interesting material relating to Samokov's mining tradition, but surprisingly little about the Samokov School of painters and woodcarvers. If you are interested in examples of this work, there are several churches in the town which are worth a visit. The **Metropolitan Church** (*Митрополитска църква; ul Zahari Zograf*) has a late 18th-century iconostasis whose intricate and delicate style is typical – plants and flowers are interwoven with a lightness of touch which seems amazing given the hardness of the medium they worked with. The **Convent of the Virgin Mary** (*Св Богородица; ul Boris Hadzhisotirov;* ① *daily*) has a lovely 19th-century painting of the Virgin Mary in the porch, but inside the murals are modern. On the road to Sapareva Banya at the village of Belyova the church has another splendid iconostasis, which still includes many representations of plants, but which is enhanced by the addition of splendid eagles and dragons.

The town's former importance as a trade centre is confirmed by some Jewish buildings: a ruined synagogue, obviously once a very substantial building, and nearby the eye-catching, blue-and-white **Sarafska House** (*Сарафската Къща; ul Knyaz Dondukov 11;* ① *09.00–17.00 Mon–Fri; adult 3lv*), in its walled yard, is the sumptuously restored home of a Jewish merchant.

BOROVETS (БОРОВЕЦ) *Telephone code: 07503*

The northern part of the Rila Mountains is the location of the oldest winter resort, Borovets, where there are views across to Mount Musala, the highest peak in the Balkans. In the 1890s Prince Ferdinand had a hunting lodge and some villas built among the pine trees (*bor*) which give Borovets its name. Naturally, his friends and those who wished to become his friends followed his lead and quite a colony was established. There are still several fine buildings from those earlier days scattered around the modern resort.

Getting there and away There are five or six daily **buses** from Plovdiv, Kostenets and Ihtiman, which stop in the old centre. Travellers from Sofia need to go to Samokov first, from where minibuses run once or twice an hour, depending on the season and time of day, to the gondola station.

🏠 **Where to stay** *Map, page 112*

None of the hotels have addresses as the streets are not named.

Hotels

🏠 **Club Hotel Yanakiev** (34 rooms, 6 apts) ⊠ 2830; e office@hotel-yanakiev.com; www.hotel-yanakiev.com. Overlooking nursery slopes. Alpine-style décor, good-sized rooms. Staff are friendly & helpful. €–€€

🏠 **Flora** (38 rooms) m 0886 306070; e hotel-flora@gbs-bg.com; www.flora-hotel.net. Centrally located, but mixed reviews for the restaurant. €–€€

🏠 **Lion** (155 rooms) ⊠ 3000; e booking@ lionhotelborovets.com; www.lionhotelborovets.

com. Comfortable, modern-style rooms. 15mins' walk from centre, but with regular ski shuttle bus. Pool & spa. Friendly, efficient staff. €–€€

🏠 **Lodge** (12 apts) ⊠ 3500; e info@ thelodgecollection.com; www.thelodgecollection.com. A nice, modern, well-maintained hotel just above the gondola station. €€

🏠 **Rila** (526 rooms) ⊠ 2295; e rila@rilaborovets.com; www.rilaborovets.com. The largest hotel in town, renovated in the late 1990s; usually booked by package groups in winter. Excellent location but rooms are basic & food & service average. The

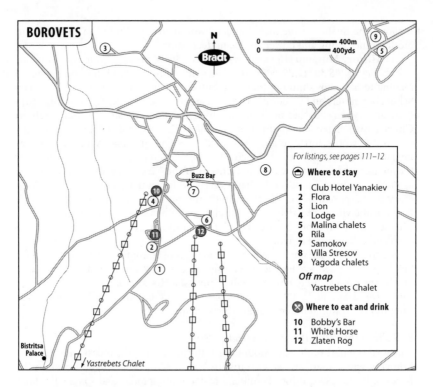

BOROVETS

N

0 ———— 400m
0 ———— 400yds

Buzz Bar

Bistritsa
Palace

Yastrebets Chalet

For listings, see pages 111–12

🛏 **Where to stay**
1 Club Hotel Yanakiev
2 Flora
3 Lion
4 Lodge
5 Malina chalets
6 Rila
7 Samokov
8 Villa Stresov
9 Yagoda chalets

Off map
Yastrebets Chalet

❌ **Where to eat and drink**
10 Bobby's Bar
11 White Horse
12 Zlaten Rog

---

hotel can also provide tourist information (m *0889 607000;* e *info@borovets-bg.com*). €€
🛏 **Samokov** (306 rooms) ☎2306; e *samokov@netbg.com; www.samokov.com*. The oldest hotel in the resort; partly renovated. Central location & good value, but rooms dated & tired. €€

Something different
🛏 **Malina & Yagoda chalets** (40 & 28 wooden chalets respectively) ☎2532; e *office@yagodavillage.com; www.yagodavillage.com*. Each

chalet has 2 rooms & a kitchen, some with sauna. Lovely location in the pine forest. €–€€
🛏 **Villa Stresov** (4 rooms) ☎02 9810482; www.villastresov.com. 1920s chalet restored as luxurious accommodation. You can book rooms singly or the whole villa. €€–€€€
🛏 **Yastrebets Chalet** (25 beds in dbl rooms or dormitories) Mountain hut at 2,369m at the upper gondola station; m *0896 715923;* e *yastrebets@gmail.com; www.yastrebets.com*. Fantastic view towards Musala peak. €

✖ Where to eat and drink *Map, above*

There are a number of cafés, bars and restaurants along the main street. Most of them have menus in English (and sometimes in French and German).

✖ **Bobby's Bar** e *info@bobbysbarborovets.com*. Bulgarian, British & Italian cuisine. €€
✖ **White Horse** Opposite the Mountain Rescue Service; m *0888 143615*. Bulgarian cuisine, grilled specialities. €€

✖ **Zlaten Rog** Opposite Rila Hotel; m *0888 994239*. Bulgarian cuisine, soups, salads & grilled specialities. €€

Nightlife The **Buzz Bar** is *the* place. It's on the main street next to Hotel Samokov and has guest DJs in the busy season. Some of the big hotels also have nightclubs, but fashions change, so watch where the crowds go.

What to see and do After World War II the 19th-century villas were used as hotels for various trade unions, but they have now been returned to their original owners. Some have become private villas, some hotels and some are falling down. **Bistritsa Palace** (⏲ *09.00–16.30 Tue–Sun; adult 12lv*), on the Malyovitsa road, was Ferdinand's hunting lodge and is now owned by his grandson, Simeon Saxe-Coburg-Gotha. Inside there are many animal trophies, woodcarvings from neighbouring Samokov and the heavy furnishings typical of the late 19th century.

In the 1960s Borovets began to develop as a modern ski resort, unfortunately influenced architecturally by the hideous constructions in the French Alps. However, its advantage is that the modern centre is compact and access to the ski areas is convenient. An additional bonus is that, unlike the two other main ski resorts in Bulgaria, Bansko and Pamporovo, the transfer time from Sofia airport is short, 1–1½ hours depending on weather conditions.

Snow cover is generally good from mid-December until April. Now a busy package holiday resort, Borovets has 58km of runs varying in length and difficulty, with something for beginners, intermediates and advanced alpine skiers. There are three main ski areas: Sitnyakovo (1,350–1,780m), Yastrebets (1,340–2,369m) and Markudzhik (2,144–2,550m). The runs at Yastrebets are considered the best and this is where international competitions are held. There are also 35km of cross-country tracks.

The lift infrastructure is well developed with a total capacity of over 8,150 people per hour, so that queuing, except possibly first thing in the morning, is not a problem. Snow cannons ensure there is always some skiing available even when nature is not providing it, and four illuminated runs are available for night skiing. Visitors booked on package holidays are offered ski packs, which include lift pass, ski and boot hire, and ski school for about £160.

BLAGOEVGRAD (БЛАГОЕВГРАД) *Telephone code: 073*

Blagoevgrad lies about midway between Sofia and Bulgaria's southern border with Greece. It is named after Dimitur Blagoev, the founder of Bulgarian Marxism, and was used as a showcase in Todor Zhivkov's time, when he entertained the diplomatic corps. It is a lively and pleasant town with a large pedestrianised centre and plenty of good pavement cafés for people-watching.

GETTING THERE AND AWAY There are **trains** (*Sofia central railway station;* ☏ *02 9323333*) from Sofia (*hourly; 2½hrs*), Dupnitsa (*8 daily; 40mins*) and Sandanski (*6 daily; 1hr 20mins*).

Several **bus** companies now operate this route. Buses (*bus station* ☏ *884009*) run from Sofia via Dupnitsa (*18–20 daily; 1hr 20mins*); Plovdiv (*2 daily; 3½hrs*) and Sandanski (*2 daily; 1hr 20mins*).

TOURIST INFORMATION A new tourist information centre opened in October 2014, but at the time of writing phone and email contact details were not available. The address is ul Georgi Izmirliev, near the American University. The town is very rich in cultural institutions, so if you are here in the evening it is worth checking what performances are available: there is a theatre, a chamber opera and the base of the Pirin Folk Ensemble, one of Bulgaria's finest.

🏠 **WHERE TO STAY** *Map, page 114*
As well as the hotels listed, private rooms can be booked through Alfatour Travel Agency (*ul Krali Marko 4;* ☏ *885049*).

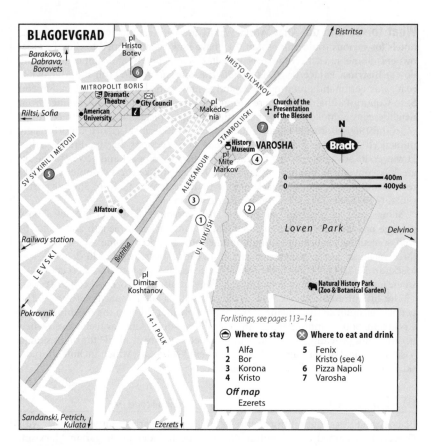

BLAGOEVGRAD

pl Hristo Botev

Bistritsa

Barakovo, Dabrava, Borovets

HRISTO SILYANOV

MITROPOLIT BORIS

Dramatic Theatre · City Council

American University

Riltsi, Sofia

pl Makedonia

Church of the Presentation of the Blessed

STAMBOLIISKI

ALEKSANDUR

History Museum   VAROSHA

SV SV KIRIL I METODII

pl Mite Markov

N

0   400m
0   400yds

Alfatour

UL KUKUSH

Loven Park

Delvino

Railway station

LEVSKI

Bistritsa

pl Dimitar Koshtanov

Natural History Park (Zoo & Botanical Garden)

14-1 POLK

For listings, see pages 113–14

🛏 **Where to stay**   🍴 **Where to eat and drink**
1 Alfa   5 Fenix
2 Bor   Kristo (see 4)
3 Korona   6 Pizza Napoli
4 Kristo   7 Varosha

Off map
Ezerets

Sandanski, Petrich, Kulata

Ezerets

🛏 **Alfa** (25 rooms) ul Kukush 7; ☏ 831122; e alphablg@hotmail.com; www.hotelalpha.net. Well presented & smart, though rooms are small. Helpful staff. **€**

🛏 **Bor** (35 rooms) ul Sv Sv Kiril i Metodii 1, Loven Park; ☏ 884075; e hotel_bor@yahoo.com. Outside the town on a wooded hillside; smartly renovated. Small pool & spa facilities. **€€**

🛏 **Ezerets Hotel** (50 rooms) bul Peyo Yavorov 2; ☏ 886611; e hotel@ezeretz.com; http://ezeretz. com. Still a popular hotel but both the restaurant & the maintenance need to improve. Outdoor swimming pool & spa. **€€**

🛏 **Korona** (25 rooms) ul Nikola Vaptsarov 16; ☏ 886633; e office@hotelkorona.info; http:// hotelkorona.info. Traditional décor, quiet location, clean & comfortable. Rooms spacious & well-equipped. **€**

🛏 **Kristo** (38 rooms) ul Komitov, Varosha quarter; ☏ 880444; e hotel_kristo@abv.bg; www.hotelkristo.com. A relatively new hotel in traditional style, with well-furnished rooms (all different) & good views, in the town's restored old quarter. Has a restaurant (see below). **€**

🍴 **WHERE TO EAT AND DRINK** *Map, above*

🍴 **Fenix** bul Sv Sv Kiril i Metodii. Traditional Bulgarian food of a high standard. Indoor & outdoor dining. **€€**

🍴 **Kristo** Hotel Kristo. Bulgarian cuisine. Nice setting in the Old Town with a terrace overlooking the church. **€€**

🍴 **Pizza Napoli** pl Hristo Botev; ☏ 34649. Great pizzas, salads, grilled meats. Popular & long-established, with efficient friendly staff. **€–€€**

🍴 **Varosha** ul Komitov; ☏ 881370. Housed in a National Revival-period building in the Old Town. Traditional Bulgarian food. **€€**

WHAT TO SEE AND DO The **Varosha** district has been beautifully restored. The **Church of the Presentation of the Blessed Virgin** (*Църква Въведение Богородично;* ☉ *daily; free*) has a distinctive red, black and white pattern on its façade and a free-standing belltower. The **History Museum** (*Исторически музей; ul Rila 1;* ☉ *09.00–noon & 13.00–18.00 Mon–Fri; adult 3lv*) has archaeological finds, a fine collection of stuffed birds and animals, and traditional costumes from the locality. Nearby craft workshops are worth a visit. Beyond Varosha, up a steep road, is the **Natural History Park** with its zoo and botanical gardens and fine views. The American University of Bulgaria is in Blagoevgrad, and during term-time the town is buzzing with life.

This area is adjacent to Macedonia and has a minor border crossing 25km to the west. It is a tobacco-growing area, and it is a common sight to see women threading the leaves on strings and hanging them up to dry.

Tobacco-growing was introduced to Bulgaria by the occupying Turks and at first tobacco was grown by them for their own use. The areas closest to the current Turkish border were the first to be planted but eventually it became a common crop all across southern and eastern Bulgaria. Though some Virginia tobacco is grown, most is Oriental. To the aficionados, different varieties are as distinctive as grape varieties are to the wine lover. However, even the non-smoker can see that the plants vary in size and colour in the different parts of the country. There are five growing areas altogether in Bulgaria and each has its own varieties. In this region, designated the Macedonian tobacco area, the local varieties are Nevrokop, Melnik and Dupnitsa. In the Plovdiv area, Ustina, with its high nicotine content, was used in the most luxurious brands, until the taste for lighter flavours prevailed. Further east the production of the historic variety Djebel-Basma has also decreased as smoking tastes have changed.

BANSKO (БАНСКО) *Telephone code: 0749*

Bansko ski resort has expanded greatly, with hotels and apartments under construction and a new golf course nearby. It is situated on a high plateau between the three mountain ranges of Pirin, Rila and the Rhodopes. As you approach the town, one of Bulgaria's most dramatic views across to the Rila Mountains is unchanged, and the heart of the Old Town somehow keeps its charm. The storks still nest on the church tower, the stone-built houses still hide behind their huge outer walls, and visitors get lost in the labyrinth of cobbled streets. In 2014, *The Daily Telegraph* placed Bansko third on its list of 'Top 20 Places for a Good Life', ahead of Paris and Tuscany, and just behind Andalusia and Gascony.

Bansko is well on the way to becoming a year-round international resort, so whether its traditions and quaintness will survive is a moot point. At least for now, much of the surrounding area is unchanged, though both Razlog and Dobrinishte have prospered thanks to their proximity to Bansko. Summer visitors will still find plenty of spectacular countryside where they can go walking, hiking, rock climbing, mountain biking, horseriding, fishing or birdwatching, or admire the wild flowers, butterflies and dragonflies in the Pirin National Park.

GETTING THERE AND AWAY There are **trains** from Dobrinishte (*4 daily; 10mins*) and Razlog (*4 daily; 15mins*). The narrow-gauge railway connects with Velingrad (*4 daily; 3hrs*) and Septemvri (*4 daily; 4hrs 20mins*).

Buses (*bus station ➘ 52157*) run from Sofia (*2 daily; 3hrs 20mins*), Razlog (*6 daily; 15mins*), Blagoevgrad (*4 daily; 2hrs*) and Gotse Delchev (*1 daily; 1hr*).

TOURIST INFORMATION The tourist information office (*pl Vazrazhdane 4;* \ 88580; e *infocenter@bansko.bg; www.bansko.bg;* ⏲ *09.00–18.00 w/days, 10.00–18.00 Sat, 10.00–14.00 Sun*) can advise on private rooms, hiking and walking routes and forthcoming events.

🏠 WHERE TO STAY Map, page 117

Many of the huge number of hotels are entirely geared to prebooked package tourists during the skiing season, and not all are open in summer.

🏠 **Bansko** (52 rooms) ul Glazne 37; \ 88054; e bansko@biscom.net; www.hotelbansko.bansko. bg. Comfortable. Pool & sauna. €€

🏠 **Bulgaria** (25 rooms) ul Hristo Matov 2; \ 88010; e hbulgaria@infotel.bg; www. hotelbulgariabansko.com. In an established part of town, so there are no building sites on the doorstep! Though the public rooms are small, they have some stylish features, including a huge open fire in winter & balconies with glass floors overlooking the indoor swimming pool. €€

🏠 **Dedo Pene Inn** (4 rooms) ul Aleksander Buinov 1; \ 88348; e info@dedopene.com; www. dedopene.com. Cosy rooms above a popular restaurant (see below). Family-run, friendly. €

🏠 **Dzhangal** (9 rooms) ul Gotse Delchev 24; \ 82661. A modern house in a quiet area; 10mins' walk from the centre. Highly recommended, warm, comfortable & friendly. €

🏠 **Elitsa** (14 rooms) ul Gotse Delchev 12; \ 88391; www.hotel-elitsa.com. Central location. Spacious rooms, very clean & cosy. €€

🏠 **Katarino Spa** (139 rooms, 46 chalets) \ 0747 89600; e office@bulgariaholidays-bg.com; www.bulgariaholidays-bg.com. About 10km from Bansko at Razlog, Katarino area, with a shuttle bus for skiers. Quiet situation. Spa recommended, but general décor a bit tired. €€€

🏠 **Kempinski Grand Arena** (159 rooms) ul Pirin 96; \ 88888; e reservations.grandarena@ kempinski.com; www.kempinski.com/en/bansko. Stunning & right next to the main gondola. Has a fitness centre, treatment rooms for health & beauty, internet, indoor & outdoor heated swimming pools, & several bars & restaurants. €€€

🏠 **Perun** (145 rooms) ul Georgi Nastev; \ 88477; e reservations@hotelperunbansko.com; www.hotelperunbansko.com. Comfortable & good value. Has outdoor heated pool, sports centre & various bars. *Mehana* & subterranean cellar bar with a wide variety of wines. €€

🏠 **Pirin** (68 rooms) ul Tsar Simeon 68; \ 88051; e hotelpirin@bansko.bg; www. hotelpirin.bansko.bg. The original Bansko Hotel, in the old part of town, has now been refurbished & renamed. Friendly staff, but food lacks variety. €€

🏠 **Pirin Golf and Country Club** (62 rooms, 9 apts) Pirin Golf Resort, Razlog; \ 0747 98200; e office@piringolfhotel.com; www. piringolfhotel.com. Not really up to 5-star standards, staff can be unhelpful, but wonderful location & views, with highly rated golf & other leisure facilities. €€€

✖ WHERE TO EAT AND DRINK Map, page 117

✖ **Chevermeto** pl Vuzrazhdane 4; \ 88080; e chevermeto@bansko.bg. Whole barbecued lamb is the speciality. €€

✖ **Dedo Pene** See above. Good food, great atmosphere, live music. €€

✖ **Molerite** ul Glazne 41; \ 88494; e molerite1792@abv.bg; www.molerite.com.

One of the biggest & most popular restaurants in Bansko. Traditional-style local cuisine with excellent service & live music. €€

✖ **Momini Dvori** pl Nikola Vaptsarov 2; \ 88076; e mominidvori@bansko.bg. On the main square. Highly recommended, traditional Bulgarian food with a modern twist & Bansko specialities. €€€

WHAT TO SEE AND DO Bansko has 75km of runs and is good for all levels of skier. Snowboarders can choose between the pistes and a fun park for freestyle boarding. Races of the Alpine Ski World Cup circuit are held here, which is a testament to the quality of the resort. There is usually good snow cover from December to April, and

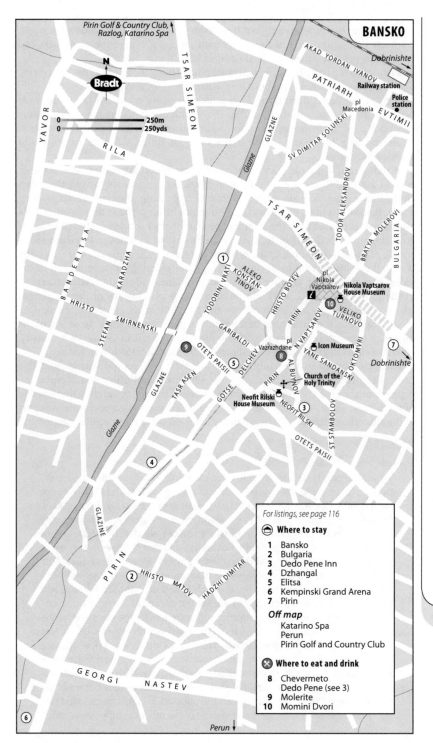

For listings, see page 116

⊖ **Where to stay**

1 Bansko
2 Bulgaria
3 Dedo Pene Inn
4 Dzhangal
5 Elitsa
6 Kempinski Grand Arena
7 Pirin

Off map
  Katarino Spa
  Perun
  Pirin Golf and Country Club

⊗ **Where to eat and drink**

8 Chevermeto
  Dedo Pene (see 3)
9 Molerite
10 Momini Dvori

snow-making machines to help out if necessary. A 7km trail, illuminated at night, connects the higher parts of the resort with the town, where the many bars and restaurants provide a lively après-ski atmosphere.

Visitors booked on package holidays are offered budget-priced ski packs covering one week's ski school, ski and boot hire, and lift pass for about £150.

Bansko prospered during the 19th century because it was on the trade route between the Aegean and the Danube. The wealth of the town's merchants, many of whom used their money to endow churches or contribute to the restoration of nearby Rila Monastery, made it the base for influential icon painting and woodcarving schools.

Walking round the old part of the town is always an adventure, as it is rather easy to get lost! There are friendly stray dogs, local residents forcing their cars along narrow cobbled alleys and plenty of appetising cooking smells wafting about. Bansko is a town of heroes from Bulgaria's history. The main square, **Nikola Vaptsarov**, is named after the poet and revolutionary executed by the pro-Fascist government in 1942. His birthplace has been opened as a **house-museum** (*дом-музей; pl Nikola Vaptsarov;* ⊕ *08.00–noon & 14.00–17.30 daily; adult 3lv*). Nearby is a craft exhibition with local rugs, carvings and paintings for sale. Uphill to the oldest part of the town, another square (Vuzrazhdane) and another statue, this time of the monk Paisii (1722–73). He was the author of a history of the Bulgarians which recounted the achievements of the two Bulgarian kingdoms, reminding the people of their almost forgotten periods of glory before the long ordeal of the Ottoman occupation. It was not widely distributed until the early 19th century, when it helped to give the growing desire for freedom a historical rationale.

Bansko's **Church of the Holy Trinity** (*Църква Св Троица*) was built at this time. The people managed to outwit the Ottoman authorities and, despite the regulations about the permitted height and size of Orthodox churches, theirs is one of the biggest in the country. Building it inside a large walled enclosure was part of the subterfuge! Inside the church many icons decorate the spacious interior and

THE MOST LOVED BIRD

Why is the only large bird living so close to people in Bulgaria the white stork, but not, for example, the golden eagle? For several reasons. The stork does not eat the same food as man does, but rather what people don't like: frogs, snakes, locusts, grasshoppers and mice. By eating mice, the stork is saving people's food and thus ensuring their love. Other reasons are that the stork cannot be eaten, that it is white (the colour of purity), and that it arrives every year at the best season (the spring) at the same time as new life and new hopes. And, indeed, the white stork is everywhere in Bulgaria. In almost all lowland villages there are nests on the chimneys, roofs, churches, occasionally in trees, and most often on the electricity pylons. For the last decade all the nests on pylons have been moved to special platforms, which are safe for the birds and for the electricity lines. Once every ten years BSPB (together with other NGOs, such as Green Balkans) organises the National White Stork Census, when all villages are visited and all nests counted. The data shows where there are most serious risks for the species and where more efforts are necessary. BirdLife International initiates the count and it is simultaneous in all other European countries of the species' range. During the last 20 years the population of this much-loved bird is slightly increasing in Bulgaria and in most of the other countries surveyed.

Pirin was declared a National Park in 1974 and covers a territory of 6,212ha. It is divided geographically into Northern, Central and Southern Pirin. The Central and Southern parts are formed mainly from marble base rock, and the flora and vegetation are similar to those of the Slavyanka Mountains. The Northern Pirin Mountains are formed by both marble and silicate base rocks, and here a real alpine flora and vegetation belt exists above 2,500m.

Pirin National Park is recognised by UNESCO as a World Heritage Site. The unique beauty of the mountain is a relief of alpine type concentrated in a small territory sculpted by marble and silicate. There are two biosphere reserves: Bayuvi Dupki-Dzhindzhinitsa and Yulen. The first is a UNESCO-designated biosphere reserve, because the flora and vegetation are unique.

The flora of Pirin includes 1,300 plant species, of which 121 are threatened and so listed in the *Red Data Book of Bulgaria*. Many of the plants growing in Pirin have a distribution restricted to the Balkan Peninsula, ie: Balkan endemics. These are **violets** (*Viola perinensis, V. grisebachiana*), **whitlowgrass** (*Drabaathoa*), **saxifrages** (*Saxifraga ferdinandi, S. stribrnyi, S. spruneri, S. sempervivum*) and **bellflower** (*Campanula velebitica*).

The highest peak, Vihren (2,914m), is located in the marble part of Northern Pirin and looks like a huge rock garden. There are 18 plant species that can be seen only on this mountain, including local endemics such as **yellow poppy** (*Papaver degenii*), **mullein** (*Verbascum davidoffii*), **rattle** (*Rhinanthus javorkae*), **knapweed** (*Centaurea achtarovii*), **locoweed** (*Oxytropis urumovii*), **pink sainfoin** (*Onobrychis pindicola*), **cabbage** (*Brassica jordanovii*) and **thyme** (*Thymus perinicus*).

As a result of glacier activity there are many U-shaped valleys and corries (cirques) at their heads, and in total 119 glacial lakes were formed 10,000–12,000 years ago, after the last glacial period in the silicate part of Northern Pirin. They are clustered in corries between 2,000m and 2,710m in altitude. Many interesting and rare beetles and butterflies can be seen here.

The towns from where you can start botanical walks in the mountains are Razlog, Bansko (towards Vihren peak or some of the glacial lakes), Dobrinishte (to some other glacial lakes) and Gotse Delchev (towards the peak, Orelek).

outside is the impressive belltower (built 60 years later) whose pealing bells don't seem to bother the nesting storks or their lodgers, the Spanish sparrows.

By the entrance to the churchyard another hero poet, **Peyo Yavorov**, is commemorated. He was a noted romantic poet who became involved in the struggle for Macedonian independence. Behind the church another **house-museum** (*дом-музей; ul Pirin 17; ⊕ 09.00–13.00 & 14.00–17.30 daily; adult 3lv*) is dedicated to **Neofit Rilski**. Although he was a monk, he played a key role in the establishment of secular education in Bulgaria, becoming the headmaster of the first such school in Gabrovo and later establishing a similar and equally renowned one in Koprivshtitsa. A leading scholar, he translated the New Testament into Bulgarian and compiled a Greek–Bulgarian dictionary. As with many of Bulgaria's smaller museums, the captions are only in Bulgarian, though curators are often keen to help when they see you are interested. It is usually a pleasure simply to be inside these historic buildings, even when some of the displays are a bit of a mystery.

In the summer the ski resort of Bansko is a gateway into the Pirin Mountains for those who want to enjoy its spectacular scenery and natural history.

Not far above Bansko, in clearings and meadows among the spruce forests or on vegetated ski runs, a wide variety of butterfly species can be found. Among the blues will be **mazarine blue, blue argus, turquoise blue, geranium argus, Meleager's blue** and **Amanda's blue**. Brilliant coppers are also common, including the **purple-shot** and **scarce coppers** and in the damper areas the **Balkan copper** which, as the name suggests, is endemic to the Balkans. The more dingy but still attractive **sooty copper** is also frequently seen here. Fritillaries are also common and include **Glanville, knapweed, heath** and **pearl-bordered fritillaries**. The **woodland ringlet** is also common.

In these meadows can be found colonies of the rare subspecific form *rebeli* of the **Alcon blue**. Look for the food plant, the cross gentian, and the butterfly may also be found in its season. Caterpillars of this butterfly only feed on the plant for a short time before being taken below ground to complete their development in the nests of certain species of red ant. When the time comes for the adults to emerge, several may do so simultaneously from the same ant nest and be found together drying their wings. This butterfly has severely declined in western Europe but is still widespread in mountainous areas of Bulgaria.

The subspecific form *baldur* of the **Idas blue** can be common here; associated with its food plants the broomlike *Chamaecytisus* bushes, which are often common in these forest clearings. This butterfly is similar to the more familiar silver-studded blue (also common in Bulgaria) and the subspecies *baldur* even more so, in that the black borders to the upperside of the male's sapphire blue wings are as broad as those of the silver-studded blue. The **black hairstreak** occurs here too; look on blackthorn or wild plum growing in clearings.

In areas where spruce and pine forests give way to scrubby mountain pine and subalpine meadows you start to see high-altitude butterfly species. These include the spectacular **Apollo**, which cruises low over ground vegetation, along with the smaller **clouded Apollo**, which can be numerous. Also here will be found a Balkan endemic, the **Balkan fritillary**, similar to but distinct from its close relative the **shepherd's fritillary**, another mountain species which is found here higher still, along with the beautiful **Cynthia's fritillary**.

At these high altitudes, spring species are often still flying in late June and early July and it is no surprise to see **orange tip, green hairstreak, Duke of Burgundy, chequered skipper** and especially **pearl-bordered fritillary**. This is one of the places in Bulgaria to see a good range of other high-altitude butterfly species. For example, 14 species of mountain ringlet (*Erebia*) occur in Bulgaria and 11 of these can be found in the Pirin Mountains, including two endemic species, the **Bulgarian ringlet** and **Nicholl's ringlet**. These chocolate-brown butterflies with orange markings fly on high alpine slopes only when the sun is shining, quickly disappearing into the grass when cloud obscures the sun. July and August are the months to see the *Erebias*.

This is an area where a wide range of habitats, from low to high altitudes, occur within a relatively short distance, making it easier for the visitor to see a wide range of species without travelling too far; added to which the spectacular mountain scenery is a wonderful tonic for any traveller. Bansko provides a good base from which many good butterfly areas can be visited.

Just off pl Vuzrazhdane is the small nunnery affiliated to Rila, and here there is an excellent **Icon Museum** (*Музей на иконите; ul Yane Sandanski 3;* ⌚ *09.00–noon & 14.00–17.30 Mon–Fri; adult 3lv*) showing the achievements of the Bansko School of painters, particularly the Vishanov and Molerov family. It is interesting to see how the artists created very lifelike features for their subjects, rather than the more stylised characteristics painted earlier. Their work can be seen in churches and monasteries all over the area.

AROUND BANSKO

Dobursko (Добърско) A fascinating excursion from Bansko is the village of Dobursko, about 20km north. It is on an interesting road passing through mountain pastures and tobacco fields. The objective is the church, Sv Sv Teodor Tiron and Teodor Stratilat, which from the outside has little to commend it, but inside are some of the finest **frescoes** you will ever see. There are scenes from the New Testament and of the saints to whom the church is dedicated, and the famous picture of Jesus apparently ascending to heaven in a space rocket!

The narrow-gauge railway Another possibility is to take a trip on the narrow-gauge railway, which runs from Dobrinishte via Bansko to Septemvri, west of Plovdiv. It was constructed by the occupying Germans in World War II to facilitate their logging activities. There are four trains a day, which travel extremely slowly (the whole journey takes 6 hours), but the mountain views are spectacular and the trip is well worth making if you have the time. See www.bgrazpisanie.com for timetables.

Belitsa (Белица) The same route is possible by car, and this has the advantage that you could pay a visit to one of Bulgaria's more unusual attractions: a **sanctuary for rescued dancing bears**. The road there is unfortunately in poor condition. In the past the bears were a common sight on the coast and at tourist attractions; I have even seen them in the centre of Sofia. It was a truly pathetic image: the powerful wild creature forced to stand on its hind legs while its Roma (usually) owner played a few derisory notes on a musical instrument for the bear to dance to. Fortunately this practice was banned in 2002. In 2000, an Austrian charity and the Brigitte Bardot Foundation established this refuge in Belitsa, formerly a mining village and now an area of high unemployment. The bears are purchased from their owners and released into a large enclosure of wooded hillside. Most were captured as cubs and would not know how to live in the wild. It is a sad tale, but with a reasonably happy ending.

SPECIAL EVENTS There are a few special events in Bansko, which you might like to co-ordinate with your visit. For a few days in mid-August **Bansko Jazz Festival** is held, and in recent years it has attracted some big names. Also musical, but of a very different kind, is the **Pirin Sings Folk Festival** held at the Predel Pass (on the way to Bansko from the Sofia–Kulata road). After the Koprivshtitsa Festival this is Bulgaria's largest folklore event and, given its location, there is a strong Macedonian influence in the songs and dances. The festival takes place in August in odd-numbered years. For both events it's best to check the dates at the **Pirin Sings Foundation** (*Pirin Pee, Dinova Kushta, Varosha, Blagoevgrad;* ☎ *80036*).

Close to Bansko, in the town of **Razlog**, the ***kukeri*** rites on 1 January are a major attraction for folklore enthusiasts. The fearsome *kukeri*, men dressed in animal skins with several large bells strung on their bodies, form a colourful and very noisy procession intended to drive away evil spirits. In 2014 over a thousand *kukeri* took part!

This is a busy border area – Greeks come to Bulgaria for shopping at good-value prices, Bulgarians love to holiday in Greece, and of course it is a major international route. However, the areas east and west of the busy main road are rural and unspoilt, fascinating for nature lovers and those with an interest in history.

KRESNA (КРЕСНА) Returning to the main road and continuing south brings you to the Kresna Gorge, a convenient and picturesque spot for a coffee or lunch break. Once upon a time there was a lone café here with a little veranda hanging over the rushing Struma River. Now there are dozens! But the riverside is still a pretty spot where martins, swallows and wagtails dart about. The various NGOs involved in conservation united to protest against the proposed motorway through this gorge, and have successfully stopped the project. As a result, a series of tunnels will be constructed (starting in 2016) so that the road traffic does not harm wildlife.

SANDANSKI (САНДАНСКИ) *Telephone code: 0746*
The spa town of Sandanski is famous for its mild temperatures, hot mineral springs and pure air, and a stay here is recommended for sufferers from bronchial and asthmatic conditions. Ironically, it is also in the centre of Bulgaria's tobacco-growing area! Its long pedestrian street is the setting for a very relaxed evening promenade, with plenty of opportunities to stop for coffees and sweet pastries of all kinds. Another good place for pleasant strolls is the large town park, with swimming and boating pools, and a wide selection of plants and trees, which thrive in the mild Mediterranean climate.

Getting there and away There are **trains** (*central railway station* ✆ *02 9323333*) from Sofia (*5 daily; 3hrs 25mins*) and Blagoevgrad (*hourly; 1hr 10mins*). The station is 4km west of the town, though there are regular buses to the centre.

Buses (*Sandanski Bus Station* ✆ *31239*) run from Sofia hourly (*2hrs 45mins*) and the route is served by several companies.

Tourist information The information centre (*ul Macedonia 28;* m *0884 898976;* e *tic.sandanski@gmail.com*) can arrange accommodation in private rooms and supply local information and maps.

BIRDWATCHING IN THE STRUMA VALLEY

The Struma Valley is situated on a secondary, but interesting, migratory flyway, where habitats are strongly influenced by the proximity of the Mediterranean. Common breeders are species such as **blue rock thrush, Orphean** and **Sardinian warbler, rock nuthatch, rock sparrow, Cetti's warbler** and **scops owl**. A very rich variety of birds can be seen during both the spring and autumn passage, especially at the marshy areas along the Struma River near Rupite, and near the village of Mursalevo. **Whiskered, black** and **white-winged terns, roller, semi-collared, collared** and **pied flycatchers** are regularly seen, especially on spring migration. The adjacent slopes of the neighbouring mountains are interesting; here **woodchat shrike, black-headed bunting** and even **Calandra lark** breed in large numbers.

⌂ Where to stay

⌂ **Aneli** (14 rooms) ul Gotse Delchev 1; ☎31844; e sandanski_aneli@mail.bg; www. aneli.hit.bg. Budget option, good-value, basic accommodation. €

⌂ **Balevurov Hotel** (20 rooms) ul Mara Buneva 14; ☎30013. Right in the centre, close to the main street & overlooking the remains of Sv Ivan Basilica. €

⌂ **Interhotel Sandanski** (296 rooms) ul Makedoniya; ☎31162; e info@ihsand.com; www. interhotelsandanski.com. Prominent building near the centre, with spa facilities & swimming pool, & next to the lovely park. €€

⌂ **Park Hotel Sandanski** (15 rooms) Hristo Smirnenski 13; ☎30206; www. parkhotelsandanski.eu. Central location, spacious rooms. Restaurant recommended. €€

⌂ **Sveti Vrach** (20 rooms) ☎32093; e booking@svetivrachsandanski.com. Wonderfully situated on a hillside with a lake & large grounds, this former government residence is about 4km from the town. Spa facilities. €€

✕ Where to eat and drink

✕ **Chevermeto** ul Lilianska 10; on the road to Popina Luka. Picturesque location with traditional cuisine. €€€

✕ **Fish & Barbecue Restaurant** Interhotel Sandanski. Fish & seafood specialities from the Aegean, plus the usual Bulgarian grills of lamb, pork & chicken. €€€

✕ **Sandanski Mehana** Interhotel Sandanski. Traditional style with live music. €€€

✕ **Surprise** bul Makedoniya 63; ☎31202. On main street. Varied traditional menu. €

✕ **Tropikana** bul Makedoniya 73; m 0898 726578. Nice location by the park. Big menu of salads, grilled meat & Bulgarian cuisine. €€

What to see and do The town is named after Yane Sandanski, one of the three main leaders in this area in the struggle for Macedonian liberation from the Ottoman Empire. The town also has links with another revolutionary from a different era, Spartacus. Sandanski was a settlement of the Thracian Medi people, many of whom were sent to work in Sicily after the Roman conquest. Local hero Spartacus, whose huge statue dominates the approach to the town, is credited with being the leader of the slave uprising against the Romans in the 1st century BC.

Although it is an ancient settlement, there is little in the modern town to reflect this apart from the **Archaeological Museum** (*Археологически музей; bul Makedoniya 55;* m *0896 713202;* ⊕ *Apr–Oct 10.00–noon Mon–Sat & 13.00–17.00 Mon–Fri, Nov–Mar 10.30–noon & 13.00–17.00 Mon–Fri; adult 2lv, free on Thu*). This is built around a Roman villa with a mosaic floor, together with votive tablets and other artefacts from the necropolis at Muletarevo. It only has captions and explanations in Bulgarian.

Sandanski may be a good base for further exploration of Bulgaria's southernmost part. For nature lovers this is a richly rewarding area (see box, pages 126–7), partly because throughout the communist era the border zone was closed off and birds, butterflies and flowers were undisturbed. The Belasitsa and Slavyanka mountains, right on the Greek border, are the habitat for a spectacular number of species.

MELNIK (МЕЛНИК) *Telephone code: 07437*

As you approach Melnik the scenery starts to change; strange bare cliffs of eroded sandstone stand guard behind the town. Quite suddenly the main street comes into view, bordering the (usually) dry river-bed running through the centre. It presents a pretty picture of whitewashed houses, trailing vines and brightly coloured flowers.

History In medieval times Melnik was a border settlement, sometimes within the Bulgarian Empire, sometimes within the Byzantine one. In the 13th century it was the capital of Alexei Slav, the independent despot who ruled much of the region, and a fortress and several monasteries were built. As a result of his influence, wealthy Greeks settled here, thus stimulating trade and investment, as well as an influx of new social and cultural influences.

During the Ottoman period Melnik was in decline until the 17th and 18th centuries, when its production of tobacco and wine made it a flourishing town of merchants, who traded all over Europe. The town expanded and houses were rebuilt on the old medieval foundations. The traditional style is of a high ground floor, usually with stone walls, and a lighter, often timber, upper floor. Below many of the houses were cellars for the famous wine. By the end of the 19th century the town had 20,000 inhabitants, whereas now there are fewer than 300. The decline during the early 20th century was partly brought about by the Balkan wars, during which Melnik was burned down and its population forced to flee, and partly by economic catastrophe when the vines were struck by the fatal phylloxera disease.

Getting there and away There is a **bus** from Sofia (*1 daily; 4hrs*), Blagoevgrad (*1 daily; 2hrs*) and Sandanski (*2 daily; 30mins*).

Tourist information There is no tourist office in the town, but the website www. melnik-bg.eu has helpful general information, and there is an email contact at e gradmelniktic@abv.bg.

🏠 Where to stay

🏠 **Bolyarka** (17 rooms, 2 luxury apts, 2 small apts) ☏ 2383; e sokolov82@mail.bg; www. bg.melnikhotels.com. Nice-looking building, family-run & very helpful & friendly. Comfortable rooms, many with lovely views of the sandstone pyramids. **€€**

🏠 **Litova Kushta** (12 rooms) ☏ 2313; e litovakushta@abv.bg; www.litovakushta.com. The newest hotel in Melnik, but in traditional style. Has an outdoor swimming pool. **€€**

🏠 **Sveti Nikola** (10 rooms) ☏ 2211; e info@ melnik-svnicola.com. Stylish modern rooms with wonderful views. Indoor & terrace dining, local specialities. **€**

🏠 **Uzunova Kushta** (10 rooms) ☏ 2270. Nicely modernised building with the added kudos of being the former Turkish prison. **€**

✗ Where to eat and drink
As well as those in the listed hotels, Melnik has a number of good restaurants.

✗ **Chinarite** m 0878 688328. Nice veranda. Good traditional food, Bulgarian music. **€€**

✗ **Mencheva Kushta** ☏ 2339. Traditional Melnik *mehana* with excellent food & nice setting. Worth trying the homemade sausage. Sometimes live music. **€€**

✗ **Sveta Varvara** m 0899 874580. Above the ruins of Sv Varvara Church, below the Kordopulov house. Nice view from the terrace. Bulgarian food, soups & salads. **€€**

What to see and do At weekends and during the main tourist season Melnik gets very busy, but luckily most parts of it are accessible only on foot and most visitors park at the entrance to the town.

Various houses are open to visitors, the most impressive being the **Kordopulov House** (*Кордопуловата къща*; ⊕ *09.30–19.00 daily; adult 2lv*) at the top of the town, with extensive views over it and the surrounding countryside. Built in 1754 by Manolis Kordopulis, a rich wine merchant, it is the largest National Revival-style house in Bulgaria with four storeys, two of which house a huge labyrinth of cellars cut into the sandstone, where thousands of litres of wine were once stored. The wine matured in enormous barrels which gave it its distinctive flavour. The story of Melnik's wine is rather interesting: it is made from the local indigenous grape, Shiroka Melnishka Loza, the broad-leaved Melnik vine, which is only grown in this area of the country. When I first visited Damyanitsa Winery many years ago, an old man who worked there recalled how every year several barrels of the wine were shipped to England for Winston Churchill, who had a particular liking for it. The upper floors of the Kordopulov House reflect the wealth of its original owner: finely carved woodwork, painted panelling and numerous large windows, some with colourful stained-glass inserts, give an air of spacious splendour. The low, cushioned seats and tables conjure up images of men relaxing and talking, probably about politics, in a smoky haze!

Across the town the **Pashova House** (*Пашовата къща;* ⊕ *09.00–noon & 13.00–16.00 Mon–Fri; adult 2lv*), where Yane Sandanski proclaimed Melnik's final liberation from the Turks in 1912, houses a small museum with costumes, jewellery and other artefacts, together with fascinating old photographs of the town in its heyday.

Melnik's troubled history is revealed by the large number of ruined churches and houses, one of which, the Bolyarskata House, is thought to have been the home of Alexei Slav. There are still several working churches, one of the most interesting of which is **Sv Sv Petur i Pavel** (*Св Св Петър и Павел*) situated on the hillside after the first bridge, which has a brightly painted iconostasis. On the other side of the river, the **Church of Sv Nikolai the Miracle-worker** (*Св Николай Чудотворец*) is imposing, with its belltower and long veranda, while inside a very fine iconostasis dominates the scene. As you wander around Melnik you may also find the ruined *konak* and Turkish baths, catch sight of a lizard darting or a tortoise pottering, or come face to face with a donkey grazing in the ruins of a house.

There is a lively trade in homemade wines and local delicacies, with stalls outside almost every house. There are also plenty of places to eat and drink along the main street. If you have time to linger here, the walk across the hills to Rozhen Monastery is very pleasant, though steep and narrow in places.

ROZHEN MONASTERY (*Роженски Манастир;* ⊕ *daily; free*) If you have walked from Melnik (about 1½–2 hours, depending on your route) you will have seen the sandstone pyramids at close quarters and have the pleasure of striding across the grassy plateau to Rozhen Monastery like a proper pilgrim.

It is a small and rather cosy place, seemingly more farmhouse than monument, and a great contrast to Rila. It was probably founded by the Melnik ruler, Alexei Slav, during the late 12th or early 13th century, and like Rila has been looted and burned many times since its foundation. The courtyard, with tiers of cells and wooden balconies, is very simple, but the juxtaposition of stone and old woodwork softened by vines and fruit trees is appealing.

The Nativity of the Virgin Church (*Св Рождество Богородично*) has 17th-century murals, which have been delicately restored, and above the entrance door there is a painting of Christ and his 12 apostles which dates from the late 16th century. Many of the paintings feature fishermen, reminding us of the area's links with Greece and the Aegean. The iconostasis is a magnificent example of the Debur woodcarving tradition, lavishly gilded and decorated with figures, flowers, fishes and flourishes. The church's greatest treasure is a miraculous icon of the Virgin and Child, which many visitors come specially to see. There is some stained glass, a rare sight in Bulgaria, which dates from 1715 and depicts secular scenes. The northwest chapel of the church is dedicated to Sv Sv Cosmas and Damian, known as the healing twins, who according to local tradition lived in Sandanski and were skilled in folk medicine. They treated people free of charge.

Some cells are furnished to give visitors an impression of monastic life over the years. The rooms are simple but with brightly coloured textiles, and for the more senior monks there were some small touches of luxury. If you happen to be visiting on 8 September, you will find the monastery celebrating its anniversary, when people from all over the region come to take part in the festivities.

Rozhen's particular contribution to Bulgaria's cultural tradition was its 14th-century school of calligraphy, where the monks copied and decorated manuscripts. A small gallery houses a fine collection of **icons**, some of which illustrate Bulgaria's spirit of resistance; for example, close examination of a picture of Sv Georgi (*Св Георги*) killing a dragon reveals a tiny Turk in the body of the dragon. The refectory, unusually, also has fragments of murals and is a fine room, reminiscent perhaps of a college dining room in Oxford or Cambridge.

Near the monastery is the **Church of Sv Sv Kiril and Metodii** (*Църквата на Св Св Кирил и Методий*), a 20th-century building housing an important icon of Sv Nikolai (*Св Николай*). Outside is the grave of Yane Sandanski, the great

BUTTERFLIES IN SOUTHWEST BULGARIA AND SLAVYANKA MOUNTAINS

The far southwest corner is the richest area for butterflies in Bulgaria, with about 80% of Bulgaria's butterfly species having been recorded here (if one includes the Pirin Mountains, nearly 90%). Here the Struma Valley runs south into Greece and eventually into the Mediterranean Sea. It provides a Mediterranean influence to the climate of the region, which is reflected in some of the plants and insects that occur here. Along the border with Greece run the Belasitsa Mountains to the west of the Struma Valley, and the Slavyanka Mountains to the east. The Slavyanka Mountains, which rise to just over 2,200m, are just south of the southern end of the Pirin Mountains.

The Mediterranean influence is reflected in the butterfly fauna in this corner of Bulgaria, which has several species not found elsewhere in the country. These are species which occur further south in Greece and other Mediterranean countries, but have also colonised this part of Bulgaria. Several of these are only known to exist in a few isolated colonies in Bulgaria. These include the **inky skipper**, the **eastern greenish black-tip** and the **powdered brimstone**. **Gruner's orange tip** is almost in this category, but has also been recorded in the Mesta Valley east of the Pirin Mountains. However, to see these species you need to know exactly where and when to go, though chance findings are always possible in such a relatively unrecorded country. Other species in this category, such as the **Mediterranean skipper** and the **white-banded grayling**, are a little more common and thus a little easier to find in their season.

A good variety of other species can be found in the warmer, drier, grassy areas and rocky slopes. These include the **Grecian** and **lesser fiery coppers**, **little tiger blue**, **eastern baton blue**, **Krueper's small white**, **Balkan marbled white**, and the **eastern wood white**, distinguished in the male from the more familiar **wood white** by the lack of white on the inside of the antennal tips. This species can be quite common in open, scrubby grassland. Both the **dusky** and **oriental meadow**

Macedonian freedom fighter, still usually bedecked with wild-flower offerings in his memory from his supporters.

Down the hill is Rozhen village, less touched by tourism than Melnik, and perhaps the more attractive for that. Its houses are a bit ramshackle, looking almost as if they are held up by the vines that scramble all over them. There are strings of peppers hanging up to dry, hundreds of bright gourds and squashes, neatly stacked winter wood and flowers blooming in boxes and tins.

RUPITE (РУПИТЕ) Despite being a popular destination, mainly for Bulgarians, this is poorly signposted and hard to find. You need to leave the E79 at Novo Delchevo, towards Petrich; Rupite will be a left turn. It is not accessible by public transport.

Rupite village is a place of pilgrimage situated in the crater of an extinct volcano. Most visitors are interested in Vanga, but others come for the hot springs or the rich wildlife.

Rupite is the birth and burial place of the famous clairvoyant Vanga. The story is that when she was a child an angel offered her the choice between sight and second sight (or clairvoyance) and she chose the latter. Her prophecies became internationally famous and her healing powers gained her a huge following. The modern church where she is buried has external frescoes by Bulgarian artist Svetlin Rusev. Controversially these show Vanga alongside Jesus Christ and the Virgin

brown occur here also and several very similar grayling species which arguably cannot be reliably identified in the field!

The Slavyanka Mountains are particularly rich in butterflies and it is possible to see at least 80 species of butterfly here in a single day. The underlying carboniferous marble rock results in calcareous soils, which support a rich flora that in turn supports many butterfly species. On the lower slopes in the herb-rich grasslands, among scrub and along the forest edge, many species can be found flying together and nectaring on the wide variety of flowers available. These include numerous **sloe** and **ilex hairstreaks**, associated with blackthorn and oak respectively, **mountain small white, large blue, Niobe** and **dark green fritillaries, Weaver's** and **heath fritillaries**.

During hot weather the males of many of these species congregate on wet patches on roadsides and tracks, in an activity called 'puddling'. Instead of taking up nectar from flowers, these butterflies are taking up mineral salts important for reproduction. Sometimes hundreds of butterflies will congregate together on a series of damp patches, with a variety of species of blue and others jostling for the best areas. Here, four species of anomalous blue occur (including Grecian and Higgins' anomalous blues), and several of these species may be seen together, along with other species such as **Idas blue, Osiris** and **small blue, false Eros blue, Escher's blue** and **Meleager's blue**, as well as more generally common species. The **nettle-tree** or **snout** butterfly is also common here and sometimes congregates in hundreds on these damp patches along with **silver-washed fritillaries, cardinals** and **large tortoiseshells**. Other damp patches will have groups of skippers on them, notably the **sandy grizzled skipper**.

This part of Bulgaria is a fabulous place to visit and boasts a wide range of different habitats within a relatively small area, making it easy to see a large number of species while being based at a single location.

Mary, something of which the Orthodox Church authorities disapprove. Inside there is a painted iconostasis but it is otherwise very plain, though some soothing bell music plays. The place does seem to have a peaceful, spiritual atmosphere, despite the many visitors. The sight of the ground steaming even on warm summer days is quite surreal; the mineral springs are a very hot 75°C.

PETRICH (ПЕТРИЧ) *Telephone code: 0745*

Petrich is a border town both with Greece and Macedonia, and it has a long tradition of profiting from this, whether sanction-busting during the United Nations trade embargo on Yugoslavia, or importing Western luxuries from Greece during the communist period. Its history is closely tied to the Macedonian Question (see box, pages 130–3) and in the 1920s and 1930s it had the reputation of being the murder capital of Bulgaria, as freedom fighters feuded with each other.

Getting there and away There are **trains** (*railway station* ☏ *23357*) from Sandanski (*5 daily; 50mins*) and Sofia (*with a change; 4 daily; 4hrs*).

Buses (*Sofia central bus station* ☏ *0900 63099*) run from Sofia (*3 daily; 3½hrs*), Kulata (*1 daily; 30mins*), Sandanski (*1 daily; 30mins*) and Blagoevgrad (*4 daily; 1hr 30mins*).

🏠 Where to stay

🏠 **Bats** (33 rooms) ul Tsar Boris III 43; ☏ 69300; e hotelbats@satline.net; www.hotelbats.com. Central location, swimming pool, small spa. Very clean, friendly, traditional-style hotel. €€

🏠 **Bulgaria** (94 rooms) ul Tsar Boris III 21; ☏ 22233. Rather dated hotel but in a wonderful position with views to mountains; open-air restaurant in a garden of mature trees. Good value. €

🏠 **Elena** (13 rooms) ul Asen Zlatarov 2A; ☏ 62101; e hotel_elena@abv.bg; www. hotelelena-bg.com. Small, modern & central hotel. €

✗ Where to eat and drink

✗ **Argilov** ul Stamboliiski 10; ☏ 22024. Classy place offering international & Bulgarian cuisine; seafood specialities; good selection of wines. €€

✗ **Raiski Kut & Yavorite** In the town park. Both serve traditional Bulgarian food, & have live music at w/ends. €

✗ **Rubin** ul Polkovnik Drangov 3; ☏ 22424. Good central restaurant. €€

What to see and do Nowadays Petrich is a quiet, dusty town surrounded by beautiful countryside. In the exceptionally mild climate fruits such as peaches and apricots, cherries and grapes, melons and kiwis are ripe early in the season. There is even the possibility of major investment in the area for olive groves, which though common in Greece do not normally flourish in Bulgaria.

There is a small **museum** (*музей; below Town Hall;* ⊕ *09.00–16.00 Mon–Fri; adult 1lv*) with a modest collection of Thracian and Roman artefacts from local excavations.

To the southwest at **Samuilovo** there are the extensive ruins of a fortress, a monument to perhaps the cruellest moment in Bulgarian history (though sadly there are other contenders for this label in the country's turbulent past). After the defeat of the Bulgarian army by the Byzantines in 1014, over 14,000 prisoners were blinded with red hot pokers, and one in a hundred was left with one eye so he could lead the others home. The Bulgarian Tsar Samuil died of a heart attack from the shock. It is hard to imagine such horrors in the peaceful pastoral landscape of today.

GOTSE DELCHEV (ГОЦЕ ДЕЛЧЕВ) *Telephone code: 0751*

This pleasant small town is reached along the beautiful valley of the River Mesta. It was established by the Romans as Nikopolis ad Nestum in the 2nd century AD. For most of its history it was known by the Greek name Nevrokop, and in the early 20th century was renamed to honour the Bulgarian revolutionary. Delchev was born in northern Greece in 1872, and was influenced by the theories of Bulgarian revolutionaries Vasil Levski and Hristo Botev. However, he applied their ideas to a different cause, that of an autonomous Macedonia which might join a future Balkan federation, but he did not seek union with Bulgaria. He was killed in 1903 in an encounter with Turkish troops before the abortive Ilinden uprising for which he had worked. He is still a popular hero in Bulgaria and Macedonia.

Getting there and away There are buses (*bus station* ✆ *23547*) from Blagoevgrad (*3 daily; 2hrs 15mins*), Bansko (*1 daily; 1hr 10mins*), Kovachevitsa (*5 daily to Ognyanovski Bani, 25mins, then a taxi*) and Sofia (*every 4hrs; 3hrs 45mins*).

Tourist information The tourist information office (*pl Makedonia 2;* ✆ *60125;* ⊕ *09.00–17.00 daily*) offers maps, listings of accommodation in private rooms and information about events.

Where to stay and eat As well as those listed below, several small places offer grills and snacks along ul Turgovska in the centre.

Baroto Complex (30 rooms, 4 apts) 3km east in the direction of Dospat; ✆ 61221; e complex_baroto@mail.bg; www.complex-baroto.com. Stylish décor, pool, good restaurant. €€

Egeya (9 rooms) bul Gotse Delchev 7; ✆ 25069. Small hotel in the centre. €

Hristov (22 rooms) ul Byalo More 4; ✆ 29113; www.hhristoff.hit.bg. Modern hotel in the centre with a swimming pool on the rooftop. €

Malamovata Kushta (11 rooms) ul Hristo Botev 25; ✆ 61230. Family hotel in a beautiful National Revival-period house. Restaurant with lovely garden & good Bulgarian specialities; probably the best place to eat. €

Nevrokop (82 rooms) ul Mihail Antonov 1; ✆ 61240; e info@hotelnevrokop.com; www.hotelnevrokop.com. Central location. Rooms were renovated in 2003, but still have the retro look. €

What to see and do A new border crossing between Ilinden, just south of Gotse Delchev, and Exochi in Greece has recently opened, which will probably benefit the town's tourist business.

Within the town the finest attraction is the **Museum of History and Ethnography**, in the **Prokopov House** (*Прокоповата къща; ul Botev 26;* ✆ *60287;* ⊕ *09.30–noon & 13.30–17.30 Tue–Sat; adult 2lv*). This is an absolutely lovely building in Baroque style, its lemon façade lavishly ornamented around each window, and with a fine metal balcony. It is a most atypical building for this area. Inside there are archaeological exhibits from Nikopolis ad Nestum – ceramics, coins and photographs. One local trade was the making of Rhodope bells; in the 19th century there were as many as 20 such workshops in the town.

Rifat Bey Kushta (*Къщата на Рифат Бей;* ⊕ *10.00–noon & 14.00–18.00 Tue–Sat; adult 2lv*) has an ethnographic collection focused on the National Revival period. Nearby is a famous plane tree, 24m high and estimated to be 500 years old.

The **Church of the Archangel Michael** (*Църквата Архангел Михаил*) was built in 1811 and is the oldest in the town. It has a fine iconostasis and a richly

Macédoine is the French word for a mixture or medley; it is also their name for Macedonia, an area known for its ethnic variety. The country now called Macedonia does not encompass the historical area which bore this name, parts of which are in Greece and Bulgaria. The modern country bears the awkward acronym FYROM, the Former Yugoslav Republic of Macedonia. One historian jokingly suggested FOPITGROBBSOSY as an alternative: the Former Province of Illyria, Thrace, Greece, Rome, Byzantium, Bulgaria, Serbia, the Ottoman Empire, Serbia and Yugoslavia.

In history studies there are many intractable 'questions'; one such was the Schleswig-Holstein Question which Lord Palmerston, the 19th-century British statesman, declared to be '… so complicated only three men in Europe have ever understood it. One was Prince Albert, who is dead. The second was a German professor who became mad. I am the third and I have forgotten all about it.' The Macedonian Question is similarly complicated and similarly misunderstood, though it is different in that no-one has forgotten all about it. It is a matter of frequent debate in Bulgaria and a subject on which many people have very strong opinions. I have attended historical conferences, normally very staid occasions, where participants have almost come to blows while discussing the subject. As a visitor you should avoid expressing an opinion on such a sensitive topic.

Ancient Macedonia was, as the mnemonic above tells us, part of the Illyrian and Thracian civilisations but, according to archaeologists who have excavated royal tombs, there was a strong Hellenistic influence before Philip of Macedon conquered Greece. Philip (ruled 359–336BC) and his son Alexander (ruled 336–323BC) took Macedonia to the peak of its influence. Alexander was a brilliant strategist and military leader who defeated the mighty Persian Empire and extended his boundaries to the Indus River. His successors gradually lost power to the rising influence of Rome, and under the Roman Empire Macedonia was again a mere province, though still bordering the Adriatic. From about the 6th century AD, migrating Slavs began settling in the Balkan region, adding to the ethnic mix.

In medieval times the area was part of the Bulgarian kingdoms which reached the three seas (Black, Aegean and Adriatic), while in 1346 the Serbian Tsar Stefan Dushan was crowned in Skopje, the capital of today's Macedonia, and described as the ruler of Serbs, Greeks, Bulgars and Albanians. The Ottoman Empire conquered the whole of the Balkans and once again national boundaries became less defined within a larger unit. So a pattern emerges: the area of Macedonia, with no clear physical boundaries, was at times part of large empires and at times part of the territory of its various neighbours when their power was in the ascendant. Its own period of glory in the pre-Christian era was never repeated.

In the 19th century the province of Macedonia was a fairly typical Balkan region where Orthodox Christians, Jews and Muslims, Greeks, Turks, Bulgarians, Albanians and Serbs lived, all subjects of the Ottoman Empire. The whole area was ethnically mixed; a town might be mainly Turkish and Greek while the countryside around it was Albanian and Slav. The rising tide of nationalism, combined with the decline of the Ottoman Empire, led to territorial rivalry in the Balkans, with each country aspiring to the boundaries it had enjoyed at the peak of its power.

In 1876, the Bulgarians launched the April Uprising and the Turks, already troubled by revolts in Bosnia and Herzegovina, Serbian and Montenegrin military intervention and Austrian diplomatic meddling, reacted furiously. The resulting 'Bulgarian Horrors' roused international public opinion, and attempts were made to force reform on the decaying empire. Two successive sultans were overthrown, but no progress was made and in April 1877 the Russians invaded Ottoman territory by crossing the Danube. Their victory allowed them to dictate terms and the resulting Treaty of San Stefano created a Big Bulgaria which alarmed both the Balkan neighbours and the other great powers who saw it as a vehicle for Russian influence. The great powers insisted on a congress to discuss the situation and the Treaty of Berlin which followed dismantled Big Bulgaria. The Macedonian area was returned to the Ottoman Empire. The rest was divided into the new principality of Bulgaria, and Eastern Rumelia was made an autonomous but vassal state of the Ottoman Empire, with its capital in Plovdiv. When in 1885 Bulgaria and Eastern Rumelia united, Serbia promptly declared war on Bulgaria, angry that Balkan borders had been changed and nervous that other territorial gains might be planned. The Bulgarians defeated the Serbs.

Macedonia's reluctant return to Ottoman rule in 1878 caused great dissatisfaction, and this spawned a liberation movement which soon became notorious for its violence, with terrorist acts and political assassinations. Often known by the acronym IMRO (sometimes VMRO), the Internal Macedonian Revolutionary Organisation was founded in 1893 by schoolteachers Gotse Delchev and Dame Gruev. Although there was consensus about winning freedom from Turkish rule, there were differences of opinion about how to achieve it. Some wanted an independent Macedonia, perhaps in some kind of federation, a possibility that would be more likely to get the support of the Great Powers than an expanded Bulgaria. However, those Macedonian emigrants who had taken refuge in Sofia thought that joining Bulgaria would be the best way to free themselves from the Ottoman Empire. The latter were known as the Supreme Macedonian Committee or supremists. They envied the strong position of IMRO in the country and set out to get control of it. Both organisations infiltrated the other and the liberation movement became increasingly divided.

Supremist military incursions into Macedonia achieved little except to incur Ottoman vengeance. Anxious to take the initiative, IMRO leaders hastily launched an uprising named Ilinden (as it was launched on the day of Sv Iliya, or Elijah) in August 1903. It was centred on the mountain town of Krushevo, southwest of Skopje, but lasted only a few weeks.

In the Balkan Wars of 1912–13 Macedonia was fought over by Greece, Bulgaria and Serbia. Each war ended with a treaty and though Albania emerged as a separate state, Macedonia did not. Its southern part, centred on Thessalonika, became part of Greece; eastern Macedonia became the western part of Bulgaria; and the northern part, a very mixed area of Albanians and Slavs, became part of Serbia. These divisions survive.

After World War I, in which it had been allied with Germany, Bulgaria found itself diplomatically isolated and unable to pursue its claims in Macedonia. Refugees from Serbian Macedonia arrived in Bulgaria and reinforced a resurgent IMRO, which urged a strong line on the Macedonian Question. This tough stance made the rebuilding of relations with their neighbours difficult for the Bulgarian government. IMRO made raids into Serbian Macedonia and carried out terrorist attacks in Bulgaria. The newly established Comintern in Moscow thought IMRO could help to destabilise the Balkans and topple the royal and reactionary rulers

continued overleaf

4

there. The differences between those in IMRO seeking to join Bulgaria and those wanting an autonomous Macedonia divided them in their dealings with the Comintern. Internecine fighting and assassinations of key figures meant that by the 1930s IMRO was ineffective as a liberation movement and had become little more than a criminal organisation, and as such it was suppressed by sending troops into the Petrich region.

When Bulgaria joined the Axis powers in World War II, it was asked to occupy Serbian Macedonia, and, after the repressive regime of the Serbs, they were welcomed. However, the eventual military success of Tito and his partisans gave them a powerful position with fellow Balkan communists. Tito hoped to use the establishment of a Macedonian republic as a carrot to entice Bulgaria into a Balkan federation which he expected to dominate. This scheme eventually came to nothing, probably to the relief of the Bulgarian government who had feared the loss of Pirinska-Makedoniya to the new republic. After 1945 the inhabitants of Pirinska-Makedoniya were given the status of a national minority (a situation which was reversed in the 1960s when Bulgaria's rulers wanted to emphasise the homogeneity of their people).

The post-war Yugoslav government was determined to reduce any lingering affection the inhabitants of Macedonia might feel for the wartime Bulgarian occupiers and neighbours, or the historic attractions of ancient Greece. Their propaganda machine worked hard to simplify history, linking the small modern republic with its own distant historic past. People were encouraged to believe in the continuity of a Slav Macedonia stretching back for centuries. The dialect of the political élite was declared to be a separate language from Serbian or Bulgarian, and the religious language Old Church Slavonic was rechristened Old Macedonian. Propaganda and facts have long been intermingled here.

The fall of communism unleashed the many unresolved ethnic problems of the Balkans, resulting in the breakup of Yugoslavia. Macedonia declared its independence in 1992 and Bulgaria recognised it immediately. Greek objections to its name (the same as part of northern Greece) delayed its recognition by the EU.

---

fretted decorative ceiling. The **Church of the Assumption of the Holy Mother** (*Църква Възнесение Богородично*) has icons from the Bansko School of painters.

LESHTEN AND KOVACHEVITSA (ЛЕЩЕН И КОВАЧЕВИЦА) These are two pretty villages northeast of Gotse Delchev. They have become very popular with Sofia weekenders and there are plenty of places to stay, ranging from the basic to the luxurious, though the state of the roads is closer to basic than luxurious. The scenery is stunning, and different from nearby Pirin; here you are in the most westerly part of the Rhodopes, with vegetation of stunted oaks, aromatic herbs and patches of tobacco.

Getting there and away There are **buses** from Gotse Delchev (*5 daily, part of the way*) but the best option is by **car**, although the road is bad. The route to Kovachevitsa passes through Leshten.

Where to stay and eat As well as the *mehana* in The White House, which is worth trying, there are also two or three places in the village where you can sit to have a drink or a bite to eat.

The new state's main problems were with its large Albanian minority whose rights to land and education in their own language were not acknowledged. The conflict in Kosovo was on Macedonia's northwest border, and Albanians in the region had close cross-border links. In 2001 Albanian insurgents began a guerrilla war with the Macedonian authorities but the Ohrid Agreement signed later that year, making some concessions to the Albanians, averted a full-scale war.

In conclusion, the Bulgarians generally believe that the Slavs who live in Macedonia are descended from the same forefathers and speak the same language as they do. They share a history from medieval times and Ohrid, now in Macedonia and a former capital of Bulgaria, was the seat of the Bulgarian Patriarchate until 1767. During Bulgaria's National Revival craftsmen from Macedonia, particularly the Debur School of woodcarving, worked in churches and monasteries all over the country. The cultural and artistic renaissance was a shared one. The religious links continued with the establishment of the Bulgarian Exarchate in 1870. Much of central Macedonia was included and the provision made that if two thirds of the population in other areas wanted to be included they could; those from Skopje, Ohrid and Bitola joined, reinforcing Bulgarian beliefs in the legitimacy of their claims to the region. The Balkan wars and both World Wars were fought by the Bulgarians primarily because of Macedonian irridenta (meaning a region historically connected to one nation, but subject to a foreign government).

Though the Bulgarians promptly recognised FYROM as a state, they do not recognise a Macedonian nation, and this antagonises their neighbours. In the last few years FYROM has conducted a concerted policy to assert its national identity by making claims to historical events, challenging and encroaching on the recognised history of neighbouring Greece and, even more so, Bulgaria. Laying claim to the Cyrillic alphabet, medieval Tsar Samuil and some 19th-century Bulgarian heroes has resulted not only in a hardening of official policy but also a gradual change in Bulgarian popular attitudes towards its neighbour, from almost universally positive in the past to sceptic at best nowadays.

In Kovachevitsa

⌂ **Bai Markovata Kushta** (2 dbl, 2 trpl rooms) ☎0752 26769; m 0899 929560; www. markovhouse.com. The first house on the right after the signpost. €

⌂ **Kapsuzov's House** m 0899 403089, 0898 296669. One of the best places to stay in Kovachevitsa: hospitable owners, excellent food. €€

⌂ **The White House** (9 dbl rooms) m 0899 886342; e ecotour@ecotourbg.com; www.

bialatakushta.com. Fully renovated traditional house with nice interior & bright, spotless bathrooms; Wi-Fi. Excellent *mehana*. €

In Leshten

⌂ **Leshten Eco Village Complex** (27 rooms in 15 houses) ☎0752 7522; m 0888 544651; e leshten@yahoo.com. Two of the houses have *mehanas* on the ground floor. The restaurant in the centre is well known for its good food. €–€€

What to see and do These villages are relaxing places for a weekend break; you can walk, or not, apart from the lovely architecture of the village houses there are no sights.

On the way you pass the meagre ruins of Nikopolis ad Nestum; it's worth stopping to absorb the feel of a place inhabited so long ago. After a spectacularly scruffy Roma village, in which the road threatens to be completely taken over by the residents' need to store huge piles of wood, park cars, donkeys and carts and dry their washing, you reach, as a contrast, the rather picturesque village of Leshten. Here weekend visitors outnumber locals.

Continuing on through a Pomak (Bulgarian Muslim) village, Gorno Dryanovo, you reach Kovachevitsa, which was used in the making of several Bulgarian films. Some of its houses are deserted, while others are being restored. It is picturesque, with huge views of Pirin. We were welcomed by an old woman who was determined to show us her house, in which she told us she lived in the traditional way. On the ground floor the heavy door opened into a big space which was essentially an indoor farmyard. There were goats energetically scrambling to get at nice new shoots of spring greenery that had been hung from a high hook, hens and enchanting day-old chicks were clucking under our feet and there was a donkey. A flight of stone stairs brought us to an open veranda, which was quite a surprise to see in the mountains, but she assured us that the winters are mild. Leading from this was the only other inhabited room, which was the kitchen, dining, sitting and bedroom, cosily decorated with bright and fluffy rugs, and a lot of vegetables hanging in strings from the ceiling. It was inevitable that she would offer us some homemade *rakiya* and *lukanka* (Bulgarian salami). We enjoyed it very much and came away with a very good feeling about this hard-to-reach village.

AROUND KYUSTENDIL

NEVESTINO (НЕВЕСТИНО) Driving towards Sofia along the E79, it is well worthwhile leaving the main road near Boboshevo, where the road and the River Struma diverge, and following the river towards Kyustendil. At Nevestino there is the loveliest bridge, Kadin Most. The construction is complex but the result is elegant perfection. It has five arches in graceful proportion and is 100m long. It was built in the late 15th century and is still in use and in good order.

In the Ottoman period this was an important trade route between Sofia and Constantinople and this bridge replaced a Byzantine one, which had been destroyed. Tradition has it that it was built at the request of a beautiful maiden, whose betrothed love lived on the other side of the river. The sultan reputedly built the bridge as a wedding gift, thus providing its name: Nevestin Most or Bride's Bridge. A separate legend recounts how one of the builders of the bridge suggested to the others that they offer a sacrifice to the river in the form of one of their wives. Whichever wife arrived first with her husband's lunch would be immured in the bridge to give it the power to stand the force of the river. This is quite a prevalent story, as many bridges have similar tales told about them.

Ivo Andrić's Nobel Prize-winning novel *The Bridge on the Drina*, set in Bosnia, is the epic story of a similar bridge, beginning with its troubled construction. Rade, the mason in charge of the work, decided they needed something to change their fortunes. Two babies, boy and girl twins, had to be found and walled into the central pier of the bridge. The mother insisted she be allowed to continue feeding them, and, according to the story, milk has flowed down the smooth surface of the masonry ever since.

KYUSTENDIL (КЮСТЕНДИЛ) *Telephone code: 078*

The road onward to Kyustendil is quiet, crossing rolling cultivated hills with distant mountain views, and passing only a few villages. The centre is poorly signed and the various attractions hard to find. Historically the town was always noted for its hot mineral springs. The Romans developed the baths and, much later, the Turks settled here, building hammams and mosques. Though these buildings give the town a little Eastern flavour, there is no Muslim population now and one mosque is falling down, while another is used as the town museum for visiting exhibitions.

Getting there and away There are **trains** (*railway station* ✆ *550623*) from Sofia (*3 daily; 2hrs 45mins*), Pernik (*5 daily; 2hrs*), Zemen (*every 2hrs; 50mins*) and Gyueshevo near the Macedonian border (*1 daily; 2hrs 45mins*).

There are **buses** (*bus station* ✆ *550141*) from Sofia (*every 4hrs; 2hrs 35mins*).

Tourist information The tourist information office (*ul Demokratsya 40;* ✆ *511166; www.tourism-kn.net*) can arrange accommodation in private rooms and provides some general information.

🏠 Where to stay

🏠 **Bulgaria** (34 rooms) ul Konstantinova Banya 3; ✆ 551200. Modern & stylish. Central. €€

🏠 **Hotel Lazur** (6 rooms) ul Kiril & Metodii 15A; ✆ 550566; e hotel_lazur@abv.bg; www.hotellazur.com. Luxury furnishings, gym, pool, sauna, restaurant with Serbian & international specialities. There's also the sister hotel Lazur 2 (9 rooms; bul Bulgaria 41; ✆ 551200). €

🏠 **Strimon Spa Club** (75 rooms) ul Tsar Simeon I 24; ✆ 559000; e strimon@strimon-spaclub.com; www.strimon-spaclub.com. Smart & luxurious place offering a variety of treatments & spa procedures. €€€

🏠 **Velbuzhd** (145 rooms) bul Bulgaria 1; ✆ 524264. Former state hotel, towering in the town centre; some rooms have been renovated. €€

✗ Where to eat and drink

✗ **Bordo** bul Bulgaria 6 & 28; ✆ 552242. Pizzas, salads, grilled meats. €

✗ **Bulgaria** Bulgaria Hotel. Rooftop restaurant for traditional grills & good views. €€

✗ **Sekoya** ul Gladstone 35; ✆ 552171. National style with garden; Bulgarian cuisine, grilled specialities. €€

What to see and do The **Vladimir Dimitrov-Maistora Art Gallery** (*Художествена галерия на Владимир Димитров–Майстора; ul Patriarh Evtimii 20;* ✆ *550029;* ⊕ *Apr–Oct 10.00–18.00 daily, Nov–Mar 09.00–17.00 daily; adult 2lv*) contains many works of the influential artist. He preferred rural life and objected to the pretensions of the art world, making a gesture against it by never signing his paintings. He particularly disliked Modernism, favouring idealised images of fresh-faced maidens amid fruits and flowers. I suspect he would not much like the ugly modern building in which he is exhibited! His popularity, combined with his trenchant views, influenced modern Bulgarian art and kept it away from new trends.

The **History Museum** (*Историческия музей; bul Bulgaria 55;* ✆ *550095;* ⊕ *08.00–noon & 13.00–17.00 Mon–Fri; adult 2lv*) has well-displayed Thracian and Roman artefacts. Captions are in English and Bulgarian.

The pleasant **main square**, pl Velbuzhd, has a memorial to Todor Alexandrov, a Macedonian freedom fighter who was assassinated in 1924. In a corner of the square is the **Church of the Virgin Mary** (*Църква Св Дева Мария*), sunk down some 4m into the ground to comply with Turkish restrictions on the dimensions and visual significance of Christian churches. It stands in a garden and has three distinctive little belltowers on its roof. Inside it is simple but with fine panelling and screen. Alongside it is the original belltower, made of wood on a stone foundation.

The old thermal baths, **Chifte Banya**, still fulfil their original function, and the Dervish Banya nearby are being restored to become a museum. Beyond the

Chifte Banya are the **Pautalia Thermae**, the Roman baths built in the 2nd century which are the second largest in Bulgaria. The Emperor Trajan was supposedly cured of a skin complaint by the local waters. During the Ottoman period the baths were converted into a mosque. Although the minaret has been taken down, the remaining building is an odd juxtaposition of Roman and Islamic styles. Near the baths is the **Pirkova Tower**, a 15th-century fortification, once part of the Velbuzhd citadel.

A local hero is commemorated in the **Dimitur Peshev House-Museum** (*Дом-музей Димитър Пешев; ul Tsar Simeon I 11;* ☏ *551811;* ⊕ *09.00–17.00 Tue–Sun; adult 2lv*). Dimitur Peshev was a politician and native of the town, who during World War II played an important role in the campaign to prevent Bulgaria's Jews (about 48,000 people) from being sent to concentration camps. The house has been set up as an exact replica of his home. It was opened in 2003, to celebrate the 60th anniversary of the successful campaign.

The hillside dominating the town, Hisarluk, is a steep walk but gives fine views and there are the ruins of both the Roman settlement and a medieval fortress. Its border position has meant that Kyustendil has changed hands many times from its Thracian beginnings. It has been noted for its mines and metalworking, which thrived under the Macedonians, Greeks and Romans, only to stagnate in the Byzantine period, its economy spoiled by wars. It revived under the Ottoman administration and was an important centre during the Hapsburg-Ottoman wars of the 17th and 18th centuries.

After exploring the town, which, on a Sunday afternoon, was almost deserted, we returned to our car to find two traffic policemen beside it. Although there was no visible sign forbidding us to park there, we were assured that we were wrong and the usual prolonged paper trail of form filling ensued. Kyustendil suddenly seemed a lot less attractive!

ZEMEN MONASTERY (ЗЕМЕНСКИ МАНАСТИР) The **Monastery of St John the Theologian** (*Манастир Св Йоан Богослов;* ⊕ *May–Sep 09.00–18.00 daily, Oct–Apr 09.00–17.30 daily; adult 3lv*) is now a museum. It is picturesquely situated in a gorge of the Struma River. There is no exact record of its foundation but its architectural style is typical of Bulgaria's earliest churches. It lacks the high surrounding walls of many other foundations and presents a rather humble outside appearance. The 12th-century church is cruciform with a small dome and an unusual-shaped roof.

The first written record is the 14th-century inscription over the gate saying that the restoration of the church and the painting of the murals had been funded by donations from the despot Deyan, ruler of the Velbuzhd area.

The murals are what make a visit to Zemen worthwhile. They date from two periods: the 11th century and the 12th–14th centuries. Much has been destroyed, but sensitive restoration in the 1970s revealed medieval masterpieces. The saints depicted are local ones: Sv Ivan of Rila, Sv Clement of Ohrid and Sv Joachim of Osogovo. The faces are in a lively, vivid style, influenced by the Macedonian rather than the Turnovo School of painting, which was the contemporary prevailing style with stiff, rather expressionless one-dimensional figures. The portraits of donor Deyan and his wife are particularly appealing. The colours are soothing blues and greys against which their clothes and halos stand out.

The monastery suffered under the Ottoman domination and its large library was destroyed. In the early 19th century, as part of the National Revival, the monastery was restored and new buildings were constructed. However, in the 20th century it declined again and ceased to function as a cloister.

Those travelling by train from Zemen to Kyustendil pass through the Zemen Gorge, some 22km long. Here the River Struma has carved through the Konyavska and Zemenska mountains creating odd-shaped rock formations, waterfalls and caves, resulting in a beautiful scene of rocks and flowing water.

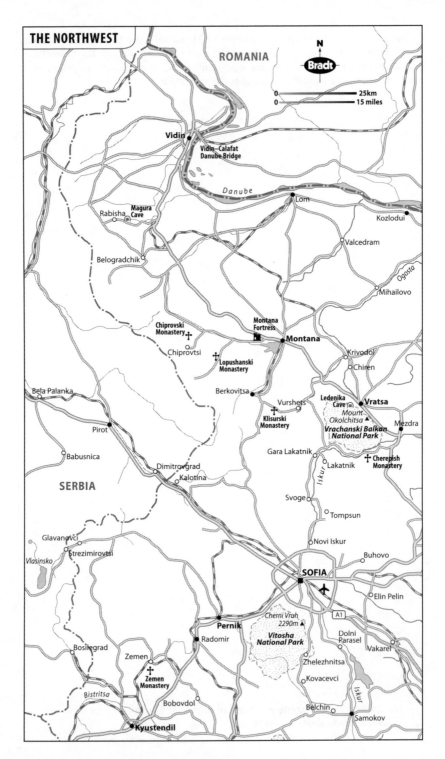

THE NORTHWEST

ROMANIA

N

Bradt

0   25km
0   15 miles

Vidin

Vidin–Calafat
Danube Bridge

Danube

Lom

Kozlodui

Magura
Cave

Rabisha

Valcedram

Belogradchik

Ogosta

Mihailovo

Chiprovski
Monastery

Montana
Fortress

Chiprovtsi

Montana

Krivodol

Chiren

Lopushanski
Monastery

Berkovitsa

Bela Palanka

Vurshets

Ledenika
Cave

Vratsa

Klisurski
Monastery

*Mount
Okolchitsa*

Mezdra

*Vrachanski Balkan
National Park*

Pirot

Babusnica

Gara Lakatnik

Cherepish
Monastery

Dimitrovgrad

Lakatnik

Iskur

Kalotina

Svoge

SERBIA

Tompsun

Glavanovci

Strezimirovtsi

Novi Iskur

Buhovo

Vlasinsko

SOFIA

Elin Pelin

A1

Bosilegrad

Pernik

*Cherni Vrah
2290m*

Dolni
Parasel

Radomir

*Vitosha
National Park*

Vakarel

Zemen

Zheleznitsa

Zemen
Monastery

Kovacevci

Iskur

Bistritsa

Bobovdol

Belchin

Samokov

Kyustendil

5

The Northwest

Although the northwest of Bulgaria is easily reached from Sofia, it is less visited than the southwest. Its main attractions are provided by nature: rock formations and caves, the **Vrachanski National Park** and, as Bulgaria's northern boundary, the **Danube**. It is a rural area with some small towns of interest, as well as monasteries and castles, and is a wonderful area for hiking and rambling. Hiring a car will make this area much more rewarding as many of the villages and monasteries are not easily accessible by bus or train.

This is the western part of the Balkan range of mountains which have given their name to the whole peninsula. Bulgarians refer to them as **Stara Planina**, the 'old mountains'. Maps and information covering this region can be hard to come by, but that is changing in response to an increased interest in activity holidays.

ISKUR GORGE (ИСКЪРСКО ДЕФИЛЕ)

There are three main routes leading from Sofia to the northwest, and the Iskur Gorge is the most attractive. The Iskur is the only river that flows from the Rila Mountains north and crosses Stara Planina to become a tributary of the Danube. The capital's sprawl continues as far as Novi Iskur, and then quite suddenly the view is transformed into spectacular mountain views, with a rushing river and cliffs of red rock.

The village of **Tompsun** clearly does not have a Bulgarian name! It commemorates Major Frank Thompson, who was killed nearby in May 1944, fighting alongside Bulgarian partisans. This is an interesting stop for me for two reasons. I studied Yugoslavia's history during World War II for my thesis, and knew that Thompson had been parachuted in to a British mission with the Yugoslav partisans near to Nish, and had made his way to Bulgaria from there. By coincidence he was dispatched on his journey by John Henniker-Major, the late Lord Henniker, who was our friend and neighbour in Suffolk. At the station there is a rather moving plaque bearing Thompson's name alongside a sculpted image of him – a young Englishman of the 1940s with a floppy haircut and a pipe. It is sad to realise that fewer and fewer people know how or why he came to die here.

The road north continues to follow the river and brings you to **Svoge**, a tidy and prosperous-looking town with various factories, including a sweet-smelling chocolate-maker! Beyond it, the road runs even closer to the river, giving glimpses of elderly grannies and grandpas tending flocks of sheep and goats as they graze on the water meadows. From Gara Lakatnik to Mezdra is the finest stretch of road with lovely views across to the cliffs of the Vrachanski National Park.

GETTING THERE AND AWAY All the **train** routes to the towns in the northwest start their journey along the Iskur Gorge, road and rail sharing the often narrow space.

There are interesting stops in the gorge before Mezdra, which is a useful junction giving access north to Vratsa and Vidin, or east to Pleven and beyond. There are trains through the gorge from Sofia to Lakatnik (*hourly; 1hr*), Svoge (*every 20mins; 35mins*) and Mezdra (*hourly; 1½hrs*).

Buses follow the same initial route through the gorge, leaving Avtogara Sofia every hour and taking about 2 hours to Vratsa. **Car** drivers will find the northwest generally a quiet and pleasant area for travelling, though many roads are in poor condition.

WHERE TO STAY AND EAT Most travellers through the gorge will not be planning to stay so close to Sofia. Gara Lakatnik has a café and food shop in the station itself, but otherwise eating and sleeping are best saved for Vratsa.

CHEREPISH MONASTERY (МАНАСТИРА ЧЕРЕПИШ) Before reaching the town of Mezdra, it is worth stopping at Cherepish Monastery, situated between the villages of Zverino and Lyutibrod. It was built during the reign of Tsar Ivan Shishman in the late 14th century. During the Ottoman occupation the monastery was destroyed and set on fire more than once.

In the 17th century there was reconstruction by Sv Pimen, who was also responsible for the very fine frescoes near the entrance to the church. These have been recently restored. In a single colour, a lovely faded red, Biblical scenes and a Tree of Jesse (genealogy of Christ) are depicted. The 19th-century frescoes by Priest Ioanikius are much more vividly coloured. This period was significant in the monastery's history and many of the recently restored buildings were built then in the National Revival style. Cherepish expanded and became a cultural and educational centre, and like many monasteries was involved in the struggle for independence, accommodating and assisting revolutionary activists when they were in the area.

Just beyond the monastery is one of the named rock formations of the Iskur Gorge called *Ritlite* ('Cart rails'), three jutting strips of rock, 200m high in places.

VRATSA (ВРАЦА)   *Telephone code: 092*

Vratsa has some beautiful National Revival-period houses, historical associations with the doomed national hero Hristo Botev and Bulgaria's subsequent liberation, and its museums have particularly rich archaeological and ethnographic collections. It's worth spending at least a day in the town. The views here are dominated by the mountains, and the town is a good base for exploring the nearby **Vrachanski Balkan Nature Park**.

Archaeological finds in the area are evidence of a prosperous Thracian civilisation, and later the Romans, recognising the strategic advantage of settling in the gorge, turned the area into a stronghold. It continued to be a place of importance as a local trading centre in medieval times, and thrived during the 19th-century National Revival period as a handicraft and commercial centre. Meat and dairy produce, cloth and gold were traded all over Europe. Ore mining produced copper, lead, zinc and silver, and gold was panned in the rivers. Vratsa was well known as a prosperous town.

GETTING THERE AND AWAY There are **trains** (*railway station* ✆ 624415) from Sofia's central railway station (*5 daily; 2hrs–2hrs 40mins*), Pleven (*connect at Mezdra for hourly trains; 1hr 20mins*), Montana (*6 daily; 1hr*), Mezdra (*7 daily; 20mins*) and Vidin (*4 daily; 3½hrs*) – these stop at Oreshets station where you can catch a bus to Belogradchik.

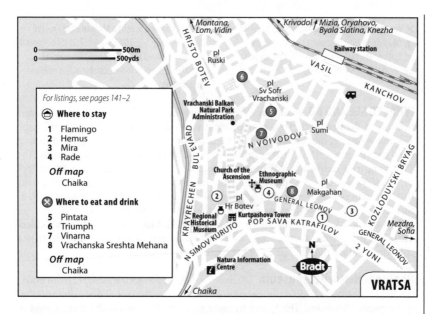

For listings, see pages 141–2

Where to stay
1 Flamingo
2 Hemus
3 Mira
4 Rade

Off map
Chaika

Where to eat and drink
5 Pintata
6 Triumph
7 Vinarna
8 Vrachanska Sreshta Mehana

Off map
Chaika

VRATSA

Buses (*bus station* ☎ *622558*) generally take less time. There are services from Sofia's central bus station (*hourly; 2hrs*), Vurshets (*5 daily; 50mins*), Montana (*1 daily; 40mins*), Oryahovo (*6 daily; 2hrs 15mins*), Botevgrad (*5 daily; 1hr 15mins*), Vidin (*1 daily; 2hrs*), Pleven (*3 daily; 2hrs 15mins*) and Berkovitsa (*1 daily; 1hr 5mins*).

The train and bus stations are adjacent and just to the east of the town centre on bul Vasil Kunchov.

TOURIST INFORMATION The **Natura Information Centre** in the Old Eski Mosque (*ul Pop Sava Katrafilov 27–29;* ☎ *660318;* e *naturacenter@abv.bg;* ⏰ *09.00–17.00 daily*) is mainly for information on the national park, ecotrails and educational routes. However, there is also material on accommodation and events in the town.

WHERE TO STAY *Map, above*

⌂ Chaika (32 rooms) 1km from Vratsa on the road to Ledenika Cave; ☎ 621369; e chaika_hotel@abv.bg; www.chaika.net. Beautiful location & views; comfortable but rather tired accommodation. €

⌂ Flamingo (14 rooms) bul Vtori Yuni 69; ☎ 662299; m 0896 111165; e kompleks_flamingo@abv.bg; http://hotelflamingo.org. Small, modern hotel 500m from the main square. €

⌂ Hemus (77 rooms) pl Hristo Botev 1; ☎ 624150; www.hotelhemus.com. Refurbished central hotel, lovely views, close to all sites & shops. €€

⌂ Mira (25 rooms) ul San Stefano 8; ☎ 666262; m 0898 558658; e mira_hotel@abv.bg; www.mirahotel.hit.bg. Family-run hotel in the centre; welcoming with good food. €

⌂ Rade (8 rooms) ul General Leonov 9; ☎ 661470. Small, modern central hotel. €

WHERE TO EAT AND DRINK *Map, above*

✗ Chaika See above. Nice location & garden. Varied menu of soups, salads, grilled & local specialities. €€

✗ Pintata ul Sofronii Vrachanski 17; ☎ 621873. Central location with a garden. Typical Bulgarian

food, soups, salads. Probably the best in Vratsa. €€

✗ Triumph ul Trayko Kitanchev 9; ☎ 661448. Near the small central park. Bulgarian cuisine, good choice of wines. Live music in the evenings. €

✘ Vinarna bul Nikola Voivodov 9/2; ☏ 663607;
📱 0878 663656; e restorant_vinarna@abv.
bg. Rather old-fashioned décor but inexpensive
traditional fare, so worth a visit. €

✘ Vrachanska Sreshta Mehana ul Krustyo
Bulgariata 62; ☏ 663607; 📱 0887 514506. Central
location, housed in 100-year-old wine cellar.
Traditional décor & food; occasional live music in
the evenings. €

WHAT TO SEE AND DO Nowadays Vratsa is still a regional centre, its palace of culture
housing a theatre, orchestra, puppet theatre, art gallery and historical museum.
The main square, named after the hero Hristo Botev, is pedestrianised and from it
runs the main street, ul Hristo Botev, bordered by pavement cafés and shops. The
17th-century **Kurtpashova Tower** is in front of the History Museum; with its lack
of windows, it gives the impression of being a small fortress. Apparently during
the Ottoman occupation there were several similar towers; they were used both as
fortified houses and as demonstrations of the status of their owners.

Just outside Vratsa to the south is **Mount Okolchitsa** where Botev was killed.
This is a place close to the heart of every Bulgarian, and every year there is a
commemoration march, retracing his route.

Regional Historical Museum (*Регионален Исторически музей; pl Hristo Botev;*
☏ *620220;* ⏲ *09.00–17.30 daily, closed noon–13.00 Sat–Sun; adult 6lv – also valid for
Ethnographic Museum*) The Vratsa treasure was found in two of the three tombs in
the Mogila mound, excavated in 1965. The tombs were made from enormous beams
joined by huge nails. A man and woman were buried in one tomb with many artefacts
for their use in a future life: a chariot with two horses in harness, silver and bronze
vessels, plus many small ornaments and pottery. Stunning gold jewellery was laid
out beside the woman, as well as a gold wreath and earrings, and many gold rosettes
which had decorated her clothing. The burials date from 380–350BC.

The oldest human skeleton found in Bulgaria is displayed here. It was found
during excavations in the village of Ohoden in 2004. It is the remains of a young
woman ritually buried in 5800BC in a special mausoleum. The burial chamber and
its contents are in a sealed showcase to protect them from pollution.

The **Rogozen treasure** is perhaps the most famous exhibit, as it has travelled
to many of the world's major museums. It consists of over a hundred silver vessels
found quite by chance by a farmer in 1985. This hoard was probably a family or
tribal treasure buried for safety in a time of difficulty and never recovered. It dates
from around 500–350BC. The decorations are of favourite Thracian themes: chariot
racing, hunting, various wild animals and goddesses, all finely wrought. There is
also an exhibition detailing the route and last days of Hristo Botev's ill-fated *cheta*
(small group of fighters).

Ethnographic Museum (*Етнографски музей; ul David Todorov 2;* ☏ *624573;*
⏲ *09.00–17.30 daily, closed noon–13.00 Sat–Sun; adult 6lv – a joint ticket for this
and the Historical Museum*) This is named after the patriot Sv Sofronii Vrachanski,
a former Bishop of Vratsa. It is a large area with seven National Revival buildings
grouped around the **Church of the Ascension** (*Възнесенска църква*). There is a
former school, fine houses, and a wealth of artefacts illustrating important aspects
of Vratsa's past.

One display explains about sericulture (the breeding of silkworms and production
of raw silk) which was begun by Turkish women at the end of the 18th century, and
the craft continued to be a local speciality with the founding of a factory here in
1896. Each cocoon produces an astonishing 2,000m of silk thread.

There are fine displays of the work of Vratsa's gold- and silversmiths from the 19th century, some jewellery and ecclesiastical artefacts, together with the craftsmen's tools. Other exhibits include pottery-making and, more unusually, phaeton building. The Orazov family were the builders of all Bulgaria's finest carriages in the late 19th and early 20th centuries. There is also an excellent collection of costumes and exhibits illustrating local customs, and a large number of brass instruments imported for village bands.

Beside the ancient wine barrels and vine-growers' tools arranged in the cellar of Zambin's house is a diploma from a tasting competition in Brussels awarding the wines of local vintner Stefan Kraskiev a gold medal. The famous 19th-century writer Aleko Konstantinov, remembered for his character the anti-hero Bai Ganyu, made a journey to this area on the new railway line. He visited the cellar and sampled the wine. 'Clear and gold, the wine's aroma is felt at three metres away and costs only two leva a bottle,' he declared appreciatively.

The dark wooden beams on all these buildings are, surprisingly, not painted but actually burned to create a black crust, which is reputed to be a more reliable deterrent to woodworm than other methods.

AROUND VRATSA The **Vrachanski Balkan Nature Park Administration** (*природен парк врачански балкан; ul Ivanka Boteva 1; \ 665849; www.vr-balkan. net*) has information on hiking, rock climbing and caving in the park.

HRISTO BOTEV 1848–76

Hristo Botev is, of all the revolutionary idealists, perhaps the closest to Bulgarian hearts. A poet, a revolutionary and a patriot, he was influenced by the writings of Russian revolutionaries, and believed in republican and socialist ideals. After attracting the attention of the Ottoman authorities by making a provocative speech in his home town of Kalofer, he joined other young exiles in Romania.

He became involved in émigré journalism, working on or founding newspapers with inspiring titles: *Freedom, Independence* and *The Banner*. His poems about freedom and liberty, heroes and revolution, were too fiery for some tastes and he fell out with fellow journalist and revolutionary activist Lyuben Karavelov.

Literary plans were put on hold when the April Uprising began in 1876, and Botev, who had no military experience, accepted the leadership of an armed band who were to cross the Danube and march to Vratsa in support of the uprising. They planned to increase their numbers on the way. Supporters in the town had sent money for weapons, which the group planned to deliver.

The scheme was obviously ill conceived, as it was not even launched until after the main uprising had been savagely suppressed. Botev's rhetoric did not win over crowds of additional fighters; indeed, parts of the route of the march were through villages not even inhabited by Bulgarians, and the inhabitants were openly hostile. The network of experienced revolutionaries which he expected to greet him was non-existent, and his threat to the Turks was negligible – they annihilated his group when they chose to.

Was Botev seeking a martyr's death? Certainly his poems expressed the wish to make sacrifices for Bulgaria. Or was he just an excitable, unrealistic young man hoping to snatch a victory and publicise the cause of freedom? Whatever his motives, he is admired and beloved by Bulgarians.

The park, Bulgaria's second largest, is well wooded with extensive ancient beech forests. It is home to many rare and endemic species, and the European bird migration route, the Via Aristotelis, crosses it. About 170 bird species inhabit the area, which is also noted for many varieties of shrubs and grasses. The landmark chalk cliffs known as Vratsata are the highest on the Balkan Peninsula, and a favourite destination of rock climbers. The karst character of the park has resulted in a landscape rich in caves, over 500 in fact.

Ledenika (*Пещера Леденика;* ⊕ *summer 09.00–17.00 daily, winter 10.00–16.00; adult 7lv*), about 15km southwest of Vratsa, was the first cave in the country to be provided with electricity and facilities for visitors. The Bulgarian word for ice is *led*; the cave is full of icicles, as well as stalactites and stalagmites. There are weird and wonderful shapes picked out by the lighting, and the acoustics are extraordinarily clear. It is very cold inside the cave all year round and the route is steep and slippery. Occasionally concerts are held here, so it's worth enquiring at the tourist office for dates. Visits are only possible with a guide and usually need about six to eight participants, but on a summer weekend this shouldn't present a problem.

Near the Ledenika Cave there is a visitor centre with a model of the Vrachanski Balkan Nature Park in the entrance hall, a 3D film hall and a small stage in front of the building.

Another interesting natural phenomenon is **God's Bridge** (*Божия мост*) near the village of Chiren to the northeast of Vratsa. This is a rock tunnel some 100m long and about 20m high and wide.

VRATSA TO VIDIN

The main road northwest to Vidin has more fine views of the Vrachanski Balkan Nature Park. There is an interesting side route to Berkovitsa via Vurshets and Klisurski Monastery. **Vurshets** is a nicely situated town with a small river and tributary streams running through it. It has always been known for its mineral baths, though now it seems a bit faded. There is a **tourist information office** at bul Republika 90A (✆ *0952 73156;* e *tic_varshets@abv.bg; www.varshets.bg*).

A few kilometres further is **Klisurski Monastery**, built on a strangely shaped, presumably manmade hill. The church is very plain, but there are pretty domestic buildings and a memorial chapel with extremely bright frescoes. Most of the frescoes we see would have started out in vivid colours but time and the smoke from thousands of candles have usually dimmed them. The frescoes here were extensively renovated in the 1990s.

BERKOVITSA (БЕРКОВИЦА) *Telephone code: 0953*

This can also be reached from Sofia over the Petrohan Pass, which at 1,420m is sometimes closed in winter, though warning road signs are displayed on the approach roads when this happens. It is quite different from the Iskur Gorge route but also attractive as it passes through the well-wooded western Balkan Mountains. On the way you pass the village of **Gintsi**, where there is a lively trade along the road in the locally renowned sheep's milk yoghurt.

Berkovitsa was a favoured health resort in communist times, both for resting politicians and athletes in training, and after a lull it is regaining favour as a destination for weekend breaks from Sofia. It is a pleasantly situated small town surrounded by orchards, and a convenient access point for hikers heading for Mount Kom.

Getting there and away There are no direct **trains** to Berkovitsa (*railway station* ✆ 88687), as the route is a branch line from Boichinovtsi. There are trains from Boichinovtsi (*3 daily; 1hr 10mins*), from Sofia to Boichinovtsi (*hourly; 2hrs 40mins–3hrs 45mins*) and from Vidin to Boichinovtsi (*4 daily; 2½hrs*).

There are **buses** from Sofia (*4 daily; 2½hrs*), Vratsa (*2 daily; 1hr 20mins*) and Montana (*every 30mins–1hr, depending on the time of day; 40mins*).

The **bus station** is to the east of the centre and the **railway station** also lies on the eastern side, about 15 minutes' walk from the centre.

Tourist information The tourist information office is at ul Poruchik Grozhdanov 11, next to Ivan Vazov House-Museum (✆ 88682; e *tic_bercovitsa@abv.bg*).

🏠 Where to stay

🏠 **Hotel Gelov** (20 rooms) ul Alexandrovska 28; ✆ 95008; e gelovhotel@dir.bg; www.hotelgelov. com. New hotel with sauna, restaurant & gym. Good views, very clean & welcoming. €

🏠 **Petar Levski Guesthouse** (3 rooms) ul Malinarka 2; ✆ 80135; m 0889 988530; e levskihouse_berk@abv.bg. Modern house with pretty garden. €

🏠 **Salvia** (10 rooms) ul Hrizantema 8; ✆ 88513; e hotel_salvia@abv.bg; www.hotel-salvia.com. Welcoming family-run hotel in the centre. Stylish rooms. €

🏠 **Starata Kushta** (13 rooms) ul Vladimir Zaimov 6; ✆ 88085; m 0888 380473, 0888 986158; e sk@viptour-bg.com; www.viptour-bg.com. Cosy, traditional-style house in the centre. €

✗ Where to eat and drink

✗ **Adashite** ul Zdravchevitsa 3; ✆ 88899; m 0886 741909. Centrally located in a renovated old house. Bulgarian & local specialities, salads, soups. €–€€

✗ **Krustevata kushta** ul Sheinov 5; ✆ 88099. Traditional food with a modern twist in an atmospheric setting in a handsome old house & walled garden. €–€€

What to see and do Berkovitsa has links with Bulgaria's national author, Ivan Vazov. His most famous work was *Under the Yoke*, describing life under the Ottoman occupation. The **Ivan Vazov House-Museum** (*Дом-музей Иван Вазов; ul Berkovitsa reka;* ☉ *08.00–noon & 14.00–17.00 Mon–Fri, from 09.00 at w/ends; adult 2lv*) was the writer's home for two years when he was appointed as a magistrate here. In the early days of independence Bulgaria was short of qualified people to hold administrative posts and those with a secondary education were much in demand. It seems that Vazov's youth and inexperience left him ill equipped for the task and, on being demoted to a lesser role in Vidin, he resigned. The gossip was that he had a scandalous affair with a widowed Turkish girl during his stay. The house has an exhibition relating to his work and the upstairs rooms are furnished in Ottoman style with low seats under a beautifully carved ceiling by craftsmen from Tryavna.

There are many examples in his writing which show that Vazov's time in Berkovitsa affected him strongly; it was where he fell in love with nature and where he spent many hours riding in the foothills of the mountains absorbing their beauty. He was fascinated by the local custom of passive resistance to the Ottoman occupiers and the wealthy Bulgarians who collaborated with them; this took the form of cairn building – rocks were thrown on chosen spots, accompanied by a curse. Apparently huge such cairns were built, and the message was clear. Vazov wrote poems about the cairns and the Turkish girl, Zihra, during his time here.

Nearby, the **Ethnographic Museum** (*Етнографски музей; ul Poruchik Grozhdanov 7;* ☉ *08.00–noon & 14.00–17.00 Mon–Fri, from 09.00 at w/ends; adult 2lv*) has displays of crafts including the local pottery. The **Nativity of the Holy Virgin**

Church (*Църква Рождество на Пресвета Богородица; ul Cherkovna*) is one of the many sunken churches of Bulgaria; it has icons by the noted painter Dimitur Zograf and a stunningly carved iconostasis, lively with lions and trumpeting angels.

Above the central square on an inauspicious-looking wooded hill is Berkovitsa's fortress, **Kaleto**. It was excavated in the 1960s, and was apparently one of several defensive buildings in this area. A visiting Englishman, John Galt, wrote in 1811: 'At a nearby hill with views of the town is located a small ancient fortress that has recently been strengthened with new facilities and a garrison for a few hundred people.' The inner and outer walls are visible, as are the remains of two Christian basilicas. The oldest parts of the fortress date from Thracian times, while at the highest point a coin from the Second Bulgarian Kingdom (1185–1396) was found.

MONTANA FORTRESS (КАЛЕТО)
North of Berkovitsa is the pleasant town of Montana. Its name reflects its Roman origins, but the town is modern, with a lovely, large, central pedestrian square full of fountains and flowers. In 2014 its restored fortress opened to visitors (*Montana Museum of History* ☏ *0963 05489; www.montana.bg;* ⊕ *daily; free*). It is on a hill in the northwestern part of the town. There is archaeological evidence that the area was settled by nomadic hunters in prehistoric times, followed by the Thracians, who left behind still-visible wide stone walls. The Romans developed the town and strengthened its defences. The fortress was destroyed at the end of the 6th century, but was later resettled by Slavs. Its position above the town has saved this interesting site, with its layers of history.

LOPUSHANSKI MONASTERY (ЛОПУШАНСКИ МАНАСТИР)
Northwest of Berkovitsa near the small village of Georgi Damyanovo, Lopushanski Monastery is in a pretty valley and a tranquil location among pine trees. It was a welcoming place where we were invited in to listen to the sung service and had a chance to admire the famous icons and iconostasis by Stanislav Dospevski. Otherwise the interior and exterior are plain with no frescoes. Outside, the walls have occasional stone reliefs which look almost pagan, depicting odd-looking animals and men. The belltower is a masterpiece of inventiveness, relying on a massive plank and homemade structure propped up by a tree. In its shade a man was sitting cleaning the shelves from the beehives nearby.

It is possible to stay here and use the monastery as a base for visiting Chiprovtsi, Belogradchik and Vidin. The monastery can provide transport and accommodation (*9 rooms*) and there is a monastery kitchen restaurant with fine mountain views (*enquire at Berkovitsa tourist information or* ☏ *0953 88682*). Ivan Vazov stayed here and wrote several chapters of *Under the Yoke*.

CHIPROVTSI (ЧИПРОВЦИ)
This village, famous for its kilim-making, is on the very edge of Bulgaria. The other side of the mountains beyond it is in Serbia. Occupying a border area meant that for many years it was rather isolated. Nowadays Chiprovtsi is an enchanting, small, old-fashioned village which has several places of interest.

Getting there and away
Chiprovtsi is not on a railway line. There are **buses** from Montana (*4 daily; 45mins*) and Sofia (*1 daily to Montana, 1hr 40mins, then connect*).

Tourist information
The tourist information office (*ul Pavleto 27;* ☏ *0955 42910;* e *tic.chiprovci@gmail.com*) in the centre has local information and can book accommodation.

Where to stay and eat

Gostopriemnitsa (10 rooms) ul Balkanska 46; ☎ 0955 42974; m 0888 299994. In a beautiful old-style house, this is a monument of culture. The restaurant serves local specialities. €

Pavlovata kushta (3 rooms) ul Pavleto 17; m 0885 614461. This is a National Revival-style guesthouse & restaurant with welcoming hosts. €

Torlatsite Hotel (4 rooms) ul Pavleto 31; m 0887 892790; e info@torlacite.com; www.torlacite.com. Centrally located with simple & comfortable rooms, very welcoming & family-run. The restaurant, with some local specialities, is popular with visitors & villagers alike. €

What to see and do Although it is beginning to be popular with Sofia weekenders, the traditional atmosphere remains and the sound that wakes you in the morning is the clanking bells of the herd of goats, one or two from each family, being led out to pasture by their herdsman. The goats seem well used to the routine as they stop off outside their own yards on the return trip in the evenings.

In some houses the colourful kilim-style rugs and carpets are still woven on a small loom or *stan*. At the **Torlatsite Hotel** carpets are on sale, and if they don't have the size or the colours you like you can order one to be specially made. They are much cheaper here than in the specialist carpet or museum shops in Sofia.

Chiprovtsi designs are mainly traditional stylised patterns reflecting village matters: vines, chickens and flowers in pots, and some have coded symbols to wish the owner good health or happiness. Oddly, despite the fact that the patterns are traditional, there is something very modern and stylish about the geometric designs and strong colours. There are over 25 patterns, some simple, some complex. The work is very skilful and creative, and each woman can produce about two or three square metres in a month. The work is double-sided, so that the rug can be turned over and another less worn or faded side shown. The weavers say the rugs, which are very densely woven and quite heavy, last for 30 years each side! Though some use modern chemical dyes, there is a move towards using the old traditional plant dyes and part of the village **museum** (*музей;* ☉ *08.00–noon & 13.00–18.00 Mon–Fri, 09.00–17.00 Sat, Sun & hols; adult 2lv*) is a garden where examples of these plants are grown. Different colours come from flowers, leaves, herbs and tree bark.

There are also some delicately made pieces of jewellery and information about carpet-making, as well as a map showing where in the Balkans Chiprovtsi gold is used. Unfortunately, there are few English labels.

Near the museum is the 19th-century **Church of the Ascension of Christ** (*Св Възнесение Господне*), which has some interesting icons, but is often closed.

Chiprovtsi is a pleasant village to potter around though there are some rather unfriendly geese near the museum! In the museum, Chiprovtsi's mining tradition is described and there is a model of the machine for cleaning the stones. The village was an important gold- and silver-mining area in the Middle Ages, using the expertise of fair-haired and Catholic immigrants from Saxony. Even under Ottoman domination the area remained a centre of Catholicism and provided young men for the priesthood. This contact with western Europe was perhaps the reason for the 1688 uprising (shown on a map in the museum), which broke out when Austrian troops were successful against the Turks. Unfortunately, Austrian progress was slow and the premature uprising was fiercely crushed by the occupiers, who burned the village to the ground and drove away the inhabitants. They also destroyed the nearby monastery to confirm that uprisings were forbidden, and it was 50 years before Chiprovtsi was resettled.

CHIPROVSKI MONASTERY (ЧИПРОВСКИ МАНАСТИР) The monastery was destroyed after the 1688 rebellion, and in its thousand-year history has been burned down and damaged many times. It was involved in several uprisings and paid the price. Nowadays it is home to large numbers of cats, a couple of fierce-looking dogs and several families of birds nesting on the hanging lamps in the church.

The buildings are mainly 19th century, with a small church which has a gold iconostasis. Locally made rugs decorate the bishop's throne. The place has a reputation for its healing powers and many people leave gifts as offerings and thanks for the prayers said daily for their cure. There is an ancient-looking tower which houses, on the ground floor, the bones of those who died in rebellions, with a chapel above, and on the third (more recently built) floor the bells are hung.

Despite its Catholic heritage, Chiprovtsi now has the reputation of celebrating events in the Orthodox calendar on a truly magnificent scale. On several saint's days each year, every neighbourhood sacrifices a lamb and cooks up a huge stew of *kurban chorba* to share in a communal feast. The day of the union of the two parts of Bulgaria, 6 September, is celebrated as a particularly important occasion. The people go to the remains of the Gushovski Monastery, known as the Archangel Michael Summer Monastery, for their blessing by the Bishop of Vidin and priests, followed by the feast. An illustrated leaflet available at the monastery shows huge crowds attending.

BELOGRADCHIK (БЕЛОГРАДЧИК) *Telephone code: 093*

The minor roads from Chiprovtsi to Belogradchik make a pleasant approach to the town. There was a fascinating big yard used by charcoal burners, each dome of wood being a perfect hemisphere, despite being made from the heaps of stiff, awkward and angular branches. Closer to Belogradchik the landscape gradually changes and the distinctive red rocks in crazy shapes dominate the view. The rock formations cover a huge area of nearly 100km².

Getting there and away Belogradchik is not on a railway line. There are **buses** (*bus station* ☎ 653427) from Montana (*1 daily; 1hr 35mins*), Oreshets (*2 daily; 20mins*) and the central bus station in Sofia (*1 daily; 4½hrs; 16lv*).

Tourist information The tourist information office is at ul Poruchik Dvoryanov 5 (☎ 653291; e ticbelogradchik@gmail.com; www.belogradchik.info).

🏠 Where to stay

🏠 **Madona** (6 rooms) ul Hristo Botev 26; ☎ 665546; e madonainn@yahoo.com; www. madonainn-bg.com. Family hotel in a quiet street with views of the fortress & rocks. Good restaurant. €

🏠 **Rai** (6 rooms) ul Ivan Stratsimir 3; ☎ 653735; m 0894 702917; e bubjordanova@ abv.bg. Opposite the bus station. Plain & simple accommodation. B/fast not inc. €

🏠 **Sasho's Guesthouse** (4 rooms) ul Poruchik Drianov 27B; ☎ 653558; e pri_sasho@ belogradchik.info. Small but nice place with lovely view towards the Kaleto fortress. €

🏠 **Skalite** (40 rooms) Vazrazhdane Square 2; ☎ 094 691210; m 0884 514154; e reception@ skalite.bg; www.skalite.bg. Centrally located with a wonderful view to the rocks from the bar. €€

✗ Where to eat and drink

✗ **Elit** ul Yuri Gagarin 3A; ☎ 654558; m 0886 676197. One of the best places to eat in the town. Bulgarian specialities in a traditional setting. €–€€

✗ **Madona** See above. Speciality dishes & traditional grills. €–€€

What to see and do For most visitors the attraction of Belogradchik is the rocky landscape. Local people have given names to the most distinctive rocks: the bear, the mushrooms, Adam and Eve, the monk, the camel, the cuckoo, the horseman and many more. Legends about the origins of the stones abound. In the past, one such story relates that there was a nunnery near the rocks. Sister Valentina, who took the veil and joined the nuns, was said to be very beautiful and rumours of her loveliness spread far and wide, even reaching a poor shepherd boy called Anton. Every night he tried to woo Valentina by playing his shepherd's pipe beneath her window. Apparently the musical Romeo was successful and Valentina fell in love with him. Later she gave birth to a child and was of course expelled from the nunnery. God's anger was turned on the convent and all the nuns were turned to stone; Valentina became a stone Madonna and poor shepherd Anton waits for his love among the stone figures.

In fact, the rock formations are a result of millions of years of geological activity as stratified rocks were covered by a sea in which river sand, gravel and clay were carried. In time these materials were joined together by silicon or sand-clay solder. Local iron oxide caused the redness. Other rocks of grey and white limestone were piled on top in some places during the Jurassic period, and because of the different levels of hardness the rocks have eroded unequally, thus creating the fantastic outlines of today. Amid this rockscape are caves and waterfalls, and the area is a haven for many unusual flowers and birds. We saw the exceptionally rare *Ramonda serbica* when we were there.

Belogradchik is situated amid the towering rocks. It is a pleasant small town with a modest **museum** and **art gallery** (*Музей и Художествена галерия;* ⊕ *09.00–noon & 14.00–17.00 Mon–Fri; both 2lv*) displaying local folklore exhibits in the former and the work of local artists in the latter. The **citadel** (⊕ *summer 09.00–18.00 daily, winter 09.00–16.30; adult 4lv*), which is built into and amid the rocks, is the destination of most visitors. Its obvious strategic significance means that it has been a fortified site since Roman times, with Bulgarians and then Turks adding to its defences. Over time it has been the guardian of the approach to the Belogradchik Pass and a Turkish garrison intended to overawe the local population.

The fortress has three parts, each of which could be defended separately, and two main gates, named Vidin and Nish, presumably because of the direction they faced. There were barracks, arsenals, food stores, a prison, water cisterns and a flour mill. It housed about 3,000 defenders, and was last used during the Serbian-Bulgarian war of 1885.

MAGURA CAVE (ПЕЩЕРА МАГУРАТА) Northwest of Belogradchik near the village of Rabisha is the amazing Magura Cave (*Пещера Магурата; check opening times in Belogradchik; adult 5lv*). It is a large underground area consisting of a main gallery with several others around it, the whole area being about 135ha with galleries some 2,600m long. The average annual temperature is 12°C, hence over time it has been the home of bears, hyenas and, nowadays, four kinds of bats. The favourable conditions meant that in about 8000BC it was inhabited by humans, probably mainly as a temporary shelter, and the earliest rock drawings date from this period.

In one of the halls evidence of a Bronze Age settlement has been found: fireplaces, stone and bone tools, weapons and many ceramic pots, jugs and cups. The tour takes you past many named formations of stalactites and stalagmites: the alpine climbers, the pipe organ, the dragon, Buddha's head and so on. Beautiful and interesting as these are, it is the paintings, over 750 of them, which particularly interest many visitors. They were apparently drawn at intervals over a very long period in prehistoric times, and were painted using bat droppings. The subjects include hunting scenes, mythological figures and rituals.

The cave also provides ideal conditions for the making of wine, so here you will find the only cellar in Bulgaria where naturally sparkling wine made by the traditional *méthode champenoise* is produced. The wine can, of course, be tasted and purchased here.

VIDIN (ВИДИН) *Telephone code: 094*

Vidin, like Petrich in the southwest, is a town close to two international boundaries, in this case Serbia and Romania. It is on the River Danube and, unsurprisingly given its important position, it has been inhabited since ancient times.

It is a regional centre, and the long-awaited Danube Bridge has, after years of being mired in disagreements and difficulties, finally been completed. It has been christened the New Europe Bridge and will be a very useful international transport link, as it should bring more tourism and other business to the northwest of Bulgaria, one of Europe's poorest areas, though the roads leading to the bridge still need considerable improvement.

HISTORY There was a settlement here in Celtic times, before the Roman invasion. After the Romans evacuated Dacia to the north, the Danube became the empire's northern frontier and its fortresses became increasingly significant. The Romans called it Bononia. During the Middle Ages the Bulgarians knew it as Budin, then Bdin. It had its period of greatest prosperity in the late 14th century when it was briefly the capital of the separate kingdom of Ivan Stratsimir. In 1396 it was conquered by the Turks. By the 16th century Vidin was the largest town in Bulgaria and one of the biggest ports on the Danube. It had another brief burst of independence under a rogue Turkish commander, Osman Pazvanoglou, who, between 1794 and 1807, declared himself the independent ruler of a large area of northwest Bulgaria. Its remoteness from the centres of power in Istanbul and Veliko Turnovo made these bids for independence possible. From about 1836, when shipping on the Danube began to develop, a profitable trade with Austria opened up. After liberation in 1878 the Turkish population left en masse and people from local villages moved in.

GETTING THERE AND AWAY There are **trains** from Sofia (*3 daily; 5½hrs*) and Boichinovtsi (*6 daily; 2hrs 40mins*). **Buses** (*bus station* \ *606190*) are slightly quicker. Services run from Sofia (*7 daily; 4–5hrs*), Vratsa (*1 daily; 2hrs*) and Pleven (*4 daily; 3½hrs*). The bus (and private Alexiev bus) and railway stations are south of the centre.

TOURIST INFORMATION The tourist information centre (*ul baba Vida 4;* \ *609498;* e *tourism.obshtinavidin@gmail.com*) has information about the town, accommodation and transport.

⌂ WHERE TO STAY *Map, page 152*

⌂ **Anna-Kristina** (23 rooms) ul Baba Vida 2; m 0878 836901; e office@annakristinahotel.com. Near the centre, in the Danube River park, this Austrian-style building from the early 1900s has been beautifully restored. Recommended for its style, service & food. €€

⌂ **Avramov** (18 rooms) ul Tsar Aleksandur II 63; \606680; m 0885 287766; e hotel_avramov@mail.bg; www.hotel-avramov.domino.bg. Centrally located with views of the Danube River, this a small, elegant & comfortable hotel, close to bus & train stations & the town centre. €€

🏨 **Bononia** (50 rooms) ul Bdin 2; ☎606031; e office@hotelbononia.net; www.hotelbononia.net. Central location, but décor tired & dated, & service variable. Restaurant. €€

🏨 **Staryat Grad** (Old Town) (8 rooms) ul Knyaz Boris I 2; ☎600023; e oldtown_vd@abv.bg; www.oldtownhotel.dir.bg. Individually designed rooms

in a beautiful, old city-centre building; welcoming owners, highly recommended. €€

🏨 **Ninov** (18 rooms, 5 apts) ul Dunavska 28; ☎600402; m 0899 906125; e hotel_ninov@abv.bg. A modern hotel by the Danube, offering fine views from the bar. It has a restaurant & is convenient to the centre. €

✕ WHERE TO EAT AND DRINK *Map, page 152*

✕ **Anna-Kristina** See page 150. Grills & kebabs, local wines. €€

✕ **Bononia** See above. Varied menu with soups, salad & local specialities. €€

✕ **Fish and Grill Dunav** m 0889 088673. On a ship across from the art gallery. Fish specialities. €€

✕ **Pizza Vivaldi** ul Naicho Tsanov 2; ☎606296. Centrally located. Pizzas, salads & Bulgarian specialities. Popular & busy in the evenings. €€

✕ **Riviera** Located in riverside park; m 0887 817640; e rivieravd@gmail.com. Extremely varied menu with Bulgarian specialities including many grills. Traditional-style décor. €€

WHAT TO SEE AND DO The **Baba Vida Fortress** (*Крепост Баба Вида*; ⊕ *08.30–17.00 Mon–Fri, 10.00–17.00 Sat–Sun; adult 4lv*), the town's chief attraction, is a vast medieval citadel dominating the riverside in the northern part of the town. This is a magnificent castle, the sort you imagine as the centrepiece in some epic film, with a dark, brooding hero and sultry heroine! It is surrounded by huge walls and a deep moat, now dry. It is perfect for scrambling about between courtyards and along ramparts; you can picture yourself peering at the Danube through gun positions trying to spot the approach of your enemies.

Construction was begun by the Bulgarians in the late 10th century on the ruins of Roman Bononia and continued over the years. It is an irregular shape, roughly rectangular, with four great corner towers. There are parts for domestic use and then the defensive area of two walls with turrets and the moat, which would have been filled with water from the river. The name of the fortress translates as 'Granny Vida's', supposedly because her father, a local *bolyar*, had ordered it to be built. A more interesting, but unconvincing, legend tells how in ancient times a king died and left his vast kingdom between the Carpathians and the Balkans to his three daughters, Vida, Kula (which means 'tower') and Gamza (the local red wine). The younger sisters married but Vida did not; instead she ruled from this castle.

The fortress is the central feature of a whole system of defences which protected the town from attack from both the land and river sides. The fortress was impregnable and able to withstand very long sieges. Much of what is visible today was part of the 17th-century reconstruction by the Turks. It escaped damage during the Russo-Turkish war of 1877–78, and is now probably the best-preserved medieval fortress in the country.

The **Archaeology Museum** (*Археологически музей*; ul Turgovska; ⊕ *09.00–noon & 13.30–17.30 Tue–Sat; adult 4lv*) is in a wooden pagoda-style 19th-century building once the Turkish *konak*, northwest of the main square, pl Bdin. A *konak* was the headquarters of the occupying Ottoman authority and would have included the residence of the governor, a garrison or barracks and a prison. The oldest exhibits are prehistoric tools made of stone and bone found in a cave near Oreshets. More interesting are finds from Ratiaria, some 25km south of Vidin near the present-day village of Archar. Mosaics and sculptures show unexpected sophistication for a place so remote from the heart of the Roman Empire. More modern displays cover the period of National Revival and the liberation struggle.

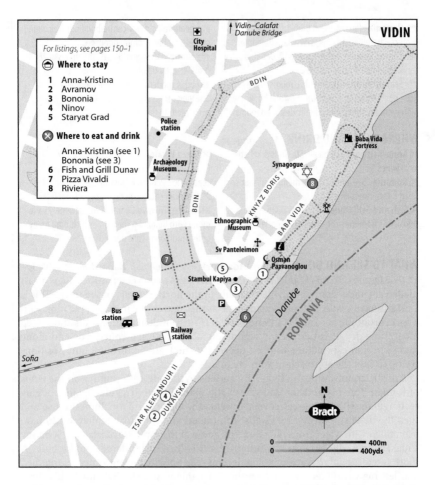

For listings, see pages 150–1

VIDIN

↑ Vidin–Calafat
Danube Bridge

City Hospital

🏠 **Where to stay**

1 Anna-Kristina
2 Avramov
3 Bononia
4 Ninov
5 Staryat Grad

❌ **Where to eat and drink**

Anna-Kristina (see 1)
Bononia (see 3)
6 Fish and Grill Dunav
7 Pizza Vivaldi
8 Riviera

BDIN

Police station

Baba Vida Fortress

Archaeology Museum

Synagogue

KNYAZ BORIS I

BDIN

BABA VIDA

Ethnographic Museum

Sv Panteleimon

Osman Pazvanoglu

7

5

Stambul Kapiya

3

1

Danube

ROMANIA

Bus station

Railway station

6

Sofia

TSAR ALEKSANDUR II

DUNAVSKA

4

2

N

Bradt

0   400m
0   400yds

The town's **park** alongside the river may remind you a little of an English park, but the vegetation is lusher and the plant varieties more exotic. The views of the Danube are very impressive. It is the second-longest river in Europe and flows through more countries than any other river in the world, nine in total: Germany, Austria, Slovakia, Hungary, Croatia, Serbia, Romania, Bulgaria and Ukraine, and four capital cities: Vienna, Bratislava, Budapest and Belgrade. It is not, however, blue. Indeed, it has serious problems with pollution. Sewage from cities, chemicals from agricultural run-off, waste from factories and bilge oil from shipping all contribute to the problem. NATO bombing during the war with Serbia caused huge quantities of oil and chemicals to enter the Danube ecosystem. In March 2006 it was announced that 62 Danube NGOs would be given funds to help them reduce pollution. The Danube regional project aims to improve the environment of the river basin, protect its waters and manage its resources for the benefit of nature and people in a sustainable manner. It will encourage information sharing and co-operation among the countries that share the river.

The main square, pl Bdin, lies to the south of the fortifications, but has no buildings of interest around it, except on the north side where you can see the **Stambul Kapiya** or Istanbul Gate, a large fortified Turkish gatehouse dating from the 18th century. In the park beside the river is the only remaining **mosque** in Vidin, named the Osman Pazvanoglou; it escaped demolition during the 1970s and 1980s and was restored in 2003. It is a beautiful building but it is rarely open. The nearby modern Church of Sv Nikolai is bright but not of interest, though in contrast behind it is the ancient and definitely not bright **Sv Panteleimon**. This is a well-preserved Byzantine building from the 12th century, restored in the 17th; it is semi-subterranean and rather dark, but there are interesting murals.

Ul Baba Vida continues towards the fortress, passing the striking but decaying and abandoned **synagogue**. Vidin had a considerable Jewish population until after World War II, when most emigrated to the new state of Israel. On a parallel street to ul Baba Vida, also leading north, there is an interesting 19th-century building, the Krustata Kazarma, a former barracks built in the shape of a Greek cross, in which the **Ethnographic Museum** is housed (*Етнографски музей; ul Knyaz Boris I;* ⏱ *09.00–17.00 Mon–Fri, 10.00–17.00 w/ends; adult 2lv*).

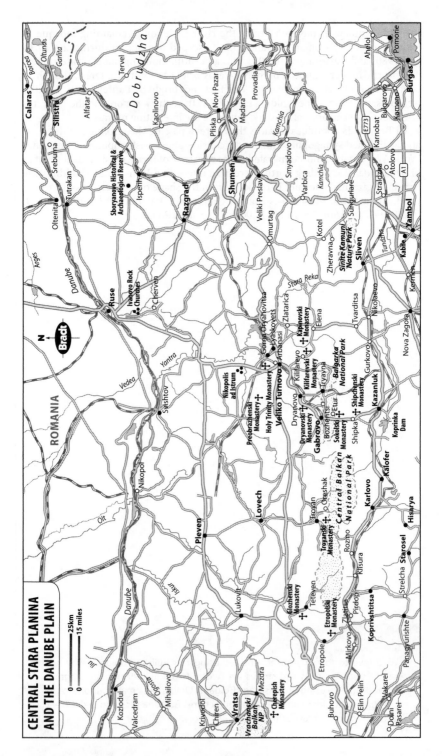

CENTRAL STARA PLANINA AND THE DANUBE PLAIN

0   25km
0   15 miles

6

Central Stara Planina and the Danube Plain

Stara Planina, or the Balkan Mountains, stretch right across the country from west to east, and in winter they can prove a formidable obstacle. In this region are three of Bulgaria's former capitals, **Pliska**, **Preslav** and **Veliko Turnovo**, making it very much the historical centre of the country. The mountain villages and remote monasteries preserved Bulgarian traditions and were involved in a series of uprisings against the Ottoman Empire. There are several interesting towns that could be used as bases from which to explore the magnificent countryside, the small mountain towns and villages, and the numerous interesting monasteries, but public transport is not much use for reaching remote monasteries and archaeological sites, so a car is essential if you want to get off the beaten track. Pleven has many monuments to events during the Russo-Turkish War of 1877–78, and Veliko Turnovo is a visually stunning city with churches, museums and nearby monasteries to visit. Shumen is well placed for exploring the old capitals of Pliska and Veliki Preslav, while Ruse, with its shaded boulevards and air of elegant Mitteleuropa, is situated on the beautiful River Danube with the Ivanovo Rock Churches and Cherven nearby. The region has four UNESCO World Heritage-listed sites: the **Madara Horseman rock relief**, the **Sreburna Biosphere Reserve**, the **Ivanovo Rock Churches** and the **Thracian tomb at Sveshtari**.

TOWARDS STARA PLANINA   *Telephone code: 0720*

ETROPOLSKI MONASTERY (ЕТРОПОЛСКИ МАНАСТИР) The monastery is 5km from Etropole, to the northeast of Sofia. It is a fine example of the important role played by the church during the Ottoman occupation. Like other monasteries it ensured the continuity of the Bulgarian literary and oral traditions, and acted as a centre for education and scholarship. While Rila and the cell schools it organised were the most important, north of Stara Planina the acknowledged centre was Varovitets, Etropole's Monastery of the Holy Trinity, which is still a working monastery. Here scribes copied important manuscripts and new books were written.

It was built in the 13th century and renovated in the 17th, but destroyed and rebuilt many times during the Ottoman occupation. There is a large five-domed cruciform church with two chapels, as well as residential buildings. There are some splendid icons and treasures such as a gold-plated ossuary and two intricately decorated silver crosses.

The drive to the monastery up wooded slopes conceals the buildings till the last moment – a nice visual surprise!

Getting there and away There are **buses** (*bus station* ☎ 62300) from Vratsa (*2 daily; 1hr*), Pleven (*3 daily; 1hr 40mins*) and Sofia (*hourly; 1hr 10mins*).

Tourist information Etropole tourist information office is at bul Ruski 88 (↘ 67335).

⌂ Where to stay Etropole is a small town with limited options.

⌂ **Etropole** (30 rooms) m 0899 887569. Just above the bus station near the centre. Convenient location, with renovated rooms. €

⌂ **Everest Kraigradski Park** (41 rooms) m 0899 887568; e hotel_everest@abv.bg; www. everestetropole.com. Modern hotel in pleasant location. €

⌂ **Podkovata** (18 rooms) About 1.5km from the centre, adjacent to the horseriding centre; m 0899 999369; www.hotel-podkovata.com/ home. Well-equipped, Wi-Fi, AC, restaurant & summer garden. €

✗ Where to eat and drink

✗ **Pri Chasovnika Bistro** Next to the historic clocktower. Bulgarian & international cuisine. Inexpensive place offering good food. €–€€

✗ **Restaurant Grishano** bul Ruski 95. Bulgarian specialities, soups, salads. €–€€

GLOZHENSKI MONASTERY (ГЛОЖЕНСКИ МАНАСТИР) This monastery of Sv Georgi the Victor (*Св Георги Победоносец*) was established in the 12th century and rebuilt in the 13th and is still functioning. It is in a spectacular elevated position above the village and looks a little like a medieval fortress.

The story is that during the Second Bulgarian Kingdom a Russian Prince, Georgi Glozh, banished by the Tatars in the 13th century, was granted land by the Bulgarian King Ivan Assen II and laid the foundations of the village Chiren Pazar and the first monastery, dedicated to the Transfiguration. In this story as well as on two seals from 1776 and 1821 the monastery is mentioned as the Kiev Monastery. The miraculous icon of Sv Georgi, for which the cloister was famous, also originated from Kiev. The legend says that the icon came from Kiev and landed on a high rock platform and the astounded prince ordered that a new monastery should be built, dedicated to Sv Georgi. Until the 1920s there were traces of ruined residential buildings and a defence tower, built in the 13th or 14th century. The monastery, a centre of culture during the 19th century, was completely destroyed by the 1913 earthquake and subsequently rebuilt on the same foundations.

The church is small and plain but the approach up steep cobbles is rather nice. Despite being in a very isolated position there were draconian parking rules firmly enforced!

TETEVEN (ТЕТЕВЕН) *Telephone code: 0678*

The town is in the pretty valley of the River Vit. It was inhabited in Neolithic times, and there are numerous Thracian tombs nearby. The earliest written reference to the town dates from the 14th century, but the settlement was centred on the Sv Iliya Monastery from the 13th century onward. Teteven had certain privileges under the Ottoman occupation, and it prospered as a crafts town until 1801, when Kurdzhaliya completely ravaged it and only the monastery and four houses (out of 3,000) survived. It was gradually reconstructed, but never regained its original prestige. Nowadays it gives a rather drab impression.

The final drama in the April Uprising took place 15km southeast of the town in the locality of Kostina. Georgi Benkovski, Zahari Stoyanov and other leaders of the revolt were betrayed, ambushed and murdered.

Getting there and away There are **buses** (*bus station* \ *52557*) from Lovech (*5 daily; 1hr 30mins*), Pleven (*1 daily; 2hrs*), Ribaritsa (*4 daily; 30mins*) and Sofia (*hourly; 2hrs*).

Tourist information The tourist information office is opposite the bus station (*ul Petko Milev Strashnia 2;* \ *95056;* e *infoc_teteven@abv.bg; www.teteven.bg*).

Where to stay

Maksim (5 rooms) ul Emil Markov 27; \ 5552; m 0899 894119. The best place to stay in the town. Centrally located, with a restaurant. Rooms have TV, fridge & are smart & comfortable. €

Olymp (72 rooms) ul Treti Mart 33; \ 52067. 400m from town centre, with a sports & spa centre. Wi-Fi, AC, fridge in rooms. €

Zdravets Balneo Complex (75 rooms) ul Petrahilya 29; m 0878 939141. This former tourist hostel has been renovated & transformed into a spa & fitness destination, though the décor is quite old-fashioned. €–€€

Where to eat and drink

Maksim Hotel See above. The restaurant here is worth trying for regional cuisine amid mock medieval surroundings! €

Mehana Vodenitsata 4km from town on road to Ribaritsa; \ 54258. Traditional *mehana*. Authentic old building with a nice outdoor garden; serves Bulgarian & local specialities. There is a folklore programme & live music. €€

What to see and do The **Museum of History** (*Исторически музей; pl Sava Mladenov 3;* \ *52005;* ⊕ *summer 09.00–noon & 14.00–17.00 daily, winter Mon–Fri; adult 2lv*) has a strong archaeological collection.

All Saints Church (*Bcu Cвemuu; ul Simeon Kumanov 15*) was built in 1843–46 and is unusually large for a church of this Ottoman occupation period. It has two bells made in Moscow, a fine carved pulpit by the Debur School of woodcarvers and an iconostasis from the Tryavna School. In the churchyard is a clocktower.

The town is a good centre for summer mountain activities and there is a limited amount of skiing in winter. It is known as a town where many traditional festivals are held throughout the year, so do ask at the tourist office. Bulgarians regard its *rakiya* as particularly fine, so that might be worth a try if you're not driving!

PLEVEN (ПЛЕВЕН) *Telephone code: 064*

Pleven is a spacious town and much of the centre is pedestrianised. A huge area of park close to the centre leads to, or houses, several of the town's attractions. There has been a settlement here since the Neolithic period and the museums have large and interesting collections illustrating Pleven's history.

GETTING THERE AND AWAY There are **trains** (*railway station* \ *822390*) from Varna (*5 daily; 5hrs*), Troyan (*2 daily; 3hrs*), Shumen (*7 daily; 3hrs*) and Sofia (*8 daily; 3hrs 20mins*).

There are **buses** (*bus station* \ *888666*) from Sofia (*5 daily; 3hrs*), Lovech (*hourly 07.00–18.00; 40mins*), Stara Zagora (*2 daily; 4hrs*), Ruse (*4 daily; 2hrs*), Gabrovo (*2 daily; 2hrs*) and Montana (*1 daily; 2hrs*). The bus station is north of the centre.

TOURIST INFORMATION The tourist information office is at pl Vuzrazhdane 1 (\ *824004;* e *tourpleven@abv.bg; http://tourinfo.pleven.bg;* ⊕ *09.00–17.00 Mon–Fri*).

🏠 WHERE TO STAY

🏠 **Balkan** (226 rooms) bul Ruse 82; ✆ 803700;
e office@hotel-balkan.com; www.hotel-balkan.
com. Old-style central hotel, shabby but good
value. Friendly staff, spacious rooms & wonderful
views on higher floors. AC, Wi-Fi. €–€€

🏠 **Gallery** (11 rooms) ul Kailuka 7; ✆ 894444;
m 0885 992289; e hotelkailaka@gmail.com.

Private hotel not far from the centre, with art
displays, stylish décor, Wi-Fi, restaurant & terrace
bar. €€

🏠 **Rostov** (97 rooms) ul Tsar Boris III 2;
✆ 805005; e hotel@rostov.bg; www.rostov.bg.
Rooms are small but have TV & fridge. Service, staff
& cleanliness can be variable. €€

✗ WHERE TO EAT AND DRINK

✗ **Paraklisa Klub** ul Knyaz Boris III 1; ✆ 820020.
Centrally situated in an atmospheric building with
a good selection of Bulgarian dishes, plus some
international fare. Very popular & busy. €–€€

✗ **Pizza Tempo** ul Dimitar Konstantinov 23;
✆ 806920; m 0879 988103. Good option; the

food is great, lots of choice but service often slow.
€–€€

✗ **Speedy Bar and Grill** ul Vasil Levski.
Western-style fast food, salads, grilled meats.
Friendly & efficient service & a good selection of
wines. €–€€

WHAT TO SEE AND DO To historians the name of Pleven resounds as one of
the great battles of the Russo-Turkish war which liberated Bulgaria. The Siege of
Pleven in 1877 is commemorated in the **Panorama** (*Панорама Плевенска епопея;
Skobelev Park;* ⊕ *09.00–noon & 12.30–17.00 daily; adult 5lv*), the only monument
of its kind in southeast Europe. This park is the actual battlefield. The Panorama
takes the form of a circular painted scene of the situation on 11 September, the
day of the third assault by the Russians and Romanians. As you enter you see the
Turkish army nearby and the Russians to the right with General Skobelev on his
white horse. Despite being refused reinforcements, Skobelev led his men into fierce
fighting. The artists have created a wonderful three-dimensional effect: the edge of
the painted scene merges seamlessly into the pieces of equipment, fighting soldiers
and injured men arranged in the foreground. There are other paintings displayed
downstairs introducing the visitor to the historical background: the Turkish Yoke,
the April Uprising and the events leading up to the war and its early stages.

The **Regional History Museum** (*Регионален исторически музей; ul Stoyan
Zaimov 3;* ✆ *822691;* ⊕ *09.00–noon & 13.00–17.00 daily; adult 2lv*) is in a huge
former barracks near the central park. There is a strong archaeological collection,
an interesting ethnographic display with exhibits connected with fishing and the
Danube (something a little different from other collections) and, not surprisingly, a
very large exhibition connected with the Russo-Turkish War.

The **Icon Museum** (*Иконна изложба; pl Sv Nikolai;* ⊕ *daily; donations welcome*)
is in the 19th-century Church of Sv Nikolai, with examples of the fine work of
several of the best-known artists including those of the Samokov, Debur and
Tryavna schools.

In the old public baths building in the park, a striped church-like pink-and-
white edifice is the **Gallery of Svetlin Rusev** (*Картинна галерия Светлин Русев;
ul Doiran 75;* ✆ *838342;* ⊕ *10.30–18.30 Tue–Sat; adult 1.50lv*). Rusev is an artist
who has collected paintings, sculptures and icons in Bulgaria and from overseas
and presented the collection to Pleven. There are works by Tsanko Lavrenov and
the well-known Vladimir Dimitrov-Maistora.

South of the town is the area called Kailuka Park. As you leave Pleven you
suddenly find yourself passing through an area of rocky cliffs quite unlike any of
the other surrounding countryside; this leads to an area of almost alpine scenery
with lovely views from the hillsides across to attractive small lakes.

LOVECH (ЛОВЕЧ)   *Telephone code: 068*

During medieval times the town was a military and trading centre. An important treaty was signed here in 1187, in which Byzantium recognised Bulgarian independence, making the establishment of the Second Bulgarian Kingdom possible. Lovech retained significant rights even during Ottoman rule, and in the 17th–19th centuries it flourished to such an extent that the Turks called it Altan ('Golden'). Schools were founded and one of the first teachers was the famous poet Petko Slaveykov.

GETTING THERE AND AWAY   The bus and train stations are close to one another, but not to the centre. There are **trains** (*railway station ☎ 634935*) from Levski (*3 daily; 1hr*), Pleven (*1 daily; 2hrs 10mins*) and Troyan (*3 daily; 1hr*).

There are **buses** (*bus station ☎ 603618*) from Kazanluk (*4 daily; 3hrs 40mins*), Pleven (*hourly 07.00–18.00; 1hr*), Troyan (*hourly 08.00–17.00; 1hr*), Veliko Turnovo (*3 daily; 2hrs*) and Vratsa (*2 daily; 2½hrs*).

TOURIST INFORMATION   The tourist information office is on ul Karakonovski 2 (*☎ 604218; e otic_@abv.bg*).

🏠 WHERE TO STAY

🏠 **Lovech** (141 rooms) ul Turgovska 12; ☎ 604717; m 0894 406895; e info@hotellovech. com; www.hotellovech.com. Former state hotel in a good location by the river, close to the historic bridge. Renovated spacious rooms. €€

🏠 **Presidium Palace** (52 rooms) ul Turgovska 51; ☎ 687501; e info@presidium.com; www. presidium.com. Currently the best hotel: centrally located, modern & smart, with a beauty centre, business centre & tourist information. Plasma TVs & Wi-Fi in rooms. €€–€€€

🏠 **Tsaryana** (24 rooms) pl Todor Kirkov 10; ☎ 600995; m 0888 556174; e tsariana@abv.bg; www.tsariana.com. Budget place to stay in the centre, with decent rooms in a nice old building. €

🏠 **Varosha 2003** (10 rooms) ul Ivan Drasov 23; ☎ 622277; m 0887 996687; e hotelvarosha@ mail.bg. Attractive, cosy little hotel in the old part of town. Family-run & friendly. Good *mehana* attached to it. €–€€

✖ WHERE TO EAT AND DRINK

✖ **Gallereya** ul Vasil Levski 25; ☎ 601055. Very tasty food & nice location, in the centre, next to an art gallery; pleasant garden. Bulgarian cuisine, traditional style. €€

✖ **Pizza Arsis** ul Targovska 22; ☎ 604341; m 0885 080933; e arsis@mail.bg. Pizzas, pasta, salads, grilled meats. Fast & efficient service, good prices. Indoor & outdoor dining. €€

✖ **Pri Voivodite** ul Marin Poplukanov; m 0888 837513. Centrally located traditional *mehana* with interesting interior. Bulgarian food & specialities. €€

WHAT TO SEE AND DO   In the centre of Lovech, astride the River Osum, is the **covered bridge** (*Покрития мост*), the only one on the Balkan Peninsula. The original was built in 1848 and there have been various restorations, the present one following the 1872 design of the master-builder Kolyo Ficheto. It has several interesting crafts shops and cafés.

The bridge links the new and old parts of the town. Overlooking the latter is a huge statue to Vasil Levski, and nearby the **Vasil Levski Museum** (*Музей Васил Левски; ☎ 601407; ◷ winter 08.00–noon & 13.00–17.00, summer 08.00–noon & 14.00–18.00, both Mon–Fri; adult 3lv*) traces his revolutionary career. When he set up his revolutionary committee here, he designated it as the central leadership and called it the Interim Government of Bulgaria. The town was liberated in 1877, but quickly recaptured by the Turks, who in vengeance killed more than 2,500 Bulgarians.

It is pleasant to stroll through Varosha, the restored old quarter which has been designated an Architectural Reserve, and up the hill towards the statue. Here, on Stratesh Hill, there is a medieval fortress where the Treaty of Lovech was signed in 1187 where Byzantium recognised the restoration of the Bulgarian Kingdom. On the same site are the ruins of Melta, a Roman fortress, itself superimposed on the original Thracian settlement.

The **Ethnographic Complex** (*Етнографския комплекс; ul Hristo Ivanov Golemia;* ⊕ *summer 08.00–noon & 14.00–18.00, winter 08.00–noon & 13.00–17.00, both Mon–Sat; adult 3lv*) consists of two neighbouring houses, Drasova and Rashova, with exhibitions of domestic life in the 19th and early 20th centuries.

From Lovech it is possible to visit the huge cave **Devetashka Peshtera** (*Деветашката пещера; 18km north*), which has an underground river and a series of lakes and waterfalls. Evidence of the caves being inhabited in the Stone, Bronze and Iron ages has been found. The tourist office has details of local excursions there.

TROYAN (ТРОЯН) *Telephone code: 0670*

Troyan gets its name from the Roman road, Via Trayana, which passed through it. Remnants of the road, with well-preserved stone paving, are visible at Beklemeto, the Troyan Pass. After the Turkish conquest, many refugees from other parts of Bulgaria moved here as it was a fairly inaccessible area. Even so it was devastated in the early 19th century in several attacks by Kurdzhaliya. In 1877 it was severely damaged by the Turkish army, but the population risked further retribution and still gave assistance to the Russian General Karkov in crossing the Troyan Pass.

GETTING THERE AND AWAY There are **trains** (*railway station* ✆ *24091*) from Levski (*3 daily; 2hrs*) and Pleven (*1 daily; 2hrs 50mins*). The **bus station** (✆ *62172*) has one daily bus to Sofia (*3hrs*).

TOURIST INFORMATION There is a tourist information office at ul Vasil Levski 133 (✆ *60964;* e *infotroyan@yahoo.com; www.troyaninfo.com;* ⊕ *summer 09.00–20.00 daily, winter 09.00–17.00 Mon–Fri*), which has information about accommodation, hiking, climbing, cycling and adventure tourism.

🏠 WHERE TO STAY

🏠 **Nunki** (15 rooms) ul Hristo Botev 138; ✆22606. Large & quiet rooms in a central location. Restaurant attached. €

🏠 **Park-hotel Troyan** (48 rooms) 500m from the centre; ✆68500; m 0878 303939. Quiet hotel in the park Kapincho. Nice location, but poor maintenance of the rooms, & at times inefficient service. €–€€

🏠 **Troyan Plaza** (57 rooms) ul PR Slaveykov 54; ✆64399; m 0885 100006; e reservations@ troyanplaza.com; www.troyanplaza.com. Most luxurious hotel with many facilities: fitness centre, restaurant & *mehana*. In the centre. €€

✗ WHERE TO EAT AND DRINK

As well as the restaurants listed below, there are also several bistros and pizza places around pl Vuzrazhdane and ul Vasil Levski, and in the hotels listed above.

South of Asenovgrad, Asenova Fortress is a striking landmark, and a steep climb rewards you with magnificent views of Plovdiv and the Thracian Plain
(o/S) page 236

above   The beautiful Preobrazhenski Monastery has colourful frescoes depicting those sinners heading for hell, including thieves, traitors and innkeepers who water down their wine! (2/D) page 177

left   Sokolski Monastery is a brightly coloured jewel, and in its yard there is a fountain designed by the famous architect, Kolyo Ficheto (2/S) page 166

below   The remote rock churches at Ivanovo are decorated with skilful, lively and expressive frescoes (ML) page 195

above & right Bachkovo Monastery is a beautiful ensemble of religious and domestic buildings with a pastoral feel. It has fine frescoes dating from different periods of its long history. (AK/D) and (v/S) pages 236–8

below With a spectacular location in the Iskur Gorge, Cherepish Monastery was an important religious, cultural and educational centre during Bulgaria's National Revival (D/D) page 140

above left One of the first of many Thracian treasures to be discovered, the much-admired Panagyurishte hoard has travelled to the world's major museums (C/D) page 204

above right Kazanluk's annual Rose Festival gives visitors the chance to sample rose liqueur or join in with some early-morning rose picking (TY/D) page 210

left Traditionally, red and white *martenitsi* are exchanged on 1 March to wish good health and welcome spring, and are worn until a stork or flowering tree is seen (ND/D) pages 26–7

below Local women chat whilst doing some handicrafts (JM/S)

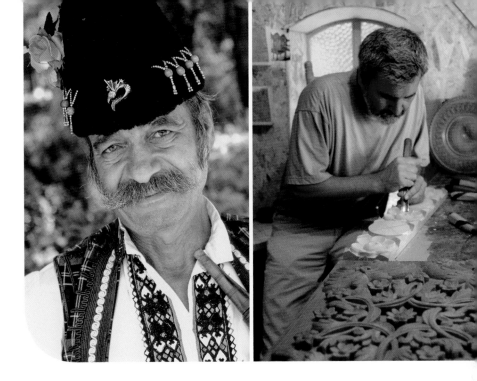

above left The traditional male costume includes a white shirt embroidered at the neck and cuffs and a black lambskin hat (*kalpak*) (H/AWL) page 30

above right Woodcarving is a traditional skill which is still very much a part of Bulgarian culture (BT)

below Wine tours are becoming increasingly popular in Bulgaria; its great variety of terrains and microclimates means it can produce many wines of distinctive characters (JL/D) pages 61–2

above **European bee-eater** (G/S) page 6

below left **The sociable white stork likes to nest in villages on churches and chimneys** (AI) page 6

below right **A rose-coloured starling – the starling character known in Britain, but with a stylish new colour scheme!** (E/S) page 220

SOFIA METRO

© Sofiiski Metropoliten

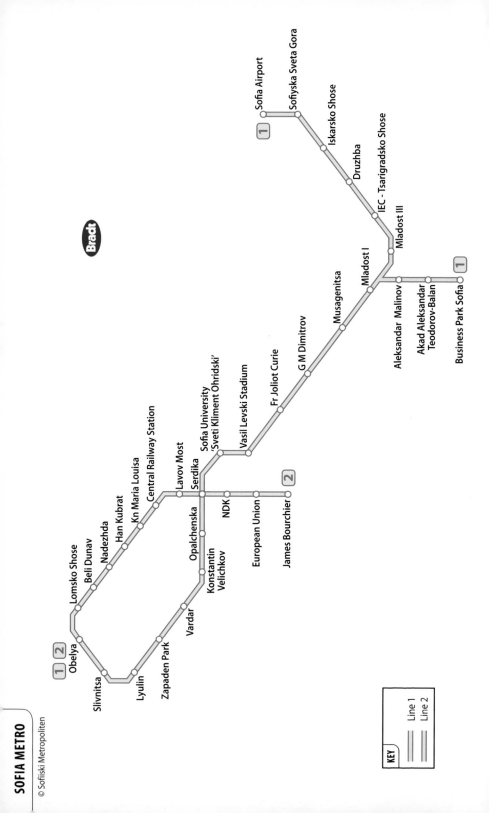

Sofia Airport

Sofiyska Sveta Gora

Iskarsko Shose

Druzhba

IEC - Tsarigradsko Shose

Mladost III

Mladost I

Aleksandar Malinov

Akad Aleksandar Teodorov-Balan

Business Park Sofia

Musagenitsa

G M Dimitrov

Fr Joliot Curie

Vasil Levski Stadium

Sofia University 'Sveti Kliment Ohridski'

Serdika

Lavov Most

Central Railway Station

Kn Maria Louisa

Han Kubrat

Nadezhda

Beli Dunav

Lomsko Shose

Obelya

Slivnitsa

Lyulin

Zapaden Park

Vardar

Opalchenska

Konstantin Velichkov

NDK

European Union

James Bourchier

Bradt

KEY

Line 1

Line 2

✗ Café Antik pl Vuzrazhdane; ☏ 60910. Generous portions of hearty food. River views from the terrace. €–€€
✗ Pri Voivodite ul General Kartsov 72. Rotary Club meeting place, so good quality traditional food & service. €€

✗ Starata Kushta ul General Kartsov 86; m 0878 123108. Nice traditional *mehana* in the centre, with a pleasant garden. Bulgarian & local specialities. €€

WHAT TO SEE AND DO The **Museum of Folk Crafts and Applied Arts** (*Музей на народните художествени занаяти и приложните изкуства*; pl Vuzrazhdane; ☏ 62062; ⊕ *09.00–17.00 Mon–Sat; adult 2lv*) has exhibitions about woodcarving, metalwork, weaving, pottery, textiles and archaeology. Troyan was always known

---

CENTRAL BALKAN NATIONAL PARK

Stara Planina is the long mountain range which separates north and south Bulgaria. The Central Balkan National Park is located in the narrowest and most massive part of the main ridge of Stara Planina, and occupies the highest part of it. The park was designated in 1991 and covers a territory of 73,262ha, including nine natural reserves: Boatin, Tsarichina, Kozya Stena, Steneto, Stara Reka, Dzhendema, Northern Dzhendema, Peeshti Skali and Sokolna. The forests included in the National Park occupy an area of about 44,000ha, and the high-mountain treeless zone covers about 29,000ha. All the natural reserves, except for Kozya Stena and the park itself, are included in the United Nations List of National Parks and Protected Areas. In addition, four of the reserves have been declared Biosphere Reserves within the Man and Biosphere (MAB) Program: Boatin, Tsarichina, Steneto and Dzhendema. Two differentiated sections can be clearly distinguished: the Zlatishko Tetevenska Mountain, with the highest peak of Vezhen (2,198m), and the Troyansko-Kaloferska Mountain, with the highest peak in Stara Planina, Botev (2,376m). The southern slopes are very steep, while the northern ones are relatively steep only in their higher parts. The park altitude varies from 600m to 2,376m. On the top of the mountain the main plant is the **mat grass** (*Nardus stricta*) and it covers the meadows. The northern and most of the eastern parts of the Central Balkan are formed of granite, gneiss and magnetite. The base rocks in the centre of the park are mainly sandstone and limestone, which reach the surface at certain points. Four of the 12 largest rivers in Bulgaria – Vit, Osum, Yantra and Tundzha – rise in the park. The treeline of the Central Balkan is rather low and varies from 1,300m on the southern slopes up to about 1,600m on the northern slopes, unlike other mountains in Bulgaria where the forest belt is at an altitude of 1,800m.

Here a lot of Balkan endemics, such as **haberlea** (*Haberlea rhodopensis*), **knapweed** (*Centaurea kernerana*), **angelica** (*Angelica pancicii*), **bellflowers** (*Campanula trojanensis, C. lanata*), and many rare plants such as *Campanula transsylvanica, Corthusa mattioli*, **daphne** (*Daphne blagayana*), **edelweiss** (*Leontopodium alpinum*) and **gentians** (*Gentiana frigida, G. punctata* and *G. lutea*) can be seen.

Stara Planina are the richest Bulgarian mountains, with about 90 species and subspecies of Bulgarian endemics, 20 of which are local. An endemic **pink primrose** (*Primula frondosa*), occurring only in Stara Planina, is the most interesting.

This park is the Bulgarian Noah's ark, not only because of its very elongated shape, but also because it has carried through the centuries some of the oldest European beech forests, home to **Ural**, **Tengmalm's** and **pygmy owls**, **white-backed woodpeckers**, **red-breasted** and **semi-collared flycatchers**, **hazel hens** and **nightjars**, and also good populations of wolf, brown bear and other animals.

The park and its surroundings is designated by BirdLife International as an Important Bird Area because of the significant numbers of the bird populations, important for the EU, but also as a site inhabited by the Globally Threatened **imperial eagle**, **saker falcon**, **corncrake** and other birds. Incredible rocky massifs are home to vital populations of **golden eagle**, **alpine chough** and **peregrine**. In the highest parts **alpine accentor**, **horn lark**, **water pipit** and other species breed in high numbers. In spite of its high protection status, the park is threatened by some plans for creating ski complexes. For information on the park and conservation activities contact Central Balkan National Park Directorate (*www.visitcentralbalkan.net*).

as a crafts town, its people making their living from ironwork, leather, textiles and ceramics. The town is still noted for its distinctive pottery, featuring the popular stylised design based on the shape of a drop of water, which is on sale all over the country. There are English captions.

The **Cherni Osum Natural History Museum** (*Прородонаучен музей Черни Осъм;* ☉ *08.00–noon & 13.00–17.00 daily; adult 3lv*), 12km southeast of Troyan, is popular with children as there are appropriate sound effects accompanying some of the exhibits. It has preserved examples of all the wildlife of Stara Planina, including a huge collection of butterflies.

AROUND TROYAN

TROYANSKI MONASTERY (ТРОЯНСКИ МАНАСТИР) The monastery (☉ *daily; free*) is undoubtedly one of Bulgaria's finest. It was established in the 16th century. Set in a wooded cobbled courtyard, it presents a perfect ensemble of timbered galleries, roofed with traditional local heavy stone slabs, and colourful external frescoes. There is a fine 19th-century church, with frescoes inside and outside by the famous artist Zahari Zograf, whose signed self-portrait is inside in the arch of a window. His brother, Dimitur, was responsible for the richly coloured icons. At present a lot of the icons are almost black from candle smoke. The iconostasis, the work of Tryavna craftsmen, is carved in walnut and includes in its delicate, three-dimensional tracery flowers, grapes and creatures such as storks, which symbolise hope, dragons representing evil, and lions epitomising strength, all favoured motifs. There is a famous miraculous icon here: the three-handed Holy Virgin. This is said to have come from Mount Athos during the 17th century, donated by a Romanian monk in thanks for the hospitality he received at the monastery.

On a visit just before Easter we were fortunate enough to hear a rehearsal for the Velikden service: four young men, in jeans and T-shirts, and a robed priest sang in wonderful harmony, all having really excellent voices. Although Orthodox services are sung morning and evening, there is something special about the major church occasions, so don't miss the opportunity to listen if you are visiting then.

Vasil Levski established a revolutionary committee here and there is a small **'hiding place' museum** (*музейна експозиция със скривалище;* ☉ *dawn to dusk; adult 2lv*) about him, which visitors can see.

Together with Bachkovo and Rila monasteries, Troyan has a special status known as Stauropegial. This exempted them from the authority of local bishops and placed them under the direct rule of Constantinople. This status was granted in 1830, perhaps in recognition of the achievements of the distinguished Abbot Parteni. The buildings form a wonderful ensemble, in which the builders have maintained a level roof line despite the uneven ground, somehow achieving a barely noticeable transition from three storeys to two. Several thriving families of kittens enjoy playing on the staircases and sleeping in the sun, unmoved by the splendour of their surroundings.

In 1873, faced by the constant threat of Turkish attacks, the monks built a small monastery in the forest nearby, Sv Nikolai the Miracle-worker (*Св Николай Чудотворец*). They used it as a hiding place for precious religious books and weapons, and as a discreet centre of cultural life.

Troyan plum brandy is very famous in Bulgaria. It is made of the Kyustendil variety of plums and served as a traditional welcome to guests. At the monastery they make a special brandy, adding a number of mountain herbs.

ORESHAK (ОРЕШАК) Nearby, the **National Fair and Exhibition of Arts and Crafts Complex** (*Комплекс национално изложение на художествените занаяти и изкуствата; pl Vuzrazhdane;* ✆ *0695 22816; www.oreshakbg.com;* ☉ *09.00–18.00 daily; adult 2lv*) is a large permanent exhibition of traditional crafts such as copper ware, textiles, rugs, ceramics, wooden objects and carvings, some of which can be purchased. Our guide here was very helpful, but the pavilions are in need of some investment and improvements.

🏠 Where to stay

🏠 **Padarski Guesthouse** (3 rooms) ul Stara Planina 105. Picturesque setting & rural surroundings with gardens, orchard & brandy cauldron! €

🏠 **Stranopriemnitsa Oreshak** (11 rooms) ul Stara Planina 207; ✆ 0695 22109; m 0887 927035. Best place to stay near the monastery, this family hotel has friendly staff. The restaurant is highly recommended. €€

🏠 **Troyan Monastery** ✆ 0695 22866; e troyanskim@abv.bg. Interesting opportunity to stay in a working monastery. The atmosphere is great but the rooms are basic & quite expensive, though they do have their own bathroom & TV. €€

✗ Where to eat and drink

✗ **Kaisera** ul Stara Planina 163; ✆ 0695 22678; m 0899 821315. Popular restaurant, offering tasty food & pleasant atmosphere. Traditional rural style, with a garden for summer dining; local trout is a speciality. €€

✗ **Pri Vancheto** Opposite the monastery. Drinks, grilled meats & salads. €

✗ **Strandzhata** ul Stara Planina; opposite the Arts & Crafts Complex; ✆ 0695 22321; m 0878

919096. Really pleasant setting, housed in an authentic old 2-storey building with nice courtyard. Very good food & service. €€

✗ **Stranopriemnitsa Oreshak** See above. An excellent choice. Furnished & decorated in old Bulgarian folk style, the restaurant has an original stone fireplace & a nice terrace for the warm days. €€

GABROVO (ГАБРОВО) *Telephone code: 066*

The exact centre of Bulgaria is at Uzana, a few kilometres from Gabrovo. The medieval town was indeed at a trading crossroads, much used by travellers heading

6

to and from the capital Veliko Turnovo. After the Ottoman conquest, refugees from the capital came to Gabrovo and the surrounding villages, and as a result the area developed as a commercial, religious and political centre.

Gabrovo has an old quarter with National Revival houses and craft shops. It was always famous for its skilled craftsmen, and the introduction of the waterwheel increased production and led to a flourishing textile trade. Economic success created a favourable climate for cultural and educational developments, such as the foundation of Bulgaria's first secondary school in 1835. Nowadays Gabrovo is an industrial town, still specialising in leather and textiles.

GETTING THERE AND AWAY There are **trains** (*railway station* ✆ *805339*) from Tsareva Livada (*6 daily; 30mins*) and Dryanovo (*1 daily; 50mins*).

There are **buses** (*bus station* ✆ *805566*) from Veliko Turnovo (*hourly 06.00–18.00; 1hr*), Dryanovo (*hourly 06.30–20.00; 50mins*), Bozhentsi (*3 daily; 30mins*), Kazanluk (*6 daily; 1hr*), Lovech (*2 daily; 1½hrs*), Pleven (*2 daily; 2hrs 10mins*), Sofia (*3 daily; 3½hrs*) and Stara Zagora (*2 daily; 2hrs 20mins*).

TOURIST INFORMATION The tourist information office is on pl Vuzrazhdane 2 (✆ *818406*; e *tour_info@gabrovo.bg; www.gabrovo.bg*).

🏠 WHERE TO STAY

🛏 **Balkan** (147 rooms) ul Emanuil Manolov 14; ✆801066; m 0879 406723; e info@hotelbalkan-gabrovo.com. Basic but clean, central & friendly. Good value. €

🛏 **Gabrovo** (20 rooms) bul Hemus 4; ✆801705; e hotelgabrovo@contact.bg. Good budget hotel, south of centre, spacious rooms. Welcoming & friendly. €

✖ WHERE TO EAT AND DRINK

✖ **Pizza La Scala** ul Radion Umnikov 3; ✆991729. Pizza, seafood & international dishes. €€
✖ **Pri Lovetsa** ul Emanuil Manolov 17; m 0899 134893. Traditional-style place with Bulgarian food & lots of salads. €€

✖ **Rest** ul Stara Planina 4; ✆876543. Very good restaurant in the centre; Bulgarian & European cuisine, along with a good selection of wines & beers. €€

WHAT TO SEE AND DO In the middle of the River Yantra, in the centre of town, is a statue of Racho the Blacksmith, standing on a rock; he is the symbol of Gabrovo and, according to legend, its founder in the 16th century.

The **Aprilov High School** (*Априловската гимназия; ul Aprilovska;* ✆ *800770;* ⏱ *09.00–17.30 daily; adult 2lv*) is a lovely building now housing a museum of education. It was endowed as a school by Vasil Aprilov, a merchant, and other Gabrovo patriots in 1835, and was the first Bulgarian secular school.

Gabrovo has a rather unusual museum, the **House of Humour and Satire** (*Дом на хумора и сатирата; ul Bryanska 68;* ✆ *807228; www.humorhouse.bg;* ⏱ *09.00–18.00 daily; adult 4lv*) where a large international collection of paintings, cartoons, photographs, sculpture and graphics can be seen. There are English captions. One area has been set aside to illustrate local humour. The people of Gabrovo are reputedly very mean: they happily take credit for inventing narrow trousers and short skirts, they carry their shoes, stop their clocks at night and cut the tails off their cats so that they don't let too much warm air out as they go through doors. One Gabrovo man put one stotinka in the church collection and challenged his friend to do better. The friend crossed himself and said: 'That was for both of us.' Aside from the jokes about meanness, there is a nice Gabrovo saying: the shortest distance between two people is a smile. Something which made me smile on one of my visits to Gabrovo was to be approached by an old man who was very keen to sell me one of his homemade axes.

The **Church of the Assumption** (*Църква Успение Богородично*), built in 1865, is a three-nave basilica with two domes, one of which serves as a belfry. The iconostasis is carved from lime, and features various floral and animal motifs.

The **Detchko House** (*Къща-музей Дечковата къща*) is a lovely, elegantly furnished, old 19th-century town house, the home of Hadzhi Detchko. It gives a glimpse of the comfortable lifestyle of a successful merchant. There are occasional concerts and exhibitions here.

The **clocktower**, a prominent landmark on the main square, was built in 1835 and is one of the highest in Bulgaria. Enthusiasts can arrange to visit the clockwork mechanism.

Baev Bridge was built in 1855 to commemorate a visit made by the Turkish sultan, Abdul Mejid; there is an inscription in Arabic on the highest part of the bridge giving his blessing to the project. The architect Mincho Stoyanov was a student of Kolyo Ficheto.

AROUND GABROVO

ETUR (ЕТЪР) *Telephone code: 066*

The interesting **Etur Architectural and Ethnographic Complex** (*Архитектурно-етнографски комплекс Етъра;* ✆ *801830; www.etar.org;* ⊕ *09.00–18.00 Mon–Fri, 09.00–17.30 Sat–Sun; adult 7lv*) was set up in 1964 by Gabrovo municipality to preserve and teach the town's traditional skills. It is a re-creation of a 19th-century village, an open-air museum. Some of the buildings have been restored on site and others moved here from neighbouring villages. There are over 50 shops or workshops. There are woodcarvers and turners, fur-dressers, bell-makers, musical instrument makers and icon painters, as well as a bakery and a tempting sweet shop. You can watch craftsmen make ceramics, braid and copper ware, and see the herbal centre where oils are produced from different herbs in the traditional Bulgarian way. Elsewhere there is a watermill and workshops for cutting timber, fulling (cleaning and thickening) cloth and making wooden boxes.

Etur is genuinely charming and doesn't feel contrived or artificial. It is a good place to see things being made which you can purchase as souvenirs if you wish. By arrangement, special demonstrations and even tuition in particular skills are possible.

There are frequent colourful folklore events at the museum so it's worth checking what's on when you plan your visit.

Getting there and away From Gabrovo **buses** 1, 7 and 8 from ul Aprilov go to the Etur Complex. Buses from Kazanluk, Plovdiv and Stara Zagora pass the Etur junction, from where it is a 2km walk. **Taxis** from Gabrovo cost 6–8lv (one-way).

🏠 Where to stay

🏠 **Perla** (6 rooms) North part of the museum complex; ✆801984. A nice little hotel; large rooms with balconies. B/fast not inc. Friendly & good value. **€**

🏠 **Stranopriemnitsa** (77 rooms) Opposite Perla; ✆801831; e stranopriemnica@etar.org. Often full of tour groups. **€**

🍴 Where to eat and drink

🍴 **Mehana Vuzrazhdane** At the upper end of the museum complex. Housed in one of the museum's buildings. A limited menu of local specialities, but excellent food. **€–€€**

✕ **Stranopriemnitsa** See page 165. Traditional setting. Efficient service, nice views. Bulgarian specialities including locally baked bread, but food is average. €–€€

SOKOLSKI MONASTERY (СОКОЛСКИ МАНАСТИР)

Nearby is the much-photographed Sokolski Monastery (⊕ *09.00–18.00 daily*), actually now a nunnery, built in 1833. External frescoes are protected by a dome roofed by what looks like a little hat with a frilly edge.

It is named after its founder Archimandrite Yosif Sokolski or, according to a different story, both he and the monastery are named after the many falcons which nest in the nearby rock crevices: *sokol* means 'falcon' in Bulgarian. The church, the Assumption of the Blessed Virgin, has icons attributed to Zahari Zograf and to the Tryavna School. The icon of the Holy Mother and Child is believed to be miraculous.

In the courtyard there is a rather elegant fountain, featuring spouts shaped like falcon's heads, by Kolyo Ficheto. The whole monastery and its frescoes have been restored in recent times.

SHIPCHENSKI MONASTERY (ШИПЧЕНСКИ МАНАСТИР)

The drive south from Gabrovo to Kazanluk across the Shipka Pass is a beautiful and dramatic one, though in fog or poor weather it offers a reminder that this mountain barrier is still formidable. The walk from the car park at Shipka Pass up to the **Freedom Monument** at the summit (*Вр Столетов, Паметника Шипка*; ⊕ *09.00–17.00 daily; free*) is also quite formidable, involving 500 steps! However, if you are lucky enough to have a clear day, the panorama is unforgettable. The monument commemorates the defenders of the pass, the 6,000 Russians and Bulgarians who resisted 27,000 Turks who were on their way to raise the siege of Pleven in 1877. Although they were so heavily outnumbered, the weather conditions were terrible and they ran out of ammunition after three days, the Russians and Bulgarians did not give in. They threw rocks, trees and corpses at the Turks, and held on at the pass until Pleven surrendered.

At the nearby restaurant you can buy the yoghurt which experts regard as the finest in Bulgaria; it is made from buffalo milk and has a very rich smooth taste.

Below the pass is the village of Shipka. As you make the steep descent you get frequent glimpses of the gold onion-shaped domes of the **Nativity Memorial Church** (*Мемориална църква Рождество Христово*; ⊕ *08.30–17.30 daily*) built to a Russian architect's design between 1885 and 1902. From the outside, set against the wooded backdrop, it looks like a vividly coloured jewel. There is gold, deep green, white and rose pink. The interior is also very ornate. It has 17 bells, 12 of which were made entirely from melted-down shell cases and shrapnel from the battlefield.

BOZHENTSI (БОЖЕНЦИ)

Bozhentsi is an architectural historical reserve (✆ 066 804462; e bozhentsy@abv.bg; ⊕ *09.00–18.00 daily*) and one of the most charming villages in the area.

According to legend, Bozhentsi was founded by a noblewoman, Bozhena, and her nine sons, who fled from Veliko Turnovo after the fall of the Second Kingdom. It flourished from the 18th century onward, its smiths, carpenters and other craftsmen trading their wares in Austria, Russia and the rest of the Ottoman Empire.

Nowadays it is not a working village; indeed, it gives the impression of being a village in a fairy tale where everyone has been put under a spell for a hundred years.

Scattered seemingly at random in a quiet valley are about a hundred wood-and-stone houses with their distinctive heavy roofs of hand-cut stone slabs. Many are whitewashed, a contrast to the dark carved wood of their verandas and gates, and the roof is topped by white chimneys. One or two are house-museums with 19th-century furnishings. The layout of each house is similar, with the high-ceilinged ground floor used for business premises, shops, cellars, stables or animal housing. The outdoor staircase leads up to the hall, off which are a guest room, a kitchen and a bedroom. Large corner fireplaces are typical of this area. The furnishings are lavish with oak panelling, carved ceilings and cupboards, and colourful rugs.

Getting there and away Bozhentsi is 17m east of Gabrovo. There are three **buses** daily from Gabrovo, taking half an hour.

Where to stay The local museum offers accommodation in five of the **village houses**. They are all 100–200-year-old cultural monuments with traditional decoration and furniture. Ask at the reception at the entrance of the village (➜ 066 804462; e bozhentsy@abv.bg; €–€€). You can book a room or a whole house.

Fenerite (12 rooms) Kmetovtsi village; ➜ 067 193267; m 0888 383125; www.fenerite.bg. Small hotel on the road to Bozhentsi (4km away). An 1865 inn nicely renovated as a hotel, with a very good restaurant attached to it. €€

Sharlopovata & Parlapulovata kushti m 0899 972917; e office@yantrabg.com; www. bhouses.com. Nicely converted into luxurious guesthouses, though access is difficult & the welcome indifferent. €€

Where to eat and drink Mehana Bozhentsi (m 0899 440639; http://mehanabojentsi.com; €) is the oldest tavern in the village and serves traditional dishes.

What to see and do The **house-museums of Grandma Rayna and Doncho Popa** (Дом-музей на баба Райна и Дончо попа; ☉ summer 09.00–18.00, winter 09.00–17.00, both daily; adult 2lv, guided tour in English 4lv) date from the late 18th and early 19th century and reveal the details of two contrasting examples of everyday life here. The former shows a frugal life, which would have been the norm, whereas the latter is the home of a wealthy wool merchant. There are also some craft workshops which are interesting to visit and where you can buy souvenirs. The cell school has interesting exhibits of survaknitsi, the twigs of dogwood decorated with popcorn, peppers, small dried fruits and ribbons, which children use to tap their elders on the back and wish them 'A Happy New Year!' There are also a wide variety of the red-and-white woollen martenitsi which Bulgarians give each other on 1 March as a spring wish for good health.

Bozhentsi is typical of many mountain villages, where the houses are sturdily built to keep out the extremes of heat and cold, using plentiful local materials such as stone and hardwoods. In the past these scattered communities would have been much more isolated than they are today, and each was a microcosm of the Bulgarian village life which famous writers such as Ivan Vazov, Yordan Yovkov and Elin Pelin have immortalised. They are as typical of Bulgaria's literary tradition as Charles Dickens is of Victorian England.

TRYAVNA (ТРЯВНА) *Telephone code: 0677*
Like several other mountain villages in the area, Tryavna was founded by refugees from Veliko Turnovo. During the Ottoman occupation some strategically important villages, of which Tryavna was one, were given exemption from the heavy burden of taxation which funded the Turkish administration. In return they were expected to guard a pass or a route. These villages therefore prospered and expanded and

many have survived intact. Others closer to major routes used by the Turks were frequently burned down or destroyed in retribution for attempted uprisings. At Tryavna they guarded the route between the Danube and Kazanluk. However, they maintained a defiant attitude by rejecting Islam and refusing to have any Turkish families in the town.

According to local legend, the town is named after the lush pastures that surround it, *treva* meaning 'grass'. Place names are often a joy in Bulgaria; we drove through Torbaluzhite (*Торбалъжите*), meaning 'a bag of lies' to reach here. The Tryavna house typically stands in its own courtyard, has two storeys and is roofed with heavy stone slabs to protect it from the snows of winter and the heat of summer. The eaves are broad and overhang the house protectively, and there are elegant wooden balconies and fine oriel windows. Although the houses are similar to those in nearby Bozhentsi, Tryavna feels like a busy little town rather than a museum.

Getting there and away There are **buses** (*bus station* ☎ *63413*) from Gabrovo once or twice an hour, between 06.30 and 19.30, taking 40 minutes.

Tourist information The tourist information office is on ul Angel Kunchev 33 (☎ *62247*; e *tourinfo-tryavna@globcom.net; www.tryavna.bg*).

🏠 Where to stay

🏠 **Art-M** (6 rooms) ul Angel Kunchev 20; m 0887 097373; e artm@artmgallery.com; www. artmgallery.com. A really good place to stay in the heart of the Old Town. Good-value stylish rooms, & a very warm welcome. €–€€

🏠 **Hilez** (20 rooms) ul Stara Planina 17; ☎66920; m 0899 932470; e info@hotelhilez. net; www.hilez.tryavna.biz. Modern hotel in the centre of the town with large, comfortable rooms. *Mehana*. €€

🏠 **Ralitsa** (31 beds) ul Kaleto 16A; ☎62262; e hotelralica@abv.bg; www.ralitsa.tryavna.biz. Big hotel complex outside town, popular with

Sofia & other weekenders. Convenient starting point for walks. €€

🏠 **Tryavna Kompleks** (59 rooms) ul Angel Kunchev 46; ☎63448; e complex.tryavna@gmail. com; www.complex.tryavna.biz. Good central location, but dated. Spa & fitness facilities. €€

🏠 **Zograf Inn** pl P R Slaveykov 1; ☎64970; m 0882 447314; e zografhotel@gmail.com; http://zograf.tryavna.biz. Recently built complex in an old style, next to the historic clocktower & the old school. *Mehana* & art galleries on the ground floor. €€

🍴 Where to eat and drink

As well as the restaurants listed here, some of the hotels above have good *mehanas*.

🍴 **Balabanovata Kushta** ul P R Slaveykov 30–33; ☎62124; m 0888 886403; www. balabanovata-kashta.tryavna.biz. Cosy little restaurant 100m from Daskalov House. Recommended. €€

🍴 **Pizza Domino** ul Angel Kunchev 36; ☎62322; http://brashlyan.tryavna.biz/domino. Pleasant atmosphere in beautiful National Revival-period

building. Always good pizzas, pasta & salads. €–€€

🍴 **Starata Loza** ul P R Slaveykov 44; ☎64501; m 0887 810257; e starata-loza@tryavna.biz; http://starata-loza.tryavna.biz. Opposite Daskalov House. One of the oldest restaurants in Tryavna, with a charming courtyard. Bulgarian & unusual local specialities. Big choice of *rakiyas*. €–€€

What to see and do The woodcarving tradition of Tryavna is well known, and the small town and its museums, church and numerous old houses present a harmonious whole, which is a pleasure to wander round. All the museums are open daily at the same times: 09.00–16.30 in winter and 09.00–18.00 in summer, unless otherwise specified. The much-photographed central square with its clocktower, built in 1814, is the hub of the town. It is worth walking along each of the cobbled streets leading off it. Across the old humpbacked bridge over the clear Trevnenska River is **Daskalov House** (*Даскаловата къща; ul Slaveykov 27;* \62166; ⊕ 09.00–18.00; *adult 3lv*). It was built in the first decade of the 19th century for Hadzhi Hristo Daskalov, a wealthy merchant who traded in rose oil and silk. The house is symmetrical in form but inside is a riot of carving: suns on the ceilings, and birds and flowers among the favoured motifs on cupboards, doors and furnishings. There are two spectacular sunburst ceilings; it is said that two rivals in the art of woodcarving, Dimitur Oshanets and his apprentice Ivan Bochukovetsa, had a bet as to who could produce the finest ceiling. History does not relate who won, but both are masterpieces. They were created between the days of Sv Georgi and Sv Dimitur (that is between May and October). All the interiors are enhanced by bright blankets, cushions and rugs. There is also a **small woodcarving museum** with examples of the craft and the tools used to create them. Flowers were the favourite motif but doves, nightingales and peacocks feature, and even exotic creatures such as camels.

The **Church of the Archangel Michael** (*Черквата Архангел Михаил; pl Kapitan Dyado Nikola;* ⊕ 07.00–noon & 15.00–17.30 daily; *adult 1lv*) seems almost smothered by its roof, perhaps because it is so low. Though destroyed in 1798, it was rebuilt by 1819 at a time when local craftsmanship was at its height. Several woodcarvers were involved in the creation of the detailed iconostasis, with its 12 intricate scenes, and there is an elaborate bishop's throne. Skilful icon painters have contributed to the elaborate effect. The Tryavna School style is characterised by its wonderful light and lacy effect, the heaviness of wood somehow lifted by the skill of the craftsmen.

The **House-Museum of Petko and Pencho Slaveykov** (*Дом-музей Петко и Пенчо Славейкови; ul P Slaveykov 50;* \ 62458; ⊕ summer 09.00–13.00 & 14.00–18.00, winter 08.00–noon & 13.00–17.00, both Wed–Sun; *adult 2lv*) has an exhibition of the works of the father-and-son writers and shows where and how they lived.

The **Old School** (*Школото; pl Kapitan Dyado Nikola 7;* \62517; ⊕ 09.00–18.00; *adult 3lv*), built in the late 1830s, was one of the first secular schools in Bulgaria. Petko Slaveykov was a teacher here. It is a very fine building currently housing a series of exhibitions including paintings and timepieces.

The town is the birthplace of the revolutionary Angel Kunchev, an associate of Vasil Levski. His **House-Museum** (*Дом-музей Ангел Кънчев; ul Angel Kunchev 39;* m 0896 755935; ⊕ summer 09.00–13.00 & 14.00–18.00, winter 08.00–noon & 13.00–17.00, both Tue–Sat) is part of the main square ensemble. The house was built by his father, obviously a skilled craftsman. Kunchev became a revolutionary at a young age, but it was his dramatic suicide that secured his place in history. He was stopped by the police when boarding a ship without a passport at Ruse. He feared he might betray his fellow revolutionaries if he was tortured, so shot himself. Levski approved of his honourable death. The museum now hosts a rich collection of Asian and African art, donated to the town by the Bulgarian sculptor Zlatko Paunov.

The **Church of Sv Georgi** (*Св Георги Победоносец;* ⊕ 07.30–noon & 14.30–17.30 daily) was built between 1848 and 1852; its woodcarvings and icons are more fine examples of local workmanship.

The **Tryavna Icon Painting School Museum** (*Музей Тревненска иконописна школа*) is housed in the tsar's chapel away from the centre. There are over 160 original works, as well as tools and paints.

Tryavna masons built churches, houses and schools in many places in Bulgaria, notably Zheravna and Bozhentsi, but also in Serbia, Turkey and other neighbouring countries. The woodcarvers were even more famous and in 1920 a vocational school was opened which still educates talented craftsmen. Their work can be seen in Gabrovo, Troyan, Arbanasi and many other towns and villages. They used a wide variety of woods: walnut, pear, sycamore, lime, birch, poplar and holm oak. The Tryavna icon painters were also famous, following the traditions of the medieval Veliko Turnovo School during the 19th-century National Revival.

In 1798 the town was almost destroyed by bandits, but its inhabitants at once began rebuilding. Tryavna was unique because of the high proportion of people who were craftsmen. Over the years the Vitanov family alone produced more than 50 well-known craftsmen, and whole families were involved in icon painting, displaying exceptional talent. The most extraordinary thing about Tryavna is not only the huge number of craftsmen who were born here, but also their considerable output and the fact that it was a phenomenon that lasted for several generations.

DRYANOVO (ДРЯНОВО) *Telephone code: 0676*

The name means 'the place of dogwood', and it has been an inhabited site since prehistoric times, as evidence found in Bacho Kiro Cave, to the west of the monastery, shows.

Getting there and away There are **trains** (*railway station* `73209`) from Ruse (*1 daily; 3hrs 10mins*) and Stara Zagora (*4 daily; 3hrs*).

There are **buses** (*bus station* `72045`) from Veliko Turnovo (*1 daily; 40mins*), Gabrovo (*hourly 05.30–19.00 Mon–Fri; 30mins*) and Dryanovski Monastery (*summer only; 3 daily; 15mins*).

Tourist information The tourist information office is on ul Shipka 65 (`98097`; e *tic_dryanovo@abv.bg*).

Where to stay

Olimp (8 rooms) ul Stefan Stambolov 44; `75395`. Small family hotel in the pedestrianised centre, with nicely furnished, clean & light rooms. **€–€€**

Park-hotel Dryanovo (72 rooms) pl Stadiona; `72245`; e parkhoteldryanovo@abv.bg; www.parkhoteldryanovo.com. Modern hotel in the centre. Excellent value. **€€**

Where to eat and drink
The restaurant of the **Park-hotel Dryanovo** (see above; **€€**) is the best place to eat. There are also several small places around the main square.

What to see and do There is a small **museum** (*музей; ul Shipka 82;* `72097`; e *ficheto@mail.bg;* 08.00–noon & 13.00–17.00 daily; adult 3lv) about the masterbuilder Nikolai Ivanov Fichev, known as Kolyo Ficheto, who was born here in 1800. He studied building from an early age, and by the time he was 36 he was universally acknowledged as a master craftsman. He had surpassed the skills of his teachers and had innovative ideas which others followed. He built bridges, churches, inns and houses, many of the masterpieces of the National Revival period.

The building of the **Church of Sv Nikolai** (*Църквата Св Николай*), a domed basilica supported by wooden columns, began in 1835 but was completed by Kolyo Ficheto. It was after this that he was recognised as a master of his trade.

The **Lafchieva House** (*Лафчиевата къща; ul Shipka 92*), built in 1840, is a three-storey wooden house constructed without the use of a single nail.

Dryanovski Monastery (Дряновски манастир) This monastery has its origins in the Second Bulgarian Kingdom in the late 12th century, but has been destroyed and rebuilt many times. It has been on this site since 1845, when its monks became involved in revolutionary activity against the Ottoman Empire. During the uprising in April 1876, rebel leaders and 200 men sheltered here. In a fierce nine-day battle in which they were heavily outnumbered, rebels and monks led by Bacho Kiro and the priest Hariton were killed and the monastery was burned down, leaving only part of the stone church. What you see now is a sympathetic reconstruction. The **monastery museum** (⊕ *09.00–17.00 Mon–Fri, 09.30–16.00 Sat–Sun; adult 3lv*) honours the rebels who died here.

Bacho Kiro Cave (*Пещерата Бачо Киро;* ⊕ *summer 09.00–18.00 daily, winter 10.00–16.00 Fri–Sun; adult 2lv*) Bacho Kiro Cave is a short walk from the monastery. Some formations are floodlit. The Stone Age pottery, flint knives and other artefacts that were found here are in the monastery museum.

VELIKO TURNOVO (ВЕЛИКО ТЪРНОВО) *Telephone code: 062*

Veliko Turnovo was the capital of Bulgaria during its period of medieval greatness (12th–14th century – Second Bulgarian Kingdom). After 500 years of subjugation under the Ottoman Empire, Veliko Turnovo was, symbolically, chosen in 1879 as the location for the meeting of the Grand National Assembly, which drew up the constitution of the newly liberated state.

Veliko Turnovo is probably the most picturesque Bulgarian city, its houses seemingly stacked up on the high banks of the sinuous River Yantra. In medieval times it was seen as second only to Constantinople in splendour, and it became a flourishing city again during the 19th-century National Revival. It is set on three hills round which the river curves and loops. Each house is perched vertiginously on a precipice, some houses actually needing to be entered through the house below them. Every building has successfully overcome major architectural problems. It is possible to walk along an alley with buildings towering above you on one side and an aerial view of a church belfry on the other. There are tantalising glimpses across to the Tsarevets and Trapezitsa hills, and wonderful views across the river to the wooded hillsides which surround the city. It is worth going down to the riverbank in the evening; here frogs croak out their courtship songs, and the houses and lights are reflected in the water. From a distance the whole improbable structure of the city looks as if it is bound together only by the fragile lacework of vines, roses and geraniums which seem to grow on, up and over the houses.

GETTING THERE AND AWAY There are **trains** (*railway station* ☏ *620065*) from Plovdiv (*1 daily direct, 3 daily with a change at Stara Zagora; 5hrs*), Gabrovo (*3 daily with a change at Tsareva Livada; 2hrs*) and Gorna Oryahovitsa (*10 daily; 20mins*).

Note that Veliko Turnovo only has a small railway station; it is better to go to **Gorna Oryahovitsa** (7km away) which is one of the main railway junctions for northern Bulgaria (☏ *826118*). Direct trains arrive there from Varna (*3 daily; 4hrs*), Ruse (*10 daily; 2hrs*), Pleven (*8 daily; 1½hrs*), Stara Zagora (*6 daily; 4hrs*) and Sofia (*8 daily; 4hrs 45mins*).

There are two main **bus stations** in Veliko Turnovo. Bus Station Zapad (*ul Nikola Gabrovski 7;* ↘ *640908*) serves buses to the countryside. To get there take buses 10, 12, 14 or 70 from the centre (4km away). There are buses from Elena (*6 daily; 1hr 15mins*), Kazanluk (*4 daily; 2hrs 20mins*), Gabrovo (*hourly 06.00–18.00; 1hr*), Kilifarevo (*6 buses daily; 50mins*), Lovech (*4 daily; 2hrs*), Sevlievo (*4 daily; 1hr*), Svishtov (*4 daily; 2hrs 40mins*), Ruse (*8 daily; 2hrs*), Sliven (*8 daily; 2hrs*) and Plovdiv (*4 daily; 4hrs*).

Bus Station Yug (*ul Hristo Botev 74;* ↘ *620014*) is closer to the centre and serves buses to Sofia and the Black Sea coast. There are buses from Sofia (*hourly; 4hrs*). Varna buses (*10 daily*) come via Shumen, taking 2 hours from Shumen and 4 hours from Varna.

There is also Etap Bus Station, which is run by a private company from outside Hotel Etar (↖ *630564*). They run hourly buses to Sofia, two daily to Varna, and one daily to Dobrich, Kavarna, Balchik and Shumen.

TOURIST INFORMATION There is a tourist information office on ul Hristo Botev 5 (↖ *622148;* e *ticvt2@gmail.com; www.velikoturnovo.info;* ⊕ *09.00–noon & 13.00–18.00 Mon–Fri*). Every day there is a free guided 2-hour walking tour of Veliko Turnovo, starting from the tourist office (m *0885 030845, 0883 369024*).

WHERE TO STAY *Map, page 173*

⌂ **Anhea** (10 rooms) ul Nezavisimost 32; ↘577713; www.anheabg.com. Central, great views, clean rooms, helpful owners. Very popular. €€

⌂ **Bolyari** (18 rooms) ul Ivanka Hristova Boteva 2; ↘606002; m 0888 378206; e boliarihotel@ yahoo.com; www.boliarihotel.com. Centrally located, built in National Revival style with numerous overhangs & wooden balconies. Great views from the rooms. Good value. €–€€

⌂ **Etar** (86 rooms) ul Ivailo 2; ↘621838; m 0888 889117; e hoteletar@hotmail.com. Unexciting place next to bus station. Some rooms renovated, good views. A possibility if everything else is booked. €–€€

⌂ **Grand Hotel Veliko Turnovo** (201 rooms) ul Alexander Penchev 2; m 936365. Rather ugly architecture, overpriced & a bit gloomy, though great views. Mainly frequented by tour groups. €€€

⌂ **Gurko** (11 rooms) ul General Gurko 33; ↘672838; m 0887 858965; e hotel_gurko@ abv.bg; www.hotel-gurko.com. One of the most popular places to stay in Veliko Turnovo, so make sure you book in advance. The rooms are big, clean & nicely furnished with fantastic views. The restaurant on the ground floor is well known for its great cuisine. €€–€€€

⌂ **Hikers Hostel** ul Rezervoarska 91; m 0889 691661; e info@hikers-hostel.org; www.hikers-

hostel.org/vt. Great views, very popular, owner offers lifts to & from bus & train stations. Spartan dormitory rooms but warm & relaxed welcome more than compensates. €

⌂ **Nomads Hostel** ul General Gurko 27; ↘603092; e info@nomadshostel.com; www. nomadshostel.com. The hosts are friendly, the b/fasts generous, relaxed ambience with enthusiasm for green lifestyle. €

⌂ **Premier** (43 rooms) ul Sava Penchev 1; ↘615555; m 0886 056565; e hotel.premier@ abv.bg; www.hotelpremier-bg.com. One of the recently built hotels, equipped with lots of facilities, including rooftop pool; helpful staff. €€€

⌂ **Tashkov Guesthouse** (3 rooms) ul General Gurko 19; ↘635801; m 0887 437419; e office@ tashkoff.com. Nicely furnished guesthouse, an excellent option for budget travellers; internet access. €–€€

⌂ **Tsarevets** (10 rooms) ul Chitalishtna 23; ↘601885; m 0886 462626; e hoteltsarevets@ gmail.bg; www.tsarevetshotel.com. Comfortable & friendly hotel close to the fortress. €€

⌂ **Yantra** (71 rooms) ul Opulchenska 2; ↘600607; e office@yantrabg.com; www. yantrabg.com. The restored former state-run hotel has comfortable rooms with great views (make sure you get a room at the back). €€€

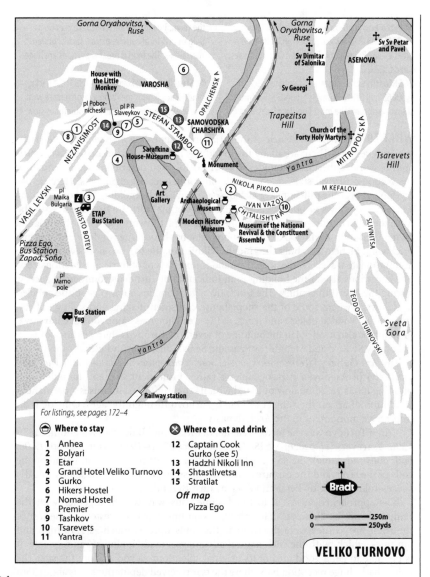

For listings, see pages 172–4

🛏 Where to stay

1 Anhea
2 Bolyari
3 Etar
4 Grand Hotel Veliko Turnovo
5 Gurko
6 Hikers Hostel
7 Nomad Hostel
8 Premier
9 Tashkov
10 Tsarevets
11 Yantra

✖ Where to eat and drink

12 Captain Cook
   Gurko (see 5)
13 Hadzhi Nikoli Inn
14 Shtastlivetsa
15 Stratilat

Off map
   Pizza Ego

N

Bradt

0 ——————— 250m
0 ——————— 250yds

VELIKO TURNOVO

✖ WHERE TO EAT AND DRINK *Map, above*

As well as the places listed below, there are also several pizza and doner kebab places along ul Nezavisimost.

✖ Captain Cook ul Stefan Stambolov 50A; ☎637909. Rather expensive fish restaurant. Still, the service is efficient & this is the only proper place to have Black Sea fish. €€–€€€

✖ Gurko See page 172. Traditional-style restaurant with Bulgarian & local specialities, & good wines; warm atmosphere. €€

✖ Hadzhi Nikoli Inn ul Rakovski 19; ☎651291; m 0879 066455; e office@hanhadjinikoli.com; www.hanhadjinikoli.com. Probably the finest dining in the finest building in the city. Modern European cuisine with a twist. Good selection of wines. €€€–€€€€

✗ Pizza Ego ul Nezavisimost 17; ☎601804; 📱 0885 044719; www.ego-vt.com. Tasty food & great views. Bulgarian & European cuisine, steaks, salads. €–€€

✗ Shtastlivetsa ul Stefan Stambolov 79; ☎600656; ul Hristo Botev 3; ☎606053; e office@ shtastliveca.com. The most popular places in the town. Two restaurants: both are very busy. Bulgarian & local cuisine, pizzas, salads, grilled specialities. The food is great & portions are huge. €€

✗ Stratilat ul Rakovski 11; ☎635313. Snacks, sandwiches & light meals on a large terrace with fine views. Always busy, service sometimes slow. €

WHAT TO SEE AND DO Much of Bulgaria's most appealing architecture dates from the 19th century. There are many fine buildings from this period in Turnovo which are the work of the master-builder Kolyo Ficheto, often described as the founder of the National Revival style, and certainly one of its greatest exponents. Here he has triumphed over the difficulties of lack of space and light by building tall houses, many with oriel windows or open arcading. Examples of his work are the **House with the Monkey**, a tall house with the little figure grimacing at the world, said to be the original owner of the house who looked like a monkey! It has handsome windows and unusual brickwork. Ficheto also built the **Hadzhi Nikoli Inn**; the top two floors were used to accommodate travellers, the arched verandas reminiscent of those at Rila Monastery. The enormous size of the building is an indication of Turnovo's commercial success during the late 19th century. The inn (now a very fine restaurant) is on the cobbled ul Rakovski, where some of the shops house craftsmen making and selling pottery, rugs, silver, wooden objects and icons, in the area known as **Samovodska Charshiya**. Ficheto was also involved in the building of several of Turnovo's churches, including Sv Nikola, Sv Sv Kiril and Metodii, Sv Spas and Sv Sv Konstantin and Elena.

The **Art Gallery** (*Държавна художествена галерия;* ⊕ *10.00–18.00 Tue–Sun; adult 4lv*) in Asenovtsi Park occupies a rather prominent site, and though a fine building it has yet to mellow or blend with its surroundings. It houses a permanent exhibition of art on the subject of Veliko Turnovo through the ages. Outside is an impressive monument to the Asen dynasty.

Veliko Turnovo was the fortress capital of the Second Bulgarian Kingdom, 1187–1396. **Tsarevets** (*Царевец;* ☎638841; ⊕ *summer 08.00–19.00, winter 09.00–17.00, both daily; adult 6lv*), the so-called royal hill, is almost made into an island by the coils of the river, and the capture of this strong strategic position made possible the successful rebellion by Petar and Asen against Byzantium in 1185.

It is approached across a fortified stone causeway which, together with the ramparts and the elements determining its outline, has been restored. The rest of the ruins are as they were discovered. The walls were as much as 12m high and 3m thick which, with the site's natural advantages, made it almost impregnable. It is possible to get a good idea of its original splendour as you explore the site. The palace had a huge reception hall where the tsar received deputations; it is about 35m by 16m, divided into three by rows of columns. On the walls there were apparently historical scenes portrayed in mosaics and frescoes.

At the summit stands the completely rebuilt Patriarchal Church, decorated with modern and rather uninspiring murals of scenes from Bulgaria's history. The views alone are adequate reward for the steep climb. Baldwin's Tower to the southeast was where the Emperor Baldwin of Flanders was imprisoned after being captured by Tsar Kaloyan during the Fourth Crusade. Nearby the execution rock was a convenient place from which to push enemies and traitors!

Sound and Light (*Звук и светлина,* or *Аудио-визуална програма Царевград Търнов - звук и светлина* in full) is a spectacular performance that takes place several times a year on national holidays and during the tourist season, though it is difficult to find out in advance when it is going to happen. Spotlights and lasers light up the Tsarevets Hill with different colours, and solemn music and church bells accompany them. The glorious history of the Second Bulgarian Kingdom is the subject. The performance can be put on especially for a minimum of 30 people (✆ 636952).

Trapezitsa (*Трапезица*), another distinct hill, is still being excavated, but it seems that here the *bolyars* and leading clergymen had their mansions and churches. The remains of many churches have already been uncovered, as well as walls and fortified gates, and some 16 churches are currently being excavated. Between Trapezitsa and Tsarevets is the **Asenova quarter** where in medieval times the artisans and lower clergy lived. The churches (✆ *620481*; ⊕ *summer 09.00–noon & 13.00–18.00 daily, winter by appointment*) still stand, though a 20th-century earthquake levelled most domestic buildings here. The stunningly restored **Church of the Forty Holy Martyrs** (*Църква Св Четиридесет мъченици*) dates from 1230. Tsar Kaloyan's grave and signet ring were discovered here, and the murals include the oldest example of an illustrated calendar anywhere in the Balkans. There are also unique stone inscriptions: one, associated with Khan Omurtag, bearing a Greek inscription, has been brought here from its original site; the other, obviously inspired by it, recounts Asen II's defeat of his Byzantine enemy and his much enlarged territories, stretching from Adrianople to Durazzo.

The clairvoyant Vanga prophesied that when this church was restored 'Bulgaria will thrive'. Its reopening after years of neglect and intermittent restoration was attended by members of the government and diplomatic corps in September 2006. It was the major cathedral of the Second Bulgarian Kingdom, built by Tsar Ivan Asen II after his victory over the Byzantine army at Klokotnitsa.

In the same district is the **Church of Sv Sv Petar and Pavel** (*Църква Св Св Петър и Павел*) with fine murals and an unusual brick façade. This was at one time (Ottoman domination) the church of the Greek bishops of Turnovo, built in

BOGOMILISM

In medieval times belief in the Bogomil heresy was widespread. It is believed to have come from the teachings of a priest called Bogomil, a name which means 'beloved by God'.

Bogomil beliefs differed from Orthodox Christianity on the origin of evil. They rejected the story of the Creation and believed that the world had been created by Satan, God's elder son. They also rejected Christ's miracles, the Sacraments, and most of the ritual of orthodoxy. They particularly disliked the symbolism of the cross, associating it with Christ's murder.

They read only the Psalms, the Prophets, the Gospels and Revelation, and used only one prayer (Our Father) which they recited over a hundred times a day. Some sects were even more extreme, experimenting with nudism as a way back to the Garden of Eden or indulging in orgies in order to be made to repent. There were many attempts to curb the heresy, particularly during the period of the Second Bulgarian Kingdom. In 1211 the Bulgarian synod met in Veliko Turnovo to discuss the problem.

However, its followers were stubborn nonconformists, their persistence meaning that the heresy spread, reaching across the Balkans into southwest and northern France and Germany, and lasted from its beginnings in the 10th century until the 15th century, when much of its area of influence became part of the Ottoman Empire.

the 13th century and many times destroyed and rebuilt, only to be damaged again by the 1913 earthquake. Among its important murals are a Tree of Jesse, and above it a masterly Dormition of the Virgin. The original portrait of Sv Ivan of Rila is here, later copied at Rila.

Sv Dimitur of Salonika (*Св Димитър Солунски*) is the city's oldest church, built in 1185 to house the icon of the saint, now restored in the style of Nesebur churches. This was where Petar and Asen declared Bulgaria's independence and were crowned. **Sv Georgi** is nearby with its well-preserved early 17th-century frescoes of the Creation and the Last Judgement.

The **Sveta Gora** (*Света гора*, 'Holy Wood') hill was famous as the site of the Turnovo Literary School. In the 14th century there were reputedly more monasteries here than on Mount Athos. Icon painters were trained here and gospels copied. The Gospels of Tsar Ivan Alexander (see box, page 178) show that painting in miniature reached new levels of artistic achievement here. Nowadays the city's Kiril and Metodii University is on this site.

The **Archaeological Museum** (*Археологическия музей; ul Ivanka Hristova Boteva 2; ＼ 601528; ⊕ summer 09.00–18.00 Tue–Sun, winter 09.00–17.00 Mon–Fri; adult 6lv*) has exhibits from Neolithic to late medieval times. The unique gold treasure from the nearby Hotnitsa archaeological site is on display here. These excavations were in the news again in summer 2006 when the oldest gold earring ever discovered in the world was found here. It dates back to 7000BC, about 2,000 years older than any previous similar find. The earring is heavy and massive weighing 4g, and so far only one has been found. Excavations continue each summer.

There are also finds, including gold and silver jewellery and ceramics, from Nikopolis ad Istrum (page 180), a Roman administrative centre some 17km north of Veliko Turnovo, and from Turnovo itself.

The **Museum of the National Revival and the Constituent Assembly** (*Музей 'Възраждане и Учредително събрание'; pl Suedinenie 1; ＼ 682511; ⊕ summer 09.00–18.00 daily, winter 09.00–17.30, closed Tue; adult 6lv*) is housed in the old *konak*. The building itself is one of Kolyo Ficheto's masterpieces. The exhibition covers the economic and political development of Veliko Turnovo in the 19th century. The setting for the Constituent Assembly, which debated and adopted the new constitution in 1879, has been recreated.

Behind this museum is another, the **Modern History Museum** (*Музей нова и най-нова история; ⊕ 09.00–17.30 Mon–Fri; adult 6lv*), in the former Turkish prison. There are exhibits about the former prime minister, Stefan Stambolov, who was born in Turnovo, and about the Balkan wars and World War I.

Sarafkina House-Museum (*Музей Сарафкина къща; ul General Gurko 88; ⊕ 09.00–17.30 Mon–Fri; adult 6lv*) is a restored house from the National Revival period now hosting an ethnographic collection, with woodcarving, pottery and textile exhibits as well as a special display about early photography. Part of the pleasure is simply being inside this amazing house, which at first appears to be two storeys high, though actually another three overhang the river. Inside there is an unusual octagonal hall with a fine ceiling and elegant furnishings.

Veliko Turnovo was at the centre of many uprisings against the Turks; in 1598 and 1686 there were uprisings in expectation of help from, on the first occasion the Austrian Emperor, and on the second, after Polish victories against the Turks, other foreign armies. On similar lines Velcho the glazier, commemorated by the **monument** in front of the Yantra Hotel, had the idea of besieging Varna's fortress in the expectation of Russian assistance. He and his fellow conspirators were captured and hanged in 1835.

The National Revival-style houses here usually have two façades because often both the front and the back face a street. The streets Gurko and Kraibrayna are two particularly good examples. It is well worth walking along **ul General Gurko**. Every vista and group of houses on this long, curving street attracts attention, yet the charm of the street is its feeling of timelessness, that these old houses on this steep cliff are almost unchanged for over a hundred years.

VELIKO TURNOVO'S MONASTERIES As a legacy of Turnovo's spiritual and cultural pre-eminence in the past, there are still 16 monasteries within 15km of the city. Once there would have been many more, but these provide plenty of opportunities for the visitor. Among the finest are Kapinovski and Kilifarevski monasteries to the south (pages 180 and 181), and Holy Trinity and Preobrazhenski (the Transfiguration), two monasteries facing each other across a lovely valley to the north.

Holy Trinity (*Св Троица;* ☉ *dawn to dusk daily*) was founded in 1371 by Patriarch Evtimii who lived here as a monk before becoming the head of the Bulgarian church in 1375. However, the buildings visible today are from a 19th-century restoration. The monastery was the base of the Turnovo Literary School, where several eminent scholars were educated. The church was built by Kolyo Ficheto. The convent is at the end of a track in poor condition, a couple of hours' walk from Veliko Turnovo.

Preobrazhenski Monastery (*Преображенски манастир;* ☉ *dawn to dusk daily; adult 2lv*) is an interesting ensemble of buildings including four churches from the 19th century: God's Transfiguration, the Assumption, Andrey Purvozvany and Lazarus' Resurrection. The belltower was built by Kolyo Ficheto.

The monastery was founded in the 14th century but destroyed by the Ottoman invaders and abandoned. The buildings here date from the early 19th century when it was refounded and both Kolyo Ficheto and Zahari Zograf were involved in its construction and embellishment. Vasil Levski found shelter here too, as in so many monasteries.

Zograf painted a famous Wheel of Life as part of the external murals. The frescoes repay study as there are wonderful morality tales here: those heading for hell include thieves, traitors, adulterers, smugglers and witches, and also millers famous for selling short measures, innkeepers for the same sin and for watering wine.

The monastery is perilously positioned on an eroding cliff; subsidence has caused some buildings to collapse but fortunately not the main church.

AROUND VELIKO TURNOVO

ARBANASI (АРБАНАСИ) They have a saying here that if you have never visited the monasteries of Rila and Bachkovo, the village of Arbanasi and drunk Bulgarian plum brandy, your life has been like an empty suitcase. Arbanasi is certainly special. It is 4.8km northeast of Veliko Turnovo, on a high plateau with views across to Tsarevets. Some say it was founded by Albanian refugees fleeing the Kastriotis rebellion in 1466; others believe that it was the summer residence of the royal court in the 13th century.

Its houses are remarkable in that each resembles a fortress from the outside, while inside it is richly decorated with woodcarvings and murals. Arbanasi reached the height of its prosperity in the 17th and 18th centuries, when there were as many as 1,000 houses. Copper, gold and silver crafts flourished here, and each spring merchants left to sell the hides, dried meats, wool, furs and wine produced here, travelling to Hungary, Italy, Poland, Russia and even Persia and India, and returning with velvets, silks and spices.

Getting there and away If you are not driving, or walking, you'll need a taxi from Veliko Turnovo for the 4.8km trip.

THE GOSPELS OF TSAR IVAN ALEXANDER

These illustrated gospels are the outstanding treasure of 14th-century Bulgaria, demonstrating the height of its medieval culture on the eve of its defeat by the invading Ottoman Empire. Both Christianity and the Cyrillic script had by then been established in Bulgaria for 500 years, but it was to be almost another 500 years before Bulgaria was free again.

These beautifully illustrated gospels were commissioned in 1355 for Tsar Ivan Alexander and completed in just one year. They were the work of a scribe called Simeon and artists from the Turnovo School. Turnovo was the capital of Bulgaria at this time, and its ecclesiastical and cultural centre, continuing the tradition of artistic magnificence established at the earlier capitals of Pliska and Preslav.

The gospels contain 367 miniatures, one of which is an outstanding portrait of the tsar and his family. They were obviously intended as a family treasure as there are many private references, as well as the fascinating palindrome, a geometric word puzzle in which the title *The Four Gospels of Tsar Ivan Alexander* can be read both forwards and backwards many times.

When Turnovo was captured in 1393, the manuscript was taken to safety across the Danube to Moldavia, from where it must have been moved again at some point to Mount Athos, to the Monastery of St Paul. This was where the young Robert Curzon saw it when he was travelling. He described it as 'one of the most curious monuments of bygone days to be found in any library in Europe'. Curzon was an enthusiastic collector and, though only 23 years old, managed to convince the Archbishop of Canterbury to write a letter of recommendation to His Holiness Patriarch Gregorios requesting that he be allowed to explore the monasteries of Mount Athos, long known as a repository of antiquities.

The gospels made an immediate impression: 'The third manuscript was likewise a folio of the Gospel in the ancient Bulgarian language and like the other two in uncial [like capital] letters. The manuscript was quite full of illuminations from beginning to end. I had seen no book like it anywhere in the Levant, and I almost tumbled off the steps on which I was perched on the discovery of so extraordinary a volume.' Later when he was offered a memento of his visit he boldly asked for the book which had pleased him the most. 'I took down the illuminated folio of the Bulgarian gospels, and I could hardly believe I was awake when the *agoumenos* [the Abbot] gave it into my hands.'

The gathering by young British aristocrats on their grand tour of the finest examples of another country's culture now seems in many ways reprehensible, though in this case it seems that it was for the best, as in 1905 a major fire destroyed much of the library of St Paul's Monastery.

The illustrations are extraordinarily lively and expressive, the colours being mainly red, blue, gold and green. The artist's skill is of the finest standard and the work highly original, but there are some similarities to the expressive and realistic portraits at Boyana Church.

For those who'd like to know more, the British Library published a short monograph, *The Gospels of Tsar Ivan Alexander* by Ekaterina Dimitrova, in 1994.

Where to stay

Arbanasi Palace (19 rooms) ☎062 630176; e reservations@arbanassipalace.bg. Rather tired-looking exterior, but still a luxurious place, favoured by wealthy Bulgarians, with excellent facilities. €€€

Bohemi (18 rooms) m 0888 378206; e kintsvet@yahoo.com; www.boliarska.com. Slightly old-fashioned style, but well-maintained & well-equipped rooms. Good value. €–€€

Where to eat and drink

Izvora ul Opulchenska 2; ☎062 627917. Popular with tour groups, so may be booked up in high season. Bulgarian & local oven-baked dishes. €€

Lyuliaka ☎062 630260; m 0885 185650. Between the main square & Konstantsaliev House, this is a good place to eat, with a nice courtyard. Bulgarian & local specialities. €€

Payaka ☎062 606810. Near the main square, this is a very good place to dine with a lovely garden. Try the local chicken stew, nettle soup & a dessert called *kadaif*, & the usual selection of grills. €€

What to see and do As in many mountain villages during the Ottoman occupation, the inhabitants secured relief from the tax burden and other privileges in exchange for guarding the nearby mountain pass. As a result the village became a prosperous one.

The **house-museums** and churches have the same opening hours (m *0885 105282;* ⊕ *summer 09.00–noon & 13.00–18.00; winter 09.00–noon & 13.00–17.00, both daily, but it is necessary to book for a visit in winter*)

The **Konstantsalieva House** (*Константцалиева къща; adult 6lv*) is one of the finest in Arbanasi, and brings together the two distinctive features of life here. The spacious rooms with their panelled ceilings, heating stoves and comfortable furnishings are evidence of an elegant lifestyle, while the built-in escape routes from two of the rooms indicate that fear of attack was a constant consideration. The house was built at the end of the 17th century, and has been enlarged and reconstructed several times during the following years, especially after the 1798 fire which gutted the village, and is typical in style. Its stone-walled ground floor was used for servants' quarters and storage; the wooden upper floor is more lavish and would have housed the family. The whole is surrounded by walls with strong, nail-studded gates.

Other houses can be visited, such as the **Hadzhiiliev** (*Хаджиилиев*), with its wonderful wooden doors, and the **Kandilarov** (*Кандиларов*), with its fine panelled ceilings including one carved with the popular sunburst design.

The churches of the two convents, **Sv Nikolai** (*Св Николай*) and the **Holy Virgin** (*Св Богородица*), are both worth visiting, as are the four other stone churches in the village which were built between the 16th and 18th centuries. They all have interesting frescoes. All are far outshone, however, by the **Church of the Nativity** (*Църквата Рождество Христово; adult 6lv*). It has a long and complicated history – the first small church was erected during the second half of 16th century and its frescoes were completed in 1597. The enlargement and redecoration of the church was done during a period of almost 90 years during the 17th century. Its humble exterior is reminiscent of a low farm building (it has no belfry), yet from the moment of entry the visitor is assailed by powerful visual images. The main church and chapel had separate areas for men (the naos) and women (the narthex), and these and the entrance are covered from floor to ceiling with over 3,500 painted figures. The subjects include the Creation, the Fall, the Tree of Jesse, Greek philosophers and the first Wheel of Life in Bulgaria, later copied by

6

Zahari Zograf at Preobrazhenski Monastery and Bachkovo. Fortunately these 17th-century frescoes have survived fire, war and other hazards intact.

LYASKOVETS (ЛЯСКОВЕЦ) Nearby Lyaskovets is a pleasant small town known to Bulgarians for its winemaking. The **Petropavlovski Monastery** (*Петропавловски манастир*) is said to have been founded in the late 12th century but the present buildings are 19th century. In the town, the **Church of Sv Dimitur** (*Църквата Св Димитър*) was built by Kolyo Ficheto using wide carved stones for the walls. A fine old building houses Bulgaria's only **Horticulture and Viniculture Museum** (*Музей на градинарството и лозарството; ul Petar Karaminchev 12;* \ *0619 922191;* ☉ *09.00–14.00 Mon–Fri; adult 2lv*), in a traditional National Revival house; your visit ends with a glass of the local sparkling wine.

NIKOPOLIS AD ISTRUM Near the village of Nikyup (*Никюп*), 20km north of Veliko Turnovo, are the extensive ruins of a Roman town (☉ *summer 09.00–18.00, winter 10.00–16.00, both daily; adult 6lv*). It was founded by Emperor Trajan to celebrate his victory over the Dacians, who lived north of the Danube. The foundations were laid in about AD110. The town had all the usual public buildings: the forum, the odeon, basilicas and fortified gates. There is a great deal still to see here and everything is well labelled in Bulgarian and English.

This became the most important settlement between the Stara Planina and the Danube. It was attacked and partly destroyed by the Goths and Slavs in the 6th century. Excavations were begun here in the 19th century by the famous archaeologist and traveller Felix Kanitz.

KAPINOVSKI MONASTERY (КАПИНОВСКИ МАНАСТИР) If you travel from the fortress of Tsarevets in Veliko Turnovo to Kapinovski Monastery, you will find another fortress but on a smaller, homelier scale. The entrance of huge heavy doors is surrounded by vibrant frescoes, a striking contrast to the stone walls and timbers. Then a flight of stairs takes the visitor to the monastery yard, itself dominated by the church and a new belltower. There was a warm welcome from the two resident monks, one of whom showed us the frescoes depicting the Day of Judgement with lively devils prodding unfortunate sinners, and ghostly images rising from their graves.

Sofronii Vrachanski was the abbot here before he became Bishop of Vratsa in 1794. He was a great figure of the Bulgarian Renaissance who promoted the use of the Bulgarian language. His literary works included the first autobiography in Bulgarian – *The Life and Suffering of the Sinner Sofronii* – and a translation of Aesop's fables into Bulgarian. These helped to develop the standard written form of the language.

The exact date of the monastery's foundation is not certain but there is evidence of a building here in the 13th century. Like many Bulgarian monasteries, it had a period of pre-eminence during the Second Bulgarian Kingdom (1185–1396), only to be destroyed under Ottoman rule. Eventually in the 17th century reconstruction was permitted, but what is visible now is largely from the 19th century, when the church and cells for the monks were built. The monastery was involved with the preparations for uprisings against Turkish rule, including the April Uprising.

ELENA (ЕЛЕНА) *Telephone code: 06151*
This is another of Bulgaria's beautiful National Revival towns, and has a fine ethnographic complex beside the prominent mid-19th-century **Church of the Assumption** (*Църква Възнесение Господне*). Much less conspicuous, but much

more beautiful, is the **Church of Sv Nikola** (*Църква Св Никола*), a 16th-century structure rebuilt around 1805, after destruction by raiding Kurdzhaliya. With frescoes covering every surface, it is so vivid and lively – a feast for the eyes. Towards the end of the Ottoman domination Elena prospered as a centre for crafts, but also maintained a strong revolutionary tradition. Its citizens participated in several uprisings during the 19th century: Velcho's plot in 1835, Captain Dyado Nikola's uprising in 1856 and the Turnovo uprising of 1862. During the Liberation War a large part of the town was destroyed by fire, though about 130 buildings from the National Revival period survive. Among the town's fine buildings is the **House-Museum of Ilarion Makariopolski** (*Дом-музей Иларион Макариополски*), whose campaign to establish a Bulgarian church free from Greek control was successful in 1870.

In the 18th and 19th centuries it was a leading crafts town, noted for its production of a coarse woollen cloth, *aba*, used to make men's jackets, and silkworm breeding. In 1843 Ivan Momchilov of Elena established the first school for training teachers in Bulgaria, which still functions.

Getting there and away There are **buses** from Veliko Turnovo (*4 daily; 1hr 15mins*), Sofia (*1 daily, 2 on Fri; 4hrs*), Gorna Oryahovitsa (*4 daily; 1½hrs*) and Sliven (*1 daily, 2 on Fri; 2hrs*).

Tourist information There is a tourist information office at pl Ilarion Makariopolski 13 (✆ *7430*).

🏠 Where to stay

🏠 **Central** (6 rooms) ul Stoyan Mihailovski 4; ✆2348; m 0886 220338; e hotel_central@elena. vali.bg. Very good value, with a restaurant. **€**

🏠 **Elena** (55 rooms) pl Ilarion Makariopolski 1; ✆3632; m 0878 277538; e elena_hotel@abv.bg; www.helkk.com/main.htm. Centrally located with reasonable prices & decent-sized rooms. **€–€€**

🏠 **Kostadinovi Kushti** (7 rooms) ul Chukani; ✆7732; m 0878 911511; e elena_hotel@abv.bg; www.k-house.com. Charming complex of 3 houses with nicely arranged rooms. The only downside is that it is outside the town. **€–€€**

✗ Where to eat and drink
As well as those listed below, there are several bistro-type restaurants around the main square.

✗ **Kyosheto** ul Yeromonah Yosiv Bradatii 11; above the main square; m 0887 247553. Bulgarian & local specialities. **€–€€**

✗ **Truhchev** ul Ivan Kirilpov 4; m 0888 643264. The usual grilled meats & salads. **€–€€**

✗ **Usoeto** ul Sheitani 13; m 0888 423203. Good Bulgarian meals. **€–€€**

KILIFAREVSKI MONASTERY (КИЛИФАРЕВСКИ МАНАСТИР) The scenery is enchanting: rolling, well-wooded hills, with a series of small villages until you reach Kilifarevski – really a nunnery not a monastery. On a recent visit, there was a sung evening service in the church so closer examination of the interior wasn't possible, though the iconostasis, carved by Tryavna craftsmen, was a fine one.

Kilifarevski was the site of a famous school in the 14th century, where literary works were translated, and at one time there were several hundred monks working here, but this potentially important place was destroyed by the Turks in 1393. Today's buildings are 19th century, based around the Kolyo Ficheto **Church of Sv Dimitur** (*Църквата Св Димитър*). There are two older chapels with 16th-century frescoes adjoining the church.

KOTEL (КОТЕЛ) *Telephone code: 0453*

This is a small mountain town with a strong revolutionary tradition. It was also the birthplace of Sofronii Vrachanski (page 180) and Georgi Rakovski (see box, page 183). Like many other mountain towns, it was at its height during the 19th century, but unfortunately a fire in 1894 destroyed many of its old houses, though about a hundred remain and are well preserved.

Getting there and away There are **buses** (*bus station* ☏ *42052*) from Sofia (*2 daily; 4½hrs*), Sliven (*6 daily; 1hr*), Burgas (*3 daily; 3hrs*), Shumen (*1 daily; 2hrs 20mins*), Plovdiv (*3 daily; 4hrs*) and Yambol (*1 daily; 2hrs*).

⌂ Where to stay

⌂ **Kotel** (25 rooms) ul Izvorska 49; m 0889 269134. Former state-run hotel, central but basic. **€**

⌂ **Starata Vodenitsa** (7 rooms) ul Luda Kamchia 1; ☏42360; m 0879 933994. Motel with popular restaurant. **€**

⌂ **Tara Guesthouse** (4 rooms) ul Novachka 6; ☏44050; m 0889 896282; e parkaliev@mail.bg; www.tara-bg.net. Small, modern & basic. **€**

✗ Where to eat and drink

Starata Vodenitsa (see above; **€–€€**) is a traditional *mehana* offering generous portions of local and Bulgarian specialities. Its location by the park is nice but a bit inconvenient as it is on the edge of town. There are also a few pizza places and traditional grills in the centre.

What to see and do The town is famous for its carpets and rugs. These are mostly kilim style with geometric patterns and strong colours such as red, black, blue and green. I have one here by my desk purchased in 1973, still in perfect condition.

The main square is dominated by the very gloomy **Pantheon** (*Пантеона;* ☏*42549;* ⊕ *winter 08.00–noon & 13.00–17.00, summer 09.00–18.00, both Mon–Sun; adult 3lv*) commemorating Rakovski. There is a small **museum** about him, Sofronii Vrachanski and other local figures.

The **Carpets and Woodcarving Hall** (*Зала дърворезба и килими; ul Izvorska 17;* ☏*42316;* ⊕ *08.00–noon & 13.30–17.30 daily; adult 3lv*) has a mixture of old and new kilims and presents a colourful scene. Kotel carpet-makers also produce *chergi*, which are usually just bright coloured stripes rather than having the complicated symbolic patterns of the kilims.

The **Ethnographic Museum** (*Етнографския музей; ul Altunlu Stoyan 5;* ☏*42315;* ⊕ *08.00–noon & 13.30–18.00 daily; adult 3lv*) is in an old house where the fairly prosperous merchant's family lived in close proximity, all eight sleeping in one room. Across the yard is the kitchen, with an impressive collection of cooking equipment.

Kotel is also known for its **folk music school** (*музикално училище*), where young people learn to play the traditional Bulgarian instruments.

ZHERAVNA (ЖЕРАВНА)

With its hilltop setting and large number of wooden houses with oversize roofs, Zheravna has a wonderful atmosphere of calm. The façades of all the 300 or so houses built in the 17th century face the sun.

There is the splendid **House-Museum of Sava Filaretov** (*Дом-музей Сава Филаретов;* ⊕ *09.00–noon & 14.00–17.00; adult 3lv*) built by Tryavna craftsmen in the 18th century, and demonstrating their typical woodcarving style on ceilings and

Rakovski was the revolutionary whose vision of Bulgaria's route to freedom probably came closest to the way it happened, though he didn't live to see it. He developed the idea of *haiduts*, or bandits, and how they had a tradition of opposition to the Turks, of living in the mountains, and thought this could be expanded and turned against the Turks, like a guerrilla war in fact. He was sentenced to death at the age of 20 for trying to invade Ottoman territory with just such a group, but he escaped to Belgrade where he formed a Bulgarian legion which fought with the Serbs against the Turks.

His idea of sending small groups of armed men to raise support among the local population was popular in émigré circles. They believed a bigger uprising would win support from the great powers. In practice this did not seem to be the case, as a small-scale uprising in 1867 had no success. This reduced Rakovski to despair, and he died later that year. His followers did not relinquish his ideas and others, notably Hristo Botev, died martyrs' deaths trying to carry them out. Rakovski was right in that when, after the massacre at Batak, the great powers finally got involved, Bulgaria won its freedom.

cupboards. Nearby, the **House-Museum of Rusi Chorbadzhii** (*Дом-музей Руси Чорбаджии; same price and opening times*) is similarly rich in brightly coloured rugs and shows the comfortable life of the merchants of Zheravna.

The house where the writer Yordan Yovkov was born has been restored, but there is not much information about him here, though the house evokes his humble origins: **Yovkov House** (*Къщата-музей на Йордан Йовков; same price and opening times*). If you are interested, the museum dedicated to him in Dobrich is the place to go.

The **Church of Sv Nikolai** (*Църквата Св Николай*) is the work of Tryavna masters and was built in 1833. It is very brightly decorated, giving the impression that the painters have just completed their work.

VELIKI PRESLAV (ВЕЛИКИ ПРЕСЛАВ)

HISTORY Preslav was founded by Khan Omurtag in AD821, and soon eclipsed Pliska. When it became the capital of the First Bulgarian Kingdom under Tsar Simeon's rule in 893, it acquired the prefix Veliki (Great). In the 10th century it was said to be the most populous town in the Balkans, and had many churches and a palace richly ornamented with paintings, precious metals and stones. It became the symbol of a new era, marking the transfer of influence from formerly pagan Pliska. Tsar Simeon transformed the grim fortress of Omurtag in style. The achievements of artists and craftsmen in decorative sculpture and painted ceramics reached new heights here.

The Exarch Ioan's description of Simeon's capital noted that when a visitor 'enters the palace and sees the high buildings and churches beautified with much stone, wood and colours, and inside with marble and copper, with silver and gold, he will not know what to compare them with, since he will never have seen such a thing in his own land.'

Preslav was razed in 972 and, though it recovered and was largely rebuilt, it never regained its former size and glory. Preslav was finally destroyed by the Turks, who used stone from it for other buildings, including Shumen's fine Tombul Mosque.

The outer part of the city was defended by strong walls and had a 'Golden' Church built in 907 with 12 marble columns, a gilded dome and mosaics (hence its name) and colourful ceramic tiles. The artists painted with ochre, green, deep red, violet and beige on cream-coloured tiles.

Simeon's interests were not just in palatial splendour, for he also invited scholars to Preslav and literature and natural sciences were studied; many translations were made from Greek into Bulgarian. Preslav became an intellectual centre from which the Bulgarian language, with its own Cyrillic alphabet, and the recently adopted Christian religion were able to spread.

GETTING THERE AND AWAY There are buses from Shumen every 4 hours taking half an hour.

WHAT TO SEE AND DO Today the visitor will find the ruins concentrated in an area of about 3km². There has been considerable restoration of the walls and palace buildings, giving some idea of its original impressiveness. The on-site **Archaeological Museum** (*Археологическия музей;* \ 053 843243; ⊕ *summer 09.00–18.00, winter 09.00–17.00, both daily; adult 3lv*) is worth visiting for its helpful plans and models. Exhibits include a gold treasure with very elaborate pieces of jewellery.

SHUMEN (ШУМЕН) *Telephone code: 054*

Shumen is almost surrounded on three sides by a plateau projecting from the Balkan Mountains. This hill above the town has been a fortified site since Thracian times. Here a Roman fortress, which guarded the route from the Danube Plain to the mountain passes of the Balkans, was built. There was a fortress on the plateau in the 12th century. The strategically important location meant that it became the site of the largest Turkish garrison town during the 500-year Ottoman occupation of Bulgaria. It was part of the empire's northern defence system, and had extensive ramparts.

During the period of the National Revival, Shumen was a thriving economic and cultural centre; here Bulgaria's first theatre and first orchestra were founded. During the 19th century Shumen offered sanctuary to various Polish and Hungarian political refugees, and there is a house-museum of the famous Hungarian revolutionary Louis Kossuth (Layosh Koshut).

The modern city still has an interesting old quarter and the largest mosque in the Balkans, and on the nearby hillside there are the ruins of the fine medieval fortress and a huge modern monument celebrating 1,300 years of Bulgaria, both clearly visible from the town.

GETTING THERE AND AWAY The bus and train stations are adjacent in the east of the town. There are **trains** (*railway station* \ 860155) from Varna (*10 daily; 2hrs*), Gorna Oryahovitsa (*10 daily; 2hrs 10mins*), Pleven (*7 daily; 3hrs 50mins*), Plovdiv (*1 daily; 6hrs*) and Sofia (*2 daily; 6½–7½hrs*).

There are **buses** (*bus station* \ 830890) from Burgas (*4 daily; 3hrs 40mins*), Varna (*11 daily; 2hrs*), Dobrich (*4 daily; 2hrs 15mins*), Kavarna (*1 daily; 2hrs 40mins*), Razgrad (*1 daily; 1hr*), Ruse (*3 daily; 2hrs 15mins*), Silistra (*3 daily; 3hrs*), Sliven (*1 daily; 3hrs*) and Sofia (*6 hourly; 5½hrs*).

TOURIST INFORMATION There is a tourist information office on bul Slavyanski 17 (\ 857773; e tic@shoumen.bg).

⌂ WHERE TO STAY

⌂ **Bohemi** (5 rooms, 3 apts & 7 lodges) ul Izvorna 20, Divdyadovo; ✆828110; m 0898 622007; e bohemy@abv.bg; www.bohemi.net. Modern hotel complex in the Divdyadovo district. It is inconvenient if you don't have a car (though you can take bus number 7 or a taxi). Excellent value, swimming pool. €€

⌂ **Shumen** (205 rooms) pl Oborishte 2; ✆800003; e office@hotel-shumen.com; www.hotel-shumen. com. Large hotel in centre opposite the mosque; business centre, excellent restaurant & *mehana*, bars, indoor swimming pool, sauna. €€–€€€

⌂ **Shumen-Rimini Club** (10 rooms) ul Haralan Angelov 2; ✆976423; m 0888 266553; e shumensint@ro-ni.net; www.riminiclub.com/ indexbg.htm. Two restored 19th-century buildings, with newly renovated, modern & very colourful rooms. Fitness & spa. €€

⌂ **Zamuka** (15 rooms) ul Vasil Levski 17; ✆800409; m 0885 237374; e zamaka@gmail. com; www.zamakbg.com. Perhaps the best value in the town. Modern hotel in the centre, close to the city park. €–€€

✗ WHERE TO EAT AND DRINK

✗ **Hotel Shumen Restaurant** See above. By reputation the best in town. The service is excellent & the views are good. €–€€

✗ **Osmarska Izba** pl Oborishte. One of the classic restaurants in Shumen, offering traditional cuisine & a good selection of wines in an authentic setting. €€

✗ **Pizza Elit** pl Slavyanski. Fast foods, pizzas & salads. €€

✗ **Popsheitanova Kushta** ul Tsar Osvoboditel 158/pl Oborishte; ✆802222; m 0896 629489; e office@popsheitanova.com. One of the best restaurants in the town. Authentic interior, varied menu with big portions of Bulgarian food, good selection of wines. €€

✗ **Stariyat Bor** ul Tsar Osvoboditel 154/pl Oborishte; ✆54807. Popular *mehana* offering Bulgarian food, soups, salads. Nice garden. €€

WHAT TO SEE AND DO Most of the fine 19th-century houses are on ul Tsar Osvoboditel, at its western end. Several are house-museums dedicated to eminent Bulgarians. Further west are two fine Turkish buildings, the **Tombul Mosque** and the **Bezesten** or covered market. In ul Stara Planina, to the north of the mosque, is the walled **Dyukmedzhian House**, a very fine 19th-century National Revival building, built for wealthy Armenian merchants.

The **Pancho Vladigerov House-Museum** (*Дом-музей Панчо Владигеров; ul Tsar Osvoboditel; ⊕ 09.00–17.00 Mon–Fri; adult 3lv*) has memorabilia from the life of the famous composer who lived during his early childhood in Shumen.

The **Dobri Voynikov House-Museum** (*Дом-музей Добри Войников; ul Tsar Osvoboditel; ⊕ 09.00–noon & 14.00–18.00 Mon–Fri; adult 3lv*) has theatrical memorabilia from the playwright's life.

The **Panayot Volov House-Museum** (*Дом-музей Панайот Волов; ul Enyu Markovski; ⊕ 09.00–17.00 Mon–Fri; adult 3lv*) commemorates a leader of the April Uprising who grew up here and perished in the River Yantra while trying to escape from the Turks.

The **Kossuth House-Museum** (*Дом-музей Кошут; ul Tsar Osvoboditel; ⊕ 09.00–17.00 Mon–Fri; adult 3lv*) is where the Hungarian revolutionary stayed for a few months in 1849.

The **History Museum** (*Историческия музей; bul Slavyanski 17; ⊕ 09.00–17.00 Mon–Fri; adult 3lv*) has a rich collection including Thracian and Roman artefacts and many finds from nearby Pliska and Preslav.

The **medieval fortress** seen from the town is on the same site as several earlier structures. The Thracians were the first to recognise the strategic importance of the site, but each succeeding power – Romans, Byzantines, Bulgars and Turks – continued to use it. During the Second Bulgarian Kingdom (1185–1396) the fortress took on its present appearance. At that time there were houses nearby but, when the Turks conquered the area, they extended the fortress and forced the townspeople to live in the valley, the site of present-day Shumen.

The **1300 Years of Bulgaria Monument** is a strange juxtaposition of various historical figures, constructed in concrete in larger-than-life dimensions, which is visible from all over Shumen. It was erected in 1981 to commemorate Bulgaria's existence as Europe's oldest nation-state.

The **Bezesten** (*Безистена*), which is in need of restoration, is a covered market built in the 16th century from large blocks of stone 'borrowed' from Preslav.

The **Tombul Dzhamiya** (*Томбул Джамия*) or mosque was built in 1744 at the instigation of Sherif Halil Pasha. He was a native of Shumen, who became a deputy Grand Vizier in the Ottoman administration in Constantinople. Obviously he remembered his home town fondly, and wanted to endow it with these fine buildings. The mosque formed part of a religious and educational complex, including a primary school, a *madrasa* and a library. Beside the entrance is a beautiful, arcaded courtyard with an elaborately decorated fountain. Inside the mosque, above the sea of rugs, there are glowing chandeliers beneath the impressive blue-and-gold domed ceiling. For many years the mosque was used as a museum, but it is now restored to its original purpose. The courtyard buildings are once again used as a school and boarding house for religious students. Shumen is an important centre for Muslims in northeast Bulgaria, many of whom travel considerable distances to attend the mosque during major Islamic festivals.

AROUND SHUMEN

PLISKA (ПЛИСКА) Pliska was the capital of the First Bulgarian Kingdom (681–1018), which adopted Christianity in 865, and enjoyed a golden age of both territorial expansion and cultural achievements until its defeat by the Byzantine Empire. Pliska was founded in the late 7th or early 8th century, and is less well preserved than its successor, Preslav, which became the capital in the late 9th century. It covered a large area, some 20km², and was protected by strategic citadels in the surrounding hills. The ruins are extensive, but nothing of any significant height remains. The museum has a helpful reconstruction. There was a concentric fortification system: an outer rampart with a moat, and inner walls with gates. These protected the houses of the *bolyars* and their temples and palaces in the centre. Between the two fortification rings were many churches and the dwellings of ordinary people.

The famous bronze rosette of Pliska with its seven rays is a symbol of the religious beliefs of the Bulgarians in the 7th–9th centuries and an indicator of their knowledge of astronomy. Here at Pliska, in 681, the date of the foundation of the Bulgarian state, Khan Asparuh is said to have put his horse's tail banner, the symbol of the steppe kingdom from which he had come, into the soil of the Slav settlement.

At Pliska there was obviously a high level of comfort: the remains of a water supply, sewerage system and the largest contemporary reservoir in Europe have been uncovered. Walking along the avenue of walnut trees, passing sleeping dogs and playing children to reach the **museum** (✆ *0532 32012;* ⊕ *09.00–17.00 daily*) it is hard now to imagine the splendour of Pliska. Even the museum, with its finds of the tools, weapons and storage pots of daily life, cannot summon up royal magnificence.

MADARA (МАДАРА) In a wooded hilly landscape between Stara Planina and the Danube, there is an unusual rocky massif, and high up on one inaccessible rock face is a mysterious carving. This is the famous **Madara Horseman** (*Мадарски конник;*

⊕ *summer 08.30–19.00, winter 08.30–17.00, both daily; adult 4lv).* It has been much eroded by wind and rain, but if you look carefully you will see that it depicts a triumphant ruler in a symbolic hunting scene. The horseman has speared a lion, probably representing a powerful enemy, with his lance. He is being followed by a dog, his loyal people, and led by a bird. In one hand he holds a wine cup. The figures are almost life-sized, and the scene covers some 40m². Madara is the only rock relief in Europe, and its unique importance was recognised by its inclusion on UNESCO's World Heritage list in 1979.

The various inscriptions, now very eroded, do not clarify the relief's origins. The oldest, from the 8th century, records a debt owed by the Emperor Justinian to the Bulgarian Khan Tervel for his help in reinstating him after he had been overthrown by conspirators. Many scholars believe that the horseman is much older than the inscriptions and represents the Thracian deity. The cup of wine in the horseman's hand is certainly evidence in favour of the Thracian connection, for the Thracians have gone down in history as warlike, wine-loving people. Experts believe the inscriptions indicate that the relief was a phenomenon which later Bulgarian rulers thought to be worth appropriating. Whatever its exact date, it is a powerful visual image and a statement of technical prowess.

Though the horseman is the main attraction, there are several other sights to see. The whole place has a feeling of great antiquity, of having been lived in since earliest times. There are **caves**, including a huge one under a mighty overhanging rock, close to a spring which is the source of the River Madara. The whole cliff face shows evidence of habitation; there were perhaps as many as 150 cells here, making it one of the largest **rock monasteries** in the Balkans.

In 2006 the **museum** (*same opening times as the rock relief*) reopened after a long period of renovation. A 2,000-year-old stone zodiac is one of the attractions. It is a sphere, 25cm in diameter, with the signs of the zodiac engraved on it – maybe priests in ancient times also tried to foretell the future. A marble tablet of three nymphs dating from Thracian times is one of the most valuable finds.

Visitors with enough energy and a head for heights can take the steep path up about 670 steps (yes, I lost count) to the top of the cliff. Here on a plateau are a ruined 5th-century fortress and two tumuli of the Thracian Getae tribe. There is a magnificent panoramic view which includes some excavated ruins, a Roman villa and a pagan temple. The wild flowers and darting lizards beside the path and on the plateau make the climb well worthwhile.

KYULEVCHA (КЮЛЕВЧА) About 3km south of Madara is this village, where Chiflik Elena (*4 rooms;* m *0887 201135;* e *office@georgievtours.com; www.chiflikelena.com*) is situated. This is a traditional homestead/smallholding where guests can experience aspects of village life. There is a kitchen for self-catering or the option of choosing from the menu of local specialities. The *mehana* is open all year round. There are flower and vegetable gardens, and themed guided walks are offered. For groups of 15 or more, folklore programmes and local craft demonstrations can be arranged.

THE LUDOGORIE

RAZGRAD (РАЗГРАД) *Telephone code: 084*
Razgrad, which developed on the site of the Roman town of Abritus, is an ancient settlement and its museums have some rich collections illustrating this. It is the main town of the Ludogorie region. The road to Isperih passes through rather beautiful, quiet, rolling, wooded countryside with huge fields.

Getting there and away There are **trains** (*railway station* ☏ *660704*) from Varna (*2 daily; 2hrs 50mins*), Gorna Oryahovitsa (*2 daily; 4hrs*) and Ruse (*6 daily; 1hr 10mins*).

There are **buses** (*bus station* ☏ *660810*) from Shumen (*6 daily; 1hr*), Isperih (*1–2 per hr Mon–Fri, 6 daily Sat–Sun; 40mins*), Ruse (*4 daily; 1hr 20mins*) and Sofia (*2 daily; 6hrs*).

Tourist information There is a tourist information office on pl Nezavisimost 2 (☏ *662324;* e *ticrazgrad@abv.bg; www.tic-razgrad.org*).

🏠 Where to stay and eat

🏠 **Accent** (13 rooms) ul Lyule Burgas 15; ☏660072; m 0888 766866; e accent_hotel@ abv.bg; www.hotel-accent.com. Traditional style, with an outdoor pool. Restaurant with Bulgarian cuisine. Friendly & helpful owners. €–€€

🏠 **Holiday Spa Ostrovche** 15km south of Razgrad towards Turgovishte, in the village of Ostrovche; m 0882 334433; e office@ostrovche. com; www.ostrovche.com. Luxury accommodation, spa, pool & tranquil location in a lime tree forest. €€

What to see and do The **Abritus Museum** (*Музея Абритус;* ⊕ *08.00–noon & 13.00–17.00 Mon–Fri; adult 3lv*) is one of the new generation of Bulgarian museums, beautifully arranged, smart and welcoming. There are plenty of interesting booklets to buy and the contents have Bulgarian and English captions. It has some major treasures on display marked as items of 'European Cultural Heritage', which the curator explained means that these are the only extant examples. There is beautiful gold jewellery and statuettes of idols, and a huge hoard of over 800 gold coins.

One of the great treasures of the museum is the Golden Pegasus, the front part of a winged horse. It is finely detailed, and perhaps was once part of a larger treasure. The winged horse, half-bird and half-horse, a fantastic mythical creature capable of extraordinary feats, has a special significance in Thracian iconography.

There is a display of items from the Sveshtari tomb: a wooden table, a glass sequin, a stone sculpture, a silver phiala (a saucer or flat bowl), gold earrings, a bronze mirror, a clay lamp and bowls and a lachrimarius (tear glass or bottle).

Abritus was the scene of fierce fighting between the Romans and Gothic tribes, hence the strong fortress walls and defensive towers. It was also a good example of Roman town planning with still-visible evidence of its water and sewerage systems. Also outside is the lapidarium, displaying larger artefacts such as tombstones, terracotta wheat containers and sacrificial altars.

At the **Ethnographic Museum** (*Етнографския музей;* ⊕ *08.00–noon & 13.00–17.00 Mon–Fri; adult 3lv*) there is a lot of very interesting material about the Kapantsi, whose clothes and customs are completely different from all around them. The museum has an astonishingly rich collection: bangles, *pafti* (the decorative buckles on women's costumes), jewellery, decorated hats for children, cushions, blankets, bags, towels and embroidered costumes for men and women.

Razgrad hosts an unusual annual festival dedicated to yoghurt! There are stalls with buckets and decorated earthenware pots full of yoghurt. Competitions are held for the best made, and a local poet has produced an *Ode to Yoghurt*. Three days at the end of July is the regular date for the event. There is folk music and dancing, and decorated donkey carts giving visitors a lift or acting as mobile shops for yoghurt and cheese.

ISPERIH (ИСПЕРИХ) *Telephone code: 08431*

Isperih is a small market town in the Ludogorie Hills, and is a convenient place from which to visit **Sboryanovo Historical and Archaeological Reserve** (*Историко-*

археологически резерват Сборяново; \ *4783;* ⊕ *09.00–16.30 Wed–Sun, closed Dec–Mar; adult 10lv).* This includes more than 140 monuments such as the ruins of prehistoric settlements, burial mounds, sanctuaries, a Thracian town, an early Byzantine castle and a medieval Turbe (Turkish tomb) and many others. For most people it is the **Sveshtari Thracian tomb** that is the main attraction.

Getting there and away There are **trains** (*railway station* \ *2047*) from Silistra (*3 daily; 2hrs*), Kaspichan (*1 daily; 1hr 40mins*) and Samuil (*4 daily; 30mins*).

There are **buses** (*bus station* \ *2111*) from Shumen (*2 daily; 1hr 40mins*), Gorna Oryahovitsa (*2 daily; 2hrs*), Dobrich (*2 daily; 3hrs*), Ruse (*4 daily; 2hrs*), Silistra (*2 daily; 2½hrs*) and Sofia (*2 daily; 6hrs 20mins*).

⌂ Where to stay, eat and drink
⌂ **Alen Mak** (23 rooms) ul Vasil Levski 79; \ 2359. Good hotel in the centre; the restaurant has a spacious garden & serves traditional Bulgarian cuisine. €

What to see and do These Thracian tombs, about 6km from Isperih, are on UNESCO's World Heritage list. There is now a very smart visitor centre here with plenty of interesting brochures to buy. There are timed entrances so you either need to book ahead, come at a quiet time (early or late in the day) or be prepared to wait.

The protected status of the area has benefited wildlife, and observant visitors may see over 40 bird species, endemic wild flowers and a variety of mammals.

The tour visits two tombs which have an ante-room and a chamber under semicylindrical domes. They have yielded fragments of vessels and weapons. The third tomb, the most interesting, is believed to be that of a ruler of the Thracian tribe, the Getae, and is called the **Royal Tomb**. This is a unique monument of Thracian-Hellenic art of the 3rd century BC. The quality of the architecture and decoration emphasise the power of the ruler for whom it was built. The mound covers a corridor leading to the three chambers of the tomb which are under a single barrel-vaulted ceiling. This is the most sophisticated roof, capable of supporting the weight of hundreds of tonnes of earth. The richest decoration is in the central chamber where the king was buried with his wife and five horses. The most striking image is of the ten caryatids, their arms raised as if to carry the roof – perhaps they are multiple images of the mother goddess. The stone figures and their clothing are extremely finely chiselled.

Nearby is Demir Baba Tekke, a Muslim shrine from the 16th century, the burial place of the revered Demir Baba. It is a simple, dignified building dwarfed by the cliffs behind it. It seems that the aura of the place was felt before Islam arrived, because Neolithic and Thracian settlements precede it. Local Muslims, known as Aliani, have traditionally been influenced by their Christian neighbours with whom they share various ceremonies here. People of both faiths tie strips of cloth to trees to ward off evil spirits.

Excavations continue here – there are over a hundred mounds! Researchers believe that the layout of the mounds is carefully calculated, mirroring the constellations of the stars. The plan of the necropolises suggests the idea of the Milky Way, the route of the soul to immortality.

ON THE DANUBE

SILISTRA (СИЛИСТРА) *Telephone code: 086*
Silistra is a pleasant town, and has a central European feel to it. This is the last Bulgarian town on the Danube; from here going east there is a land frontier with

Romania. The town, mentioned in a written document in the year AD106, was an administrative centre and customs station, known as Durostorum. It developed as a self-governing municipium, the second-highest grade of town, and in the 2nd century AD reached the high point of its development. Apparently there were magnificent public buildings, villas, public baths, basilicas and the usual sophisticated water supply. Later, Slav settlers and then Bulgarians arrived, and the town continued to change hands many more times. Its strategic position on the Danube means that it is a settlement of long standing through which many conquerors have passed. Local historians say no Bulgarian town had more changes of government; even in the 20th century Romanian claims, peace treaties, transgressions and negotiations caused several more changes.

Silistra is a major port for the agricultural produce of Dobrudzha – grain, grapes and apricots.

Getting there and away There are **trains** from Isperih (*3 daily; 1½hrs*), Kaspichan (*1 daily; 2½hrs*) and Samuil (*3 daily; 2hrs 15mins–2hrs 30mins*), the main junction.

There are **buses** (*bus station* ✆820280) from Ruse (*hourly; 2hrs*), Veliko Turnovo (*1 daily; 3hrs 40mins*), Shumen (*3 daily; 3hrs*), Dobrich (*5 daily; 2hrs 15mins*) and Sofia (*7 daily; 7hrs*).

⌂ Where to stay

⌂ **Bartimex** (10 rooms) ul Kapitan Mamarchen 20; ✆820111; m 0896 695603; e bartimex@mail. bg. Small hotel near the harbour & not far from the centre. **€**

⌂ **Drustar** (44 rooms) ul Kapitan Mamarchev 10; ✆812200; e drustar@hoteldrustar.com; www.hoteldrustar.com. Very smart hotel in the heart of the town, with a Danube River view. **€€–€€€**

⌂ **Zlatna Dobrudzha Complex** (67 rooms) ul Dobrudzha 1; ✆821357; http://tour-istar. domino.bg. Modern hotel located in the centre; has restaurants & bars. Also offers motorboat cruises. **€–€€**

✗ Where to eat and drink

✗ **Geran** ul Baba Tonka; ✆851498. Offers Bulgarian & international cuisine, along with live music. **€€**

✗ **Zlatna Dobrudzha Pizzeria** See above. Offers the best pizzas in the area, also a big variety of salads & a good selection of wines. **€€**

What to see and do The **Art Gallery** (*Художествената галерия; pl Svoboda;* ✆822039; ⊕ *08.00–noon & 14.00–18.00 Mon–Fri; adult 1.50lv*) has works by Zlatyu Boyadzhiev and Vladimir Dimitrov-Maistora. It is in the former school building which was used as an administration centre between 1920 and 1940, when Silistra was under Romanian rule.

The **Archaeological Museum** (*Археологическия музей; bul Simeon Veliki 72;* ⊕ *08.00–noon & 14.00–18.00 Mon–Fri; adult 1.50lv*), in a former bank, is full of interesting exhibits from Durostorum including a unique 1st-century sundial with a relief of Orpheus playing his lyre to a group of appreciative animals; other artefacts include gold jewellery, a funeral chariot, coins and seals.

The **Abdul Medzhid Turkish Fort** (*Меджиди табия – Турската крепост*), the best preserved in Bulgaria, is now used as a museum with statues, sundials and other Roman finds. There are fine views across the Danube to Romania.

Silistra's most important asset is its 4th-century **late Roman tomb** (*Късно Римска гробница; enquire at the Archaeological Museum about access*). By this time, the Romans were on the defensive against the Goths from the north, yet the wall paintings are at a high artistic level. The wealthy couple are in the centre, accompanied by servants and a candelabra to light the way into their next life. There are hunting scenes on the ceiling, clearly influenced by Thracian art, and illustrations of birds, animals and flowers. The most striking image is of two peacocks, but the whole tomb is very vivid and colourful. The construction of the tomb is similar to others, but the fact that the whole of the interior is painted is unusual for this period. The tomb was discovered in 1942, but in 1968 further excavations unearthed a 3rd-century burial of a high official who had been interred with a four-wheeled chariot, four horses and funerary vessels and weapons. The chariot was richly decorated with small statues in bronze, and two swords were ornamented with rubies and other precious stones.

The **Kurshumlu Mosque** (*Куршумлу джамия*), dating from the 16th century, has a very beautiful interior, with floral patterns decorating the walls and ceiling.

SREBURNA (СРЕБЪРНА) The Sreburna Biosphere Reserve is about 16km west of Silistra and 1km south of the Danube. It covers some 650ha and has been a protected area since 1948, and on the UNESCO World Heritage list since 1983. The reserve has a **natural history museum** (*природонаучен музей;* ⊕ *09.00–noon & 14.00–18.00 daily; adult 3lv*) near the lake, which has various stuffed birds and local mammals such as badger, deer, marten and boar. There is also a tower with special birdwatching facilities for visitors.

The first impression is of peace and stillness, but once the view to the lake is studied through binoculars or a telescope, the activity of the varied wildlife becomes clear. In the late 19th century the Hungarian traveller Felix Kanitz wrote: 'I have seen the Eldorado of wading birds.'

In summer the lake is almost covered by water lilies and huge floating islands of reeds and rushes, which provide nesting sites. Though it is famous for its birds, Sreburna is also home to flowers, grass and water snakes, tortoises, fish, frogs, insects and butterflies.

RUSE (РУСЕ) Telephone code: 082

Though the Danube forms most of Bulgaria's northern border, in recent history it has often acted less as a barrier and more as a link with the styles and culture of central Europe. Ruse owes its splendid Baroque appearance to the influence of Vienna and Budapest. It has spacious squares, elegant boulevards and a fine opera house. Many buildings have been restored in recent years. It is a busy river port with one of the two Bulgarian bridges across the Danube. It is also an important cultural centre, a lively city and a useful base for a variety of nearby attractions, including the Ivanovo Rock Churches and Cherven.

GETTING THERE AND AWAY There are **trains** (*railway station* ✆ *820222*) from Varna (*2 daily; 4hrs*), Gorna Oryahovitsa (*9 daily; 2hrs*), Sofia (*7 daily; 6–7hrs*) and Stara Zagora (*5 daily; 3hrs*).

There are **buses** (*bus station* ✆ *828151*) from Varna (*3 daily; 4hrs*), Dobrich (*2 daily; 2hrs 15mins*), Veliko Turnovo (*6 daily; 2hrs 40mins*), Silistra (*hourly; 2hrs*), Sofia (*14 daily; 5hrs*), Razgrad (*5 daily; 1hr 15mins*), Pleven (*2 daily; 2½hrs*) and Svishtov (*hourly; 2hrs*).

TOURIST INFORMATION There is a tourist information office on ul Aleksandrovska 61 (✆ *824704;* e *tic@tic.rousse.bg;* ⊕ *09.00–18.00 daily*).

These areas are famous as the site of the only **Dalmatian pelican** breeding colony in Bulgaria, and for big colonies of **glossy ibis**, **spoonbill**, **herons**, **egrets** and **pygmy cormorant**, also **ducks**, **greylag goose** and many **passerines**. More than 156 breeding species were recorded in Sreburna Lake around the end of the 20th century. In milder winters the lake is an important roosting place for waterfowl and it is possible to see **white-tailed eagle** then. The other wetlands along the River Danube are the marshy areas Kalimok, Malak Preslavets, Garvan, Momin Brod and Orsoya, as well as the islands of Kosuy, Vardim and Tsibar. During the migration and breeding season they are full of interesting bird species. On most of the marshes colonies of **whiskered tern** occur, and **purple heron**, **ferruginous duck**, **garganey**, **marsh harrier** and **little bittern** can also be seen. In the adjacent areas common breeders are **roller**, **Levant sparrowhawk**, **bee-eater** in huge colonies, **grey-headed woodpecker** and **lesser grey shrike**.

WHERE TO STAY *Map, page 193*

Anna Palace (25 rooms) ul Knyazheska 4; 825005; e hotel@annapalace.com; www. annapalace.com. In a lovely historic mansion, central, views of the Danube. **€€**

Bistra & Galina Complex (39 rooms) ul Asparuh 8; 823344; e info@bghotel.bg; www. bghotel.bg. Part of the Best Western chain. Well-equipped & comfortable business hotel, recreation centre with swimming pool, jacuzzi & gym. **€€–€€€**

City Art Hotel (20 rooms) ul Veliko Turnovo 5; 519848; e office@cityarthotel.com; www.

cityarthotel.com. Stylishly renovated 19th-century hatmaker's shop, with colourful décor, each room is different. Close to centre & to the Danube. **€€**

Pension Petrov (4 rooms) Zapaden Park Prista; 222401. Traditional guesthouse & *mehana*. **€**

Riga (157 rooms) bul Pridunavski 22; 822042; m 0882 920092; e office@hotel-riga. com; www.hotel-riga.com. The largest hotel in the city on the riverbank, great variety of rooms, but not all updated. **€€**

WHERE TO EAT AND DRINK *Map, page 193*

Bamboo In the courtyard of City Art Hotel, see above; 870555. Chinese restaurant, still something of a novelty outside Sofia & the resorts. **€**

Chiflika ul Otets Paisii 2; 828222. Most popular restaurant in Ruse. Bulgarian food mainly, excellent selection of wines & other drinks. The service is fast & efficient, even when it's busy. **€€**

Leventa Complex 862880. Stylish restaurant in the old fort, reopened after

renovation. High standards of food & wine. Ruse Wine House is also here. **€€–€€€**

Pizzeria Nano bul Rodina 80; 846171. Fast food, salads, pizzas, grilled meats. **€€**

Strandzhata ul Konstantin Irechek 5; 821185. Traditional *mehana*, Bulgarian food, pleasant setting & interior. **€€**

Vienna bul Pridunavski 54; 828435. BBQ, seafood, fish & chips. River views. Excellent service & presentation. **€€**

WHAT TO SEE AND DO The Romans built the fortress of Sexaginta Prista, the city of 60 ships, to guard the northern frontier against marauding tribes from across the Danube. Barbarian invasions in the 6th and 7th centuries destroyed the fortress and the population took refuge some 25km south, where they established the town of Cherven. This was later destroyed by the Ottoman occupiers, who re-established Ruse, making it an important military and strategic centre, known as Ruschuk. It was then larger than Sofia, and had more factories, inhabitants, consulates and

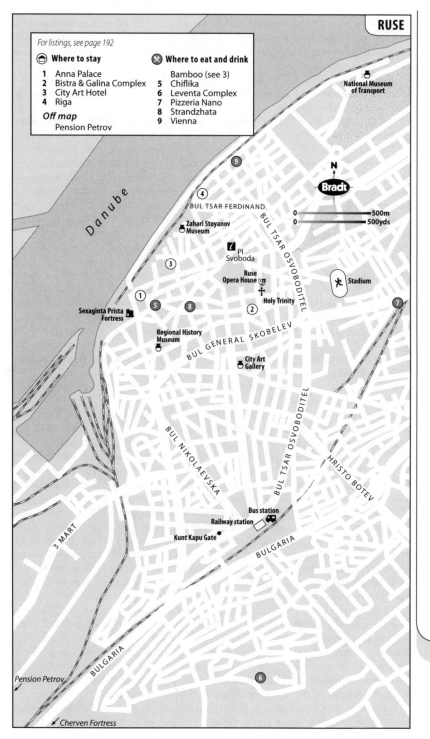

For listings, see page 192

Where to stay
1 Anna Palace
2 Bistra & Galina Complex
3 City Art Hotel
4 Riga

Off map
Pension Petrov

Where to eat and drink
Bamboo (see 3)
5 Chiflika
6 Leventa Complex
7 Pizzeria Nano
8 Strandzhata
9 Vienna

National Museum
of Transport

Danube

BUL TSAR FERDINAND

Zahari Stoyanov
Museum

Pl
Svoboda

Ruse
Opera House

Holy Trinity

Stadium

Sexaginta Prista
Fortress

Regional History
Museum

BUL GENERAL SKOBELEV

City Art
Gallery

BUL NIKOLAEVSKA

BUL TSAR OSVOBODITEL

HRISTO BOTEV

3 MART

Bus station

Railway station

Kunt Kapu Gate

BULGARIA

BULGARIA

Pension Petrov

Cherven Fortress

500m
500yds

banks. The Nobel Prize-winning author Elias Canetti lived here in the late 19th century when the town was home to a really cosmopolitan mixture of races and religions. 'Everything I experienced later in life had already happened in Ruse,' he wrote in his autobiography.

The **fortress** (*Римска крепост Сексагинта Приста*; ⊕ *09.00–17.00 daily; adult 2lv*) has some 3rd-century defensive walls still standing and a few decorated tombstones, and fine views of the Danube.

On the riverfront, which unfortunately is not particularly attractive, the **Zahari Stoyanov Museum** (*Музея на Захари Стоянов; bul Pridunavski 15;* ⊕ *09.00–noon & 14.00–17.00 Mon–Fri; adult 3lv*) is interesting. As a young man, Stoyanov was inspired by the dramatic suicide of revolutionary Angel Kunchev at Ruse. Kunchev was caught leaving the city without a passport, and, fearing that under torture he would reveal secrets of the clandestine network he worked with, he shot himself after shouting out: 'Long live Bulgaria!' Stoyanov was in Georgi Benkovski's rebel group in Koprivshtitsa (page 201) and his later account of the uprising, describing the various leading figures, is an important contemporary record. He married a daughter of Baba Tonka Obretenova. Granny Tonka was strongly influenced by Georgi Rakovski, and allowed her home to be used by rebels both as a meeting place and arms store. She was a major figure in revolutionary Ruse. There is information about her in the Stoyanov museum, which also commemorates other rebels such as Panayot Hitov.

The **Regional History Museum** (*pl Aleksandur Batenberg 3;* \ *825002; www. museumruse.com;* ⊕ *09.00–18.00 daily; adult 4lv*) is on a lovely square, and in a splendid building: the former palace of Prince Aleksandur Batenberg. One of the finest exhibits is the Thracian Borovo Treasure, but there are other ancient and Roman artefacts, as well as more modern exhibits from Ruse's 19th-century heyday.

The splendid **Ruse Opera House** (*Русенска опера; pl Sv Troitsa*), built in 1949, is really impressive. It hosts various music festivals and, thanks to its reputation, is able to attract well-known performers.

Holy Trinity (*Св Троица; ul Gorazd*) is a three-aisled church dating from 1764 and noted for its exceptional icons. It replaced the sunken church built in 1632, and displays more self-confidence with its Russian-influenced elaborate style.

The **City Art Gallery** (*Градската художествена галерия; ul Borisova 39;* ⊕ *09.00–13.00 & 14.00–18.00 Tue–Sun*) mainly displays the work of local artists, but has some works by Zlatyu Boyadzhiev. Nearby is the **Kunt Kapu Gate** (*Aleya Osvobozhdenie 60A*), the only part of the Turkish fortress which is still standing.

Ruse is the home of the **National Museum of Transport** (*Национален музей на транспорта и съобщенията; ul Bratya Obretenovi 5;* ⊕ *10.00–noon & 14.00–17.00 Mon–Fri; check at the tourist office; adult 4lv*), based in a railway station which was built by a British company in 1866. This was the original route of the Orient Express before the line from Vienna to Istanbul via Belgrade and Sofia was opened in 1888. Passengers used to travel from Budapest to Bucharest, then to Giurgiu, take a ferry across to Ruse, a train to Varna and then a ship to Istanbul.

This was the country's first railway line; building work started in 1864 and was completed in 1866. It is about 250km long and apparently presented many engineering problems because of rocky and marshy terrain. One of the Barkley brothers (there were four, all involved in international engineering projects) designed the station which is now the museum's home. Engines and carriages are on display, as well as royal train compartments from the old Orient Express. There are also examples of the first telegraph and telephone equipment.

Ruse is a city where it is a great pleasure simply to stroll along the main boulevards, the long vistas across squares towards elaborately decorated houses encouraging the visitor to explore. There are plenty of pavement cafés to relax in, and it is worth sampling the famous local apricot juice.

AROUND RUSE

IVANOVO (ИВАНОВО) The **Ivanovo Rock Churches** (*Скалните църкви край Иваново; Regional History Museum, Ruse* \ 082 825002; ☉ *Apr–Nov 09.00–18.00 daily; adult 5lv*) are in the beautiful valley of the Rusenski Lom River, about 25km south of Ruse, in a remote place which is quite difficult to find. The river runs through soft limestone, and has formed almost inaccessible cliffs. Here, in the 12th century, hermits first made their cells. Seclusion was a characteristic feature of medieval monastic life, though sometimes these places became well known for their spirituality and attracted royal or aristocratic interest, as at Ivanovo. As a result the religious colony grew in size and the generous donations of its patrons meant that the best artists could be commissioned to work here. There was thus the strange paradox that during the 13th and 14th centuries these desolate places became a veritable treasure trove of art.

The murals show a high degree of skill, though they were painted in a very limited space and on a poor surface. They are full of light and life, showing many figures in expressive and dramatic poses against an architectural background. They are in marked contrast to traditional Byzantine art, which portrays stiffer and more formal figures in strong colours. Here light and warm colours predominate. As at Aladzha (on the coast near Golden Sands resort), the monks here were Hesychasts, silent and ascetic, yet they were surrounded by art which is almost sensuous. The figures have shape, with muscles and form clearly depicted, the clothes are fluid and draped and, unusually, there are even a number of naked figures. The frescoes are the achievement of unknown masters of the Turnovo School, and there are many Bulgarian inscriptions. They were placed on UNESCO's World Heritage list in 1979.

CHERVEN (ЧЕРВЕН) Cherven was first settled by refugees from Ruse in the 6th century. During the Second Bulgarian Kingdom it developed as an important religious, trade and military centre. The **Citadel** (*Цитаделата;* \ *as Ivanovo above;* ☉ *Mar–Nov 09.00–18.00 daily; adult 4lv*) has some recently excavated streets and churches, and the ruins are very atmospheric. Cherven reached its zenith during the 13th and 14th centuries, by which time the fortress had already spread over the whole area of the rocky ridge and was divided into two parts, with the citadel at the highest and least accessible place and the town in the other section. The palace was built with huge cut rocks: the walls were very thick, and the whole area covered was 180m². Six churches have been unearthed. The fortress was completely surrounded by walls fortified with towers and bastions.

After the Ottoman conquest, Cherven lost its *raison d'être* and fell into disrepair. However, it is still the best-preserved medieval fortification in Bulgaria, and as such has starred in various films.

SVISHTOV (СВИЩОВ) *Telephone code: 0631*
This is the only town of significance between Vidin and Silistra. It is near the site of the Roman city of Novae, established in the 1st century AD and fortified as part of Emperor Justinian's defensive system in the 6th century AD. However, by the beginning of Ottoman rule it had declined to just a few houses. Its advantageous hilltop position on the River Danube meant that it attracted emigrants and it developed as a major trading town of the Ottoman Empire. The Russo-Turkish

War of Liberation began here in June 1877; the town was once again completely destroyed but it was immediately rebuilt and maintained its significance.

Getting there and away Svishtov is at the end of a branch **railway** line from Levski (*4 daily; 1½hrs*) on the Sofia–Varna route.

There are **buses** from Veliko Turnovo (*4 daily; 2hrs 40mins*), Ruse (*hourly; 2hrs*) and Pleven (*10 daily; 1hr 20mins*).

Tourist information There is a tourist information office at ul Dimitur Hadzhivasilev 2 (✆ *60371;* e *info@visitsvishtov.com; www.svishtov.org*).

🏠 Where to stay and eat

🏠 **Hotel Pri Popa** ul Georgi Tishev 4; ✆41650; www.pripopa.com/index.php. Friendly, comfortable accommodation, offering good-value spacious rooms. Walking distance from centre in a quiet location. Good food. The owner runs boat trips on the Danube on his boat *Odyssey*. €

🏠 **Manastira Complex** (15 rooms) 2km west of Svishtov; ✆41010; m 0878 316702; e manastira_sv@abv.bg; www.manastira.com. Picturesque location. Traditional *mehana*, with jacuzzi & wine-tastings. €

What to see and do Built in 1640, **Sv Dimitur** (*Св Димитър*) has a wooden cross with a silver handle and an inscription in Old Church Slavonic, and interesting woodcarvings. **Sv Sv Petur and Pavel** (*Св Св Петър и Павел*), built in 1644, is remarkable for its murals. The **Transfiguration Church** (*Св Преображение*), built in 1836, has a fine Tryavna iconostasis. The **Church of the Holy Trinity** (*Св Троица*) was built in 1867 by Kolyo Ficheto and is considered one of his finest creations. The curving lines of the roof were presumably intended to reflect its proximity to the rippling waters of the Danube.

The **Aleko Konstantinov House** (*Къщата-музей Алеко Константинов*; ✆60467; ⊕ *08.00–noon & 13.00–17.00 Mon–Fri; adult 2lv*) is painted a cheery pink. Konstantinov was a humorous writer and creator of Bulgaria's favourite rogue, Bay Ganyu, a travelling pedlar selling rose oil and rugs. The house is furnished in Viennese style and contains the rather gruesome exhibit of Konstantinov's heart, complete with bullet hole. He was shot by mistake when assassins attacked a travelling companion.

Nearby is the **Ethnographic Museum** (*Етнографския музей; ul Georgi Vladiki 14; same times & price*) which displays some very fine folk costumes and an especially large collection of *pafti*. These are the often beautifully wrought belt buckles which are an important part of women's traditional dress. It is said that their purpose was to distract men's eyes from other parts of the body!

There is a small **Archaeological Exhibition** (*Археологическа експозиция; same times & price*) which has finds from nearby Novae, where excavations take place every summer.

7

The Valley of the Roses and Sredna Gora

This is the heartland of Bulgaria. The central valley, bounded by Stara Planina to the north and the Sredna (Central) Gora Mountains to the south, lies east of Sofia and reaches almost to the coast. The Sredna Gora Mountains are forested hills rather than rocky peaks, and in some ways resemble the neighbouring Rhodope Mountains. It is an ancient place of habitation: at Stara Zagora **Neolithic** dwellings from about 6000BC have been discovered. The **Thracians** also settled here and the landscape is dotted with their burial mounds, some of which have recently been excavated with exciting results. The **Romans** also liked this sheltered area and based a walled city at Hisarya, where there are many mineral springs.

For Bulgarians the area is indelibly associated with the **April Uprising** of 1876; the famous first shot was fired in Koprivshtitsa, and some nearby towns were the birthplaces of revolutionaries such as Hristo Botev and Vasil Levski.

The valley is a main east–west route for many drivers (though quieter since the completion of the Sofia to Burgas motorway) and for train and bus passengers travelling from Sofia to the coast, but there are plenty of reasons to stop along the way.

SREDNA GORA

KOPRIVSHTITSA (КОПРИВЩИЦА) *Telephone code: 07184*

The town is noted for its 19th-century National Revival architecture, but its origins are in the 14th century. Its earliest inhabitants seem to have been a mixture of people fleeing from the Ottoman invasion. There were *bolyars* (feudal noblemen) fleeing from Veliko Turnovo and Bulgarian villagers from regions where the occupation was the most oppressive. The town thrived, and the settlers were known as good stockbreeders and craftsmen. Unfortunately the prosperous town attracted the attention of the Turks, who looted and burned it several times. Each time it was restored and by the 19th century it reached its apogee.

There are beautiful homes, often decorated with furnishings imported from central Europe, or by paintings of places the wealthy merchants visited on their travels. There are schools, churches, fountains and bridges, all privately funded.

The people of Koprivshtitsa participated in several uprisings, but it is the final one, which began on 20 April 1876, that is commemorated everywhere in the town, in the names of streets and bridges.

Getting there and away There are **trains** from Sofia (*5 daily; 2½hrs*), Burgas (*1 daily; 7hrs with connections at Karlovo & Anton*) and Karlovo (*4 daily; 1hr 10mins*). It is important to note that the station is 10km from the town and that in practice there are not always connecting buses or waiting taxis.

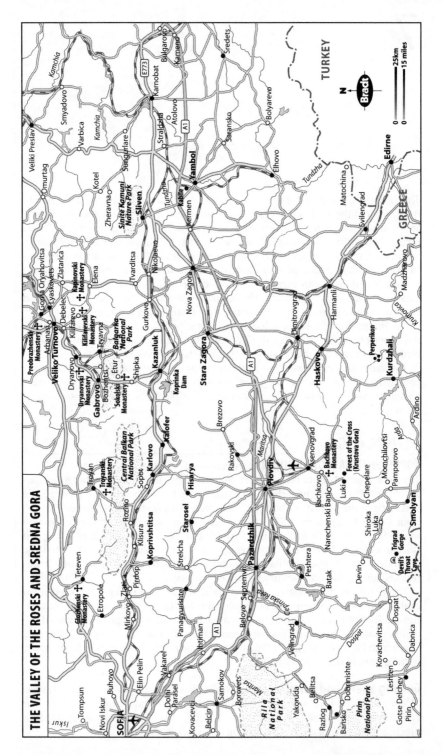

THE VALLEY OF THE ROSES AND SREDNA GORA

TURKEY

N

Bradt

0 ___ 25km
0 ___ 15 miles

From Sofia there are **buses** from the central bus station (☎ *0900 63099; 3 daily; 2hrs 40mins*) and from Poduene bus station (*2 daily; 2hrs 40mins*). There are also buses from Pirdop (*3 daily; 45mins*) and Plovdiv (*1 daily*).

By **car** this is an easy day trip from Sofia or Plovdiv, or a nice diversion from the east–west route through the Valley of the Roses.

Tourist information If the tourist information office (*pl 20th April 6;* ☎ *2191;* e *info@koprivshtitza.com; www.koprivshtitza.com;* ⊕ *Apr–Oct 09.30–17.30, Nov–Mar 09.30–17.00, both daily*) is closed, go to the museum ticket office next door (☎ *2180*). The tourist information office can arrange private rooms. Unless it is festival time, it is unlikely that everywhere will be booked up.

🏠 Where to stay *Map, page 200*

🏠 **Bashtina Kushta** (14 rooms) ul Hadzhi Nencho Palaveev 32; ☎3033; e info@fhhotel.info; www.fhhotel.info. Modern hotel built in traditional style; close to the centre. Excellent restaurant with local specialities. Welcoming and efficient staff. €

🏠 **Hadzhiite Hotel Complex** (12 rooms) ul Hadzhi Nencho Palaveev 15; ☎2123; m 0889 070077; www.hadjiite.bg. This newly built hotel resembles the Kableshkov House. It sits in a lovely yard with an old unrestored house, some huge striking pines & sheltered outdoor dining. The rooms & bathrooms are spacious & very comfortable. €

🏠 **Karagyozov House** (6 rooms) ul Ivan Dzhartanazov 4A; ☎2018; m 0889 862386;

e karagyozovhouse@abv.bg; www. karagyozovhouse.com. Centrally located in a beautiful old house. €

🏠 **Kozlekov House** (20 rooms) ul Georgi Benkovski 8; m 0879 891077; e info@ hotelkozlekov.com; www.hotelkozlekov.com. Central location; modern hotel with spacious rooms. Excellent value. €

🏠 **Panorama** (15 rooms) ul Georgi Benkovski 40; ☎2035; m 0888 531441; e hotel@ panoramata.com; www.panoramata.com. Very attractive, family-run hotel with light, clean rooms & good views; excellent service & hospitality. *Mehana* on the ground floor. €

✗ Where to eat and drink *Map, page 200*

✗ **20 April Mehana** pl 20 April; m 0887 590322. Traditional style. Bulgarian cuisine & local specialities. €€

✗ **Chuchura** ul Hadzhi Nencho Palaveev 66; ☎2712; m 0888 347770; www.mehana.eu. Good food, mainly Bulgarian specialities, salads, soups. €–€€

✗ **Dyado Liben** ul Hadzi Nencho Palaveev 47; ☎2109. Across the bridge from the main square. Oldest & most emblematic *mehana* in a beautiful old

building with garden. Bulgarian & local specialities: try the nettle soup & local sausage. €€

✗ **Lomeva Kushta** ul Hadzhi Nencho Palaveev 42; m 0879 433031. Traditional Bulgarian food, salads, grilled meats at reasonable prices. €–€€

✗ **Pod Starata Krusha** ul Hadzhi Nencho Palaveev 76; ☎2163; m 0887 349901. Small but nice restaurant with excellent cuisine, soups, salads & grilled meats. €–€€

What to see and do Koprivshtitsa is a place that deserves to be thoroughly explored – not just the house-museums, lovely as they are, but all the little alleyways. There are stone water fountains (*чешми*) to discover, fascinating details such as door handles to notice, and a variety of unusual colours on the houses: deep blue, cinnamon brown, light blue, yellow and a wonderful dusty violet. There are monuments and statues, and in summer the hills all around are a sea of wild flowers and a source of wild strawberries, raspberries and other fruits.

The town is the birthplace of several well-known Bulgarians. Some of the house-museums recount their lives and display artefacts connected with them. Three such examples are the Karavelov, Kableshkov and Benkovski houses. The **Koprivshtitsa**

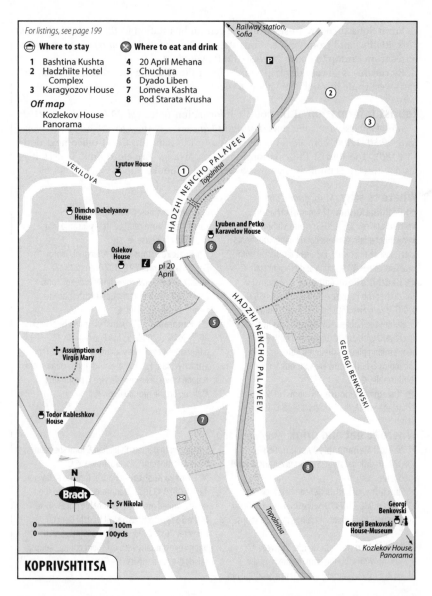

For listings, see page 199

Where to stay

1 Bashtina Kushta
2 Hadzhiite Hotel
   Complex
3 Karagyozov House

Off map
   Kozlekov House
   Panorama

Where to eat and drink

4 20 April Mehana
5 Chuchura
6 Dyado Liben
7 Lomeva Kashta
8 Pod Starata Krusha

Railway station,
Sofia

P

VEKILOVA

Lyutov House

HADZHI NENCHO PALAVEEV

Topolnitsa

**Dimcho Debelyanov
House**

**Lyuben and Petko
Karavelov House**

**Oslekov
House**

pl 20
April

HADZHI NENCHO PALAVEEV

**Assumption of
Virgin Mary**

GEORGI BENKOVSKI

**Todor Kableshkov
House**

N

Bradt

Sv Nikolai

0 — 100m
0 — 100yds

Topolnitsa

**Georgi
Benkovski**

**Georgi Benkovski
House-Museum**

*Kozlekov House,
Panorama*

KOPRIVSHTITSA

House-Museums (2180; *Debelyanov & Kableshkov* ⊕ 09.30–17.30 *Tue–Sun;
Lyutov, Karavelov & Benkovski* ⊕ 09.30–17.30 *Wed–Mon; individual houses 5lv,
joint ticket for all 5 10lv; English-speaking guided tours of all the museums available,
15lv)* have each got a special charm and, as they are scattered around the town, a
visit to all of them gives you a good itinerary for a walk.

The earliest houses, in a very simple style, were built of wood and only one
storey. Most of these were destroyed in the 1793 attack by Kurdzhaliya. One
example remains: the Pavlikenski House. Those built in the first half of the 19th
century, of which the Benkovski House is a good example, were two-storeyed with
a veranda and sturdy doors. In the second half of the century the houses were larger

and much more lavish. They had many windows, elaborate carvings and decorated ornamental niches (*alafrangas*), following the Plovdiv tradition.

Images of the **Oslekov House** are frequently used to illustrate the beauties of Koprivshtitsa. Built in the mid 19th century for a wealthy merchant, its columns of cedar of Lebanon and the painted façade are very striking. Inside there are many frescoes and beautiful carved wooden ceilings. The contents of the house are now in the local museum as the house has been returned to its original owners. It can still be visited (*3lv*) but is no longer included in the group ticket.

Nearby is the **House of Todor Kableshkov**, which was built in 1845. It is a perfect example of the symmetrical house designed around a circular central hall. There are wonderful ceilings, some of the most elaborate in the town, as well as carved doors and cupboards. Kableshkov was a participant in the uprising and wrote the famous Blood Letter. This was a message to the leaders in nearby Panagyurishte to say that the uprising had begun, and was signed with the blood of the first Turk killed in the battle for the *konak*.

The **Dimcho Debelyanov House** is a tiny blue building with wooden verandas, shaded by huge pine trees. It was the home of the lyrical poet Dimcho Debelyanov, whose grandfather built it in 1830. The exhibition inside has books and manuscripts about the poet's work. In the garden, and also in the churchyard, is the moving statue by Ivan Lazarov of Debelyanov's lonely mother waiting for her son to come home from the war in Greece, where he was killed in 1916.

On the other side of the river is the **Lyuben and Petko Karavelov House** ensemble. There are three buildings, described as the winter house, the summer house and the farm building. The winter house, built in 1810, is the oldest, the farm building followed and the summer house was completed in 1835. Lyuben was a revolutionary and writer, and his brother was a prominent politician who served as prime minister and in other posts after the liberation.

The large printing machine on display, which Lyuben used while in exile in Romania to print revolutionary leaflets, booklets and proclamations, later played another historic role: it was used in Veliko Turnovo to print the first Bulgarian constitution.

The unmissable huge statue of a revolutionary on horseback is of **Georgi Benkovski**. It stands on five enormous stones which symbolise the five centuries of the Ottoman occupation. His home nearby is another museum, built in 1831. The house, with its huge verandas, is typical of the so-called craftsman's guild style. Benkovski was said to be a fiery and passionate man who was the leader and strategist of the uprising.

KOPRIVSHTITSA NATIONAL FESTIVAL OF FOLK SONG AND DANCE

Held every five years on the first or second weekend in August (the next will be in 2015) in this historic museum town, this festival almost resembles a medieval pageant, except that half of those attending are in modern dress. Amateur groups and soloists from all over Bulgaria perform their local music, dance and rituals, and have already been through preliminary auditions to reach this competition. It takes place along a 2km linear site above the town on several separate stages. Accommodation in the town is a must in order to join in the late-night spontaneous entertainments. There is a smaller festival held annually in mid-August.

For those who develop a taste for Balkan folk music, a useful CD supplier is at www.music-bulgaria.com.

The final house-museum open to the public is the beautiful **Lyutov House**, the pinnacle of Koprivshtitsa's building achievements. It was built in 1854 and sold to the merchant Lyutov. The painted scenes show how far the town's merchants travelled: Istanbul, Venice, Alexandria and Cairo. Apart from these fascinating murals, there are lavish painted niches and borders, featuring flowers and stylised patterns. Inside there is an exhibition of a very typical traditional Koprivshtitsa craft: the making of richly decorated felt carpets.

AFTERNOON IN KOPRIVSHTITSA

In 1988 I wrote about Koprivshtitsa for a competition in *The Independent* newspaper. The idea was to write about a 'real' holiday, which went beyond the standard two-week sun-and-sand tower-block package: walking in the Black Forest, lost in France, getting your kicks on Route 66, flying down to Rio, losing your heart in San Francisco – the choice was yours. This was my contribution.

'You are the only English people here,' she said as she stamped our registration cards. We had the beautiful small town in the Sredna Gora Mountains to ourselves. That afternoon I wandered through the siesta-silence with my son, both happy to return to our favourite places. The stream ran summer shallow, but still purposefully, to the River Topolnitsa, passing under stone and wooden bridges. Heaven for a small boy in wellingtons, with a stick and a bucket. Another little boy appeared from a house across the bridge. His mother hovered momentarily on the doorstep, I smiled and apparently passed the test, for she smiled in return and left us. Two four-year-olds with no words in common spent an hour in complete, if splashy, harmony. Then it was time for our ice cream, a daily highlight which was never missed. I returned little Vladko to his grandmother, who was dozing on the wooden bench against the front wall of the house.

As we walked through the narrow alleys, we heard the sound of a violin repeatedly playing a few haunting notes. We passed the cobbler's shop and the rug-makers, the parked donkeys and carts, several groups of hens and even three cows making their own way out to the pastures. We crossed the stream where a youth brigade was mending the bridge, and reached the main square.

After the briefest pause at our favourite water fountain, we arrived at Nikolai's café. We were greeted as old friends, a table was found when all had seemed full, and a coffee, two mineral waters and a large ice cream soon appeared. The quiet and the heat of the afternoon were over, the pace quickened. People walked, talked and shopped; the restaurants opened, and the appetising smells of Bulgarian cooking charged the air. We watched and absorbed it all, until friends came and it was time to concentrate on multilingual conversations.

Our evening stroll often took us through the churchyard, where the statue of a sad mother waiting for the return of her son from the war attracted Rupinka's attention. It is a local custom, and ours too, to cheer her with a small bunch of wild flowers.

On the way down the hill that evening, I had the satisfaction of being asked by a Bulgarian for directions to the square and of knowing both the answer to his question and how to say it.'

There were over 600 entries in the competition and this won first prize. A lot has changed in nearly 30 years, but Koprivshtitsa is still my favourite place.

By the mid 19th century and as a result of its material prosperity, the town was playing an important part in Bulgarian cultural life. It had established two schools and in the second, founded in 1837, followed what was then a new idea of older pupils helping to teach younger ones.

The town also has two churches. The **Assumption of the Virgin Mary** (*Успение Богородично*), built in 1817, replaced the one burned down by Kurdzhaliya at the end of the 18th century. The icons and woodcarvings are by well-known craftsmen including Zahari Zograf. The iconostasis and pulpit are particularly elaborate. The church itself is inconspicuous as the Ottomans required, and it is painted bright blue, like many of the nearby houses, to avoid drawing attention to itself. The prominent belltower was added much later.

The so-called new church, built in 1844 and dedicated to **Sv Nikolai** (*Св Николай*), was funded by wealthy families in the town. Sv Nikolai is the patron saint of those who travel by sea or make long and hazardous journeys, so he was an obvious choice for the well-travelled merchants of Koprivshtitsa.

A fine stone bridge in the centre of the town is named as the Bridge of the First Rifle Shot. There are dozens of bridges here, as the River Topolnitsa runs through the town and is fed by several tributary streams, all crossed at intervals by stone humpback bridges. In the main square a mausoleum and ossuary are dedicated to those who fell in the uprising.

Apart from the museums there are many other beautiful houses in the town, strictly preserved in their appearance, but not open to the public. Even new houses in the town have to comply with regulations about style and erect the traditional big-roofed gate to their yards.

There are many stone fountains dotted around the town, their positions carefully chosen so they could be seen from a distance or perhaps from two directions. They are not fountains in the English sense; there is no jet of water, but rather a piped water supply to a stone trough, sometimes quite simple and sometimes more refined and decorated. They were a convenient supply of water for horses and cattle, but also served as social meeting places at the end of the working day.

It is known that the town enjoyed certain privileges of self-government and reductions in taxes. According to local legend this was because an early settler was a beautiful woman from Rila, who persuaded the sultan to grant her authority in Koprivshtitsa and for the town to have certain privileges traditionally denied to subject Christians: the right to ride fine horses, wear high-quality clothes and carry weapons.

Apart from the fascination of the town, its lovely setting with old forests and mountain pastures means there are a variety of walks in the Sredna Gora. The tourist information office has leaflets.

PANAGYURISHTE (ПАНАГЮРИЩЕ) *Telephone code: 0357*

The town was, like its neighbour Koprivshtitsa, deeply involved in the April Uprising; indeed, a short-lived provisional government was declared here before the insurrection was suppressed. In Koprivshtitsa the wealthy *chorbadzhi* bribed the *bashibozuks* not to burn down the town. However, in Panagyurishte they did burn it down and today the town is mainly modern, though there are plenty of memorials to the events of 1876.

In many ways the towns have a similar history, as Panagyurishte also had privileged status as a military town under the Ottoman Empire, allowing it self-government and exemption from certain taxes. Here, too, education and culture thrived in the 19th century.

Getting there and away There are **trains** from Plovdiv (*every 4hrs; 2hrs*) and from Sofia (*via Plovdiv; 2 daily; 5hrs 10mins*).
There are **buses** (*bus station* ✆ *3383*) from Sofia (*every 2hrs; 1hr 45mins*).

⌂ Where to stay

⌂ **Bonbon** (3 rooms) ul Tsar Osvoboditel 8; ✆4727; m 0888 420188. A small & basic B&B close to the centre. €

⌂ **Kamengrad** (28 rooms) ul Pavel Bobekov 2; ✆6287; m 0879 801901; e complex_ kamengrad@abv.bg. This is the centrally

located former state hotel, with renovated rooms. €–€€

⌂ **Tavernata Hotel Complex** (11 rooms) ul Georgi Bozadzhiev 24; ✆6639; m 0887 758578. Family-run hotel close to the bus station. Good restaurant. €

✗ Where to eat and drink
As well as the places below, the listed hotels also have restaurants.

✗ **Pizza Maldini** ul Georgi Benkovski 24; ✆2334. Offers pizzas & salads & is a good place for a drink. €–€€

✗ **Starata kushta** ul Bunai 6; ✆3508; m 0895 620690. Bulgarian & European cuisine, soups, salads. Pretty setting, with a garden. €–€€

What to see and do The main square has views across to the massive **Memorial to the April Uprising**. The broad processional staircase leading to it passes the **Church of the Virgin Mary** (*Черква Дева Мария*), which was partly burned down by the Turks. This is perhaps the more moving memorial as its interior still bears the scars. Some murals just inside have been left showing fire damage, but the rest was redecorated in the 1890s with many brightly coloured scenes from the life of the Virgin Mary.

There are a few old buildings which escaped destruction and these house the **Town Museum** (*Градскиямузей; ul Raina Knyaginya; e histmuzpan@abv.bg; ⊕ 09.00–17.00 Tue–Sun; adult 2lv*), which has an ethnographic section and weaponry and materials relating to the uprising. There is also a **House-Museum of Raina Knyaginya** (*Дом-музей Райна Княгиня; ul Oborishte 5; ⊕ 09.00–17.00 Tue–Sun; adult 2lv*), a heroine of the uprising.

You may remember the name of Panagyurishte as one of Bulgaria's famous gold hoards. The Thracian treasure was discovered in 1949. There are nine vessels of 23-carat gold, weighing over 6kg. Scenes and figures from Greek mythology are depicted in fine detail. It is now displayed in Plovdiv Archaeological Museum.

STAROSEL (СТАРОСЕЛ) East of Panagyurishte via Strelcha the road brings you to Starosel, previously a typical dusty village of the region, now famous for its Thracian tombs.

Getting there and away There are **buses** from Plovdiv (*5 daily; 1½hrs*).

⌂ Where to stay and eat

⌂ **Starosel Winery Complex** (28 rooms) m 0897 870908; e hotel@starosel.com; www. starosel.com. Traditional style in a modern

setting, with a restaurant, spa & wine-tasting tours. €€

What to see and do The **tombs** (*Тракийски гробници; ⊕ May–Sep 09.00–18.00, Oct–Apr 10.00–16.00, both daily; adult 3lv*) are respectively about 3km and 6km from the village.

Why did the Thracians build such elaborate tombs? The answer lies in their religion and mythology. The Greek historian Herodotus wrote that the Thracians had a strong belief in the afterlife. They believed their king was also a god, who was going to rise from the dead and come back to his people. Meanwhile he needed a special place for his body until this time came. The construction of the tomb had to be secure enough for the king and his treasures, but also needed to give him the opportunity to leave the tomb when he returned to his people. This is the reason why all Thracian tombs have stone doors.

In the year 2000, one of the most significant examples of Thracian monumental architecture was discovered. A huge stone tomb of magnificent proportions was found: this is the Chetinyova tomb, about 6km from Starosel. The building was covered by a 20m-high mound. The entire tumulus is surrounded by a 265m-long wall made out of 4,000 or so massive and smoothly hewn stone blocks. A processional staircase flanked by two smaller staircases leads to an impressive platform in front of the entrance.

The construction consists of two successive chambers decorated with geometric motifs in bright colours, imitating the architectural elements of a Greek temple. The main hall is round, vaulted and the ceiling is supported by ten Doric semi-pillars, each carved with ten vertical flutes. In the inner walls there are incorporated ornate stone plates and the dome is decorated with a frieze in red, black, green and blue. The tomb had been plundered repeatedly, but there remained some pieces of a gold funerary wreath, gold buttons and Greek pottery, testifying to the richness of the missing grave offerings. In the antechamber were found the skeletons of two horses, killed when the tomb was originally sealed to accompany their master in his journey to the world beyond.

There is a theory that the complex probably belonged to the Thracian King Sitalk I, from the 5th century BC. He was one of the most powerful Odrysian kings whose territory was situated between the Black Sea, the Danube River and the Rhodope Mountains. From ancient sources it is known only that he had an annual income of 800 talents and that he was courted by Athens and Sparta. In 429BC he invaded Macedonia with an army of 150,000 men. This was certainly a huge army, but it should be borne in mind that authors in those times often tended to exaggerate numbers, as this was their way of emphasising somebody's importance and power.

Closer to Starosel is the Horizont tomb which was originally a Thracian temple, later used as a tomb for an unknown Thracian ruler, who was buried in the traditional style with armour and weapons.

If you are driving between Starosel and Hisarya, you will pass through the village of Staro Zhelezare, where there is a small museum in a beautifully restored old house, displaying local crafts and traditions, and selling some handmade items. Worth a visit!

HISARYA (ХИСАРЯ) *Telephone code: 0337*

Further east is Hisarya, a spa since ancient times. You can buy its mineral water all over Bulgaria. The town is still noted for its clean air and its mild climate, as it is protected on each side by mountains. The earliest inhabitants were the Thracian tribe of Bessi, followed by the Macedonians, but it was under the Romans that it particularly thrived. Their city, which they called Augusta, had huge walls, wide streets, villas, baths and an amphitheatre. The walls in particular are still a feature of the town. It was destroyed by the Crusaders and during the Ottoman invasion, though later, in the 17th century, the Turks realised the value of its resources and restored it.

Getting there and away There are **trains** from Plovdiv (*3 daily; 45mins*). There are **buses** (*bus station* \ *0337 62069*) from Plovdiv (*hourly; 1hr*), and Karlovo (*5 daily; 35mins*).

Tourist information There is a tourist information office at bul Gurko 14 (\ *62141;* e *hissar_infotour@abv.bg; www.hissar.org*).

⌂ Where to stay

⌂ **Augusta Spa** (160 rooms) bul Gurko 3; \62255; m 0887 333849; e augusta.marketing@ gmail.com; www.augustaspa.com. In the eastern part of the town. Not central but near the mineral springs; some rooms are renovated. €€–€€€

⌂ **Hisar Spa** (106 rooms) bul Gurko 1; \62782; e hissarhotel@abv.bg; www.hotelhissar.com. The biggest hotel, with renovated rooms, spa facilities, open-air swimming pools & restaurant. Very busy. €€–€€€

⌂ **Paradise** (8 rooms) ul Ilin Paunov 2; \65521; e vzidarova@abv.bg; www.hotelrai.hit. bg. Small hotel with spa facilities & an open-air swimming pool nearby. €

✕ Where to eat and drink

There are many inviting *mehanas* and restaurants along the main street, ul Gurko. The listed hotels also have restaurants.

✕ **Cesar** ul Hristo Botev 37; m 0899 272530. Traditional *mehana* with interesting interior & courtyard. Bulgarian grills & European cuisine. €–€€

✕ **Chinar** ul Augusta 17; \62370. Pretty setting in a beautiful garden. Rich menu with over 30 salads, grilled specialities & locally baked bread. Very popular. €€

✕ **National** ul Gurko 12; \62580; m 0879 448733. Traditional Bulgarian cuisine. €€

What to see and do The town has a small **Archaeological Museum** (*Археологически музей; ul Stamboliiski 8;* \ *62796;* ⊕ *09.00–noon & 13.00–16.30 daily; adult 2lv*) displaying Neolithic idols, stonework, coins and ceramics from all the periods of the settlement. The 15th to 18th centuries seem to be mainly represented by weaponry, indicating the unstable nature of life under the Ottoman occupation. There is also an ethnographic display of local costumes and crafts.

The **fortress**, dating from the 4th century, covers 30ha, but the walls and gates are all that remain. Archaeologists believe there were as many as 43 towers along the fortress walls, which were 2–3m thick; it must have been quite an impressive sight. The building technique bonded stone and brick with red mortar, creating a sort of sandwich effect. The **Camel Gate** is the image usually used to illustrate the town, so named either for the camels who passed through on trade routes, or because it looks like a camel.

About 100m to the west is a 4th-century basilica, and a similar distance to the south is the 6th-century **Church of Sv Stefan**. There is also a 4th-century **Roman tomb** with a mosaic floor and frescoed walls.

EAST TOWARDS KAZANLUK

SOPOT (СОПОТ) *Telephone code: 03134*

Travellers through the Valley of the Roses begin on an interesting stretch of road with fine views of Stara Planina, and a series of small towns which make worthwhile short stops. The first of these is Sopot, the birthplace of Ivan Vazov, the author of *Under the Yoke*, which is regarded as Bulgaria's national novel. It tells the story of the Ottoman occupation, or yoke, from the perspective of a small town, Byala Cherkva, which is the old name for Sopot, on which it is clearly based.

During the National Revival period the town became known for various high-quality crafts: silk, gold, *gaitan* (a special braid used on national dress), leather and rose oil. Lying as it does on a major route it was frequently attacked and burned, by irregular Turkish troops and brigands in the years of occupation, and by Ottoman troops during the war of liberation.

Getting there and away There are **trains** from Sofia (*3 daily; 3½hrs*), Zlatitsa (*1 daily; 1hr 15mins*), Koprivshtitsa (*1 daily; 35mins*), Karlovo (*6 daily; 10mins*) Klisura (*1 daily; 30mins*).

There are **buses** every half-hour from Karlovo.

Tourist information There is a tourist information office on ul Ivan Vazov 34 (\ *8651;* e *sopot@sopot-municipality.com; www.sopot-municipality.com*).

Where to stay and eat The most central hotel is **Shterev** (*30 rooms; ul Ivan Vazov 2;* \ *8674;* m *0886 277181;* e *sopot_reception_shterev@abv.bg;* €) There aren't many places to eat in the town except the restaurant of the hotel and a few cafés in the centre.

What to see and do The childhood home of Ivan Vazov is now a **house-museum** (*дом-музей;* \ *8650;* ⊙ *08.30–17.00 daily; adult 2lv*). It is on the main square, where there is also a bronze statue of the writer. The house is a comfortable middle-class home with some pieces of furniture and china of good quality. There is also an exhibition of his documents, photographs and copies of his novels in various languages.

KARLOVO (КАРЛОВО) *Telephone code: 0335*
A few kilometres further east, Karlovo is also the birthplace of a national hero, Vasil Levski (see box, page 17). It is not an ancient town, but it is a very pleasant one, with some fine National Revival houses in its old quarter. Here there are over a hundred houses with the typical carved wooden ceilings and frescoed walls, standing in their yards protected by big gates. Approaching the town from the east or west, you'll be greeted by the largest number of vans for sale that you could ever wish (not) to see.

Getting there and away There are **trains** from Burgas (*1 daily; 4–5hrs*), Koprivshtitsa (*1 daily; 40mins*), Plovdiv (*hourly; 1hr 40mins*) and Sofia (*2 daily; 2–3hrs*).

There are **buses** from Sofia (*2 daily; 3½hrs*), Plovdiv (*1–2 per hr; 1hr 25mins*), Kalofer (*1–2 per hr; 30mins*) and Hisarya (*5 daily; 35mins*).

Where to stay
El Paraiso (9 rooms) ul Todor Kableshkov 3; \ 94305; m 0886 580895; e info@elparaisohotel-bg.com; www.elparaisohotel-bg.com. In the upper part of the town; rooms with lovely views; good service. €

Hanut (10 rooms) ul General Kartsov; \ 95337; m 0888 304694; e info@hotelhanat. com; www.hotelhanat.com. Central family hotel with very good *mehana*. €

Shterev (39 rooms) pl 20 Yuli 1; \ 93380; m 0886 277188. Good location on the main square, but not all rooms are renovated & it's not great value. €

Where to eat and drink
The Club ul Pliska 5; \ 96929. Good cuisine, both Bulgarian & European. €

Edno Vreme ul Rakovska 9; \ 95019. Probably the best eating place in the town, with a rich menu & fine setting in an old house with big yard & authentic terrace. Mainly Bulgarian & local specialities. €€

✖ **Vodopad** ul Vodopad 41; ☏ 93127. Picturesque location by a waterfall on the outskirts. Traditional grills. €

What to see and do The small **Historical Museum** (*Историческимузей; ul Vuzrozhdenska 4;* ☏ *0335 94728;* ⊕ *09.00–noon & 13.00–17.00 Tue–Sun; adult 0.50lv*) is in the old school, near the Levski statue.

The **Church of the Holy Virgin** (*Черква Св Дева Мария*) has a particularly intricate iconostasis decorated with double-headed eagles and frescoes featuring Levski in ecclesiastical robes, surrounded by clerics.

STARA PLANINA WALKS

It is hard to make just a day walk in this huge and diverse mountain chain. The difficulty is also that the Balkan Mountains rise in height fairly aggressively, which means that you have to climb quite a way to get anywhere. However, once you are on the ridge itself, it is excellent: almost flat and spectacular because you are virtually walking on the border between north and south Bulgaria.

I would recommend trying one of the eco-paths in this mountain for a day walk. There are examples in the following places:

From **Kalofer Monastery** in the Byala Reka area, an eco-trail begins from the monastery and this is where you can leave your car. Start behind the monastery and descend to the small river. Then follow the trail and you will see and experience some beautiful nature! This is a circular trail, which means that in about 2 hours you will be back and can have a picnic.

Troyan Pass can be reached from the village of Kurnare in south Bulgaria or from the town of Troyan in north Bulgaria. This is the highest mountain pass in Stara Planina, at some 1,550m. And you are actually on the ridge, so from the mountain pass you can walk either west or east with no significant gain or loss in height.

If you walk west in 2–3 hours you can reach the Kozai Stena Nature Reserve, where the rare edelweiss can be seen from mid-July to mid-August. Then return the same way back to Troyan Pass. The path is marked with red marks and you need only follow them.

If you walk east in 2 hours you can reach a small shelter house called Eagle's Nest. Here you can stop for a picnic and then return the same way. As in the previous description, the path is marked with red marks and you need only follow them.

If you are driving, for either walk you can park your car at the monument representing a huge arch, which stands just above the pass.

Sinite Kamuni Nature Park, just north of the town of Sliven, is a real jewel, famous for its fauna and also for the huge diversity of butterflies.

From Sliven you can drive to the chair-lift and ride all the way up to the park. Or you can drive, following the signs for Karandila, which is the region where most hotels are. Before you leave the town, call at the tourist information centre, which can provide you with maps, books and other information.

It is best to begin your walk from the final station of the chair-lift. The most interesting direction is to the west of the station to Golyamata Chatalka peak, which is easy to climb. From this peak you will have a complete 360° panorama.

The **Vasil Levski House-Museum** (*Дом-музей Васил Левски; ul General Kartsov 57;* ✆ *93489;* e *v_levski_museum@mail.orbitel.bg; www.vlevskimuseum-bg. org;* ⊕ *08.30–13.00 & 14.00–17.00 Mon–Fri; adult 2lv*) has several rooms around a courtyard with exhibits illustrating Levski's life and beliefs. Here you can see the humble origins and Spartan surroundings of his youth: low plain wooden furniture and nothing decorative. A separate gallery has paintings of Levski and some interesting old photos of his fellow freedom fighters. A lock of his hair is displayed in a small chapel almost as a holy relic. There are English captions.

KALOFER (КАЛОФЕР) *Telephone code: 03133*

According to tradition the town was founded by a rebel leader, Kalifer Voivoda (voivoda meaning leader of a group of militia). The Turks were unable to suppress his activities so they did a deal allowing the fighters to settle in the area as long as they did not attack Turkish trade caravans. The rebels captured some maidens from the town of Sopot and established themselves in Kalofer, which became known as a wealthy town and a cultural and commercial centre.

Tourist information There is a tourist information office on the main square (✆ *5988; www.visitcentralbalkan.net*) but this is mainly for information about hiking in the Central Balkan National Park.

Getting there and away There are **trains** from Burgas (*1 daily; 5hrs*), Sofia (*2 daily; 2–3hrs*) and Karlovo (*3 daily; 10mins*).

There are **buses** from Karlovo (*1–2 per hr; 30mins*).

Where to stay Two small hotels offer comfortable basic accommodation.

⌂ Sandevata Kushta (4 rooms) ul Sevlievska 66; ✆ 5857; m 0876 578677. €

⌂ Tsutsovata Kashta (5 rooms) ul Bluskova 7; ✆ 5483; e cucovata@abv.bg; www.cucovata.com. €

✗ Where to eat and drink

✗ Kalofer Mehana Near the central square; m 0898 743851; www.balkanibg.com/tavern. htm. Authentic old building with a garden. Bulgarian specialities, soups & salads. €

What to see and do Kalofer's chief claim to fame is as the birthplace of national hero Hristo Botev (see box, page 143). There is a statue of Botev in the main square and behind him is a view of the highest peak in the Balkan Mountains, which is named after him. The **Town Museum** (*Градския музей; just off the main square;* ⊕ *08.00–17.30 Tue–Sun; adult 2lv*) has a major exhibition about Botev, though there are no English captions. Outside is his birthplace, a humble cottage, across the square from the old schoolroom where his father, and briefly Botev himself, taught.

There are several attractive stone bridges over the River Tundzha, which runs through the town. While we were sitting on one for a rest we saw two dippers fishing; it was fascinating to watch them standing on a small rock studying the water, and then suddenly diving in.

KOPRINKA DAM (ЯЗОВИР КОПРИНКА) This dam, just to the west of Kazanluk, was built in the late 1940s by volunteer brigades, and is a pleasant, peaceful spot. Beneath its waters lies the Thracian city of Sevtopolis, the city of King Sevt III, which was thoroughly studied before being submerged. There is a suggestion that the city could be separated from the waters of the dam by a surrounding wall, and become a tourist attraction to be visited by boat. It is certainly an exciting idea, though probably a very expensive one!

KAZANLUK (КАЗАНЛЪК) *Telephone code: 0431*

Kazanluk is almost the geographical centre of Bulgaria and it is a crossroads for travellers, with important north–south and east–west routes meeting here. It is known as the centre for rose oil extraction and more recently for the archaeological discoveries in its vicinity.

In June, Kazanluk and other nearby towns host the annual Rose Festival, an event largely geared to tourists but which does provide a lot of picturesque photo opportunities. There are chances to sample a variety of rose products: rose-petal jam, rose-flavoured Turkish delight (*lokum* in Bulgarian), rose liqueur and even rose brandy on some occasions, although this is rare. Enthusiastic visitors can join tours to participate in early morning rose picking or visit one of the old-fashioned distilleries. The smell of roses is everywhere – sometimes rosewater is substituted for ordinary water in the decorative fountains or even sprayed from a light aircraft on those below. A Rose Queen is chosen and there are processions, parades and dances.

TOURIST INFORMATION The tourist information office is at ul Iskra 4 (✆ *62817;* e *stour@kazanlak.bg; www.kazanlak.bg).*

GETTING THERE AND AWAY There are **trains** from Burgas (*2 daily; 3hrs*), Sofia (*3 daily; 3–4hrs*) and Karlovo (*hourly; 1hr*).

There are **buses** (*bus station* ✆ *63200*) from Gabrovo (*9 daily; 1hr*), Stara Zagora (*9 daily; 1hr*), Sofia (*6 daily; 3½hrs*), Plovdiv (*5 daily; 2hrs*), Hisarya (*1 daily; 1hr*), Burgas (*2 daily; 3hrs 10mins*) and Veliko Turnovo (*4 daily; 1hr 20mins*).

🏠 WHERE TO STAY

🏠 **Chiflik** (6 rooms) ul Knyaz Mirski 28; ✆ 81411; m 0898 948454; e reserve@hotelchiflikakazanlak. bg; www.hotelchiflikakazanlak.bg. Small friendly family-run hotel near the park & Thracian tomb. €

🏠 **Grand Hotel Kazanluk** (150 rooms) pl Sevtopolis 1; ✆ 63210; e info@hotelkazanlak-bg. com; www.hotelkazanlak-bg.com. Centrally located; renovated rooms in former state-owned hotel. €€

🏠 **Palas** (30 rooms) ul P Stainov 9; ✆ 62161; e info@hotel-palas.com; www.hotel-palas.com.

Modern hotel close to the centre; the best option for staying, although it's usually booked up for the Rose Festival period. Smart spacious rooms. €€

🏠 **Rosa** (21 rooms) ul Rozova Dolina 2; ✆ 50005; m 0888 671958; e info@hotelrozabg.com; www. hotelrozabg.com. Central location above offices. Rooms rather small. Roof terrace with great views. €€

🏠 **Teres** (10 rooms) ul Lyubomir Kabakchiev 16; ✆ 64272; www.hotelteres.com. Brightly coloured rooms, friendly service; restaurant. €–€€

✗ WHERE TO EAT AND DRINK

✗ **Chiflik** See above. Good *mehana* offering national dishes & plenty of soups & salads. €–€€

✗ **Lucky restaurant** ul Gurko 8; ✆ 63180. Popular restaurant. Recommended for traditional Bulgarian fare. €–€€

✗ **New York Pub and Grill** pl Sevtopolis; ✆ 62464; m 0888 721264; ⏰ 10.00–23.00. The

most popular place in town. Sit for a drink with the locals in the evening or have pizza, salad or traditional Bulgarian food. €–€€

✗ **Rozarium** In the Rozarium Park in the centre; ✆ 63009. Unique location & atmosphere in the park with the roses. Varied menu with reasonable prices. €–€€

WHAT TO SEE AND DO The **Iskra Historical Museum** (*Исторически музей Искра; ul Sv Sv Kiril i Metodii junction with ul P Slaveykov;* ✆ *63762;* ⏰ *09.00–17.30 daily;*

adult 4lv) is part of the same building as the **Art Gallery** (*Художествена галерия; same opening times and price*). There are no English captions but a brochure is available in various languages including English.

According to a map, there are about 3,000 Thracian tombs in Bulgaria, and 150 around Kazanluk. This is an excellent museum with some really exciting treasures, including amazing intricate gold jewellery from a small mound at Shipka and Golyama Kosmatka. Many of the displays concern Sevtopolis and the weapons, pottery and coins found there.

Upstairs in the Art Gallery there are mainly modern works and some icons. There is also an interesting section on the making of rose oil. Astonishingly the oil has arrived in the space age, as US space shuttles are lubricated with Bulgarian rose oil because it is resistant to all temperature changes. Rose oil, despite its name, is not a liquid. At 20°C it takes the form of crystals and is stored at 10°C in

THE BULGARIAN ROSE

The rose's origin can be traced back to the ancient and evergreen dendriform roses, growing in the woody and humid provinces of China and India.

In the 12th and 13th centuries the oil-bearing rose was brought to Europe from the Middle East. In 1270, at the time of the Crusades, Count Breuer selected the famous *Rosa damascena* from the area of Damascus, Syria. This rose was found to grow exceptionally well in the sub-Balkan valleys of Bulgaria along the southern slopes of the Balkan range and the Sredna Gora Mountains. It was this rose which ensured that the Kazanluk region came to be known as the **Valley of the Roses.** The favourable climate of the valley, with its characteristic mild winters and a long spring with light rains, high humidity and abundant morning dew, are ideal for growing the oil-yielding rose and creating its unique aroma.

Rosa damascena from the valley of the Shiraz River in Persia reached the Kazanluk Valley via Syria and Adrianople, and its spread continued during the centuries of the Ottoman Empire. There are two documents preserved from those years: the first is an ordinance of Sultan Murad III (1574–95) to the chief gardener of Adrianople, in which he gives the order that roses from the gardens there should be sent to the gardens of the old palace in the Ottoman capital; the second documentary evidence is in the travel notes of the famous traveller Hadzhi Khalfe, in which he points out that in 1650 rosewater was in great demand in the busy market of Adrianople.

The first Bulgarian attar of roses appeared on European markets as early as the end of the 17th century to meet the needs of the developing perfumery industry. In the beginning it was a small cottage industry and initially involved small domestic stills comprising a copper cauldron from which water-cooled pipes dripped the greenish-yellow rose oil. It became big business early in the 19th century. The high-quality Bulgarian rose oil brought its representatives scores of medals and diplomas from world exhibitions, shows and fairs.

The rose flowers are picked in the course of a month, from the middle of May to the middle of June from 05.00 to about 10.00, before the sun gets too high in the sky, as it can quickly evaporate up to half of the oil. Between 3,000 and 5,000kg are required to make one litre of attar, leaving a residue of rosewater and pulp which is used to make medicaments, flavourings, jam and liqueurs.

a high-security vault in Sofia. Each container is sealed with a special wax stamp of which there is only one copy. This tight security is necessary because of the very great value of the oil, known as 'Bulgaria's gold,' and the risk of counterfeiting with an inferior-quality product.

The **Kazanluk Tomb and Museum** (*Казанлъшката гробница и музей; Tyulbe Park, northeast of the centre near Kulata Ethnographic Complex;* \ *62817; replica* ⊕ *09.00–17.00 daily; adult 2lv*) provides an alternative to seeing the real thing, which is kept closed to preserve it from pollution and damage. The frescoes are remarkable and well worth visiting. The fluidity of the lines, the folds of the clothes, the blowing hair of the groom, the way that each horse is painted as an individual, with a tilted head here and a knowing look there, indicates that this decoration was the work of a great master or his pupil, who travelled to the area for this commission (see box, below). There is also a Turkish tomb in the park, that of the first Ottoman governor of Rumelia, who was killed in battle here.

The **Kulata Ethnographic Complex** (*Етнографски комплекс Кулата; ul Knyaz Mirski;* ⊕ *08.00–noon & 13.00–18.00 daily; adult 3lv*) shows the home of a

THE VALLEY OF THE THRACIAN KINGS

If you want to get to know the ancient culture of the Bulgarian lands you should visit at least one of the Thracian tombs. They are not as famous or as huge as the Egyptian pyramids, but they represent a unique material culture, still not sufficiently examined and still full of mysteries.

One of the most famous monuments of Thracian art and architecture is the Kazanluk tomb. When it was discovered in 1944 the tomb was the first in the Valley of the Roses. Now it seems it is part of a whole Thracian necropolis, because recently in the region another 12 tombs have been found, each of them with different construction plans and a variety of styles of decoration. For this reason some now refer to the area as 'The Valley of the Thracian Kings'. The necropolis was probably connected to Sevtopolis, the capital of Odrysae, the most famous Thracian kingdom in antiquity. Sevtopolis, though almost fully preserved, is now covered by the waters of Koprinka Reservoir.

We may never know who the people buried in these tombs really were. It is doubtful that all of them were Thracian kings, but certainly most were a part of the Thracian nobility. The tombs were built between the end of the 5th and the beginning of the 3rd century BC. Those worth visiting include the mound of the Golyama Kosmatka, the tombs of Muglizh, Helvetia and Shushmanets and the tumulus of the Gryphons. Most of them were looted in late antiquity or medieval times; unfortunately even nowadays there are still treasure hunters destroying cultural monuments.

It doesn't happen often, but sometimes the archaeologists are lucky enough to discover an untouched tomb. A good example of this is the Golyama Kosmatka. It is assumed that the great Thracian King Sevt III, from the 4th century BC, was buried here, together with his armour, weapons, gold and silver vessels and amphoras, and with a golden wreath on his head.

THE KAZANLUK TOMB Most other recently discovered tombs have decorations that are in a very poor state of preservation, or almost fully destroyed, so the Kazanluk tomb remains the one with the most spectacular and well-preserved wall paintings. When it was discovered, the Kazanluk tomb was already empty, probably having peasant, some wooden buildings storing agricultural implements and carts, and the National Revival-style home of a wealthy rose-oil merchant.

The **Church of the Assumption** (*Възнесение*), just off the main square, has another wonderful iconostasis by the master craftsmen from Debur.

About 3km north of Kazanluk is the **Institute of Roses, Essential and Medical Cultures and Museum of Roses** (*Институт за розата и етеричномаслените култури и музей на розата; bul Osvobozhdenie 49;* \ *62039;* ⊕ *summer 09.00–17.00 daily; adult 3lv*). The gardens supposedly have examples of every variety of rose, but they are not arranged for display. The museum has no English captions but the photographs of the oil-making process are interesting. There is a sweet-scented souvenir shop.

There are now several excavated mounds, which can be visited around Kazanluk; for some it is necessary to make arrangements at the Iskra Museum. The **Golyama Kosmatka** mound has been developed for tourists, and is well signposted, with parking and a useful selection of guidebooks. The archaeologist Georgi Kitov's *The Valley of the Thracian Rulers* is a mine of information for the enthusiast. It was

been robbed in antiquity. The interior style and the building techniques indicate that the tomb was built during the last decades of the 4th century BC.

In 1977, it was included in UNESCO's World Heritage list. An exact replica has been built next to the original tomb for the general public to visit.

The building has an interior brickwork wall and an exterior wall of hewn ashlar held together with clay, and, like most other tombs from the period, it consists of three chambers. The first room is the antechamber, which normally contained some of the gifts needed for the afterlife; very often these included a chariot, one or more sacrificed horses and sometimes even slaves, who had to accompany the dead person into his next life. The next chamber is a narrow corridor, or *dromos*, which was constructed for the preservation of some of the smaller items, such as vessels and food. The antechamber and the corridor would have been decorated with murals, but those in the antechamber have been totally destroyed. In the corridor on opposite sides are two friezes, representing a procession of soldiers. On the eastern wall there is a meeting between two military commanders, followed by their slaves; on the western wall you can see one of the warriors kneeling, and holding up a long curved knife in his right hand, beside a standing man. Both friezes are painted in warm colours, typical of Classical and Hellenistic art, such as Pompeian red, black and white, with different shades of ochre predominating.

The third chamber, the burial chamber itself, is circular and richly decorated, its false dome topped by a granite keystone. The frieze in the burial chamber is the largest and shows a ceremonial celebration, a scene which was very popular in ancient art. The central personalities are a dignitary and his wife, sitting in front of a table with various dishes on it. They are surrounded by a procession of men, women and horses, each of the people carrying a different gift. There are a variety of interpretations of the meaning of the scene, the most popular being that it represents the dead Thracian king or dignitary and his wife in their afterlife, where they would find eternal happiness. The ancient authors mention that the Thracians had a deeply held belief in the afterlife, and went so far as to celebrate when somebody was dying, because he or she would be saved from their sufferings on earth.

his find, in 2004, of the solid gold life-size mask, or *phiala*, weighing over 600g, that really excited people. It is a remarkable face – not a death mask but that of a vigorous strong man. There is a story that after drinking from a gold vessel at a feast the ruler suddenly raised it against his face, transforming flesh and blood into pure gold, and presumably convincing his people that he was a very powerful figure chosen by the gods. The roof of the tomb is one huge granite slab.

At **Malkata** tumulus a necklace judged the most exquisite ever found in Thrace was discovered, indicating that this may also have been a royal burial site.

STARA ZAGORA (СТАРА ЗАГОРА) *Telephone code: 042*

There has been a city here since the 6th century BC, and Thracians, Romans and Turks have left their mark. Its situation at the crossroads of two important trading routes and in a fertile agricultural area ensured that it would always be a settlement, and that it would be fought over by successive conquerors. Its inhabitants were active during the National Revival period and in the struggle for liberation. Nowadays it is known for its numerous lime trees, its grid-pattern straight streets and the number of 20th-century poets, such as Geo Milev and Kiril Hristov, who lived and worked here. The Ayazmo Park is one of the beauties of this agreeable city.

GETTING THERE AND AWAY This is a busy transport hub. There are **trains** from Burgas (*5 daily; 2hrs*), Plovdiv (*5 daily; 2hrs*), Sofia (*5 daily; 4hrs*), and Ruse (*3 daily; 6hrs*). The railway station is on ul Gerasim Papazchev 20 (☏ *626752*), about five minutes' walk from the bus station.

There are **buses** from Burgas (*hourly; 3hrs*), Varna (*5 daily; 5hrs*), Veliko Turnovo (*7 daily; 3hrs*), Kazanluk (*6 daily; 45mins*), Sofia (*hourly 05.00–19.00; 4–6hrs*), Plovdiv (*1–2 per hr; 1½–2hrs*) and Sliven (*1–2 per hr; 1hr 35mins*) **The bus station** is on bul Slavyanski 64 (☏ *605349*).

TOURIST INFORMATION The tourist information centre is on bul Ruski 27 (☏ *627098*; e *tic@starazagora.bg*).

🏠 **WHERE TO STAY** *Map, page 215*

🏠 **Elegans** (20 rooms) ul Petko Slaveykov 54; ☏636606; m 0885 656606. Friendly hotel in the centre with comfortable rooms at reasonable prices. €–€€

🏠 **Ezeroto** (16 rooms) ul Bratya Zhekovi 60; ☏600103; m 0879 545707. Good place in a parkland setting near the centre, and close to bus & railway stations. Modern style, nicely furnished. Restaurant. €€

🏠 **Forum** (13 rooms) ul Hadzhi Dimitar Asenov 94; ☏631616; m 0886 631616; e reservations@ hotelforum.bg; www.hotelforum.bg. Centrally located hotel in a restored 1891 house that is a

'monument of culture'. Very good restaurant (see below). €€

🏠 **Uniqato** (16 rooms) ul Sava Silov 36; ☏661155; m 0888 661155; e reservationa@ uniqato.com; www.uniqato.com. Centrally located. The best place to stay in the city; very nice rooms, excellent service. The hotel restaurant is one of best in Stara Zagora (page 215). €€

🏠 **Vereya** (115 rooms) ul Tsar Simeon Veliki 100; ☏919373; e hotel_vereya@yahoo.com; www. hotel-vereya.com. Largest hotel, on the main square with its many bars & cafés; central location. Now modernised as a stylish business hotel. €€–€€€

✖ **WHERE TO EAT AND DRINK** *Map, page 215*

✖ **Forum** See above. Beautifully presented & stylish, mainly modern Bulgarian & some

international cuisine. Good selection of wines. €€–€€€

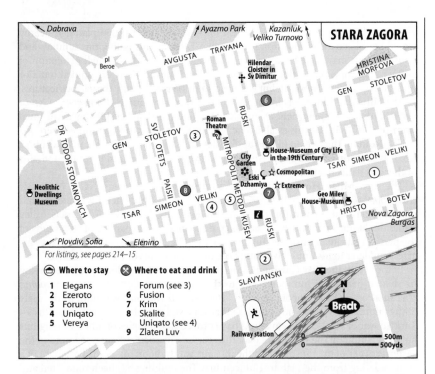

For listings, see pages 214–15

Where to stay

1	Elegans
2	Ezeroto
3	Forum
4	Uniqato
5	Vereya

Where to eat and drink

	Forum (see 3)
6	Fusion
7	Krim
8	Skalite
	Uniqato (see 4)
9	Zlaten Luv

✕ **Fusion** ul Ivan Shishman 64; 644999. In the centre. Nice setting, with garden. International cuisine. €€

✕ **Krim** bul Ruski 30; 250021. Centrally located with original interior decoration. Varied menu. €€

✕ **Skalite** ul Pop Mincho Kunchev 96; 980981. Central. Three different zones: pizzeria, tavern & winter garden. Bulgarian & international cuisine. Excellent choice of good wines. €–€€

✕ **Uniqato** See page 214; 641164. One of the best restaurants in the city. Bulgarian, Italian & European cuisine. Wide choice of excellent wines. €€

✕ **Zlaten Luv** ul Ivan Shishman 58; 651010; 11.00–02.00. Attractive restaurant in the centre; interesting interior. Varied menu with local specialities & international cuisine. €€

NIGHTLIFE

☆ **Cosmopolitan** bul Tsar Simeon Veliki 107; 602581; 22.00–05.00 daily. Big, busy club. Programme includes both guest DJs playing electronic music & Bulgarian pop-folk stars.

☆ **Extreme** bul Tsar Simeon Veliki 108; m 0888 655345. Two halls with pop-folk & house & techno music.

WHAT TO SEE AND DO The **House-Museum of City Life in the 19th Century** (Дом-музей на Градския бит през 19-ти век; ul Dimitur Naumov 68; 919214; 09.00–noon & 14.00–17.00 Tue–Sun; adult 2lv) is in a distinguished old house furnished as a typical middle-class home.

The **Neolithic Dwellings Museum** (Музей на неолитните жилища; in the grounds of the district hospital, ul Dr Todor Stoyanovich; 600299; 09.00–noon & 14.00–17.00 Tue–Sat, also Sun in Jul/Aug; adult 3lv) houses the remains of two small homes from around 6000BC. This is one of the most important Neolithic sites in Europe. The larger dwelling measures 6m by 5.2m and the smaller 5.2m by 3m. Their walls would have been of wattle and daub, the roofs of thatch, and the floors levelled with wet clay. The hearth provided heat for cooking and a raised platform nearby would have been a cosy position for sleeping. There are intriguing tiny animals and houses which may have been toys for children. There is also a small exhibition of pottery and implements, but it is not labelled in English. There are guided tours or you can buy a helpful booklet, but you need some help to identify the various features.

The **Hilendar Cloister** is in the yard of **Sv Dimitur Church** (*Катедрален Храм Св Димитър; ul Pop Bogomil 1*) and has exhibits about Vasil Levski's stay in the town from 1855 to 1858, and his establishment of local revolutionary committees here.

The **Roman Theatre** on ul Mitropolit Metodii Kusev was built in the 3rd century AD. It is sometimes used for performances. Immediately behind it are the remains of thermal baths from the 2nd century AD.

The **Geo Milev House-Museum** (*Къща-музей Гео Милев; ul Geo Milev 35;* *623450; ⊕ 09.00–noon & 13.00–17.00 Mon–Sat; adult 4lv*) depicts his home life, and memorabilia are displayed, together with some exhibits about other local poets. Milev wrote the famous poem *September* which denounced the massacre of thousands of the participants in an unsuccessful uprising in 1925. His radical views led first to his arrest and later to his untimely death, possibly at the hands of the secret police.

In the centre the **City Garden** is a lovely park, always full of local people enjoying its shaded paths and fountains. The **Eski Dzhamiya** or Old Mosque (*Старата Джамия*) on ul Tsar Simeon Veliki (⊕ *10.00–18.00 Tue–Sat*) was built in the early 15th century. This is the only building that survived the city fire during the Russo-Turkish war of 1877–78. Excavations have proved that temples of different religions have been built on the same spot over the years: a Thracian cult pit was found in the eastern corner of the mosque, and the mosque was built on top of the basement of a church dating from the 11th to 12th century. The building has been renovated and is a Museum of Religions.

Nearby are the old and new **opera houses**. Stara Zagora was the first city outside Sofia to have its own opera house, and it still has a fine reputation, not least because the world-famous Boris Hristov began his career here.

Ayazmo Park is in the northern part of the city. It is something of a botanical garden and has numerous different species of tree. It is a pleasant place to walk and there are also sport and leisure facilities and a small zoo. In late June or early July a Roma Music Festival is held here.

NOVA ZAGORA (НОВА ЗАГОРА) Telephone code: 0457

Nova Zagora is at the hub of an area of Thracian archaeological finds. There are 26 prehistoric settlements here, of the type known as village tumuli, of which the best known is probably Karanovo, west of the town off the Plovdiv road. This is an astonishing site – a gigantic layer cake of history. The mild climate and fertile soil attracted settlers to the area from the 7th millennium BC. The production of sophisticated artefacts was made possible by the juxtaposition of copper deposits and the highly skilled metalworking abilities of the settlers. These combined to give the brilliant culture of the Chalcolithic and Bronze ages.

GETTING THERE AND AWAY There are **trains** from Burgas (*5 daily; 2½hrs*), Varna (*5 daily; 4hrs 10mins*), Plovdiv (*hourly; 3hrs*), Sofia (*5 daily; 6hrs*), Stara Zagora (*hourly; 35mins*) and Yambol (*1 hourly; 45mins*).

There are **buses** (*bus station* \\ *22196*) from Stara Zagora (*hourly; 30mins*), Plovdiv (*6 daily; 2hrs*), Burgas (*2 daily; 2½hrs*), Sliven (*2 daily; 30mins*) and Sofia (*18 daily; 4hrs*).

TOURIST INFORMATION The tourist information office is on ul 14 January 52 (✆ 64310; e office@bcnzagora.org).

🏠 WHERE TO STAY

🏠 **Dragon Hut** (7 rooms) 8km north of Nova Zagora in the foothills of Sredna Gora; ✆ 64272. Family hotel, welcoming place, rural location in the pine forest. Outdoor pool. *Mehana.* €

🏠 **Soli Invicto** Elenovo village, 15km south of Nova Zagora; ✆ 0445 00412; m 0889 066330;

e sales@soliinvicto.bg; www.soliinvicto.bg. Boutique hotel in the middle of vineyards. Modern stone-&-timber building, stylish rooms, amazing views. Infinity pool. Wine-tasting & restaurant. Worth a detour. €€

✖ WHERE TO EAT AND DRINK

✖ **Merkurii** ul San Stefano 3; ✆ 62969. Traditional, Bulgarian dishes. €€

✖ **Yanitsa Restaurant** pl Svoboda 7; m 0878 622647. Good traditional food. €

WHAT TO SEE AND DO The tell (or mound) at Karanovo, at a height of 12m, is the biggest in southeast Europe. The site shows the different stages of development. The earliest level of habitation is from 6000BC when the inhabitants practised pastoral agriculture, hunting and fishing; the earliest dwellings were made of woven sticks covered in mud. In the Stone Age, two-storey houses were built and stone walls were constructed around the village to protect it. Tools and implements were made of horn, and stones were used for grinding corn. Some animals were kept as domestic animals although others continued to be hunted. Flint was used in tools; copper and later bronze were also worked for tools, but in time were used for ornamentation. Pottery was made and fine decorations were painted on the red background.

In the Chalcolithic Age, pottery was made in more elaborate and unusual shapes, sculpted by special knives. Statuettes were at first usually of women, reflecting their status as mother goddess, but in time more were made of men, reflecting a major cultural shift, important for Bulgaria and all early history.

As you approach the site it is horseshoe shaped because that is how the hillside mound was excavated. On the top, more excavations are taking place and from there two or three Thracian mounds and a barrow are visible nearby; there are apparently 15 or so in the immediate area.

The richness of Thracian culture attracted many conquerors: the Macedonians, the Romans and the Byzantine Empire.

Nova Zagora Historical Museum (*Исторически музей, НоваЗагора; pl Svoboda 3;* ✆ *63154;* e *museum_nz@abv.bg;* ⊕ *09.00–noon & 14.00–17.00 Tue–Sat, 14.00–18.00 Sun; adult 2lv*) was established in 1926 and has a strong archaeological collection. In particular the museum has some remarkable rescued Thracian chariots. It was a widespread custom to bury chariots when their owners died, but because they were so beautifully decorated many have been sought and found by treasure hunters. The equipment and chariots had been used, as there is often evidence of repairs, but the Thracians believed in the afterlife and therefore took with them possessions which they thought would be useful. It seems that the horses were harnessed to the chariots and taken to the place of the funeral where a large pit was dug out. Then chariots were driven in and the horses were killed, their bodies heaped up on one side. Rituals were carried out over the chariots but not the horses, judging by the placing of vessels. Then the chariots were put in the central place and partly dismantled. All the chariots found so far were drawn by two horses and had either two or four wheels. Those found at Karanovo had many bronze decorative elements, while at Korten, a village near Karanovo, the four-wheeled chariot is the biggest that has ever been found. These burials date from around 3000BC.

SLIVEN (СЛИВЕН) *Telephone code: 044*

The town first became important between the 7th and 11th centuries, because of its strategic position on the route by water from the Danube to Istanbul. From the 11th century it was known as Sliven, which means a confluence: that is, of the three rivers that flow through the town and the three winds that blow from the three passes of the Balkan Mountains. It has always kept its Slav name and indeed was a privileged town under the Ottoman Empire, as it was known for its protection of the mountain pass.

GETTING THERE AND AWAY There are **trains** (*railway station* 622614) from Burgas (*6 daily; 2hrs*), Sofia (*3 daily; 5hrs 15mins*), Kazanluk (*6 daily; 2hrs*), Karlovo (*4 daily; 2½hrs*) and Karnobat (*5 daily; 45mins*).

There are **buses** (*bus station at ul Hadzhi Dimitur;* 662629) from Burgas (*1–2 per hr; 2hrs*), Varna (*3 daily; 3½hrs*), Veliko Turnovo (*8 daily; 3hrs*), Plovdiv (*6 daily; 3hrs*), Stara Zagora (*10 daily; 1hr 15mins*) and Sofia (*10 daily; 5hrs*).

TOURIST INFORMATION The tourist information office is at ul Tsar Osboboditel 1 (611148; e *infotourist@sliven.bg; www.infotourism.sliven.bg*).

🏠 WHERE TO STAY

🏠 **Central** (47 rooms) bul Tsar Osvoboditel 6; 501700; m 0882 001002; e reception@hotel-park-central.bg; www.hotel-park-central.bg. Modern hotel in centre; clean rooms & friendly staff. €€

🏠 **Imperia** (48 rooms) ul Panayot Hitov; 667599; e hotel.imperia.sliven@gmail.com; www.hotelimperia.net. On the outskirts of Sliven so more suitable for travellers with a car; stylish rooms, swimming pool, restaurant serving Bulgarian food with a modern twist. Very good value. €

🏠 **National Palace** (34 rooms) ul Velikoknyazhevska 31; 662929; m 0889 819911; e hotel@nationalpalace.bg; www.nationalpalace.

bg. Probably the best hotel in the city, with a friendly atmosphere. *Mehana* on ground floor (see below). €€

🏠 **Sliven** (88 rooms) pl Hadzi Dimitar 2; 624056; e sliven.hoteltower@gmail.com; www.hotel.sliven.net. Former state-run hotel. Rooms need renovation but it's right in the centre. Good option for budget travellers. €

🏠 **Toma** (6 rooms) ul Velikoknyazhevska 27; 623333; e office@hoteltoma.com; www.hoteltoma.com. Original 1856 house with *alafranga* decoration, carved ceilings & authentic details. Bathrooms squeezed in to old building and rather small. Central, can be noisy. €€

✖ WHERE TO EAT AND DRINK

✖ **Evrika** ul Rakovski 48; 622233. Central location in a handsome old house. Varied menu with international cuisine; good choice of wines. €€
✖ **Karakachanska Kushta** ul Panayot Hitov 1; m 0878 889939. Central location with fantastic atmosphere; garden. Bulgarian food. €€
✖ **Pri Fabrikadzhiyata** In the courtyard of the National Palace Hotel (see above). Smart restaurant with well-presented traditional dishes. Live music sometimes. €

✖ **Pri Hadzhyata** ul Yordan Kyuvliev 11; 625062. Central location with traditional atmosphere. Indoor & outdoor dining. Bulgarian food & local specialities; the stuffed trout is worth trying. Good choice of wines. €€
✖ **Toma Inn** See above. Offers mainly Bulgarian food & traditional specialities. €€
♀ **Club Areka** bul Hristo Botev 23; 089 868 5975; ⊕ 17.00–06.00 daily. It is more of a bar than club, but there is a great party atmosphere.

WHAT TO SEE AND DO During the 19th century Sliven was known for its production of fine-quality textiles. The first textile factory in Bulgaria was built here in 1836, and it is still an impressive building. Sliven is known to Bulgarians as the town of the hundred *voivodi*. They were the local leaders of the resistance to the Ottoman Empire during Bulgaria's struggle for freedom in the late 18th and early 19th centuries. They were rather like Britain's Robin Hood, and there are many tales about their exploits.

The town centre is an attractive car-free area, with plenty of lively cafés and shops, and a remarkable 1,000-year-old oak tree which somehow survived a great fire in medieval times. The main square is named after the hero Hadzhi Dimitur, and there is a statue of him to the northeast of the tall Hotel Sliven. There is also a **house-museum** (*дом-музей; ul Assenova 2;* \ *622496;* ⊕ *09.00–noon & 14.00–17.00 Mon–Fri; adult 2lv*) dedicated to him across the river by the covered market, incongruously sited amid tower blocks. There are no English captions but it is a fine old house in a courtyard which was once an inn run by the hero's father. It is set up to replicate the house as they would have lived in it. By the tender age of 20 he had become the standard-bearer for Panayot Hitov, another Sliven hero, and fought in various guerrilla raids from Romania into Bulgaria, meeting his death at the hands of Turkish troops when only 28.

The **History Museum** (*Исторически музей; ul Tsar Osvoboditel 18;* \ *622494;* ⊕ *09.00–noon & 14.00–17.00 Mon–Sat; adult 2lv*) is also in a fine building. There are no English captions but the archaeological exhibits, coin collection and weapons are interesting, as is the material about the *voivodi*. There is also a collection of exhibits from nearby Kaloyanovo, where a Thracian ruler was buried with his horse.

The local beauty spot is the **Blue Rocks** (*Сините камъни*), where stony slopes with small trees and shrubs provide a home for butterflies, birds and wild flowers. In the evening light the rocks look grey-blue, hence the name. The area can be accessed by a scenic road, by the chair-lift (⊕ *08.30–17.30 daily; 6lv single, 10lv return*) or by walking. The chair-lift theoretically works shorter hours in winter and there are occasional breaks for maintenance in spring and autumn. It's worth checking at the tourist office before you set off.

The unusual rock formation, the **Ring**, a jagged arch, is associated with several legends. Local sailors supposedly tied their boats up here during the flood, and couples who walk through the arch will be in love forever.

YAMBOL (ЯМБОЛ) *Telephone code: 046*

Yambol is another ancient settlement as the number of burial mounds in the area indicates. Finds from the Rasheva and Marcheva mounds are in the local museum, in the National History Museum in Sofia and even in the Louvre in Paris. The predecessor of the modern town was the ancient site of Kabile (pages 222–4).

GETTING THERE AND AWAY There are **trains** (*railway station* \ *662626*) from Burgas (*5 daily; 2hrs*), Varna (*5 daily; 3½hrs*), Plovdiv (*4 daily; 3hrs*), Stara Zagora (*hourly; 1hr 20mins*) and Sofia (*5 daily; 5–6hrs*).

There are **buses** (*bus station* \ *661914*) to Ruse (*4 per week; 6hrs*), Burgas (*6 daily; 1hr 35mins*), Sliven (*1–2 per hr; 1hr*) and Elhovo (*hourly; 1hr*).

⌂ WHERE TO STAY

⌂ **Diana Palace** (54 rooms) ul Ivan Vazov 2; \ 664807; e dianapalace@mail.bg; www. dianapalace.com. Primarily for business guests, but good central location & comfortable rooms. **€–€€**

🛏 **Kabile** (56 rooms) ul Turgovska 35; ☏680000; m 0894 704490. Central, modern hotel complex with a lot of facilities. Friendly staff, good b/fast selection. €–€€

🛏 **Mercury** (11 rooms) ul Indzhe Voivoda 68; ☏664292; m 0896 786977; www.hotel-merkurii. com. Cosy, small hotel. Very good value. €–€€

🛏 **Tundzha** (60 rooms) ul Buzludzha 13; ☏662771; e hotel.tundzha@gmail.com; www. yambolsite.com. Remnant from communist period, but with renovated rooms & very good central location. €

✗ **WHERE TO EAT AND DRINK** There are many restaurants and pizzerias along the main pedestrian street, Turgovska.

✗ **Kushtata** ul P Parchevich; ☏663292. Traditional *mehana* in the centre offering Bulgarian cuisine, soups, salads & grilled specialities. €–€€

✗ **Strandzhata** ul Angel Kanchev 4; ☏661114. Central location. Traditional specialities, soups, salads. €–€€

WHAT TO SEE AND DO In the town centre is a remarkable building, the **Bezesten** (*Безистен; pl Osvobozhdenie*), built in the late 15th century as a covered market. It was surrounded by the minarets of 11 mosques, of which only one, the Old Mosque (*Старата джамия*) survives. The **Church of Sv Georgi** (*Черква Св Георги*) dates back to 1737 and was at the centre of the struggle for religious and national freedom. It has a beautiful iconostasis by master woodcarvers from Debur. The town's **Museum of History** (*Историческимузей; ul Byalo More 2;* ⊕ *08.00–noon & 14.00–17.00 Mon–Fri; adult 2lv*) has a large collection of archaeological exhibits, ceramics and local crafts.

Yambol is at the heart of the Thracian Valley wine region, well known for its quality red wines. Travellers through the region will see hectares of vineyards, some well cared for and some overgrown and neglected. Try to sample some wines from Yambol, Sakar and Sliven while you are in the region.

BIRDWATCHING NEAR SLIVEN AND KARNOBAT

The Sliven and Karnobat areas are representatives of the sub-Balkan plains and embrace the southern slopes of the eastern Balkans and some wetlands in the lower parts. Sliven Plain is the region where, in a limited area, you can see within an hour **long-legged buzzard, imperial eagle, golden eagle, lesser spotted eagle, booted eagle, goshawk**, and sometimes **steppe eagle**, together with several other commoner species of birds of prey. They are all attracted by the numerous colonies of suslik there. Similarly, in the Karnobat area, near the former Straldzha Marsh and Tserkovski Reservoir, **Montagu's harrier, corncrake** and **long-legged buzzard** breed, as do **stone curlew, tawny pipit, Isabelline wheatear** and **roller**, as well as enormous colonies of **rose-coloured starling** in some years. In Tserkovski Reservoir interesting water birds can be seen, including **Dalmatian pelican** and **red-breasted goose** in colder winters. It is designated by BirdLife International as an Important Bird Area. To the south of the town of Sliven are the flooded forests along the Tundzha River, examples of European 'jungle' vegetation. Colonies of **herons** and **egrets** can be seen in the two small reserves here, and also **black kite, grey-headed** and **middle-spotted woodpeckers** and other woodland birds.

There is an old Bulgarian legend saying that when the hailstorm appears in the sky, the imperial eagle takes off to fight with it to save its eaglets. Later on people realised that a cross was formed by the white shoulders of the flying bird. These two things combined to make Bulgarians consider the eagle a sacred bird. There used to be hundreds of nests everywhere in the country, often on solitary trees within arable fields, just metres from the working farmers! Fewer than 100 years were enough for the imperial eagle to reach the edge of extinction in the country. When BSPB started its special programme for saving the eagle, there were about ten pairs left. After almost 20 years that number increased to 17, but this is a lot taking into consideration the increasing developments, land transformation and increasing human disturbance. BSPB guards most of the nests during the entire breeding season, and recommended virtually all nests to be included in Natura 2000 protected areas (however, this did not happen for economic reasons). Efforts to save the last lords of the air continue and will continue in spite of the difficulties. Thanks to the conservation work the imperial eagle can still be seen, especially in the areas of Sakar, Sliven and other sites.

AROUND YAMBOL

ATOLOVO (АТОЛОВО) Northeast of Yambol, close to the town of Straldzha, is the small village of Atolovo. This was established in 1926 to receive ethnic Bulgarian refugees from Greek Macedonia and Eastern Thrace. It received assistance from the Save the Children Fund and financial support from the 8th Duke of Atholl, hence the name. Tsar Boris III attended the inauguration ceremony. British volunteers helped to build the houses, a cultural centre (*chitalishte*) and a church. Having travelled to this remote place out of curiosity about the British connection, I was surprised to discover another one. The water supply (*cheshma*) bore an English inscription: Major Anthony Buxton of Horsey Hall, Great Yarmouth, England. Perhaps there is a family link with the Buxton brothers after whom a district and boulevard in Sofia are named?

ELHOVO (ЕЛХОВО) *Telephone code: 0478*
South of Yambol is the small town of Elhovo, in the heart of a big vine-growing area. Archaeologists have found implements and ceramics from the Neolithic period, and there are Thracian burial mounds nearby. The Romans fortified the settlement, calling it Oruditsa ad Burgum, and used it as a staging post between Kabile, present-day Yambol, and Adrianople (present-day Edirne). It was part of the Byzantine and Bulgarian empires before being occupied by the Turks.

Getting there and away There are **buses** from Yambol (*hourly; 1hr*) and Burgas (*2 daily; 1½hrs*).

Tourist information The tourist information centre is on ul Targovska 23 (\ *81073;* e *info@elhovo.org; www.elhovo.org*).

Where to stay and eat Two small hotels offering basic accommodation.

☗ **Iznenada** ul Yanko Bakalov 10. €   ☗ **Smokinya** ul Indzhe Voivoda 2; \ 88618. €

What to see and do If you are travelling through the town it is worth stopping to visit the excellent **Ethnographic Museum** (*Етнографския музей*; ⊕ *08.00– noon & 13.30–17.30 Mon–Fri; adult 1lv*). The topics covered include agriculture, viticulture, architecture, hunting and fishing, clothes and jewels, textiles and embroidery, handicrafts and folk art. Particularly interesting are the late 19th-century costumes, as they include less familiar styles worn by refugees to this area from Odrin and Aegean Thrace. There are some fascinating old photos of people in similar costumes. There is also a big collection of *pafti*, the decorative buckles from women's belts. There is an amazing toy water buffalo made of sticks, string and sweetcorn husks, and huge *kukeri* headdresses nearly 2m high. One of the museum's most prized possessions is a map, one of only three in the world, showing costume areas; for example, it shows the southernmost limit of the area where women wear two aprons, the easternmost limit of the soukman tunic and so on.

Unfortunately there are no English captions, though there is a useful guidebook on sale with some text in English.

KABILE (КАБИЛЕ) Kabile was originally a Thracian town, from the 2nd millennium BC. Each successive occupier of this site built on top of the buildings they found here, or appropriated the stones for new structures of their own nearby. The colour-coded plan at the entrance shows clearly the continuity of occupation, the successive layers of buildings and the different inhabitants. It is easy to see that

THE VINE-GROWERS' YEAR

Vines can live for up to 100 years, but their best productivity lasts for about 50 years. Until the vine is about four years old, productivity is negligible, from the age of five to 35 it is on an upward curve, and thereafter, from about 35 to 55 it is declining.

The annual cycle coincides roughly with the calendar year. In **January** and **February** the vine is resting and during this time pruning takes place. The purpose of pruning is to remove inefficient shoots, and give the vine the best shape for the next season's growth. As in most vine-growing countries, this is an important occasion in village life, and there are many rituals and customs associated with it.

Each region has variations, but most celebrate 14 February as the Day of **Trifon Zarezan**, the so-called patron saint of vine-growers. Traditionally everyone involved in winemaking dresses in their finest clothes and, accompanied by musicians playing Bulgarian folk instruments, goes to the vineyards. Many wear symbolic flowers: wild geranium (for good health) and boxwood (an evergreen shrub for longevity). The people choose a leader of the festivities, perhaps the oldest vine-grower or someone who is seen as the best vine-grower, and he opens the festivities by symbolically pruning vines in different parts of the vineyard and pouring wine over them to encourage a fruitful vintage. The pruned twigs are often woven together and worn by the men across their shoulders. When people return to their village, wine is served to the leader of the festivities and other guests. A few drops of wine are customarily spilled on the ground to encourage fertility both in the vineyard and in the village. The festivities normally continue until well into the night!

In **March**, the vine begins to show signs of life, and a clear liquid starts to flow from the pruning cuts. In **April**, when a temperature of about 10°C is reached, the buds begin to break and leaves begin to appear.

in ancient times this hillside was a distinctive landmark, and that its possessors would control the area and the routes passing through it.

It was conquered in the 4th century BC by Philip of Macedon, father of Alexander the Great, who made it into a powerful stronghold. It was important because of its strategic position – close to the Tundzha River and on the important route from Augusta Trayana (Stara Zagora) to Adrianople (Edirne). There is a wealth of written evidence supporting the existence of the city and its importance as a major crossroads. It was described as a typical Greek *polis*, with the usual city layout of a main square surrounded by all the necessary administrative and business buildings, accessed by four main gates, one from each point of the compass. Interestingly, there is in the main square an altar to one of the most respected Greek gods, Apollo, who was also an accepted hero to the Thracians.

The Romans defeated the Macedonians in the 2nd century BC, and from this period there have been very rich finds of coins which were cut in the city, giving evidence of a well-organised and active mint. Many other finds, such as Greek pottery and seals, show active trading links with the Hellenic world. So Kabile at this time was an important staging post on the way to the coast, to Adrianople (Edirne) and Constantinople (Istanbul). When the area became part of the Byzantine Empire, Kabile's role was as a defence against barbarian invaders from the north. It was they who almost entirely destroyed it in the year AD583. Thereafter it continued its existence as a simple, unimportant settlement until the 14th-century conquest by the Turks.

By the end of **May** flowering should have been completed. When the flower opens, fertilisation can take place. Occasionally if conditions are not quite right (too cool or too humid) the flower is not totally fertilised and the bunches will have a smaller number of grapes. At first the grapes are very small, very bitter and very green. This condition lasts until about July.

By **July** the vine should have reached maturity, in that it could now reproduce itself. But the vine-grower is looking for more than reproduction – he wants ripe grapes! During July the grapes begin to change colour: the green turns to a yellowish colour in white varieties and to pink for red varieties – only at this stage can the nonexpert tell red grapes from white. In addition the grapes begin to lose acidity and accumulate sugar. The number of hours of sunshine at this point is important. This process continues during September, and the grapes increase in colour and sweetness, their skins softening during this ripening stage.

Some time in **late September, October** or even **early November**, the vine-grower will decide that the time is right to harvest the grapes. The bunches are cut by hand and taken in carts and trailers to the winery for processing. The faster this procedure is carried out the better; even a day's delay in the movement of ripe fruit can cause mould to form which can be tasted in the finished wine. The grower will bear in mind the end product required. Early harvesting gives a light, fresh wine; later harvesting gives a wine of deeper colour and higher alcohol content. Normally grapes which cannot be immediately processed are crushed and conserved as juice until the winery is ready to start with the fermentation process.

And thus the year ends: in **November** the vine leaves begin to harden and then wither and fall. As winter approaches the sap accumulates in the stem and sustains the plant during the winter until the vine's year starts again.

Archaeologists have been working here for many years, and believe there is still much of interest waiting to be discovered.

There is a small **museum** (⊕ *summer 08.00–20.00, winter 10.00–16.00, both daily; adult 1lv*) which shows the cultural life of the Thracians. Many pottery utensils, oil lamps and items of jewellery reveal the Thracian decorative style. Some items – bronze and marble statuettes, mirrors, votive plaques and decorations for chariots – are particularly skilfully made.

Bulgaria
awaits you

BULGARIA

www.bulgariatravel.org

8

Plovdiv, the Rhodopes and the Thracian Plain

Southern Bulgaria is dominated by the beautiful Rhodope Mountains and the fertile Thracian Plain. Plovdiv, Bulgaria's second city and a picturesque rival to Sofia, has the UNESCO-protected **Old Town** with its fascinating mixture of Classical ruins, mosques and National Revival-style architecture. Nearby is the beautiful **Bachkovo Monastery** and, further south into the mountains, **Pamporovo** ski resort and picturesque villages such as Shiroka Luka and Momchilovtsi. Further east the Turkish influence is evident in towns like Haskovo, Harmanli and Kurdzhali. Bulgaria's southern border area has some stunning scenery, for example at **Trigrad Gorge**, while to the east the Thracian Plain is one of the main wine-producing areas of the country and a fertile agricultural land. There have been some fascinating recent archaeological discoveries, for example at **Perperikon**. Near **Madzharovo** there is a nature reserve which is a spectacular area for observing birds, butterflies and flowers.

THE OLD ROAD FROM SOFIA TO PLOVDIV

The small town of **Ihtiman** (*Ихтиман*) used to be the home of Bulgaria's only golf course but there are now several others around Sofia, on the coast and at Bansko. The Air Sofia Golf Club and a horseriding centre are on the outskirts, making this a popular day or weekend break from Sofia.

Belovo (*Белово*) is the base of a large paper factory and the main street is the place to stock up on inexpensive toilet rolls! **Septemvri** (*Септември*) is a railway junction where you can connect with the scenic narrow-gauge railway up to Bansko and Dobrinishte.

Pazardzhik (*Пазарджик*), or as it used rather exotically to be known, Tatar Pazardzhik, is a dusty town with almost impenetrable signposting. I have been here several times, driving with various Bulgarian friends, and we have never succeeded in leaving the town without one or two U-turns.

Pazardzhik was originally settled by Crimean Tatars and one of the largest horse and camel fairs in the Ottoman Empire was held here. It still has a daily market, though fruit and vegetables rather than livestock predominate. It has a pleasant old quarter with some National Revival houses obviously influenced by the sophisticated examples in Plovdiv. The **Church of the Virgin Mary** (*Св Богородица*), also 19th century, is still being restored but you can go in to see the really wonderful Debur School iconostasis, carved in walnut.

Opposite the church is the **House-Museum of Stanislav Dospevski** (*Къщата-музей на Станислав Доспевски*; ⊕ *09.00–noon & 14.00–16.00 Mon–Fri; adult 2lv*). Dospevski (1826–76), one of the country's best-known artists, was born in the town. His icons and murals are particularly fine. The enigmatic portrait of his sister

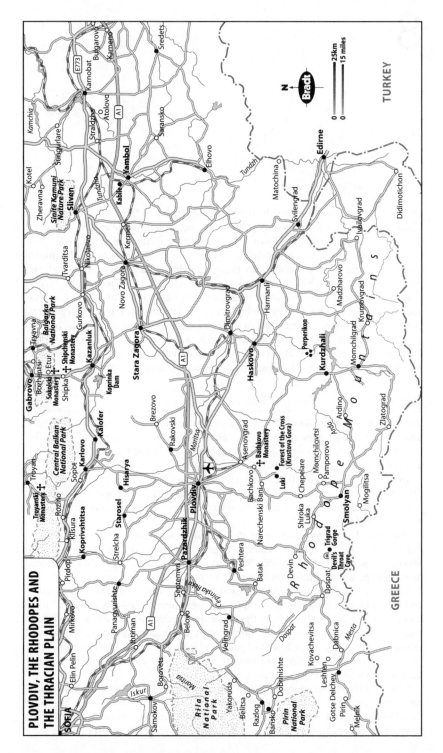

PLOVDIV, THE RHODOPES AND
THE THRACIAN PLAIN

TURKEY

GREECE

has earned the picture the title of the Bulgarian *Mona Lisa*. Dospevski took part in the April Uprising and was imprisoned in Istanbul, where he died.

Nearby, the **Ethnographic Museum** (*Етнографския музей; ul Kiril i Metodii 4; ⊕ 09.00–17.00 Mon–Fri, 10.00–17.00 Sat; adult 2lv*) is well worth visiting. It is in the town's largest 19th-century house. Pazardzhik makes a pleasant stop for a stroll around and a coffee or lunch.

PLOVDIV (ПЛОВДИВ) *Telephone code: 032*

With its attractive Old Town, Plovdiv is often considered more appealing than Sofia, though nowadays it seems to lack something of the buzz that characterises the capital. Known as Philippopolis in ancient times, and Filibeto by the Turks, Plovdiv has Classical remains, Byzantine churches, mosques and some of the country's finest National Revival domestic buildings. Much of its charm lies in the incongruous juxtaposition of ancient, medieval and modern. It is also an excellent base for exploring the Rhodope Mountains and villages.

HISTORY Approaching from the north it is easy to understand why Plovdiv is an ancient settlement, as its hills rising from the Thracian Plain are the most significant natural landmark. It sits on both banks of the Maritsa River and has been a commercial and transport centre over the centuries. The climate is particularly favourable, with an early spring, a hot summer and a mild winter. Its strategic importance made it the target for invaders, and each new occupier has left their mark.

Excavations on Nebet Tepe hilltop show evidence of a Thracian settlement from around the 12th century BC; still visible are some of the dry-stone walls and steps and a quadrangular tower. You can also see a *poterne* (secret exit) which was added in the 6th century AD, leading down to the river, and a water reservoir from medieval times. There are also imposing 10m-high fortress walls from the 12th to 14th centuries going down the eastern side of the hill.

In 341BC Philip II of Macedon conquered the town and renamed it Philippopolis after himself. The Thracian fortress was surrounded by new walls and defended until the Romans captured it in AD46. They called it Trimontium ('Three Hills'), and built the theatre, stadium and forum, the remains of which are still visible today.

A period of darkness and destruction followed as the wealthy town was plundered and destroyed by Goths and Huns, but a new period of reconstruction followed during the two Bulgarian kingdoms.

The Ottoman conquest saw yet more destruction, but the town's obvious strategic significance meant that the Turks eventually rebuilt the town and used it as a regional centre of government. As the town grew in economic, strategic and religious importance, its inhabitants prospered and the wealthiest built the beautiful timber-framed houses which lean across the steep, narrow, cobbled streets of the Old Town.

The treaty of San Stefano in 1878 envisaged Plovdiv as the capital of the newly liberated Bulgaria, as it was ideally placed, central, and already a commercial centre. However, the revision of the treaty at the Congress of Berlin was dominated by the Western powers who feared the expansion of Russian interests in the Balkans. They divided Bulgaria into two parts: the new principality of Bulgaria and the province of Eastern Rumelia which was to remain under the influence of Turkey, with Plovdiv as its capital. The two united in 1885 on 6 September, a date which is still celebrated as a national holiday. By then Sofia was established as the new capital, and Plovdiv remains a splendid second city.

8

GETTING THERE AND AWAY

By train Travellers by train will find that the **central railway station** in Plovdiv (*bul Hristo Botev 31A;* ✆ *622729; http://bdz.bg*) is very well organised, with signs and timetables in English. There are trains from Sofia (*14 daily; 2½–3hrs*), Burgas (*6 daily; 4½–5½hrs*), Asenovgrad (*hourly; 25mins*), Pazardzhik (*16 daily; 30–45mins*), Septemvri (*16 daily; 50mins–1hr*), Karlovo (*hourly; 1hr 20mins*) and Svilengrad (*3 daily; 3½hrs*).

There are daily **international** trains from Istanbul (*11hrs*).

By bus There are **three bus stations** in Plovdiv. The best way to get to **Avtogara Sever** (North) (*ul Dimitur Stambolov 2;* ✆ *953011*) is by taxi. There are buses from Veliko Turnovo (*3 daily; 4½hrs*) and Koprivshtitsa (*1 daily; 2½hrs*).

Avtogara Rhodope (*ul Makedonia, behind the central railway station – just follow the underground passage next to the entrance;* ✆ *657828*) serves destinations in the Rhodope Mountains. There are buses from Smolyan (*hourly; 2½–3hrs*), Devin (*2 daily; 2hrs 20mins*), Gotse Delchev (*1 daily; 4hrs*), Madzharovo (*1 daily; 4hrs*), Pamporovo (*8 daily; 2hrs*), Kazanluk (*2 daily; 1½hrs*), and Zlatograd (*3 daily; 4hrs*).

Avtogara Yug (South) (*bul Hristo Botev 47;* ✆ *626937*) serves the rest of the country and international lines. It is close to the railway station; just follow bul Hristo Botev and it is 500m on the left-hand side. There are buses from Sofia (*1–2 per hr; 2hrs 20mins*), Asenovgrad (*every 30mins; 30mins*), Blagoevgrad (*3 daily; 3hrs*), Burgas (*2 daily; 4½hrs*), Varna (*2 daily; 7hrs*), Karlovo (*1–2 per hr; 1hr 20mins*), Pazardzhik (*1–2 per hr; 40mins*), Svilengrad (*2 daily; 3hrs*), Sliven (*5 daily; 3½hrs*), Stara Zagora (*4 daily; 2hrs*) and Hisarya (*14 daily; 1½hrs*). In summer there are buses to the seaside resorts.

There are **international** buses from Istanbul (*daily; 5hrs*), Athens (*daily; 25hrs*) and Thessalonika (*5 daily; 15hrs*).

By car The quickest way to reach Plovdiv by road is to take the E80 motorway which passes through pleasant rolling countryside until it reaches the Thracian Plain. This does mean that several small but quite interesting places are missed, so if time is not a priority it is more pleasant to follow the old route to Plovdiv, road number 8. The railway line also follows this latter route.

TOURIST INFORMATION The tourist information centre is at pl Tsentralen 1 (✆ *656793;* e *info@tourismplovdiv.org; www.tourismplovdiv.org*).

⌂ WHERE TO STAY *Map, page 229, unless otherwise stated*

To enjoy Plovdiv at its best, avoid coming during the two main trade fairs in spring and autumn, as hotels and restaurants are full, everywhere is crowded and prices are inflated.

Hotels

⌂ **Dafi** (20 rooms) ul Kapana G Benkovski 23; ✆620041; e office@hoteldafi.com; www. hoteldafi.com. On a quiet street near the Old Town. Good value, friendly & comfortable. €–€€

⌂ **Hebros** [map, page 233] (10 rooms) ul K Stoilov 51; ✆260180; e hebrosh@tourism.bg; www.hebros-hotel.com. Luxury boutique hotel in an old mansion on the edge of the Old Town. €€€

⌂ **Leipzig** (122 rooms & suites) bul Ruski 70; ✆654000; www.leipzig.bg. Multi-storey building in a quiet residential area not far from the centre; very stylishly & colourfully renovated. Good garden restaurant. €€

⌂ **Novotel Plovdiv** (321 rooms) ul Zlatyu Boyadzhiev 2; ✆934444; e reservation@ novotelpdv.bg; www.icep.bg. Business hotel, with sports facilities such as indoor & outdoor pools,

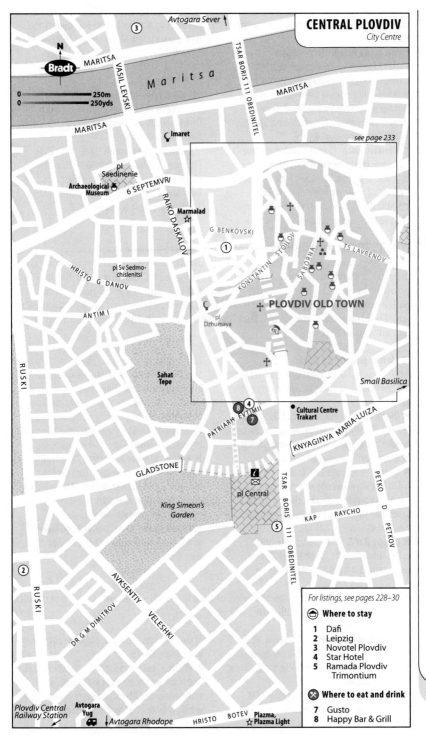

see page 233

CENTRAL PLOVDIV
City Centre

Avtogara Sever

MARITSA

M a r i t s a

MARITSA

MARITSA

VASIL LEVSKI

TSAR BORIS 111 OBEDINITEL

0   250m
0   250yds

Imaret

pl Saedinenie

Archaeological Museum

6 SEPTEMVRI

RAIKO DASKALOV

Marmalad

G BENKOVSKI

KONSTANTIN STOILOV

SABORNA

TS LAVRENOV

HRISTO G DANOV

pl Sv Sedmo-chislenitsi

ANTIM I

PLOVDIV OLD TOWN

pl Dzhumaya

RUSKI

Sahat Tepe

Small Basilica

Cultural Centre Trakart

PATRIARH EVTIMII

KNYAGINYA MARIA-LUIZA

PETKO

GLADSTONE

King Simeon's Garden

pl Central

TSAR BORIS 111 OBEDINITEL

KAP   RAYCHO

D   PETKOV

RUSKI

AVKSENTIY VELESHKI

DR G M DIMITROV

Plovdiv Central Railway Station

Avtogara Yug

Avtogara Rhodope

HRISTO   BOTEV

Plazma, Plazma Light

For listings, see pages 228–30

Where to stay

1   Dafi
2   Leipzig
3   Novotel Plovdiv
4   Star Hotel
5   Ramada Plovdiv Trimontium

Where to eat and drink

7   Gusto
8   Happy Bar & Grill

Plovdiv, the Rhodopes and the Thracian Plain   PLOVDIV

8

sauna & tennis courts, but not much atmosphere. €€€€

🏠 **Ramada Plovdiv Trimontium** [map, page 233] (158 rooms) ul Kapitan Raicho 2; ☎605000; e reservations.plovdiv@bgprincess.com; http://plovdiv.bgprincess.com. Often described as a Stalinist monster, but it does have elegance & style, & has been lavishly refurbished. Spacious rooms. Central position. €€€€

🏠 **Renaissance** (5 rooms) pl Vuzrazhdane 1; ☎266966; e info@renaissance-bg.com; www.renaissance-bg.com. Combines National Revival style with a really warm welcome. €€€

🏠 **Star Hotel** (48 rooms) ul Patriarh Evtimii 13; ☎633599; e reservation@starhotel.bg; www.

starhotel.bg. Very central. No-frills budget hotel on the main street. Modern rooms at reasonable rates. €

Hostels

🏠 **Hikers Hostel** [map, page 233] ul Saborna 53; m 0896 764854; www.hikers-hostel.org/pd. Offers rooms & dormitories in an interesting old house in the Old Town. €

🏠 **Plovdiv Guesthouse** [map, page 233] (10 rooms) ul Suborna 20; ☎622432; e info@plovdivguest.com; www.plovdivguest.com. Dormitories with 4, 8 or 10 beds. Also in the Old Town, bright, clean & welcoming. €

✗ **WHERE TO EAT AND DRINK** *Map, page 233, unless otherwise stated*

There are countless cafés and restaurants all over Plovdiv, those in the Old Town offering a particularly pleasant dining experience. **I Claudius Café** has the best position in town, right next to the Roman stadium, and is a good place for lunches, coffee or snacks. The **Arena Café** is well positioned overlooking the Roman theatre, and **Dzhumayata Café** serves Turkish coffee and sweet pastries right next to the entrance to the mosque.

✗ **Alafrangite** ul Kiril Nektariev 13–17; ☎620983; www.alafrangite.eu. A must-see in the Old Town in an interesting old house with lovely garden. €€€

✗ **Diana 1** ul Dondukov 2; ☎623027; m 0888 747968; ⊕ 24hrs; www.dayanabg.com. Part of a popular chain, 5mins' walk from centre, folk style, local specialities, prompt service. €€

✗ **Gusto** [map, page 229] ul Otets Paisii 26; ☎623711; www.gustobg.com. Opposite Star Hotel. Bistro-type restaurant close to the main pedestrian street. Pizzas, salads, soups, grilled meats. €€

✗ **Happy Bar & Grill** [map, page 229] ul Patriarh Evtimii 13; m 0888 181073; www.happy.bg/bg/our_restaurants.

html?restaurant=bulgaria_plovdiv. Next to Hotel Star. The first Bulgarian fast-food chain. Offers a big variety of salads, grilled meats & soups. Very good service. Also a good place for a drink. €

✗ **Hebros** See page 228; ☎625929. Innovative Bulgarian cuisine using seasonal, fresh & unusual ingredients, formal & attentive service. €€€

✗ **Puldin** ul Knyaz Tseretelev 3; ☎631720. Housed in the former Mevlevi Hane dervish monastery, only the dancing hall of the whirling dervishes remains nowadays. Noted for its excellent local specialities. €€€–€€€€

✗ **Renaissance** See above. Fish, grills & unusual specialities, good choice of wines. €€–€€€

NIGHTLIFE Kapana area, to the west of tsar Boris III Obedinitel, and north of pl Dzhumaya, is the hub of Plovdiv's nightlife.

☆ **Konushnite na Tsarya** ul Suborna 40; m 0899 448896; ⊕ 09.00–02.00. Open-air stage during the summer for live music in the Old Town, bar & café. Popular & busy.

☆ **Marmalad** ul Bratya Pulyevi 3; m 0898 653753; ⊕ 09.00–02.00. Very popular place in Kapana area. Ground-floor bar, & downstairs one

of the best clubs in the city. Bulgarian bands in the week. DJ parties Fri–Sat.

☆ **Plazma** bul Hristo Botev 82; ☎0889 993333. One of the best house clubs in Bulgaria, with world-renowned DJs playing every w/end. Great setting & fantastic atmosphere. **Plazma Light** is the pre-party place in the same building.

WHAT TO SEE AND DO Plovdiv is divided into two main parts, the **Old Town** (*Старuя град*) on the hills and the newer part, which has some Roman and Ottoman sites of interest. The modern central area of Plovdiv is south of the river and at the foot of the Old Town. There is a long main pedestrianised shopping street, ul Knyaz Aleksandur I Batenberg, with many clothes shops, cafés and fast-food outlets. This links pl Tsentralen, where the post office and Hotel Ramada Plovdiv Trimontium face one another, and pl Rimski Stadion (also popularly known as Dzhumayata), where the 14th-century Friday Mosque is situated. This is the route for evening strolling, which is fun to watch from a pavement café or to join in. At various points along the street, lower levels have been exposed showing Roman remains amid the modern city. Across the square from the Hotel Ramada Plovdiv Trimontium there are marble paving stones and colonnades from the 3rd-century Roman **forum**.

Further along ul Knyaz Aleksandur I, in front of Dzhumaya Mosque, an excavated section of the **stadium** (*Римскuя стадuон*) once used for chariot racing and gladiators' contests can be seen. The marble seats and track are easy to pick out, as are the bases of the columns which supported the aqueduct bringing water from the Rhodopes to the large reservoir on Taxim Tepe. The stadium could seat 30,000 people and must have been a spectacular sight. A new entrance and an information centre have been opened (⊕ *Apr–Oct 09.00–18.00, Nov–Mar 09.00–17.30; free for now, currently no future ticket price available; http://oldplovdiv.com/en/tickets*). There is a model of the stadium in the centre of the square (pl Rimski Stadion), with explanations in Bulgarian and English.

The three hills of the Old Town are Nebet Tepe, Taxim Tepe and Dzhambaz Tepe. On nearby Sahat Tepe the old Ottoman clocktower, one of the few surviving Turkish buildings, is built of hexagonal granite blocks surmounted by a wooden belltower. From here you can see across to the huge Soviet Army memorial, known as Alyosha, on the Hill of the Liberators.

The Old Town is lovely just to wander round, with photo opportunities at every turn. The **Roman Theatre** (*Антuчен театър*; ⊕ *same times as the stadium; adult 6lv. There is also a combined ticket (15lv) for any 5 museums or houses*) is perhaps the greatest attraction. During the summer there is a season of opera and classical music concerts here. It seats over 4,000 spectators in a semicircle of 11 tiers, set into the hillside. The backdrop to the stage is a façade of Ionic columns and statues which is, of course, a work of restoration but sympathetically done.

The **Ethnographic Museum** (*Етнографскu музей; ul Dr Chomakov 2;* ☏ *625654;* e *ethnograph@abv.bg; www.ethnograph.info;* ⊕ *summer 09.00–18.00, winter 09.00–17.00, both Tue–Sun; adult 5lv*) is in a beautiful old house, dating from 1847. Probably Plovdiv's most photographed building, it was built for a rich Greek merchant, Argir Kuyumdzhioglou. Sometimes on a summer evening there are chamber music performances in the garden; a small fountain adds its music, and the slightly sour smell of box trees and the sweeter perfume of roses complete the sensory experience. The museum opened in 1962, and has a rich collection illustrating local skills such as the making of tobacco, wine and cheese, textiles and weaving, costumes, folklore traditions and music. The house itself is a joy to be inside, especially if you are lucky enough to catch it at a quiet time. The ceiling in the main upstairs hall features a stunning rosette and sunburst pattern. Outside, the roof sweeps in voluptuous curves, and ornate gilt wreaths decorate its façade.

Another handsome building, **Dr Chomakov's House** (*Домът на Д-р Чомаков; ul Suborna 18;* ⊕ *summer 09.00–18.00, winter 09.00–17.30, both daily; adult 3lv*), has a permanent exhibition of the paintings of Zlatyu Boyadzhiev (1903–76), who

Boyadzhiev (1903–76) was born in the village of Brezovo, near Plovdiv. His work can be divided into two distinct periods. At first he painted in a classical manner, his favourite subjects being pictures of village life; these are affectionate portrayals of typical scenes: markets, shepherds with their flocks and traditional celebrations.

In 1951 he suffered a debilitating stroke which left his right-hand side completely paralysed. Gradually he taught himself to work with his left hand and, after a few years, he started to paint again. During this second period, he completely changed his style, introducing grotesque imagery, child figures and vibrant, expressive colours. Some of his most famous paintings are *Brezovo Village*, *At the Table* and *Two Weddings*. A large number of his paintings are shown in the exhibition arranged in Dr Chomakov's House in Plovdiv.

painted many scenes of Bulgarian village life. He is regarded as one of the country's most eminent and original artists.

Also on ul Suborna is a 19th-century pharmacy shop, **Apteka Hipokrat**, now a museum (*Аптека Хипократ;* ⊕ *09.00–17.00 Mon–Fri*). In practice it is often closed but you can still look through the windows at the furnishings, jars and bottles.

The **Hisar Gate** (*Хисар капия*), the eastern gate in the old fortress wall, is another famous sight. It dates from the 12th- to 14th-century period of reconstruction, but is on Roman foundations. Nearby are the ruins of a round tower, showing the typical alternate brick and stone bonded layers of Byzantine construction.

The National Revival-style buildings in Plovdiv are at a more sophisticated level than those in the small towns and villages; here the difficulties of building on steep narrow streets have been confronted and defeated. Upper storeys are larger than lower ones, making up for lack of space at street level, and at times it seems that they almost meet above your head. The 19th-century builders displayed great creativity and their 150 or so old houses and churches are a harmonious whole.

Many of Plovdiv's house-museums are open to the public nowadays, though they are fairly similar so most visitors will be happy just to visit two or three. Check locally for reduced-price tickets for several museum visits.

The **Balabanova House** (*Балабановата къща; ul Konstantin Stoilov 57;* ⊕ *09.00–17.30 daily; adult 5lv*) is a tall, three-storey maroon-coloured house, named after its original owner, a wealthy merchant. It was built early in the 19th century and is now used as a cultural centre, where concerts, meetings and exhibitions take place. It has been furnished with authentic period items like those the house would originally have contained. Nearby, beyond a fountain, is **Hindlian House** (*Къщата на Степан Хиндлиян; ul Artin Gidikov 4;* ⊕ *09.00–17.00 Mon–Fri; adult 5lv*), built between 1835 and 1840. This masterpiece retains its original wall and ceiling paintings of Venice and Constantinople. There was once a rosewater fountain in the wall of the main room – how exotic! The original owners were Armenian merchants who travelled widely, and there is a felicitous continuity in that the **Sv Kevork Armenian Church** (*Арменската църква;* ⊕ *10.00–17.30 Mon–Fri, 10.00–13.00 Sat–Sun*) is nearby and is used by a few remaining Armenian families. Wine-tasting places can be reserved in the refurbished cellar downstairs.

On ul Kiril Nectariev the house of **Veren Stamboulyan** is noted for its painted decorative niches, known as *alafrangas*. A prominent building is the symmetrical

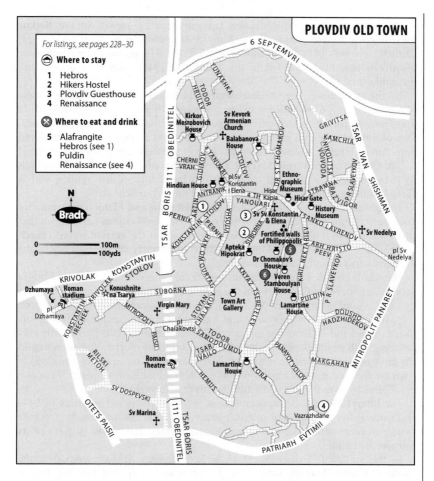

For listings, see pages 228–30

⬛ **Where to stay**

1 Hebros
2 Hikers Hostel
3 Plovdiv Guesthouse
4 Renaissance

❌ **Where to eat and drink**

5 Alafrangite
  Hebros (see 1)
6 Puldin
  Renaissance (see 4)

Lamartine House (*Къщата на Ламартин; ul Knyaz Tsertelev;* ⊕ *by appointment only*), named after the French poet, who stayed here in July 1833 while writing *Voyage en l'Orient* and recovering from an attack of cholera. There is a small museum in his memory.

The warren of streets is an artist's and visitor's dream but the mapmaker's nightmare. Wandering rather than map-reading is probably the best approach, allowing you to follow tempting paths at will. Along some streets ancient fortress walls from Byzantine times can be seen, often included in the next layer of building, as on **ul Vitosha**, where there is a wonderful view of several houses each resting on different heights and styles of old wall. The large blocks date from Roman times and others are Byzantine.

There are several small museums in the Old Town, of which the **History Museum** (*Исторически музей; ul Tsanko Lavrenov 1;* ⊕ *09.00–noon & 13.00–17.00 Mon–Sat; adult 3lv*) covering the period of the National Revival is perhaps the most interesting. It is in **Dimitur Georgiadi House**, a fine building with elegant proportions and magnificent oriel windows. The exhibits show the resistance to Turkish rule and the activity of revolutionary leaders such as Rakovski, Levski and Botev.

The work of noted artist Tsanko Lavrenov can be viewed in the **Kirkor Mesrobovich House** (*Къщата на Киркор Месробович; ul Artin Gidikov 11; ⌚ 09.00–noon & 14.00–17.00 Mon–Fri; adult 3lv*). His pictures of 19th-century Plovdiv were actually painted in the 1930s and 1940s; they have a beautiful, dreamlike quality.

In the new town the **Archaeological Museum** (*Археологически музей; pl Suedinenie 1; ☎ 633106; www.archaeologicalmuseumplovdiv.org; ⌚ 10.00–17.30 Tue–Sun; adult 5lv*) has a rich collection, particularly of coins, icons and incunabula. One of Bulgaria's famous gold treasures, that found at Panagyurishte, is displayed here. After a lengthy reconstruction, this is an excellent, visitor-friendly museum.

The **Church of the Virgin Mary** (*Св Богородица; ul Mitropolit Paisii*) was built in 1844, replacing a medieval church. It is a large, three-aisled basilica, with a carved iconostasis by the Stanishev brothers of the Debur School.

The oldest church is dedicated to **Sv Sv Konstantin and Elena** (*Църквата Св Св Константин и Елена; ul Suborna 24; ⌚ daily*). Excavations have shown that there was a church on this site in the 4th century, but the current walled church is 19th century. There is a striking gold-plated iconostasis, and many icons by the extraordinarily talented artist Zahari Zograf.

The whole church is a riot of colour, with floral patterns in the porch and bright geometric patterns and scenes from the gospels inside.

The Dzhumaya or **Friday Mosque** (*Джумая джамия*) probably dates from the 14th century. It is a very large and fine building with beautiful floral motifs inside. It was and is the major mosque in Plovdiv. Its minaret is particularly eye-catching, with its diagonal pattern of red bricks on white mortar. Visitors who find the mosque open are welcome to enter. Northeast of the mosque was traditionally a bazaar area and it is still busy with shops, cafés and stalls, which continue across the footbridge over the River Maritsa towards the Novotel Hotel.

The **Imaret Mosque** (*Имарет джамия; ⌚ daily after noon*) was built in 1444 and named after the *imaret* or pilgrim's accommodation that was nearby. It stands in a small garden and has been restored in recent years. The twisted patterns on its minaret are striking.

In the so-called Archaeological Underpass (*Подлез Археологически*) is the **Cultural Centre Trakart**, sometimes described as the ancient building Eyrene (*☎ 631303; www.trakart.org; ⌚ summer 09.00–19.00, winter 10.00–18.00 daily; adult 2lv*). This was once a wealthy home and there are extensive mosaic floors, preserved *in situ*; one image is that of a female head surrounded by geometric patterns and the name Eyrene also in mosaics. She is said to be Penelope, the goddess of peace, adopted by early Christians as St Eyrene. There are other remains and artefacts on display. This place is also used as a performance space for concerts and events.

Another archaeological site is sheltered within in a red, modern building, opened in 2014. This is the **Small Basilica** (*Малка базилика на Филипопол; bul Knyaginya Maria Luiza 31A; m 0876 662882; www.romanplovdiv.org/en; ⌚ 09.00–18.00 daily; adult 5lv*), the remains of a Christian church dating from the 5th–6th century. The mosaics depict birds and animals. There is a raised platform giving a good overview, and a short video (in English) about the history.

Plovdiv hosts spring and autumn **international trade fairs** (*международни панаири*) exhibiting consumer goods in spring and industrial goods in autumn, as well as smaller annual events such as Vinaria, the wine-trade fair. The first fair was opened with a volley of celebratory gunfire on 15 August 1892. Thirty-six wooden pavilions, some from Vienna and Paris, were erected in what is now the central park. The most luxurious pavilion was from Karlovo – no doubt

THE STORY OF MAVRUD

During the reign of Khan Krum (AD803–14) a law was passed ordering the destruction of vineyards in an effort to curb excessive drinking. According to legend, one of the Khan's lions escaped from his cage, causing widespread panic. A young man called Mavrud captured and killed the lion. The khan wanted to reward the youth, but asked first for the secret of his strength. Mavrud and his mother were reluctant to explain, until they were reassured that no harm would come to them. They admitted that they had broken the law about destroying all their vines, and had kept one, from which the mother had made the wine which had given Mavrud his strength and courage. The khan was so impressed that he rescinded his law and allowed vineyards to be re-established. Mavrud lives on as the name of one of Bulgaria's indigenous grapes, from which one of the best-quality red wines is produced.

it displayed rose oil, Bulgaria's gold. The pavilion from Pazardzhik was barrel shaped and inside visitors could sample good wines from that region, while the Varna pavilion foresaw the country's potential for tourism. That first fair lasted 75 days! Nowadays the spring and autumn fairs last for only five days, but are the largest events of their kind in the Balkans.

INTO THE RHODOPE MOUNTAINS

Heading south from Plovdiv near the airport and the village of Krumovo is the **Museum of Aviation** (*Музей на Авиацията*; \ *032 636677*; e *airmuseum.bg@ abv.bg*; *www.airmuseum-bg.com*; ⊕ *summer 09.00–17.00, winter 09.00–16.00, both Wed–Sun; adult 2lv*). There are indoor exhibits on the history of aviation in Bulgaria, and outdoors there are numerous examples of military planes. Enthusiastic guided tours are available.

ASENOVGRAD (АСЕНОВГРАД) *Telephone code: 0331*

Many visitors will want to explore the Rhodope Mountains, but even those with little time should make an excursion to Bachkovo Monastery. The first town of interest on the way is Asenovgrad, some 20km southeast of Plovdiv. Most Bulgarians will know the town as the home of Mavrud wines, and you should try some during your visit. It is a substantial wine, good with hearty meals like stews, and it can age, unlike most Bulgarian wines which are best drunk young.

The town is nicknamed 'Little Jerusalem' because of the large number of monasteries in its vicinity. There are also numerous Thracian mounds in this area.

Getting there and away There are **trains** (*railway station* \ *22970*) from Plovdiv every hour, taking 30 minutes.

There are **buses** (*bus station Ivan Vazov Str 36*; \ *64071*) from Plovdiv (*1–2 per hr; 30mins*), Bachkovo (*1–2 per hr depending on time of day; 15mins*), Chepelare (*hourly; 1hr 20mins*) and Smolyan (*hourly; 2hrs 15mins*).

🏠 Where to stay

🏠 **Asenovets** (17 rooms) pl Nikolay Haitov 3; \ 62277; m 0888 272297; e hotel_asenovets@ abv.bg. This is the formerly state-owned hotel in the centre of town; some of the rooms are renovated. Good location is its main advantage. **€–€€**

🏠 **Chiflika** (8 rooms, 2 studios) Gornovodensko Shose 13; m 0897 455466; www.hotelchiflika.com. Not central, but overall a pleasant & welcoming small hotel, though it can be noisy at w/ends. €€

🏠 **Hotel Nic** (15 rooms) ul Zahari Stoyanov 6; ☎64888; e reservation@hotel-nic.com; www.hotel-nic.com. A 5min walk from the centre, with modern, well-equipped rooms. €€

✗ Where to eat and drink

✗ **Ambelino** pl Trakia; ☎63345; m 0877 474700. Outdoor tables. Good salads. In a pleasant setting. €€

✗ **Aqua** ul Hristo Smirnenski 14; m 0898 600085. Eye-catching aquarium inside. Bulgarian & international cuisine. €€

✗ **Stanimaka** ul Tsar Ivan Asen II 13; ☎67932. Traditional *mehana*. €€

What to see and do Asenovgrad's mild climate, fertile soil and position beside one of the main passes across the mountains means it has been a settlement since Thracian times. It was an important staging post on the route to the Aegean Sea, though it was known as Stanimaka (meaning 'a narrow defended pass') from around the 11th century until 1934, when it was renamed in memory of Tsar Ivan Asen II, who completed the building of the nearby fortress.

The **Palaeontological Museum** (*Палеонтологическия музей*; ☎ 63736; ⏰ 08.30–17.00 Mon–Fri, 10.00–16.00 Sat; adult 2lv) has fascinating animal skeletons from nearby excavations, including a mammoth and a tiger. There are also large collections of fossils. The museum is a branch of the National Museum for Natural History in Sofia. The **Historical Museum** (*Исторически музей*; Nikolay Haitov 1; ☎ 62250; ⏰ 08.30–17.00 Mon–Fri, 10.00–16.00 Sat; adult 2lv) has three sections, archaeology, National Revival and ethnography. The **Ethnographic Exhibition** (*Етнографски музей*; ul Stanimaka 34; ☎62250; ⏰ 08.30–17.00 Mon–Fri) presents the domestic life of a well-to-do urban family of the 19th century.

The **Church of the Holy Virgin** (*Св Богородица*) has ceiling frescoes by the famous Zahari Zograf. There is a miracle-working icon of the Virgin Mary which is taken each year to Bachkovo Monastery in a religious procession 25 days after Easter.

The **Church of Asenova Fortress** (*Църквата при Асеновата крепост*) is a distinctive landmark and from it there are wonderful views to Plovdiv and the Thracian Plain. It is possible to drive part of the way to the fortress but then the walk to the church is steep and can be slippery. The church has been well preserved and the frescoes are interesting, though they have damaged faces. The fortress itself has almost disappeared; just the remains of an odd tower and some crumbling walls are visible.

BACHKOVO MONASTERY (БАЧКОВСКИ МАНАСТИР) After Asenovgrad in the gorge of the River Chepelare, just beyond the pleasant hilltop village of Bachkovo, is the monastery of the same name. The approach is up a short path through some souvenir stalls selling honey, jams, wooden items, postcards and so on. This is Bulgaria's second-largest monastery; it is less vivid than Rila Monastery, its colours softer and its buildings more gently rounded, but it is still a most impressive ensemble.

History Bachkovo Monastery was founded in 1083 by two Georgian brothers, Grigoriy and Abasius Bakuriyani, who were military officers of the Byzantine Empire. From that era the ossuary church still remains with remarkable interior murals, some dating from the 11th century, one of which is said to depict Grigoriy. This ancient building stands apart from the present monastery on a mountain slope. Bachkovo became a major centre during the Second Bulgarian Kingdom (1185–1396); both Tsar Ivan Asen II and Tsar Ivan Aleksandur were donors and, during the reign of the latter, Bachkovo was considerably extended. It was frequently looted, burned and desecrated by the Turks, but each time it was restored. It was substantially reconstructed in the 17th century, and has several new buildings and many murals from the 19th century.

Getting there and away There are **buses** from Asenovgrad (*1–2 per hr depending on time of day; 15mins*), Chepelare (*1–2 per hr; 1hr 20mins*) and Pamporovo (*1–2 per hr; 1hr 10mins*).

⌂ Where to stay, eat and drink
Many visitors to Bachkovo will be on a day trip from Plovdiv, but it is possible to stay both in the monastery and in the vicinity.

⌂ **Bachkovo Monastery** ✆0332 72277. Basic rooms with no hot water are a few leva cheaper than those with it. The unusual experience of sleeping in an active monastery makes up for the lack of creature comforts! **€**

⌂ **Dzhamura Hotel/Restaurant** (11 rooms) Near the river; ✆0332 72320; www.djamura.com. Good restaurant. **€**

⌂ **Eco** (8 rooms) Across the river from the monastery; m 0899 995957. Clean, quiet & comfortable. **€**

✗ **Vodopada Restaurant** Near the monastery entrance; m 0890 120556, 0878 810822. Picturesque setting, garden with a waterfall & pool where you can catch your own trout for lunch. **€€**

What to see and do The monastery (⊕ *06.30–21.00 daily; free*) is entered through a small door which leads you into the cobbled courtyard. The harmony and beauty of the buildings, despite their different ages, is striking, and even when the monastery is busy with visitors there is a calm and serene atmosphere. Trees and flowers, grazing sheep, foraging hens and playful kittens add a pastoral feel.

There are galleried domestic buildings with open wooden verandas, guest rooms and the lovely refectory (*трапезария; adult 6lv*), inside and outside of which there are murals, some by pupils of Zahari Zograf, who himself painted the panorama of Bachkovo on the refectory's northern wall, depicting the miraculous icon being taken out. Beyond the refectory another courtyard, not at first noticeable, is sometimes open. This gives access to Sv Nikolai (*Св Николай*), with the well-preserved Zahari Zograf painting of the Last Judgement which includes various notables of 19th-century Plovdiv, dressed in the style of the day, heading for Hell. There are three figures in the upper left corner of the painting in the narthex – the portraits of the Abbot, the Plovdiv Bishop and Zahari Zograf himself.

The main church, **The Dormition of the Virgin** (*Св Успение Богородично*), was built in 1604 and is again a feast of frescoes, with those in the belltower's porch giving a lively impression of the horrors in store for sinners. The beautiful icon of the Holy Virgin was brought from Georgia and dates from the 14th century. It has the main role in various festivals at the monastery: the August celebrations of its name day and an occasion known as Prepolovenie, 25 days after Easter. On the latter occasion the icon is taken in procession to three small adjacent chapels in the nearby hills, about half an hour's walk away. The route, in fact, makes an interesting short walk. Starting from the monastery gate you pass the Church of Sv Troitsa, the ossuary church, with its medieval frescoes and portrait of Tsar Ivan Aleksandur, who was one of the monastery's donors. This is usually locked to protect its treasures. Beyond it, signs to Chervenata Stena, established as a nature reserve in 1962, bring you to one of the finest protected areas in Bulgaria, where rare birds like rock thrush, golden eagle and peregrine may be seen, as well as orchids and butterflies. Characteristic trees are black fir, pine, spruce and maple.

SOUTH OF BACHKOVO MONASTERY About 45km south of Asenovgrad near the town of Luki is the **Forest of the Cross**, Krustova Gora (*Кръстова гора*). This is revered as a holy place by Bulgarian Christians. There was once a monastery here which was burned down by the Turks, who also massacred its monks. From time immemorial it has been regarded as a place of healing. Those who spend the night here before the Feast of the Movement of the Holy Cross, on 14 September, believe they will be cured of their illnesses. In 1995 a new church was built and a lane leads from it to the place of worship of the Cross; along it are 12 chapels, one for each apostle.

NARECHENSKI BANI (НАРЕЧЕНСКИ БАНИ) The road continues south into the Rhodope Mountains; it is busy with trucks which are hard to overtake on the winding road, so it is best to be patient and admire the scenery. Narechenski Bani is a straggling village known for its therapeutic waters. One of its springs has the highest level of radioactivity in Bulgaria. About 20km further on there is a lovely quiet side road beside a stream which leads to the Wonderful Bridges, Chudnite Mostove (*Чудните мостове*). These are natural rock formations of truly impressive size, formed when an earthquake destroyed a cave. Along the road to the bridges there is a wealth of flowers and birds.

CHEPELARE (ЧЕПЕЛАРЕ) *Telephone code: 03051*
This small town has developed into a modest-sized ski resort on the coat tails of its better-known neighbour 6km to the south, and is a good base for hiking or mountain biking in summer. It has a unique **Museum of Speleology and Karst** (*Музей по спелеология и българския карст; ul Shina Andreeva 9A;* 3041; *www. terranatura.hit.bg;* ⊕ *09.00–noon & 13.30–17.00 Mon–Sat; adult 3lv*) with displays about local caves and the various artefacts and creatures found in them.

Getting there and away There are **buses** from Plovdiv (*hourly; 1hr*) and Smolyan via Pamporovo (*hourly; 1hr*).

Tourist information The tourist information office is at ul Dicho Petrov 1 (8178; e *tic@chepelare.bg; www.tourism@chepelare.bg;* ⊕ *08.30–12.30 & 13.30– 17.30 Mon–Fri*). They can also advise on private rooms.

Where to stay and eat Most of the private hotels in the town have restaurants.

Ivan (13 rooms) ul Progres 6; 3113; e hotel_ivan@abv.bg; www.hotel-ivan.hit.bg. Surrounded by a pleasant garden with a large area for children to play; the snack bar offers national & local dishes. €

Martin (9 rooms) ul Kiril Madzharov 23; 2194; e martin_hotel@yahoo.com. Located not far from the centre & about 1km from the ski lift; there is a cosy *mehana*, and a summer garden with BBQ serving national & local *rodopski* dishes. €

Phoenix (15 rooms) ul Murgavets 4; 3408. Central, inexpensive & well kept. Traditional-style restaurant. €

Rodopski dom (53 rooms) ul Perelik 13–15; 0240 10565, 0240 10515. Light, clean, comfortable rooms. €€

Vanaleks aparthotel (7 apts, 3 studios, 2 rooms) ul Zdravets 17; 3010; http://vanaleks. alle.bg. Guests can enjoy the comfort of their suite or apartment combined with the hotel facilities such as the restaurant & garden; playground for the children. €€

🏠 **Vila Mechi Chal** (8 rooms) Upper lift station at an altitude of 1830m; m 0879 991809; www. mechichal.com/web. Wonderful views & peace & quiet; rooms offer accommodation for 2, 3 & 4 persons; there is a restaurant, sauna & free Wi-Fi. €€

✗ **Kostovski Han** ul 24 May 48; ☎ 3063; m 0898 720764. Traditional food from the Western Rhodopes. €

PAMPOROVO (ПАМПОРОВО) *Telephone code: 03021*

Pamporovo used to be Bulgaria's best-known resort, but it has been overtaken by Bansko, which has developed very rapidly in the last few years. It has 37km of runs, 18 lifts and several new and some refurbished places to stay. It is situated at a height of 1,650m, with the highest ski run starting from 1,926m. There is a strong Mediterranean climatic influence, providing more than 120 sunny days during the winter season. The average snow cover is 150cm.

Pamporovo is also being developed and in summer there is usually some building going on. It is, however, still in a beautiful area of old spruce forests, rich in wild flowers, birds and butterflies, and makes a convenient base for exploring the Southern Rhodopes.

Unlike Bansko, which is a proper mountain town which has become a ski resort, or even Borovets, which has some history based around the former hunting lodges built there in the late 19th century, Pamporovo is a purpose-built ski resort. It is definitely a package-holiday destination and can be noisy with bar-crawling Brits. It is, however, a well-designed resort, easy to get around and with a good range of skiing for all abilities, though it is particularly appealing to beginners and young families because of its sunny climate. Travelling on a package holiday gives access to competitively priced ski packs (lift pass, ski and boot hire and ski school for around £150).

The television tower, Snezhanka (🕒 *09.00–16.30 daily*) is a useful landmark for both skiers and hikers and has a café with fantastic views.

GETTING THERE AND AWAY There are **buses** from Sofia (*every 2hrs; 4hrs*), Smolyan (*hourly; 30mins*), Plovdiv (*hourly; 2hrs*) and Devin (*4 daily; 1½hrs*).

🏠 **WHERE TO STAY** *Map, page 240*

🏠 **Dafovska** (34 rooms) ☎ 0309 59700; e dafovska_hotel@yahoo.com; www. dafovskahotel.com. Central location, friendly & helpful staff, good b/fast options, great views. €€
🏠 **Malina Cottages** (120 beds in 30 chalets) m 0888 137007; www.malina-pamporovo. com. Wooden self-contained chalets in the forest, smart, modern & well-equipped. A good choice for families. €€

🏠 **Murgavets** (92 rooms) ☎ 0309 58310; e office@sharlopov.eu; www.murgavets-bg.com. Well-equipped hotel, gym, spa, playground & pool. Central. €€
🏠 **Orlovets** (98 rooms & 7 apts) ☎ 0240 10565; e booking@orlovets.com; www.orlovets.com. Popular, modern, family-friendly hotel; good food. €€€

✗ **WHERE TO EAT AND DRINK** *Map, page 240*

Most of the listed hotels also have restaurants.

✗ **Bai Panayot's Chevermeto** ☎ 8338. Pamporovo's best-known restaurant, always popular. Grilled & spit-roasted meats a speciality. €€

✗ **Chanovete** ☎ 0309 58212; m 0889 815503. Traditional style, with Bulgarian cuisine. €€
✗ **Gloria Mar** m 0893 550055; contact@ gloriamar-bg.com. Fresh fish dishes, international cuisine, fine dining. €€€–€€€€

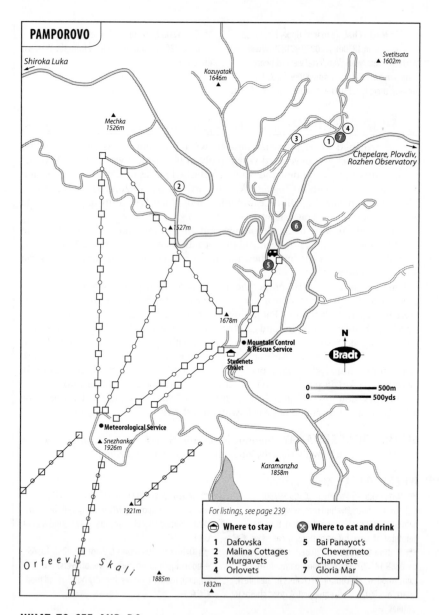

PAMPOROVO

Shiroka Luka

Svetitsata
▲ 1602m

Kozuyatak
1646m
▲

Mechka
1526m
▲

③ ④
① ⑦

Chepelare, Plovdiv,
Rozhen Observatory

②

▲ 1527m

⑥

⑤

▲ 1678m

● Mountain Control
& Rescue Service

▲ Studenets
Chalet

N

Bradt

0 ———————— 500m
0 ———————— 500yds

● Meteorological Service

▲ Snezhanka
1926m

Karamanzha
1858m
▲

▲ 1921m

For listings, see page 239

🍽 **Where to stay**   ✖ **Where to eat and drink**

1	Dafovska	5	Bai Panayot's
2	Malina Cottages		Chevermeto
3	Murgavets	6	Chanovete
4	Orlovets	7	Gloria Mar

O r f e e v i   S k a l i
▲ 1885m

1832m
▲

WHAT TO SEE AND DO This is an area with strong musical traditions; folk instruments include the bagpipes (*gaida*) and the shepherd's pipe (*kaval*). You may be able to see some performers in one of the local restaurants. For the real enthusiast, the Rozhen Festival held nearby in August is a folklore feast; this is usually held on the last weekend in August, but check at a local tourist office. The white-domed **Rozhen Observatory** (*Националната астрономическа обсерватория Рожен;* ☎ *8357*) can be seen from far off, its position a testament to the purity and clarity of the air here. It is possible to arrange a visit and see the huge telescope but it is only in use at night, so visitors can't sample the view of the night skies.

AROUND PAMPOROVO

MOMCHILOVTSI (МОМЧИЛОВЦИ) *Telephone code: 03023*

This picturesque hilltop village just off the main road from Chepelare to Smolyan was one of the first villages in Bulgaria to develop the idea of rural tourism in small family-run hotels, a concept which in the past was rather unusual, as tourists were generally assumed to prefer purpose-built large hotels. That Momchilovtsi continues to offer this kind of accommodation, and that practically every small town and village also does so now, is evidence of a successful idea!

Though it is 1,200m above sea level, Momchilovtsi has a mild climate as it is protected from cold winds by higher ridges around it. Untypically, the village has many young people. The Momchil Adventure Sports and Tourism Centre offers many recreational facilities to them and to visitors. Guides can be hired for hiking, photo safaris, caving and fishing. There are a variety of mountain-biking routes

Getting there and away For minibus or taxi connections to Pamporovo, check locally. There are also buses from Smolyan (*5 daily; 2hrs 20mins*).

Tourist information The tourist office (\ *2803;* e *tic_momchilovtsi@abv.bg; www.momchilovtsi.info;* ⊕ *09.00–noon & 13.00–17.00 daily*) can also advise about private rooms.

Where to stay, eat and drink These are village houses with rooms to let: hospitable and friendly with plain accommodation.

⌂ **Harmonia** (9 rooms) \ 2311. **€**
⌂ **Pei Surtse** (3 rooms) \ 2832; m 0898 406718. **€**
⌂ **Rodopchanka** (6 rooms) \ 2863. **€**

⌂ **Shipkata** (6 rooms) \ 2204. **€**
✕ **Restaurant Momchilovtsi** In the centre. Offers typical Rhodope specialities at very good prices. **€**

What to see and do There is a small **Ethnographic Museum** (*Етнографски музей; ul Byalo More;* \ *2272;* ⊕ *09.00–17.00 daily; adult 1lv*) where you can find out about the village's lifestyle, history and traditions. The beauty of the area has been an inspiration to painters and artists, and their work can be seen in the art gallery.

The village is close enough to use as an alternative base to Pamporovo; it is peaceful and relaxing, and a favoured resort of wealthier Bulgarians, as evidenced by the number of modern villas which have been built here.

Villages such as this are ideal for sampling some traditional Rhodope specialities such as *kachamak* (polenta), *patatnik* (potato pancakes) and *Rhodopski klin* (a pastry filled with eggs and rice). The spit-roasted lamb is also a favourite traditional dish.

SMOLYAN (СМОЛЯН) *Telephone code: 0301*

If Smolyan seems a long and straggling place (over 10km actually!) that is because it is an amalgamation of four smaller places: Ustovo, Raikovo, Smolyan and Ezerovo. It is a regional centre and a bustling town. A huge cathedral, the second largest in the country, has recently been built here. The area is like much of the Rhodopes: a mixture of Christians and Pomaks – you sense some competitive church- and mosque-building in the villages. It's a good alternative base to Pamporovo, not only for skiers but also for those wanting to explore the southern borderlands.

GETTING THERE AND AWAY There are **buses** (*bus station* ✆ *63104*) from Plovdiv (*hourly 06.00–19.00; 2½hrs*), Sofia (*5 daily; 4hrs*), Mogilitsa (*2 daily; 1hr*), Devin (*5 daily; 2½hrs*), Momchilovtsi (*5 daily; 2½hrs*), Zlatograd (*6 daily; 1hr*) and Smilyan (*4 daily; 1hr*).

TOURIST INFORMATION The tourist information office is at bul Bulgaria 5 (✆ *62530;* e *toursmolyan@abv.bg*).

⌂ WHERE TO STAY
⌂ **Hotel Smolyan** (136 rooms) bul Bulgaria 3; ✆ 62019; m 0882 933365; e hotelsmolyan@ gmail.com; www.hotelsmolyan.com. Convenient & good value, but very dated. €

⌂ **Pamporovata kushta** (8 rooms) Dobrik voivoda 9, Ezerovo; ✆ 68043; http://pamporov.hit. bg/menu.html. Guesthouse located in Ezerovo above Smolyan. Great hospitality. The owner has a wealth of local knowledge, including how Pamporovo got its name from one of his ancestors. €

⌂ **Sekvoya** (6 rooms) ul Studenets 25; ✆ 63085; e sekvoia@abv.bg; www.sekvoya-sm.hit.bg. Family-run hotel, though away from the centre. Good value. €

⌂ **Sokolitsa** (29 rooms) ul 1 Mai 47; ✆ 63143; e shumcov@mail.orbitel.bg; www.sokolitsa. domino.bg. Lovely location, gardens, indoor & outdoor dining. €

✗ WHERE TO EAT AND DRINK
✗ **Konaka** ul Shipka 7; ✆ 65515. Traditional tavern in Raikovo. Bulgarian & local specialities. €
✗ **Pizza Lucia** bul Bulgaria 57; ✆ 63334. Also soups, salads & grilled specialities. €
✗ **Riben Dar** ul Snezhanka 16; ✆ 63220; www. riben-dar.com/bg/index.html. Hard to find

but worth the effort. Aegean & freshwater fish specialist. €
✗ **Rodopski Kut** bul Bulgaria 2; ✆ 62853; http://rodopskikat.com. Central, good for local specialities. €

WHAT TO SEE AND DO Although it is a modern town, Smolyan has some interesting attractions including the Planetarium, the Art Gallery and the Historical Museum, which is of real importance. Nearby the Smolyan Lakes are worth exploring and are good for having a picnic with a picturesque view. Those furthest from Smolyan show less evidence of your untidy predecessors!

The **Planetarium** (*Планетариума; bul Bulgaria 20;* ✆ *83074; www.planetarium-sm.org;* ⊕ *09.00–18.00 Mon–Sat; adult 5lv*) is about 200m west of the centre of the town, near Hotel Smolyan. There are shows in various languages, but if you want a non-Bulgarian version a quorum of ten must be reached and an hour's notice given. Actually the show is visually spectacular and perhaps for nonexperts the Bulgarian version will be fine.

The **Historical Museum** (*Исторически музей; ul Dicho Petrov 3;* ✆ *62727; www. museumsmolyan.eu;* ⊕ *May–Sep 09.00–18.00, Oct–Apr 09.00–noon & 13.00–17.00, both Tue–Sun; adult 5lv*) is a short, steep walk up some steps across from the central hotel. It is very extensive so be sure to allocate an afternoon to it. It has English captions. There are many archaeological exhibits beginning with the Palaeolithic period, including a Thracian helmet with elaborate cheek guards. There are also ethnographic exhibits covering weaving, woodcarving and ironwork, as well as costumes from folk festivals including fantastic *kukeri* masks. Traditional architecture is illustrated with photographs of fine local examples from Shiroka Luka and Mogilitsa. Local folk music instruments such as bagpipes (*gaidi*) and lutes (*tamburi*) are displayed. There are also typical Rhodope rugs – the tufted goat's hair ones known as *halishta*, and the woven kilim style, *chergi*. It is colourful and well presented.

The **Art Gallery** (*Художествена галерия; ul Dicho Petrov 5, next to the Historical Museum;* \ *62328;* ☉ *09.00–17.00 daily; adult 3lv*) has a collection of nearly 2,000 works, including some fine Rhodope landscapes and works by local, national and foreign artists.

The **Pangalov House** (*Пангаловата къща; ul Veliko Turnovo*) is a very fine tall National Revival-style town house, but it is not open to visitors.

In July 2006, **Sv Vissarion Smolyansky** was consecrated. It is the second-largest Orthodox Church in the Balkans, after Sv Aleksandur Nevski Memorial Church in Sofia, and has room for 500 worshippers.

NORTH AND WEST OF SMOLYAN

From Smolyan there is a nice excursion west on mountain roads to the two small towns of Dospat and Devin, the Trigrad Gorge and the village of Shiroka Luka.

SHIROKA LUKA (ШИРОКА ЛЪКА) This village is about 13km from Pamporovo and is the focus of excursions from there, but it is not spoilt and remains a genuinely interesting architectural ensemble, with over 60 preserved National Revival-period houses.

Getting there and away There are **buses** from Smolyan (*4 daily; 45mins*), Pamporovo (*4 daily; 20mins*) and Devin (*4 daily; 1½hrs*).

Tourist information There is a tourist information office in the central square (\ *03030 2220;* m *0899 465770;* e *pesponedelnik@abv.bg*).

🏠 Where to stay

🏠 **Kalina** (6 rooms) ul Kapitan Petko Voivoda; m 0888 784897; e hotelkalina@abv.bg; http://shirokaluka-kalina.com. Rhodope-style rooms & tavern (see below). €

🏠 **Sgurovska Kushta** (5 rooms) ul Kapitan Petko Voivoda 117; m 0887 942004; www.zgurovskihouse.hit.bg. Comfortable, rustic style. €

🏠 **Shiroka Laka** (25 apts and 12 rooms) ul Chukata 1; \ 03030 2121; e reservations@shirokalaka.bg; www.shirokalaka.bg. Large hotel with spa, nightclub & restaurant with wonderful views. €€€

✖ Where to eat and drink

✖ **Kalina Mehana** See above. Good variety of local specialities, homemade brandy & red wine. Live folk music sometimes. €

✖ **Pri Slavchev Mehana** m 0888 784897. Local specialities in the centre of the village. Sometimes live music. €

✖ **Sgurovska Kushta Mehana** \ 0889 448201. See above. Also offers Bulgarian specialities. €

What to see and do The style of the village houses is asymmetric and the demeanour sturdy, as it needs to be with the heavy stone-flagged roofs. There are some fine old humpbacked bridges along the main street. The **Kalaidzhiyska House** (*Калайджийската къща; opens on request, check at tourist office*) contains an ethnographic collection and art gallery. The contents are fairly typical: milk churns, cheese-making equipment, local costumes and musical instruments, but it is well displayed and worth a visit.

The **National School of Folklore Arts** (*Национално училище за фолклорни изкуства*) specialises in music, and if you are arriving on an organised tour this will include a performance by the students.

There is an annual bagpipe festival (first Sunday in August) and several other musical competitions and events, including the wonderfully named 'Kukeri Festival on Dog's Monday' which is apparently held on a Sunday, the first in March.

The 19th-century **Church of the Assumption** (*Църква Успение Богородично*) is a National Revival-period church with naïve frescoes on that favourite theme of sinners being prodded into Hell by demons, and a rather splendid Elijah being propelled to Heaven in a chariot belching out clouds of smoke.

DEVIN (ДЕВИН) *Telephone code: 03041*

This is a nice small town, noted for its spa treatments, and perhaps more famously for its eponymous mineral water. Dating from Thracian times, like many Rhodope settlements it suffered during the period of forcible conversions to the Muslim faith in the 17th century and many inhabitants fled; in the early 20th century there were two major fires causing devastation. In 1912 when the town was finally

THE RHODOPE MOUNTAINS

The Rhodopes are mountains with mystic charm, giving an incredible impression of space and peace. On the rounded hills of the Western and Central Rhodopes, dark and cool spruce forests alternate with lush meadows full of wild flowers. The region of the Eastern Rhodopes is quite different but no less interesting with respect to the flora. Here the Mediterranean influence is significant.

The wildlife of the Rhodopes is fantastic, with 20 natural reserves. During the glacial periods the lowlands were covered by grass vegetation and the tops of the high mountains were either glaciated (Rila and Pirin) or covered by 'snow hats' (Vitosha). At that time in the small hidden valleys of the Rhodopes which enjoyed a milder climate, small groups of trees were preserved. These trees later became venerable forests. The Rhodopes have sheltered some Tertiary relicts, plants that several million years ago were widely distributed and now are preserved only here and there. An amazing plant that has the ability to hibernate is the **haberlea** (*Haberlea rhodopensis*). Plants can dry out completely and after some years in moist conditions they come back to life. Haberlea grows on the shady and damp rocks in Trigrad Gorge, at Chudnite Mostove, the Rock Bridges, and in the valley of the River Chaya.

There are many endemic plants in the Rhodopes, some of them only seen in these mountains: **Rhodopean sandwort** (*Arenaria rhodopaea*), **Rhodopean moon carrot** (*Seseli rhodopaeum*), **Rhodopean violet** (*Viola rhodopaea*), **Rhodopean mulleins** (*Verbascum decorum, V. juruck*), **Rhodopean scabious** (*Scabiosa rhodopensis*). Others occur here and there on the Balkan Peninsula as well: **saxifrages** (*Saxifraga sempervivum, S. stribrnyi, S. ferdinandi-coburgi*), **Greek mountain tea** (*Sideritis scardica*), **mullein** (*Verbascum humile*), **bellflowers** (*Campanula lanata, C. jordanovii, Trachelum rumelianum*). The Eastern Rhodopes, together with the Strandzha Mountains, are the country of the **orchids** in the spring. Enthusiasts can admire fine populations of orchids in the Western Rhodopes as well, on wet meadows according to their flowering periods, some appearing in early spring while others bloom a bit later.

liberated and became part of Bulgaria, people from nearby villages settled here and it developed into a regional centre. It makes a pleasant base for exploring the nearby caves and gorges.

Getting there and away There are **buses** (*bus station* ✆ *2077*) from Dospat (*daily; 1hr*), Smolyan (*2 daily; 2½hrs*), Plovdiv (*2 daily; 2hrs 20mins*), Sofia (*1 daily on Mon/Wed/Fri/Sun; 4½hrs*), Trigrad (*daily; 30mins*) and Yagodina (*daily; 40mins*).

Tourist information There is a tourist information office on ul Osvobozhdenie 5 (✆ *4161*).

🏠 **Where to stay and eat** Several cafés and restaurants are located along the main street. Also the restaurants of the listed hotels offer very good food.

🏠 **Devin Spa** (56 rooms) ✆2498; e office@ spadevin.com; www.spadevin.com. One of the best spa hotels in the area; various services & helpful staff. Central. Popular & busy restaurant. €€

🏠 **Elit** (14 rooms) ul Yundola 2; ✆2240; e reception@elite-devin.com; www.elite-devin. com. On the pedestrianised main street, modern & well-presented rooms. €

🏠 **Ismena** (23 rooms) ul Goritsa 41; ✆4872; e spa@ismena.bg; www.ismena.bg. On the outskirts of the town, a modern villa with high-quality fixtures & fittings. €€

🏠 **Orpheus** (210 rooms) ul Tsvetan Zangov 14; ✆2041; e reservations@orpheus-spa.com; www. orpheus-spa.com. Luxury spa, fitness centre, sports facilities & 2 restaurants. €€

What to see and do There is a small **museum** on the main square (🕐 *10.30–12.30 & 13.30–17.30 Tue–Sat; adult 2lv*) with an exhibition on Rhodope folklore.

DOSPAT (ДОСПАТ) *Telephone code: 03045*

From Devin there is a scenic mountain road to Dospat, situated at the southern end of a large dam. This is a quiet and remote area, rich in wildlife, particularly flowers and butterflies.

Getting there and away There are **buses** (*bus station* ✆ *2249*) from Plovdiv (*2 daily; 3hrs 45mins*), Pazardzhik (*1 daily Mon/Wed/Fri; 3hrs*), Devin (*2 daily; 1hr*) and Gotse Delchev (*one daily Mon/Wed/Fri; 1½hrs*).

Where to stay and eat

🏠 **Diamond** (27 rooms) ul Trakia 10; m 0897 974051; e hoteldiamant@abv.bg. Business hotel, garden restaurant with soups, salads & local specialities. Gym, jacuzzi, sauna. €

🏠 **Tihiat kut** (25 rooms) ul Rhodopi 5; ✆2082; http://tihiatkut.com. Located 50m from the Dospat Dam its rooms give a nice view to the lake; as the name of the hotel suggests it offers a relaxing, quiet atmosphere; garden restaurant; free parking. €

TRIGRAD GORGE (ТРИГРАДСКОТО ЖДРЕЛО) *Telephone code: 03040*

From the road between Devin and Dospat there is a turning to Trigrad, the village itself lying beyond the spectacular gorge.

Getting there and away There is one daily bus from Devin, taking half an hour.

🏠 **Where to stay and eat** Most of these small hotels have restaurants serving local specialities, and are in the upper part of town. They all offer simple rooms furnished in the traditional style.

8

🏠 **Arkan han** (5 apts & 11 rooms) m 0886 908912; e office@arkantours.com; http:// arkantours.com/bg/page/hotel_arkanhan. €€
🏠 **Crystal** (5 rooms) ☎ 2279. €

🏠 **Silivryak** (7 rooms) ☎ 2220; www. hotelsilivryak.vibs.bg. €
🏠 **Zdravets** (6 rooms) ☎ 3291; m 0889 180040. €

What to see and do At some places it is possible to pull off the narrow road and it is certainly worth doing this, not just to better admire the towering crags and peer down into the river below, but also to examine the cliffs more closely. In spring you can see the rare *Haberlea rhodopensis* growing in the crevices of the rocks. This is a Bulgarian endemic and an amazing plant which can 'hibernate'. When there is no water it just shuts down, if necessary for several years, but it revives when sufficient rain falls. There are other wild flowers, butterflies and birds, including the celebrated wallcreeper.

At one point the river disappears into a huge cave known as the **Devil's Throat** (*Дяволското гърло*; m *0889 052208;* ⊕ *10.00–16.00 Wed–Sun; hourly guided tours; adult 6lv*). This popular attraction is accessible along a short tunnel. You can hear the sound of water roaring before you see the mighty waterfall as it disappears into the earth. The cave is enormous, and home to many bats! When you leave you can walk to a viewpoint and see where the Trigradska River goes underground; it is quite a spectacle and easy to understand how local legend associates this with Orpheus coming back from the underworld. Further on beside the road the river reappears, apparently calmed by its subterranean adventure.

Nearby at Yagodina, in the Buinovo Gorge, there is another cave (*Ягодинска пещера; same entrance fee and opening times*) which has regular tours lasting 45 minutes. You see about 1km of the huge 10km cave system. It is cold and wet inside so dress appropriately. There are interesting illuminated formations to see, and artefacts from the prehistoric cave dwellings here.

Real enthusiasts should contact the caving club in Trigrad, Peshteren Club Silivryak, run by the owner of the Silivryak Guesthouse, who can arrange caving, horseriding and hiking; in summer there are English-speaking guides.

BATAK (БАТАК) *Telephone code: 03553*
From Dospat or Devin there are quiet roads to Batak, the western road passing two large reservoirs, but no villages. There are mature pine forests for most of the way,

---

BIRDS IN THE TRIGRAD GORGE

Trigrad Gorge is famous because it is probably the easiest place in Europe to see the **wallcreeper**. It is a common bird in every high European mountain. The problem is that to see it there, you must walk miles on almost vertical mountain paths, jump over stones, often surprised by snowfall even in June, and have a lot of other 'sharp' experiences on the way to this beautiful target.

It is impossible to describe the scenery of the gorge, where 500m-high cliffs come close together; you have to be here to feel and touch this magic. But the wallcreeper, seen often only minutes after arrival, and at just a few metres distance, creeping on the stone wall or flying like a giant butterfly over the valley, can make even this magic something minor. **Peregrine**, **dipper**, **serin** and many other bird species are just an added bonus. For the plant lovers the fantastic **burnt-tip orchid** can offer the same delight as the wallcreeper for the birders. And the natural charm of the little village of Trigrad will definitely make you want to come again and again.

and some wonderful drifts of orchids in a boggy area. We once travelled that way on a dark and heavy day, which, before we reached Batak, broke out into the most dramatic thunderstorm. We arrived in this sad place almost in darkness, although it was early in the afternoon. Somehow it seemed fitting.

History The region was inhabited in antiquity and perhaps its name comes from the nearby Batashko Marsh. It grew in size as Christians trying to escape the forcible conversion to Islam settled here. It was repeatedly destroyed by Kurdzhaliya and each time was rebuilt. In the early 19th century it had become quite prosperous, its people being timber workers and sheep farmers. In 1813 the Church of Sv Nedelya was built, which became the centre of the tragedy which unfolded in Batak some 60 years later.

The April Uprising against the Ottoman occupation began in Koprivshtitsa, but it soon spread to many other towns and villages. It was unfortunately not well co-ordinated and was quickly and viciously suppressed. More than 200 men, women and children were herded into the church and burnt alive, 3,000 more were massacred in the churchyard, and nearly 2,000 more in the town.

An Irish-American, J A MacGahan, writing in the *London Daily News*, broke the news and this is an extract from his horrifying account:

> We entered the town. On every side were skulls and skeletons charred among the ruins… We entered the churchyard. The sight was more dreadful. The whole churchyard for three feet deep was festering with dead bodies partly covered – hands, legs, arms and heads projected in ghastly confusion. The church was still worse. The floor was covered with rotting bodies quite uncovered. There were 3,000 bodies in the churchyard and church. In the school, a fine building, 200 women and children had been burnt alive.

All Bulgarians have known this dark episode in their history since their schooldays, and that other terrible massacres occurred in nearby towns: Kalofer, Karlovo, Sopot and others. The Ottoman yoke was heavy and long, and it still casts a shadow.

Many eminent people from around the world became involved in the protest, Victor Hugo, Oscar Wilde, William Gladstone and Leo Tolstoy among them. The British prime minister, Disraeli, comes out of this episode very poorly. He at first dismissed the accounts of the massacres as an exaggeration, wishing for pragmatic reasons to continue Britain's alliance with Turkey. The realisation that the news was true prevented him from supporting Turkey in the war with Russia, but didn't stop his manoeuvres at the subsequent Congress of Berlin. There the newly liberated Bulgaria was divided, with the regions of Macedonia and Thrace remaining within the Ottoman Empire and the southern part of Bulgaria becoming the Turkish protectorate of Eastern Rumelia.

Getting there and away There are **buses** (*bus station* ☏ *2328*) from Sofia (*Mon, Wed & Fri; 4hrs*), Plovdiv (*3 daily; 2½hrs*), Pazardzhik (*3 daily; 1hr 20mins*) and Velingrad (*3 daily; 1hr*).

Where to stay and eat There aren't many hotels in Batak itself. You could try the **Kolarov House** (*ul Todor Kolarov;* m *0877 075995; www.batak-bg.com/tur_spalnya. htm;* €), which has 23 beds in dormitories. Several holiday places are situated around the **Batak Reservoir** outside the town in Tsigov Chark area. All the hotels have restaurants (€–€€).

🛏 **Aida** (16 rooms) 📞 2343; e reservations@
hotelaida.bg; www.hotelaida.bg. Close to the dam
& 500m away from the ski tracks; restaurant & a
café indoors & outside; children's playground. €€
🛏 **Eterno** (15 rooms) 📞 2841; e hoteleterno@
abv.bg; http://hotel-eterno.com. Facing the dam;
picturesque restaurant with a garden; good starting
point for other interesting places in the area. €€
🛏 **Katalina** (22 rooms) 📞 03542 3366;
e vilen_complex_katalina@abv.bg; http://
katalina-bg.com. The complex offers

accommodation in 5 family villas & rooms in
the 2 hotels; each villa has a private terrace & its
own kitchen, but guests can also taste the local
speciality dishes of the restaurant. There's also a
rent-a-bike service. €€
🛏 **Sezoni** (24 rooms) 📞 2350; e seasons.bg@
gmail.com; www.seasons.bg. Located 3km from
the centre of the resort, facing the dam with its
rooms & terraces; a relaxing centre with sauna;
offering a wide selection of local dishes; starting
point for tours to the mountains. €€

What to see and do The **museum** (*музея; on main square;* ⊕ *09.00–17.00 daily,
closed noon–13.00 in winter; adult 3lv*) tells of the massacre and other stories in
Batak's history. It is probably best to visit the museum first, because the church gives
such a powerful impression it is hard to absorb anything else afterwards.

The exhibition begins with Thracian finds and continues with the beginnings of
resistance encouraged by the church, the hopes for religious autonomy and eventual
freedom, by following the route of literacy and education. The Turks apparently
regarded the town as a hotbed of outlaws, notably Voivod Strakhil, whose portrait
is here. The museum has two cherry tree cannons used by the rebels; it is hard to
imagine them being effective against the Turks, but their very existence brought
down the vengeance of the bashibozuks (irregular soldiers of the Sultan, their
name means 'broken heads' in Turkish). The international outcry focused attention on
the failings of the 'Sick man of Europe' (the Turkish Empire) and was the catalyst
for the Russo-Turkish War of 1877–78.

Visitors to the **Church of Sv Nedelya** (*Храмът Св Неделя*) today find an ossuary
and museum; there are marks on the wall of bullets, cuts from *yatagans* and fire. It is
impossible not to be moved by this small place which witnessed such horrors. The
museum staff will open the church if you find it locked.

The museum staff will also open the small **Ethnographic Museum** on request.
The **Art Gallery** (*Художествената галерия; ul Apriltsi;* ⊕ *same times as History
Museum above*) is in an old National Revival house.

VELINGRAD (ВЕЛИНГРАД) *Telephone code: 0359*

The town was formed from the old Pomak villages of Kamenitsa, Chepino and
Ludzhene.

The surrounding area and the Western Rhodopes is the region of the Pomaks
(Bulgarian-speaking Muslims, nowadays more usually called Bulgarian Muslims).
Their origins are disputed but most agree that they are ethnic Bulgarians who
converted, or were forcibly converted, to Islam in the 15th century after the Ottoman
occupation was fully established in this area. They are thus different from ethnic
Turks who were brought from different parts of the huge empire to settle in areas of
Bulgaria. Other Turks will be descendants of the original occupiers who remained
after the liberation. Some historians dispute the forcible conversion and say that
these people were voluntary converts, hoping to secure economic advantages. This
theory has etymological backup, as the word *pomak* may derive from *pomagach* or
helper. Whatever the motives of the original converts, it is undeniable that some of
their descendants became the vicious perpetrators of horrors such as that at Batak.

The area has always been rich and fruitful, with its two rivers, its wooded hills and
its mineral springs. Historically there are traces of Thracian, Roman and Byzantine

settlements. Nowadays Velingrad is a well-known spa visited by more than 200,000 people each year. There are more than 70 springs of different temperatures, which are beneficial for liver, stomach and skin disorders. It is an attractive town, currently receiving considerable investment and development.

Velingrad is also at the hub of the revival of regional crafts; souvenirs such as wooden toys and textiles can be seen and purchased at the business centre.

The town, which seems to have avoided the post-communist renaming frenzy, is named after Vela Peeva, who was active in the revolutionary and workers' movement during World War II. Its most famous son is the world-renowned opera singer Nikolai Ghiaurov.

Getting there and away There are **trains** (*railway station* 📞 *52141*) from Septemvri (*4 daily; 1½hrs*) and Dobrinishte (*4 daily; 3½hrs*).

There are **buses** (*bus station* 📞 *53073;* 📱 *0898 714952*) from Sofia (*3 or 4 daily; 3½hrs*), Plovdiv (*3 daily; 2hrs*) and Pazardzhik (*8 daily; 1hr*).

Tourist information The office is at pl Svoboda (📞 *58401; www.velingrad.bg*).

Where to stay At weekends the hotels are often full, so it's wise to book ahead.

Aquatonik (96 rooms) ul Nikola Vaptsarov 122; 📱 0878 441685; e reception@aquatonik.com; www.aquatonik.com. Good-value spa with friendly staff. €€€

Dvoretsa (106 rooms) ul Tosho Staikov 8; 📞 56200; e reservations@dvoretsa.com; www.dvoretsa.com. A former government residency, this is the poshest place in Velingrad. In the centre of town, next to an attractive landscaped park area. Has a spa. This is old-style communist grandeur, with enormous public rooms, now fully modernised. Go for a coffee if a stay is too expensive, as it is fascinating to see. €€€

Tabakovi (5 rooms) ul Hristo Smirnenski 31; 📞 59877; e info@hoteltabakovi.com; www.hoteltabakovi.com. Family-run hotel, good value. €

Velina (51 rooms) ul Dr Doshnikov 14; 📞 53412; e reception@hotelvelina.com; www.velinahotel.com. Wonderful location in the forest. Spacious rooms, spa treatments & restaurant of high standard. €€

Velingrad (78 rooms) bul Saedinenie 50; 📱 0884 770387; www.grandhotelvelingrad.com. Excellent location, variety of spa therapies, welcoming & relaxing. €€€€

Where to eat and drink There are several restaurants along the two main streets, Suedinenie and Asparuh.

Bonzhur bul Suedinenie 111; 📱 0887 450029. Popular central restaurant. €–€€

Chevermeto By the central outdoor pool; 📞 29661. Bulgarian & local specialities in traditional style. €€

Omar Tavern bul Suedinenie 500; 📞 57803. Generous portions, traditional Bulgarian. €–€€

Pizza Venezia ul Han Asparuh 23; 📞 57903. Pizzas, salads, grilled meats. €

What to see and do Velingrad is primarily a spa and there are few other attractions. The Kleptouza Karst Spring has been diverted into a pretty lake in the middle of an attractive park in the Chepino district of the town. There are shady walks, rowing boats and pedalos, cafés and restaurants, or bring a picnic.

PESHTERA (ПЕЩЕРА) The small town of Peshtera is known for the eponymous *mastika* produced here, and for the famous **Snezhanka Cave** (*Пещерата Снежанка;* ⊕ *summer 09.00–17.15 daily, winter 10.00–16.00 Mon–Fri*). This is 5km to the southwest, on the Batak road. It is called Snezhanka (meaning 'Snow-white') because of the white calcite rock formations in many beautiful shapes, one of which is in the form of a girl, perhaps Snow White from the fairy tale. The cave is not particularly large, only 145m long, but it is very densely decorated with stalactites and stalagmites, and there are several separate halls. You will need to walk for about half an hour from the car park to the cave.

SOUTH FROM SMOLYAN

For many years I wanted to go to **Mogilitsa** (*Могилица; tourist office* \ *0301 62530;* e *mogilitza@abv.bg;* ⊕ *09.00–17.30 daily*) to see the *konak*, so often used as an illustration in guides to Bulgaria. It can now only be seen from outside. There was a long stretch of about 15km of unmade road, but it always looked as though it was leading somewhere! Mogilitsa for some reason does not feature on any road signs, but once we had arrived there were plenty of helpful signs. The *konak* was just as beautiful as I'd expected, though smaller, and the grounds around it were not well cared for.

Known as the Agushevi Konak after the landowning family who built it, it displays many characteristics of Rhodope-style architecture. It consists of three connected courtyards, each of which has both residential and farming premises. There would have been a courtyard each for the father and his two eldest sons and their families. Each has been altered over the years yet it remains a harmonious whole. There are many chimneys and, reportedly, 221 windows! The most eye-catching feature is the tower decorated with floral paintings. According to legend, the creator of this beautiful building had his hand cut off so that he could not make anything else to rival it.

A fortified house such as this would have been built by a wealthy merchant, the owner of huge flocks of sheep. The Agushevs used this as a winter residence and apparently had a summer one of similar grandeur which has not survived.

The interior, which unfortunately can no longer be visited, was very spacious and comfortable with many large, panelled rooms with carved ceilings. Different woods were used: pine, cherry and walnut. Lattice-work screens protected the women's privacy, and meant that they did not have to be veiled all the time. A huge hall for receiving guests was designed to impress. There are workrooms upstairs where the wool was dyed and processed.

Uhlovitsa Cave (*Пещерата Ухловица;* ⊕ *09.00–17.00 daily*) is near the village of Mogilitsa, and is well signposted. It is a very steep climb to the entrance but the cave has a wonderful formation like a waterfall, which goes down into a lake, the lights making it sparkle like diamonds. There are also many odd-shaped formations and caverns. There are several other caves near Mogilitsa.

Nearby is **Smilyan** (*Смилян*), a village known by Bulgarians for its giant-sized beans, often sold on the roadside. Though the word is that there are more Smilyan beans for sale than there are being grown! The village is also known for its brand of yellow cheese.

SMOLYAN TO KURDZHALI

This route passes through a former mining area: Rudozem, Ardino and Madan. Gold, silver, copper and iron were mined here. These towns prospered in communist times as heavy industries needed the ore, but in the post-communist era the economic difficulties, competition from overseas and falling world prices for metal meant that most mines were closed by the late 1990s.

ZLATOGRAD (ЗЛАТОГРАД) *Telephone code: 03071*

This former mining town is well worth the detour. It is Bulgaria's most southern town, a settlement even in Thracian times. There are many rock sanctuaries and tombs nearby. During the Ottoman occupation in the late 17th century, the forcible conversion to Islam took place. Many local people adopted Islam to save their families, but they retained their Bulgarian ethnicity. Relations between Christians and Muslims in this area have always been harmonious.

Getting there and away There are **buses** (*bus station* ✆ 2013) from Sofia (*3 daily; 5½hrs*), Plovdiv (*5 daily; 4hrs*) and Smolyan (*4 daily; 1hr*).

Tourist information The nearest tourist information office is in Smolyan.

⌂ Where to stay and eat

⌂ **Aleksandur** (16 rooms) ul Stefan Stambolov 40; ✆4166; www.eac-zlatograd.com/en/home. New spa hotel; the restaurant has regional specialities. €–€€

⌂ **Flora** (12 rooms) ul Bulgaria 90; ✆4494; e info@hotelzlatograd.com; www.hotelzlatograd.com. Modern, family-friendly hotel. €

⌂ **Koruchevata Kushta** (6 rooms) In the Ethnographic Complex. A simply furnished old house. €

⌂ **Pachilova Kushta** (8 rooms) ul Evgenya Pachilova 4; ✆4166. Another old house in the Ethnographic Complex, beautifully restored, with modern facilities. €

✗ **Mehana Belovidovo & Pri Vodenitsata** Both serve local specialities, & are situated in beautifully restored old houses. €

What to see and do During the period of National Revival, Zlatograd developed as an exporter of wool, goats' hair, hides and furs, and local stockbreeding flourished. In 1834 the prosperous town built a large church, a school and many fine houses which combined the National Revival style with Rhodope architectural traditions. A special feature of the houses is their round white chimneys. The roads were cobbled, and beautiful bridges were built. To mark the establishment of the Bulgarian Exarchate in 1870, they built the **Church of Sv Georgi** (*Църквата Св Георги*) in 1871–72, which contains several icons brought from Mount Athos. The brave freedom fighter Delyo Voivode was from the town. As a local hero, he was commemorated in many legends and songs; one of the latter was chosen to represent our planet together with a Beethoven symphony, and is on board the *Voyager 1* probe in its journey of 60,000 years to the star AC+793888. The **Church of the Assumption** (*Успение Богородично*) is surrounded by a wall and is, like so many Bulgarian churches, dug into the ground to avoid being conspicuous.

In recent years the central area, where over a hundred National Revival-period buildings remain, has been well restored on the initiative of a local businessman. The **Zlatograd Ethnographic Complex** (*Етнографскиареален комплекс*; ✆4166; www.eac-zlatograd.com; ◷ 09.00–noon & 13.00–18.00 daily; adult 2lv) includes an open-air museum, many craftsmen's workshops where souvenirs are made and sold, *mehanas* serving Rhodopean specialities, and a café where rye coffee is made in a traditional way by heating it on hot sand. The workshops include a carpenter, goldsmith, tailor, braid-maker, weaver, coppersmith, saddler and cutler.

The museum has exhibitions of costumes, looms and tools from the locality. This is the only place in Bulgaria where both the small, traditional, horizontal *stan* or loom and a large vertical one for making big carpets and blankets can both be seen working. There is a lovely display of a bride's trousseau, which demonstrates her skill and eye for beauty.

Across the river there is also a watermill museum, **Vodenitsata**, with a water-driven fulling machine – basically four very noisy mallets beating the rough cloth.

ARDINO (АРДИНО) On a different road between Smolyan and Kurdzhali, the small town of Ardino is worth a visit. In these eastern Rhodope villages the majority of the population are Muslim, and minarets become part of the landscape. Ardino is a neat town, with the River Arda flowing through its centre. The mosque has two minarets and looks almost new, though it was built in the 16th century and restored in 1976. The church is modern and also well kept. If the mosque is open it is worth looking in to see the beautiful murals.

What to see and do The famous **Devil's Bridge** over the Arda is beyond Dyadovtsi, north of Ardino, about 1½ hour's easy walk along a forest road, not waymarked. Its beauty and symmetry and its perfect reflection in the clear water of the river are a special sight. The bridge, built in the 15th century, is 66m long, 3.4m wide and 8.5m high. It has been used in various historical films. On one of the keystones of its central vault there is a small hexagonal impress known as Solomon's seal; nothing similar exists elsewhere in Bulgaria.

East of Ardino, **Momchilgrad** was the scene of violent clashes in 1984–85 when local Turks reacted against the enforcement of name-changing to Slav names (page 19). In that clash 40 people died, but community relations are now good and there is no feeling of tension in the town.

The area east of Momchilgrad has many ruined fortresses which changed hands countless times between the rival Bulgarian and Byzantine empires. It is perhaps for this reason that Tatul's particular significance was not at first realised.

TATUL SANCTUARY (ТРАКИЙСКОТО ОБРОЧИЩЕ ТАТУЛ) As we approached the sanctuary, 10km east of Momchilgrad, we suddenly smelt the rich, sweet scent of carnations, *karamfil*, which grow wild here. A Hermann's tortoise was crossing the road in a leisurely fashion, but luckily there was no traffic. At Tatul there are the remains of a medieval fortress with a partly preserved tower, the ground floor of which was used as a water reservoir. A Thracian sanctuary has been excavated nearby, two rock tombs and some niches and steps having been cut into the rock. Some archaeologists believe that the sanctuary was dedicated to Orpheus, as a rock tomb discovered in 2004 was said to be his. Another theory is that the drainage channels from the tombs imply human sacrifice rather than burial, but there is also the possibility of the channels being connected to the making of wine, as at Perperikon. Orpheus apparently requested to be buried between earth and sky, and Tatul is plainly visible to men and highlighted by the sun, so some believe this could be his burial place.

KURDZHALI (КЪРДЖАЛИ) *Telephone code: 0361*

This pleasant town sits between two large reservoirs. Before you reach the town if you are travelling southeast from Asenovgrad, you begin to see a change in the scenery, particularly after the village of Komuniga. It is a drier, rockier landscape with fewer trees and more scrubby bushes. The road from Kurdzhali to Haskovo is surprisingly busy as this area is where many of the Turkish minority live, and where a lot of trade with Turkey is carried out. It has benefited from Turkish investment in the road infrastructure to facilitate the commerce.

Like so many Bulgarian towns, Kurdzhali is an ancient settlement and there are traces of Thracian, Roman, Byzantine and Bulgarian inhabitants. It is thought to have got its name from a governor of the town, Kurdzhi Ali. Although it was briefly liberated in 1878, after the Congress of Berlin it became part of the Turkish protectorate of Eastern Rumelia, and when that, against Turkish wishes, united with Bulgaria in 1885, Kurdzhali was given to Turkey as a compensation, remaining part of the Ottoman Empire until its demise in 1912. It then became the main town of the tobacco-growing and processing industry, and for a time a metallurgical centre. Nowadays it is increasingly used by tourists who come to the area for the archaeological sites and for the rich wildlife.

GETTING THERE AND AWAY There are **trains** (*railway station* ✆ *61226*) from Dimitrovgrad (*4 daily; 2hrs*), Momchilgrad (*4 daily; 30mins*) and Plovdiv (*2 daily; 4hrs*).
There are **buses** (*bus station* ✆ *26792*) from Ardino (*5 daily; 1hr*), Zlatograd (*5 daily; 1hr*), Krumovgrad (*10 daily; 40mins*), Plovdiv (*12 daily; 2½hrs*), Ivailovgrad (*2 daily; 3hrs*) and Sofia (*12 daily; 4½hrs*).

WHERE TO STAY

🏠 **Arpezos** (74 rooms) ul Republikanska 46; ✆ 60234; e hotel_arpezos@mail.bg; www. arpezos.com. Central location; old-fashioned tower-block style, but renovated. **€**

🏠 **Perperikon** (27 rooms) ul Volga 3; ✆ 67140; e hotel@perperikonbg.com; www.perperikonbg.

com. Comfortable modern hotel. Central location with swimming pool. **€€**

🏠 **Ustra** (57 rooms) ul General Delov 1; ✆ 64722; e hotel_ustra@mail.bg; www.ustra-tour.com. Quiet location, large clean rooms, good value. **€**

WHERE TO EAT AND DRINK

✕ **Arpezos** See above. Varied menu of local & Bulgarian specialities. Sometimes live music. €–€€

✕ **Meatsa** ul Hristo Botev; ✆ 67799; www. komplex-meatsa.com. Definitely the best restaurant in the town. €–€€

✕ **Seven Blackberries** ul Konstantin Stoilov 16; ✆ 36428. Bulgarian cuisine, grilled specialities. Live music. €–€€

WHAT TO SEE AND DO The **History Museum** (*Исторически музей; east of ul Republikanska;* ✆ *63587;* ⊕ *09.00–noon & 13.00–17.00 Tue–Sun; adult 4lv*) is a really splendid one. It is on the outskirts of town in an impressive building, the former Turkish *konak*.

For the archaeologists there are artefacts from Thracian times, including some fine jewellery; for those interested in natural history there is a whole floor devoted to minerals, crystals and photographs of rock formations.

The ethnographic sections are particularly rich with very fine jewellery and a great variety of costumes. The local patterns are quite different from those in the Western Rhodopes. There are literally dozens of *chorapi* (*плетени чорапи*), the thick woollen socks worn by women. A fascinating area is devoted to reconstructions of various workplaces, so there is a tailor, a shoemaker, a coppersmith, a dairy and a charcoal burner. The tobacco section shows the various shapes in which the leaves were packed for transport.

There are many examples of boiled-wool rugs, very dense and serviceable. Another interesting display is of the different shapes and patterns of loaves baked for special occasions such as weddings, Easter and St George's Day.

The **Art Gallery** (*Художествената галерия; ul Republikanska;* ✆ *23619;* ⊕ *09.00–noon & 14.00–17.30 Tue–Sun; adult 3lv*) has icons and works by Vladimir Dimitrov-Maistora, Dechko Uzunov and Svetlin Rusev.

Kurdzhali is close to the famous Perperikon archaeological site, near which are several unusual rock formations that you could visit if you are driving. There are **stone mushrooms** (near Beli Plast), a **stone forest** (near Tatul), a **broken mountain** (near Vodenicharsko) and even a **stone wedding** (near Kurdzhali).

EAST OF KURDZHALI

This is an area of *mahali* or hamlets; if you look at the map you will see numerous small places marked, far more than in other areas, but most are tiny. The village names around here are rather fascinating: some translated ones are Idiot, Wild Plum, Slave Village and Beardless Ones! It is also an area of outstandingly rich wildlife; in 5 minutes after leaving Perperikon we saw black-headed bunting, crested lark, black storks, bee-eater and roller.

The countryside is of rolling hills, very open with just low bushes and a few small trees. For nature lovers with a car any roads to Madzharovo, Krumovgrad and Ivailovgrad are worthwhile. The butterflies, birds and flowers are everywhere and it pays to stop frequently. Studen Kladenets Reservoir is also interesting for

WHAT WAS PERPERIKON?

Perperikon (*www.perperikon.bg*) is one of the archaeological sites in Bulgaria that truly deserves to be seen. It is an adventure through natural stone, ancient walls and mystical forests. It involves a bit of climbing and will intrigue both specialists and enthusiasts.

So, if you feel fit and ready to take the challenge, bearing in mind that in the summer it could be rather hot, then you will have the chance to explore an archaeological complex where the first human presence dates from 7000 years ago – the end of Eneolithic age – and continued until the 14th century AD.

What attracted people to this exact place? First of all, it is naturally fortified by mountains. Secondly, it lies 2km from the ancient gold mines near Stremzi village. Places so ideally situated were considered sacred, and usually sanctuaries were placed there. This is the case with Perperikon, which is thought to be the biggest megalithic ensemble in the Balkans. The first signs of religious practices here date from the early Iron Age, at which time an impressive round altar with a diameter of almost 2m was hewn in the rocks. The earliest niches, probably dating from the same time, were specifically used for the sacred process of producing grape juice and later on wine.

But what do the ancient sources say about Perperikon? The first written evidence that probably relates to Perperikon is from the father of history, Herodotus. Describing the campaign of the Persian King Xerxes against the Greeks in 480BC, he provides interesting information about one of the most famous sanctuaries of antiquity. There was said to be an oracle whose predictions were as trustworthy as those of the oracle at Delphi. This mysterious sanctuary was situated somewhere in the Rhodope Mountains. Later in the 4th century BC that mysterious sanctuary was where Alexander the Great was predicted to become the conqueror of the ancient world. After him, in the 1st century BC, the same prediction was made for Augustus.

Was Perperikon really this sanctuary? Excavations in recent years show a whole architectural complex consisting of a fortress and an acropolis containing a palace with a sanctuary. It is clear that the visible ruins are from different periods but birdwatchers. There is a huge dam wall, like something from an action scene in a James Bond film; there were even divers in black wetsuits working there when we passed – rescuing the hero, perhaps?

This is the most Turkish area of Bulgaria; the Turkish language is widely spoken and many people don't speak or understand Bulgarian. The faces are quite different: a broader brow, weather-beaten skin and the build is shorter and more solid. The people are reserved; we even saw one woman who was working in the fields take to her heels when my (male) driver got out to ask the way.

There are fascinating cliff faces pitted with manmade niches of different sizes; the smaller ones probably held gifts for the gods, while larger ones were graves.

The soil is poor and tobacco is virtually all that grows. There are a few sheep and cattle, their herdsmen accompanied by fierce-looking Anatolian shepherd dogs, with enormous spiked metal collars on. They are used to protect the sheep against wolves. We rounded a corner and saw several on the bank beside the road, dozing in the sun; nearby a foolhardy suslik poked its nose out, but only for a moment.

Further east beyond Ivailovgrad there are significant remains of the **Roman Villa Armira** (*Римската Вила Армира;* \ *036 616026;* ⊕ *09.00–noon & 13.00–18.00*

some of them are still difficult to date exactly. Nevertheless the complex clearly had great importance through the ages.

The walls of the fortress that surround the hills are massive. On the top of the hill is the acropolis. Some of its buildings have not been identified and their function is not clear. Their ground floors were constructed and hewn into the rocks and the holes for their doors can still be distinguished. The streets are perfectly preserved, so the visitor can easily walk among these mysteries. A pagan temple, probably connected to Dionysus, covers the eastern part of the acropolis, and in the 4th– 5th century AD it was converted into a church. This is the reason for the addition of a semicircular apse to the eastern end, and a portal to the western part. The almost untouched pulpit is richly decorated with carved stone ornaments. An eagle with wings broadly spread out can clearly be seen on the rocks. It bears five inscriptions in Greek that are yet to be explained, but archaeologists suppose they are liturgical writings. The church probably existed until the 12th century, when it was destroyed by barbarian invaders. A path through a covered colonnade leads the way from this temple to the acropolis, and some of the columns are preserved.

In the excavated areas on the hill two gates were discovered, on the east and west sides. The western gate has a rectangular bastion. To the south, 30m under the acropolis, lies the most impressive complex, which is believed to be the palace or the great sanctuary of the oracle. A visitor enters the building through a narrow 100m passage that ends at a complex fortification with two gates. It covers a magnificent territory of about 1,700m² and consisted of at least two floors. Only the ground floor is preserved today, with 50 rooms hewn into the rocks. Around 30m from the surface of the palace are the remains of a huge hall, called the ceremonial hall. All around there are benches, a throne, other niches for unknown purposes, and a very interesting system of canalisation. In the western part of the palace two crypts were found, the first with five sarcophagi and the second with 15. They were robbed, most likely in antiquity, so we shall never know who these important people were. The material evidence shows that the complex flourished mainly in Roman times.

daily; adult 5lv), which has been taken as a wine name by local producers. The wine is worth trying! The villa was a large one, built during the second half of the 1st century AD. This is the most richly decorated and substantial private house (even palace) of the Roman period discovered in the Bulgarian lands. The villa was at the centre of an estate; the occupant was probably the governor of the surrounding area who received the status of a Roman citizen to reward his good service to the Romans. He was given the right to create this villa, its gardens and pools, and he did this during the period AD50–70. It was vandalised by the Goths at the end of the 4th century but several exquisitely detailed, large mosaic floors survive.

MADZHAROVO (МАДЖАРОВО) At Madzharovo there is a **reserve** and **visitor centre** (m *0885 516633;* ☺ *10.00–18.00 daily; adult 2lv*) run by the Bulgarian Society for the Protection of Birds. It is situated by the bridge over the Arda, just off the road. There are interesting interactive displays in the visitor centre and a small café. Guided walks and a visit to the nearby vulture feeding station can be arranged. With a telescope or good binoculars you can see Egyptian and griffon vultures and golden eagles. The vultures feed on carrion which is provided for them, picking the corpses completely clean. The reserve is encouraging the breeding of what was once

MADZHAROVO FOR BUTTERFLIES

Madzharovo is adjacent to the Arda River, surrounded by the spectacular rocky peaks of the Eastern Rhodope Mountains in the central part of southern Bulgaria, not far from the Greek border. The mountains rise to just over 750m near Madzharovo, to nearly 900m further west near the Studen Kladenets Dam, and soon rise to over 1,000m still further west. Though lacking altitude, these are certainly mountains with attitude! They are rocky, with steep craggy peaks, cliffs and scree, and are stunningly beautiful. They are partly bare rock and partly clothed with deciduous trees and scrub interspersed with open, scrubby, herb-rich grassland, little or none of which has been agriculturally improved. Among the forest and scrub are numerous glades bursting with flowers, many of which are characteristic of, and some endemic to, the Balkans.

Many butterfly species can be seen here that are still common in many parts of Bulgaria. In the meadows a wide range of skippers, blues, fritillaries and other butterflies will be encountered in their season, June and July being the months when the largest number of species are on the wing. Here you will encounter various skippers such as the distinctive **yellow-banded skipper**, the **orbed red-underwing** (or Hungarian) **skipper** and **sandy grizzled skipper**. Fritillaries are everywhere and include **spotted** and **lesser spotted fritillaries**, **knapweed**, **heath** and **Glanville fritillaries** and the ubiquitous **Queen of Spain fritillary**. Several large fritillaries are also found here: **high brown**, **Niobe** and **dark green fritillaries**. On the woodland edges, **twin-spot** and **marbled fritillaries** are frequent, as is the **southern white admiral**. In the woodlands, **silver-washed fritillaries** and the spectacular **cardinal** may be common. Blues include **Mazarine**, **green-underside**, **Amanda's**, **Meleager's** and **Chapman's blue**. **Silver-studded blues** can be abundant in some of the shorter grasslands. **Sloe** and **ilex hairstreaks** may be plentiful in the right places associated with their food plants, blackthorn and oaks.

This part of Bulgaria is a good place to see a range of species whose European distribution is restricted to southeast Europe. Among the more spectacular species to be found here is **Freyer's purple emperor**, an elusive butterfly which can be a common type of sheep, the *karakachan*, named after the nomadic people who kept them in huge numbers in the past.

Getting there and away There are **buses** from Haskovo (*2 daily; 2hrs*).

⌂ Where to stay and eat

⌂ **Arda** (8 rooms & 8 apts) near Dolno Cherkovishte village; m 0884 101001; www.complexarda.com. Idyllic location, gym, sauna, pool, restaurant. **€–€€**

⌂ **BSPB Centre** (3 rooms) m 0885 516633. Peaceful location but shared bathroom facilities. **€**

⌂ **Rai (29 rooms)** ul Dimitar Madzharov 48; ☏03720 2230; www.hotelraibg.com. Modern & comfortable rooms. A good restaurant with generous portions. **€**

HASKOVO TO SVILENGRAD

HASKOVO (XACKOBO) *Telephone code: 038*

This is a pleasant town, but it is not much visited by tourists, who tend to pass through it either on the way to Plovdiv or to the border at Svilengrad (*Свиленград*).

found in association with the willows that line parts of the Arda River. However, the male can be seen when it comes down to the ground to find minerals on damp sandy patches, which are frequent on the exposed shingle areas of the river-bed. They are also partial to the excreta of carnivorous mammals (a habit it shares with other emperor species).

The **eastern festoon** can be seen almost anywhere in this region in June. Similar in size to the **swallowtail** and **scarce swallowtail** (both common here) the festoon's characteristic flight is recognisable even from a moving vehicle. The distinctive spiky caterpillars of this species, and those of the earlier-flying **southern festoon**, can readily be found on patches of *Aristolochia*, which often grow on patches of wasteland and the rough edges of fields and woodlands.

One of the most common species of shrub in this region is the Jerusalem or Christ's thorn (*Paliurus spina-christi*). Its fragrant yellow blossoms colour the rocky hillsides in June attracting, among other insects, jewel-like, green chafer beetles to its pollen and nectar. This is the larval food plant of the delightful **little tiger blue** butterfly, which inhabits hot rocky valleys among the rocky mountains and hillsides where the food plant grows, such as dry river-beds.

Another species associated with scrub is the **lattice brown**, a large distinctive species that often hides among scrub during the heat of the day. However, it is easily disturbed, whereupon it usually flies only a short distance to a nearby patch of scrub and immediately disappears from sight. If approached carefully they can usually be viewed closely.

The hot, steep, dry rocky slopes of the Eastern Rhodopes are habitat for the **Krueper's small white**, a very distinctive species. Although closely related to the common cabbage whites, this one feeds only on *Alyssum* species.

Those who have the privilege to visit the Madzharovo area are entranced by its beauty, its atmosphere, the sense of going back in time, and of course its rich wildlife and especially, at the right season, the sheer abundance of its flower-rich meadows. All combine to entice visitors to return.

Its centre is, however, rather a nice mixture of old Bulgarian National Revival houses and some Ottoman streets, all overlooked by the elegant minaret of the mosque.

Getting there and away There are **trains** (*railway station* ✆ *624125*) to Dimitrovgrad (*2 daily; 30mins*) and Momchilgrad (*2 daily; 2hrs 20mins*).

There are **buses** from Sofia (*1–2 per hr; 5hrs*), Plovdiv (*1–2 per hr; 1½hrs*), Kurdzhali (*hourly 05.00–17.30; 50mins*), Svilengrad (*hourly; 1hr 20mins*), Ivailovgrad (*1 daily; 3hrs*), Krumovgrad (*1 daily; 4hrs*) and Stara Zagora (*hourly; 2hrs 20mins*).

Tourist information The tourist information centre is at bul Rakovski 1A (✆ *666444;* e *tourism.haskovo@gmail.com; www.haskovo.com*).

What to see and do There is an attractive central square, pl Svoboda, around which cafés and shops cluster. There is not a great deal for the visitor to do, but the Eski Dzhamiya, the **Old Mosque** (*Старата джамия, Ески джами*), actually the oldest in the Balkans, is welcoming. It was built in 1395, in the earliest years of the occupation. The **History Museum** (*Историческия музей;* ⊕ *09.00–17.00 Mon–Fri; adult 2lv*), just off the central square, has a good collection of early coins, both Roman and medieval. There are Iron Age vessels and weapons, and an ethnographic section devoted to local trades, tobacco, cotton and silk. Exotic crops like aniseed and sesame were also grown in this area. The years of Ottoman occupation are rather bypassed, but there is interesting material from the National Revival period, including documents about the fair at Uzundjovo, which was the predecessor of today's Plovdiv Fair.

Paskaleva Kushta (*Паскалевта къща; ul Episkop Sofronii 3;* ⊕ *09.00–noon & 14.00–17.00 Mon–Fri; free*) is an old house furnished with authentic pieces and housing a small art gallery. It is named after its original owner who was a publisher.

The famous revolutionary Vasil Levski set up one of his committees in the town and the legendary freedom fighter **Kapitan Petko Voivoda**, recalled in many folk songs, was from this region. There is a statue to his memory.

Northwest of Haskovo is a village whose name resonates in Bulgarian history, **Klokotnitsa**. It was the scene of a major battle in 1230 between the Bulgarian Tsar Ivan Asen II and Theodore Comnenus, the Byzantine ruler of a large territory extending to the Greece–Albania border. It was a big victory for the Bulgarians and their tsar was afterwards acknowledged as the tsar of the Bulgarians and Greeks.

South of Haskovo, on the Kurdzhali road, is the village of **Konush** (*Конуш*). The recently discovered Thracian tomb there was probably that of a high-ranking Thracian aristocrat; the red lines painted along the joints of the stone blocks are related to the god, Zagreus. The tomb is dated from the end of the 5th and the beginning of the 4th century BC. The entrance to the mound was found and inside were spearheads, chain fragments from a hauberk (coat or tunic of chain mail) and some unique wooden hearts, possibly used as decoration of a bed or throne. The discoveries made the national newspapers in 2006, not just because the many recent discoveries have excited Bulgarians about the fascinating ancient history of their lands, but also because apparently in their excitement the archaeologists broke one of their own most important rules. Normally before they begin work they offer wine to the gods, but this time they forgot. On the first morning the archaeologist, Dr Kitov, cut his leg, severing an artery and requiring an emergency operation. Visitors are warned: 'Be careful when you walk about, because the gods always take what belongs to them!'

About 19km northeast of Haskovo, between the villages of Aleksandrovo and Simeonovgrad, is another wonderful archaeological discovery: the Aleksandrovo tomb (❧ *666444; www.alexandrovo.com; May–Oct 09.00–17.00, Nov–Apr 08.00–16.00, both Tue–Sun; adult 4lv*). It dates from the 4th century BC and is a prime example of Thracian culture. It has impressive, monumental proportions. The frescoes are very well preserved and give a lot of information about Thracian weapons, clothing and rituals. In 2009 the adjacent Thracian Art Museum, built with the aid of Japanese donations, was opened. Here, an exact replica of the Aleksandrovo tomb can be studied. The museum also houses artefacts from other archaeological sites in the region, including an amazing collection of gold jewellery, from 4500–4000BC.

HARMANLI (ХАРМАНЛИ) This is a quiet, dusty town, which feels remote despite its proximity to the truck-laden E80. Its most famous sight is the humpback bridge which, despite its name in English, is beautiful. The Grand Vizier who ordered its construction was pleased with the result, according to the effusive dedication: 'He ordered an arch like a rainbow to be built over the River Harmanli... and alleviated rich and poor alike from their sorrows.' This was built in the early period of the Turkish occupation in the early 16th century. From the same date is a ruined wall from a caravanserai. The town's name comes from the Turkish for threshing mill;

THE EASTERN RHODOPE MOUNTAINS

This is a paradise for birds of prey. A considerable part of these mountains were identified by BSPB and designated by BirdLife International as an Important Bird Area (IBA) of European and Global significance. Of 39 raptor species inhabiting Europe, 37 have been seen in the Eastern Rhodopes. You can see the four European vulture species (with the exception of the Egyptian vulture) all year round, especially at the feeding stations in the area, managed by the second BSPB Conservation and Information Centre: Eastern Rhodope Vulture Centre (m *0885 516633;* e *vulturecenter@bspb.org*). Some wetland birds, including **pygmy cormorant**, **whooper swan** and other waterfowl, can be seen in winter. During the period of migration, though not so spectacular as over Burgas, the passage of birds of prey, including **red-footed falcon**, **herons** and **egrets**, but especially **passerines**, takes place throughout the area. Among the most interesting breeding species are the **chukar**, **sombre tit**, **rock nuthatch**, **blue rock thrush**, **Isabelline** and **black-eared wheatear**, **masked shrike**, **eastern Bonelli's warbler** and a large variety of the Mediterranean-type warblers. **Scops owl** and **little owl** can often be seen in the towns and villages. There is an amazing density of some species such as **black stork**, **Ortolan bunting**, **hawfinch**, **barred warbler** and others.

The extremely rich biodiversity of other wildlife (butterflies, beetles, dragonflies, amphibians, reptiles, bats and other mammals) and plants (especially orchids) is another specific quality of these mountains. Here the field conservation actions (artificial feeding of vultures and the monitoring of the breeding sites of rare birds) were started in 1984 and subsequently organised by BSPB professionally and on a large scale for the entire area of the Eastern Rhodopes, thanks to the BSPB Vulture Centre in Madzharovo. Over 20 new protected areas were designated in the area, not just for birds, but also to protect rare plants, bats and other wildlife.

8

THE BULGARIAN PHOENIXES

Once upon a time, there were four species of vultures living in Bulgaria. All of them were often seen flying over the capital of the country, attracted by the many slaughterhouses and by their relatives behind the cages of Sofia Zoo. Some of them even nested near the capital: the **giant black vulture** on old trees in Sofia Plain and the **griffon vulture** on the cliffs of Vitosha Mountain. That most insolent of birds, the **Egyptian vulture**, was breeding, not in Sofia, but in the very centre of Plovdiv, on the rocky hills within the city. No, this is not a picture from medieval times, but from the first part of the 20th century! But as usually happens, such a good thing didn't last. Clever people decided that all birds of prey were harmful, as they eat the same food as man, and mass extermination began. As a result, by 1970 just a few tens of breeding pairs of Egyptian vultures survived in the whole country. Then Mother Nature decided to give the vultures a chance – slowly the griffons and even the black vultures started to be seen again, often just single birds at various places in the country. Just after the first nest of the griffon vulture was found in the Eastern Rhodopes in 1985, the mass emigration of ethnic Turks left the birds without their main source of food – the flocks of hundreds of thousands of sheep, goats and cattle, which produced enough carcasses every day for them to survive. Bulgaria was going to lose its vultures again if the conservationists were not there to start artificial feeding of the flying giants. It was therefore organised on a professional and regular base by BSPB, which for this purpose created its own Vulture Centre in Madzharovo. The effects were immediate: griffon vultures' nests increased from one or two to 35 or 36. Moreover, for the first time in Bulgarian history, an extinct species, the black vulture, was restored. In 1993 the first nest with young was found just a few kilometres from one of the BSPB 'vulture restaurants'.

the area was a major corn grower supplying the Ottoman armies. Both Harmanli and nearby Svilengrad were major silkworm breeding centres.

Getting there and away There are **trains** from Plovdiv (*1 daily; 2–3½hrs*) and Svilengrad (*3 daily; 30mins*).

There are **buses** from Haskovo (*3 daily; 40mins*), Ivailovgrad (*1 daily; 2½hrs*), Svilengrad (*5 daily; 40mins*) and Plovdiv (*2 daily; 2½hrs*).

SVILENGRAD (СВИЛЕНГРАД) For admirers of Turkish bridges there's another at **Svilengrad**, the Mustafa Pasha Bridge across the River Maritsa. This is a mighty structure nearly 300m long, with 13 arches. It was designed by Sinan, the architect of many glorious mosques in Turkey, and built in about 1540. The town was known as Mustafa Pasha until 1912, when it was renamed Svilengrad from *svila*, meaning 'silk'. Just beyond Svilengrad is the main crossing point to Turkey, Kapitan Andreevo, and nearby a minor crossing into northeast Greece. Situated as it is, bordering two other countries, Svilengrad's population is a mixture of all three. Many Greeks settled here after 1913 when some population exchanges were carried out. Anyone fascinated and horrified by this extraordinary attempt to impose population order on the diversity of the former Ottoman Empire should read Louis de Bernières's *Birds Without Wings*. Set at the time of Gallipoli, the collapsing Ottoman Empire and the conflict between Greeks and Turks which was unleashed, de Bernières focuses on a single small village in which Christians and Muslims had lived in harmony for centuries; there were deep friendships and even love across the religious divide. World War I intruded and destroyed a whole way of life.

Getting there and away There are **trains** (*railway station* ☏ *0379 73012*) from Plovdiv (*3 daily; 3–4hrs*) and **buses** from Harmanli (*5 daily; 40mins*), Haskovo (*7 daily; 1hr*) and Kapitan Andreevo, on the Turkish border (*5 daily; 20mins*).

What to see and do From Svilengrad by car you can visit **Mezek** (*Мезек*), close to the Greek border, where there is an important archaeological site. Historically it was linked with earlier settlements of present-day Edirne, just over the Turkish border. There are the remains of a medieval fortress and nearby an Iron Age settlement and necropolis have been discovered. In 1908, in the mound embankment a villager found a life-sized bronze statue of a wild boar. A large and beautiful tomb was also discovered by chance in the 1930s; it contained a great number of pieces of jewellery and other artefacts such as the Mezek collar and candelabrum, which are thought to be of Greek origin. The tomb, shaped like a beehive, has a 20m corridor, two rectangular rooms and a round burial chamber. Bronze artefacts were discovered inside. It is said to date from the 4th century BC and to have been that of a Thracian ruler. The tomb can be visited (⊕ *10.00–17.00 daily; adult 2lv*).

Also accessible only by car and 40km northeast of Svilengrad, right on the Turkish border, is Matochina. This is a remote place, rich in historical and natural beauty. There is a magical view of the ruins of the medieval fortress, Bukelon, above the village. Nearby is a 10th-century rock church. The region is of great importance to environmentalists, as there are many rare species such as imperial eagle, eagle owl, jackal and many types of orchids and butterflies. For this reason the Green Balkans NGO has developed a field and visitor centre there. To arrange a visit or find out more, contact the Levka conservation information centre (m *0885 609289*; e *ggradev@greenbalkans.org*).

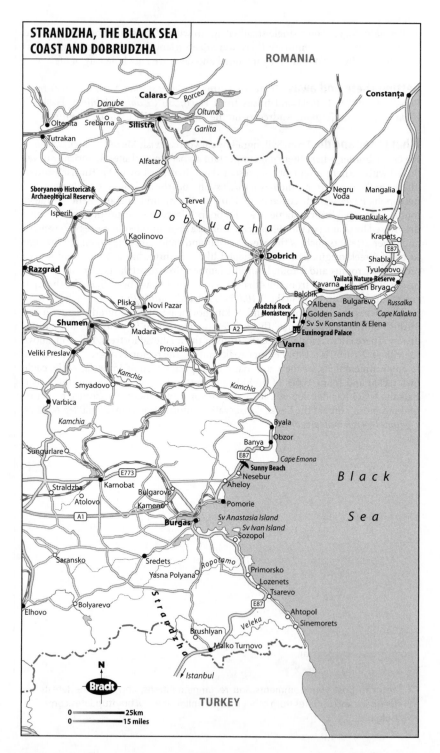

STRANDZHA, THE BLACK SEA COAST AND DOBRUDZHA

ROMANIA

Constanţa

Calaras
Danube
Oltenita
Srebarna
Tutrakan
Silistra
Borcea
Oltuna
Garlita

Alfatar

Sboryanovo Historical & Archaeological Reserve
Isperih

Tervel

Dobrudzha

Negru Voda
Mangalia

Durankulak

Krapets
E87
Shabla
Tyulenovo

Kaolinovo

Razgrad

Dobrich

Yailata Nature Reserve
Kavarna
Kamen Bryag
Balchik
Pliska
Novi Pazar
Aladzha Rock Monastery
Albena
Bulgarevo
Russalka
Shumen
Golden Sands
Cape Kaliakra
Madara
Sv Sv Konstantin & Elena
A2
Euxinograd Palace
Provadia
Varna

Veliki Preslav

Kamchia

Smyadovo
Kamchia

Varbica

Kamchia
Byala
Obzor
Banya
Cape Emona
Sungurlare
E87
Sunny Beach
Nesebur
B l a c k
E773
Aheloy
Straldzha
Karnobat
Bulgarovo
Pomorie
S e a
Atolovo
Kameno
A1
Burgas
Sv Anastasia Island
Sv Ivan Island
Sozopol

Saransko
Sredets
Primorsko
Yasna Polyana
Ropotamo
Lozenets
Tsarevo
Elhovo
Bolyarevo
E87
Ahtopol
Sinemorets
S t r a n d z h a
Brushlyan
Veleka
Malko Turnovo

N
Istanbul
Brabt

TURKEY

0 ———— 25km
0 ———— 15 miles

9

Strandzha, the Black Sea Coast and Dobrudzha

This juxtaposition brings together one of the most remote parts of Bulgaria with one of the busiest and most built up. The **Strandzha Mountains**, especially when approached from the west, seem a long way from any major centres. This is an area of rolling hills, many stunted oak trees and little clearings. Villages are few, small and scattered. The coast still has some large, unspoilt, beautiful areas in the north, particularly in **Dobrudzha**, and in the extreme south, but development is taking place at a great rate. Tourists from the UK, Ireland, Germany, Poland, Scandinavia and Russia come in their thousands, attracted by the sunny climate, clean beaches, watersports and affordable prices. The **mega-resorts** of Golden Sands, Albena and Sunny Beach are the main attractions, but many smaller, pretty villages are joining in and a ribbon of development is taking place. Even so, there are deserted beaches to be found and good places for walking and birdwatching. Bulgaria's coast still has something to offer everyone.

IN THE STRANDZHA MOUNTAINS

BRUSHLYAN (БРЪШЛЯН) *Telephone code: 05952*
In a low-key way the small village of Brushlyan in the Strandzha Mountains is encouraging tourism. It has been designated an architectural and ethnographic reserve, as it is the site of Strandzha's best-preserved village houses. Several small but very interesting museums have been established.

Getting there and away There are **buses** from Burgas (*2 weekly; 1hr 50mins*).

Tourist information There are offices at neighbouring Malko Turnovo and Tsarevo (pages 265 and 268). Staff at the Brushlyan museums are helpful too.

Where to stay and eat
Complex Sarmashik (21 rooms) \3460; m 0888 441836; www.sarmashik.bg. Smart hotel in the centre, built in the old style; hotel rooms & cottages. Good restaurant. €

Gergana Nakova Guesthouse (3 rooms) m 0887 762741. Local cuisine & hospitality, with a garden & BBQ. €

Kushtata Guesthouse (3 rooms) \4158. With a garden, veranda & BBQ. €

What to see and do The **Museum in the Old School** (*Старото манастирско училище*; ⊕ *10.00–17.00 daily; joint ticket for all the museums, adult 3lv*) has been set up as it once was, with goat- or sheepskins for the children to sit on. A sandbox was used as a sort of blackboard. Children came when they were 12 years old and they 'wrote' on wax slates which could be cleared by warming them at the fire. In the late 19th century they were taught four basic subjects: mathematics, natural sciences, geography and grammar. From modest beginnings with six students, the school grew to 60. In winter they studied all day, but in the other seasons they would have spent part of each day helping in the fields. Their lunch bags hang empty on the wall.

Next to the school in a little yard is the very low **Church of Sv Dimitur** (*Църквата Св Димитър*) and a belltower. It is a working village church, with a simple patterned wooden ceiling and a basic modern wooden iconostasis. There are a few 18th-century Greek-style icons and some modern Bulgarian ones. The curator pointed out a Strandzha-style icon of Sv Georgi, a rather lively image with an unusual blue-green background drawn from nature rather than traditional iconography. Both the Orthodox Greek and Russian icons usually have a gold background colour. At the back there is a separate area for women and children to worship.

The **Village House Museum** (*Музей на селския дом*) is rather well hidden but worth visiting. The various types of local houses are illustrated: one-storey wooden houses, or two-storey houses, often accommodating animals on the ground floor.

The friendly curator can tell you all about family life in this house which, despite its small size, was home to parents and 12 children. They lived and slept in one room, sleeping on the floor, and eating at a *sofra* or low table; the father had a stool and everyone else sat on cushions. Their food was lentils, beans, cheese and salads; meat was rarely eaten, not because it was unavailable but because it couldn't be preserved. So for special occasions a whole animal would be roasted and eaten and shared with other families.

Everything from clothes to tools was homemade. The house was always very hot because of the animals below and because the fire was constantly lit for cooking and baking. As if raising 12 children was not enough, the mother would normally do needlework in the evenings, as all their clothes would have been homemade. The shoes were made of incredibly hard leather which had to be soaked overnight so that they were soft enough to put on in the mornings.

The curator gives a fascinating glimpse of village life. Water had to be collected from 1km away. Girls traditionally did this task and dressed up to do so, wearing a flower behind their ear; boys took the horses to water at the same time. If the boy

STRANDZHA NATURE PARK

The mountains in Strandzha Nature Park are of low elevation, but their geographical situation and geological history make them one of the most interesting plant areas. This is also true of the Black Sea coast nearby. Here there remain many evergreen trees and shrubs from the Tertiary period. This means that the flora and vegetation is of really ancient origin, or in other words, that glaciation affected this territory less.

The main part of the distribution range of flora and vegetation occurring here is in Asia Minor and the Caucasus. Strandzha is at the western limit of their range, so this is a bonus for visitors, who can see here plants from further east, such as **oriental beech** (*Fagus orientalis*), **Caucasus nettle-tree** (*Celtis caucasica*), **Colchian holly** (*Ilex colchica*), *Laurocerasus officinalis*, *Vaccinium arctostaphylos*, **squill** (*Scilla bythinica*), **pontian fritillary** (*Fritillaria pontica*) and the relicts – **pontian rhododendron** (*Rhododendron ponticum*) and **pontian daphne** (*Daphne pontica*). This is also the best area for orchids.

Sakar is a picturesque hilly mountain area near the borders with Greece and Turkey. It is sparsely populated, which makes it an ideal destination for those looking for solitude in the wild. Sakar has three designated Natura 2000 sites, which aim to preserve the region's unique natural resources. The southern part of Sakar also falls within the European Green Belt – an international ecological network of regions of preserved biodiversity on either side of the old Iron Curtain.

Sakar is one of Bulgaria's richest biodiversity regions – here nature lovers can enjoy the great variety of birds, such as imperial eagle, long-legged buzzard, black kite, hoopoe, European roller and masked shrike, for example. The Green Balkans NGO is running a successful reintroduction project for the globally threatened lesser kestrel – the small and graceful falcon that once used to be a common species in Bulgaria. The area is also home to many mammal species such as golden jackal, red fox and suslik, as well as reptiles, including the European legless lizard, European worm snake, Hermann's tortoise, Greek tortoise, centipedes and scorpions. It is rich in wild orchids, peonies, pheasant's eye, peacock anemone and many others.

Cultural and historical places of interest, including medieval fortresses, rock churches, Thracian cliff sanctuaries and dolmens, can also be seen here.

took the flower and asked to drink the water it was a sign that he liked the girl and might be a pretext for courtship.

Nearby the **Museum of Farm Implements** (*Музей на селско-стопанските инструменти и пособия*) has a huge variety of implements, including carts, ploughs, a threshing floor with a 'sledge' (which was pulled by water buffalo), tethers and sieves. There are tools for giving the water buffalo a pedicure, and a prod to make them move. It is a fascinating place.

MALKO TURNOVO (МАЛКО ТЪРНОВО) *Telephone code: 05952*

A few kilometres further on from Brushlyan is Malko Turnovo, and beyond that a crossing into Turkey. In communist times this was a sensitive border, and tourism was not encouraged. However, the town has interesting museums and is a good base for exploring the Strandzha Nature Park.

Getting there and away There are **buses** (*bus station* \ *2060*) from Burgas (*6 daily; 2hrs*).

Tourist information The tourist information office is at pl Preobrazhenie (\ *3017;* m *0886 647201;* e *tic_mtarnovo@mail.bg; www.malkotarnovo.org*).

Where to stay and eat

Hipokrat (25 rooms) \ 2814. Pleasant small hotel. €

Kovach Inn (5 rooms) Ethnographic Complex, Kovach, 2km from Zvezdets; m 0878 705484. Cosy rooms, *mehana* with traditional Bulgarian cuisine. €

Nadka Vulkova Guesthouse (2 rooms) \ 2575. Traditional style. €

Sveti Nikola (7 rooms) ul Dyado Blago 3; m 0878 226234. Simply furnished, small hotel. €

✕ Restaurant Ribarnika Zvezdets; m 0885 916144; e info@ribarnika.net. Part of a fish farm, so excellent fresh fish. €

✕ Restaurant Veselyatsi \ 2788. Local specialities. €€

What to see and do Malko Turnovo rather surprised us because, as we stopped to get our bearings, we found ourselves beside a huge, almost Georgian-looking, town house made entirely of wood, which had a sign saying it was the Catholic Exarchate. The **Historical Museum** (*Исторически музей; ul K Petkanov 1A;* ↘ *3664;* ☉ *summer 08.00–17.00 Mon–Fri, 09.30–noon & 14.00–17.00 Sat–Sun, winter 08.00–noon & 13.00–16.00 Mon–Fri, by appointment Sat; adult 4lv*), which was our destination, occupies an ensemble of three buildings. There are five exhibitions: archaeology, modern history, icons, ethnography and nature, with some English captions.

There is a rich collection of Thracian pots and some interesting photos of excavations. A map shows the numerous burial mounds in the area. The Catholic influence locally, which had surprised us, was attributed by the curator to Bulgarian patriotism, a reaction to the political supremacy of the Muslim Turks and the religious dominance of the Orthodox Greeks. Many Bulgarians left the area when it was excluded from the newly liberated country. Some headed for Varna and set up a Strandzha Society and a campaigning newspaper there. A whole room is devoted to the Ilindensko-Preobrazhensko Uprising of 1903 (see box, pages 130–3).

The next house in the museum has some fine icons from this area, including Sv Modest, the patron saint of animals, an unusual figure in iconography.

The third house has an exhibition by the Bulgarian Swiss Biodiversity Conservation Programme about the Strandzha Nature Park, with plenty of interactive learning opportunities for Bulgarian children. Phoning a bird to hear its voice was great fun.

AROUND MALKO TURNOVO North of Malko Turnovo is Petrova Niva, where a large monument commemorates the Bulgarians who lost their lives in a battle with the Turks during the Ilindensko-Preobrazhensko Uprising in 1903. In August each year there is a memorial ceremony here.

The area around the town is rich in Thracian megalithic monuments and necropolises. At Mishkova Niva, 13km southwest of Malko Turnovo, there are the remains of a domed tomb, Roman villa and a mound necropolis. Visits can be arranged at the tourist information office.

Strandzha is noted for its tales and myths. One concerns an Egyptian goddess, Bast or Bastet, with the body of a woman and the head of a cat or lion. At the foot of Gradishte peak, near Mishkova Niva, there is a cave entrance to some mysterious tunnels. According to the local story, in 1980 an ancient map was discovered. Archaeologists reported the find to Lyudmila Zhivkova, the daughter of Bulgaria's ruler, who was then minister of culture. She in turn took the map to Vanga, the famous clairvoyant, who saw an alien race living here many centuries ago, so an archaeological expedition was launched. They found, in a tunnel deep in the mountain, stones of black granite carved with men's profiles, and a dodecahedron which they believed was some kind of data carrier like a modern microchip. The finds were sent for analysis to Germany, where they disappeared without trace. The following year researchers camping nearby saw two luminous figures, one enthroned, appear on the rocks. Zhivkova's sudden death brought the exploration to an end. All that can be seen today is the entrance cave and a ruined stone cat's head. Strange energy is said to be emitted from the cave, and this is thought to be the reason for the fact that no grass grows on Gradishte's somewhat unnaturally symmetrical peak. Could it be Bast's tomb? Or just the tunnels of an abandoned mine?

Strandzha Nature Park, established in 1995, covers an area of 2,226km² and is the largest protected area in the country. There are four nature reserves within the park.

THE MASKED FOREST 'BANDIT'

He is masked, very secretive and always keeps to the oak forests. You may pass at a metre's distance from him not realising that he is here. And you *will* get very excited when he suddenly appears in front of you. If you are a birdwatcher, of course, as the talk is about the masked shrike! This could happen now at quite a lot of sites in the south of the country, but until 1960 nobody had seen this magnificent bird in Bulgaria. It was just not living here. However, due to the natural extension of its range from the south, at some point the masked shrike appeared here, quite successfully occupied part of the Bulgarian lands and now is a real birding 'delight'. It is, indeed, not easy to spot it. Unlike the other shrikes, the masked shrike keeps to the forest canopy, although in more open, lighter forests it is sometimes seen in small valleys. Because of this, even when you know that a pair is in the area, it may sometimes take half an hour to find the birds. This creates a real feeling of gambling, adding some more adrenalin to the adventure!

The road from Malko Turnovo to the coast crosses the Veleka River, which in the past has flooded very seriously, with whole trees beached in fields far from the riverbank. Huge trees had been uprooted as if they were matchsticks.

On the way is the village of Bulgari, which is traditionally associated with the Strandzha ritual of Nestinarstvo, a dance performed on fire embers. The dancers appear to be in a trance as they move to a loud rhythmic drumbeat clutching an icon. In this village it is performed on the day of Sv Sv Konstantin and Elena on 21 May. However, it has become something of a tourist attraction and you can see it performed at folklore restaurants in other areas of Bulgaria and at other times of year.

THE SOUTHERN COAST

SINEMORETS (СИНЕМОРЕЦ) _Telephone code: 0550_
This remote village has always been known for its wonderful beach and as the base for a relaxing holiday. Recently hotels and apartments have been built, though further south the beaches are still quiet.

Getting there and away Sinemorets can be reached by **bus** from Burgas (*1 daily; 3hrs*), or **minibus** from Ahtopol, about 10–15 minutes away.

Where to stay and eat
⌂ **Casa Domingo** (45 rooms) ul Dunav 73; ☎ 66093. New complex with range of rooms including studios. Outdoor pool. Seafood & Mediterranean specialities beautifully presented in the restaurant. Set in pretty gardens. Welcoming family hotel. **€–€€**

АHTOPOL (АХТОПОЛ) _Telephone code: 0590_
The road from Malko Turnovo reaches the coast at Tsarevo. To the south there are four villages before the Turkish border, but there is no crossing. Ahtopol, a Greek colony in ancient times, is the largest of these villages. It remained a part of the Ottoman Empire until 1913, and at that time the population was mainly Greek, but with the population exchanges it was taken over by Bulgarians. Staying here is a good option if you want to explore the quieter southern beaches and the beautiful estuary of the River Veleka at Sinemorets.

9

Getting there and away There are **buses** from Burgas (*1 daily; 1hr 20mins*) and Sinemorets (*3 daily; 10mins*). In summer there are also minibuses from Zapad bus station in Burgas to Ahtopol.

Where to stay

🏠 **Ahtopol** (15 rooms) ul Ivan Vazov 21; m 0885 904636; e hotelahtopol@abv.bg; www. hotelahtopol.hit.bg. Family-run hotel in the centre of town; comfortable rooms. €–€€

🏠 **Escada Beach** (81 rooms) ul Georgi Kondulov; 62035; m 0887 147100; e eskada@ dir.bg; www.hoteleskada.com. Modern hotel offering pleasant spacious rooms with pool or sea views. €€

🏠 **Lola Garden** (9 rooms) ul Preobrazhenska 7; 62020; e office@lolagarden.com; www.

lolagarden.com. Hospitable hosts, central position, sea views. €–€€

🏠 **Valdi** (11 rooms) ul Cherno More 22A; 62320; m 0888 877076; e hotelvaldi@hotmail. com; www.hotelvaldi.com. Beautiful view, near the beach. Welcoming family hotel. €–€€

🏠 **Villa Alexandrovi** (7 rooms) ul Cherno More 4; 62488; m 0889 971772; www.villa-alexandrovi.hit.bg. Setting in landscaped gardens in the centre of town, variety of rooms & villas. Bar & BBQ. €

Where to eat and drink

✖ **Calypso** Neptun 18; m 0888 139961. Stylish restaurant, generous portions of local specialities. €–€€

✖ **Morsko Oko** ul Cherno More 29; 62361; m 0889 593493; e info@seaeye-bg.com; www. seaeye-bg.com. Lovely location with fantastic views. Good food; fish specialities. €

What to see and do Ahtopol, like many early settlements, is situated on a small peninsula, around which there are several shingle beaches protected by rocky headlands. There is a small **museum** (*музей*; ⊕ *irregularly Tue–Sun; adult 1lv*) which gives some information about the original Greek settlement. There is also a small but still active fishing harbour, and new developments including a marina.

TSAREVO (ЦАРЕВО) This is a small town built on two picturesque peninsulas, with a pleasant harbour and a park beside the sea. In communist times the town was known as Michurin, named after a famous Soviet scientist, and many locals still use this name. It was a favoured resort of Bulgaria's royal family in the late 19th and early 20th centuries. There has been a lot of new hotel development, some oversize and ugly, though the town centre is still attractive.

Getting there and away There are **buses** from Burgas (*12 daily; 1hr*), Ahtopol (*3 daily; 10mins*) and Sinemorets (*3 daily; 20mins*).

Tourist information The tourist information office is on ul Mihail Gerdzhikov 2 (*52162; m 0888 592801*).

Where to stay and eat

🏠 **Diana** (15 rooms) ul Hristo Botev 2; 0554 240068; e hoteldiana@abv.bg; www.hoteldiana. hit.bg. Located in the centre, next to Sv Tsar Boris Church; sea view. €

🏠 **Villa Victoria** (9 rooms) ul Shipka 13; m 0894 488188; e villa_viktoria@abv.bg; www. villaviktoria-bg.com. Modern hotel with pleasant rooms. €

🏠 **Zebra** (40 rooms) ul Han Asparuh 10A; 0293 60046; e zebra@mail.orbitel.bg; www. hotel-zebra.com. Modern building; spacious rooms. Sea views. Great value. €€

✖ **Ribarska Sreshta** kv Basiliko 510. Popular fish restaurant beside the harbour. Part of the hotel of the same name. €€

What to see and do Tsarevo was known in the past for its boatbuilding, which was facilitated by its sandy coastline and access to plentiful Strandzha oaks. Its history is documented in the small **History Museum** (*Исторически музей; in the Holy Trinity Church, Св Троица;* ⊕ *09.00–noon & 15.00–20.00 Sun–Fri; free*).

The road north passes Lozenets, Kiten and Primorsko, all formerly used mainly by Bulgarians staying in accommodation provided by their employers, known as rest homes (*почивни домове*). However, refurbishments and new developments are changing this previously sleepy area.

Inland from Primorsko, there is an interesting side road to **Yasna Polyana** (*Ясна поляна*). This small village is known well beyond Bulgaria's boundaries to those who admire the work of Leo Tolstoy. It is named after his birthplace and has a library and a museum explaining the beliefs of his followers.

About 5km north of Primorsko is Begliktash, the oldest Thracian megalithic sanctuary found so far on the coast. From about the 8th to 4th centuries BC this was a sanctuary connected with the fertility cult of the mother goddess. There are impressive dolmens, a rock labyrinth and special stones for votive offerings. It is near the former Perla residence and can be reached from the Svetilishteto parking area by walking for about 20 minutes.

Travelling north there is construction everywhere, though between places there are gaps and some stretches of beach with no development. There appears to be no regard for nature or for the long-term attractiveness of a beautiful coastline. Hotels of Las Vegas-like proportions are squeezed in next to more normal-sized neighbours, or, worse still, suddenly appear on the horizon, dominating what was once a pleasant view.

North of Primorsko and before Dyuni, the road crosses the Ropotamo River and you can take short river cruises from here, either inland or to the sea, but only when enough people have arrived to satisfy the captain! It is a rather scruffy area but the boat trip is nice, especially in spring. Here and on the Kamchia and Veleka rivers exists a strange natural phenomenon, known as Longoza, or European jungle. For about 30km inland from their estuaries in the Black Sea there are dense areas of trees with trailing, climbing lianas.

Walks in the area are signposted from the road.

DYUNI (ДЮНИ) This holiday village was constructed in 1987; it is built around Alepu Bay and replicates older-style buildings in a modern way. It is well equipped for sports, but a busy road separates some parts of the complex from the sea.

SOZOPOL (СОЗОПОЛ) *Telephone code: 0550*

The town centre is still charming but the surroundings are a huge mushroom growth of new hotels. This town was also an ancient Greek colony, known as Apollonia. Named after Apollo, the god of healing, it was a thriving centre trading inland and by sea. It was attacked by the Romans and destroyed in 72BC, and its famous bronze statue of Apollo, which was 13m high, was taken as booty to Rome, from where it has long since disappeared. Sozopol ('Town of Salvation') was renamed in the 4th century and eventually settled by Slavs. It remained a small fishing village until the Ottoman occupation, during which it lost its position as the area's main port to Burgas.

In its heyday as a powerful trading centre it was also known for its cultural life, a tradition maintained to this day. Each September the Apollonia Arts Festival takes place, with classical, folk, jazz and pop music and literary events held at a variety of venues. This is one of the major such events along the coast. Perhaps because of this, Sozopol is said to be a favourite resort for many Bulgarian artists and writers.

GETTING THERE AND AWAY The bus station (*ul Khan Krum*) is between the old and new parts of the town. There are **buses** from Burgas (*1–2 per hr 06.00–20.30; 40mins*) and from Ahtopol (*2 daily; 50mins*).

WHERE TO STAY As well as the hotels listed below, Sozopol has a huge number of houses offering private rooms. There are signs everywhere in the Old Town and along ul Republikanska in the new part.

⌂ **Art Hotel** (11 rooms) ul Kiril i Metodii 72; ✆24081; www.arthotel-sbh.com. Quiet location at the end of the peninsula. Comfortable rooms, sea views. This old house is the property of the Bulgarian Artists' Union, hence its name & stylish décor. €€

⌂ **Diamanti** (20 rooms) ul Morski skali/ Valnobor 8, in the Old Town; ✆22640; m 0888 260911; e contact@hoteldiamanti.com; www. hoteldiamanti.com. Quiet situation with sea views. Good restaurant. €€

⌂ **Lola** (23 rooms) ul Vihren 32; ✆22232; m 0889 998999; e office@lolahotel.com; www. lolahotel.com. 10mins on foot from the centre; comfortable rooms & friendly staff. €€

⌂ **Vadzho** (11 rooms) ul Vihren 41; ✆23185; m 0888 247720; e office@hotelvadjo.com; www. hotelvadjo.com. Beautiful location with sea view. €–€€

✕ WHERE TO EAT AND DRINK
✕ **Kirik** ul Ribarska 77; ✆42860. Good place to try fresh Black Sea fish. €€

✕ **Ksantana** ul Morski skali 7; ✆22454. Another good place to try the local fish specialities or just grilled meats & salads. €€

BOAT TRIP TO SV IVAN ISLAND

From Sozopol port it is possible to take a boat across to Sv Ivan Island, about 1km from Sozopol (*1 hourly between 09.00 and 17.00; 15lv*). It was inhabited by the Thracians and conquered by the Romans in 72BC. After Bulgaria became Christian, a monastery and other buildings were constructed on the ruins of a Roman temple. The early Christian basilica of Sv Bogoroditsa and the monastery became a major cultural centre, distributing religious texts translated there from Greek. A period of mixed fortunes followed, with abandonment then reconstruction. In the 13th century the monastery was renovated and a new church named St John the Baptist was built and became an important centre. A royal wedding took place in 1308 and the monastery received a royal charter.

During the Ottoman conquest the monastery was destroyed. In the Russo-Turkish war of 1828–29 it was used by the Russians as a field hospital. A lighthouse constructed in 1884 still stands. In recent times the discovery of the remains of John the Baptist were reportedly found on the island. Archaeological research in the 1980s found the remains of two churches, a royal residence, a library, some fortified walls and several monastic cells.

The island is also important for its wildlife, and over 70 species of birds nest here, including several unusual gulls. For this reason no visits can be made during their spring nesting season.

✗ **Neptun** ul Morski skali 45; ☎ 22735; m 0888 212691. Reliable cuisine & fantastic views. €€
✗ **Viaturna Melnitsa** ul Morski skali 27; ☎ 22844. The most emblematic place in town,

easily recognised by the huge windmill at the back. Nice setting & panoramic views. Food tasty & reasonably priced. €€

WHAT TO SEE AND DO The **Archaeological Museum** (*Археологически музей; ul Khan Krum 2;* ☎ *22226;* ⊕ *summer 09.00–17.30 daily, winter same hrs Mon–Fri; adult 4lv*) is well worth visiting. Exhibits are well arranged and labelled in English and Bulgarian. It has a very fine collection of Greek ceramics. Apollonia was noted for its early production of silver coins, around 520BC, on which symbols of the sea were engraved, such as a crayfish and an anchor.

The town has a large number of 19th-century wooden houses, built on lower floors made of stone. Its cobbled streets and the glimpses of the sea as you stroll around are very picturesque. Behind the stone walls there are gardens shaded by vines and fig trees. Unlike Nesebur, which it resembles in many ways, Sozopol has few churches, as they were destroyed by the Turks in the 15th to 19th centuries. The Christian population replaced them with small chapels. The **Church of the Holy Virgin** (*Църквата Св Богородица; ul Anaksimander 13;* ⊕ *daily, keys from the Archaeological Museum during the working day if it is closed; adult 1lv*) crouches so low in the ground that it managed to escape destruction. It is from the late 15th century. It has a bishop's throne and an iconostasis by the famous craftsmen of Debur.

Sozopol has two beaches; Harmanite to the south is the larger and better equipped.

BURGAS (БУРГАС) *Telephone code: 056*

This is Bulgaria's fourth city in size, and second port. It is busy and industrial, but like Varna it has beautiful wooded gardens along the seafront. There is a pedestrianised main street with lots of pavement cafés, and some older buildings among the modern ones.

Like most places on the coast, Burgas was a Thracian and then a Greek settlement; the latter called it Pirgos, meaning 'tower', hence its current name. It was a fishing port for centuries, and developed significantly in the 20th century after the arrival of the railway line from Plovdiv and the expansion of its port.

The town is small enough to explore on foot, the main pedestrian street, ul Aleksandrovska, linking the bus and train stations in the south with the shops and cafés.

To the east is the large Primorski Park, which is perfect for strolling, sitting and stopping for food or coffee. It is well maintained with flower-beds, trees and fountains. The nearby beach is often busy, but it is not as attractive as ones at the resorts nearby.

GETTING THERE AND AWAY There are **trains** from Sofia (*6 daily; 6½–8½hrs*), Plovdiv (*7 daily; 5–6½hrs*) and Karnobat (*14 daily; 50mins–1hr 20mins*).

There are two main **bus** stations in Burgas. **Yug Bus Station** (☎ *842692*) is next to the railway station and is for buses along the coast. There are buses from Sarafovo (*every 30–40mins; 25mins*), Pomorie (*1–2 per hr; 35mins*), Sunny Beach (*every 40mins; 45mins*), Sozopol (*hourly 06.00–20.00; 45mins*) and Tsarevo (*3–9 daily depending on season; 1½hrs*).

Zapad Bus Station (*ul Maritsa 2;* ☎ *831427*) is for **buses** from the Burgas district. There are buses from Yambol (*1 daily; 2½hrs*), Elhovo (*1 daily; 2½hrs*), Malko Turnovo (*3 daily; 2hrs 20mins*) and Sredets (*5 daily; 40mins*).

TOURIST INFORMATION There is a tourist information centre at ul Hristo Botev at the entrance to the underpass in front of the Opera House (✆ *825772*; e *tic_burgas@ burgas.bg; www.tic.burgas.bg*).

⌂ WHERE TO STAY *Map, page 273*
Hotels

⌂ **Aqua** (302 beds) bul Demokratsya; ✆ 833535; e burgas@aquahotels.com; www.aquahotels.com/ bourgas/bg. Good business hotel. Can be noisy with wedding parties at w/ends. €€–€€€

⌂ **Astoria** (17 rooms) ul Kiril i Metodii 38; ✆ 820670; m 0888 543090; www.infotour.org/ bourgas/astoria.html. A 5-storey block in a quiet residential area, a short walk to Primorski Park & the North Beach. Good location, budget option. €–€€

⌂ **Bulgaria** (172 rooms) ul Aleksandrovska 21; ✆ 841291; e HotelBulgaria@bginfo.net; www. bulgaria-hotel.com. The landmark of the town; a popular place to meet as it is right in the centre of the city. Some of the rooms have been renovated. €€

⌂ **Doro Burgas** (12 rooms) ul Sredna Gora 28; ✆ 820808; e info@hoteldoro.com; http:// hoteldoro.com. Stylish new hotel in boutique style, with a variety of rooms. Quietly situated just a short walk from Primorski Park. €€

BURGAS WETLANDS: THE BIRDING MECCA

This area is attractive to birdwatchers all the year round. There is a complex of closely related coastal lakes, lagoons, salinas, marshes, wet meadows and sea shore, situated at the westernmost point of the Black Sea. Access is easy as they are near Burgas, one of Bulgaria's biggest towns, well connected by rail and road, and with an airport. The large variety of wetland habitats (and also rocky and steppe ones in the vicinity), the position in the middle of one of Europe's busiest migratory flyways, the Via Pontica, and the existence of a system of protected areas may satisfy even the most discriminating birding tastes. All the main wetlands of the complex were identified by BSPB and designated by BirdLife International as Important Bird Areas (IBAs) of European and Global significance. The BSPB Poda Conservation and Information Centre (✆ *850540*; e *poda@bspb.org; www.bspb-poda.de*) makes available the latest news about the presence of 'hot birds' in the area. Top winter species are the **white-headed duck**, **Dalmatian pelican**, and sometimes **red-breasted** and **lesser white-fronted goose**. During the migration period you can see spectacular flocks of **white pelican**, **white stork** (up to 20,000 birds in a single flock!), **lesser spotted eagles** (more than 1,000 in just an hour in September), **Levant sparrowhawk** (flocks of tens of birds), together with rarities such as **spotted**, **steppe** and **imperial eagle**, **pallid harrier** and other birds of prey. Almost all European wader species can be seen together with a rich variety of terns and gulls, roller, wryneck and big numbers of passerines of different species, including large numbers of **red-breasted flycatcher**. During the breeding season **collared** and **black-winged pratincoles** may be seen, as well as **eagle owl**, **glossy ibis** and **spoonbill**, together with many other typical species for southeast Europe. The Burgas Wetlands are the place where, in 1988, the first modern conservation field activities in Bulgaria were started by BSPB (artificial rafts to help the breeding of rare birds like avocet, Sandwich tern and others). Since then many direct conservation actions have been carried out by governmental institutions and non-governmental organisations (NGOs): the designation of new protected areas, development and implementation of management plans and species conservation measures.

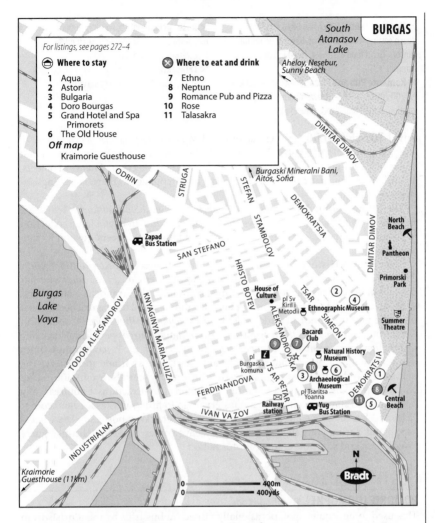

For listings, see pages 272–4

Where to stay
1. Aqua
2. Astori
3. Bulgaria
4. Doro Bourgas
5. Grand Hotel and Spa Primorets
6. The Old House

Off map
    Kraimorie Guesthouse

Where to eat and drink
7. Ethno
8. Neptun
9. Romance Pub and Pizza
10. Rose
11. Talasakra

South Atanasov Lake

Aheloy, Nesebur, Sunny Beach

Burgaski Mineralni Bani, Aitos, Sofia

Zapad Bus Station

Burgas Lake Vaya

House of Culture

pl Sv Kiril i Metodii

Ethnographic Museum

Bacardi Club

pl Burgaska komuna

Natural History Museum

Archaeological Museum

pl Tsaritsa Yoanna

Railway station

Yug Bus Station

North Beach

Pantheon

Primorski Park

Summer Theatre

Central Beach

Kraimorie Guesthouse (11km)

0   400m
0   400yds

N

Bradt

Grand Hotel and Spa Primorets
(67 rooms) ul Knyaz Aleksandur Batenberg 2;
📞 812345; e info@hotelprimoretz.bg; www.
hotelprimoretz.com. Well situated, overlooking
Primorski Park; luxuriously renovated, spa &
wellness facilities. 5-star but service not always
friendly & efficient. €€€€

Hostels
Kraimorie Guesthouse ul Valnolom 19A,
Kraimorie; m 0889 374973; e contact@kraimorie.
com; www.kraimorie.com. Good location & good
value. Friendly, helpful owner. €
The Old House ul Sofronii 2; m 0879
841559; e burgashostel@abv.bg. Some rooms with
2 beds, some with 3 or 4; shared bathrooms. Near
Primorski Park & rail & bus stations. €

✕ WHERE TO EAT AND DRINK *Map, above*

In summer there are restaurants and clubs in Primorski Park and on the beachfront.

✕ **Ethno** ul Aleksandrovska 49; m 0887
877966. Unexciting looking place, but very

popular & the food, service & presentation are
excellent. €€

✕ Neptun Central Beach; m 0878 101788. Beach setting: think sound of waves & beautiful sunsets. Good food & service. Need to book in summer. €€

✕ Romance Pub and Pizza ul Alexander Veliki 4; ☎ 0700 20011; e office@pizza-romance.com. Central location, & food highly recommended. €–€€

✕ Rose ul Bogoridi 19; m 0897 200000; nice setting in an old building; seafood & Mediterranean specialities. €€

✕ Talasakra bul Bulair 37; ☎ 843717. Central location, good food, excellent service. €€

WHAT TO SEE AND DO The **Archaeological Museum** (*Археологически музей; ul Aleko Bogoridi 21;* ☎ *843541;* ☉ *summer 09.00–17.00 daily, winter closed Sun; adult 4lv*) is in a 19th-century school building. It has a large collection of nautical objects, as well as an unusual wooden Thracian burial sarcophagus. There is an English-language leaflet.

The **Ethnographic Museum** (*Етнографски музей; ul Slavyanska 69;* ☎ *842586;* ☉ *summer 09.00–17.00 Mon–Sat, winter closed Sat; adult 4lv*) has a large collection of costumes from the Strandzha Mountains including fire dancers' costumes from Bulgari.

The **Natural History Museum** (*Природонаучен музей; ul Konstantin Fotinov 20;* ☎ *843239;* ☉ *summer 09.00–17.00 Mon–Sat, winter closed Sat; adult 4lv*) has displays of local flora and fauna, including that found in the Strandzha Nature Park.

Sv Anastasia Island has recently opened for tourists, and can be reached by boat from the pier in Primorski Park (*3 daily, check departure times locally; adult 12lv. Note: from summer 2015 the new passenger terminal at Burgas port will be working so this departure point may change; check at tourist office*). In communist times this was used as a prison, but in medieval times it was an island monastery. The monastery and church, with its restored 19th-century murals, a museum (*adult 6lv*), a shop selling herbs and a restaurant are among the attractions. Enquire locally if you want to stay in a cell in the monastery or go to http://anastasia-island.com.

Burgas has an active cultural life and it's worth checking posters to see what is happening during your stay. Hotels usually have copies of the free listings guide *Programata* and some other tourist information.

NORTH OF BURGAS

POMORIE (ПОМОРИЕ) *Telephone code: 0596*
This used to be a quiet spot, occasionally visited on bus trips by the tourists from Sunny Beach, but Cinderella has definitely joined the party, and all the outskirts have been developed with large hotels. It is known for its mineral spa and mud treatments, for the production of wine and brandy, and for its vast salt-pans.

Getting there and away There are **buses** (*bus station* ☎ *32592*) from Burgas (*1–2 per hr 06.45–22.00; 25mins*), Sunny Beach/Nesebur (*every 30–40mins; 30mins*), Varna (*4 daily; 2hrs*), Plovdiv (*4 daily; 4hrs 10mins*) and Sofia (*6 daily; 6½–7hrs*).

Tourist information The tourist information office is at pl Kiril i Metodii (☎ *22278;* e *tourism@pomorie.org*).

⌂ Where to stay
⌂ Pomorie ul Yavorov 3; ☎ 22440; e ih-pomorie@pomonet.bg; www.pomonet.bg/ih-pomorie. Near the beach & town centre, with most rooms renovated. Has a sea view, health centre & swimming pool. €€

🏠 **St George** (98 rooms) ul Peyo Yavorov 15; \24411; m 0885 274884; e office@ st-george-bg.info; www.st-george-bg.info. Central, with sea view, swimming pool, spa & beauty centre. €€–€€€

🏠 **Swiss House Pomorie** (6 apts) ul Yordan Yovkov 12; \22295; m 0889 583456; e toscheff@tiscali.ch. Modern, clean & friendly, on a pedestrianised street, 200m from the beach. €€

✗ **Where to eat and drink** As well as those listed below, there are also plenty of places along the main pedestrian street of the town.

✗ **Izbata** At the entrance to Pomorie by the town sign, on the right-hand side if you are travelling from the south, awkward to reach without a car; \29600. Housed in one of the original wine cellars of the local winery. Bulgarian cuisine & fish specialities. Live music at w/ends. €€

✗ **St George Restaurant** \22440. See above. Varied menu: Bulgarian, seafood & international. €€

What to see and do The older part of Pomorie is situated on a rocky peninsula. Its beach has sand which is black due to the magnetic compounds in it; this is used in mud treatments at the sanatorium. The nearby lagoon is famous for its production of salt by evaporation. The seascape here, especially at dusk, is astonishingly beautiful. There is a small **Museum of Salt** (*Музея на солта*; ⊕ *Jun–Sep 08.00–18.00 Mon–Fri & 10.00–18.00 Sat, Oct–May 08.00–16.00 Mon–Fri; adult 2lv*) illustrating the process.

Pomorie Lake is a natural hyper-saline lagoon north of Pomorie. Humans have turned part of the lake into salt-pans for centuries, and medicinal mud is extracted from the bottom. The lagoon's situation along the large bird flyway the Via Pontica makes it a bird paradise. More than 270 bird species are recorded at the site and it is one of Bulgaria's most important breeding sites for the following species: Sandwich tern, avocet, black-winged stilt, Kentish plover, common tern, little tern and shelduck. Thanks to the waterbird habitat restoration carried out by the Green Balkans NGO, Sandwich tern numbers have increased from six to more than 2,000 pairs.

Specific hyper-saline conditions create a habitat for highly adapted flora and fauna like glasswort and brine shrimps, complemented by the 5km sand spit with dunes harbouring specific plants like sea rocket, sand-pit knapweed and sea holly. The successful preservation of the area's natural heritage is recognised by the inclusion of Pomorie Lake in the Ramsar Convention's List of Wetlands of International Importance and by the designation of two Natura 2000 sites.

At Green Balkans's state-of-the-art **Pomorie Lake Visitor and Conservation Centre** (*ul Solna 15; adjacent to the Salt Museum;* \22333; e *dpopov@greenbalkans. org;* ⊕ *summer 09.00–21.30 Tue–Sat; adult 2lv*) you can find information about all aspects of biological diversity, ecotourism trails and how the Pomorie Lake Complex looks after protected areas.

The **Monastery of Sv Georgi the Victorious** (*Св Георги Победоносец*) was destroyed many times by the Turks, but it was always rebuilt and we were told it was never deserted by its monks. According to the local legend, a Turk called Selim Bey came to live here in the late 17th century. He was very wealthy but suffered from an unknown and incurable disease. He dreamed that there was life-giving water in his courtyard. When he dug down he found a stone plaque with the image of Sv Georgi on it. He lifted the plaque and water spurted out. This water healed him and he was so impressed by this demonstration of God's power that he and his family became Christians. He built a chapel in honour of the saint near the miraculous fountain. The fountain is still flowing and the plaque can be seen. The monastery has colourful flowers and shrubs in its courtyard gardens, enlivening otherwise rather plain buildings.

Pomorie also has a Thracian domed tomb (*Тракийската гробница; 4km west of Pomorie near Europa Camping;* ✎ *22008;* ⊕ *09.00–noon & 14.00–18.00 daily; adult 3lv*) from the 2nd to 4th centuries AD; although this was the Roman period, an important Thracian person was buried in this tomb. It is a whole complex dedicated to one person, including a tomb, a sanctuary and a courtyard. The influence from Roman mausoleums is also visible. You enter along an arched corridor about 20m long, with two rectangular rooms alongside. The tomb itself is circular, with a diameter of 11.5m, supported by a central column. It is an unusual mushroom shape built of brick.

AHELOY (АХЕЛОЙ) This growing village, south of Nesebur and Sunny Beach, is situated on the River Aheloy, a famous place in Bulgarian history. Near the mouth of this river Tsar Simeon defeated the Byzantines who had invaded the country in 917. It was a resounding victory. A contemporary historian recounted that half a century later there were still piles of bones to be seen. There is a monument commemorating the event.

NESEBUR (НЕСЕБЪР) *Telephone code: 0554*
The beauty of Nesebur is threatened by its proximity to Sunny Beach. In high season it is very busy, and stalls, cafés and restaurants vie for the visitor's attention. Yet even then actually, if you walk away from the centre, it is still just possible to get a feel for this little peninsula as it once was. This small space was home to as many as 40 churches constructed between the 5th and 17th centuries, many of which remain in part or whole.

History Nesebur is one of the oldest settlements in Europe, with traces of Thracian settlement in the 2nd millennium BC. During the time of ancient Greece it was known as Mesembria, and was part of the Roman Empire in the 4th to 6th centuries. It retained this name until about the 11th century. Then, as Nesebur, it changed hands many times between the Byzantine and Bulgarian empires in the 12th and 13th centuries, but in the 14th, when it remained Bulgarian, it flourished, and many of its most interesting sites are from this time.

Getting there and away There are **buses** (*bus station* ✎ *22633*) from Sunny Beach (*every 15mins; 10mins*), Burgas (*every 30mins; 40mins*), Varna (*7 daily; 2hrs*) and Sofia (*7 daily; 7hrs*).

Tourist information The tourist information office is at ul Mesembria 10 (✎ *29346;* e *visitnessebar@abv.bg; www.visitnessebar.org*).

Where to stay All the prices are for the high season; off season there are serious discounts and rates are negotiable. Private rooms in the old part of town are a good bet if you are on a budget, there are signs everywhere and people offering rooms stand around at the bus station.

⌂**Marina Palace** (125 rooms) ul Ivan Vazov 7; ✎20600; m 0888 111440; e marinapalace@ pirgos.com; www.marinapalacebg.com. Between the new part & the Old Town. Advance booking essential in high season. **€€€**

🏠 **Morska Perla** (6 rooms) ul Tsar Simeon 4; ☎ 45606. Comfortable rooms, AC. Friendly staff, good location. €€

🏠 **Rony** (9 rooms) ul Chaika 1; ☎ 44000; e hotelrony@mail.bg; www.hotelrony.com. Excellent location, friendly staff. Very good value. €€

🏠 **Sveti Stefan** (19 rooms) ul Ribarska 11; ☎ 43603. Opposite Church of Sv Stefan, some rooms with a view of it. AC, helpful staff. €€

🏠 **Trinity** (15 rooms) ul Venera 8; ☎ 46600; e info@trinity-nessebar.com; www.trinity-nessebar. com. Picturesque hotel in traditional style, great sea views. Clean, comfortable & secluded. Restaurant specialises in seafood. €€–€€€

✕ Where to eat and drink

✕ **Kapitanska Sreshta** ul Mena 22; ☎ 42124; m 0886 657826; www.kapitanska-sreshta. com. Nesebur's emblematic restaurant is in a picturesque old house, but can be overcrowded with tourist groups. Bulgarian & international, seafood. Sometimes live music. €€

✕ **Neptun** ul Neptun 1; m 0896 704405; e ttopalov@abv.bg. On a quiet street looking towards the sea. Great place for seafood. €€

✕ **Zornitsa** ul Mesembria 28B; ☎ 45231. Lovely place with sea view. Go early as it gets busy in the evenings. Bulgarian & international cuisine, seafood. €€

What to see and do After crossing the causeway with its wooden windmill, once a common sight on the coast, you see the town gate and the ruins of some outer walls, layers surviving from Greek, Roman and Byzantine eras.

The numerous churches dotted around the peninsula are the wealth of Nesebur, many in the traditional local style with bands of white stone alternating with red brick, often decorated with blind arcading, ceramic discs and rosettes.

The **Holy Pantocrator Church of Christ** (*Църквата Христос Пантократор; ul Mesembria*) is quite close to the town gate. It dates from the 14th century and is one of the best-preserved medieval churches in Bulgaria. The shape is cruciform and domed, and the stone and brick exterior is decorated with ceramic inserts. The frieze of swastikas always attracts the attention of visitors; the swastika is an old religious symbol based on the form of a Greek cross. There is usually an exhibition by local artists inside the church.

St John the Baptist (*Църквата Св Йоан Кръстител; ul Mitropolitska; adult 3lv*) from the 11th century lies beyond. Its form is transitional between the cruciform dome and the earlier basilica style. It too is currently used as an art gallery.

Just beyond is the 17th-century **Church of Sv Spas** (*Църквата Св Спас – Св Възнесение Христово; ul Aheloi; ⊕ 10.00–17.30 Mon–Fri, 10.00–13.30 Sat–Sun; adult 3lv*). Inside there are colourful frescoes of scenes from the life of Christ and the Virgin Mary; it is interesting to see these murals because, although they were painted during the Ottoman occupation, they seem confident and vibrant.

Further on and to the left are two churches from the 13th century, the **Archangels Michael and Gabriel** (*Архангели Михаил и Гавраил; ul Hemus*) and **Sv Paraskeva** (*Св Параскева; ul Hemus; adult 3lv*), both with richly decorated outer walls.

The **Old Metropolitan Church** (*Старата Митрополия Св София; ul Mitropolitska passes through its square*) from the 5th century is the oldest church in Nesebur. It represents the first wave of church building here and is a three-nave basilica with huge supporting columns. It was restored in the 9th century, and there are mosaics remaining from different periods.

The **New Metropolitan Church** (*Новата Митрополия Св Стефан; ul Ribarska; ⊕ 09.00–noon & 14.00–18.00 daily; adult 5lv*) is also a three-aisled basilica, with 16th- and 18th-century additions. The well-preserved frescoes are particularly interesting; the oldest is from the 11th century, but most are 16th century. There is a fine 17th-century iconostasis and a richly carved 18th-century bishop's throne.

The architectural masterpiece **Sv Ivan Aliturgitos** (*Св Йоан Алитургетос; ul Ribarska*), meaning St John the Unconsecrated, is close to the harbour and entrance gate. This church is beautifully adorned and its striking silhouette is often used in photographs to demonstrate the skill of local church builders. The details are fascinating: patterns of mussel shells, images of the sun, decorative plaques, crosses and even four-leafed clovers. This was built in the 14th century, but much damaged by the 1913 earthquake.

No less beautiful are the 19th-century houses, stone-built at ground level, with larger upper floors of wood. The **Kapitanska Sreshta** (*Капитанска среща*) restaurant is a fine example.

The **Archaeological Museum** (*Археологически музей; ul Mesembria 2A; *\46019; ☉ 09.00–13.00 & 14.00–19.00 Mon–Fri, 09.00–13.00 Sat, 14.00–18.00 Sun; adult 5lv*) is well worth a visit. There are English captions to the archaeological exhibits, which include coins, pottery, votive plaques and jewellery.

The **Ethnographic Museum** (*Етнографски музей; ul Mesembria 34; *\ 46012; ☉ 09.00–13.00 & 14.00–19.00 daily; adult 3lv*) is in a typical old Nesebur house, and worth visiting for that reason alone, but there are also interesting exhibits of costumes and textiles.

There are combination tickets, covering visits to several sites, at reduced prices.

The old part of the town has been an architectural-historical reserve on UNESCO's World Heritage list since 1983. This status is under threat due to constant infringements by builders, including in the listed area.

SUNNY BEACH (СЛЪНЧЕВ БРЯГ)

Slunchev Bryag in Bulgarian, and Sonnenstrand to the many German visitors, is, with Golden Sands in the north, the main destination for package-holiday visitors. As both were developed early on, they have the advantage of really prime locations. Sunny Beach is a massive 8km beach, wide and gently sloping, very safe for swimming or paddling. There are hundreds of hotels of all categories, but the previous target of family-friendly holidays has been superseded by a party atmosphere, with clubs and parties for young people, and celebrities and famous DJs performing at the clubs and bars.

GETTING THERE AND AWAY There are **buses** to Burgas (*every 30mins in summer; 45mins*) and Varna (*every 30mins in summer; 2hrs*).

TOURIST INFORMATION This can be found at Complex Melodie opposite Sea Sanatorium (m *0899 888282*; e *contact@info-sunnybeach.com*).

WHERE TO STAY AND EAT The hotels are completely geared to package tourists who fly into Burgas airport, and as most are on full-board the restaurant options are not particularly exciting. Prices are as much as 50% lower in the shoulder season, May/June and September/October. However, some facilities may not be open outside high season. In general, independent travellers will do much better for accommodation and restaurants in Nesebur.

FROM SUNNY BEACH TO VARNA

The coast from south of Nesebur to north of Sunny Beach and Sv Vlas is built up solidly. Sv Vlas has been developed very insensitively, though its hotels do have a lovely view across the bay to Nesebur. Only the area beyond this, formerly a military zone, has stopped the developers. **Banya**, a small town, has some new villas, but still has an identity. There are vineyards around the town and a new winery has been built.

Obzor is a well-kept place, clean and decorated with flower-beds and hanging baskets, though to the north there are huge new hotels. At **Goritsa** the road turns inland, and the route is well wooded. **Kamchia**, a turning off the main road, is an attractive river estuary with Longoza Forest. This mixture of marsh and forest has dense almost tropical undergrowth. The ancient trees are covered with a variety of climbers, forming a canopy. The area around the river, on which boat trips can be taken, is scruffy, but can be interesting for birdwatchers, who look for hawfinch and tawny pipit here in spring.

VARNA (BAPHA) *Telephone code: 052*

Varna is bustling, smart and well kept. It is the third-largest city in Bulgaria and the largest on the coast. However, whereas Burgas is commercial and industrial, Varna is a naval and commercial port. Varna is on the same latitude as resorts such as Monte Carlo, Nice and Cannes. It has always had a cosmopolitan feel, sailors on shore leave joining the evening promenade along shady boulevards, lined by dignified 19th- and early 20th-century buildings, and adding something to it with their unfamiliar ceremonial uniforms. There are important historic sights and an Archaeological Museum of major significance. The Primorski Park, extensive gardens beside the sea, and lively shopping and nightlife make it a good alternative to staying in a resort, and it also has lovely beaches!

GETTING THERE AND AWAY   There are **trains** (*railway station* ✆ *630414*) from Ruse (*2 daily; 4hrs*), Plovdiv (*3 daily; 7hrs*), Sofia (*6 daily; 7–8hrs*) and Shumen (*8 daily; 1½hrs*).

There are **buses** from Sofia (*1–2 per hr; 7hrs*), Veliko Turnovo (*20 daily; 4hrs*), Burgas (*9 daily; 2hrs*), Shumen (*6 daily; 1½hrs*), Ruse (*4 daily; 4hrs*), Silistra (*2 daily; 2½hrs*) and Kavarna (*10 daily; 1hr 20mins*). The bus station is at ul Vladislav Varnenchik 158 (✆ *448349*).

There is also the private bus station Mladost (*ul Dobrovoltsi 7;* ✆ *500039; 200m from the main bus station*). There are minibuses from Dobrich (*15 daily; 50mins*), Kavarna (*1 daily; 1hr*) and Balchik (*8 daily; 50mins*).

TOURIST INFORMATION   The tourist information office is on pl Sv Sv Kiril i Metodii (✆ *820689;* e *office@varnainfo.bg*).

WHERE TO STAY   *Map, page 281*
Hotels

Best Western Prima (10 rooms) ul Tsar Samuil 5; ✆ 609809; e prima@bestwesternvarna. com; www.bestwesternvarna.com. Small hotel in quiet area near main street & Sea Gardens; AC & internet. €€€

Graffit Gallery bul Knyaz Boris I 65; ✆ 989900; www.graffithotel.com. Art gallery within the hotel, with suitably stylish & individual rooms. For the restaurant, see page 280. €€€

Grand Hotel London (24 rooms) ul Musala 3; ✆ 664100; m 0893 378147; e londonhotel@ galeriahotels.com; www.londonhotel.bg. As grand as its name & a really lovely hotel, built over 100 years ago & elegantly restored. A hotel from a different era, with comfort & service to match. €€€

Odessos (94 rooms) bul Slivnitsa 1; ✆ 640300; e info@odessos-bg.com; www. odessos-bg.com. Wonderful location on the edge of Primorski Park. Clean & comfortable; staff friendly but service can be slow. Restaurant. €€–€€€

🛏 **Panorama** (57 rooms) bul Primorski 31; ✆687300; e hotel@panoramabg.com; www. panoramabg.com. Modern hotel, stylishly furnished, close to the seafront. Fitness centre, bar & internet. €€

🛏 **Splendid Boutique** (26 rooms) ul Bratya Shkorpil 30; ✆681414; m 0888 887164; http:// boutiquesplendid.net. Another very good luxurious hotel in the centre, in a restored 19th-century building, with views across to the cathedral. €€

🛏 **Voennomorski Club** (36 rooms) bul Vladislav Varnenchik 2; ✆617965; m 0892 606814. Budget place with basic facilities but central & cheap. Rooms are clean & comfortable. €

Hostels

🛏 **Flag Varna Central Hostel** 4th floor, Bratya Shkorpil 13a; m 0897 408115; e flagvarna@gmail. com; www.varnahostel.com. Long-established & popular hostel. €

🛏 **Gregory's Backpackers Hostel** Zvezditsa, ul Fenix 82; ✆379909; e info@hostelvarna.com; www.gregorysbackpackers.com. Highly rated for friendly atmosphere & good value. €

✗ WHERE TO EAT AND DRINK *Map, page 281*

✗ **Di Wine** ul Bratya Shkorpil 2. Excellent wine list as the name implies, & meals can be light snacks or full-scale dinners of steaks or game, or cheaper grills. €€€

✗ **La Pastaria** ul Dragoman 45; ✆632060. Pleasant setting. Italian food; big variety of salads. Very popular. €€

✗ **Pri Monahinite** bul Primorski 47. Good for roast & grilled meats, decent selection of wines. Unusual setting near a small church. €€

✗ **Red Canape** ul Knyaz Boris I 65; m 0882 005005.The restaurant of the Graffit Gallery Hotel (page 279). Beautifully presented French & Mediterranean cuisine & Black Sea fish. €€€

NIGHTLIFE In summer the most fashionable bars are near the beach along Kraibrezhna Aleya.

WHAT TO SEE AND DO Varna was an inhabited place even before the Greeks established the colony of Odessos in about 580BC. Later, under the Romans and their successors, the Slavs, Varna became a major port trading with Constantinople, Venice and Dubrovnik. In 1393 it was captured by the Turks, who made it an important military centre.

The 19th-century **Cathedral of the Assumption of the Virgin** (*Катедрална храм Св Успение Богородично; pl Mitropolitska Simeon; ⊕ 08.00–22.00 daily; entrance by donation*) is an imposing landmark, which contains a finely carved iconostasis and bishop's throne from the famous Debur School of woodcarving, some interesting murals and stained glass.

The 2nd-century **Thermae** (*Термите; ul San Stefano & Han Krum;* ✆ *600059;* ⊕ *summer 10.00–17.00 Tue–Sun, winter same times Tue–Sat; adult 4lv*) are the remains of the largest Roman public building in Bulgaria. Enough has been revealed by archaeologists to give a good impression of the original layout, though some parts remain hidden under nearby streets. Coming across an extensive ancient building amid the streets and houses of a modern city is not unusual in Bulgaria, but it is always a delight.

This enormous building implies a great confidence in the builders, for it must have needed an army of slaves both to build it and to tend its furnaces. Ancient Odessos was obviously a place of importance. The thermae were built on even older foundations in the 2nd century AD, water being provided by aqueduct. Nearby would have been temples and a marketplace. Here and there you can still see small areas of mosaic which, together with the decorative fragments of marble from columns and capitals, indicate that this was a very ornate building. There was

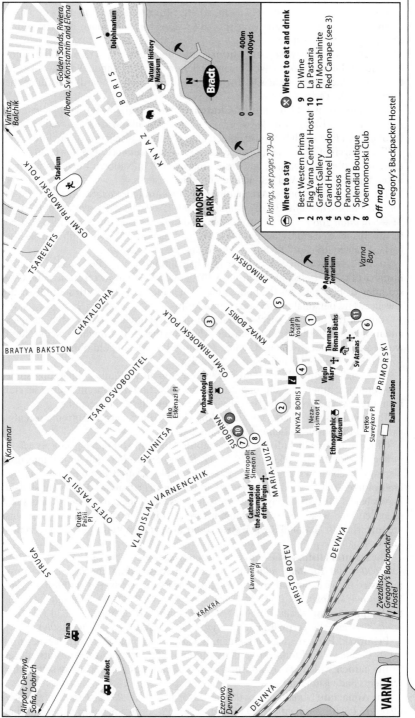

VARNA

Where to stay (For listings, see pages 279–80)

1 Best Western Prima
2 Flag Varna Central Hostel
3 Grafit Gallery
4 Grand Hotel London
5 Odessos
6 Panorama
7 Splendid Boutique
8 Voennomorski Club

Off map
Gregory's Backpacker Hostel

Where to eat and drink

9 Di Wine
10 La Pastaria
11 Pri Monahinite
Red Canape (see 3)

Golden Sands, Riviera,
Albena, Sv Konstantin and Elena

Vinitsa,
Balchik

Dolphinarium

Natural History
Museum

B O R I S

PRIMORSKI
PARK

K N Y A Z

0   400m
0   400yds

Stadium

TSAREVETS

OSMI PRIMORSKI POLK

CHATALDZHA

BRATYA BAKSTON

PRIMORSKI

Aquarium,
Terrarium

Varna
Bay

KNYAZ BORIS I

TSAR OSVOBODITEL

Kamenar

SLIVNITSA

Ilko
Eskenazi Pl

Archaeological
Museum

SUBORNA

Ekzarh
Yosif Pl

Virgin
Mary

Thermae
Roman Baths

Sv Atanas

PRIMORSKI

Neza-
visimost Pl

Ethnographic
Museum

Petko
Slaveykov Pl

Railway station

OTETS PAISII ST

STRUGA

Otets
Paisii Pl

VLADISLAV VARNENCHIK

Mitropolit
Simeon Pl

Cathedral of
the Assumption
of the Virgin

MARIA-LUIZA

Laventiy
Pl

KRAKRA

HRISTO BOTEV

DEVNYA

Zvezditsa,
Gregory's Backpacker
Hostel

Airport, Devnya,
Sofia, Dobrich

Vama

Mladost

Ezerovo,
Devnya

DEVNYA

VARNA

a large meeting hall called a *palaestra*, where citizens discussed matters of public interest, as well as the baths with special sections for cold, warm and hot water, changing rooms and shops.

The destruction may have been from Gothic invasions or as a result of the major earthquake here in AD544 which caused a tidal wave to engulf Varna. This is a fascinating and atmospheric site. There are a few information boards explaining the purpose of the various rooms.

The unobtrusive 17th-century **Church of the Virgin Mary** (*Черквата Св Богородица; ul Han Krum 19*) has a bold iconostasis, an intricately carved bishop's throne and a fine small belltower, added after Ottoman restrictions were lifted.

The **Church of Sv Atanas** (*Православен храм Св Атанас;* ⊕ *09.00–17.30 daily*) dates from the 13th century, but was rebuilt in 1838 in National Revival style. It is noted for its icons, carved ceiling and gilded iconostasis.

The pride and joy of the **Archaeological Museum** (*Археологическия музей; ul Mariya Luisa 41;* ✆ *681030;* ⊕ *summer 10.00–17.00 Tue–Sun, winter same times Tue–Sat; adult 10lv*) is the oldest worked gold in the world. The museum is housed in the former Secondary School for Girls, and has over 55,000 exhibits from the earliest Palaeolithic, or Old Stone Age, to the late Middle Ages.

In 1972, excavations in the Varna Chalcolithic Necropolis revealed a large number of gold artefacts from around 4000BC. These are now on show here. One stunning display case has the bones of a tribal leader arranged with skilfully made jewellery and personal possessions around him.

Some of the finds are displayed behind magnifying glass to show the complex and minute details of the craftsmanship. These are the items thought to be the oldest worked gold so far discovered. There are more than 2,000 gold objects, weighing some 6.5kg. The gold is nearly pure, 23.5 carat.

Other exhibition halls contain Greek and Roman antiquities, including some fine ceramics, funerary sculptures and a large collection of icons, including several from the Tryavna School; there is also medieval jewellery and weapons.

There is a display of artefacts, including clay fertility charms, from the recently excavated Eneolithic settlement at Durankulak.

Other museums include the **Ethnographic Museum** (*Етнографския музей; ul Panagyurishte 22;* ✆ *630588;* ⊕ *10.00–17.00 Tue–Sun; adult 4lv*), with interesting displays of costumes and jewellery, and examples of folk customs such as the embroidered masks used in the *kukeri* and *survakari* rituals, and different shaped loaves baked for festival days. There are displays about local trades and crafts such as agriculture, weaving, winemaking, fishing and iron-smelting, and some rooms are furnished in National Revival style. There are some captions in English, French and German.

The **Natural History Museum** (*Природонаучен музей; Primorski Park;* ✆ *618011;* ⊕ *10.00–17.00 Tue–Sun; adult 4lv*) focuses on coastal flora and fauna. For those interested in live exhibits there is a cluster of interesting nearby possibilities: the **Zoo** (*Зоологическа градина; Primorski Park;* ⊕ *summer 08.00–20.00 daily; adult 1.50lv*); the **Dolphinarium** (*Делфинариум;* ✆ *302199; shows at 10.30, noon & 15.30 Tue–Sun; adult 20lv*); and the **Terrarium** (*Терариум;* ⊕ *09.00–20.00 daily; adult 1.80lv*).

Primorski Park, or the Sea Garden, is Varna's own holiday resort. It has a fine sandy beach, colourful flower gardens and fountains, cafés and restaurants, all set in the garden which was established in 1862. The trees make a shady setting for residents and visitors alike.

The **Aquarium** (*Аквариум;* m *0879 473275;* ⊕ *summer 09.00–19.00 daily, winter 09.00–15.00 Tue–Sun; adult 4lv*) was built in 1912, its façade being rather unusual as it features bas-reliefs of oysters and other sea creatures. The main hall has a large collection of both freshwater and saltwater creatures, and there are further exhibits about the Black Sea and its flora and fauna.

Varna has a small part in the Dracula story, as it was from here that the vampire travelled in his coffin from Transylvania to England.

Varna hosts an annual busy programme of classical music and opera at a variety of venues. Enquire at the tourist office or your hotel, or check the listings in *Programata*.

Further from the centre, a granite **monument** commemorates the Battle of Varna, which took place in 1444. Some 30,000 Crusaders were waiting to sail to Constantinople when they were attacked by 120,000 Turks. The Polish King Ladislas was killed in a bold attempt to capture the Sultan Murad, and the subsequent retreat foreshadowed Christendom's general retreat before the advancing Ottomans.

West of Varna is a natural phenomenon known as the **Stone Forest** (*Побитите камъни*). The first impression is of a ruined temple, but scientists have discovered that it is a geological formation of stalagmites, some 50 million years old. A large area (800m x 120m) is covered by stone columns and stumps, some as high as 10m. A few have animal shapes and others have smaller rocks balancing on them to give a mushroom effect. Close up, the columns are particularly interesting as they have a porous honeycombed surface with many fossils and molluscs embedded.

THE COAST NORTH OF VARNA

SV SV KONSTANTIN AND ELENA (СВ СВ КОНСТАНТИН И ЕЛЕНА) This is one of the oldest resorts on the coast and is fairly quiet. There is more of a mixture of accommodation as there are private hotels here for the employees of various state bodies, and some small hotels too. There are several beaches, but they are small coves, which create a cosier atmosphere.

EUXINOGRAD PALACE (ДВОРЕЦА ЕВКСИНОГРАД) This former royal residence looks like a French chateau. It was constructed in 1882 to the designs of an Austrian architect. Its name means 'hospitable'. The development of its park began in 1890, when over 200 different species of plants, shrubs and trees from the Mediterranean, Asia and South America were chosen by Tsar Ferdinand. These extensive grounds are still well kept, and there is also a private beach.

It is now a government-owned hotel where you can stay (*www.travel.government. bg*), though in the past it was reserved for official visitors. There is a picturesque winery building where Euxinograd wine and brandy are bottled.

RIVIERA (РИВИЕРА) These were hotels for the *nomenklatura* in communist times and this is still a fabulous place to stay (✆ *052 386815; www.rivierabulgaria. com*). There is beautiful parkland which surrounds the various four- and five-star hotels, and through which you can stroll to the beach. There are several restaurants (including a very good one specialising in fish), tennis courts, several spa centres, a kindergarten and various attractions for children, an outdoor pool and a huge indoor swimming pool with an opening roof.

GOLDEN SANDS (ЗЛАТНИ ПЯСЪЦИ) This is a big, lively resort with a 24-hour lifestyle. There are a lot of clubs, bars and restaurants and, in high season, a lot of drunken tourists. Early and late in the summer it is quieter and you can see what a nice setting it has on a wooded hillside. The 4km beach is well groomed and there are countless hotels but, as at Sunny Beach and Albena, they are prebooked for package tourists. Prices in all the resorts are considerably higher than in other parts of Bulgaria, but there are plenty of activities for all ages, including a water park which is very popular.

About 4km away is the **Aladzha Monastery** (*Аладжа манастир;* ⊕ *09.00–18.00 daily; adult 5lv*). Here the monks' cells and rooms were hewn out of the soft white limestone cliff. This was a retreat or a refuge, not a confident statement of conviction like Rila or Bachkovo. The medieval murals are few and faded, though they must once have been striking and colourful enough to have earned the monastery its name, which means 'multicoloured' in Turkish.

There are two floors, reached now by a metal staircase; the upper has a chapel and some small cells, the lower a church and several rooms and cells. The remaining 14th-century murals are said to be of the Turnovo School. The monks who chose this place were Hesychasts, who believed in a life of physical immobility and silence. This practice was introduced to the monasteries of Mount Athos by Gregory of Sinai, and thus the Bulgarian monks from Zograf and Hilendar learned of it. It is this contemplative inactivity which is irreverently described as navel-gazing. Even today this is a peaceful place, a surprising find so close to the busy resorts.

Everything is signed and labelled in English.

ALBENA (АЛБЕНА) This resort is named after the heroine in a story by Yordan Yovkov, a popular writer of short stories which were often set in northeast Bulgaria. This is a spacious resort which has not succumbed to building frenzy. It has always been noted for its well-landscaped gardens. Many hotels are right on the beach and most have been renovated over recent years. This is a good choice for family holidays, as there are numerous entertainment options for children, as well as good sporting facilities.

About 10km from Albena is the village of Obrochishte, a village where, historically, dervishes lived. There is a tomb and mausoleum here.

BALCHIK (БАЛЧИК) *Telephone code: 0579*

The town was founded in the 6th century BC. Later it was known as Dionysopolis, after the god of wine. In certain lights both sea and sand gleam silver, giving the area its name, the Silver Riviera. There is a picturesque harbour area, and from the jetty it is fascinating to watch shoals of tiny fish darting about in the clear water, while larger individual fish lurk in a predatory fashion in the shadow of small boats.

This town, always the nicest on the north part of the coast, is still lovely. There are some old Ottoman houses and some from the National Revival period.

GETTING THERE AND AWAY There are **buses** (*bus station* ⟋ *74069*) from Varna (*hourly 06.30–18.30; 1hr*), Dobrich (*1–2 per hr 07.15–18.30; 45mins*), Kavarna (*4 daily; 30mins*), Sofia (*2 daily; 9–10hrs*) and Albena (*every 15–30mins; 20mins*). Ask at the tourist information centre about local minibus routes.

TOURIST INFORMATION There is a tourist information office at ul Primorska 25A (⟋ *76961;* e *tic_balchik@balchikinfo.org*).

⌂ WHERE TO STAY

⌂ **Esperansa** (4 rooms) ul Cherno More 16; ⟋75148. Near the port. Guesthouse with shared bathroom. Budget option. **€**

⌂ **Lotus** (35 rooms) ul Primorska 12; ⟋72195; e office@lotos-hotel.com; www.lotos-hotel.com. Good location on seafront, but maintenance needs to improve. **€€**

🛏 **Mistral** (42 rooms) ul Primorska 8B; ☎ 71130; e reservation@hotelmistralbg.com; www.hotelmistralbg.com. Good views, friendly staff, spacious rooms. €€–€€€

🛏 **Valeo** (28 rooms) ul Samara 6; ☎ 77029; e sales@wtc.bg; www.hotelvaleo.com. Friendly basic hotel. €€

✖ **WHERE TO EAT AND DRINK** There are numerous restaurants, pizzerias and cafés along ul Primorska.

✖ **Francis Drake** Restaurant of the Mistral Hotel. Sophisticated fish dishes. €€€
✖ **Korona** In the Cultural Centre Dvorets; ☎ 76847; m 0885 775520. Atmospheric place with sea views. €€

✖ **Lotus** See page 284. Popular place to eat, with reliable Bulgarian & international food. €€

WHAT TO SEE AND DO The chief attraction is **Queen Marie's Palace** (*Дворецът на Кралица Мария*) and the surrounding **Botanical Garden** (*Ботаническата градина;* ☎ *76849;* ⊙ *summer 08.00–20.00, winter 08.30–18.30, both daily; adult 10lv*). Its name is Quiet Nest (*Тихото гнездо*). It's a popular destination for coach trips from the resorts, so it's worth arriving early or late in the day if you can. The palace is small, more like a villa, and sports a minaret. It was built in the 1920s by the Romanian queen, when this northern area of Bulgaria was part of Romania. Marie was a granddaughter of Queen Victoria, and was born in England in 1875. She wrote some fiction and her memoirs in English, and used the villa as a summer residence. The story is that the elderly queen had a young Turkish lover.

There is a lot to see in the 10ha of gardens that are set on a steep hillside and descend in six terraces to the sea, supposedly one terrace for each of the queen's children. There are many different shrubs, roses and flowers set among streams, waterfalls and ornamental channels. There is a rock garden, a formal French-style one with clipped box cones and geometric beds, and an astonishing collection of cacti. Interspersed are stone thrones, seats, pillars and ornaments collected by the queen, or given to her as gifts. There are trees here that are more than 300 years old.

KAVARNA (КАВАРНА) *Telephone code: 0570*

Kavarna is the port from which much of Dobrudzha's grain is exported and nowadays it seems to have adopted a new role as the host of many pop music events. Two sights dominate the view: first, the huge cliff which appears to have been neatly sliced off, and, secondly, the huge, ugly, concrete grain silos. These are apparently too expensive to remove, so a clever solution, which works particularly well at night, has been to decorate and illuminate them. They look a little like the turrets of some medieval castle!

Three golf and spa complexes – Thracian Cliffs (*www.thraciancliffs.com*), Black Sea Rama (*www.blacksearama.com*) and The Lighthouse (*www.lighthousegolfresort.com*) – have been developed in this area. Famous players have designed the courses, which all benefit from wonderful locations near the sea.

GETTING THERE AND AWAY There are **buses** (*bus station* ☎ 82390) from Balchik (*4 daily; 30mins*), Varna (*14 daily; 1hr 15mins*), Dobrich (*1–2 per hr; 1½hrs*) and Sofia (*3 daily; 7hrs*). There are also minibuses to Bulgarevo, Rusalka and Shabla.

TOURIST INFORMATION This can be found on ul Dobrotitsa 27 (☎ 81818).

🏠 WHERE TO STAY

🏠 **Denitsa** (40 rooms) Ikantuluka area; ☎88017; e hotel-denitsa@icon.bg; www. hoteldenitsa.com. Modern hotel with sea view; swimming pool & sauna. €€

🏠 **Kavarna** (37 rooms) ul Delfin 8; m 0885 070002; e reception@hotel-kavarna.com. Located in Kavarna Bay, with fitness centre, sauna, swimming pool. €–€€

🏠 **Monako** (35 rooms) ul Prostor 24; ☎82130; m 0888 203450. Beautiful panoramic sea view, but in need of renovation. Friendly hosts. Good cooking with local specialities, homemade wine & *rakiya*. €

🏠 **Venera Hotel** (19 rooms) ul Chaika 6A; ☎87003; e hotelvenera@hotmail.com; www. venera-bg.eu. Comfortable hotel & a restaurant with a panoramic view. Just metres from the sea. €

✖ WHERE TO EAT AND DRINK

✖ **Bulgarka** On the beach; m 0887 864768. Bulgarian cuisine. €€

✖ **Morska Sreshta** On the beach; m 0889 253501. Bulgarian & international cuisine, grilled specialities, Black Sea fish. €€

✖ **Pizza Di Mare** ul Georgi Kirkov 1; ☎85150. Pizzas, salads, grilled meats. €€

WHAT TO SEE AND DO Kavarna has several small museums of interest, but opening times are a bit erratic. In the **History Museum** (*Исторически музей; ul Chernomorska 1;* ☎ *82150;* ⊕ *08.00–noon & 14.00–18.00 Tue–Sun; adult 3lv*) there are artefacts from Thracian and Greek settlements and information about the earthquake which in the 1st century BC dropped most of the ancient town into the sea.

Dobrudzha and the Sea Museum (*Експозиция Добруджа и морето; ul Chernomorska 1B;* ⊕ *summer 08.00–noon & 13.00–17.00 Tue–Sun, irregularly in winter; adult 3lv*) is housed in a restored medieval baths. Amphoras, stone anchors, coins and some Thracian gold treasure are displayed.

The **Ethnographic House** (*Етнографска къща; ul Sava Ganchev 16;* ☎ *050178;* ⊕ *08.00–noon & 13.00–17.00 Mon–Fri; adult 3lv*) is in a restored old house and shows the lifestyle of a moderately prosperous Kavarna family of the 19th century.

NORTH OF KAVARNA

The far north is much quieter, both in terms of traffic and development, though the environmentalists have a battle on their hands with the builders of wind turbines which pose a big threat to migrating birds.

At Bulgarevo, the village between Kavarna and Kaliakra, there is an information centre with interesting displays where you can find out about birdwatching in the area.

A side road leads to **Cape Kaliakra** (*Нос Калиакра; admission 3lv when kiosk is manned*), with its prominent red cliffs rising 60m above the sea. According to local legend, 40 girls, the only survivors of a Turkish attack, tied their long plaits of hair together and jumped to their deaths, rather than be raped by the victors. The red stains in the cliffs are said to be from their blood. Today it is a much more peaceful place, with an interesting small archaeological museum, the ruins of an ancient fortress and a small chapel which has recently been restored. The chapel is named after Sv Nikolai.

A legend tells how Sv Nikolai saved the crew of a ship which had been tossed about by the stormy sea until they had reached the point of exhaustion. They believed he would save them and he did. They prayed to thank him, the patron saint of seamen, and then went to their homes. Sv Nikolai was about to take some rest when he was attacked by robbers, and he retreated towards the sea. A miracle happened: as he ran, the earth extended further into the sea. Some say he was saved and some that he perished, but the result was the big finger of land jutting into the sea which is Cape Kaliakra.

In summer 2006, archaeologists found the burial site on Cape Kaliakra of a dwarf 110cm tall. In ancient times such people were believed to be touched by the gods; ordinary mortals thought that they had supernatural powers to compensate for their physical handicaps. The dwarf must have died in some kind of tragedy as the grave was under a burnt down house. Excavations are continuing here each summer. In the National History Museum in Sofia a huge gold ingot is displayed which was found off Cape Kaliakra. Is this the sought-after Golden Fleece?

Also in 2006, a monument to Admiral Fyodor Ushakov was unveiled at Kaliakra to commemorate Russia's great naval victory over the Turks. This, and the Bulgarian navy's successful attack on an Ottoman gunboat in 1912, are also the subjects of displays in the small museum in one of the caves (⊕ *mid-May to mid-Oct 10.00–19.00 daily*). Some very finely crafted medieval jewellery is also exhibited here.

NORTH OF KALIAKRA

At **Russalka** (*Русалка*) there is a romantically situated holiday villa complex on a rocky bay. Beyond this the road is increasingly quiet, passing through small villages where flocks of geese and turkeys graze. Sunflowers, vines and corn grow in the rolling wooded countryside.

Kamen Bryag (*Камен бряг*) is the typical shoreline of the northern coast. This quiet spot is frequented by hippies and backpackers who spend the summer in the caves or camping nearby.

Yailata Nature Reserve is a strange spot, a large area which seems to have sunk below the level of the surrounding plateau. It is a haven for all kinds of flowers and grasses. Caves in the surrounding cliffs were ancient dwellings from the 5th millennium BC, and sanctuaries, necropolises, faded medieval inscriptions and markings are fascinating to those interested in history and willing to negotiate the almost invisible tracks down the steep slopes. Nearby there is a ruined Roman fortress. According to legend, Orpheus was born near here and learned to play such beautiful music from the bird songs he heard.

At **Tyulenovo**, a tiny village, you can have a free mineral water treatment by standing under the flow from big black barrels.

SHABLA (ШАБЛА) This is a small, quiet town. It has a nice little church, built in 1853, with a splendid sounding name, **Sv Haralampiy** (*Св Харалампий*), and there are some fine icons inside. There is a former government residence in which you can stay; for information see the website www.travel.government.bg. The residence has a good fish restaurant. Shabla has a long sandy beach, but its exposed position catches the wind and there are hazardous currents. North of here is steppe, with thin, poor soil, on which in spring there is the most spectacular carpet of assorted and colourful wild flowers.

Cape Shabla is Bulgaria's most eastern point, and on it stands the country's oldest lighthouse. Shabla Lake is another bird reserve.

DURANKULAK (ДУРАНКУЛАК) This is the last village before Romania. The lake here is one of the most attractive coastal ones, separated from the sea by a narrow sand strip. It is slightly salty because of the penetrating seawater. The whole area is currently quiet and sleepy and a haven for birds. The village also attracts archaeologists because scientists regard this place as Bulgaria's Troy.

Getting there and away There are buses from Kavarna (*4 daily; 35mins; 5lv*).

Where to stay, eat and drink

Branta Birding Lodge (10 rooms); ul Durankulak 120; m 0887 308753; e info@ branta-tours.com; www.birdinglodge.com. Well positioned for birdwatchers, but also appreciated by those seeking peace & quiet in a coastal location. Plain, comfortable rooms. €

✗ **Ezeroto** 50m from Durankulak Lake; m 0887 607202. Fish & grills. €

✗ **Golden Fish** Right beside the lake at the north end, access along a rough track from the main road; m 0898 777070. Very popular restaurant with fish specialities, freshly caught from the lake. €

What to see and do On the big island in Durankulak Lake archaeologists have excavated a settlement mound or tell which was inhabited in the 6th millennium BC. In this **Archaeological Park** (*Археологически парк*) you can see the oldest monumental structure in Europe and a temple dedicated to Kibela, the great mother goddess from the Helenistic period (3rd–4th century AD). Here, too, is the largest Eneolithic settlement ever discovered; excavations have revealed a necropolis with over 1,200 graves, in which gold and copper artefacts were found, indicating active trade with other regions.

DOBRUDZHA (ДОБРУДЖА)

This flat fertile plain is the granary of Bulgaria, occupying the northeast corner of the country from Dobrich to the Romanian border and beyond. It has huge skies, rolling fields of wheat and barley and areas of woodland. In the villages, ducks, geese, goats and sheep graze near ponds with their attendants musing nearby. Older women are sometimes seen multi-tasking by spinning threads from fluffy bundles of wool and child-minding as well.

The Dobrudzha occupies the southwestern extremity of the Eurasian steppes; historically this was a route frequently used by invaders, and it was always found to be difficult to defend. The Ottoman Empire found the area quite depopulated after years of lawlessness, and resettled it with Turks, who still form a significant minority of the population here and in the Ludogorie, the low hills to the north of Razgrad and Shumen. Gradually Bulgarians settled here, and by the early 20th century they were in the majority. Between 1913 and 1940 the area was ceded to Romania, which encouraged Romanian-speaking Vlachs to settle here (Vlachs were traditionally nomadic sheep farmers). To this day it is an ethnically diverse part of Bulgaria.

DOBRICH (ДОБРИЧ) *Telephone code: 058*

Dobrich was formerly known as Tolbuhin after the Russian Field Marshal who liberated the area in 1944. In fact, many road signs continue to refer to it as Tolbuhin. Dobrich was the name given to the town after its liberation from the Turks; it was named after Dobrotitsa, a feudal ruler of Dobrudzha. Under the Ottoman Empire it was known as Hadzhioglu Bazardzhik, after the merchant who first settled here. It was known for its annual horse fair, and horse-breeding is still carried on. Dobrich is at the crossroads of the rich agricultural region of Dobrudzha, and is its administrative centre.

Getting there and away There are **trains** (*railway station* ✆ 602281) from Sofia (*1 daily; 9½hrs*) and Varna (*5 daily; 2hrs*).

The **paddyfield warbler** may easily be seen… in India, for example. But if you want to do this in Europe, Bulgaria is the westernmost country in its range – not everywhere, but just the northernmost marshes along the Black Sea: Durankulak and Shabla. It is a friendly guy – easily seen in May, when it constantly sings from the tops of the reeds, providing an excellent opportunity to take a photograph or to record its specific song. And it is not necessary to walk far to reach the place – just a few hundred metres from the car park. The presence of several other warblers make comparison and identification of this rarity easy.

There are **buses** (*bus station* \ 690120) from Albena (*hourly; 1hr*), Balchik (*hourly; 1hr 40mins*), Burgas (*1 daily; 3½–4hrs*), Ruse (*2 daily; 5hrs*), Varna (*1–2 per hr; 1hr*), Kavarna (*1–2 per hr; 2½hrs*), Silistra (*7 daily; 2hrs 15mins*) and Sofia (*6 daily; 8hrs*).

Tourist information There is currently no tourist office in Dobrich, but for information on the town go to www.dobrich.bg.

Where to stay

Bulgaria (104 rooms) pl Svoboda 8; \600226; m 0885 993883; e hotel@bulgaria-dobrich.com; www.bulgaria-dobrich.com. Old high-rise hotel in the centre; sports centre, panorama restaurant, bars, pool & casino. **€**

Sport Palace (45 rooms) bul 25 Septemvri 1A; \603622; e sportpalace@tur-sport.com; www.sportpalas.tur-sport.com. Convenient for the centre, in the park; fitness & beauty centre, sauna & swimming pool. **€**

Stariya Dobrich Inn (7 rooms) ul Dr Konstantin Stoilov 18; \690200; m 0879 601014. In the Ethnographic Museum Complex. Cosy guesthouse with traditional furniture. **€€**

This is an area which combines the shoreline, including the main Bulgarian cliffs, with some of the biggest coastal wetlands in the country and with the largest remains of steppe territories. In addition, the region is situated on the Via Pontica migratory flyway. This is a dream combination for every birdwatcher, especially bearing in mind the proximity of the area to the Danube Delta and other Romanian wetlands, from where in severe winters all water birds come to find unfrozen wetlands. In such winters over 72% of the world population of the **red-breasted goose** have been recorded on the Shabla and Durankulak lakes. Large crop fields also provide food during the winter for the **lesser white-fronted goose**. This is an area where **great** and **little bustard** may be observed, as well as **spotted eagle**. The migration period is also very rich in birds: raptors, pelicans, storks, herons and egrets, and a wide variety of waders and passerines. The area is famous for the intensive migration of the **quail**, **corncrake** and **red-footed falcon** (which also breeds there). The region is very special for breeding birds, as it is the furthest west in Europe for the breeding of such species as **paddyfield warbler** and **pied wheatear**. The abundance of **Calandra lark**, **short-toed lark**, **stone curlew** and **tawny pipit** is impressive. Cape Kaliakra is one of the best Bulgarian sites for sea birdwatching.

✗ Where to eat and drink

✗ **Gergana Mehana** ul Raiko Daskalov 2; m 0888 307122. Bulgarian specialities, good service. €€

✗ **Seasons Bistro** ul Bulgaria 4; ✆601606. Variety of grilled meats, salads, soups; fast service. €€

✗ **Starata Kushta** bul 25 Septemvri 14; ✆29114. Bulgarian cuisine & good atmosphere. €€

✗ **Stariyat Dobrich** In the Ethnographic Complex; ✆601590. Traditional *mehana* with good food & local specialities. €€

What to see and do The **Yovkov Museum** (*Дом-паметник Йордан Йовков; ul General Gurko 1;* ✆ *602213;* ⊕ *08.00–noon & 13.00–17.00 Mon–Fri; adult 2lv*) is an exhibition about the famous writer Yordan Yovkov (1880–1937) who was born in Zheravna. He taught in the primary schools of Dobrudzha, living with village families and gaining an insight into their lives. He married the daughter of one of his host families. Later, working at the embassy in Bucharest, he wrote several volumes of short stories about village life and characters. There is another house-museum of Yovkov – the house of his wife. It is here that the couple were married in the 'large' room and the writer started his first post-war short novel.

The **Art Gallery** (*Художествена галерия; bul Bulgaria14;* ✆ *602215;* ⊕ *09.00–noon & 13.00–17.00 Mon–Fri; adult 2lv*) is one of the best regional art collections. It has several exhibits by well-known Bulgarian painters such as Zlatyu Boyadzhiev, Dechko Uzunov and Vladimir Dimitrov-Maistora.

The **Old Dobrich Ethnographic Complex** (*Етнографски комплекс Стария Добрич; ul K Stoilov 18;* ✆ *602642; www.dobrich.org;* ⊕ *summer 09.00–18.00, winter 08.00–17.00, both Mon–Fri; free*), just off the central square, houses traditional workshops including weaving, wood-turning and gold-working. Within the complex the **Archaeological Museum** (*Археологическия музей;* ✆ *603256;* ⊕ *08.00–noon & 13.00–17.00 Mon–Fri; adult 2lv*) has many exciting finds from Durankulak's necropolis, including gold treasures and fine ceramics.

Appendix 1

LANGUAGE

BULGARIAN ALPHABET The present-day Bulgarian alphabet, last reformed in 1945, consists of the following 30 Cyrillic letters, all of which, except one, 'ь', have higher, capital, and lower case. When written in script, some letters like 'T' take an unexpected form in lower case like 'm':

Letter	Script	Sound	As in
А, а	*А, а*	[a]	anglia
Б, б	*Б, б*	[b]	big
В, в	*В, в*	[v]	voice
Г, г	*Г, г*	[g]	good
Д, д	*Д, д*	[d]	dog
Е, е	*Е, е*	[e]	echo
Ж, ж	*Ж, ж*	[zh]	measure
З, з	*З, з*	[z]	zero
И, и	*И, и*	[i]	in
Й, й	*Й, й*	[y]	yes
К, к	*К, к*	[k]	kilo
Л, л	*Л, л*	[l]	left
М, м	*М, м*	[m]	more
Н, н	*Н, н*	[n]	nut
О, о	*О, о*	[o]	hot
П, п	*П, п*	[p]	park
Р, р	*Р, р*	[r]	rye
С, с	*С, с*	[s]	soft
Т, т	*Т, m*	[t]	tom
У, у	*У, у*	[u]	cool
Ф, ф	*Ф, ф*	[f]	fab
Х, х	*Х, х*	[h]	high
Ц, ц	*Ц, ц*	[ts]	tsar
Ч, ч	*Ч, ч*	[ch]	cheese
Ш, ш	*Ш, ш*	[sh]	sheep
Щ, щ	*Щ, щ*	[sht]	ashtray
Ъ, ъ	*Ъ, ъ*	[u]	up
ь	*ь*	[y]	mayor
Ю, ю	*Ю, ю*	[yu]	you
Я, я	*Я, я*	[ya]	yard

VOCABULARY
Hi there!

Hello	*Zdraveite*	Здравейте
Good day	*Dobur den*	Добър ден
Good morning	*Dobro utro*	Добро утро
Good evening	*Dobur vecher*	Добър вечер
Good night	*Leka nosht*	Лека нощ
Good bye	*Dovizhdane*	Довиждане
How are you?	*Kak ste?*	Как сте?
And you?	*A vie?*	А вие?
Fine, thanks	*Blagodarya, dobre*	Благодаря, добре
What is your name?	*Kak se kazvate?*	Как се казвате?
My name is…	*Imeto mi e…*	Името ми е…
Do you speak English?	*Govorite li angliyski?*	Говорите ли английски?
I do not speak English	*Ne govorya angliyski*	Не говоря английски
Do you speak Bulgarian?	*Govorite li bulgarski?*	Говорите ли български?
I do not understand Bulgarian	*Ne razbiram bulgarski*	Не разбирам български

Be polite

Please	*Molya*	Моля
Thank you	*Blagodarya*	Благодаря
Sorry	*Suzhalyavam*	Съжалявам
Excuse me	*Izvinete*	Извинете

Let's agree

yes	*da*	да (= a horizontal shake of the head)
no	*ne*	не (= a nod of the head)
good	*dobur*	добър
bad	*losh*	лош

Enquire

Who?	*Koy?*	Кой?
What?	*Kakvo?*	Какво?
How much?	*Kolko?*	Колко?
How many?	*Kolko?*	Колко?

Going anywhere?

Where?	*Kude?*	Къде?
Where is the hotel?	*Kude e hotelut?*	Къде е хотелът
Do you have a vacant room?	*Imate li svobodna staya?*	Имате ли свободна стая?
Where is the restaurant?	*Kude e restorantut?*	…ресторантът?
… the shop?	*… magazinut?*	… магазинът?
… the pharmacy?	*… aptekata?*	… аптеката?
… the toilet?	*… toaletnata?*	… тоалетната?
How can I get to the airport?	*Kak moga da stigna do aerogarata?*	Как мога да стигна до аерогарата?
… the bus station?	*… do avtogarata?*	… до авто-гарата?
… the railway station?	*… do zhe pe garata?*	… до ж.п. гарата?
left	*lyavo*	ляво
right	*dyasno*	дясно

There are some variations in the standard Latin spelling of Bulgarian words, centring on the letter 'ъ' which is pronounced like the 'u' in 'up', although others define this as the sound of 'a' as in 'across'. The result is that when transliterated it varies. I have used the former throughout the book.

The Bulgarian alphabet does not include the letter 'x', and its sound is instead represented by 'ks', for example in 'Aleksandur'. The letter 'ж' is equivalent to the 's' in 'measure' and represented by the letters 'zh'. The letter 'ц' is the sound of 'ts' as in 'tsar'.

Hotel websites and email addresses are usually individual interpretations and may vary from these examples!

The correct practice for naming churches dedicated to two saints is to repeat the abbreviation for saint. Hence Sv Sv Konstantin and Elena – **Св Св Константин и Елена**.

straight on	*napravo*	направо	
back	*nazad*	назад	
east	*iztok*	изток	
west	*zapad*	запад	
north	*sever*	север	
south	*yug*	юг	
ladies (toilets)	*zheni*	жени	
gentlemen	*muzhe*	мъже	

Numbers

one	*edno*	едно	1
two	*dve*	две	2
three	*tri*	три	3
four	*chetiri*	четири	4
five	*pet*	пет	5
six	*shest*	шест	6
seven	*sedem*	седем	7
eight	*osem*	осем	8
nine	*devet*	девет	9
ten	*deset*	десет	10
twenty	*dvayset*	двайсет	20
fifty	*petdeset*	петдесет	50
hundred	*sto*	сто	100
thousand	*hilyada*	хиляда	1,000

They also talk about it

weather	*vreme*	време	
warm	*toplo*	топло	
hot	*goreshto*	горещо	
cold	*studeno*	студено	
ice	*led*	лед	
wet	*vlazhno*	влажно	
dry	*suho*	сухо	
rain	*duzhd*	дъжд	
snow	*snyag*	сняг	
fog	*mugla*	мъгла	

Appendix 1 LANGUAGE

A1

sunny	*slunchevo*	слънчево
cloudy	*oblachno*	облачно
wind	*vyatur*	вятър
storm	*burya*	буря
degrees	*gradusa*	градуса
centigrade	*tselziy*	целзий
spring	*prolet*	пролет
summer	*lyato*	лято
autumn	*esen*	есен
winter	*zima*	зима

When?

When?	*Koga?*	Кога?
now	*sega*	сега
later	*posle*	после
immediately	*vednaga*	веднага
tomorrow	*utre*	утре
yesterday	*vchera*	вчера
quickly	*burzo*	бързо
slowly	*bavno*	бавно
day	*den*	ден
night	*nosht*	нощ
light	*svetlo*	светло
dark	*tumno*	тъмно
Monday	*ponedelnik*	понеделник
Tuesday	*vtornik*	вторник
Wednesday	*sryada*	сряда
Thursday	*chetvurtuk*	четвъртък
Friday	*petuk*	петък
Saturday	*subota*	събота
Sunday	*nedelya*	неделя
week	*sedmitsa*	седмица
last week	*minalata sedmitsa*	миналата седмица
next week	*sledvashtata sedmitsa*	следващата седмица
January	*yanuari*	януари
February	*fevruari*	февруари
March	*mart*	март
April	*april*	април
May	*may*	май
June	*yuni*	юни
July	*yuli*	юли
August	*avgust*	август
September	*septemvri*	септември
October	*oktomvri*	октомври
November	*noemvri*	ноември
December	*dekemvri*	декември
month	*mesets*	месец
next month	*sledvashtiya mesets*	следващия месец
last month	*minaliya mesets*	миналия месец
year	*godina*	година
next year	*dogodina*	догодина

last year	minalata godina	миналата година
hour	chas	час
minute	minuta	минута
New Year	Nova godina	Нова година
Christmas	Koleda	Коледа
Easter	Velikden	Великден
Bayram	Bayryam	Байрям
birthday	Rozhden den	Рожден ден
name day	Imen den	Имен ден

Eating and drinking

restaurant	restorant	ресторант
tavern	mehana	механа
canteen	stol	стол
self-service	zakusvalnya	закусвалня
café	kafene	кафене
bar	bar	бар
pub	kruchma	кръчма
menu	menyu	меню
The menu, please	Menyuto, molya	Менюто, моля
mineral water	mineralna voda	минерална вода
sparkling water	gazirana voda	газирана вода
tap water	cheshmyana voda	чешмяна вода
wine	vino	вино
The wine list, please	Vinenata lista, molya	Винената листа, моля
What would you recommend?	Kakvo shte preporuchate?	Какво ще препоръчате?
I will have…, please	Za men…, molya	За мен…, моля
red wine	cherveno vino	червено вино
white wine	byalo vino	бяло вино
dry wine	suho vino	сухо вино
semidry wine	polusuho vino	полусухо вино
sparkling wine	iskryashto vino	искрящо вино
beer	bira	бира
lager	svetlo pivo	светло пиво
dark beer	tumno pivo	тъмно пиво
bottle of beer	butilka bira	бутилка бира
draft beer	nalivna bira	наливна бира
rakiya	rakiya	ракия
mastika	mastika	мастика
juice	sok	сок
ayran (yogurt drink)	ayran	айран
fizzy drink	gazirana napitka	газирана напитка
ice	led	лед
straw	slamka	сламка
glass	chasha	чаша
carafe	kana	кана
soup	supa	супа
tarator (yogurt soup)	tarator	таратор
salad	salata	салата
meze	meze	мезе

starter	*predyastie*	предястие
grill	*skara*	скара
chicken	*pile*	пиле
pork	*svinsko*	свинско
beef	*teleshko*	телешко
lamb	*agneshko*	агнешко
side order	*garnitura*	гарнитура
fish	*riba*	риба
bread	*hlyab*	хляб
slice of bread	*filiyka hlyab*	филийка хляб
toast	*prepechen hlyab*	препечен хляб
roll	*pitka*	питка
butter	*maslo*	масло
pudding	*desert*	десерт
vegetarian	*vegetariansko*	вегетарианско
chilli	*lyuto*	люто
hot	*goreshto*	горещо
cold	*studeno*	студено
salt	*sol*	сол
vinegar	*otset*	оцет
sugar	*zahar*	захар
milk	*mlyako*	мляко
sweetener	*zaharin*	захарин
honey	*med*	мед
tea	*chay*	чай
herb tea	*bilkov chay*	билков чай
coffee	*kafe*	кафе
breakfast	*zakuska*	закуска
lunch	*obyad*	обяд
dinner	*vecherya*	вечеря
the bill	*smetkata*	сметката
The bill, please	*Smetkata, molya*	Сметката, моля
change	*resto*	ресто
Keep the change	*Zadruzhte restoto*	*Задръжте ресто̀то*

Love thy neighbour

neighbour	*sused*	съсед
	komshiya	комшия (Turkish)
It is noisy	*shumno e*	шумно е
quiet	*tiho*	тихо
vicious dog	*zlo kuche*	зло куче
friendly	*druzhelyuben*	дружелюбен
grumpy	*surdit*	сърдит
tidy	*pribran*	прибран
dirty	*mrusen*	мръсен
rubbish	*bokluk*	боклук
Did you pick your grapes?	*Obra li grozdeto si?*	Обра ли гроздето си?
Is the wine ready?	*Stana li vinoto?*	Стана ли виното?
She is milking the cows	*Tya doi kravite*	Тя дои кравите
The lift doesn't work	*Liftut ne raboti*	Лифтът не работи
The roof is leaking	*Pokrivut teche*	Покривът тече

Who is ringing the door bell?	*Koy zvuni?*	Кой звъни?
Who's knocking?	*Koy chuka?*	Кой чука?
postman	*poshtadzhiyata*	пощаджията

Shopping

shop	*magazin*	магазин
market	*pazar*	пазар
kilo, kilogram	*kilo, kilogram*	кило, килограм
half a kilo	*polovin kilo*	половин кило
quarter kilo	*chetvurt kilo*	четвърт кило
100 grams	*sto grama*	сто грама
open	*otvoreno*	отворено
closed	*zatvoreno*	затворено
money	*pari*	пари
bank notes	*banknoti*	банкноти
coins	*moneti*	монети
ATM	*bankomat*	банкомат
Bulgarian lev	*lev*	лев
5 leva	*pet leva*	пет лева
10 stotinki	*deset stotinki*	десет стотинки
How much?	*Kolko struva?*	колко струва?
receipt	*razpiska*	разписка
(exchange) rate	*(obmenen) kurs*	(обменен) курс
buy	*kupuva*	купува
sell	*prodava*	продава

Aches and pains

headache	*glavobol*	главобол
(I have) sunstroke	*slunchasal (sum)*	слънчасъл (съм)
(I have a) hangover	*mahmurliya (sum)*	махмурлия (съм)
flu	*grip*	грип
high temperature (fever)	*visoka temperatura*	висока температура
pharmacy	*apteka*	аптека
doctor	*lekar*	лекар
nurse	*sestra*	сестра
ambulance	*lineyka*	линейка
medicine	*lekarstvo*	лекарство

Help

fire	*pozhar*	пожар
fire department	*pozharna*	пожарна
police	*politsiya*	полиция
ambulance	*burza pomosht*	бърза помощ

Things wise (or not) old men say

Бели пари за черни дни	White money for black days (Saving for a rainy day)
Бяга като дявол от тамян	Running away like the devil from incense

Всяко чудо за три дни

Every wonder for three days
(Seven-day wonder)

Вълк в овча кожа

A wolf in sheep's skin
(A wolf in sheep's clothing)

Гладна мечка хоро не играе

Hungry bear doesn't dance

Гони дивото – изпусна питомното

Chasing after the wild – missing the tame

Ден година храни

Day feeds the year

Дума дупка не прави

Word makes no hole
(Sticks and stones may break my bones,
    but words will never hurt me)

Казана дума хвърлен камък

Spoken word is a stone thrown

Една лястовица пролет не прави

One swallow does not make a spring

За вълка приказват а той в
    кошарата

Speak of the wolf and he's in the sheepfold
(Speak of the devil)

Запънал се като магаре на мост

Stuck like a donkey on a bridge

Здрав като камък

As solid as a rock

И вълкът сит и агнето цяло

Both the wolf is fed and the sheep intact
(Have your cake and eat it)

Капка по капка – вир става

Drop by drop – fills a dam

Който хвърчи високо пада ниско

He who flies high falls low

Който пее зло не мисли

He who sings thinks no evil

Котка по гръб не пада

The cat never falls on its back

Между два стола

Between two stools

Много баби – хилаво дете

Many grannies – sickly child
(Too many cooks will spoil the broth)

Мокър от дъжд не се бои

The wet does not fear the rain

На лъжата краката са къси

A lie has short legs

По дрехите го посрещат, по ума
    изпращат

They meet him by his clothes and send
    him off by his brains
(Don't judge a book by its cover)

Приятел в неволя се познава

You'll know a friend in times of trouble
(A friend in need is a friend indeed)

Рано пиле рано пее

Early bird sings early
    (Early bird catches the worm)

Тихата вода е най-дълбока

Quiet water is the deepest
(Still water runs deep)

Хлопа му дъската

His plank is banging
(He's got a screw loose)

Чупи – купи

Breakers – buyers

Appendix 2

GLOSSARY

Alafranga	Usually used to describe painted walls and niches in National Revival-style houses, but also more generally the influence of Western styles on traditional decoration, from *à la française*.
Banya	Mineral baths; in place names it means spa.
Bashibozuks	Turkish militia used to put down and avenge uprisings against Ottoman rule.
BDZh	Bulgarian railways.
Bey	Local Turkish governor.
BGN	Bank and exchange bureau abbreviation for Bulgarian leva.
Bolyar	Bulgarian nobleman in medieval times, and *bolyarka* is a noblewoman.
BSPB	Bulgarian Society for the Protection of Birds.
bul	Abbreviation for boulevard.
Caravanserai	Place where travelling merchants stayed during Ottoman times.
Chardak	Veranda or balcony.
Charshiya	Street with many craftsmen and workshops.
Cherga	Handwoven rug.
Cheshma	Stone drinking fountain.
Chorbadzhiya, Chorbadzhii (pl)	Village leaders or rich people in Ottoman times. It literally means soup makers, and was used in a disparaging way to imply they were collaborators with the occupiers.
C-x	Abbreviation for *Complex*, ie: housing complex, a residential area of modern blocks.
Dvorets	Palace.
Dzhamiya	Mosque.
Gradina	Garden, sometimes park.
Hadzhi	Someone who has made a pilgrimage, either to Jerusalem for Christians or to Mecca for Muslims, used as a surname prefix.
Haiduk	Bandit, outlaw.
Haidutin	Also, confusingly, outlaw, but used to describe 19th-century guerrilla freedom fighters against the Turks.
Hali	Indoor market.
Halishte	Fluffy blanket.
Han	Inn or caravanserai.
Hizha	Literally 'mountain hut', but most offer hikers simple accommodation and food.
House-Museum	Former home of a famous Bulgarian, turned into a museum commemorating them.

Iconostasis	The screen in Orthodox churches behind which is the sanctuary. It is often beautifully carved and the centrepiece of the church.
Janissaries	Boys who were taken in childhood from Christian subject peoples in the Ottoman Empire under the infamous Blood Tax (*devshirme*). They were taught to be fanatically loyal élite soldiers.
Khan	King or leader of early Bulgarians. After Christianity was adopted in 865, they were known as tsars.
Kilim	Handwoven woollen carpet.
Konak	Local headquarters of the Ottoman administration, including the governor's residence, a barracks and a prison.
Knyaz	Prince.
Krepost	Fortress.
Kuker	Mummer. Man dressed in an elaborate costume with a tall headdress, animal skins and numerous animal bells, who, originally according to pagan ritual, drives away evil spirits and ensures a good harvest, traditionally nowadays at events in January and the beginning of Lent.
Kurdzhaliya	Turkish outlaws who, particularly in the late 18th and early 19th centuries, ransacked and set fire to towns.
Mahala	Hamlet in the countryside, or neighbourhood in a town.
Manastir	Monastery.
Mehana	Tavern.
Minder	Low seating around the walls of a room.
Mogila	Burial mound.
Most	Bridge.
National Revival	During the late 18th and 19th centuries, while still under the Ottoman Empire, the Bulgarian Renaissance or National Revival took place. There was an upsurge in national awareness and a cultural revival. Domestic and church architecture of the time features woodcarving and murals of wonderful craftsmanship.
Pametnik	Monument.
Pazar	Market.
Peshtera	Cave.
Planina	Mountain.
pl	Abbreviation for *ploshtad*, town square.
Pomaks	Bulgarians who converted to Islam under the Ottoman Empire.
Pop	Priest.
kv	Abbreviation for *Quarter*, a residential area of a town, sometimes a historic part.
Raya	Turkish derogatory name for their Christian subjects, meaning the herd.
Reka	River.
Selo	Village.
Shose	Avenue or highway, from the French *chaussée*.
Sofra	Low table.
Sv	Abbreviation for Sveti meaning Saint or Holy. Sveta is the feminine form.
Mogila	Mound of earth which when excavated reveals successive layers of human habitation. The Thracian Plain has many examples revealing Stone and Bronze Age settlers.
ul	Abbreviation for *ulitsa*, a street.
UNESCO	United Nations Educational, Scientific and Cultural Organization.
Varosha	Central quarter of an old town, often now the part restored as a visitor attraction.

Appendix 3

FURTHER INFORMATION

BOOKS
Travel
Crane, Nicholas *Clear Waters Rising* Penguin, 1997. A mountain walk across Europe.

Eames, Andrew *Blue River, Black Sea* Black Swan, 2009. A journey along the Danube to the Black Sea, with a section on Bulgaria.

Hall, Brian *Stealing from a Deep Place* Minerva, 1989. A cycling tour of southeast Europe, with a section in Bulgaria.

Leigh Fermor, Patrick *The Broken Road, from the Iron Gates to Mount Athos* John Murray, 2014. The long-awaited third part of his walk to Istanbul.

Hamilton, Jack *The Good Balkans: Adventures Between Old and New Bulgaria* Wild Man Books, 2007. Entertaining travels and encounters.

Vitaliev, Vitali *Borders Up!* Scribner, 2000. An alcohol-themed travelogue by an observant Russian journalist, with a section on Bulgaria.

History and background
Ascherson, Neal *Black Sea* Hill and Wang, 1996. Eastern European history from Herodotus to the demise of communism.

Crampton, R J *A Concise History of Bulgaria* CUP, 2006. The definitive account.

Crossbill Guides *The Eastern Rhodopes: Nestos, Evros and Dadia – Bulgaria and Greece* KNNV Publishing, 2013. In-depth study of this remote area. In two parts, the first gives a detailed description of the geology, history, flora and fauna, and the second provides practical information about walks, drives and travellers' tips.

Magris, Claudio *Danube* Harvill Press, 2001. A cultural history of the riverain countries.

Pavlowitch, St K *A History of the Balkans 1804–1945* Longman, 1999. The Balkan countries as they fought for liberation from the Ottoman Empire and attained independence, before the next major realignment caused by World War II.

Trankova, Dimiana; Georgieff, Anthony; Matanov, Professor Hristo *A Guide to Ottoman Bulgaria* Vagabond Media, 2011. A beautifully illustrated tour around Bulgaria, visiting important buildings from the Ottoman era, some still in use either for their original purpose or a new one, and some in ruins. The text explains the buildings and places, and reminds us that in the Balkans, where borders have often changed, history is multilayered and interlocking, All who have lived here have left their contribution.

Trankova, Dimiana; Georgieff, Anthony *A Guide to Jewish Bulgaria* Vagabond Media, 2011. Similar to the above, but emphasising the Jewish contribution to Bulgaria's towns and cities.

Winchester, Simon *The Fracture Zone: A Return to the Balkans* Viking, 1999. Reflecting on the geological meeting of two tectonic plates, which was also the boundary of two great empires, with a small section on Bulgaria.

Fiction

Akunin, Boris *Turkish Gambit* Random House, 2006. Spy story set against the background of the Russo-Turkish war of 1877–78.

Andrić, Ivo *The Bridge on the Drina* Harvill Press, 1994. Winner of the Nobel Prize for Literature, a fascinating insight into life in the Ottoman Empire.

Barnes, Julian *The Porcupine*. Random House, 1995. Satirical account of the trial of a deposed communist leader, based on Bulgaria's Todor Zhivkov.

Bradbury, Malcolm *Rates of Exchange* Picador, 2003. The amusing story of a British Council lecture tour of the communist country Slaka, which bears some resemblance to Bulgaria.

Dasgupta, Rana *Solo* Fourth Estate, 2009. An unusual novel about the life and daydreams of a 100-year-old Bulgarian man.

Haitov, Nikolai *Wild Tales* Peter Owen Ltd, 1983. Short stories set in the Rhodope Mountains.

Kostova, Elizabeth *The Historian* Little, Brown & Co, 2005. An exciting, labyrinthine tale of a young woman's search for the truth about the Dracula story.

Littell, Robert *October Circle* Faber & Faber, 1993. Atmospheric thriller set in the Cold War period.

Radichkov, Yordan *Hot Noon* Sofia Press, 1975. Short stories set in the northwest of Bulgaria. Village life and the changes brought about by socialism.

Vazov, Ivan *Under the Yoke* Pax Publishing, 2005. Bulgaria's national novel describing the uprising of 1876.

Yovkov, Yordan *The Inn at Antimovo and Legends of the Stara Planina* Slavica, 1990. Short stories of village life during the Ottoman occupation.

USEFUL WEBSITES

www.bulgariatravel.org Official Tourism Portal of Bulgaria.

www.gov.uk/government/organisations/foreign-commonwealth-office Country profile from the British Foreign Office.

www.gov.uk/knowbeforeyougo Know before you go travel advice.

www.government.bg Bulgarian Government website.

www.bta.bg Bulgarian News Agency.

www.bgmaps.com Maps of Bulgaria and the big Bulgarian cities, with some useful addresses.

www.rooms.bg Online booking of accommodation from small villages to the capital city, tips on nearby sightseeing and activities.

www.visitsofia.bg/index.php?lang=en Sofia city guide.

www.programata.bg Online cultural guide for the five biggest Bulgarian cities.

www.historymuseum.org National Museum of History.

www.bulgarianmonastery.com Bulgarian monasteries.

www.tripadvisor.co.uk Hotels, restaurants and visitor attractions reviewed.

40 Years of Pioneering Publishing

In 1974, Hilary Bradt took a road less travelled and published her first travel guide, written whilst floating down the Amazon.

40 years on and a string of awards later, Bradt has a list of 200 titles, including travel literature, Slow Travel guides and wildlife guides. And our pioneering spirit remains as strong as ever – we're happy to say there are still plenty of roads less travelled to explore!

Bradt...take the road less travelled

Index

Pages in **bold** indicate main entries; those in *italics* indicate maps

women travellers *see* safety
Yagodina 41, 246
Yavorov, Peyo 27, 119
yoghurt 64, 144, 166, 188 *see also* cuisine

Zemen Monastery 136–7
Zheravna 182–3
Zlatograd 251–2

INDEX OF ADVERTISERS